CROSSKEY, William Winslow. Politics and the Constitution in the history of the United States. v.3: The political background of the Federal Convention, by William Winslow Crosskey and William Jeffrey, Jr. Chicago, 1981 (c1980). 592p index 53-7433. 27.00 ISBN 0-226-12138-0. CIP

The important introductory volume (misleadingly numbered Volume 3) for Crosskey's monumental *Politics and the Constitution* (2v., 1953). Crosskey left the current volume in a nearly completed state; Jeffrey completed the first of Crosskey's chapters and added a valuable introductory chapter of his own. In this chapter Jeffrey describes the basic thesis of volumes 1 and 2 and tries to bolster Crosskey's startling thesis that the Framers intended a unitary, national government rather than the federal system in which Congress plays a relatively co-equal role with the states. The present volume describes the political theory and political history of the Revolutionary era and the Confederacy, with a view to providing the background of the Constitutional Convention of 1787. (Crosskey apparently intended to write a fourth volume analyzing the Convention itself.) The account is in the same vein as the earlier volumes, with a strong emphasis on newspaper accounts, correspondence, and other contemporaneous expressions of opinion. The argument throughout is aimed at demonstrating the inexorable triumph of the idea of nationalism, and it involves another of Crosskey's rather fantastic attacks upon the reliability of the posthumous materials of James Madison regarding the Constitution. Indeed, this eccentric, cranky, and obtuse volume may be too easily dismissed by historians. It contains much that is new and a great deal that ought to be seriously considered by contemporary scholars. Unfortunately, there are no references to materials published since 1953, nor is there any attempt to address the multitude of specific criticisms brought by reviewers of the first volume. *Politics and the Constitution* is one of the most remarkable scholarly monuments in American constitutional history, and it deserves to be taken much more seriously than heretofore has been the case. For all four-year college and university libraries.

Politics and the Constitution
in the History of the United States

I smelt a Rat.
PATRICK HENRY

Politics and the Constitution
in the History of the United States

VOLUME III

The Political Background of the Federal Convention

WILLIAM WINSLOW CROSSKEY
and
WILLIAM JEFFREY, JR.

THE UNIVERSITY OF CHICAGO PRESS

CHICAGO & LONDON

THE UNIVERSITY OF CHICAGO PRESS, CHICAGO 60637
THE UNIVERSITY OF CHICAGO PRESS, LTD., LONDON

The late WILLIAM WINSLOW CROSSKEY
was professor of law at the
University of Chicago.

WILLIAM JEFFREY, JR., is professor
of law at the University of
Cincinnati.

Library of Congress Cataloging in Publication Data (Revised)

Crosskey, William Winslow.
  Politics and the Constitution in the history of the
United States.

  Vol. 3 by W. W. Crosskey and W. Jeffrey has special
title: The political background of the Federal Convention.
  Includes bibliographical references and indexes.
    1. U. S.—Constitutional law. 2. U. S. Supreme Court.
3. U. S.—Constitutional history.   I. Jeffrey,
William, 1921–   II. Title.
KF451.C7   342'.73'029   53–7433
ISBN 0–226–12138–0 (vol. 3); 0–226–12134–8 (3-vol. set)

TO THE

CONGRESS OF THE UNITED STATES

IN THE HOPE THAT IT MAY BE LED TO CLAIM

AND EXERCISE FOR THE COMMON GOOD OF THE COUNTRY

THE POWERS JUSTLY BELONGING TO IT

UNDER THE CONSTITUTION

Contents

PART III

POLITICS AND EVENTS LEADING UP TO THE FAILURE OF THE ANNAPOLIS COMMERCIAL CONVENTION OF 1786

PART IV

POLITICS AND EVENTS LEADING UP TO THE AGREEMENT OF CONGRESS AND THE STATES TO THE MEETING OF THE FEDERAL CONVENTION OF 1787

PART V

THE PUBLIC MIND ON THE EVE OF THE FEDERAL CONVENTION

APPENDICES

Preface

IN HIS preface to the two volumes of this study published in 1953, Professor Crosskey gave notice that "considerably more [text] than is now offered" was already in draft. He also ventured the prediction that a "long time [would] elapse before the remainder of the book [would be] ready." The materials announced in those prefatory remarks as being then in draft are at long last in the reader's hands.

The wide-ranging researches reported herein are exclusively those of Professor Crosskey; only in a very small number of instances have I completed references or supplied citations. The language in which these researches are published, however, reflects revisions made by the present writer. After his father's untimely death, John Crosskey, Esq., of the Hartford, Connecticut, bar, delivered into my charge the research notes, photostats, and transcripts left by his father, together with a much-revised typescript for nearly all of the present volume. After making the few rearrangements in the text that were indicated by Professor Crosskey's manuscript notations, I prepared two additional chapters. While Chapter I hereof is entirely my own writing, I incorporated several major fragments from Professor Crosskey's typescript into the text of Chapter II. For the rest, I revised the entire typescript along the lines on which Professor Crosskey had been working. To those readers who detect differences, from the first volumes, in a modest number of technical details, most particularly in the style of capitalization and in the system of cross-references in the notes, I think it right to point out two facts: first, some editorial fashions at the University of Chicago Press have changed during the past quarter-century, and, second, horrendous increases in printing costs are an unavoidable fact of present-day life.

I first heard Professor Crosskey expound his views of the nation's constitutional history at the University of Chicago Law School in the Winter Quarter of 1942. Following my return to the University of Chicago as a student after service in World War II, our friendship deepened, and I witnessed at first hand—indeed, I typed and retyped some of the chapter drafts for—the final stages of the writing of the first two volumes.

After his retirement from the University of Chicago, Professor Crosskey was a visiting professor for a semester at the University of Cincinnati Law School, and plans for a collaboration to complete *Politics and the Constitution* began to take form. Fate, however, decreed otherwise. We enjoyed one summer's work together at his home in Woodbridge, Connecticut, but early in the succeeding January Professor Crosskey's labors were at an end.

To have seen his book into print was a final, melancholy task. To have been his student, his friend, and his collaborator was the greatest of fortunes and the highest of honors.

William Jeffrey, Jr.

Cincinnati, Ohio
April 17, 1980

Introduction

Note to the Reader

Italics in quoted materials in this book are, in all cases, those of the present authors, unless the contrary is in some way indicated in the particular instance. Small capitals, on the other hand, are, in all cases, those of the original authors whose writings are quoted. Such quotations are marked in the usual way, by double quotation marks; but such marks are also used to mark words being talked about and, occasionally, to mark words suggested as the meaning of some source item or some word being talked about. Brackets are used to mark insertions or changes in source materials and other quotations. These are of various kinds. The insertions have mostly been made to supply missing or illegible words or letters, in manuscripts. Some, however, are merely explanatory; but where such explanations are at all long, they have generally been put in, in dashes, at breaks in the quotations. Changes in quoted materials have, in general, been made in the interest of brevity or readability, or both. The changes consist, sometimes, of the substitution of a pronoun for a noun or a phrase; or, sometimes, of a noun or a phrase for a pronoun, where the meaning of the pronoun is not clear without an extended quotation. In the latter case, if the noun or phrase is taken from the source material, as is usually the case, the fact is indicated by quotation marks within the brackets. The other changes consist, in the main, of changes in the tense of verbs, to preserve the proper sequence in the general discourse in which the quotations appear; or of changes of words like "these" and "hereto" to "th[o]se" and "[t]hereto," or the like, to avoid disturbing shifts for the reader in the point of view. Footnotes have been used sparingly, chiefly to supply the full text of documentary material too long for full quotation in the text, and too short to justify printing as an appendix. A full citation to all other materials employed in the discussion will be found in the notes collected at the end of this volume.

CHAPTER I

The Constitution of 1787:
An Introductory Review

1

THE first two volumes of this study in American legal and constitutional history were published by the senior author almost exactly a quarter of a century ago. The consequent interval of time would appear to have generated a need for this introductory chapter, for readers of the present volume will fall into three reasonably well-defined groups. Some readers, who then read those first two volumes, now remember the main lines of the argument, the principal conclusions about the original and intended meanings of the Constitution, and much of the evidence adduced in support thereof; readers in this group will find very little to their purpose in this chapter. The two remaining groups of readers consist, on the one hand, of those who have read the first two volumes but at present do not recall the argument, the evidence, or the conclusions with sufficient confidence to proceed without some retrospect, and, on the other hand, of those who have never read the first two volumes. Our purpose in this introduction is to provide for those readers who may find themselves in these last two groups some outlines of a general framework in terms of which the arguments, the evidence, and the conclusions to be presented in this volume will be more readily comprehensible.

The tumultuous reception which greeted the initial volumes of *Politics and the Constitution* suggested, with a fair measure of cogency, that their author had at least touched, if, indeed, he had not severely lacerated, an unusually sensitive nerve in a respectable number of students of American constitutional and legal history, from at least three major disciplines: law, history, and political science.[1] In these United States—as, of course, in a great many other countries throughout the period of recorded history—political views and a tangled mass of "received" notions concerning the nation's historical traditions have been—in fact, they quite clearly remain—very closely and inseparably intertwined. At least one of the safely predictable consequences of that fact is this: any suggestion that divergent or, even worse, "revisionist," views are not only possible but indeed are supported by a considerable body of evidence, has been, and will be, met with howls of

3

outrage, charges of the suppression of evidence, and sundry other distressful sequelae.

This phenomenon of intertwined political viewpoints and "received" notions about our constitutional history has often been exhibited in a particularly virulent form in this country because, from a very early date in our national history, American political parties and their leaders have sought to drape their merely partisan views in the sheltering mantle of what politicians and sundry other great leaders ritually refer to, in solemn and awestruck phrase, as the "intentions of the Framers." Quite predictably, the adjective "constitutional" has come to serve as something very much more than a neutrally descriptive label; it has become the ultimate word in the positive evaluation of any legislative measure, while the reiterated public employment of its antonym has developed into one of the more reliable techniques for consigning its target into the remotest regions of political and legal untouchability.

The materials presented to readers of the intitial volumes of *Politics and the Constitution* were, and in fact still are, of a nature to suggest a comprehensive reassessment of the conglomerate of received traditions concerning our national Constitution. Continuing and fortifying the earlier discussion, the volume now in the reader's hands will in all likelihood stimulate a similar reaction. Some review of the basic conclusions which have been reached thus far regarding the intended meanings of the Constitution appears to be essential for the two groups of readers earlier mentioned. Relying upon frequent references to the previous volumes for more extensive discussions and the evidence relevant to particular points, the present chapter is devoted to such a summary review..

2

For most readers, this essential introduction or review will be most profitably launched with a brief treatment of a broad issue, almost "philosophic" in character, an issue which is quite clearly fundamental to the entire project undertaken in *Politics and the Constitution*.

This fundamental issue was a subject for remark by the unrivalled master among English legal historians, Frederic William Maitland, in his inaugural discourse as Downing Professor of the Laws of England, in Cambridge University.[2] To his audience, Maitland propounded the instance of a lawyer finding on his table a case involving rights of common which sent him to the Statute of Merton. "But is it really the law of 1236," Maitland asked, "that he wants to know? No, it is the ultimate result of the interpretations set on the statute by the judges of twenty generations."[3] In one basic sense, the first two volumes offered the mirror-image of something very like this; relegating to a distinctly subordinate position what Professor Maitland characterized as "the interpretations set on [the document] by the judges of twenty generations," they sent the reader to the Constitution of 1787.

"[The] process by which old principles and old phrases are charged with a new content," Maitland went on, "is from the lawyer's point of view an evolution of the true intent and meaning of the old law; from the historian's point of view it is almost of necessity a process of perversion and misunderstanding." Having, in this sentence, put his finger unerringly upon the issue most relevant to the present discussion, Maitland proceeded to an elaboration of the point. "Thus we are tempted to mix up two different logics," he said, "the logic of authority, and the logic of evidence. What the lawyer wants is authority and the newer the better; what the historian wants is evidence and the older the better."[4] In the perspective thus supplied by Maitland's pellucid formulation of the problem, a major share of many readers' reactions to the first two volumes in this study becomes more understandable. Accustomed as those readers had become by then, to considering legal and constitutional questions almost exclusively in terms of "authority," the presentation of a massive body of "evidence" supporting the contrary view could, and in many instances did, have an extremely unsettling impact upon those readers.

The foregoing remarks bring up for our consideration a further aspect of the relationship between "evidence" and "authority"—or "law" and "history"—which deserves explicit statement for the reader. At what point, if any, should these two things be blended? When, and to what extent, should "historical evidence" be accepted and acted upon as "legal authority" or "precedent"? As the reader will easily perceive, this question is basically political in its nature, and, given the nature of "politics," people may, and they do in fact, differ widely regarding the proper response to be made to it.

This next, closely related proposition is, surely, also clear: whatever the response, it cannot in any way obliterate the deeply rooted difference between the historian's "evidence" and the lawyer's "authority." In other words, should historical evidence expose some "received" constitutional premise or legal dogma as being based on either inadequate or completely imaginary foundations, the conclusion does not automatically, or even immediately, follow that the "received" constitutional premise or legal dogma should thenceforth be abandoned. Legislatures are not obliged in any way to abandon their long-established practice of carefully and deliberately considering the entire range of the aspects presented by any problem they may be called upon to handle in the course of human events. Nor are courts, having at their disposal the direction of the public force, suddenly to be converted by any kind or amount of historical evidence into "amorphous dummies, unfit receptacles of judicial power."[5] On the other hand, scholars in the fields of legal and constitutional history, should, wherever possible, avoid the overly facile acceptance of "history" as written by judges, a task which the judges perform as an ancillary to their appointed task of deciding disputes. This sort of scholarly reliance upon, and too-rapid approval of, "history" which has been carefully confected to shore up a previously reached judgment, can only produce what Maitland warningly characterized as "a mixture of legal dogma and legal history," and this, as he correctly pointed out, "is in general an unsatisfactory compound." "The lawyer must be orthodox," Maitland cheerfully conceded, "otherwise he is no lawyer; an orthodox history," Maitland believed, was a "contradiction in terms." "If we try to make history the handmaid of dogma she will soon cease to be history."[6]

Keeping in mind the foregoing background materials, we now turn to a concise summary of the more than a thousand pages in the first two volumes of *Politics and the Constitution*.

3

As the starting point for this enterprise, we may appropriately begin with the motto of those volumes. Drawn from an essay published by the late Associate Justice Oliver Wendell Holmes, Jr., the motto reads as follows: "We ask, not what this man meant, but what those words would mean in the mouth of a normal speaker of English, using them in the circumstances in which they were used."[7]

As delineated in broad outline by Justice Holmes's language, then, two major inquiries are comprehended in the general plan of *Politics and the Constitution*. The first of these involves research into the meaning of the language used in the Constitution, an inquiry in which the words are dealt with in precisely the same way as they are handled by the makers of dictionaries, i.e., simply as linguistic units, the "counters" of thought and speech. At this stage of the analysis, attention is focused on the words considered rather "generally," without any reference to their specific employment by individual speakers or writers. The other major inquiry contemplates research into the real-life context—the political, economic, and intellectual conditions or situations—within which identifiable individuals did actually use the specific language appearing in the Constitution which the nation thereafter accepted by a process of ratification.

Many of the pages in the first two volumes are occupied by matters other than those referred to in the preceding paragraph. The determination of what the words of the Constitution "would mean in the mouth of a normal speaker of English" constitutes, of course, a significant part of the volumes published in 1953, and marks the completion of the first of the two major branches contemplated in the plan of this study. Any readers of those earlier volumes who may have taken up the present volume in the pleasant anticipation of additional "philological" or "linguistic" researches will, regrettably perhaps, be disappointed.

The other portion of those two volumes, however, is devoted to the presentation and analysis of many of the moments in our national history when the original and intended meanings of the Constitution, as delineated elsewhere in the volumes, were altered or departed from.[8] The great majority of these instances involve decisions rendered by the Supreme Court of the United States, and the introduction and analysis of these materials, although neither designed nor offered as a comprehensive presentation of the course of American constitutional history since 1789, will, as the writers believe, provide sufficient guidance for any readers who may develop some interest in learning when, where, and how "things got off the track."

The second major inquiry outlined by the motto taken from the late Justice Holmes focuses our attention on "the circumstances in which [the words] were used." Compendiously viewed, these "circumstances" consist of the entire proceedings of the Federal Convention, which held its sessions at the State House in Philadelphia from May to September during the hot summer of 1787. Contemplating this matter from a somewhat less comprehensive perspective, readers will recognize that the very human delegates to the convention (Thomas Jefferson's measured characterization of them was "demigods")[9] could not, and they did not, assemble at Philadelphia with blank minds, nor did the delegates write upon some *tabula rasa*. A significant part of the "circumstances," therefore, consists of a great variety of events, trends, and contexts—military, political, economic, and cultural—particularly from the eleven-year interval between the Declaration of Independence and the assembly of the delegates at Philadelphia. The volume now in the reader's hands is devoted to the presentation and analysis of this half of the "circumstances in which" the Framers used the words which appear in the Constitution. The remaining half of the "circumstances" is constituted by the details of the debates and the drafting which took place once the "Grand convention" had been called to order by General George Washington, its duly elected presiding officer, on May 25, 1787. Presentation and analysis of this complicated mass of materials is projected for the fourth and concluding volume of *Politics and the Constitution*.

4

There are several reasons for beginning with the broad topic of the national power over commerce. This power, obviously, is one of the more important nonmilitary powers of Congress, and if the present-day interpretation of the Constitution on this important subject can be shown to be quite without warrant in any thing which the Framers of that document did or said in it, readers will be far more likely to find credible the view that other parts of the Framers' great document have been likewise misconstrued or interpreted in a sense quite the reverse of that intended by the Federal Convention or the special conventions which ratified the Constitution in 1787–88.

Another reason for thus beginning lies in the senior author's reaction to the then (and still) prevalent "interstate" theory of the meaning of the Commerce Clause, when he first heard it expounded in his student days at law school. In a basic sense, this reaction was the remote origin of the entire project of these volumes. He thought it unreasonable to split up governmental power over the nation's economic order in such a fashion, nor did the phrase "Commerce among the several States" seem apt language for the expression of what modern lawyers mean by "interstate commerce." Some few years later, upon the enactment of the securities and exchange legislation of President Franklin Delano Roosevelt's "New Deal," the senior author became the "office expert" on these laws in the Wall Street law firm where he was then practicing law. Their complicated scheme of incidence having re-aroused his former skepticism about the "interstate" theory of the Commerce Clause, he thereupon read, for the first time, the entire report of *Gibbons* v. *Ogden*, which in its uncut version occupies the first 240 pages in the ninth volume of Henry Wheaton's law reports. Despite current legend to the contrary, the *Gibbons* case did not espouse the "interstate" theory. Furthermore, the uncut report of Daniel Webster's elaborate argument in the case was seen to embody viewpoints which had not only been much neglected in the many subsequent decades but were, moreover, widely at variance with the "received" orthodox views. One thing led to another, his researches broadened, and the results were presented for interested readers in the first part of Volume I of *Politics and the Constitution*.

A very important share of this Part One is allotted to the creation of a specialized "dictionary" of eighteenth-century word usage. In the light of our concern with a particular clause in the Constitution, the first part of this dictionary is given over to the discussion of the eighteenth-century usage of "commerce" and its synonyms.[10] This survey of both American and British sources comprehends the "commercial writers" of the time, a host of pamphlets, and a multitude of newspaper items. On the basis of this considerable mass of specific items of recorded usage, not related to the Constitution and therefore free of possible bias or other partisan coloration, the term "commerce" is shown to have referred generally to the "entire body of gainful enterprise in which people are or may be engaged."

The second significant contribution made by the specialized dictionary contained in this part deals with a second crucial element in the Commerce Clause. The lexicographical research provided the demonstration that eighteenth-century Americans used the word "state" in a vividly societal, multitudinal meaning, as referring to the "people" of a "state." This had been—indeed, it still is—the British usage, but American usage, reflecting post-Independence need and custom, has come to diverge from this "societal" meaning. Among other materials, a remarkable body of cogent evidence is introduced, exemplifying the use of *plural* verbs with the singular noun "state," e.g., "The *state* of Pennsylvania *have* have justly considered themselves as holding the balance between the southern and northern interests," or, "The *state* of Virginia *are* involved to an amount almost incredible in debts to the British merchants, which were not cancelled according to their hopes by the treaty of peace."[11]

Less directly linked to the words of the Commerce Clause, the third essential contribution presented in this specialized dictionary of eighteenth-century usage involves the terms "police," "polity," and "policy." Despite surface appearances, these three words are not interchangeable synonyms; only the first two share the quality of synonymy. "Police" (or "polity") refers to the preservation of good order, with particular reference to the public safety, utility, and convenience. "Policy," on the other hand, is the phase of government concerned with the "general" affairs of a nation, i.e., those affairs that affect a nation "in the aggregate." The grand divisions of "policy," then, were "commerce" and "war, peace, and diplomacy," and all of these taken together constituted the entire *political* interest of a nation. In contrast, the "civil" powers of government were those dealing with the affairs and derelictions of individuals. The "civil" magistrates, of course, are much engaged in an essential portion of this great work, nowadays commonly referred to as "the administration of justice." The allocation of the "dispensation of justice," as between the major fields of "police" and "policy," was a matter of individual choice by eighteenth-century writers, who were under the necessity of specifying their individual views for their readers, in those cases where their discussion of the distribution of governmental powers made this specific distinction relevant.[12]

The primary, and possibly novel, conclusion that the Constitution's grant of the power "to regulate Commerce . . . among the several States" would, *on the basis of this language alone*, vest in the Congress a complete and unfragmented power vis-à-vis the nation's entire economic order may raise this question in the mind of the reader: Was there something in American history prior to the Federal Convention which produced a different meaning for this collocation of terms? For any readers who may have felt some doubt on this point, Volume I offered a consideration of some phases of the pre-Revolutionary controversy with Great Britain, and most particularly an analysis of the famous *Letters from a Farmer* published in 1767 by John Dickinson, and, more briefly, Dickinson's pamphlet of 1774, entitled *An Essay on the Constitutional Power of Great Britain over the Colonies in America*. In the course of the discussion, the glaring inconsistencies between Dickinson's statements in these two writings were shown to be the sequelae of tricks and sophistries to which Dickinson had been compelled by the "logic" of events in the pamphlet warfare in which Dickinson was then participating.[13]

On the assumption, however, that Dickinson's later statements do not compel the conclusion that there had been no change in the American understanding of a "Power to regulate Commerce," further evidence was introduced for the skeptical reader. This evidence was drawn from the papers of James Duane, relating to certain important actions taken by the members of the First Continental Congress, in the autumn of 1774.[14] The question then most particularly confronting the men of that Congress was this: How are the powers of government to be divided between the colonies, on the one hand, and the royal government in Great Britain, on the other? The answer to this interesting question, as finally adopted in the fourth of that Congress's Resolutions on Rights and Grievances, was that the colonies "[were] entitled to a free and exclusive power of legislation in their several provincial legislatures, . . . in all cases of taxation and internal polity, subject only to the negative of their sovereign, in such manner as [had] been [t]heretofore used and accustomed." There was, however, additional language regarding this distribution of governmental powers. "From the necessity of the case, and a regard to the mutual interest of both countries," the resolution continued, "[the colonies] cheerfully consent[ed] to the operation of such acts of the British parliament, as [were] bona fide, restrained to the regulation of [their] external commerce, for the purpose of securing the commercial advantages of the whole empire to the mother country, and the commercial benefits of its respective members; excluding every idea of taxation, internal or external, for raising a revenue . . . without their consent."[15] The proposed division follows the line between the colonies' "external" or foreign commerce, and their "internal" or domestic commerce, not even remotely contemplating any subdivision within the whole mass of the latter.

Despite the foregoing discussion, based largely on statements by political leaders of that time, the possibility exists that the *general* understanding of "commercial regulation" among the *people* of America had been in some way affected by the later and more sophistical phase of the pre-Revolutionary controversy. A review of the newspaper and pamphlet discussions of wage fixing and price fixing during four war-years of the American Revolution, 1777, 1778, 1779, and 1780, shows this possibility not to have been realized in fact. The evidence indicates, with great cogency, that such phrases as "the regulation of commerce" and "the regulation of trade" still had precisely the comprehensive meaning for the great generality of the American people that those phrases had had for John Dickinson in 1767 and for James Duane in 1774.[16] From this evidence, the conclusion follows that there is no reason for supposing that the words "to regulate Commerce . . . among the several States"—the words which were in fact employed by the Framers in 1787—were understood as having any meaning different from their then ordinary meaning.

The evidence in the first volume considered to this point came from the years prior to the Federal Convention of 1787. The rather arresting conclusion as to the meaning of the Commerce Clause, dictated by this body of materials but so completely at variance with the dogmas entertained at the present day by the Supreme Court of the United States, incurs the risk of seeming to have made its first appearance in these volumes. For the purpose of dispelling this risk, the remaining portions of the first part of Volume I were devoted to a wide-ranging review of materials, from the years *after* 1787, discussing early interpretations of the national commerce power,[17] more specifically as these were involved in the campaign for the ratification of the Constitution; the question of congressional power to incorporate the Bank of the United States; the "burning issue" of a national program of road- and canal-building; and the famous case of the New York steamboat monopoly, which in turn gave rise to the even more famous opinion of Chief Justice John Marshall in *Gibbons* v. *Ogden*.[18]

5

The Commerce Clause of the Constitution is not the only provision incorporated by the Framers in that document which relates, in a highly significant manner, to this nation's vast and complex economic order. Among the Constitution's many other provisions respecting this extensive subject, there are three clauses which are important, not only for the reason just mentioned, but also because they are singularly relevant to the allegedly fundamental and much-debated question which has come to be phrased, in these latter days, as "the division of powers between the national and the state governments." Their importance in this latter connection grows out of the fact that each of these three clauses contains explicit and quite extensive limitations on the powers of the state governments. Their Constitutional* meaning and significance, which the reader may find rather striking, are in no degree altered or diminished by the long-prevalent, minimal awareness of their existence and comprehension of their importance.

The first of these three significant clauses is the Imports and Exports Clause, which reads as follows: "No State shall, without the Consent of the Congress, lay any Imposts or Duties on Imports or Exports, except what may be absolutely necessary for executing its inspection Laws: and the net Produce of all Duties and Imposts, laid by any State on Imports or Exports, shall be for the Use of the Treasury of the United States; and all such Laws shall be subject to the Revision and Controul of the Congress."[19]

Analyzing this clause in terms of the eighteenth-century meaning of its key words, we may begin by noting that in 1787 the meaning of the terms "imports" and "exports" was not narrowly confined to the nation's *foreign* commerce. The contemporary evidence supporting this view is almost infinite in its abundance. There are countless advertisements in the newspapers from eighteenth-century American seaport towns which speak of products or commodities as "just imported." Using the correlative noun, "imports," for example, southern newspapers could and did refer to "Philadelphia Flour," "Maryland Flour," "Connecticut Beef," and "Potatoes, Apples, Onions... from Rhode Island." Northern newspapers printed advertisements of such "Imports" as "Super-fine Maryland Flour," "Carolina Rice," and "Carolina Pork."[20]

Perception that the Imports and Exports Clause was originally intended as applying to the entire body of gainful economic activities pursued in the United States, and as not being limited in its applicability to the foreign trade component of that activity, will stimulate the reader's interest as to the antecedent conditions which could and did lead the Federal Convention to

---

*The words "Constitutional" and "Constitutionally," when capitalized herein, are to be understood as having direct reference to the provisions of the document.

incorporate such a clause in the Constitution. The best-known of these antecedent abuses is the constant "gouging" to which certain of the American states were subject, in the years prior to 1787, under the impost laws of neighboring states. North Carolina, for example, was subject to the tariff exactions of its southern neighbor, South Carolina, and its northern neighbor, Virginia. New Jersey, often referred to as "a keg tapped at both ends," was similarly subject to the levies of New York, for the eastern part of the state, and Pennsylvania, for the western part of the state. Finally, Connecticut, another "keg" like New Jersey, was subject to levies by New York and Massachusetts.[21] Some comprehensive remedy for these undesirable situations was greatly desired, and the Convention provided precisely that kind of remedy in the Constitution.

The second considerable contribution made by the Imports and Exports Clause to the reader's grasp of the orginally intended structure of governmental powers respecting the nation's economic order will become apparent from a brief inspection of its terms. In the first place, the consent of the Congress—and in the exercise of its discretion, of course, Congress could Constitutionally *withhold* this essential consent—is required for *all* state duties or imposts on imports or exports. The clause then carefully spells out the single exception from this earlier blanket provision, the exception tightly confining *any* state duties or imposts on imports or exports to those which would be "absolutely necessary for executing [the State's] inspection Laws." To employ briefly the "multitudinal" eighteenth-century idiom referred to in an earlier section, no state are required by the Constitution to submit themselves to the importation of, or incur the commercial risks or disadvantages incident to the exportation of, impure, adulterated, or substandard foodstuffs. In other words, the states are clearly authorized to levy *only* those imposts or duties which will defray, for example, such costs as inspectors' salaries, essential testing equipment, and necessary buildings. The states, however, are not to generate so much as one penny's worth of "revenue" from their duties or imposts. This interpretation is absolutely unavoidable, for the clause continues and expressly provides that "the net Produce of all these Duties and Imposts shall be for the Use of the Treasury of the United States." Readers may quite possibly find it a mind-boggling exercise to contemplate the incalculable millions of dollars which, after nearly two centuries of history, the states unquestionably owe the United States Treasury pursuant to this explicit provision of the Constitution.

The final language of the clause in question subordinates this entire machinery ("all such Laws"), with its throng of potential (and currently realized) evils,[22] to "the Revision and Controul of the Congress," with the unmistakable result that Congress could then, and still may today, do as they please about "interstate trade barriers." The continuance of these noxious schemes for the "Balkanization" of the nation, with their concomitant and expensive paraphernalia of "border patrols," "checkpoints," and all the rest of it, will be accurately perceived, proximately, as the choice and therefore the responsibility of the Congress, and, remotely, as the responsibility of those citizens who participate in the Constitutionally provided biennial electoral process.

The second of the three clauses to be discussed at this point is the Ex-post-facto Clause, which provides in blunt and unrestricted language that "no State shall pass any ex post facto Law." Among the three clauses under discussion in this section, this clause is unique by reason of the existence, elsewhere in the Constitution, of a parallel prohibition directed against the Congress of the United States.[23]

Whatever ex-post-facto laws were, then, the Framers undeniably intended them to be completely impossible under the Constitution, at both the national and the state levels of the government. In its literal meaning, an ex-post-facto law is any civil or criminal *retrospective* law, i.e., a law made after the doing of the things to which it relates and retroacting upon them.

Many readers may have felt some shock when they finished reading that last sentence, for until now they will most probably have entertained the unquestioning belief that the phrase "ex-post-facto laws" refers to *criminal* legislation only. This narrower meaning, however, was not the current meaning of the term when the Constitution was drawn at Philadelphia in 1787.

As a matter of fact, some of the most important antecedent events that led the Framers to include these two clauses in the Constitution had been of a *civil* character. The extreme dishonesty of some of the states' legislative acts—for example, the so-called "pine-barren law" of South Carolina, or the paper-money acts of Rhode Island—had been such as greatly to enhance the desirability of prohibiting such measures in the future.

As George Mason of Virginia, a delegate to the Federal Convention, predicted, however, the general prohibition against ex-post-facto legislation was the first Constitutional limitation to fall;[24] indeed, it did so before the national government was ten years old. The destructive surgery was performed on the national Ex-post-facto Clause, and by necessary logical consequence on the state Ex-post-facto Clause, by the Supreme Court of the United States in the famous case of *Calder* v. *Bull.*[25] In an opinion masterfully contrived by Associate Justice Samuel Chase, the meaning of these clauses was cut down to their present coverage of *criminal* ex-post-facto legislation *only.*

Closely paralleling the Imports and Exports Clause in this respect, the Ex-post-facto Clause is particularly illuminative of the intended generally subordinate position of the states in the total governmental scheme, as designed by the Framers of the Constitution. Whether civil or criminal, *all* state legislation of a retroactive character was completely prohibited. The parallel prohibition against the national legislature proved, unfortunately, to be one of the least wise measures of the Framers. The fact remains, nevertheless, that in this vast field of retroactive legislation, in no way limited in its potential subject-matter, the states were originally subjected to an unlimited Constitutional prohibition. The intended thrust of the Ex-post-facto Clause as against state legislative power will be seen to be of particular significance when it is connected with the third of the three clauses, to which we now turn.

This is the famous Contracts Clause, which provides that "no State shall . . . pass any . . . Law impairing the Obligation of Contracts."[26] If the reader has been influenced by the Supreme Court's decisions under this clause, or, rather, its decisions purportedly so-based, the clause will appear at first glance to apply only to contracts which have been "previously formed." There must be such a previously formed contract, the reader has probably been taught to believe, if there is to be any "Obligation" which *can be* "impair[ed]." In the ordinary use of the English words employed by the Contracts Clause, however, it is perfectly possible for "the Obligation of Contracts" to be "impaired" by a law that is passed *before* the making of the particular contracts which are affected by the law thus enacted. What, for example, would be meant by a provision that "no State shall pass any Law impairing the Actionability of violent Torts"? Does this mean that the torts whose actionability is in question must have been committed *prior* to the enactment of the legislation? Clearly, such is not the meaning. The reader will see the close parallel between the linguistic expressions here involved, for the "obligation" of contracts consists precisely in the "actionability" of breaches of those contracts. In other words, the "obligation of Contracts" within any particular legal system at any particular time is the resultant of all the then existing laws relating to the subject of contracts. Any law which, by making it more difficult to become "bound" by a contract, has the effect of diminishing the obligation of contracts in its totality "impairs the Obligation of Contracts" as of the time in question.

The language of the Contracts Clause, however, does not support the conclusion that *all* state legislation regarding contracts is prohibited. To state the issue in the simplest terms, what the states could, in 1789, and still can, do under this clause would be to enact legislation which *enhances* "the Obligation of Contracts." A state could, for example, by abolishing its local statute of frauds, greatly enhance "the Obligation of Contracts," or a state might abolish any requirement of consideration in the making of a contract, and such abolition of the requirement of consideration, by making it easier for persons to bind themselves through entering into contracts, would enhance "the Obligation of Contracts."

A further significant feature of the Contracts Clause, however, is that a parallel prohibition against the impairment of contractual obligation by the *national* legislature is *not* contained in the Constitution. In other words, if the states are prohibited from *all retroactive* legislation by the Ex-post-facto Clause, and the states are additionally prohibited from *all prospective* impairments of the obligation of contracts, the conclusion directly follows that Congress has an *exclusive power* over contracts legislation, subject to the unprohibited sector of state legislation just referred to in the preceding paragraph. When the reader recalls the extensive scope of contract legislation, and its fundamental connection with the whole field of the regulation of "Commerce among the several States," the natural conclusions are that the power of Congress "to regulate Commerce, with foreign Nations, and among the several States and with the Indian Tribes" is *exclusive* of state legislation, and, further, that the Constitution itself provides oblique internal evidence of the intended complete coverage of the nation's gainful economic activities.[27]

6

The foregoing materials may have suggested to readers the high probability that other articles, clauses, and provisions of the Constitution have, in the course of our nation's history, come to be interpreted as having a meaning very different from their meaning as intended by the Framers. The present section is the first of three which will be devoted to a brief survey ranging widely over the entire Constitution, a survey based on the unimpeachable view so cogently and concisely stated by a late member of the Supreme Court that "the Constitution itself, and not what [the] judges have said about it, is the ultimate touchstone of constitutionality."[28] The three sections will be devoted, in turn, to the three great "departments" of the national government, and the reader's particular attention will be directed to those specific provisions relating to the respective departments in which the greatest departures from the original and intended meanings have occurred.

One of the factors which exert important influence on the contours of any document will be the rules of interpretation generally followed at the time when the document is drawn.[29] Since the late eighteenth century, there has been a considerable change in American legal theory concerning this subject. In other words, were draftsmen to sit down at the present day to write a constitution for the United States, they would proceed in a very different fashion from that which was in fact pursued by the Framers in 1787. Almost surely, they would end up producing a document closely resembling the opaque language of insurance policies or corporate debentures.

One of the most striking differences is the reliance, by the eighteenth-century draftsmen, on the use of general words and general expressions. This was particularly the case in documents addressed to public understanding, as was obviously the case with the Constitution. Within this framework of general language, specific exceptions, qualifications, and provisions were inserted as the draftsmen felt them to be necessary, but of the modern, generally felt compulsion to leave virtually nothing to logical inference there were very few traces.

One of the rules of legal interpretation, fashionable in the eighteenth century, and perhaps equally fashionable at the present day, is the rule that *every* word of a document is to be given *some* significance.

The next point is somewhat more technical. Everyone recognizes that the congruence between "words" and "things" is not always complete. In his famous *Commentaries,* Blackstone phrased the matter in this language: "In general laws, all cases cannot be foreseen; or if foreseen, cannot be expressed: some will arise that will fall within the meaning, though not within the words, of the legislator; and others, which may fall within the letter, may be contrary to his meaning, though not expressly excepted. These cases out of the letter, are often said to be within the equity of an act of Parliament; and so, cases within the letter are frequently out of the equity."[30] The device employed, in the process of interpretation, to achieve or establish congruence between words and the things they refer to is termed the "equity of the statute," and, obviously, this will appear in two types. Blackstone's category of "cases within the letter, but out of [the legislator's] meaning" will be handled by the equity of "restraint," while Blackstone's other category, cases "within the [legislator's] meaning though not within [his] words," will be dealt with by using the equity of "fulfillment."

Another technique available in the eighteenth century, though much fallen out of use since that time, was the device of a preambular statement, in general terms, of the "purpose" or the "intent" of the draftsman.[31] Documentary interpretation is necessarily confined to the draftsman's language; no interpreter is expected or required to launch into either speculation or mind reading concerning any "purpose" or "intent" which the draftsman did not see fit to embody in words. Recourse to preambular statements, where available, would obviously be of great assistance to the interpreter in determining whether the equity of "restraint" or the equity of "fulfillment" is appropriate in interpreting the particular text before him.

A consideration of the Constitution will highlight the relevance of the foregoing materials. The Constitution, of course, has precisely the kind of preamble just referred to. This preamble recites the purposes, aims, objects, or goals which "We, the People" intend to achieve by adopting the Constitution. There are six verbs and six direct objects, as follows: "to form a more perfect Union; to establish Justice; to insure domestic Tranquility; to provide for the common defence; to promote the general Welfare; and to secure the Blessings of Liberty." These broad goals represent the tasks the people intended their government to perform, and the general proposition is abundantly clear that the Constitution confers upon the national government powers fully adequate to the accomplishment of these purposes. Suppose, for a moment, that the Constitution consisted *only* of the Preamble, articles simply establishing the three departments and governing election or appointment to them, and an article regulating amendments. Is it not clear that this excessively concise document would vest powers in the government adequate to the accomplishment of the Preamble's stated purposes or goals? Is it not equally clear that the addition of all the other detail, which the Constitution does in fact contain, does *not* have the effect of rendering the Preamble substantively inoperative?

The next step in the analysis is crucial. At the end of the list of congressional powers in Section 8 of Article I of the Constitution, there appears what was referred to during the ratification campaign as the "sweeping clause" and is today referred to as the Necessary and Proper Clause. After granting power to Congress "to make all Laws which shall be necessary and proper for carrying into Execution the foregoing Powers [of Congress]," the clause proceeds to grant to Congress an identical law-making power with reference to "all other Powers vested by this Constitution in the Government of the United States, or in any Department or Officer thereof." Two distinct classes of powers are clearly contemplated by this last provision: first, the powers vested in the separate departments or officers of the government, and, second, the powers vested in the "government of the United States" considered in the collective sense as the whole governmental structure. The only place within the four corners of the Constitution where any powers are explicitly vested in the government of the United States *as a whole* is, of course, the Preamble, whose language we have just looked at, with its six verbs and six direct objects.

It is important, in this connection, for readers to perceive that the Constitutional language just examined does *not* "sweep" into the hands of Congress *all* governmental power. For example, despite the preambular statement of the purpose of "establish[ing] Justice," this language does not empower Congress to decide particular lawsuits. That power is conveyed elsewhere, by the Constitution's grant of "the judicial Power" to the national judicial system. What the language does mean, however, is that if there is any statutory enactment necessary and proper to assist the courts of the entire country in the discharge of their duties, Congress is completely empowered (subject to all explicitly stated limitations in the Constitution) to enact any and all such laws.

We may consider another of the stated preambular objects of the government, namely, the "insur[ing of] domestic Tranquility." The language of the Necessary and Proper Clause does *not* confer on Congress any power to act as the conservator of the nation's internal peace and quiet. That function goes to the President, under the Constitutional grant of "the executive Power," together with presidential duty to "take care that the Laws be faithfully executed." Again, however, should the President stand in need of some legislative enactment in connection with his Constitutionally prescribed duties of "insur[ing] domestic Tranquility," the Congress is completely empowered, always subject to whatever explicitly stated limitations may appear elsewhere in the document, to provide such "necessary and proper" assistance to the President.

As we continue with our analysis of the Preamble of the Constitution, we note that two of the objects there stated are not explicitly assigned to any department or officer of the government, namely, the "form[ation] of a more perfect Union," and the "secur[ing of] the Blessings of Liberty." The nature of these two objects, obviously, is such that no single department or officer of the government possesses special competence in these areas. This is not to say, however, that no officer or department could ever have any occasion to derive direction or support for his or its work from these preambular elements.

The two preambular objects which remain for discussion, however, *are* explicitly stated in the Constitution to be express objects of the powers of Congress. The language which does this appears in Section 8 of Article I, which provides that the Congress shall have power "to pay the Debts and provide for the Common Defense and general Welfare of the United States."[32]

Throughout much of our national history, this language has been construed as stating the *purpose* of the immediately preceding grant of the power "to lay and collect Taxes, Duties, Imposts and Excises." The Constitution contains several provisions expressed in language which is conclusive against this "purposive" view.

As a matter merely of the wording of this provision, the reader will note that the phrase "in order to" does *not* precede the phrase "to pay the Debts." More important, however, is the fact that any interpretation of this clause as being expressive of the purpose of taxation generates severe and needless logical snarls and inconsistencies, rendering the Common Defence and General Welfare Clause either redundant or completely nugatory. Both of these results are improper under the rules of interpretation fashionable in the eighteenth century as well as the present day.

The congressional power granted by the language immediately following the Common Defence and General Welfare Clause is the power "to borrow Money on the credit of the United States." This language is quite unrestricted in its scope, which means that money may be "borrow[ed] on the credit of the United States" for any purpose which Congress may please, whether or not such purpose contributes to the common defense and general welfare of the nation. Any money thus borrowed, however, obviously constitutes a "Debt" of the United States, but Congress under its explicit debt-payment power can discharge those debts, and the unavoidable result is, therefore, that the Common Defence and the General Welfare Clause is rendered *nugatory*, completely ineffective as a limitation on the congressional power to tax.

To the reader, a way around that difficulty might seem to be found by resorting to the interpretive technique previously described in this section as the equity of "restraint." By this means, the borrowing power could be "restrained" to the objects recited in the Preamble to the Constitution. The difficulty is that the adoption of that view renders the Common Defence and General Welfare Clause *redundant*, for if this "restraint" can be brought in with reference to the borrowing power, it can equally well be brought in with reference to the taxing power. Since the Common Defence and General Welfare Clause *already* appears in the document, however, the importation of such "restraint" from the Preamble renders the clause a piece of purely redundant folly.[33]

No rule of legal interpretation, in the eighteenth-century or at the present day, compels the interpreter of any document to arrive at such indefensible and unsatisfactory results. He has had either to become entangled in a logical snarl, which there is no ground for attributing to the Framers, or—and this is directly violative of a rule of interpretation—in effect he has had to discard some parts of the draftman's language.

On the other hand, an interpretation of the Common Defence and General Welfare Clause as a separate and substantive grant of power to the Congress easily avoids all of these difficulties. Once more, the conclusion does *not* follow from this grant of inexhaustible power, under the Common Defence and General Welfare Clause, that the Congress of the United States may enact whatever legislation it pleases. This conclusion is unmistakably compelled by the many other words which appear in the document, to every word of which *some* meaning must be given, under both eighteenth-century and contemporary rules of interpretation.

As an illustration of this last point, we may consider the congressional power conveyed in the third grant of power following the Common Defence and General Welfare clause, namely, the power "to establish an uniform Rule of Naturalization, and uniform Laws on the subject of Bankruptcies throughout the United States." When these two clauses are read together they ground the unimpeachable conclusion that Congress may not Constitutionally enact a *non* uniform law of bankruptcy, however much in fact, or in the opinion of Congress, such a law would "provide for . . . the general Welfare of the United States."

Having gone this far in examining the list of congressional powers in Section 8 of Article I of the Constitution, we believe this phase of the discussion is appropriately rounded out with a consideration of the entire list of congressional powers.[34]

The long-prevalent orthodoxy embraces the belief that the powers of Congress were included in this "catalog" for the purpose of securing them to Congress as against the states. The general fact of the matter is quite otherwise. Surveying the catalog of congressional powers in its entirety, we perceive there are three factors, in varying combinations, which account for the appearance of the congressional powers in Section 8 of Article I.

One of the most important of these factors was the scope of the prerogatives of the British monarchy.[35] Of the problems which confronted the delegates to the Federal Convention, one of the most troublesome was how to fashion a republicanized and thoroughly Americanized counterpart of the British king. Many of the kingly powers, which would pass under an unrestricted general grant of "the executive Power" to the President, the Framers did not intend any American President to have. In the framework of the general language and the structure of the Constitution, the Framers had to introduce explicit language allocating these particular powers to the department which they wished to have them. A few examples of this are the congressional power "to promote the Progress of Science and useful Arts, by securing for limited Times to . . . Inventors the exclusive Right to their respective . . . Discoveries"; the power "to raise and support Armies"; and the power "to provide for calling forth the Militia to execute the Laws of the Union, suppress Insurrections, and repel Invasions."

A second factor which exerted considerable influence on the contents of the catalog of congressional powers was the prior existence of certain of these powers, in the same or different form, in the hands of the Continental Congress, under the Articles of Confederation.[36] Briefly stated, the situation in which the Framers found themselves was this: Since these powers were dealt with in what we may term the "old" or the "former" constitution, it was the part of wisdom for the Framers to make explicit provision with respect to these already-existing powers. At the very least, their specific action would preclude all potential arguments to the effect that, since the (old) Continental Congress possessed the power, and the new Constitution makes no reference to the power, the proper conclusion must therefore be that the "new" Congress does not possess the power in question. Under this category we may include such congressional powers as the power "to borrow Money on the Credit of the United States," "to coin Money, regulate the Value thereof, . . . and fix the Standard of Weights and Measures," and "to provide and maintain a Navy".

The third factor which influenced the powers as listed in the catalog was specfically dictated by the stylistic needs of the draftsmen. In a number of instances, they wished to state limitations on the powers of Congress, and in order to have some grammatical element to which the desired limitations could be attached, the corresponding grant of power had to be made explicit.[37] The important point in the present connection is that the reader clearly perceive the necessity of this procedure, for this necessity existed, *whether or not* any other language in the catalog conferred on the Congress general legislative power "to provide for the common Defence and general Welfare of the United States."

Many of the powers of Congress that appear in the catalog in Article I were inserted there for more than a single reason. Without multiplying examples, we may consider one item in the list of congressional powers which neatly combines two of these reasons. Congress is given a power "to constitute Tribunals inferior to the Supreme court." The first reason for its inclusion is to supply language to which the words of limitation can be attached: Congress may *not* establish tribunals which are *superior* to the Supreme Court. The second reason for its appearance is to remove the power from among the powers of the President and to transfer it to the Congress. The traditional learning, as recorded in Blackstone's *Commentaries*, held that the British king was the "fountain of justice" and therefore had the exclusive power to establish courts.[38] This being one of the royal powers the Framers did not wish any American President to have, the power was explicitly transferred to the Congress.

Readers need hardly be reminded that not all of the powers granted to Congress appear in Section 8 of Article I of the Constitution. The document refers to "all legislative powers *herein* granted." There are three Congressional powers granted at other points in the Constitution, and a particular analysis of these will throw considerable light on the quantum of the national governmental powers as provided for by that document.

The first of these powers relates to congressional power over the national electoral process. Section 4 of Article I deals with "the Times, Places and Manner of holding Elections for Senators and Representatives."[39] The Constitution provides that regulations of these matters "shall be prescribed in each State by the Legislature thereof"; at that point, the prevailing orthodoxy fails even to read the Constitution's language. Despite this firmly indurated custom of fragmented textual analysis, we cannot here avoid pointing out that the Constitution immediately goes on to provide that "the *Congress may* at any time by Law *make or alter* such Regulations, except as to the Places of chusing Senators." Only the third of those three nouns used by the Framers to specify the objects of this power needs to be explained in order for the reader to see that, once any state legislature has prescribed the *date* for the election, and the *places* where votes shall be cast, the legislature must, if their regulation of the franchise is to be meaningful, let alone effective, eventually answer the question of *who* is to appear on the prescribed date and cast their ballots at the prescribed places. Once the ambit of the required state legislation has been grasped by the reader, the correspondingly broad ambit of congressional power becomes crystal clear, as does the extremely narrow ambit of paramount state power over the *locale* of its legislature's meetings.

The Framers' pattern of provisions on the important subject of the national franchise deserves particular attention, as the first example of a device we shall see the Framers employing in other instances. The Constitution expressly lays on the state legislatures a duty to legislate: they "shall" prescribe regulations on this subject. However, Congress is expressly granted a power in effect to *rewrite* state enactments on the subject, or, should some state ever refuse to enact legislation regarding these topics, Congress may step in and *supply* the omission by national statute, except for the unique case of paramount state power: Congress may *not* prescribe where a state's legislature shall meet, for, as the reader will recall, the state legislatures were the bodies which "chose" the senators, under the original scheme.

A second example of this device, namely, placing state governments under a *duty* to do some particular thing, and giving Congress the *option* to legislate regarding the whole field, is supplied by Section 1 of Article IV. This appears from the language: "Full Faith and Credit *shall* be given in each State to the public Acts, Records, and judicial Proceedings of every other State.

And the Congress *may* by general Laws prescribe the Manner in which such Acts, Records and Proceedings shall be proved, and the Effect thereof."[40]

Article IV also supplies the third example of congressional powers conveyed by the Constitution in places other than section 8 of Article I. Section 4 of Article IV reads as follows: "The United States shall guarantee to every State in this Union a Republican Form of Government, and shall protect each of them against Invasion; and on Application of the Legislature, or of the Executive (when the Legislature cannot be convened) against domestic Violence."[41] Analysis of this constitutional provision returns us directly to the structure we earlier examined, namely, the combination of preambular language and the Necessary and Proper Clause. The Republican Government Clause is a clear example of a power *vested by this Constitution in the Government of the United States*, for no single department is particularly or exclusively charged with responsibility in the premises.

The subject-matter of the clause will repay our attentive consideration. Steering clear of a mass of metaphysical speculation, we can see that a "Republican Government" is, obviously, a government in which the franchise is broadly available. This does not mean that every person should be entitled to vote: there exists no cogent reason why children should have the vote nor is there any compelling necessity that persons suffering the misfortune of mental derangement should exercise the franchise. When the franchise is *not* in the hands of the great majority of qualified voters, however, the "Republican" character of a government is clearly impaired or reduced. The clause under discussion has commonly been thought to become applicable only when some citizen becomes possessed in an advanced degree of kingly ambitions, but it is surely an obvious thing that the powers of the national government properly come into play much earlier. ("An ounce of prevention. . . . ") Not to put too fine a point on the matter, "the Blessings of Liberty" are not "secured," as recurrence to the Constitution's Preamble will remind us, when the government sits on its hands and allows some political leader or even a political machine to become the government of a state, very largely as a result of tampering with the franchise. Once again, we emphasize the fact that the customary failure by the national government to exercise its many and extensive powers under the Republican Government Clause cannot in any way alter what the Constitution provides or the proper inferences therefrom regarding what has come to be referred to, in stately phrase, as "the delicate balance of our federal system."

The fact of the matter is this: the Constitution establishes no such fantasy as "the delicate balance of our federal system." In view of the existence of far-reaching and general congressional legislative powers, however, one important matter remains, which we must be on guard against misunderstanding. To state the point in the plainest terms, the possession by Congress of the kind of legislative power just described does not, *without additional language*, operate to deprive the states of their pre-1787 legislative powers. The small handful of *complete* interdictions of state power are specifically provided for in the Constitution ("No Sate shall . . ."). What the state governments *did* lose, by the people's adoption of the Constitution, however, was their pre-1787 "sovereignly" character. In other words, unless the Constitution provides for a specific interdiction of state legislation after 1789, state legislatures continue to enjoy the same ambit of legislative power, but this power now survives only until Congress has enacted its own legislation in the premises. At that juncture, as the result of the operation of the Supremacy Clause, state legislative power is *pro tanto* done away with, so long as the congressional legislation remains unrepealed and "occupies the field."

In summary, then, when the explicit Constitutional grant to Congress of power "to make all Laws which shall be necessary and proper for carrying into Execution" "all . . . Powers vested by [the] Constitution in the Government of the United States" is connected up with the Supremacy Clause, which completely subordinates the state governments and every state official, whether legislative, executive, or judicial in character, to the enactments of the national legislature, our earlier conclusion that the Constitution vests a general national legislative power in Congress, subject only to the tiny handful of detailed limitations stated in that document, is seen to be very greatly fortified.

7

The second of the great departments built into their Constitutional system by the Framers is, of course, the Executive, whose powers are vested in the President of the United States. The figure delineated in Article II of the Constitution is the British monarch, after being thoroughly democratized and Americanized at the hands of the delegates to the Federal Convention. As an early "states'-righter" most judiciously phrased the matter, "the student cannot fail to have remarked how many of the important prerogatives of the British Crown [were] transferred from the executive authority, in the United States, to the supreme national council in Congress."[42] The fashioning of this character, particularly with reference to the mode of his selection, was one of the most troublesome problems encountered during the proceedings at the Federal Convention. There is more than a little irony in the fact that the "foetus of a monarchy," about which fears were so eloquently voiced during the Convention's deliberations, by Virginia's Governor Edmund Randolph,[43] should have come close to achieving birth, during the last four or five decades of our history, in what has been so tellingly labeled "the imperial presidency"—this, despite the multitude of detailed provisions, in Article II and elsewhere in the Constitution, designed to prevent precisely that event.

In its broad outlines, Article II exemplifies the general scheme of draftsmanship employed by the Framers, namely, a general grant of power, followed with a mass of whatever specific provisions, limitations, and qualifications the Framers regarded as essential or desirable.

As a further exemplification of the technique of draftsmanship employed in handling the constitutional grant to Congress of "all legislative Powers," the reader will observe of Article II that, despite the vesting of a general grant of "the executive Power," specific powers are nevertheless expressed as belonging to the President, for the purpose of attaching some limitation to them. Three examples will be sufficiently illustrative of this point. First, the executive power to make treaties is specified as belonging to the President, thereby providing a grammatical basis for attaching the important anti-regal qualification that two-thirds of the senators present shall concur in the making of the treaties. Second, the normal appointing power of any executive is stated, to supply a basis for attaching an anti-monarchical limitation, namely, the requirement of the Senate's advice and consent. Third, the presidential power to grant reprieves and pardons for offenses against the United States is expressed, to supply a basis for stating the exception, namely, cases of impeachment.

Finally, we may also note in Article II a third instance of the Framers' employment of the same device, namely, the establishment of a duty incumbent on some branch of the government respecting some particular matter, coupled with the vesting of power in the Congress to legislate at their option regarding the same matter. The President "*shall*... appoint... all other Officers...whose Appointments are not...otherwise provided for...: but the Congress *may* by Law vest the Appointment of inferior Officers, as they think proper, in the President alone, in the courts of Law, or in the Heads of Departments."

We should also remember, in this scrutiny of the National Executive, that some very important Constitutional provisions concerning the presidential office do not appear in Article II. Our reference, obviously, is to the Constitutional provisions governing the President's participation in the national legislative process. These detailed provisions are brought together with the major body of provisions governing the congressional phase of this subject in Section 7 of Article I. The provisions respecting the President's veto power are particularly significant in the Constitutional delineation of the *intra*-governmental distribution of powers. In the face of a lengthy historical record to the contrary, every American school child is taught that our national government is a government of "three equal and coordinate branches." The Constitutional clauses now under discussion go a very long way in destroying this fairy tale, for there cannot be, nor has there ever been, the slightest doubt that Congress is empowered to override a presidential veto, and on numerous occasions has in fact done so, with the required special majority of both houses. Where one branch of the government can override another branch, any suggestion that those branches are co-equal and coordinate, merits only one appropriate adjective: ridiculous.

8

We come now to a consideration of the third great department of the national government, namely, the Judiciary. Our analysis of Article III will involve us in the examination of material rather more technical in its nature than is true in the cases of the other two departments which we have considered in the immediately foregoing pages. Our difficulties are enhanced by the fact that, from the very establishment of the national government, several important parts of Article III have never functioned—or been allowed to function—in anything remotely resembling their intended scope and plenitude. Understanding of Article III, at the present day, is also severely hampered by the fact that, as a result of the interaction of several highly complicated factors, the Supreme Court of the United States has for many years indulged in actions which are described with great accuracy by some phrases from the General Confession in the Book of Common Prayer. Not only have the Justices "done those things which [they] ought not to have done," but they have also "left undone those things which [they] ought to have done." This much-debated issue of "judicial review" will be the subject for discussion in the next section of this chapter.

The great purpose of the Framers in setting up the machinery described in Article III of the Constitution was, naturally, to provide a department of government charged primarily, though not exclusively, with what the Framers referred to in the Preamble as the "establish[ment] of Justice," for "[them]selves and [their] Posterity." As an important auxiliary to this highly desirable purpose, the Framers envisioned a pervasive reform of American legal systems as inherited from the late eighteenth century, a nationwide reform which, under their plan, was to have been achieved in the normal case-by-case process of judicial decision.

Several features of the American states' legal systems of 1787 form the background and supply the motivation for the reform thus contemplated by the Framers.[44] To begin with, these systems exhibited a high degree of diversity. The various colonial and state legislatures had been in operation over widely varying periods of time, and the issues to which they had directed their attention as well as the responses they had enacted during these varying intervals had been rather divergent. The statutory portions of the states' legal systems inevitably displayed an extreme heterogeneity.

The rules that formed a part of the colonial and state legal systems, of course, had not been produced exclusively by these legislatures. No colonial or state legislature had enacted a comprehensive code of law, and a wide array of questions had arisen which were therefore decided by the colonial and state courts on the basis of English "common law." This judicial activity constituted one of the most important phases of the phenomenon compendiously referred to as the "reception of English law" in the American colonies.

"What shall be admitted and what rejected, at what times, and under what restrictions," said Sir William Blackstone in his famous *Commentaries*, "must, in case of dispute, be decided in the first instance by their own provincial judicature, subject to the revision and control of the king in council."[45] The first American law reports were not published until 1789, and, as a consequence of their absence, the judicially created segments of American colonial and state legal systems were highly fragmentary, very imperfectly and inaccessibly recorded, and therefore most difficult to apply and to administer. Again, as in the case of the statutory components, the precise scope and detailed rules of this "American common law" exhibited a very considerable degree of diversity. The gradual introduction of system and order into this vast inherited conglomerate was an important part of the Framers' contemplated reforms.

Section 1 of Article III reads as follows: "The judicial Power of the United States, shall be vested in one supreme Court, and in such inferior Courts as the Congress may from time to time ordain and establish. The Judges, both of the supreme and inferior Courts, shall hold their Offices during good Behaviour, and shall, at stated Times, receive for their Services, a Compensation, which shall not be diminished during their Continuance in Office." We have here the first series of provisions which then were, and today still are, fundamental to the reforms contemplated by the Framers. The issue of judicial tenure and independence had been a matter for growing dissatisfaction in the American colonies ever since the middle of the eighteenth-century. Specific complaints on this topic had been included, the reader may remember, in the Declaration of Independence. The Framers, therefore, improved their opportunity, and prescribed permanent tenure and irreducible salaries for all the judges in their new national judicial system.

This section again shows the Framers providing considerable flexibility for congressional law-making, as quite clearly appears in the striking difference in the auxiliary verbs which they employed. Section 1 contains four instances wherein "shall" is employed, with its mandatory or imperative meaning, and only one instance wherein "may" appears, with its sharply contrasting permissive character. The result is that Congress is under a Constitutional duty to establish the Supreme Court of the United States, while enjoying an untrammeled option respecting the establishment of inferior federal tribunals.

Finally, the reader will note, in this section, the second appearance of the adjective "inferior" (its first appearance occurred in Section 8 of Article I). This repetition discloses the Framers' great concern to fortify, by Constitutional provisions, the "judicially supreme" position of their new Supreme Court, the single Constitutionally required holder of the national judicial power. With respect to all state courts and with respect to any other national courts, which Congress might or might not establish, the Supreme Court was to have and to exercise a judicial supremacy in the appellate decision of disputes, whether "at law" or "in equity."

The intended scope and the full dimension of the Framers' plans for the great purposes, referred to in previous paragraphs, namely, the "establish[ment] of Justice" and a comprehensive reform of American law, are carefully spelled out in Section 2 of Article III.[46]

The subject of this section, as of Section 1, is "the judicial Power" of the United States. We take as clear the proposition that judicial power is, and can be, exercised only in the actual decision of disputes ("Cases" and "Controversies") and, further, that these disputes will present two kinds of questions, namely, those of "Law" and of "Fact." An inspection of the catalog of cases, set forth in Section 2, in which the national "judicial Power" must be exercised, by direction of the Constitution, discloses the two broad categories employed by the Framers. These categories are defined in terms either of the subject-matter of the dispute or the identity of the parties to the dispute. One category, indeed—a response to particular circumstances of the late eighteenth century, but of vestigial significance at the present day—is defined by elements from *both* of these categories: "Controversies between Citizens of the same State claiming Lands under Grants of different States." The further plain fact is that these two large categories are not mutually exclusive nor are they cumulative in their requirement. In other words, whenever the *subject-matter* of some dispute brings it within the mandatory extent of the national judicial power, the parties' identity is without significance; conversely, whenever the *parties' identity* brings some dispute within the mandatory extent of the national judicial power, the subject-matter of their dispute is irrelevant.

The first extremely comprehensive category of cases to which the national judicial power must extend, is described by the following Constitutional language: "all Cases, in Law and Equity, arising under this Constitution, the Laws of the United States, and Treaties made, or which shall be made, under their Authority." The textually unavoidable consequence of this clause, interpreted in the eighteenth-century meanings of its language, is that there is *no* subject-matter, whether it be "legal" or "equitable" in its nature, which is beyond the intended reach of "the judicial Power of the United States."

The first branch of this initial category will, of course, include "all Cases, in Law and Equity" involving the meaning of the Constitution. This provision supplies the major share of whatever very slender Constitutional basis exists for "judicial review" of congressional enactments. Its effect, obviously, is not confined to this very narrow topic, however, for it sweeps within the mandatory ambit of "the [national] judicial Power" a vast number of cases presenting questions which do not, in any sense whatever, involve limitations on the powers of Congress, as, for example, cases arising under the Full Faith and Credit Clause.

With reference to both the recited preambular object of "establish[ing] Justice" and the contemplated legal reform, however, the second subcategory under this grant of judicial power is of vastly greater importance. This second category sweeps into the mandatory ambit of final decision by the Supreme Court of the United States "all Cases in Law and Equity arising under . . . the Laws of the United States," and this Constitutional language covers, *in addition to* all cases arising under congressional *statutes*, all cases involving every conceivable topic, subject, or branch of the *common law*, without exception.[47] Perhaps some readers, aware of a long line of decisions by the Supreme Court of the United States that adopt the contrary of this position, will be left breathless by the final part of the last sentence. The indisputable fact which wipes out any supposed Constitutional textual basis for the Supreme Court's view, however, is that this clause, when first reported to the Federal Convention by its Committee of Detail, was by its explicit language *limited* to cases arising under "laws passed by the legislature of the United States."[48] This provision in the committee's draft constitution came on for discussion by the Federal Convention on August 27, 1787. On that date, according to James Madison's famous notes, John Rutledge, of South Carolina, moved that the phrase "passed by the legislature" be struck out, and this motion was unanimously approved by the convention.[49] That the Framers, of whom a considerable number were professional lawyers, were not in any way hampered by ignorance or confusion regarding the existence of at least two varieties of "Laws," namely, statutory law and judicial or common law, admits of no doubt whatever. No construction, it seems clear, can correctly be placed on this undeniable action of the Federal Convention other than a recognition of the common law as one of the "Laws of the United States."

This conclusion is greatly strengthened by the language employed by the Framers in another part of the Constitution, namely, the Supremacy Clause.[50] In this latter clause, supreme-law status was conferred on "this Constitution, and the Laws of the United States *which shall be made* in Pursuance thereof, and all Treaties, made or which shall be made." Obviously, Congress is the only agency which can "make" laws in this sense (despite the deterioration of American juristic thought which has been and continues to be so very productive of pervasive confusion on this point); equally obvious is the fact that this language of Article VI *retains* the precise restriction which, on August 27, 1787, the Framers unanimously struck out of the draft version of Article III reported by the Committee of Detail.

The limited space available for this summary view of the Constitution's provisions respecting the national judicial system precludes discussion of the complete list of categories included in Section 2 of Article III. One category of the disputes defined in terms of the identity of the parties, i.e., the so-called "diversity jurisdiction," however, does require our particular attention. The Constitution extends "the [national] judicial Power" "to Controversies . . . between Citizens of different States," language which may appear to have no provision for those disputes which may arise "between Citizens of the *same* State." Under other language of Article III, however, machinery exists for supplying this apparent deficiency, and a brief consideration of the potential operation of the system will show what is meant, as well as make clear the great care and precision of the Framers in this matter.

Let us, then, suppose a case involving some point of common law, e.g., a question in the law of torts, which has arisen under this so-called "diversity jurisdiction." No congressional statute, or state statute, or local ordinance is involved in any way. Article III clearly requires that the Supreme Court of the United States "shall" determine this lawsuit, i.e., decide its constitutent questions of "Law" or of "Fact," and that it shall do this "supremely." For the second step in our example, let us suppose that the same point of common law now arises in a dispute between two citizens of the *same* state. By way of strengthening the example, we shall also assume that this second dispute has come up for decision in a *state court*. Whichever way this point of common law was settled by the Supreme Court in the prior case, in the mandatory exercise of its "diversity-of-citizenship" jurisdiction, one or the other of the parties in this second litigation will inevitably wish to argue that the earlier Supreme Court precedent is binding in the litigation now being considered. That precise question, namely, whether the Supreme Court's common-law precedent is binding on the state court in this second litigation, is itself, in the normal use of the English language, literally, a "Case, in Law or Equity, arising under [the] Constitution"—the very first branch of this Constitutionally mandatory jurisdictional category of "the [national] judicial Power."[51]

As the reader will at once perceive, this language "rounds out" the system, and enables the Supreme Court of the United States to maintain a uniformity in American case-law on a nationwide basis, thereby very greatly contributing to the achievement of the preambular object of "establish[ing] Justice." The fact will bear repeating that, should the Congress be of the opinion that the common-law rule, thus uniformly maintained throughout the country, does *not* contribute to "the establish[ment] of Justice," the Congress may, under its undoubted power "to make all Laws necessary and proper" to carry into execution the powers vested in *any other* officer or *department* of the government, namely, the national judiciary, alter that case-law rule by enacting a federal statute, thereby furnishing to all courts throughout the country a new rule for the decision of such cases in the future.

Nor will this further fact escape the reader's notice: this new statute activates the machinery of the Supremacy Clause, for, as the language of that clause makes unmistakably clear, congressional statutes form a part of the supreme law of the land and are binding on "the Judges in every State," "any Thing in the Constitution or Laws of any State to the Contrary notwithstanding." Should any judge in a state court not apply the congressional statute properly, that decision is, amongst other things, one of the "Cases in Law or Equity, arising under th[e] Constitution" and, all such "Cases" being within the mandatory ambit of the national judicial power, a channel is open to the Supreme Court to maintain nationwide uniformity in the judicial interpretation of the statute.

The final language of Section 2 of Article III that requires attention at this point in our discussion provides for a congressional power which at the present time is very generally misunderstood in many quarters. The problem involves the Supreme Court's appellate jurisdiction, "both as to Law and Fact," a jurisdiction from which the Congress has power to make "Exceptions."[52] As we have seen is true of many other sections of the Constitution, this section authorizes for Congress a considerable measure of flexibility in the arrangement which Congress establishes pursuant to the Constitution. With reference to this particular issue, Congress operates in the context of the Constitutional mandate that "in all cases affecting Ambassadors, other public Ministers and Consuls, and those in which a State shall be a Party, the Supreme court shall have original Jurisdiction." The reader will note that the word "only" does *not* appear in this Constitutional language.

The general misunderstanding, already referred to, involves the immediately following provision, which appears in these words: "In all the other Cases before mentioned, the Supreme Court shall have appellate Jurisdiction, both as to Law and Fact, with such Exceptions, and under such Regulations as the Congress shall make." The misunderstanding stems from incorrectly regarding as identical two things which are very different: (1) the "appellate Jurisdiction" of the Supreme Court, and (2) the "judicial Power" of the United States. Despite the undeniably extensive area of overlap between these two things, Congress is Constitutionally empowered to make "Exceptions" from the former *but not from the latter*. The contrary interpretation, which has grown to be so generally favored in these latter days, has generated, among other results, the completely *un*constitutional assignment of the decision of cases arising under federal statutes to what are known as "administrative tribunals," not a single one of which possesses the Constitutionally required attributes of permanent tenure and irreducible salary. Nor is that the end of the matter. In precisely the extent of this *un*constitutional assignment of the decision of disputes to administrative tribunals, the "judicial Power of the United States" does *not* extend, in the face of an explicit Constitutional mandate to the contrary, to "*all* Cases" arising under the [statutory] Laws of the United States." Finally, any interpretation which obviously requires the belief that competent draftsmen will go through a lengthy process of carefully defining in abundant detail the arrangements they intend to establish regarding the nation's judicial power, expressing this all in terms of a mandatory "shall," and then proceed by their final words to give one of the departments of government a Constitutional power to make unmitigated hash out of their carefully delineated system, is a demonstrably unsound interpretation.

The reader may well ask, then, what kind of an "Exception" could Congress Constitutionally make from the Supreme Court's "appellate jurisdiction"? The answer to that question is this: Congress could transfer some branch of the Supreme Court's appellate jurisdiction over to its "original Jurisdiction," for while the Court's "original Jurisdiction" cannot be *reduced* from its Constitutionally prescribed ambit, that ambit can be *increased*. In short, the Framers gave us a system in which the Supreme Court's Constitutionally granted supremacy may be postponed but not, at least not Constitutionally, destroyed. Congress may ordain and establish inferior tribunals as it wishes, and it may make exceptions of "Fact" such as those exemplified at the present day by the required jurisdictional amount for bringing a suit in the federal district courts, but any scheme whose effect is to withhold the "supreme" determination of any issues of questions of "Law" by the Supreme Court of the United States thereby infringes, in a clearly unconstitutional fashion, the undoubted Constitutional provision that "the [national] judicial Power shall extend to all *Cases in Law and Equity*, arising" in the many categories specified by Article III of the Constitution.

9

The foregoing summary review of the original and intended meanings of the Constitution provides the reader with the main outlines of the Constitutional system, an essential background for our discussion of the persistent and much-debated question of "judicial review." The necessity for this discussion arises, not so much from its role as designed and intended by the Framers, but from the vastly inflated and highly destructive role which judicial review of congressional enactments has played, and continues to play, in American constitutional doctrine and practice. This role may have the unfortunate consequence of misleading the reader into two quite erroneous views, first, that that Framers set up the Supreme Court to decide finally what the Constitution means, and, second, that careful attention to the words of the Constitution is, consequently, a misdirection of the reader's interest and energies.

One quantitatively significant aspect of this question of "judicial review," namely, the Supreme Court's review of the acts of the state legislatures, we may omit entirely from this discussion, for the Supremacy Clause in Article VI, after specifying the three constituent parts of "the supreme Law of the Land," goes on to provide that "the Judges in every state shall be bound thereby, any Thing in the Constitution or Laws of any State to the Contrary notwithstanding," and concludes by binding "Members of the several State Legislatures and all executive and judicial officers...of the several states" "to support [the] Constitution."

The reader should also take care, lest his judgment be wrenched into distortion by the Supreme Court's long-established practice of reviewing acts of Congress for "constitutionality." Our present subject being the Constitution of 1787, "and not what [the] judges have said about it,"[53] the distinction introduced earlier in this chapter,[54] namely, between "law" and "history"—or between "authority" and "evidence"—is of particular relevance at this point. If the reader begins to sense the possible emergence of the conclusion that, over the years of our national history, the Supreme Court's performance has been what can only be characterized as a lengthy career in the distortion, misconception, and misconstruction of the Constitution of the United States, that conclusion must simply be faced, without anger, tears, or lamentations.

Regardless of the particular label employed for the description of judicial review, whether this word be "duty," "power," "right," or whatever, the Constitution clearly contemplates the possibility, within a very much *narrower* ambit than is generally recognized at the present day, of a Supreme Court decision that some piece of congressional legislation is "unconstitutional." Fundamentally, this possibility results from the Constitution's provisions regarding the components of "the supreme Law of the Land." As one of those three elements, the Constitution contains very specific limitations on some few of the powers of Congress. In the foregoing pages, we have discussed some of these specific limitations, as well as the several elements of the Constitution which vest Congress with general legislative power "to provide for the common Defence and General Welfare of the United States," always subject, of course, to any specifically expressed limitations on the other particular powers of Congress. As the reader will see from glancing at the text of the Constitution, these very specific limitations are, in general, not the kind of restrictions which Congress would, with any frequency, be much interested in transgressing. Why, for instance, should Congress enact a *non*uniform bankruptcy law? For another example, what desirable purpose would be served by establishing "Tribunals" which are *not* inferior to the Supreme Court?

Let us assume, however, that a majority of the members in each of the houses of Congress disobey their solemn oath "to support [the] Constitution," and squarely in the face of the Constitutionally based objections which, we may quite safely assume, will have been urged in committee hearings, in the press, and on the floor of each house, approve a bill which transgresses one of these few specifically stated limitations. Let us assume, further, that the Executive violates the Constitutionally prescribed presidential oath "to preserve, protect, and defend the Constitution" and, instead of vetoing the bill, signs it into law.

At a date subsequent to this rather melancholy cumulative record of undeniable misbehavior by national lawmakers, the congressional statute is invoked by a party to some litigation in which the particular statutory point is unmistakably involved, and in due course this litigation comes before the Supreme Court for final determination by that tribunal. Confronting two flatly contradictory rules within the corpus of "the supreme Law of the Land," the Supreme Court clearly has no choice in this instance but to "support [the] Constitution," as each of the Justices, for many years, has solemnly sworn to do, and therefore to deny effect to the "unconstitutional" congressional enactment which has come before them.

Unimpeachable though this decision by the Supreme Court undeniably is, however, it may prove not to be the end of the matter. Let us now take this hypothetical case one step further, and suppose that the Congress, instead of bowing to this decision, takes serious umbrage and decides, as it were, to put the Supreme Court "in its proper place." In the subsequent committee deliberations regarding the ways and means of carrying their purpose into execution, two lines of strategy will form the topics of discussion. The following brief analysis of this committee's deliberations will highlight for the reader the extremely vulnerable situation of the Supreme Court in this hypothetical "grave constitutional crisis."

In the first place, the Supreme Court's position is vulnerable because there is no Constitutional specification of the *number* of its members. Those readers who can remember the business, from having lived through the years in question, or who have subsequently read or heard about it, will entertain no doubt as to the complete constitutionality of the proposal to "pack" the Supreme Court, offered forty years ago by the late President Franklin Delano Roosevelt. The fact will bear emphasis, that the political desirability, the political wisdom, of President Roosevelt's proposal is not under discussion at this point. The prior fluctuations in the number of Supreme Court justices, and several instances of particular appointments made to the Court, combine to make unmistakably clear that "packing" the Supreme Court was not one of President Roosevelt's many innovations, and that he was not to be the last President to conduct political experiments along these fascinating lines. In other words, having shown itself "obstreperous" in our hypothetical case of an "unconstitutional" congressional enactment, the Supreme Court can be taught to know its place by being "packed" with a sufficient number of "right-minded" justices.

Should this line of strategy, for whatever reason, be deemed ineligible, the committee could choose to attack through the second vulnerable point in the Supreme Court's position. This second vulnerability grows out of the ineluctable fact that the members of the Supreme Court are in no way exempted by the Constitution from the power of impeachment, which as a matter of equally ineluctable fact, rests in the hands of Congress, and, as we have lately been informed by a President who was in a position to speak authoritatively about these matters, Congress can impeach for whatever reason it pleases.[55] The melancholy fact that employment of this salutary device was apparently rejected in practice at an early date in our national history is completely devoid of significance in the present connection, for our concern is with the Constitution which was given us by the Framers in 1787, not with the subsequent developments purportedly under that document. In brief, then, belief that the Framers could have set up such an extremely vulnerable agency as a "guardian" of the Constitution, or as a "watchdog" against the very agency that can move against it with such lethal impact, plainly stretches credibility to the breaking point.

A third, and perhaps subordinate, aspect of this problem deserves brief attention at this point. Whatever beliefs or views the reader may entertain regarding the class structure of this nation in the late eighteenth century, no grounds exist for imputing to the Framers any wish to incorporate in their proposed national governmental system such a thoroughly undemocratic element as the Supreme Court, with lifetime appointments (during "good Behaviour") at Constitutionally irreducible salaries, has come to be. In the first place, the Framers entertained no illusions whatever about any special competence on the part of judges concerning the wisdom or the desirability of legislative measures.[56] Moreover, the Framers were much more democratic than that. One of the great reforms of the legislative branch in the system as proposed by the Framers was the direct popular election, every two years, of one of the houses in the national legislature. This constituted a very considerable advance over the British parliamentary system, as this was then known to the Framers. The reader should entertain no doubt that the Framers were concerned that no rotten pocket boroughs, a phenomenon in the contemporary English scene with which they were fully familiar, should develop within this nation. They manifested their concern by their provisions in the Constitution for a decennial enumeration of the population, and reapportionment in the House of Representatives to reflect that decennial census. In addition, the Framers, as we know, vested in Congress a general superintending power over the general soundness and the proper functioning of the electoral system in this country, with their provisions about regulating the "Times, Places, and Manner of holding Elections for Senators and Representatives." Finally, the Framers made it a duty incumbent upon "the United States"—necessarily, "the government of the United States"—to "guarantee to every State in [the] Union a Republican Form of Government," and vested the government of the United States with a plenitude of all the legislative, executive, and judicial powers necessary and proper for the achievement of this very desirable object. In the face of these many arrangements for a "republican government," to espouse the view that the Framers would, on the one hand, set up a thoroughly democratic system, delineated in copious detail, and then, on the other hand, set up a very tiny oligarchy of merely appointive judges with permanent tenure and irreducible salary to overturn the work of this democratic national legislature, is in effect to accuse the Framers of suffering a severe case of schizophrenia. Such an accusation has not the slightest basis, in the Constitution or anywhere else.

The palpable want of fit between the Constitution's system of government and the doctrine, practice, or institution of judicial review of acts of Congress, as this exotic and carcinogenic plant has blossomed in these latter days, has had the effect of stimulating some students to discover or, rather, to confect either a defense of, or a rationale for, that institution.

One branch of this frenetic activity has been the ransacking of the materials of history in a search for pre-Constitutional "precedents" for judicial review. The end result of this intensive canvassing is a handful of no more than nine different cases, from eight different states. In a chapter of the second volume in this series, these nine cases were fully reviewed for the reader.[57] The essential substantive point which emerges from that analysis is that the subject-matter involved in the two or three authentic precedents represented legislative attempts to invade the courts' own prerogatives under the constitutions of those states; in other words, attempts to restrain the courts from the discharge of their peculiar functions in the way that was required by those constitutions.

This brings us to the principal area with respect to which the Framers contemplated judicial review of congressional legislation. This matter goes particularly to enforcing the Constitution, as against Congress, with respect to the contours of the national judicial system. The reader will recollect the extended series of mandatory provisions in Article III of the Constitution. The rights of "the [national] judicial Power" which grow out of these provisions, were given it by direct act of the people in the Constitution. The indicated conclusion would, then, appear to be that the Framers expected the Supreme Court, as the *one* required holder of "the judicial Power of the United States," to exercise its Constitutionally vested rights without regard to any acts of Congress which would unconstitutionally interfere with them. The historical fact that the Supreme Court has never fully done this cannot alter in the slightest degree what the Constitution says, or what the duties of the national judicial system, under its provisions, actually are.[58]

If, for a moment, we extend our view beyond the original Constitution of 1787, and consider the amendments shortly thereafter incorporated in the Constitution, the reader will notice how very many of the amendments known as the Bill of Rights are concerned with the exercise of judicial power, most particularly in matters of the administration of criminal law sanctions. The amendments, of course, form a part of "the supreme Law of the Land" and are, therefore, binding upon all government officials, on both national and state levels. All disputes which raise the question of official observance of, or compliance with, these limitations are, of course, and in the most literal sense of the words, "Cases, in Law or Equity, arising under this Constitution," and *all* of these cases are, as the reader knows, within the mandatory reach of the national judicial power. Despite the expanded area for judicial review of both congressional statutes and state legislative enactments, most of the Bill of Rights consists of limitations on power which legislatures will not frequently be greatly interested in transgressing. Should the nation, as the result of profound changes in the cultural traditions which now support the privileges and immunities of American citizens, ever reach the point where legislators *are* greatly interested in transgressing these limitations, the existence of the amendments, the Supreme Court, and judicial review will have not the slightest impact upon the course of affairs.

10

The subject of our discussion, in the preceding pages, is the Constitution of 1787, *not* "what [the] judges have said about it." Very shortly after the ratification of the Constitution, as readers are well aware, a number of amendments were adopted, and one of the amendments may generate a major obstacle to readers' comprehension of the Constitution of 1787. The amendment in question, of course, is the Tenth Amendment, which reads as follows: "The powers not delegated to the United States by the Constitution, nor prohibited by it to the States, are reserved to the states respectively, or to the people." The generally received orthodox view at the present day is that this amendment makes impossible the existence of general national legislative authority in the Congress. The matter clearly deserves our further attention.[59]

We may begin by considering briefly some remarks made, in the House, by a representative from Virginia, on June 8, 1789, when he moved the propositions which were to become the first ten amendments. "I find, from looking into the amendments proposed by the State conventions," said Mr. Madison, "that several are particularly anxious that it should be declared in the constitution, that the powers not therein delegated should be reserved to the several states. Perhaps words which may define this more precisely than the whole of the instrument now does, may be considered as superfluous. I admit," James Madison went on, "they may be deemed unnecessary; but there can be no harm in making such a declaration, if gentlemen will allow that the fact is as stated. I am sure I understand it so, and do therefore propose it."[60] We have, then, Madison's explicit statement that, in proposing this particular amendment, he quite literally intended no change from the original Constitution of 1787 which had, less than a year before he spoke, been adopted by the people of the United States.

The first thing to be considered in our analysis of the Tenth Amendment is the undeniable fact that the words "expressly" and "exclusively" do *not* appear in the amendment. This absence, however, is not the result of ignorance or inadvertence on the part of its draftsmen, for during the progress of Mr. Madison's amendment through the legislative process, in the House as well as in the Senate, several attempts were made by the opponents of the measure to insert the word "expressly" in the amendment. As its final text shows, however, their attempts did not meet with success. The insertion of the word "expressly," meaning a specific grant of power, would, of course, have operated to revive the infamous Article II of the Articles of Confederation, in which the word *did* appear. The purpose and the effect of that Article II had been to preclude any use of the "equity of fulfilment" in interpreting the Articles of Confederation, and was itself one of the thoroughly unsatisfactory arrangements which had finally led to the meeting of the Federal Convention.

The second fact about the Tenth Amendment which requires attention is that the word "retained" does *not* appear in it; the word which does appear is "reserved." The draftsmen of the amendments were obviously aware of the existence of the word "retained," for they used the word in the Ninth Amendment. This amendment reads as follows: "The enumeration in the Constitution, of certain rights, shall not be construed to deny or disparage others retained by the people." The significance in this choice of language for the Tenth Amendment lies in a difference between the two verbs which is more clearly apparent in a rather traditional situation, namely, the conveyance of real property, where an easement or a right of passage over one part of the real estate ends up, as it were, in the hands of the grantor. If the right-of-way was in existence *prior* to the conveyance in question, the grantor is said to "retain" the easement; if, however, this right-of-way or easement was created *for the first time* in the conveyance in question, the language in the conveyance speaks of "reserving" the easement.

With this background, we may turn to the language of the Tenth Amendment. The amendment speaks of powers *not* delegated, and this fact at once raises the obvious question, What powers *are* delegated? As the reader is aware, the powers delegated by the Constitution to the national government are broad, comprehensive, and quite general in their character. We refer, of course, to the power resulting to the national government under the Preamble, and most particularly to Congress, under the Common Defence and General Welfare Clause, read in conjunction with the Necessary and Proper Clause, which latter explicitly grants power to Congress to make laws to assist the carrying into execution of all the powers vested by the Constitution in the government of the United States or in any officer or department of that government. When all-inclusive powers of that extensive character have been delegated, the conclusion follows that there is, literally, nothing left which the amendment could possibly "reserve" to the states. The reader will at once perceive that Mr. Madison meant exactly what he had said: he proposed no change in the Constitutional scheme as it stood at the moment when he moved what were to become the first ten amendments.

To state the point concisely, then, the received meaning of the Tenth Amendment is based almost entirely on a kind of verbal sleight-of-hand. If the process of interpretation is begun from the premise that the national government is a government of strictly enumerated, narrowly confined, fragmentary grants of power, many of which were given to secure the powers as against the states, the inevitable consequence of that erroneous premise is a mind-set, a preemptive predisposition, which leads to a severely distorted interpretation of the Tenth Amendment.

We conclude our description and analysis of the Constitution as it came to us from the hands of its Framers in 1787. What the Framers had done, in large outline, was to return to the familiar pre-Revolutionary British imperial system, substituting Congress for Parliament, the American presidency for the British monarchy, and, undoubtedly influenced by Montesquieu's theories, setting up a third, but far from coordinate and equal, branch of the government. This American, national, and republicanized substitute for the English, colonial, and monarchical system of the pre-Revolutionary days was not the repository of fragmentary, partial powers, as present-day "constitutional" dogma would have us believe, but instead was quite generally empowered to achieve the six great objects stated by the people in the Preamble to their Constitution, subject to the tiniest handful of particular and specific restraints on the powers of the new national legislature. The chapters and pages which follow recount the history of the events, institutions, and politics that together constitute the background of the Federal Convention of 1787, whose members drafted, and offered to their fellow citizens for their ratification, a Constitution with the character and contours which have been sketched for the reader in this chapter.

Part I
The Articles of Confederation

CHAPTER II

The Early Attempts to Devise a Governmental System: Herein of the First and Second Continental Congresses

1

THE full-length portrait of *The British Empire before the American Revolution*, which we have from the pen of its distinguished historian, the late Lawrence Henry Gipson, occupies thirteen stately volumes of text, notes, maps, and plates. The creation of this multivolume classic engaged its author for almost half a century, from the formulation in 1924 of his original plan for the series to the publication in 1967 of its concluding volume. A rich conspectus of meticulously researched and lucidly presented detail, Professor Gipson's masterful series provides a broad-dimensioned background for the problem with which the present volume is concerned, a problem which is appreciably narrower in scope.

The problem just mentioned is fundamental to the subject of these volumes, for the Constitution of the United States was unquestionably the ultimate response made by the American people to a crisis which developed, over a period of little more than ten years, from what initially appeared to be a small rift in the web of the British imperial system into a full-scale rending of that fabric—the declaration and subsequent achievement of American independence by military action. Any history must necessarily be commenced at some point in space and time, so the appropriate baseline for this volume is a sketch, unavoidably compressed within narrow limitations of space and detail, of the British imperial system, with particular reference to the British colonies on the Western Atlantic littoral, around the middle and late 1770s.

As a matter of fact, the unqualified label of "system" may suggest to the reader overtones which are rather more "systematic" than is entirely appropriate for the description of an entity which was so thoroughly permeated by asymmetry and variation. As is true of the development of virtually every human social system, the growth of this imperial structure was never systematic, nor could it have been so, thanks to the multitude of independently varying elements—institutional, economic, military, and personal—whose complicated interaction created the structure. From the perspective of an appropriate level of general outline, however, we believe it possible to describe adequately the structure of the British imperial system, and the place therein of the thirteen American colonies.

41

As a sequel to the "Glorious Revolution" of 1689, and certainly after 1696, the statute books of Great Britain clearly and unambiguously provided that the overarching, supreme element of this highly variegated system was the British Parliament. Embodying the official doctrine, the statute particularly declared "that all laws, by-laws, usages, and customs, which shall be in practice in any of the plantations, repugnant to any law, made or to be made in this kingdom, relative to the said plantations, shall be utterly void and of none effect."[1] On this basis, and by the midpoint of the eighteenth century, the British Parliament's exercise of its all-embracing jurisdiction had produced an extensive list of particular statutes. Reflecting the now-familiar gap between "law on the books" and "law in action"—if we may, for the moment, use language quite undreamt of in the eighteenth and previous centuries—all of these parliamentary statutes, however, even when considered in their totality, did not form a body of legislation completely and factually coextensive with the Parliament's potential jurisdiction, as claimed in Great Britain and, in very considerable parallel measure, recognized in the American colonies.[2]

In their thinking about this accumulated imperial "pattern," the great majority of colonial Americans exhibited a more or less untroubled acceptance, indeed, most probably, an unthinking and serenely unreflective acquiescence, until 1765. In that fateful year, however, the colonists received a rather rude shock, when the British Parliament enacted the Stamp Act, intending thereby some measure of relief for the British taxpayers who were at the time staggering under the immense costs of what Professor Gipson has called "the Great War for the Empire,"[3] then recently concluded by the Treaty of Paris in 1763. For our present inquiry, we need not consider in detail the circumstances surrounding the enactment of this measure, or the resistance exhibited toward it in the American colonies, which led to its repeal by the British Parliament.

Beyond any serious doubt, however, the most significant element in the entire series of transactions was the occasion provided for the Parliament—whose attention was now, for the first time, forcefully directed to the point in question—to "crystallize" the relevant element in the "official" orthodox doctrine regarding the British imperial system, at least as the Parliament was pleased to conceive of this doctrine. The British Parliament, which for so long had seemed to the colonists to be their friend, had committed an act which Americans, for a variety of personal as well as political reasons, came to regard as most "unfriendly." Parliament, it was true, had repealed the Stamp Act, to rather general rejoicing by the American colonists. However, Parliament had thereupon, in the next succeeding act as printed in the British statute book, crystallized their thoughts in the famous "Declaratory Act," in the following measured language: "That all his Majesty's colonies and plantations in America have been, are, and of right ought to be, subordinate to and dependent upon the Imperial Crown and Parliament of Great Britain; who have full power and authority to make laws and statutes of sufficient validity to bind the Colonies and people of America, subjects of the Crown of Great Britain, in all cases whotsoever."[4]

On the American side of the Atlantic, however, the general state of affairs never completely returned to the pre-1765 position. The years immediately following the British Parliament's repeal of the Stamp Act were in general marked by a relative calm on both sides of the Atlantic. This uneasy calm was eventually to prove thoroughly deceptive, for in the year 1773, the British Parliament, with a view to improving the deeply troubled affairs of the British East India Company, enacted the so-called "Tea Act."[5] Despite its well-intentioned motivation (when regarded from at least some viewpoints), this parliamentary enactment was a major factor in triggering the famous Boston Tea Party of December 17, 1773, with its notorious but entirely lawless destruction of some hundreds of chests of the East India Company's tea. Less than a decade previously, Parliament had been prepared to, and did in fact, repeal one of their enactments. In this new instance, however, having only recently taken a line of high and therefore inflexible principle, by staking out their unlimited claim of power to bind the American colonies "in all cases whatsoever," Parliament did *not* repeal the "Tea Act."

Quite the reverse. Parliament's reaction was manifested in a series of angry enactments which came, relatively promptly thereafter, to be compendiously referred to by the colonists as the "Intolerable Acts." There were, in all, five parliamentary statutes thus characterized, three of which were of immediate concern to the citizens of Massachusetts only, while the remaining two were of great interest to all American colonists.

Of the three enactments dealing directly with the Province of the Massachusetts Bay, the first, enacted on March 25, 1774, was the Boston Port Bill.[6] Under its terms, the port of Boston was closed, as of June 1, 1774, to all vessels bound to or from the port, with the exception of vessels from other parts of America carrying necessary food and fuel to the inhabitants. This "blockade"—and no milder term can be accurate—was to be carried out by the British navy, and would continue in effect until such time as the town's citizens should pay for the tea destroyed in the "Tea Party" held in the previous December, and make other specified satisfactions to royal officials and other sufferers in the Boston disorders.

The second statute, formally entitled an "Act for the Impartial Administration of Justice"—bluntly referred to by the affected citizens as "the Murder Act"—conferred on the colony's governor authority to transfer to some other colony, or even to England, the trial of any magistrate or other person, indicted in Massachusetts for murder or other capital crime, where the alleged offense had been committed in the performance of the accused's duty and where, in addition, it appeared to the governor that a fair trial could not be obtained within the colony. The statute also provided for the compulsory attendance, at public expense, of all witnesses desired either by the prosecutor or the accused.[7] The act would seem to have been a more or less routine measure of government—an attempt, in the existing circumstances, to secure a fair trial for accused persons of the classes specified in the act—but, in the excited propaganda of the times, it was attacked as unmitigated tyranny.

The third of the parliamentary statutes designed for theMassachusetts Bay Colony, however, exhibited a very different character. Under its terms, a rough and heavy hand was exerted for the purpose, as disclosed in the statute's title, of "the better Regulating the Government of Massachusetts-Bay."[8] This "better Regulation" took the form of various nullifications and alterations of the provincial charter for Massachusetts. Chief among these innovations was the provision that the members of the governor's council of Massachusetts should no longer be elected by the General Court, but should thenceforth be appointed by the King and hold their offices "for and during the [royal] pleasure." In addition to this most unwelcome rearrangement of the province's governmental structure, the act provided that the judges of the inferior courts, the province's attorney general, all sheriffs, and sundry other officials should be appointable, and removable, at the royal governor's pleasure. Finally, and this was the most inflammatory and devastating innovation of all, the act provided that no town, district, or precinct meeting of the citizenry should thereafter be held without the governor's express consent.

That such parliamentary action came rather speedily to be characterized as "intolerable" in *all* of the American colonies should not surprise the reader. Eight years previously, the British Parliament had stated its claim to the power to legislate bindingly for the colonies "in all cases whatsoever." And now this new statute was at hand to provide an unblinkable instance of precisely what was included in this asserted power. The "intolerability" consisted not so much in the royal appointment of the governor's council, for many of the other colonies had long known such a system, but rather in the unilateral exercise of power affecting so directly and so intimately the political system of the colony. If this specific example were within the ambit of "all cases whatsoever"—and the reader cannot entertain the slightest doubt but that it was included—then no great effort on the part of any American colonist was required to grasp the fact that literally nothing, including the basic right to choose representatives to any or all of the colonial legislatures, was secure.

The first of the two parliamentary statutes of great interest to *all* American colonists was the Quartering Act,[9] which provided that, regardless of the locations of barracks in the colonies, troops might be forcibly quartered, for the immediate future, "where[ver] their presence [might] be necessary and required." In view of its intended generality of application throughout the colonies, this act appeared in rather plain terms to betray a parliamentary expectation of general trouble and a firm intention on the part of the home government to employ military force everywhere.

Contributing far more to the feeling of "intolerability," however, the other act, passed "to make more effectual provision for the government of the

[Canadian] province of Quebeck," most probably seemed to the great majority of American colonists the most amazing, not to say "intolerable," of this entire series of enactments by the British Parliament.[10]

Despite its characterization by colonial Americans as "intolerable," the Quebec Act is in one sense incorrectly included among the responses made by the British Parliament to the disorders in the province of the Massachusetts Bay. Rearrangements in the system of government for the province of Quebec had been under consideration in Parliament for some time prior to the outbreak of disorder at Boston.[11] Due in considerable measure, then, to the quite fortuitous timing of its enactment, the Quebec Act assumed its prominent position in the parliamentary enactments familiarly referred to as the "Intolerable Acts."

The Quebec Act was a fairly complex piece of legislation. Considering first what we may term its purely "provincial" aspects, its provisions introduced several fundamental alterations in the governmental system which had been established for the province at the conclusion of the war with France. Under the royal proclamation of 1763, the provincial governor had the power to summon a representative assembly and to legislate with its consent, together with the consent of the provincial council. This element of popular representative participation in provincial government was replaced with a power which enabled the governor to legislate simply with the consent of the council. Again, the royal proclamation had made provision for the introduction of English law into the province, and this was now discarded and replaced with the old civil law of France. One immediate consequence of this particular alteration was the revival of the previous onerous seigneurial rights which the *noblesse* of Quebec had enjoyed against the peasantry. A change of a much more disturbing character under the Quebec Act was that the sanctions of the British government were lent to all the "accustomed dues and rights," within the province, of the Roman Catholic clergy, though carefully limited "to such persons only as sh[ould] profess the said religion."[12]

However disturbing or ominous this pattern of pervasive rearrangements may have appeared to American colonists throughout the length of the Atlantic seaboard, colonial Americans perceived a massive threat in the last of the provisions in the Quebec Act to be noted here. Suddenly and without notice, the Quebec Act added to that province all of the land in what is now the Canadian province of Ontario plus all of the lands north and west of the Ohio River in the region known to Americans as the Northwest Territory. Great Britain had long laid claim to much of this territory as forming parts of its various American coastal colonies. The colonists themselves, of course, had so regarded these lands, and while these rich acres had for the moment been technically reserved from further settlement by the colonists (the Proclamation Line of 1763), the lands were generally regarded as a future field for American expansion. Now, under the "intolerable" Quebec Act, the coastal colonies were to be generally confined to their limits as these existed in 1774, hemmed in along their western borders by a province featuring an arbitrary system of government and a population the majority of which adhered to the Roman Catholic persuasion, a faith, quite surprisingly, to be henceforth fostered under the British aegis—in short, a system so very "un-British" in many of its aspects as to seem unbelievable to the majority of eighteenth-century Americans.

2

Strongly motivated by their perceptions of the threat embodied in this series of parliamentary enactments, which the Congress would shortly characterize as "a system formed to enslave America,"[13] all of the colonies, except Georgia, sent delegations to the sessions of the First Continental Congress, which met in Carpenter's Hall, Philadelphia, from September 5 until October 26, 1774. Despite the caution-breeding novelty of this meeting, and the tensions inherent in the initial stages of almost any human collaboration, this Congress, during its relatively short life, managed to complete a number of elegant and important epistolary enterprises, together with some few other pieces of more substantial business. Although a complete review of the transactions of this Congress is obviously neither necessary nor appropriate for the purposes of the present volume, three acts of the Congress, all of which were widely known throughout the country at the time, are particularly relevant to the project of this book.

On Wednesday, September 28, 1774, almost precisely at mid-point in the life of the Congress, Joseph Galloway, a delegate from Pennsylvania, could restrain himself no longer. He had "long waited with great patience," Galloway said, "under an expectation of hearing some proposition which should tend to [the] salutary and important purpose [of restoring harmony between Great Britian and the Colonies]."[14] Instead of this, and "to his great mortification and distress," a month had been spent in "fruitless debates on equivocal and indecisive propositions." Galloway thereupon proceeded to voice his sentiments "without the least reserve" and, having done this, laid before the Congress the famous Galloway Plan.[15] Writing in exile some six years after the event, Galloway reports that "warm and long debates immediately ensued on the question, Whether [the plan] should be entered in the proceedings of Congress, or be referred to further consideration.... The question was at length carried by a majority of one Colony."[16] Despite this narrowly favorable vote, however, the Congress did not subsequently deliberate on the plan thus submitted to them; indeed, Congress directed that the plan and the order be erased from the minutes of the Congress.[17] This fact, in conjunction with the further fact that the Tory position has generally incurred the opprobrium and neglect of American historians, has strongly tended to divert students' attention away from several very significant features of the Galloway Plan.

When the First Continental Congress convened, the political discussion conducted until then in pamphlets and in newspaper columns, had reached the point at which action, rather than further mere talk, was required. Recent events had imparted new dimensions of reality and urgency to the discussion, and in these altered circumstances the Galloway Plan had the distinction of being the first blueprint of a new governmental system to be considered, however briefly, by an American public body of truly "continental" scope.[18] This priority of consideration, and the majority vote, so very eloquent of the state of much of the public mind at the time, clearly warrant us in analyzing the plan.

Whatever his reason, Joseph Galloway had not fully developed his plan into a detailed scheme for meeting the difficulties which had led to the assembling of the First Continental Congress. Despite this absence of full details, however, the large outlines of the plan are sufficiently delineated in the surviving records for our present purpose.

The basic element in his plan, as formulated by Galloway in its opening paragraph, was "that a British and American legislature, for regulating the administration of *the general affairs of America*, be proposed and established in America, including all the said colonies; within, and under which government, each colony shall retain its present constitution, and powers of regulating and governing its own internal police, in all cases what[so]ever."[19]

With a view to providing a body of materials sufficient for consideration and discussion by the Congress, Galloway proceeded to unveil for his listeners a series of proposals for "a President-General, to be appointed by the King, and a grand Council to be chosen by the Representatives of the people of the several colonies, in their respective assemblies, once in every three years," and included specific provisions on the time and places of meeting of the Grand Council. Not surprisingly, Galloway left unspecified the numbers and proportional shares in the representation of this Grand Council.

The text of the plan next gives Galloway's other, and significantly expanded, statement detailing the jurisdiction of the American branch of the proposed British-American legislature. "The President-General, by and with the advice and consent of the Grand-Council," Galloway went on, "[shall] hold and exercise all the legislative rights, powers, and authorities, necessary for regulating and administering *all the general police and affairs of the colonies*, in which Great-Britain and the colonies, or any of them, the colonies in general, or more than one colony, are in any manner concerned, as well civil and criminal as commercial."[20]

The broad and comprehensive jurisdiction projected by Galloway for his proposed American "Parliament" is unmistakable and undeniably clear. In addition to a plenary grant of "*all* necessary legislative rights, powers, and authorities," Galloway's language ("regulating and administering") clearly discloses an anticipation of an "executive" (or bureaucratic) apparatus for "administration." The phrase "general police" will certainly extend to good order, public health, safety, and convenience, and a term more comprehensive than "affairs" was not easy to find, in 1774, nor is such a term any easier to find today. Nonetheless, Galloway went into considerable detail in spelling out the proposed coverage.

His employment of three adjectives—"civil and criminal [and] commercial"—leaves virtually nothing beyond the ambit of the American "Parliament's" power. Greatly fortifying this interpretation, we have Joseph Galloway's meticulous specification of the various combinations of parties which could be interested or "concerned" in the foregoing three kinds of "affairs": "Great-Britain and the colonies;" "Great-Britian and any of the colonies"; "the colonies in general"; or "more than one colony." Furthermore, Galloway's Plan neither requires nor even faintly suggests that the relevant "affairs" must be enterprises of great pith and moment: "any manner" of concern, however slight, would be sufficient. In the light of these broad-gauged jurisdictional boundaries, the interpretation of Galloway's word "affairs" as comprehending such "concerns" or "matters" as the common defense, the general welfare, and the domestic tranquility appears to be an obvious step, of neither great size nor great difficulty.

Despite the unquestionably comprehensive ambit of the powers of the proposed American "Parliament," however, these powers, at first glimpse, were not to be coextensive with the power which had been claimed by the British Parliament, seven years previously, in the Declaratory Act, namely, the power of legislating with "sufficient validity to bind" the colonies "in all cases whatsoever." Under Galloway's Plan, each colony was to enjoy the power of "regulating and governing its own *internal police*, in all cases what[so]ever."[21] The reader's understanding of this provision will be much facilitated by brief reference to the dictionary of eighteenth-century political terms presented in the first volume of this series.[22] This consultation will sufficiently fortify readers against interpreting Galloway's term "police" as being synonymous with the whole field of "policy" and will make clear, instead, that the term is limited to matters of "public health, safety, convenience and good order." Needless to say, readers will not fall into the anachronism inherent in any interpretation of Galloway's allocation of the field of "internal police" in terms of the vastly inflated meaning of "the police power of the states," as confected some seventy years later by the Supreme Court of United States.[23] Absolutely nothing of this latter meaning was intended or foreseen by Galloway in fashioning or proposing his famous plan. This conclusion is unavoidable, for in his opening paragraph, already quoted for the reader, Galloway had specified that "each colony" would be *within, and under* [the proposed British-American] government." Thus, even the "retained" power of each colony to "regulate its internal police" would be "under," and therefore "subordinate to," the proposed British-American Parliament.

In short, then, the first plan discussed by an American public body in the context of a considerable quantity of favorable opinion, on September 29, 1774, contemplated an American legislature, many of whose features were quite obviously modelled along the lines of the British Parliament, possessing a broad and comprehensive jurisdiction, with individual colonies (or states) having an ill-defined, but clearly subordinate, jurisdiction over their separate constitutions and matters of "internal police," i.e., matters of public health, safety, convenience, and public order.

3

Sixteen days after its attention had been briefly drawn to the Galloway Plan of Union between Great Britain and the Colonies, the Continental Congress expressed its collective mind on certain phases of the general problem which had been so very recently addressed by Joseph Galloway. Congress took this action on October 14 by adopting the Resolutions on Rights and Grievances. There were ten numbered resolutions regarding the rights, and all except two of the resolutions were adopted unanimously.[24]

Our present concern is with one of those nonunanimous resolutions, namely, the fourth. In this resolution, the Congress, in behalf of the colonies (because, as the Congress were careful to assert, the colonies were "entitled"), laid claim to "a free and exclusive power of legislation in their several provincial legislatures . . . *in all cases of taxation and internal polity*." This exclusive power was, however, "subject only to the negative of their sovereign, in such manner as ha[d] been [t]heretofore used and accustomed."[25] Interestingly enough, the Congress, though stubbornly refusing to expend any more time or effort on Joseph Galloway's plan, was quite clearly prepared to adopt some of that statesman's phraseology, adding to it specific language to make their claim, and consequently their jurisdiction, *exclusive* and not concurrent (as Galloway had proposed) and to expand their jurisdiction expressly to include (as Galloway had *not* proposed) "all cases of taxation."

Other language in this fourth resolution remains to be analyzed. The history of the drafting of the language now to be considered was recounted in full detail in the first volume of this series,[26] and that discussion need not be repeated at this point. What is important is that readers perceive the continuing influence upon draftsmen of inherited patterns of thought. "From the necessity of the case, and a regard to the mutual interest of both countries," the resolution announced, "we cheerfully consent to the operation of such acts of the British Parliament, as are bona fide, restrained to the regulation of our *external commerce* [for the purpose of securing sundry commercial advantages and benefits]; excluding every idea of taxation, internal or external for raising a revenue on the subjects in America, without their consent." As the reader will remember, Galloway's Plan had contemplated a joint British-American parliament, but not the slightest trace of such an arrangement appears in the language just quoted. Upon reading this resolution in his newspaper, a cynic might have suggested that this concession or relinquishment was simply a clear-eyed recognition of the realities of the colonists' situation: there was no American navy at the time, but even then His Britannic Majesty's frigates were on station outside of Boston harbor, and, undoubtedly, additional ships could and would be dispatched from the home islands, should any need for them arise. At any rate, the resolution contemplated a division of the whole body of American "commerce" into two parts, external and internal, and "cheerfully" confided the whole of America's external commerce to the British Parliament.

The resolution just reviewed, as readers will have noticed, made no reference whatsoever to the "internal" commerce of the colonies. The highly interesting question of what action should be taken with reference to this important subject-matter was answered by the Continental Congress with gratifying promptness. Appointed very shortly after the presentation of the Galloway Plan, a committee charged with the preparation of a plan for carrying into effect the nonimportation, nonconsumption and nonexportation policies previously resolved on by the Congress, had reported to that body on October 12, 1774.[27] After spending three days in considering this committee's plan, Congress approved the report on October 18, and "the Association" was ordered to be transcribed for signature by the several members. This being done, the Association was read and signed on October 20.[28] In its actual, de facto character, that act was nothing but a comprehensive set of commercial regulations, as readers will easily perceive from an examination of some of the things which were thereby done.

For one thing, the Association forbade the importation of any goods from Great Britain or Ireland, either directly or indirectly; the importation of East India tea from any part of the world; the importation of molasses, syrups, paneles,[29] coffee, or pimento from the British plantations or from Dominica; the importation of wines from Madeira or the Western Islands; all foreign indigo whatsoever.[30] By another provision of the Association, the prices to be charged for goods of the foregoing kinds, which were already within the country, were fixed at the prices customarily charged for them during the preceding twelve months; and by another, it was directed "that all manufactures of [America] be sold at reasonable prices."[31]

Frugality, economy, and industry were to be encouraged by all citizens, "in [their] several stations," and agriculture, arts, and the country's manufactures (especially the manufacture of wool) were to be promoted. "Every species of extravagance and dissipation" (carefully exemplified by the Association as being "horse-racing, all kinds of gaming, cock-fighting, exhibitions of shews, plays and other expensive diversions and entertainments") were to be "discountenance[d] and discourage[d]."[32]

An essential ingredient in any scheme of regulation, of course, is the provision for sanctions to make the system effective, and to this phase of the matter the Continental Congress gave their full attention. For the enforcement of the other Articles of the Association, the Congress provided, in the eleventh Article, that committees of "observation" and "inspection" should be chosen in every county, city, and town, throughout the country, by the persons qualified to vote for representatives in the local legislatures. Having been chosen, these committees were to "publish" in the local newspapers notices of violations of the Association by any person within the relevant jurisdiction, in order that "such foes to the rights of British-America [might] be publicly known, and universally contemned as enemies of American liberty" and thereafter effectively ostracized.[33] In addition, these committees were to adopt such "farther regulations" as they might think proper for carrying the Association into effect.[34]

The foregoing regulations of the commerce of the colonies, it is clear, were not cast in the usual terms of legislative action. Instead, as the name of the act implies, they were cast in terms of "agreement" and "association." In the case of many persons, however, the "agreement" involved was of the kind which lawyers call *"in invitum"* (i.e., without consent, or against the will); and in what might be termed "the enacting clause" of this strange "agreement," the language was that "we [the delegates of the several colonies . . . deputed to represent them in a Continental Congress] do, for ourselves, and *the inhabitants of the several colonies, whom we represent*, firmly agree and associate, as follows. . . . "[35] What followed consisted, inter alia, of the regulations set forth in the preceding three paragraphs. Recalling that the "compact" or agreement" theory was at the time the accepted theory underlying government; that, as Noah Webster said, "the *association* of all the individuals of a community [was] called the state";[36] and that the rules of this particular "Association" of all the individuals of America were to be enforced by commercial boycott and other means against every person on the continent, whether they associated and agreed *or not*, readers will feel no doubt that one of the very first things done by the Continental Congress was to undertake a comprehensive regulation of the country's *entire commerce*, foreign and domestic.

This view of the Association was immediately taken by the Tory writers who attacked the First Continental Congress, in the fall and winter of 1774–75; and while the Whigs, at first, generally eschewed this view, they soon came around to it and themselves began to speak of the Continental Congress as actually "governing" and of the articles of the Association as "laws of the country," or "continental acts," or "continental regulations," which had to be observed.

As early as November 28, one of the more famous pamphleteers, Samuel Seabury, stated the Tory position in his *The Congress Canvassed* (New York, 1774). The Congress, he said, had not done at all what it had been expected to do. It had made no real effort to "form [a] reasonable and probable scheme of accomodating our unhappy disputes with the mother country." Instead, it had "spent near, or quite, two months" stirring up trouble and *"exercising an assumed power of legislation.*" "Should any person choose to controvert this last position, I appeal," said Seabury, " to the *Association* published by [the Congress], under the signature of their own names. Every article of this instrument was intended by them to have the force of a law. They have indeed used the *soft, mild, insinuating* term of *recommending* their laws to our observance, instead of the authoritative phrase of 'Be it enacted, &c.' because their authority was not yet firmly settled. But they have *solemnly bound themselves and their constituents*—by whom they affect to mean inhabitants of the colonies, from Nova-Scotia to Georgia—. . .*to adhere firmly to their Association;*—they have appointed their officers [i.e., the committees] to carry it into execution, [and] they have ordained penalties upon those that shall presume to violate it." After citing various parts of the Association to prove his points, Seabury concluded with the hope "that you [i.e., "The Merchants of New-York," to whom the pamphlet was addressed] want no more proof, that the regulations of the congress have, and were intended to have, the force of laws."[37]

The same view of the actions of the Continental Congress was taken in Massachusetts by Daniel Leonard, in the series of letters signed by *Massachusettensis*, published late in 1774 and early in 1775. "The delegates," said Leonard, "erecting themselves into the States-General or *supreme legislature* of all the colonies from Nova-Scotia to Georgia, do not leave a doubt respecting their aiming, in good earnest, at independency: *This they did by enacting laws.*" "They call it an association, but it has all the constituent parts of a law." After an analysis of the Association, Leonard addded: "Here we find the congress enacting laws,—that is, establishing, as the representatives of the people, certain rules of conduct to be observed and kept by all the inhabitants of these colonies, under certain pains and penalties—such as masters of vessels being dismissed from their employment;—goods to be seized and sold at auction, and the first cost only returned to the proprietor, a different appropriation made of the overplus;—persons being stigmatized in the gazette, as enemies of their country, and excluded the benefits of society, &c."[38]

At first, the dislike of the Tory view that Congress had "legislated" was not universal among the Whigs. In answering the Reverend Seabury's strictures on this head, Alexander Hamilton asked, in his pamphlet *A Full Vindication of the Measures of Congress*, of December 15, 1774: "Pray, did we not appoint our delegates *to make regulations for us?*" Hamilton also took occasion to say, "I trust there is no danger that the prices of goods will rise much, if at all. The same Congress that *put a stop to* the importation of them, has also forbid raising the prices of them. The same committee that is to regulate [i.e., "govern" in the sense of "enforcing"] the one, is also to regulate the other." At a slightly later point in his discussion, Hamilton added: "If the next Congress should think any *regulations* concerning the courts of justice requisite they will make them; and proper persons will be appointed to carry them into execution, and to see that no individuals deviate from them."[39]

4

Most appropriately, the second essay at finding or formulating a plan of government to replace the scheme embodied in the British imperial system was made by the most widely renowned scientist and inventor then living in the American colonies, Dr. Benjamin Franklin. When Dr. Franklin launched his experiment in the Second Continental Congress, however, the circumstances in which the planning of governments was conducted had quite perceptibly changed from the circumstances prevailing in the not too distant past. By Friday, July 21, 1775, the colonists had learned of the British government's completely negative reaction to the various dispatches and measures issuing from the First Continental Congress. The tension-ridden situation in the Province of Massachusetts Bay had continued to deteriorate, seemingly at a somewhat accelerated pace, to the point where the "shot heard 'round the world" had been fired at Lexington on April 19. On June 14, the Second Continental Congress had taken steps for the formation of an American Continental army,[40] and on the following day had appointed Colonel George Washington as commanding general of the Continental forces.[41]

Introduced in these greatly altered circumstances, Dr. Franklin's plan inevitably exhibited a perceptibly higher degree of sophistication than had been manifested in the plan which Joseph Galloway had submitted to the First Continental Congress. Unquestionably, Franklin's draft of a plan became the starting point of the Continental Congress's protracted labors in devising a new scheme of government, so his blueprint of government deserves our careful consideration.

The second of Franklin's draft articles of confederation, remarkably foreshadowing the Preamble to the Constitution of the United States, provided that the United Colonies should enter into "a firm League of Friendship with each other, binding on themselves and their Posterity, for their common Defence against their Enemies[,] for the Security of their Liberties and Propertys, the Safety of their Persons and Families, and their *mutual and general Welfare*."[42]

"The Power and Duty of the Congress," as the subsequent Article V provided, "shall extend to the Determining on War and Peace, to sending and receiving ambassadors, and entering into Alliances, [the Reconciliation with Great Britain]; the Settling all Disputes and Differences between Colony and Colony about Limits or any other cause if such should arise; and the Planting of new Colonies when proper."[43]

Having thus addressed at least some of the more pressing problems then confronting the Congress, or likely to do so in the immediate future, Franklin proceeded, in the second paragraph of this fifth Article, to offer an explicit statement of the scope of congressional powers. "The Congress," he proposed, "[should] also make such general ordinances as tho' necessary to the *General Welfare*, particular Assemblies cannot be competent to: viz. those that may relate to our *general Commerce;* or general Currency; to the Establishment of Posts; and the Regulation of our common Forces."[44] Two matters incorporated in this article are sufficiently important to the subject of the present book to deserve particular discussion at this point.

First of all, this language in the fifth of his draft articles secures to Benjamin Franklin the distinction of being the first to propose a strictly American commerce power of "continental" scope, a power extending to the regulation of every kind of gainful economic activity engaged in by the American people.

That the commercial power contained in Franklin's plan had the scope just indicated is certain. In the first place, this view of that power accords with the ordinary meaning of the phrase "general commerce" which Franklin used.[45] The ordinary, comprehensive sense of "general commerce" was an old and well-established sense, during the whole of Franklin's lifetime; and while the phrase did occasionally have meanings of narrower generality in certain contexts,[46] it is highly unlikely that Franklin would have used the term without explanation, as he did in his plan, had he intended it to be understood in one of these occasional, narrower senses.

The probability that Franklin used "general commerce" in its ordinary sense is greatly enhanced by the fact that he had employed this phrase in referring to the same subject on another, closely related occasion. At that time, Franklin had been in London as agent for certain of the American colonies. He had formed a friendship with William Strahan, a well-known English book-publisher and printer, who shortly afterwards became a member of Parliament. Strahan had written to Franklin, inquiring as to what measures the latter thought were necessary to bring to a "speedy and happy conclusion" the existing disputes between Great Britain and the colonies. In the course of this letter, written on November 21, 1769, Strahan had explained that he had reason to believe those in authority intended "to relieve the colonies from the taxes complained of."

In his reply, dated November 29, 1769, Franklin expressed his hope that Strahan's information was correct, and that there might soon take place a general repeal of "all the laws that [had] been made for raising a revenue in America by authority of Parliament, without the consent of the people there." "The supremacy of [Parliament]," Franklin went on, "will be best preserved by making a very sparing use of it, never but for the evident good of the colonies themselves, or of the whole British Empire; never for the partial advantage of Britain to their prejudice. By such prudent conduct I imagine that supremacy may be gradually strengthened and in time fully established; but otherwise I apprehend it will be disputed, and lost in the dispute." Franklin then added the remark in which he used the term "general commerce" in the comprehensive sense which has been exemplified above. He said: "At present the colonies consent and submit to [the "supremacy" of Parliament] for the regulation of *general commerce.*"[47]

Our inference as to the meaning of Franklin's "general commerce" in this letter is based upon a number of collateral circumstances. First, it should be observed that this remark of Franklin's is the only statement, in his letter to Strahan, indicative of any consent, or submission, on the part of the colonies, to the authority of the British Parliament. Yet Franklin says in his letter that he thinks *the colonies* would be satisfied if Parliament should "put [them] *precisely* in the situation they were in before the passing of the late Stamp Act." Clearly, then, Franklin regarded all the colonial acts of Parliament before the Stamp Act as "regulations of *general commerce.*"

The facts in question, however, do not stand alone. There is the additional fact that John Dickinson, in his *Letters from a Farmer*, had described the earlier acts as "regulations of trade" and conceded that they were within the power of Parliament.[48] There is the fact that Franklin himself, in May of 1768, in a preface to the London edition, had presented the "Farmer's Letters" to the British public as an expression of "the *general sentiments** of the inhabitants [of the colonies]."[49] Finally, there is the fact that James Duane, in the First Continental Congress, was soon to speak of the earlier acts as "regulations of commerce."[50] When these additional facts are brought to view, doubt that Franklin regarded the earlier parliamentary acts as "regulations of general commerce" is entirely unwarranted. This means that, in his letter to Strahan, Franklin used the term "general commerce" in the emphatically comprehensive sense in which the term was ordinarily used; and when they remember that, in his letter, Franklin was speaking of the colonial powers of Parliament; that the colonies' "connection with Britain" was treated in the Franklin plan as having come to an end; and that the "General Congress" provided in that plan was plainly intended to take the place of Parliament in its relation to the colonies, readers will feel very little, if any, doubt that Franklin used the phrase "general commerce" in the same comprehensive sense in his plan, in stating the powers of his proposed new congress, as he did when he spoke, in his letter to Strahan, of the preexisting colonial powers of Parliament.

We should add, however, that Franklin himself did not approve, nor did he suppose that the colonists generally approved, all the colonial acts of Parliament prior to the Stamp Act. For example, Franklin did not approve the hat-making and felt-making statute of 1732; or the iron-splitting and steel-making statute of 1750; or the gaol-emptying statute of 1718.[51] In common with a great many other Americans of his time, however, Franklin was so convinced of the necessity of a central imperial power over all kinds of "commerce" that he was unwilling to contest Parliament's power in this regard, and was instead content merely to attack the wisdom of particular parliamentary acts which the colonists found obnoxious. In answer, then, to another inquiry of Strahan's, as to whether Parliament could return to the situation before the Stamp Act, without "encourag[ing] the violent and fac-

*Franklin's emphasis.

tious part of the colonists to aim at still further concessions from the mother country," Franklin answered that he thought Parliament could do so. "There may," said he, "be a few among [the colonists], that deserve the name of factious and violent, as there are in all countries; but these would have little influence if the great majority of sober reasonable people were satisfied." He then added: "If any colony should happen to think some of your *regulations of trade* are inconvenient to the general interest of the empire, or prejudicial to them without being beneficial to you, they will state these matters to Parliament in petitions as heretofore, but will, I believe, take no violent steps to obtain what they may hope for in time from the wisdom of government here. I know of nothing else they can have in view. The notion that prevails here of their being desirous to set up a kingdom or commonwealth of their own is, to my certain knowledge, entirely groundless."[52]

The foregoing statement, readers will remember, was made in 1769. With the passage of time, and the continuance of the dispute between the colonies and Parliament, the final part of it became untrue. As of the date Franklin made it, however, his statement was entirely accurate and thoroughly in accord with the sentiments of most Americans at the time. The fact that Franklin and these other Americans, most of whom were, like Franklin, thoroughly displeased with some of Parliament's commercial acts, should nevertheless have been willing, not only in 1769, but as late as 1774, to concede the complete power of power of Parliament over all kinds of "commerce" is solid evidence, again, that belief in the necessity of centralized regulatory power in the field of commerce was very common and very strong among Americans, at least until the eve of the American Revolution. This being true, the fact that Franklin proposed such a comprehensive commercial power for his independent American congress is in no way extraordinary or unexpected.

The other significant matter included in Franklin's fifth Article was the draftsman's explicit grant of power to the proposed congress to "make [whatever] general ordinances [might be] necessary to the General Welfare," a grant of power explicitly conveyed, even though the "mutual and general Welfare" of the United Colonies had already been stated, in the preceding second Article, as one of the general purposes of the Confederation. This idea of "mutual and general Welfare" appeared in other Articles as well. Pursuant to the fourth Article, for example, dealing with "the more convenient Management of [the] *general Interests*, Delegates [should] be annually elected in each Colony to meet in General Congress at such Time and Place as [should] be agreed on in the next preceding Congress." Article VI contained a provision that "all Charges of Wars, and all other general Expenses to be incurred for *the common Welfare* [should] be defrayed out of a common Treasury." The plan then went on to specify the proportions of the contributions to this "common treasury," carefully providing (in complete accord with the First Congress's Resolution about exclusive power in all cases of taxation and internal polity) that "the Taxes for paying the proportion [should] be laid and levied by the Laws of each Colony."[53]

The perennially troublesome question of relations with the Indian tribes engaged Franklin's attention in two separate articles of his plan. Under the tenth Article thereof, no colony was to engage "in an offensive War with any Nation of Indians without the Consent of the Congress," which body should "first consider the Justice and Necessity of such War."[54] Article XI went into considerable detail concerning "a perpetual Alliance offensive and defensive," the ascertainment of the limits of the Six Nations, and the regulation of trade with the Indians. This last provision occasioned still another reference to the "general Welfare," in its provision that "all purchases from [the Indian tribes should] be by the Congress for *the general advantage and benefit* of the United Colonies."[55]

One important part of Franklin's plan remains to be considered. This element consists of his proposal regarding a matter which was for many reasons to prove an enduring political issue throughout our national history. We may at this point usefully recall the provision in Joseph Galloway's plan respecting this hardy perennial: "Each colony shall retain its present constitution, and powers of regulating and governing its own internal police, in all cases whatsoever." Obviously adopting Galloway's language as his point of departure, Franklin recast the provision in a more flexible form, as the reader will perceive from this language of his draft Article III: "Each Colony shall enjoy and retain as much as it may think fit of its own *present* Laws, Customs, Rights, Privileges, and peculiar Jurisdictions within its own limits; and may amend its own Constitution as shall seem best to its own Assembly or Constitution."[56]

To many readers, this article may seem to constitute a rather clear provision for state territorial sovereignty. Such a view of the article, however, connot be taken without flatly disregarding the important word in it, here printed in italics. That word indicates that the purpose of the provision was to crystallize the colonies' existing status as parts of a whole; there was no intention whatever to *extend* their separate "Laws, Customs, Rights, Privileges, or peculiar Jurisdictions." The provision is to be read, therefore, as a retention of only those laws, custom, rights, privileges, and peculiar jurisdictions which the colonies "enjoyed" as of the date when Franklin proposed his plan. *At that date*, as we have already seen, no right, privilege, or peculiar jurisdiction had been claimed for the separate colonies *except* in the fields of "taxation and internal polity." In those two fields, a claim of separate and exclusive right had been advanced in the Resolutions on Rights and Grievances, adopted by the First Continental Congress on October 14, 1774.

Unlike the plan proposed by Joseph Galloway in the previous fall, Franklin's plan was backed by some of the most ardent revolutionaries in the Congress. Thomas Jefferson, by his own explicit statement, was one of these,[57] but beyond the fact of Jefferson's support no positive information exists as to the exact identity of Franklin's coadjutors. Naturally his opposition came from the conservative group, which had favored the Galloway plan in the preceding autumn. To these men, the Galloway plan had seemed attractive, because it included union with Great Britain as an essential element. On this point, the Franklin plan, inevitably reflecting the march of political events, and perhaps to some degree anticipating them, differed rather sharply.

This difference is articulated in Article XIII of Franklin's plan, which provided that the articles were to be proposed to the several provincial conventions or assemblies for their consideration, and, if the articles were approved, these groups were "to impower their delegates to agree to and ratify the same in the ensuing Congress." "After which," the Franklin plan went on, "the Union thereby established [was] to continue firm till the Terms of Reconciliation proposed on the Petition of the Last Congress to the King [were] agreed to." After specifying three additional events as conditions precedent, the Franklin plan continued: "on the Arrival of these Events the Colonies [shall] return to their *former Connection* and Friendship with Britain: But on Failure thereof this Confederation [was] to be perpetual."[58] Confronted with this blunt language in his draft articles, the conservative group almost instinctively opposed Franklin's plan as tantamount to a declaration of independence.[59]

This attitude of the conservatives was fully understood by Franklin and his friends, and for this reason Franklin's plan was not at first proposed as a subject of formal consideration. Instead, it was offered as something for the delegates to turn over in their minds, and as a basis upon which to construct a more perfect plan, when and if confederation should become desirable. The Franklin plan was thus not pushed within the Congress, when first presented,[60] and, in the event, many of its provisions were to be absent from the Articles of Confederation which Congress finally submitted to the states some two years later.

Readers may perhaps suppose that, in these circumstances, the proposals contained in Benjamin Franklin's plan were out of line with the general trend of American opinion and therefore constituted matters of only slight interest or importance. In forming any judgment upon this point, however, one should bear in mind other circumstances besides those just mentioned. Earlier in this chapter we saw that Joseph Galloway, less than a year before, had been able to interest something like half the members of the First Continental Congress in a plan which called for a joint British-American power extending to all civil, criminal, and commercial affairs of interest to Great Britain and the colonies or to some combination of these. We know also that James Duane had been able to deadlock the same Congress on a proposal to concede a purely British power extending to all "trade" or "commerce" of every kind,[61] and that this deadlock had finally been resolved in the Resolutions on Rights and Grievances wherein the Congress had "cheerfully consented[ed] to the operation of such acts of the British Parliament as [were] bona fide restrained to the regulation of [the colonies'] external commerce." Finally, we have just seen that the Congress to whom Franklin's proposals were submitted had previously, almost exactly nine months to the day, moved in a comprehensive fashion to regulate the *entire* commerce of the country, foreign and domestic, by means of "the Association." In the light of this background, Franklin's proposal of a continental American legislature with power "to make general ordinances necessary to the General Welfare" and in particular to regulate the "general Commerce" of the country, and the support given to his proposal by men like Thomas Jefferson, appear in their proper character: as particularly striking evidence that, at the period in question, some kind of generally empowered national legislature was widely regarded among men of all shades of opinion regarding independence as being an essential feature of any acceptable scheme of government.

CHAPTER III

The Public Discussions of Forming a
Continental Government in the Spring of 1776:
Thomas Paine and John Adams

FOR about ten months after Franklin proposed his plan on July 21, 1775, little was done in the Continental Congress on the subject of confederation. The Franklin plan was circulated to some extent among the colonies, and the available evidence indicates that opinions about it "out of doors" were probably about what they had been in the Congress. In some colonies, as in Virginia, the plan apparently was shown only to "the knowing ones";[1] but in North Carolina it was actually brought before the provincial congress, and on September 4 voted down as "not at present Eligible." In form at least, the substance of the Franklin plan was thus not disapproved; but the local congress thought that "the Association of the Colonies," of the previous autumn, should be "further relied on for bringing about a Reconciliation with the Parent State," and that "a further Confederacy ought only to be adopted in Case of the last Necessity."[2] In Massachusetts, on the other hand, men were readier to act; and on December 19, 1775, James Warren, president of the local congress, wrote impatiently to Samuel Adams, inquiring when the country was "to hear of your Confederation proposed in your last Session." "Is it not time," he pointedly asked, "to have the Constitution of our *supream Legislative* accurately fixed and fully established and known?"[3]

Exactly what James Warren meant when he referred to Congress as the "supream Legislative" of the country, it is not now possible, with complete certainty, to say. Some clues, however, exist in Warren's letters, and these indicate that he had in mind, if not a completely sovereign, at least a very ample, continental power. There is, for example, the desire he expressed in a letter to John Adams, on November 5, 1775, for a continental "test" act, or act controlling the right to vote in all the colonies;[4] there is the expectation *and desire*, which he expressed in a letter to Samuel Adams, on June 21, 1775, that the Continental Congress should "regulate the Constitution of all the Colonies";[5] and there is his reference to "Coin and *Commerce*," in a letter to John Adams, on August 11, 1776, as "matters of great importance, which the Continental Congress, before it should adjourn, had still to act upon."[6] A modern mind, steeped in the usual version of the history of this period, will naturally find it difficult to credit to a man like Warren ideas of the foregoing kind, because Warren was one of those who bitterly opposed the adoption of

60

the Constitution in 1787, and it is only natural to assume that his ideas were localistic at this earlier time as well.

Warren, however, was much like another well-known anti-federalist of 1787, Richard Henry Lee, of Virginia. Lee, like Warren, desired at this time that the Continental Congress should draw the constitution of all the colonies. These sentiments appear in a letter he wrote to John Adams on May 18, 1776. In the course of his letter, Lee queried the "fitness" of the then recent action of the Virginia convention in "reserv[ing] to [that] colony the power of forming its own government." "Would not a uniform plan of government," Lee went on to ask, "[a plan] prepared for America by the Congress, and approved by the colonies, be a surer foundation of unceasing harmony to the whole?"[7] The reader should also note that Lee fought to the bitter end in the Continental Congress for a power in the Congress under the Articles of Confederation, to act in all cases for the general welfare of the country. Whatever men like Lee and Warren may have thought at a later time, it is clear that they were, in the beginning, fully in favor of continental government.

The foregoing suggests that the account usually given of the way things went in connection with the Declaration of Independence and the Articles of Confederation can hardly be completely true. Desire for continental union and continental government must have been commoner than is generally supposed, and the truth is that this desire was one of the principal springs of the American Revolution. The meeting of the Albany congress of 1754 is a well-known fact; the early sentiments in favor of a continental supreme court have been referred to;[8] and the readiness with which the general legislative (as distinct from the taxing) power of Parliament was conceded in the early years of pre-Revolutionary controversy can be explained by the widespread belief that some kind of power to make general regulations for all the colonies was necessary. Men like Stephen Hopkins, of Rhode Island, made definite suggestions as to continental regulations that Parliament should adopt; and to those familiar with the ills of the time, it will not seem strange that one of the commonest suggestions made by such men was the taking of some action to establish an American continental money.[9] James Otis, also, in 1764, seems plainly to have had the necessity of continental government in mind when, in arguing the necessity of parliamentary power, he said, in his *Rights of the British Colonies Asserted and Proved*, that "it [was] barely possible, the time [might] come, when the real interest of the whole [might] require an act of Parliament to annihilate all [colony] charters."[10] In the early years even the handful of writers who denied the power of the existing Parliament very generally conceded the necessity of some kind of government over the colonies as a whole. To meet this need, these radicals proposed that either an American parliament be established for continental purposes, or the British Parliament be reformed so as to make it representative of the Empire as a whole.

As the pre-Revolutionary controversy wore along, however, more and more men became convinced that Parliament, as it existed, could not be trusted to make American regulations; that American representation in Parliament was really impracticable for geographical, if for no other reasons; and that Great Britain would never consent to a separate American continental legislature. As men attained to these beliefs, of course, they turned into advocates of American independence, but to suppose that men who thought in these ways became "states'-righters" is the crudest sort of error.[11] On the contrary, their greatest concern was that the country should not fall apart into separate states, and independence result in ruin. Fear that this might occur, it is needless to say, was also common among the Tory group, and among the group that hesitated between the Whig and Tory positions. For this reason, a great part of the newspaper and pamphlet controversy when independence became imminent was concerned with the effect which independence would have in promoting continental government or bringing about colonial separatism and disunion. The Tory writers constantly appealed to the fear that independence would convert the country into a group of petty, warring states, which would lie at the mercy of the Old World's rapacity. The advocates of independence, on the other hand, maintained that a close continental union was the country's great need; that only through independence could such a union be achieved; and therefore, that independence should be immediately declared.

Among the writings in which this argument was pressed, none was more important than Thomas Paine's famous pamphlet, *Common Sense*. A clarion call to American independence, *Common Sense* spoke emphatically for the independence of "the Continent," and not for the independence of thirteen petty states. "The authority of Great Britian over *this Continent*," the pamphlet declared, "is a form of government, which sooner or later must have an end." "As to government matters, 'tis not in the power of Britain to do *this Continent* justice: the business of it will soon be too weighty and intricate to be managed with any degree of convenience, by a power so distant from us and so very ignorant of us." "The most powerful of all arguments is that nothing but independence, *i.e., a Continental form of Government*, can keep the peace of *the Continent* and preserve it inviolate from civil wars." "The infant states of the Colonies . . . , so far from being against is an argument in favor of independence." "Youth is the seed-time of good habits as well in nations as in individuals. It might be difficult, if not impossible, to form *the Continent* into *one government* half a century hence. The vast variety of interests, occasioned by an increase of trade and population, would create confusion. Colony would be against Colony. Each being able would scorn each other's assistance: and while the proud and foolish gloried in their little distinctions, the wise would lament that the union had not been formed before. Wherefore the present is the true time for establishing it." Paine therefore called for "an open and determined DECLARATION FOR INDEPENDENCE."[12]

Paine also argued that "the Colonies [had already] manifested such a spirit of good order and obedience to *continental government* as [was] sufficient to make every reasonable person easy and happy on that head." But then he immediately added, in a somewhat different vein, that "if there [was] any true cause of fear respecting independence it [was] because no plan [of an independent government was] yet laid down." He therefore urged the immediate calling of "a Continental Conference," for the purpose of framing "a Continental Charter." Paine suggested that the conference should consist of "twenty-six members of Congress, viz: two for each Colony; two members from each House of Assembly, or Provincial Convention; and five representatives of the people at large [in each province]." The representatives of the people were to be chosen by the qualified voters and—the reader will have observed—were to outnumber the representatives of the two interested groups of colonial and continental politicians. As for the continental charter to be adopted by this convention, Paine suggested that it should contain, among other things, provisions for "securing freedom and property to all men, and above all things the free exercise of religion"; provisions "fixing the number and manner of choosing members of Congress, and Members of Assembly [in the several "provinces"]"; and provisions for "drawing the line of business and jurisdiction between [these bodies]—always remembering that our strength and happiness is *continental*, not provincial."[13]

Despite Paine's final cautionary words, and the strong continentalist tenor of his whole pamphlet, his last agendum may perhaps suggest to some modern minds that Paine had in view some such "dual system of government" as that which the Constitution is widely supposed to have established. The reader should therefore clearly understand that Paine had in view no such thing. In fact, Paine deplored the influence of the separate colonies in the affairs of "the Continent," and desired to end that influence by taking the election of congressional delegates away from the assemblies and colonial "congresses" and vesting that function in the people themselves.[14] This suggestion, we shall presently see, met with the same widespread popular support as Paine's other proposals. Beyond this change, Paine desired that the business of the "provincial" legislatures should be "wholly domestic"; that their constitution should depend upon a "continental Charter"; that they should be unicameral in structure, "with a president only"; and that their business should be "subject to the authority of a Continental Congress."[15] Precisely what Paine meant by his last proposal is, however, not entirely certain. It was open, no doubt, to the interpretation that Paine desired for the Continental Congress power to act in single "provinces" for "purely local" purposes; but, on the other hand, it may only have meant that Paine desired for the Congress "supream" power over every "province" in all cases of "continental" concern. It should be remembered, in this connection, that Paine was not a lawyer; and layman-like, he was inexact. At all events, whichever of the two foregoing was Paine's meaning, he clearly did not want what has come to be described in impressive phrase as "our dual form of government."

Paine's obscurity on the point last mentioned; his proposal of a continental conference; and his contempt for the checks and balances of the British constitution were apparently the causes of the only public dissent from his position which was of any importance. The dissent in question, which did not actually mention Paine's pamphlet, was an anonymous pamphlet from the pen of John Adams; and the importance of Adams, along with a failure to take into account all the facts as well as all the issues involved, has apparently led to a rather general belief, in modern times, that Paine's proposal of a continental government was unpopular. Such, however, was emphatically not the case; and apart from procedure, and checks and balances, the difference between John Adams and Thomas Paine—if any there really were—was a difference between a power extending to *all* cases of continental importance and a power extending to all unexcepted cases of *every* kind whatsoever.[16]

That John Adams was anything but a disbeliever in continental government is sufficiently shown, if any such showing be necessary, by the fact that Adams had actually anticipated Paine, by about five months, as a public advocate of independence and a continental constitution. Adam's prior public advocacy of a continental government had occurred in consequence of the British interception of two confidential letters which Adams had written on July 24, 1775. The letters, which were addressed to Mrs. Adams and Adams's friend, James Warren, of Massachusetts, were communicated by the British to the Tory printers; and through their printing of the letters,[17] Adams quite unintentionally became the first public advocate of the aggressive ideas for which Paine's pamphlet stood forth in the middle of the following winter. In his letter to his wife, Adams had spoken of the labors which Congress had before it as "prodigious." "[They] *have a constitution to form for a great empire*," he said, "at the same time that they have a country of fifteen hundred miles extent to fortify, millions to arm and train, a naval power to begin, an extensive commerce to regulate, numerous tribes of Indians to negotiate with, [and] a standing army of twenty-seven thousand men to raise, pay, victual, and officer." In his letter to Warren, Adams complained of John Dickinson's obstructive tactics in Congress; referred impatiently to Dickinson as "a great fortune and piddling genius"; and declared that Dickinson had "given a silly cast to [the Continental Congress's] whole doings." "We ought," declared Adams, "to have had in our hands, a month ago, *the whole legislative, executive, and judicial of the whole continent*, and have completely modelled a constitution." These "ideas of independence" set forth in these letters, (which Adams never denied but, instead, seemed very proud of)[18] compel the conclusion that, on the issues in which we are interested, Adams in fact enthusiastically agreed with Paine and with James Warren and, on most points with Bejamin Franklin,[19] also, on the date when his intercepted letters were written. That date, it is worth noting, was July 24, 1775—just three days after Franklin had first presented his plan of confederation to the Congress, and only just a few weeks, as we shall presently see, after the provincial congress of Massachusetts had signified its complete willingness to submit to any "general plan" of government which the Continental Congress might "direct".[20]

In view of these various facts, it is not surprising that, when *Common Sense* was published in the following winter, Adams's first reaction to it was one of complete approval: he probably forgave Paine's contempt for his own pet device of checks and balances and considered it improbable that this part of Paine's pamphlet would be approved. Adams first encountered *Common Sense* about February 1, while passing through New York on his way back from Massachusetts to Congress. He purchased a copy of it there, and sent it home to Mrs. Adams; and then ten days after his arrival in Philadelphia, he wrote to her, calling her attention to it. It was written, he said, "in vindication of doctrines which, there [was] reason to expect the further encroachments of tyranny and depredations of oppression [would] soon make the common faith."[21] Mrs. Adams read the pamphlet and wrote to Adams that she, for her part, was "charmed" with it. "I want to know," she added, "how [its] sentiments are received in Congress."[22] Adams replied, on March 19, with fainter praise than formerly, declaring its "notions and plans of continental government were not much applauded." "This writer," he now complained, "has a better hand in pulling down than building [and] seems to have very inadequate ideas of what is proper and necessary to be done in order to form constitutions for single colonies, as well as a great model of union for the whole."[23] From the mere face of these comments, it is hardly possible to say whether Adams—or, indeed, others in the Congress—objected to more than the sketchiness of Paine's notions and the novel mode of proceeding which he had proposed. There is other evidence, however, on the basis of which these questions can be certainly answered.

For one thing, John Adams's letters show that he was anxious to build on the existing de facto union under Congress. To throw the whole question of continental power into a continental conference organized in the manner Paine had proposed could therefore not have seemed to him other than a step backward. "We are united now," Adams was to say a few weeks later, in a jubilant letter to James Warren, on April 16, "and the Difference between Union and Confederation is only the same with that between an express and an implied contract."[24] Adams was to find, at a still later time, when he urged this argument in Congress, that, to the men who later came to that body, as well as to some who had been there longer, the difference between having, and not having, things down in black and white was a very great difference, indeed. In April of 1776, Adams of course did not foresee all the effects independence would have upon the makeup of Congress, so he was, at that time, happy and serene.

Beyond Adams's eminently sensible desire to build on the existing de-facto situation, it is clear that by the spring of 1776 he had come to hold very definite ideas as to the precise process that should be followed by the colonies in their transition from a dependent to an independent state. The change was to be accomplished not at one fell blow, as Paine had proposed, but gradually. Forgetful of his own impatient letters of only a few months before, Adams declared in a letter to Mrs. James Warren, on April 16, that he had "*ever* thought it the most difficult and dangerous Part of the Business Americans have to do in this mighty Contest, to contrive some Method for the Colonies *to glide insensibly*, from under the old Government, into a peaceable and contented submission to new ones."[25] The method he had come to approve was, first, to set up governments in the several colonies, not too different from the respective old ones; next, to confederate; and finally, to declare the colonies "a sovereign state, or a number of confederated sovereign states"—Adams seemed to think it made little difference which.[26] Entertaining these ideas, Adams naturally objected to Paine's proposal of an abrupt and wholesale procedure. "There [was] Danger of Convulsions," he said, "but [he] hope[d], not great ones."[27]

Besides Adams's objections to Paine's procedure, he also objected—and very strongly—to what he called Paine's "crude ignorant Notion of a Government by one Assembly." This complaint however, made in a letter to James Warren, on May 12, referred *not* to Paine's proposal of continental government as such but (as the context of the letter makes entirely clear) to Paine's desire to get away from a second legislative chamber and the executive veto. As we shall presently see, these suggestions of Paine's had been taking well among the people in certain parts of the Union, and Adams, who disapproved such ideas with all his heart, was disturbed. Paine was "a keen Writer," he told James Warren, "but very ignorant of the Science of Government." And Adams was afraid he would "do more Mischief, in dividing the Friends of Liberty [over the forms of Government], than all the Tory Writings together."[28]

Beyond the foregoing, there is not a line in any of Adams's private letters in the nature of an objection to any of Paine's ideas, nor is there in these letters the slightest suggestion of doubt as to the eminent desirability of a continental congress with ample powers. Quite the contrary.[29] Still, in certain letters that Adams wrote for political purposes early in the spring of 1776, he speaks as if he had not really made up his mind whether any kind of continental constitution was desirable. One of these letters, originally written for his fellow delegate in Congress, George Wythe, of Virginia, was published in Philadelphia, in April, as an anonymous pamphlet, under the title of *Thoughts on Government*. The pamphlet is the one important public dissent from Paine's position earlier referred to. Devoted almost exclusively to the problem of forming governments in the separate colonies, and to the necessity of including checks and balances in them, when formed, the pamphlet contains, towards the end, the following offhand-sounding paragraph:

If the colonies should assume governments separately, they should be left entirely to their own choice of the forms; and *if* a continental constitution should be formed, it should be a congress, containing a fair and adequate representation of the colonies, and its authority should *sacredly be confined* to these cases, namely, war, trade, disputes between colony and colony, the post-office, and the unappropriated lands of the crown, as they used to be called.[30]

Adams described this pamphlet, or letter, in a communication to his wife, on May 27, as having been "calculated for a meridian at a great distance from New England."[31] A short while earlier, he had, it appears, "calculated" another such letter for a "meridian" at an even greater distance from New England, in which the following even stranger-sounding paragraph appeared:

We have heard much of a continental constitution; I see no occasion for any but a congress. Let that be made an equal and fair representative of the Colonies; and let its authority be confined to *three* cases—war, trade, and controversies between colony and colony."[32]

This earlier letter had been written for William Hooper and John Penn, of North Carolina, where Franklin's plan had been voted down in the preceding autumn. This fact, perhaps, had as much to do, as did North Carolina's greater distance from New England, with the even fainter continentalism which Adams's North Carolina letter contained.

After Adams's Virginia letter had been published in pamphlet form, Adams heard from John Penn, who in the meantime had returned to North Carolina. Penn wrote "that he [had] heard nothing praised in the Course of his Journey, but Common Sense and Independence. That this was the Cry throughout Virginia. That North Carolina were making great Preparations for War, and were determined to die poor and to die hard if they must die in Defence of their Liberties. That they had repealed, or should repeal their Instructions to their Delegates against Independence. That South Carolina had assumed a Government . . . [and] 'in short, [that] the Vehemence of the Southern Colonies [was] such as [would] require the Coolness of the Northern Colonies, to restrain them from running to Excess.' "[33] Penn's letter seems to have reassured Adams on the state of sentiment in the South, and at the same time to have induced in him a feeling that his pamphlet had been slightly miscalculated. This seems the only explanation of the letter he wrote to his friend, James Warren, when he sent him a copy of the pamphlet. In this letter he was at great pains to explain how it came to be written and for whom exactly it had been intended. It was a pity, he added, that the pamphlet had not been printed from another version of his letter, which unfortunately has not survived. This Adams had written for and given to Jonathan Dickinson Sergeant, of New Jersey; "for that," he declared "[was] larger and more compleat, perhaps more correct." "The Design, however, [had been] to mark out a Path, and putt Men upon thinking." "I would not," he concluded, "have this Matter communicated."[34] In his May 27 letter to Mrs. Adams, Adams disclosed a similar anxiety that his authorship of the pamphlet should not become common knowledge in New England. The pamphlet was "a hasty, hurried thing," he said, "and of no great consequence." "It [had] contributed," he believed, "to set people thinking upon the subject, and in this respect [had] answered its end. The manufacture of governments having, since the publication of [the pamphlet], been as much talked of as that of saltpetre was before." "If [the pamphlet had] done no good, it [would] do no harm."[35]

The "talk" of "the manufacture of governments," which Adams spoke of, had in fact gone considerably beyond his own limited suggestions for continental government; with but few exceptions the proposals advanced were for a continental government empowered to act generally for the continental welfare, and not a power "sacredly confined," as Adams had suggested, to a few particular subjects. That the suggestions thus made were, moreover, entirely to Adams's own liking appears from a letter he wrote Mrs. Adams, on July 11. In this letter Adams promised that he would soon be coming home. He had been of use, he thought, while Congress had been engaged in "gradually erecting and strengthening governments under the authority of the people, turning their thoughts upon the principles of polity and the forms of governments, framing constitutions for the Colonies separately, and *a limited and defined Confederacy for the [whole]*." But these matters would soon be completed; and there would then be little business in Congress "but what [would] be either military or commercial; Branches of knowledge and business for which hundreds of others in [Massachusetts were] much better qualified than [he]." And, so, he concluded, he should "soon ask lieve to come home."[36]

From this Adams letter it is plainly evident that, when he wrote it, Adams was satisfied with the confederation then in prospect; and since the letter was written just the day before the first committee draft of the Articles was reported in Congress,[37] this must mean that Adams was satisfied with that committee draft. Adams, it is true, was not a member of the committee which produced that draft, but Samuel Adams and Stephen Hopkins were,[38] and it is not to be supposed that John Adams, with these two friends among its members, was in any way ignorant of what was going on in this committee. It is true, also, that Adams referred to the committee draft as "a limited and defined Confederacy," but this simply means that the confederacy for which it provided was "a limited and defined Confederacy," as these words then were understood. It was confederacy "limited" to the "defined" objects of "the common defence," "the security of liberty," and "the mutual and general welfare of the United Colonies"; a confederacy in which the role of each separate colony was "defined" as, and "limited" to, "the regulation and government of its [own] *internal police*, in all matters that should not interfere with the [confederacy]"; and a confederacy wherein the Congress of the United Colonies was restrained from "interfer[ing] in the *internal Police* of any

Colony, *any further* than such *Police* [might] be affected by the [Confederacy]." A confederacy so drawn would not, of course, according to the ideas of a later time, have been "a limited and defined Confederacy," but it *was* such a confederacy according to the ideas of 1776. It was a confederacy having the same ample power for continental purposes that Adams had seemed to desire in his intercepted letters of the year before.

If in the spring of 1776, then, there was any real difference between John Adams and Thomas Paine on the question of the scope of continental power, such difference arose out of the desire of the lawyer Adams to keep each colony's "*wholly* domestic" concerns—i.e., those matters of "internal police" which did not "interfere" with the "confederacy"—entirely free of continental authority. Perhaps the layman Paine had not meant more, since he had intended to retain the assemblies. If, however, Paine did not mean more, his use of the words "*wholly* domestic" had been most unfortunate, for his proposal had thereby been made to sound like a proposal to subject the local assemblies "in all cases whatsoever," even when continental objects were not in any way concerned. This was too much like the claim of Parliament made ten years earlier, and from such a proposal, but *not* from a proposal of general power to act for the continental welfare, John Adams undoubtedly dissented. For the benefit of any unsatisfied reader, we may add that Adams's later behavior in Congress, in the winter following, fully substantiates the view of his position which is here expounded. That behavior in Congress will be considered fully at a later point in this book.

CHAPTER IV

The Public Discussions of Forming a Continental Government in the Spring of 1776: The Less Well-Known Writers

APART from John Adam's rather artful *Thoughts* on the subject of government, only two Whig dissents from Paine's proposals in *Common Sense* are discoverable among the public discussions in the spring of 1776. One of these was a brief item signed "Marcus Brutus," which appeared in *The* [Hartford] *Connecticut Courant* on June 17. During the spring of that fateful year, a considerable clamor had arisen in Connecticut for the immediate popular election of members of Congress.[1] "Brutus" attempted to answer this clamor. The persons who had been concerned in it, said "Brutus," had "inadvertently imbibed a wrong idea of a Continental Congress." "Should [the Congress] be invested with any considerable powers of legislation, then by all means let the freemen choose them: But if they [were] to be considered as a Grand Committee, appointed by the several colonies, to execute certain purposes for the good of the whole, then the assemblies ought to appoint them." Why this should be, "Brutus" did not say. His real reason for opposing popular elections may perhaps be discerned in his later assertion thet the Congress, "if chosen by the freemen, . . . would stand upon at least an equal footing with our ancient colonial legislature." They might then "gradually assume all the powers of government, till at length the *distinct* liberties and prerogative of the whole [i.e., of all the] United Colonies [would] suffer a total dissolution." That would mean—though, again, "Brutus" did not say why—that the Continental Congress would have "a larger share of legislative authority, than it would be safe to entrust in the hands of any one set of men whatever." The thirteen free and independent colonies would then "melt down (under an absolute power of their own making) into one common mass of vassalage." This kind of writing, which completely disregarded the essential nature of representative government and aimed, by simple assertion, to arouse in unthinking men a fear of national government, was a common phenomenon in 1787 and 1788, when the Constitution was before the country for adoption. It has, of course, been common throughout our subsequent history, but in 1776 it was rare, indeed.

The one other Whig dissent from Paine's proposals was a rather elaborate series of letters by "An *Independent* Whig," which appeared in *The New York Journal* in February and March. This series of letters is chiefly remarkable for the extremely uncandid method pursued by its author. He plainly desired *not to seem* to differ too much with Paine, lest he thereby impair Paine's influence for independence, yet at the same time the "Whig" did his level best in his "independence" to discredit what Paine had had to say in favor of continental government, and to confuse the public mind upon this subject as much as he could. He therefore began with disarming praise of Paine's popular pamphlet and then passed over to insidious attack upon what it had had to say about a new form of government. What Paine had said, remarked the "Whig," was so extremely "rude and indigested" that he hardly could believe it came "from the masterly penman of Common Sense." But then, he pointed out, that author himself had professed to offer his "'hints'" only "'as an opening into the business'" and to hold "'no other opinion of them [himself], than that they [might] be the means of giving rise to something better.'" The "Whig" thereupon set about providing that "something better." He intimated that he agreed with Paine in certain things; in particular, that he agreed *in what Paine had not said at all:* that "the first step towards a Continental Charter [was] the getting the governments of the several Colonies." Paine's actual desire, we have already seen, was to form the continental and provincial governments tothether and to make them all depend upon a single charter of continental scope.

The "Whig" next observed that he also agreed—and this, Paine had in fact said—that the business of the assemblies should be "wholly domestic." "But there [were]," said the "Whig," "many objections to [having their business] 'subject to the authority of the Continental Congress.'" "The authoritative interference of Congress, with *the internal police* of a colony, might produce a worse war than the present—a civil war among ourselves." In this prognostication many readers would suppose, the "Whig" next observed, he "had an eye to religion," and despite the fact that Paine had declared it "the duty of government to protect all conscientious professors [of religion]," and further maintained that there was "no other business which government [had] to do therewith," the "Whig" said that he "readily acknowledged" religion was what he meant. He then went on to intimate that toleration was not enough, that what he really feared, under Paine's scheme of government, was a continental establishment. Despite the fact that the "Whig" said he agreed the business of the assemblies should be "wholly domestic," he gravely declared that "the extent and nature of [the legislative powers to be given to Congress] required close and long consideration in the public representative body of every colony." What Paine had proposed would, the "Whig" declared, have the effect of making the Congress "King of America." Paine's proposals were therefore exceedingly dangerous. All knew that the Continental Congress, as then set up, had no legislative power at all; and it was not to be supposed that *that* congress would "assume" such power (as, of course, the local "congresses" and "conventions" were then busily doing or getting ready to do) "till they [had] been expressly authorized [to do so] by their Constituents, whether Assemblies or Provincial Congresses." It may be added that the "Whig" also opposed per-capita voting in the Continental Congress, and the popular election of delegates. The delegates, he said, should have power only to do particular things in accordance with specific and detailed instructions from the local legislatures. "And yet," the "Whig" inscrutably declared, "if our worthy delegates know it to be the mind of their Constituents, they may declare Independence, and as *the Grand Council of the Continent*, direct our operations during the [ensuing] contest."[2]

Now, the reader should not assume that "The Independent Whig" (if, indeed, he was a Whig) and "Marcus Brutus" were the only "states' rights" men at that time in the country. There undoubtedly were others. For a very cogent reason, not very difficult to surmise, most such persons, however, kept silent. The reason was that *Common Sense* was sweeping the country. First published in Philadelphia on January 9, 1776, the pamphlet sold, according to Paine's contemporary statement, to the number of one hundred and twenty thousand copies within three months;[3] in addition, it was published in various newspapers. In a population of less than three million persons, the significance of such a circulation can hardly be mistaken: nothing else that was published in the spring of 1776 could *possibly have had anything like the same influence*. Washington said, a few weeks after its initial publication, that *Common Sense* was "working a powerful change in the minds of men [on the subject of independence]";[4] and many other important men of the time thought the same.[5] In assessing the significance of these opinions, we should not forget that one of Paine's arguments—one of his fundamental and principal arguments—was that a continental government was America's great need; that only through independence—immediate independence—could such a continental government be achieved; and, therefore, that independence should without further delay be declared. If Paine convinced the American people upon this subject, it is hard to doubt that he convinced them because they believed with him that a *continental* American government was needed.

This conclusion would be highly probable merely on the basis of the numbers in which Paine's pamphlet sold. There is other evidence corroborative of such a conclusion. For *Common Sense*, as already intimated, gave a great fillip to the discussion of plans for instituting the kind of government the pamphlet proposed. In this discussion, "independence" and "continental government" were linked together in the same manner in which Paine had linked them; and views which, a short time before, had been sporadic and somewhat furtively expressed, suddenly became open and generally expressed.

The significance of all this must have been apparent to the men who saw it: "Independence" was being urged upon the American people, with definite expectation that the government to follow would be "continental" and "supreme." The "states' rights" men were content to see this happen; content to hang back or merely to increase the hue and cry for "Independence"; content to bide their time; and then when at last it came, to attempt to pluck "states' rights" from out the confusion and disorder that "Independence" almost certainly would temporarily entail.

Fairly typical of the reaction to Paine's pamphlet among disinterested Whigs was that of Joseph Hawley, the leading figure in the Revolution in the western part of Massachusetts. Quite as important in his state, while his health continued, as the Adamses and the Warrens were, Hawley was a man of vision and great determination, a man whose fame should be known much better than it is to present-day Americans.[6] His reaction to Paine's pamphlet is to be seen in a letter he wrote on February 18, 1776, to Elbridge Gerry, one of the Massachusetts delegates in Congress. In the course of his letter Hawley explained that he had just read *Common Sense.* "Every sentiment [in it]," he said "has sunk into my well prepared heart." In particular, he told Gerry, he agreed with Paine that, "without *an American Independent Supreme Government & Constitution,* wisely devised and designed, well established and settled, [America would] always be but a rope of sand."[7] "Independence," he added in another letter, written two days later, "is the only way to union."[8] In a third letter to Gerry, written on the first of May, Hawley again came back to his subject because, as he said, "[his] hand and heart [were] full of it." "There will," he insisted in this third letter, "be no abiding union without [a declaration of independence]. When the Colonies come to be pressed with taxes, they will divide and crumble to pieces. Will a Government stand on recommendations? It is idle to suppose so. . . . Nay, without a real Continental Government, our Army will overrun us, and people will, by and by, sooner than you may be aware of, call for their old Constitutions. . . . For God's sake, let there be a full Revolution, or all has been done in vain. *Independency and a well planned Continental Government,* will save us."[9]

Views similar to Hawley's, which obviously resembled those of James Warren, of Massachusetts, were not long afterwards expressed by John Langdon, sometime a member of the Continental Congress and later a delegate to the Federal Convention from New Hampshire. "I am very happy," he said in a letter he wrote on the first of July, "at the near approach of an American Constitution. For Heaven's sake, let there be an appeal to the Continental Assembly from every government in every thing of moment relative to government matters,—for it sometimes happens that a majority of Assembly do great Mischief."[10] On the twenty-eighth of the same month, he wrote again to the same correspondent, Josiah Bartlett, one of the delegates from New Hampshire to the Continental Congress, to say that "it [had] always appeared to [him] to be good policy hitherto, not to interfere with the internal Policies of any Colony; but [that] the Matter [was] now very Different as the whole Continent [had] taken Government." "The Congress," he again suggested, "will no doubt *act as a legal body* and no doubt *interfere in any Government* that seems to go wrong."[11]

Sentiments such as the foregoing, which have survived in private letters, are in no way different from those expressed at the time in the public prints. Thus, on March 7, a writer under the pseudonym "Salus Populi," in *The* [Philadelphia] *Pennsylvania Journal*, pointed out exultantly that a de facto union was already in being, despite the fact that "a constitutional union" had so far been "impracticable" because of the veto power of royal governors, and despite the fact that "the [British] Ministry and their Tory friends [had] exerted their utmost influence to prevent any kind of union, and to break it afterwards," "All Colony distinctions," this writer went on, "are now at an end; and cursed will he be who endeavours to revive them." "And can any be so stupid," he inquired, "as to believe that they who remain united without law, without authority, and without restraint, merely because they know it to be their interest, will break that union when it shall be established under *a Continental Legislature*, and supported by publick authority?" "On the contrary, every cause of quarrel [will then] forever subside." "America will be the country, and all of us as much one people as the inhabitants of any one Colony are at present."[12] This address was copied in *The New York Journal* on March 28, and together with other writings of "Salus Populi" was also published in New York as a pamphlet.[13]

Similar views were expressed on April 29 by one "F.A.," a writer in *The Boston* [Massachusetts] *Gazette*. According to him, there were but three procedures open to the colonies: "to submit unconditionally to the mercy of Parliament; to be again dependent on the footing of 1763; or to set up *a* Government"—that is, *one* continental government—"of our own." Of the two alternatives to independence, the first, said "F.A.," was impossible. "The second [was] more specious; but would prove," he thought, "not much less distructive." His reason for this view discloses once more, as do so many of the writings of 1776, how potent the desire for "Continental Government" was in bringing about the final decision for "Independence." "Should we revert to our former dependence," said "F.A.," "that power, which has attempted to conquer us by force, will doubtless employ her policy to divide us, though a reconciliation were made, the most perfect of its kind; because it is her interest to keep us divided." He also urged that, even "if Great Britain should use no endeavours to divide us, Colony [would] naturally be jealous of Colony, while we [had] *no Continental Supreme Legislature* to connect our separate interests." "That spirit of union in which we are so happy at present, once broken, cannot be easily re-established. Reason tells us, that thirteen powerful States as these Colonies will, separately, be fifty years hence, unconnected of each other—nay, worse, jealous of each other—never yet were, and probably never will be united. . . . 'Tis next to a miracle to bring over the inveterate in an ancient, the interested in a rich, and the parties in a numerous people, *to an entire and solid union*." "Independence now," he seemed to argue in effect, meant one American empire, and consequent peace and happiness in the future; but continued "dependence" meant, he declared, that "several distinct Empires [would] be set up fifty years hence," and that "perpetual discord, obstinate rivalry, and ambitious contests for dominion, [would] follow." He concluded by observing that "those who [could] not subscribe to [his] opinions had better see them at large in that excellent pamphlet, *Common Sense*, from which," said he, "they are for the most part taken."[14] Unless desire for continental union had been rather widespread, arguments like those of "F.A." and "Salus Populi" would obviously not have been offered.

In *The New York Packet* for March 21 there appeared a more detailed sketch of a new American government. The sketch appeared in an item entitled *An Address to the Freeborn Sons of America in General, and of Connecticut in Particular.* The writer of the address appears to have been a thoroughgoing and extreme democratic republican and desired that the whole new government, from top to bottom, might be selected in both continent and province by vote of the people. "As American independence is now seriously thought of, it is high time" he said, "*to attend to the dictates of common sense*, and to be laying the plan for a more sound Constitution and scheme of Government among ourselves." "To accomplish this," the address continued, "the present happy Continental union must, by a solemn stipulation or confederation of all the Colonies, be established and ratified to endure till time shall be no more." "A standing Congress [must be] agreed upon, something in the form of the present, *to be chosen by the freemen of the Colonies*, to be entrusted with *a superintending power over them* for the time being [i.e., during some stipulated term of office], to decide disputes and adjust differences that may arise between one Colony and another; to prepare for war, or settle peace, as occasion shall require; *and to direct all commercial and Continental affairs*, &c." As for the "internal policy of each Province," which was to be under a popularly elected governor, council, and local assembly, it was spoken of as relating to "*civil* and *judicial* affairs."[15] This phraseology (obviously reminiscent of James Duane's "exclusive provincial Legislation in each Colony respecting . . . internal Polity, and comprehending the Dispensation of Justice, both civil and criminal") would not, under eighteenth-century usage, have included such "political" affairs as war, or peace, or commerce, either internal or external;[16] accordingly, war and peace and "*all* commercial and Continental affairs" were specifically confided to the Continental Congress under the plan of union proposed by this writer.

Now, the suggestion has been made that continental government was desired at this time by the aristocratic classes; that they relied upon this as a means of checking the people; and that the people at large and men of democratic views had no real interest in such a government.[17] The truth is that advocates of continental government were found among men of all classes, with the single exception of a certain class: the local politicians, who hoped to profit in position and substance from the augmentation of local power. Out of all the writers who favored continental government in the spring of '76, there was only one who did not in the plainest terms discover strong democratic leanings: Carter Braxton, of Virginia.[18] Long active in Virginia politics; a delegate at the time to the Continental Congress and, afterwards, a signer of the Declaration of Independence, Braxton was, nevertheless, not a man precisely of democratic views, and when John Adams's *Thoughts on Government* were published, Braxton undertook to answer them. His answer, under the title *An Address* ["by a Native"] *to the Convention of the Colony and Ancient Dominion of Virginia*, was first published in Philadelphia in late April or early May,[19] and then afterwards reprinted in the early part of June in Dixon and Hunter's [Williamsburg] *Virginia Gazette*.[20] Braxton's particular bias is disclosed by his proposal of handing over the control of legislation in Virginia to a governor and council, chosen to hold office during good behavior. His proposed division of power between states and nation, however, was essentially the same as that proposed by the last-mentioned writer in *The New York Packet*.

The constitution suggested by Braxton for the colony of Virginia was described in his pamphlet as one for Virginia's "internal government and police." The phrase "internal government and police," in eighteenth-century usage, was not so definite as the phrase "internal police"; why Braxton used the word "government" along with "police" is hard to say. That he intended little, if any, more than the other pamphleteers is plainly evinced by what he had to say on the subject of continental power. In turning to that phase of his subject, Braxton observed that "the next object of inquiry [was] how a *superintending power over the whole continent* [should] be raised, and with what powers invested." "Such a power," he declared, "[was] confessed on all hands to be necessary, as well for the purpose of connecting the Colonies as for the establishment of many general regulations to which the Provincial Legislatures will not be competent." He therefore urged that a permanent Continental Congress should be set up, with "power to adjust disputes between Colonies, [and] regulate the affairs of trade, war, peace, alliances, &c." Although this Congress, according to Braxton, was not "to interfere with the *internal police or domestick concerns* of any Colony," it was, nevertheless, to be fully competent to pass "such general regulations, as, though necessary for the good of the whole, [could] not be established by any other power."[21]

Despite his later "states rights" activities and his aversion in 1785 to a national power over commerce, the division of power which Braxton had in mind when he wrote this pamphlet seems clear enough. To some present-day readers, however, his statements may not seem consistent. Should this be the case, the seeming inconsistency is easily resolved by a careful examination of Braxton's language. He said quite plainly that, in addition to "internal police," the only sphere to be reserved to "the *internal* government of Virginia" was Virginia's "*domestick* concerns"; and Virginia's "domestick concerns" comprehended, of course, *only* those matters, whether *territorially* internal or not, which were of "concern" (that is, of "interest" or "importance") to Virginia *alone*. Any seeming inconsistency in Braxton's scheme is therefore dependent on taking his word "internal" in the now familiar and usual, but by no means inevitable, intraterritorial sense. If the word is taken as Braxton seems to have meant it—that is, as a synonym for his word "domestick"—there is no inconsistency or difficulty whatever. Briefly, then, Carter Braxton in 1776 apparently desired the same continental power to "regulate commerce" and to act on "*all* continental affairs," which the writer in the *New York Packet* had set forth in his projected plan of union. If the reader will compare Braxton's phrases with the phrases used in Benjamin Franklin's plan, he will find it difficult to believe that Braxton's division of power was not set down with Franklin's plan before him.

In concluding our consideration of Braxton's pamphlet, we should add that, on its publication, it was promptly attacked by Richard Henry Lee. It was, said Lee, "a contemptible little Tract," whose "confusion of ideas, aristocratic pride, contradictory reasonings, [and] evident ill design, put it out of danger of doing harm." It "betrayed," he added, "the little Knot or Junto from whence it proceeded."[22] In the absence of other evidence, this attack by Lee would of course tend to discredit any inference of general inclination toward the division of power between "continent" and "province" which Braxton proposed. As we have already intimated, however, the fact is that Lee himself, along with at least a majority of the Virginia delegation, fought to the bitter end in the Contintental Congress for precisely such a division of power when the Articles of Confederation were being drawn.[23] Apparently Lee's wrath must have been aroused by some other feature of the Braxton pamphlet, namely, the proposal contained in the pamphlet for handing over control of legislation in Virginia to a governor and council elected to serve during good behavior. This same feature also aroused the ire of Patrick Henry.[24]

Our next example of what was being said to the people in the public prints is a writer of more democratic persuasion: one "J.R.," in *The* [Hartford] *Connecticut Courant.* A whole series of writers had been busy in that paper, throughout the spring, advocating the immediate popular election of members of Congress.[25] "J.R.'s" contribution appeared toward the end of the series, in the issue of *The Courant* for June 10. His discussion began with a declaration that it was "absolutely necessary for the people's safety [that they should] retain in their own hands an effectual check [upon the authority of Congress]." "If the Delegates [should continue to be] appointed by the provincial assemblies, then in case they [should] mis-conduct, encroach upon and invade the rights of the people, the people [would] have no certain means of redress: they [might] change their Assemblies but this [might] not alter the Delegates." The difference between assemblies' choosing judicial and executive officers and constituting continental legislators was "too obvious to need a moment's reflection." Judicial and executive officers were not "supreme," but "to constitute legislators with power to make other legislators, [was] erecting a supreme authority upon a supreme authority; the former elective only by the latter, and totally out of reach of the people." Such an arrangement was dangerous and ought not to be continued. On the other hand, the local legislatures, in "J.R.'s" opinion, were entitled to have some control over the Continental Congress, to protect their own legislatural rights. "J.R." therefore proposed that the delegates to Congress be made "accountable" for "abuse or mis-use" of their powers, not only "to their constituents [i.e., the people], by being dropt at the next election, but also to the General Assemblies of their respective colonies, and be liable to be recalled or displaced, for gross negligence, or rather criminal conduct." This notion, that the delegates to Congress, though elected by the people, should be "amenable to the respective assemblies, for any unjust encroachments on [the Assemblies'] rights," was a common notion in Connecticut at the time in question;[26] and the fact is of interest, because the device of a "structural check" in favor of the states was one of the essential elements in the proposals made by the Connecticut delegation in the Federal Convention of 1787. That structural check, it is also interesting to note, was coupled, in the Connecticut proposals then made, with a general, undefined legislative power for Congress.[27]

In the plan of "J. R.," such an undefined general power was likewise proposed for the Continental Congress. "The power of the General Congress must extend," said he, "*to all matters of general concernment*, as making war and peace, sending and receiving ambassadors, levying troops and paying them, constructing a navy, and every other thing proper and necessary for the safety of the whole; to form general regulations respecting maritime affairs; to decide all controversies between colony and colony relative to their limits or boundaries; and to superintend and regulate every other matter and thing that concerns the whole, and doth not come within the territorial jurisdiction of any particular assembly."[28] "J.R.'s" language in his final clause may seem to some readers to preclude the view of his power which has just been set forth. Any reader laboring under the Supreme Court's theory of the "police power" of the states, the modern notions of the conflict of laws, and the long "states' rights" aberration in our national history, will find it easy to assume that the "territorial jurisdiction of a particular assembly," which "J. R." mentioned, was a jurisdiction that was intraterritorially all-inclusive. Such an interpretation, however, is quite unnecessary and unwarranted. Even an incorporated village has a "territorial," though it has not an all-inclusive, jurisdiction. Furthermore, such an interpretation of "J. R.'s" words would make utterly impossible the kind of continental power which he expressly said he desired. This would be true because, under such an interpretation of his words, no continental power would be possible that would "extend to *all* matters of *general concernment*," and this for the simple reason that none would then be possible which would extend to *any* such matters *of an intraterritorial kind*. That would mean, among other things, that under "J. R.'s" scheme there could not have been any uniform, nationwide laws in the field of commerce to promote and facilitate the nation's internal business; and this despite the obvious "general concernment" which would lie behind such laws, and despite the fact that no nationwide law of any kind could ever be "within the territorial jurisdiction of any particular assembly." In view of the fact that the phrase in question is often used, even at the present day, in senses which are not comprehensive, the warrant for an all-inclusive intra-territorial interpretation of "territorial jurisdiction" in "J. R.'s" power is completely imaginary. Although "J. R." might, no doubt, have made a better selection of words for his twentieth-century public, the reader will have no real doubt about what "J. R." wanted, or what his eighteenth-century readers knew that he wanted: a general power in the Continental Congress to do whatever the continental welfare required.[29]

Our final example from the discussions carried on before the people in the spring of '76, is a series of three essays, entitled *The Interest of America*, which was published over the signature "Spartanus" by some writer in New York. The writer in question was the most unfriendly to continental power (if unfriendly he can truly be called), of any of the writers who then were urging the country to independence and continental government. The essays in question first appeared in *The New York Journal*;[30] then in *The* [Philadephia] *Pennsylvania Packet;*[31] and finally in *The* [Portsmouth, N. H.] *Freeman's Journal.*[32] In the course of the second essay, "Spartanus" said: "The important day is come, or near at hand [when] America is to assume a form of Government for herself." "[This] is the most important [affair] that ever was before America. In my opinion, it is the most important that has been transacted in any nation for some centuries past. If our civil Government is well constructed and well managed, America bids fair to be the most glorious State that has ever been on earth. We should now at the beginning lay the foundation right." In the opinion of "Spartanus," this "right foundation" required the establishment in America of "a well-regulated Democracy." By "a well-regulated Democracy" "Spartanus" meant "an annual or frequent choice of magistrates, who, in a year, or after a few years, are again left upon a level with their neighbours." This, he thought, was "most likely to secure the privileges of the people." "I speak," he said, "chiefly with respect to the Legislature; [and] we should by all means avoid several branches of [it], because a plurality [of branches] causes perpetual contention, and waste of time." An executive veto of legislation he thought "absurd." He was further of the opinion that "America [ought to] consist of a number of confederate Provinces, Cantons, Districts, or whatever they may be called"; that each of these should have "a distinct Legislature"; but that all should also be "united in a General Congress." As for his notions of the proper division of power between "continent" and "province," he thought that each province ought to have, not complete power "within itself," but "as much power within itself as possible"; or, as he elsewhere put it, "as much power and liberty within itself as [would] consist with the good of the whole [continent]." "The General Congress," "Spartanus" also observed, "should not interfere or meddle with provincial affairs more than needs must. Every Province should be left to do as much within itself as [might] be; and every Province should allow each County, yea, and each Town, to do as much within themselves as possible." "Small bodies," he declared, "[could] manage affairs much easier and cheaper than large ones."

From the foregoing quotations "Spartanus" was obviously a man who entertained strong prejudices in favor of local government. Notwithstanding this fact, however, he readily conceded that there were "some things [that would have to] be left to the General Congress." Of these, he gave some examples, and it is interesting to note that his examples were at least as numerous, despite his prejudices, as those given by any of the other writers previously mentioned. They were war, peace, "*some maritime laws,*" "*general regulations respecting trade,*" currency, diplomacy, Indian affairs, the settlement of interprovincial disputes, the forming of new provinces, and the sale of new lands.[33] It should be noted, too, that the paramountcy of "the good of the whole"—by which he meant "the good of the whole" continent—ran like a refrain through "Spartanus's" whole discussion. He clearly assumed a power in each of his "provincial Legislatures" to control its towns and counties "for the provincial good," and a similar power in his "General Congress" to "interfere and meddle with Provincial affairs" whenever "the good of the continent" should require it. The reader can see then, that like the other writers herein noticed, "Spartanus" too was arguing in substance for a plan of the kind Benjamin Franklin had proposed in the preceding years; of the kind Thomas Paine, in all probability, had meant to advocate; and of the kind which James Warren, Joseph Hawley, John Langdon, Richard Henry Lee, Thomas Jefferson, and various other prominent revolutionaries desired: a plan of a "General Congress" for "the more convenient Management of General Interests" of America, with power to pass "such general Ordinances as, tho' necessary for the general welfare, particular Assemblies, [from the municipal and local nature of their powers, could] not be competent to [pass]."

The foregoing materials fairly indicate the nature of what was being said in the public press of America upon the subject of continental government in the spring of 1776. All the more extended discussions and detailed plans have been given to the reader, with the exception of one plan that was apparently garbled in the printing, and one discussion that could not be found complete. These are referred to in the notes.[34] In addition, there were a good many shorter squibs of similar tenor. Some examples of these will also be found in the notes.[35] The total bulk of these various discussions was small, of course, when compared to the bulk of the discussions which took place around 1787 when the Constitution was formed. Despite this fact, the discussions in question are believed to have reflected accurately the general state of public desire on the question of continental *versus* local government in the spring of

1776; and this, even though the suggestions contained in the discussions were totally disregarded when the confederation was later formed. The factors which led to this unfortunate result will be considered hereafter. As for the rather small total bulk of the discussions in the spring of 1776, it is accounted for, in part, by the fact that at that time there were only about one-third as many newspapers in the country as there were in the period around 1787; in part, by the fact that a good many of this much smaller total number of papers were Tory papers; in part by the fact that a large proportion of the American people were uninterested in a new continental government since they were satisfied with the continental—or, rather, the imperial—government they had; and, most of all, by the fact that the writing of such items as those herein given was an act of treason against the existing government. Because of this fact, only the bolder spirits among the Whigs spoke out; and not even these spoke out until John Adams unintentionally, and Thomas Paine deliberately, had led the way.

After independence was declared, there appeared in the papers a fair number of complaints about the way things went in the forming of the government; to complete the picture of popular sentiment, it will be well to look at one or two of these complaints. There were not so many of them as there had been of plans in the antecedent period; the war was then absorbing the energies of the patriotic, and the unpatriotic were busy in other ways. The character of the complaints that we shall look at, taken with the actual events of later years, are nevertheless sufficient to suggest quite compellingly that the usual tale to the effect that "states' rights" and the Articles of Confederation, as eventually drawn, were the heart's desire of the American people of that time exhibits a rather minimal congruence with the facts of the matter.

The complaining, mostly in the form of very brief paragraphs in the various newspapers, began in the period when the revolutionary state governments were being formed. There were complaints that the delegates to Congress were not elected by the people; complaints that the legislatures and conventions presumed to instruct Congress; complaints that the formation of the state constitutions was not postponed until Congress had formed the confederation; complaints that it was unfair, in any case, to act while so many of the staunchest patriots were in the army; complaints that the state constitutions were not being submitted to the people; and complaints of the character of the various state governments which thus were being formed.

The most interesting and lengthy of the complaints which appeared at this early period is the complaint of one "Philo-Alethias," of the state of Delaware. Like most of the writers heretofore mentioned, "Philo-Alethias" appears to have been a thorough-going democrat and a man who was interested, according to his lights, in the lasting welfare of his country. His views appeared in *The* [Philadelphia] *Pennsylvania Journal*, on October 23, 1776, and in *Dunlap's* [Baltimore] *Maryland Gazette*, on November 5. "Philo-Alethias" began by observing that, when he first had seen "that Independence was unavoidable, safe and honourable to the colonies," he had thought to himself: "There can be no trouble about New Forms of Government. The experience, wisdom and circumstances of these states, plainly point out the Congress to be the *primum mobile* and supreme directress of all momentous affairs in peace, as well as war, and the last resort, unto which appeals must lie to all who think themselves aggrieved by any Courts, or Assemblies below." Those assemblies, he had therefore supposed, would "remain as heretofore, with only some change of names and terms, unless the necessity or justice of things, [should] require some small alterations, as the wisdom of Congress, that is, of all the States by their annually chosen Representatives, [might] judge necessary."

"Thus," said he, "it then appeared to me and others." But "traitors," he bluntly declared, had since been busy in the various colonies, "compleating every little State into a separate policy [sic]."[36] In addition, the forms which, in general, had been set up were "too complex" and contained "too many jarring wheels within themselves." Of the state of Delware, he complained particularly that "they [had] made their form of government, without any appeal to the people, or hearing any objections, or giving any appeal to Congress." But the really "dangerous" feature of the Delaware constitution, and most of the others that he had seen, was "their too great self sufficiency, and want of connection with the great whole." "These states," he declared, "must be *one government*, or we are undone." "Before our little states became independent of each other and looked to the Congress as the animating soul of *one great American Republic*, how great the union, how happy the whole!—But now how changed!"

"Instead therefore of leaving ignorant men to contend about forms of Government, endangering our ALL at stake, by disunion among ourselves, why do we not remove the eclipse, and restore the Congress to *the supreme power of all affairs* at once? This is a simple Government.—The most simple is the best." "What need for all this costly parade of Governors, Counsels, and privy Counsels? cannot every Assembly do all the little common affairs within itself, and in all greater matters receive orders from the grand Counsel or Congress, which should also be the dernier resort to settle all greater difficulties of an internal nature?" "A grand Congress, chose annually by the People (not by their Representatives) would contain the united abilities and virtues of all these colonies in one great republic." "This would excite the prompt obedience and fidelity and public spirit of a willing people, no longer bent under the yoke of oppression by little tyrants in their own little and wrangling States." "*This simple and plain system* [would] contain no seeds of disease or decay; would connect all America in every liberty that Freemen wish for; and would probably last as long as time itself."

Despite the course of events, the "continental" ideas espoused by "Philo-Alethias" continued to be shared by men in other states, as is indicated by certain proposals which were advanced by one signing himself "Eleutheros," "an Inhabitant of Massachusetts-Bay," in *The Boston Gazette*, of December 22, 1777. This was but a little before the Articles of Confederation, as finally agreed upon in Congress, were at last published to the country.[37] "Eleutheros" deeply deplored the activity of those who had been busy, as he said, "concerting separate Forms of governing Separate States." Their work had "certainly left wide space for reformation when the tranquil hour of reflection [should once more] arrive." "Nothing", he said, "[was] more to be wished than that such a form of government [might] be hit upon for the whole as [would] effectually secure Freedom and Justice for every member, *efface all divisional lines between Province and Province*, and absorb all Party Names and separate Interests into *one great Commonwealth*." To accomplish this end, "Eleutheros" proposed that "all distinctions of States, Counties, Districts &c. and all divisions other than [certain divisions specially designed for instituting the proposed "great Commonwealth" should] be forever laid aside", and that "the whole CONTINENT [should] be reduced to *one Republic* with one general code of laws, one currency, one treasury, one fleet, one army, one interest, one heart and soul, all regulated by one CONGRESS." All America, he proposed, should be divided into separate towns, none of which, however, was to contain less than one hundred families. Each of these towns was to be a corporation, and, as an indication of the limited sense in which "internal police" was then used, it is interesting to note that each of these towns was to have the power of making "the laws of *its own internal police*."[38] These laws, however, were to be subject to disallowances at "the next ensuing convention of the century," to which the town belonged. The "century," which was to consist of one hundred contiguous towns and was therefore to be a relatively small aggregate of men, was to be the only legislative unit between town and continent. Thus, he apparently hoped that what was later the "esprit de corps" of the separate states—i.e., the old colonies—in the Federal Convention, would be destroyed. The "convention," consisting of one member for each hundred families, elected by the male heads of families in the various town, was to be "the supreme authority of the century, *under Congress.*" "Congress" was to consist of one delegate from each "Convention" and, besides powers of general legislation and taxation, was to have power "to ratify or annul all acts of any convention." By this scheme, which was elaborated considerably beyond this brief outline, "Eleutheros" hoped that the many evils which had already resulted from the setting-up of the new state governments might be brought to an end.

At the present day, it is, of course, easy to assume that "Eleutheros" and "Philo-Alethias" and the various other writers herein mentioned were impractical, visionary men, and that their "continental" ideas were not very widely entertained. Such ideas, however, are know to have been held by men like George Washington[39] and Henry Knox,[40] and a great many other very practical men, who were not, by reason of their memberships in the army, in a position at the moment to speak out; and such ideas persisted, as we shall see, through the whole troubled period of the Revolutionary War and the uncertain period which succeeded it. Then, when the Federal Convention was finally convened in 1787, ideas of this kind were repeatedly advocated, during the deliberations of that body, by men like Gouverneur Morris and James Wilson; Alexander Hamilton and Roger Sherman; Gunning Bedford and James Madison; George Read and John Dickinson; William Paterson and David Brearley; and Rufus King and various others. The ideas in question, it is clear, must have been rather widely held; beyond this fact, there can be no doubt, in the light of the materials here presented, that *the people* of the country had actually been led to "Independence" on the basis of such ideas in the spring of '76.

CHAPTER V

The Public Discussions of Forming
A Continental Government in the Spring of 1776:
The Views of the "State" Representative Bodies

IF WE now turn from the discussions in the public prints to the proceedings of the various provincial congresses, legislatures, and conventions, the conclusions indicated by the character of the public discussions are appreciably strengthened. Even at this early date, the proceedings in these "state" bodies were unquestionably affected by the usual desire on the part of such bodies to increase their own importance. As a consequence, the evidence to be found in their proceedings is not in certain cases as clear as that to be found in the discussions carried on before the people. Nonetheless, the evidence in their proceedings indicates that the prevailing expectation among these bodies was that the Continental Congress would be the "supream Legislative" of the country, at least in everything except matters of state "internal police." Some of the evidence unquestionably goes even further; some of it, in a vague way, not quite so far; but clearly the great weight of the evidence is as we have stated.

In this connection, one of the earliest significant items is a motion presented upon the first assembling of the provincial congress of the colony of New York. The motion was made on May 23, 1776, by Isaac Low, and seconded by Gouverneur Morris, who, twelve years later, was to take a leading part in the doings of the Federal Convention. The motion proposed the local congress should resolve, as its "opinion," that *implicit obedience ought to be paid to every recommendation of the Continental Congress for the general regulation of the Associated Colonies"*; but that the local congress was nonetheless "competent to all matters relating to [New York's] *internal police*" and "ought freely to deliberate and determine on all [such matters]." After some debate, it was determined that the motion ought not then to be put;[1] two days later the congress also postponed a motion to approve the proceedings of the First Continental Congress of the preceding fall.[2] Instead, "A Plan of Accomodation between Great Britain and the Colonies" was drawn up (as already related) and submitted to the New York delegates in Congress on June 28. The plan embodied a set of ideas not very different from those advocated by James Duane in the First Continental Congress in the previous autumn.[3] In other words, the efforts of Isaac Low and Gouverneur Morris at

85

the moment came to nothing. Nevertheless, their motion is of great interest, first, because it shows that local power over state "internal police," as then understood, could not have been considered as inconsistent with *indefinite* continental power for the "*general* regulation" of the colonies, and, second, because it shows how very ample in scope was the continental power, for which at least some of the revolutionary group of the time were working. It may be added that the New York provincial congress continued to be a drag on the revolutionary movement to the very end, and that the Declaration of Independence finally went through before the New York delegates received authority to concur in it. After the die was cast, however, New York responded through a Revolutionary congress with approval, and with full authority for continental action in the scope that Isaac Low and Gouverneur Morris had earlier thought to be desirable.[4]

Another early act, very significant in the present connection, was the application made by the provincial congress of Massachusetts, for the Continental Congress's "most explicit advice" on the local body's "taking up and exercising [in Massachusetts] the powers of *civil* government." The application was made on May 16, 1775, shortly after the assembling of the Second Continental Congress. The necessity for the proposed action was represented by the Massachusetts congress as being "most pressing." Massachusetts had long been deprived of important charter rights, in consequence of the act of Parliament "for better regulating the Massachusetts government" passed in the preceding summer.[5] Much serious difficulty had arisen therefrom, which had been borne "hitherto," the local congress said, only because it had seemed improper to "take up government" without "the advice and consent" of the "sister" colonies. The application concluded with an assurance to the Continental Congress that the local congress was ready and willing either to "submit to such a *general plan* as [the Continental Congress might] *direct*," or in the alternative to make every effort to establish in Massachusetts "such a form of government as [would] promote . . . *the union and interest of all America.*"[6] The Massachusetts application was thus a rather urgent hint that some plan of continental government was now in order. As we have seen from various earlier bits of evidence, however, much of "the Continent" was still not ready in 1775 for what seemed desirable in Massachusetts. So, on June 9, the Continental Congress, to the dismay, apparently, of many members of the Massachusetts congress, ignored the suggestion of that local body that that local body should itself assume the powers of government in Massachusetts and "advised," instead, that the people of the colony should elect an assembly in the accustomed mode and in other ways seek "to conform, as near as [might] be, to the spirit and substance of [their] charter" and carry on government as best they could, "until a Governor, of his Majesty's appointment [should] consent to govern the colony, [as its charter required]."[7] Massachusetts' prodding of the Continental Congress thus produced extremely little in the way of response. The direct assumption of government by the local congress was disapproved, and the Massachusetts suggestion of a "general plan" was left entirely untouched by the Continental Congress. Franklin's plan of confederation, however, was offered in the Congress only a short while later, and it is not unlikely that the Massachusetts urging of a "general plan" played some role in producing that result. In any case, the Massachusetts application is certainly of interest as showing the desire for continental government that existed in Massachusetts at this early date, and also the belief of its local congress at this time that the local governments should be set up in accordance with "directions" from what was coming to be known as "the superintending power of the continent."

This view of the relation of the Continental Congress to local government, while not universal at the period in question, was nevertheless very common, indeed. Evidence tending to establish this has already been introduced, and there is much more surviving of similar tenor. For example, there are certain statements in a report by a committee of the Georgia provincial congress, which had been charged in April 1776 with the preparing of "a temporary Constitution" for that colony. "Before any general system or form of Government can be concluded upon," the committee said, "it is necessary that application be made to the Continental Congress for their advice and directions." The adoption of certain temporary "Rules and Regulations" only, was recommended by this committee "to preserve rules, justice, and order"—which sounds very much like "internal police" or "polity—"until the further order of the Continental Congress, or of this or any future Provincial Congress."[8]

As further evidence that the "provincial" governments were regarded as subject to "the superintending power of the continent," we may cite, from the other end of the country, the application made by the New Hampshire provincial congress, on October 18, 1775, for "advice and direction" from the Continental Congress "with respect to a method for *administring Justice* [in New Hampshire] and regulating [that colony's] *civil police.*"[9] The language of this New Hampshire application is noteworthy, being so plainly reminiscent of the language used by James Duane in the First Continental Congress in the preceding autumn; and reminiscent also of the usage to be found in Blackstone's *Commentaries* and the translation of Vattel's *Le Droit des Gens*, referred to in the first volume of this study.[10] In the light of this usage, the function of local government was, it seems quite clear, conceived rather narrowly by the New Hampshire congress, and even a government to discharge this narrow function was to be formed, according to the New Hampshire ideas of the time, under "continental advice and direction."

The Continental Congress responded to the New Hampshire application on November 3, 1775. With characteristic caution, it recommended to the provincial congress the calling of "a full and free representation of the people" and suggested "that the representatives [so elected], if [they] should think it necessary, [should] establish such a form of government, as, in their judgment, [would] best produce the happiness of the people, and most effectually secure *peace and good order in the province*, during the continuance of the dispute between Great Britain and the colonies."[11] Unless "the happiness of the people" is to be understood in this recommendation as expressing a desire on the part of the Congress to disunite the colonies and destroy the existing de facto union, the government suggested to New Hampshire would appear to be one merely to secure local "peace and good order"; in other words, for the objects of "justice" and "police," or simply "police," if "police" is understood in the sense in which it included "justice."[12] This was the sense in which the recommendation was understood in New Hampshire, as is evident from the recited "objects" of the temporary government thereafter set up in pursuance of Congress's resolution. The objects were expressly stated to be "the securities of the lives and property of the inhabitants of the Colony" and "the preservation of peace and good order." It may be added that this temporary constitution of New Hampshire also stipulated that the provisions therein made for the election of the colony council, and probably those for the appointment of certain other officers, were conditioned upon the fact that "the Continental Congress [should] give no instruction or direction to the contrary."[13] The limited and subordinate character of local government, as that subject was understood in New Hampshire in 1775, seems therefore quite certain. There is further evidence to the same effect relating to New Hampshire which will be noted later.

A recommendation similar to that made to the New Hampshire congress was also made to the congress of South Carolina on November 4; [14] and though a contrary view has been expressed by at least one historian,[15] the recommendation seems to have been understood in South Carolina exactly as it was understood in New Hampshire. The contrary view has been based on the fact that the temporary constitution, set up in South Carolina in pursuance of Congress's resolution, included, *inter alia*, powers of war, peace, and general treaty. The provision for these powers is assumed to have been inconsistent with an expectation that binding power would be possessed within these fields—to say nothing of any other fields—by the Continental Congress. The preamble to this South Carolina constitution, however, declared that the new government had been created because it was "indispensably necessary, . . . until an accomodation [could be had] of the unhappy differences [with] Great Britain, [that] some mode should be established . . . *for regulating the internal polity of* [the] *Colony.*[16] Five days later this definitely declared purpose of this professedly temporary government was repeated in an address to the president of the colony by the legislative council and general assembly.[17] These facts cannot be conjured away, and since it is manifestly impossible, upon any straightforward interpretation, to give the term "internal polity" any meaning that will include war, peace, treaties in general, and other "external" affairs (to say nothing of other "political" affairs of nonexternal characters), clearly some view should be taken of this old document which will give some sensible effect to the contemporary declarations of its purposes. Such a view is not very difficult to formulate. Just three days before it adopted the new constitution, the South Carolina congress had voted, on March 23, to authorize the colony's delegates in the Continental Congress " to concert, agree to, and execute *every* measure which they . . . , together with a majority of [that] Congress, [should] judge necessary, *for the defence, security, interest, or welfare of [South Carolina] in particular and of America in general.*"[18] When this authority was given, it was known, of course, that some plan of union was in the offing if a settlement with Britain was not soon effected; and the new constitution itself provided that "the Resolutions of the Continental Congress [then] *of force* in [the] Colony, should so continue *until altered or revoked by them.*"[19] In addition, the new constitution also provided that all resolutions of the then present or any former local congress should continue in effect until altered by the provincial congress, which was thenceforth to be known as "the legislature of the colony."[20] The resolution of three days earlier was thus certainly incorporated into the new constitution by reference; and the expectation that the Continental Congress would be vested with general power "for the defence, security, interest, and welfare . . . of America in general" is therefore perfectly clear. The powers of the local government in fields other than "internal polity" must, accordingly, have been intended to be exercised under the "direction" of the Continental Congress as "the superintending power of the continent"; that is to say, they were expected to be so exercised to the extent that the Congress had then succeeded, or should thereafter succeed, Parliament in that role. This understanding, that there was temporarily, and might be permanently, an American continental government having indefinite power for "general" purposes (albeit, perhaps, a power "to act on the [colonies] only in their collective capacities")[21] is the only fact of present interest. There may very well have been a complete failure to comprehend the difficulties and problems of continental organization, but we can entertain no doubt that in South Carolina in the spring of 1776 there was a desire for and an expectation of a continental government having indefinite "general" powers.

The recommendation made by Congress to New Hampshire and South Carolina was repeated to the convention of Virginia on December 4.[22] The facts in relation to the Virginia attitude on continental power will be brought out fully a little later. For the present, it is sufficient to say that there is nothing to show that Virginia's understanding of the resolution of Congress was in any way different from that of the two states to which it previously had been made. The final recommendation to all "the United Colonies" to establish revolutionary governments wherever needed[23] was passed in the Continental Congress on May 10, 1776. Such governments were recommended as would "in the opinion of the representatives of the people [in the several colonies] best conduce to the happiness and safety of their constituents in particular, and America in general."[24] After a protracted debate, a preamble was added to the resolution on May 15, which declared that the recommendation was made because it appeared "necessary" that "the exercise of every kind of authority under the [British] crown should be totally suppressed, and all the powers exerted, under the authority of the people of the Colonies, *for the preservation of internal peace, virtue, and good order*, as well as for the defence of their lives, liberties, and properties, against the hostile invasions and cruel depredations of their enemies."[25] The delegates in Congress, we may feel quite certain, did not debate for five days over nothing. The preamble must, therefore, have been regarded as having some operative force.

The language of this resolve could undoubtedly have been better chosen—at least for the understanding of the present day. This much is obvious: "the preservation of internal peace, virtue, and good order" (briefly, "internal police") *plus* "the defence of life, liberty, and property against the enemies of the colonies" (briefly again, "common defence") did *not* on any theory add up to "the exercise of every kind of [government] authority." Yet the fact remains that the words of Congress clearly implied that the governments to be formed in the several colonies were to be governments for "police" purposes only; and that it was also implied that "common defence" and, indeed, everything except "police" had already been taken care of. These things would have seemed quite clear to an American of 1776, and had he been asked *how* the "common defence" had been taken care of, he would unhesitatingly have said: "By the setting-up of the Continental Congress." An American of that time would have been fully aware that the Congress had begun actively to provide for "the common defence" about a year before. At that time the army around Boston had been taken over; Washington had been appointed to the supreme command; and various other steps had been taken to organize and support "the continental forces raised, and to be raised, for the defence of American liberty."[26] As for "the regulation of commerce," an American of 1776 would have said that the Continental Congress had been governing that subject de facto ever since the forming of "the Association" in the fall of 1774. He would also have called to any questioner's attention the fact that as recently as April 13, 1776, the Continental Congress had fixed the price to be charged for such Bohea tea as could legally be sold under the Congress's earlier regulations; and had directed, at the same time, that "other teas" (i.e., green teas) should be sold "at such a price as [should] be regulated [i.e., fixed] by the committees of the town or county"—*not* the colony or state—"where the tea [was] sold."[27] Our American would also have pointed out that still more recently, on April 30, the Congress had adopted another resolution, in which, in order to encourage "adventurers" to run the then-existing British blockade, it had declared that *"the power* of the committees"—for whose election the Congress, not the state, had called in "the Association"— "to regulate the price of goods (in other instances than the article of green Tea) *ought to cease."*[28] With these very recent measures on the books of Congress, an American of 1776 would have asked how there could be any doubt as to who was to regulate commerce. He might have explained, moreover, to any questioner that "the regulation of commerce" was a "political" matter, a matter of "general concern"; that *all* matters of "general concern," including not only "the common defence" and "the regulation of commerce" but the sending and receiving of ambassadors, the making of treaties, the settling of interprovincial disputes, and a great many similar subjects were expected to be vested, and if America was to be an independent nation, *must* be vested, in the Continental Congress; that it was quite unnecessary for Congress to go into all this in its resolution of May 15; that "the common defence," the matter most recently taken over by Congress, was of course the national affair then uppermost in mind; and that on no possible view could any intention be spelled out of the resolution regarding the formation of the new "state" governments that those governments should be formed for *any* purpose whatsoever, except that of state "internal police."

The foregoing considerations are something more than speculations, as is apparent from the materials already introduced, particularly from those presented in the two previous chapters. To those materials, furthermore, certain others should be added. We may begin with discussions that appeared in *The* [Hartford] *Connecticut Courant* in the spring of 1776, when some of the merchants in that vicinity began to disregard what were referred to in *The Courant* of March 25 as "*the regulations* of Congress" and "*the laws* of our country." The writer who used these expressions meant by them the various "commercial" provisions of "the Association" of 1774. It was being said, according to the account he gave, that "the Association" had become obsolete when the sword was drawn; that the controversy with Britain had now to be settled with that weapon, and not with such "commercial" weapons as "the Association" had sought to employ. "But let me ask," inquired this writer, "What the sword will profit us if "*our union* is dissolved, which will unavoidably take place, if we refuse to acknowledge *the authority of the Congress.* If any part of the Association is [now] of so little consequence, surely we might expect a dispensation from *the same authority* by which it was originally recommended."

A little later in the spring another writer complained in the same paper of the lack of regard around Hartford for the price on Bohea tea, as fixed by Congress on April 13. According to his account, the Hartford merchants were seeking to justify their behavior in this instance on the theory that Congress's resolve of April 13 had been superseded by its resolve of April 30, by which Congress had terminated "the power of the committees to regulate the price of goods (in other instances than the article of *green* Tea)." This latter resolve, the merchants maintained, left the price of Bohea tea, a *black* tea, unregulated: an argument which of course assumed the power of Congress to regulate the subject. The writer in *The Courant* went on to show that the resolve of April 13 was in fact still unquestionably effective. "*The regula-*

tion of Bohea tea was never put by Congress into the hands of any committee whatever. A former resolve prohibited the use of it, except in [the case of what was in the country when "the Association" took effect, and what might thereafter be part of any cargoes taken by ships of war or privateers belonging to the colonies]. It was judged too important a matter for any body *save the supreme* to interpose, direct, and meddle further in, than to grant licenses *under continental restrictions.*" The importation of such tea was still prohibited, moreover, because of its source; and since the recited purpose of the resolution of April 30 was to promote the importation of articles it was desired to import, there was nothing "which could lead an attentive and unprejudiced mind to conclude that *Congress* intended to repeal or supercede *its own regulation* of the price of [Bohea tea]." But it would no doubt be asked, the writer went on, "why so much bustle about Bohea tea when the future importation of it [was] *prohibited* [by Congress]; why [might] not the traders undisturbed sell [what little there was in the country] at any price." "Rather ask," he replied, "why may not the traders violate every resolve of Congress?" "Has not Congress fixed the price of Bohea tea? *And did it not fall within their province to do it?* Is it not proper to execute their resolves, to enforce them by every justifiable means in our power? Are we not bound to adhere strictly to their measures, and strengthen their authority?" "There is not one," he concluded, "will lay his negative *publickly* upon these questions." And, it may be added, no one did.[29]

Vestiges of the view expressed in these items from *The Connecticut Courant* can be found even after the Articles of Confederation in their final form had been proposed to the states. As late as May 26, 1779, such a view was expressed in an article which appeared in *The* [Trenton] *New Jersey Gazette* of that date and was repeated in a reprint thereof which appeared on January 31, 1780, in *The* [Poughkeepsie] *New York Journal*. The article in question dealt with the vexatious problem of regulating wages and prices. By the time this article was written, regulation by uniform state action had been tried; found unsuccessful; and temporarily abandoned, partly on the plea by Congress that price-fixing retarded imports. The author of the item, seizing upon this plea, advocated the direct regulation by Congress of the prices of labor and all domestic commodities. "Surely," he argued, "the Supreme Power that governs the United States, can with one resolution, draw the line of limitation for all the prices of internal produce, manufactory and labour, leaving importation free, [and] only restraining engrossing, &c. [in the case of imported goods]." "I expect to hear", he added, "that trade will regulate itself. I know it will in ordinary cases, but we are concerned in an extraordinary one; a case of the first magnitude, in which the lives, liberties, and every thing dear to three millions of people, are at stake." At the dates when the item was published in the Trenton *Gazette* and the Poughkeepsie *Journal*, the Articles of Confederation had not, of course, as yet been adopted.

The foregoing items from the press of the time manifestly tend to prove that the understanding of Congress's resolution of May 15, 1776, was that set forth above. Apart from these items and the other materials previously introduced, cogent evidence to the same effect will be found in the response which the resolution elicited in the various colonial congresses and conventions. In the congress of New Jersey, for example, it was resolved, on June 21, that "pursuant to the recommendation of the Continental Congress of the 15th of May," a government should be set up "for regulating the *internal police* of [the] colony."[30] Since "the recommendation of Congress" had spoken only of "internal peace, virtue, and good order", it would seem pretty clear that these three things, on the one hand, and "internal police" on the other, were to the New Jersey congress one and the same. In Delaware and Pennsylvania, the same understanding of Congress's resolution appeared in certain provisions inserted in the constitutions there formed in response to the resolution of May 15, whereby the function of local government was stipulated. The people of those states, these provisions declared, were to have "the sole, exclusive, and inherent right of regulating [their own] *internal police.*" Despite the fact that the limited technical senses of "internal police" herein explained were thoroughly familiar, nothing beyond "internal police" was claimed.[31]

The general prevalence of the expectation that "internal police" would be the role of the states is also evidenced by the character of the instructions in regard to independence and confederation, which were issued at about this time to most of the delegations in the Congress.[32] The right of the "state" bodies to issue such instructions was disputed by some, as we have noted, but the instructions *were* issued, and they are part of the evidence in the case. Thus, on June 15, New Hampshire instructed its delegates "to join with the other Colonies, in Declaring The Thirteen United Colonies, *a* Free & Independent *State*," but stipulated that "the regulation of [New Hampshire's] *Internal Police* [should] be under the Direction of [its] own Assembly."[33] New Jersey made a like reservation in its authorization of independence and confederation on June 22;[34] Maryland, after some characteristic balkiness, finally did the same;[35] and the Pennsylvania Assembly, on June 14, while giving full authority to the Pennsylvania delegates "to concur . . . in forming *such further Compacts* [i.e., beyond "the Association"] between the United Colonies as [might] be judged *necessary for promoting the liberty, safety, and interests of America,*" reserved to the people of Pennsylvania "the sole and exclusive right of regulating [their own] *internal Government and Police.*"[36]

The phrase "regulating internal Government" in this Pennsylvania reservation is a phrase that may seem to some readers open to the interpretation that it was meant to reserve all territorially internal affairs. The key to what was intended by the phrase is undoubtedly supplied by a resolution adopted on June 24 by the Pennsylvania Conference of Committees, which had been called in compliance with the congressional resolution of May 15. In the resolution of the Conference, that body signified its willingness "to concur in a vote of the [Continental] Congress declaring the United Colonies free and independent States, provided *the forming* [of] *the Government,* and the regulation of the internal police of this Colony be always reserved to the people of the said Colony."[37] In the light of this second Pennsylvania reservation, there can be little doubt as to what the Pennsylvania Assembly meant in the earlier reservation by "the right of regulating internal Government," as distinct from "the right of regulating internal Police." The Assembly meant "the right of the people of Pennsylvania to set up, and alter at will, a constitution, or form of government, for the purposes of internal police." As a matter of fact, this interpretation of the first Pennsylvania reservation is in full accord with what was then the ordinary meaning of the phrase "to regulate government," a phrase much in use at the time. Its most famous—or, rather, its most infamous use—was in the title to the parliamentary act of 1774, "for the better regulating the government of Massachusetts-Bay."[38]

The right covered by this phrase, though it may possibly have been intended to be implied in some of the simpler, "internal police" reservations made by other states, was nevertheless reserved in more specific terms by several of the colony legislatures and conventions. Rhode Island, for example, instructed its delegates to "take the greatest care to secure to [it], in the strongest and most perfect manner, its [then] established form, and the powers of Government, so far as [they] related to [its] internal police and conduct of [its] affairs civil and religious."[39] Virginia, for another, stipulated that "the power of forming Governments for and the regulations of the internal concerns of [each] Colony [should] be left to the respective legislatures."[40] And Connecticut wished to save to the local legislatures "the administration of Government and the power of forming Governments for, and the regulation of the internal concerns and police of each Colony."[41] Ample justification for particularizing this right of "regulating, or forming, governments" was, no doubt, thought to arise from the prior claim to the right by the British Parliament; from the May 15 action of the Continental Congress in recommending to the colonies the forming of new governments for "police" purposes; and from the known previous view of states like Georgia, New Hampshire, and Massachusetts, as well as certain individuals in Virginia, that the setting-up of local governments even for this limited purpose should be subject to continental "direction."[42]

The reservations of Connecticut and Virginia may well evince the beginning of an overt desire among the local politicians of those states for authority in other fields besides "internal police." At any rate, the term "internal concerns," appearing in the reservations made by those two states, could certainly be taken to cover more ground than "internal police." This is especially clear in the case of Connecticut, for in its reservation the term "internal concerns" was used not as a substitute for, but in conjunction with, the term "internal police."[43] These facts, however, are easily overestimated. For a just understanding, they should be considered in context with other facts relating to these states which are undoubtedly of equal importance.

The behavior of the Connecticut governor and legislature, in connection with the convention of the New England states, heretofore mentioned, which met at Providence, in December 1776, precludes this view, in the case of Connecticut;[44] and in the case of Virginia such a view is even harder to take, because of the persistent support given by the Virginia delegation in the Continental Congress to the original draft of the Articles of Confederation. That original draft, the work of the Continental Congress of 1776, included, as already intimated, power to act in all cases for the common defense, the security of liberty, and the general welfare of the United States.[45]

In connection with the foregoing Virginia reservation, which may be a source of trouble to some present-day readers, it may be well to say a few words more about the difference between the sense in which the term "internal concerns" was used in these old discussions and documents of the eighteenth century, and the sense in which lawyers use that term today. In statements of Commerce Clause doctrine, the term is ordinarily used to denote business phenomena of an "intrastate", that is to say, "intraterritorial" character. This use of the term—apparently the result of an anachronistic misinterpretation of some of John Marshall's pronouncements in *Gibbons* v. *Ogden*,[46]—is in actual fact a sophistry. The noun "concerns" does not mean "phenomena" or "occurrences"; it means "things of importance." The word "internal," as has already been pointed out, was in the eighteenth century—as indeed it still is today—a common synonym for "domestic." "The internal concerns of a state" were, then, "the things of domestic importance to a particular state." In a certain sense this category, however, is all-inclusive, for everything that is of "general concern," or "general importance," to two or more states is also, in a certain sense, of "domestic, or internal, importance" to each of them. When, therefore, a term like "the internal concerns of a state" is used in discussions of the division of power under systems of compound government, particularly when it appears in context with terms like "general concerns" or "the general welfare," the only rational meaning which the term can have is that of "things of importance to one state *only*." If the phrase in question is taken in any more inclusive sense, then the term "general welfare" or general concerns," as the case may be, cannot be given the meaning it obviously should have. The conclusion therefore follows that a reservation like the one made by Virginia in 1776 was not at all inconsistent with willingness to vest in the Continental Congress power over "*all* matters *whatsoever* of general concern." "Internal police," as then technically understood, was a narrow, closed category; "internal concerns" was a broad and open, *but qualified*, category, which included *everything whatsoever*, which was *not* of "*general* concern." The persistent misreading of the term "internal concerns," it may be added, is merely another of the reasons for the general failure to comprehend the kind of government generally desired in this country at the period under discussion.

The one reservation of "states' rights," in the spring of '76, which at all resembled the great abuse which "states' rights" later became, was the reservation made by the congress of North Carolina. Though completely agreeable to independence, by the spring in question, the North Carolina congress was apparently not ready to go very far in the way of union with the other colonies. At any rate, in authorizing its delegates to concur in declaring independence from the mother country, the North Carolina congress carefully stipulated for "*the sole and exclusive* right of *forming* a Constitution and *Laws* [i.e., apparently, *all* laws] *for* [*North Carolina*]." It expressed, however, a willingness "to meet the Delegates of the other Colonies," but only "for such purposes as [should] be [t]hereafter pointed out."[47] Such a reservation could, to be sure, actually mean almost anything or nothing, but the consistently indifferent or antinational record of North Carolina in the early years of our national history,[48] and its exceedingly rural and dispersed backcountry character at the time in question,[49] lead to the suspicion that the reservation did probably signify an unwillingness to go very far in confederation.

In contrast to this rather grudging attitude of North Carolina, the other two states of the extreme South made no reservation whatever in favor of "states' rights." True, Georgia admonished its delegates "never [to] lose sight of the peculiar situation of the Province [which they] represented[ed]," but this probably referred to its weak and exposed military position, for in handsome terms Georgia authorized its delegates "to propose, join, and concur, in *all* such measures as [they should] think calculated *for the common good.*"[50] South Carolina, as we have seen, gave full power to its delegates to act "for the defence, security, interest, or welfare of [South Carolina] in particular and of America in general."[51] As for the colony of New York, which had long been one of the most backward in the revolutionary movement, it finally, on July 9, authorized its delegates "to consent [to] adopt *all* such measures as they [might] deem conducive to the happiness and welfare of the United States of America."[52]

The reader can thus see that, although trouble was undoubtedly brewing in the spring and summer of 1776, men believing in general government must still have been in control in most of the "state" legislatures, congresses, and conventions. Although there were also signs, no doubt, of beginning local jealousy and budding personal ambition in some of these bodies, the men in the Continental Congress of 1776 must have believed the people, as distinct from these local elected bodies, would support them in limiting the role of the states more closely than some of the bodies in question seem to have desired. As a matter of fact, in the scheme of confederation drawn up by that famous Congress, the role of the states was limited more closely. To begin with, that role was limited prima facie in the precise mode in which the role of the separate colonies had been limited in the Resolutions on the Rights and Grievances of the Colonies adopted by The First Continental Congress in the fall of 1774. This prima facie limitation—to "taxation" and "internal police," or "polity"—was in accord with what most of the "state" bodies who spoke, were asking; the domain of state power thus delimited, however, was then qualified by power in the Continental Congress to interfere with the "internal police" of a state in any case in which the objects of the confederation were concerned. As the reader will remember, these objects were "the common Defence," "the Security of Liberty," and "the general Welfare," so the resulting qualification was certainly very considerable. The scheme of power thus tentatively agreed upon in the Continental Congress undoubtedly accorded with the instructions given by the Virginia legislature to the Virginia delegates; and also with the instructions given to their delegates by the legislatures of New York, Georgia, and South Carolina. Without question, Massachusetts (which, however, had not actually spoken on the subject in over a year) was also agreeable to what was proposed; and the same was quite certainly also true of New Hampshire, New Jersey, Connecticut, and Rhode Island.[53] On the other hand, the reservations of "internal police" in Delaware and Maryland and Pennsylvania were absolute and emphatic, and could certainly have been construed as not actually authorizing what was done. As for North Carolina, we have just seen that its provincial congress conceded in advance nothing at all. The Continental Congress of 1776 did, quite clearly, go somewhat beyond what some of the "state" political bodies were asking; but did not go at all beyond the ideas which had been presented to the people in the spring of '76, as to what lay ahead in the event—by no means universally desired—that the connection between Great Britain and America should be brought to an end.

CHAPTER VI

The First Two Drafts of the Articles of Confederation: Plans of General National Power for Congress

THE subject of confederation was listed among items of unfinished business in the Continental Congress on December 23, 1775.[1] Then, on January 16, 1776, under the leadership of Benjamin Franklin, an effort was made to induce the delegates actually to take up the subject of confederation and do something about it. The proposal was again opposed, however, by the conservative forces, under the joint lead, this time, of William Hooper, of North Carolina, who had probably had something to do with the unfavorable action on Franklin's plan in North Carolina in the previous fall, and John Dickinson, an old-time rival of Franklin's in Pennsylvania politics, who, like Hooper and others, was still hopeful of reconciliation with the mother country. As a result of the opposition of the conservatives, Franklin's effort failed;[2] but, by the middle of May, most of the conservatives, including Dickinson, had become convinced that independence was inevitable, and therefore were ready, and indeed urgent, to proceed with the adoption of a continental constitution as a necessary measure before independence should be declared.[3] The motion for independence was finally presented by Richard Henry Lee, of Virginia, on June 7; and at the same time, Lee also proposed "that a plan of confederation be prepared and transmitted to the respective Colonies for their consideration and approbation."[4] The original expectation seems to have been that independence would be declared and a plan of confederation announced at about the same time.[5] Accordingly, a committee to draft a declaration of independence was appointed on June 11, and a committee to draw up a confederation, on the day following.[6] In the process of drafting the confederation, however, unexpected difficulties arose, which, with the thinness of attendance in Congress beginning in the early autumn, and the press of other business in that body, delayed the announcement of a plan of confederation for nearly a year and a half. By that time, the makeup of Congress had considerably changed; its standing and renown had become somewhat impaired; and these factors, plus others to be presently explained, produced features in the plan as finally announced which made that plan very different from the one originally drawn up and desired by the Congress that declared American independence.

Of the work of the committee of the twelfth of June 1776, not much is known. Five days after its appointment, Josiah Bartlett, of New Hampshire, one of its members, remarked in a letter to John Langdon that "some difficulties [had] arisen," and that he "fear[ed] it [would] take some time before [the plan of confederation would] be finally settled." He added by way of explanation: "The affair of voting, whether by Colonies as at present, or otherwise, is not decided, and causes some warm disputes."[7] The Franklin plan had raised this point by proposing that voting should be by delegates, and that each colony should have one delegate "for every 5000 Polls" as determined by a census triennially taken.[8] The disputes in the committee were apparently settled adversely to this proposal; in the plan of confederation that issued from the committee on July 12 (known generally as "the Dickinson draft"), it was provided that voting should be by states; and each state was left free to send and support in the Congress as many delegates as it chose.[9]

Apart from the Bartlett letter just noticed, the only comment on the work of this committee known to exist is contained in a letter written by Edward Rutledge, of South Carolina, another member of the committee, to John Jay, of New York, on June 29.[10] Rutledge, then young and inexperienced—he was only twenty-seven years old—was much out of humor when he wrote the letter. The reason is perfectly clear in what he wrote: in the activity of the committee, Rutledge was simply not getting everything he wanted. The New England men, apparently abetted by men from the Middle States and probably by those from Virginia and other states,[11] were getting the better of Rutledge and those, if there were any at this time, who agreed with his views.[12] "The Force of [New-England] Arms," Rutledge declared in his letter, "I hold exceeding Cheap, but I confess I dread their overruling Influence in Council. I dread their low Cunning, and those levelling Principles which men without Character and without Fortune in general possess, which are so captivating to the lower class of Mankind, and which will occasion such a fluctuation of Property as to introduce the greatest disorder."

As to what the New England men and others had been doing in the committee to arouse so much ire, Rutledge told Jay that a plan of confederation had been drawn up by John Dickinson, who was not from New England. "[But] unless it's greatly curtailed," he declared, "it can never pass, as it is to be submitted to Men in the respective Provinces who will not be led or rather driven into Measures which may lay the Foundation of their Ruin." And "nothing less than Ruin to some Colonies" would be the consequence, he said, "if the Plan now proposed should be adopted." "The Idea of destroying all Provincial Distinctions and making every thing of the most minute kind bend to what they call the good of the whole,[13] is in other terms to say that these Colonies must be subject to the Government of the Eastern Provinces." And so, he concluded, "I am resolved" (and this seems to have been a purely personal resolution) "to vest the Congress with no more Power than what is absolutely necessary."

Despite this young man's firm resolve—a resolve from which he completely recovered, when he had become a few years older—the committee apparently went on in the course which was causing him such acute distress. In the draft confederation as eventually reported by the committee, the power of Congress was quite as ample as it had been in Franklin's plan. The scheme of draftsmanship, to be sure, was somewhat altered: the role of the states was more plainly marked out, and the things implied and the things expressed were different from what they had been in Franklin's plan. Despite these changes, the power that resulted to Congress under the Dickinson draft was, for all practical intents and purposes, the same power to act for "the general welfare" of the country that Franklin had provided in a somewhat different way in his plan of the previous summer.

Thus, the "objects" of the confederation, in the Dickinson draft, were "the common Defence," "the Security of Liberty," and "the mutual and general Welfare" of the entire country.[14] The "objects" under the Franklin plan had been the same, except that Franklin had also mentioned "the Security of Property and "the Safety of [the "colonies'"] Persons & Families."[15] These "objects", which the reader will at once see were aspects of "police," or "polity," were omitted in the Dickinson draft; apparently their omission was part of a studied effort by the Dickinson committee (presumably in response to the resolutions already noted as adopted in certain of the states) to mark out more clearly the role the separate states were to have. Further efforts to this end can likewise be discerned in certain changes made by the committee, in what has heretofore been termed "the States' Rights provision" of the Franklin plan. By that provision, the reader will remember, "each Colony [was to be permitted to] enjoy and retain as much as it [might] think fit of its own present Laws, Customs, Rights, Privileges, and peculiar Jurisdictions within its own Limits; and [to] amend its own Constitution as [should] seem best to its own Assembly or Convention."[16] In the Dickinson draft, this provision was abbreviated to one allowing "each Colony [to] retain and enjoy as much of its present Laws, Rights, and Customs, as it [might] think fit"; but the Dickinson draft went on to add specifically that "each Colony reserve[d] to itself the sole and exclusive Regulation and Government of its *internal Police*, in all Matters that [should] not interfere with the Articles of this Confederation."[17] One of these "Articles" was the second "Article," by which the colonies united for the objects above stated. In the Dickinson draft, this specific, but qualified, reservation of the domain of "police" was further fortified, and likewise extended specifically to the field of taxation, by another provision therein that "the United States assembled" (i.e., "the Congress") should "never impose or levy any Taxes or Duties, except in managing the Post-Office, nor interfere in the *internal Police* of any Colony, *any further* than such Police [might] be affected by the Articles of this Confederation."[18] The terms of this prohibition implied, of course, that the Congress *might* "interfere" in all matters *not* comprehended in "taxation" or in "internal police"; and if one bears in mind the limited sense in which "internal police" was understood in the eighteenth century, this implication would seem to have meant, among other things, that the Congress *might* "interfere" in all matters of "commerce," whether internal or external, which, we have seen repeatedly, was *not* comprehended with the concept of "police" as then understood.[19] We should note, too, that the terms of the prohibition also implied that Congress *might* "interfere" even in matters of "internal police" in cases wherein the Articles of Confederation "affected" that "object." This would seem to mean "in those cases wherein either 'the common Defence', 'the Security of Liberty', or 'the mutual or general Welfare' of the United States was concerned." The reader will readily comprehend why Edward Rutledge was complaining that, under the Dickinson draft, "everything" was being "ma[d]e to bend to what they called the good of the whole." The committee was, in effect, proposing—just as Franklin had—a national power of "mak[ing] such general Ordinances as, tho' necessary for the general Welfare, particular [colonial] Assemblies [could] not be competent to [pass]."[20]

The foregoing interpretation of the Dickinson draft is confirmed by the comment and action of contemporaries. That Edward Rutledge agreed with the above interpretation, we have already seen. According to Rutledge, the Dickinson draft involved "the Idea of destroying all Provincial Distinctions and making every thing of the most minute kind bend to what [was called] the good of the whole." "The good of the whole," we scarcely need add, was merely "the mutual and general Welfare" by another name.

Besides the angry testimony of Edward Rutledge, who was greatly displeased with the plan, there is the testimony of James Wilson, of Pennsylvania, a member of the Congress who liked it. His views on the subject were aired in the Federal Convention, eleven years later, in debate over the necessity of vesting the Congress under the then contemplated new Constitution with a general negative upon all state laws. The remarks of Wilson, made on June 8, were recorded by Robert Yates, John Lansing, James Madison, and Rufus King. According to these sources, which are all in substantial agreement, Wilson insisted that a "national Government implie[d] the Idea of an Absorbtion of State Sovereignty." He accordingly maintained that "a definition of the cases in which the Negative should be exercised, [was] impracticable," and that "one general excepting clause"—such, presumably, as the "internal-police" exception in the Dickinson draft—"must therefore apply to the whole." "Discretion," he said, "[would have to] be left on one side or the other" and he thought it would "be most safely lodged on the side of the National Government." This scheme of things, he went on to explain, was the idea originally entertained in the Continental Congress, where the Articles of Confederation had been drawn. "In the beginning of our troubles, Congress themselves [had been] as one state." "Among the first sentiments expressed in the first Congress, one was that Virginia is no more; that Massachusetts is no more; that Pennsylvania is no more; &c. That we are now one nation of brethren." "This language"—which had been Patrick Henry's—"continued," he said, "for some time." *The original draft of the confederation was drawn on* [*this*] *idea*, and the [confederation] concluded on how different!" "Dissentions or state interests . . . gradually crept in after the formation of the [state] constitutions." It was then, said Wilson, that "jealousy & ambition began to display themselves. Each [state] endeavoured to cut a slice from the common loaf, to add to its own morsel, till at length the confederation became frittered down to the impotent condition in which it now stands." "Congress in compliance with [the] Wishes of Individual States and from an accomodating Disposition lost those Essential Powers without which a general Government was a mere Sound." All this, Wilson told the delegates, could be seen by "review[ing] the progress of the articles of Confederation thro' Congress & compar[ing] the first & last draught of it."[21]

It is obvious from the foregoing remarks, that James Wilson took the view of the Dickinson draft which is here presented. If his remarks were evidence of his own views only, they would be important; but the reader must remember that Wilson's remarks were openly made in the Federal Convention before prominent men from all parts of the country who were well-informed about the occurrences of which Wilson spoke. Not one of these men, if we may believe the records that have come down to us, undertook to contradict Wilson's account of the framing of the articles in the smallest particular.[22] This fact will appear the more significant when this further fact is brought to view: in the assemblage addressed by Wilson there sat two members of the congressional committee which had drawn up the original Dickinson draft. These men were John Dickinson, representing the State of Delaware, and Roger Sherman, of Connecticut. Sherman spoke immediately before Wilson, in the debate referred to; Dickinson, immediately after him. Dickinson agreed with Wilson in all respects. "It was impossible," he said, "to draw a line between the cases proper & improper for the exercise of the negative." "There can be no line of separation dividing the powers of legislation between the State & General Governments. The consequence is inevitable: there must be a supreme & august national Legislature."[23] Sherman, on the other hand, had expressed the belief that "the cases in which the negative ought to be exercised, might be defined"; or, at any rate, that "a trial at least should be made for that purpose."[24] He also objected, at another time, to the Virginia formula of affirmative power which up to that time the convention had approved. This Virginia formula was as follows:

That the National Legislature ought to be impowered . . . to legislate in all cases to which the separate States are incompetent, or in which the harmony of the United States may be interrupted by the exercise of individual Legislation.[25]

This Virginia formula, partly reminiscent of the formula which had appeared in the Franklin plan of 1775, which Sherman had helped to change in 1776, was thought by Sherman to be "too indefinite."[26] Yet Sherman was anything but a strict enumerationist where the affirmative powers of Congress were concerned, for he fully agreed that "it would be hard to define *all* [these powers] by detail."[27] And so, on July 17, after the equal vote in the Senate had finally been secured, Sherman finally proposed to the convention, along with an enumeration of national powers which included a power over commerce in the words now used in the Constitution, the following substitute for the Virginia formula of general power:

That the National Legislature ought to be empowered . . . to make laws binding on the People of the United States in *all* cases which may concern the *common interests of the Union:* but not to interfere with the government of the individual States in any matters of internal police which respect the governments of such States only, and wherein the *general welfare of the United States* is not concerned.[28]

This substitute formula received the immediate support of James Wilson,[29] and the substance of it was finally recommended for inclusion in the Constitution, on August 22, by the Committee of Detail, of which Wilson was a member.[30] Inferentially, then, this Sherman formula embodied the kind of "one general excepting clause applying to the whole" which Wilson had recommended to the convention in his speech of June 8. More important, as the reader will see, this Sherman formula is *the sum and substance* of the interpretation of the Dickinson draft of the Articles of Confederation which is here presented. Sherman had helped to substitute the Dickinson draft for the Franklin plan of confederation, eleven years before. Confronted once more with what was the equivalent of the Franklin formula in the Federal Convention, Sherman proposed once more to substitute for it, in brief and explicit form, the same formula of power which he previously had helped to substitute for it, in somewhat more diffuse and implicit form, in the Dickinson draft. Such behavior argues complete understanding of the Dickinson draft by Roger Sherman, and the understanding of the Dickinson draft which Sherman had is the interpretation of that draft presented here: "internal police" was the field of the states; even in that field, however, the nation might act when the "general Welfare" of the nation or, for that matter, its "common Defense" or "the Blessings of Liberty" were concerned.

The Dickinson draft of the Articles of Confederation was reported to the Continental Congress on July 12, 1776. Eighty copies of it, "and no more," were thereupon ordered to "be immediately printed, and deposited with the secretary, who [was then to] deliver one copy to each member [of the Congress]." It was also resolved "that the printer be under oath to deliver all the copies, which he shall print, together with the copy sheet, to the secretary, and not to disclose either directly or indirectly, the contents of the said confederation; [and] that no member [of Congress] furnish any person with his copy, or take any steps by which the said confederation may be reprinted, and that the secretary be under the like injunction."[31] In due course the articles, as reported, were printed, and the Congress resolved itself into a committee of the whole, and proceeded, between July 22 and August 20, to go through the articles, one by one, and to make in them such changes as appeared desirable.[32]

Of the work of this committee of the whole, not much more is known than is known of the work of the Dickinson committee. From various letters written by members of the Congress around the end of July, it appears that the mode of representation in Congress, and the method of voting therein, again came up and proved again to be extremely troublesome. Other matters that gave trouble were the closely related question of state quotas of contribution to the national treasury and—what, we shall see, was the fundamental difficulty in the whole business—the claim of certain states that their territories extended to the Pacific Ocean, or, as it was then usually put, "to the South Seas."[33] As late as August 9, one member, Samuel Chase, of Maryland, seemed in despair over the difficulties these issues had created. "When we shall be confederated States," he said, in a letter he wrote," I know not. I am afraid the Day is far distant. Three great difficulties occur—The Mode of Voting, whether by Colonies, or by an equal Representation; The Rule by which each Colony is to pay its Quota, and the Claim of several Colonies to extend to the South Seas. A considerable diversity of opinion prevails on each Head."[34] The statements in the letters of other members—John Adams, Thomas Jefferson, and Abraham Clark—are to the same effect.[35] None, other than Edward Rutledge in his petulant complaint about the Dickinson committee, makes any objection to, or any mention of trouble over, the general extent and character of congressional power. Rutledge, it may be added, was still complaining about the confederation on August 19, the day before the committee of the whole completed its labors. The confederation, he then said, was "a Devil that the Colonies [could] never agree to." In the letter he wrote, however, he intimated quite plainly that, in the views he took, he had very few sympathizers in the Congress.[36]

Besides these statements to be found in contemporary letters, there exist two sets of notes, each very far from complete, of the debates in this committee of the whole Congress. One of these sets of notes was taken by John Adams, the other by Thomas Jefferson. Neither contains anything to show that, apart from its application to western lands, the power of Congress was a troublesome question before this committee. Adams, it is true, records an objection from South Carolina to the grant to Congress of power to regulate the trade and other affairs with the Indians, but the objection does not appear to have been very strenuously urged, and it was not successful.[37]

In the end, subject to the exception hereafter noted, no change was made in the Dickinson draft that had any tendency to diminish the power which was to belong to Congress. The recital of the "objects" of the confederation came through the deliberations of the committee quite unchanged. The "states' rights" provision was *not* enlarged but instead reduced to a simple reservation of "sole and exclusive" power over "internal police" in "all matters that [should] not interfere with the articles of this Confederation." With the exception of powers relating to the western lands, none of the particular powers of Congress specified in the Dickinson draft was omitted from the draft of the committee of the whole. Final decision on the western lands was, moreover, simply postponed. As for the provision in the Dickinson draft which forbade Congress to impose or levy taxes and duties, except in connection with the post office, and that which forbade it to "interfere," in ordinary cases, in the "internal police" of the states, these provisions were omitted altogether.[38] Apart from the question of the western lands, this committee of the whole Congress of 1776, it would seem, was rather well agreed as to the power which they, the Congress, should have. Since we can hardly suppose they would draft a plan which they did not think would be adopted, we must suppose that the plan they drew was in accord with what they thought was the real sentiment of the country.

CHAPTER VII

The Revolutionary Changes in
The Articles of Confederation in the
Final Draft of 1777

THE draft of the Articles of Confederation which resulted from the revision by the committee of the whole Congress of 1776 was reported on August 20. Eighty copies of the new draft were thereupon ordered to be printed "under the same injunctions as the former articles were printed," and to be delivered to the members of the Congress "under like restrictions as formerly."[1] The intention was that the articles should then "undergo one operation through Congress more before they [were] sent to the several States for confirmation."[2] This "operation" was postponed, however, because of the pressure of other business, and because of the thinning-out of attendance in the Congress in the late summer, in consequence of the departure of many members for their homes. About the first of October, an effort was made to obtain the return of these absent members;[3] and Edward Rutledge then did some letter-writing on his own account to obtain the attendance of particular members who, he seems to have supposed, would agree with his views.[4] Attendance continued to be rather poor, however, through both October and November. About the middle of the latter month, William Hooper, who had long been the sole North Carolina representative in Congress—"the Packhorse of the State," as he styled himself—complained very bitterly of being "compelled to a constant, unremitting attendance" in Congress in order to maintain a quorum there, "neither Georgia, Maryland, Delaware, or New York, having for some time past, been represented."[5] Toward the end of November, the situation began to mend a little, but on December 12 the near approach of the British to Philadelphia caused the Congress to flee to Baltimore. A week was lost by this removal, and after the removal the thinness of attendance began all over again. Some members had remained in Philadelphia for the conduct of congressional business there; some states continued to display indifference about maintaining their congressional representations; and some of the delegates, perhaps, were deterred from attendance by their own great dislike of "the dirty, boggy hole"[6] in which Congress was sitting.

The sessions, nevertheless, were continued in Baltimore until February 27, 1777. Congress then returned to Philadelphia and resumed its sessions there on March 12. Toward the end of the Baltimore period, some new

106

delegates had begun to arrive, and various of the delegates who had been in attendance all through the trying winter of 1776-77, and some for many months before, began to take their departure. This process of change in the makeup of Congress continued after the return to Philadelphia, and by April 25, when the Congress transformed completely the character of the proposed confederation, most of the men who had taken part in the production of the first two drafts of that document in the preceding summer were no longer members of the Congress. Thus, of the committee of thirteen that had produced the original Dickinson draft, only two—Roger Sherman and Samuel Adams—were still in attendance. Of some forty-eight members who were in attendance some or all of the time while the Dickinson draft was under consideration in the committee of the whole, thirty-one had left the Congress. The remaining seventeen holdover delegates made up about half the Congress, as that body was constituted on April 25, and their distribution among the states was such that they could not have controlled more than about that proportion of the voting strength in Congress on the date in question.[7] The reasonable inference is that the Congress of that date must have been badly divided on the subject of continental power, if the newer delegates represented to any considerable degree a new point of view upon this subject.

That various of the newer delegates did represent a new point of view upon this subject, there can be little doubt. In the first place, most of the new delegates, unlike their predecessors, were appointees under the recommendation of Congress of the preceding May. The changes made as a result of this recommendation were, it is true, to a certain extent, superficial ones. As already indicated, the revolutionary governments had previously existed in the form of provincial "conventions," "congresses," and "committees," which operated by "agreement," or "association," through town and county committees of "safety," "correspondence," "inspection," and "observation," and contrived, by persuasion and intimidation, to make their decisions, and the decisions of the Continental Congress, a kind of law de facto in the different colonies. Indeed, it was said in the Continental Congress in 1777 that "the modern governments"—meaning the new state governments— "[had] not half the vigilance or authority that the conventions and committees [had] formerly had."[8] Nevertheless, the conventions, congresses, and committees had not, in general, claimed to be the lawful local governments; and they had not in fact been complete and perfected governments. Their avowed purpose had been the securing of united action by Americans to vindicate what were conceived, or at least declared, to be American constitutional rights. Professedly, the ultimate object of all these bodies, and of the Continental Congress as well, had been the effecting of some kind of amicable settlement with the mother country, a settlement that would assure to the colonies a free future within the Empire. There is no reason to suppose these professions were not in considerable measure candid and true, and because they were, to some extent at least, candid and true, many conservatives participated in the proceedings of the revolutionary bodies with a view to accomplish this stated object, up to the very day when independence was declared.[9] No doubt others, believing the real object of some of the leaders was independence, participated in the proceedings in hope that they thereby might help to postpone or prevent that dreaded event.[10] In any case, the result was a slowing down of the radical movement for independence, and a strong conservative shading in the First Continental Congress and also in the Second, in its initial composition, as we already have observed.

Once independence was declared, however, the situation changed sharply: thereafter participation was a clear act of rebellion. No loyalist could countenance such an act as that, and neither, we may suppose, could many conciliatory and many timid men who were perhaps not entirely unsympathetic to the idea of American independence. Such men, therefore, ceased to take part in the revolutionary proceedings as soon as the revolutionary character of those proceedings was unequivocally declared, and where they did not cease of their own accord, they were in most cases compelled to cease by the revolutionary party. This occurred, indeed, to some extent even before independence was delcared; yet it is natural to suppose intimidation increased against all weak-kneed groups at the moment when the final plunge was made. In addition to this, the formation of the revolutionary governments and the actual Declaration of Independence made the exclusion of the conservatives easier and more effective. As adherents of Britain, they could thereafter be treated as enemies of the country, and their exclusion accomplished under the forms of law. This was done through the so-called "test acts," which disfranchised all who declined to renounce their British allegiance. However the matter be viewed, then, the formation of the revolutionary state governments and the Declaration of Independence will certainly have produced a great and sudden lessening of conservative influence.[11] This effect of these events, it also seems clear, was certain to manifest itself sooner or later in changes in the makeup and sentiments of the Continental Congress. And if the number of the outright loyalists and of the near-loyalists, or timid and undecided men, are kept in view (each of which groups, according to John Adams, constituted about one-third of the country),[12] the certainty is that, by the date in which we are interested, the Continental Congress had ceased upon many issues to be truly representative—even if it had once been representative—of the country as a whole. For, upon any issue as to which there was agreement between the loyalists, the near-loyalists, and any considerable proportion of the revolutionary group, there was likely, as a result of the complete squeezing-out of the first two groups, to be divergence in sentiment between the majority in the Congress and the majority in the country.

Among the issues affected by the foregoing factors, the issue of general versus local government unquestionably was one. Those who were conservatives on the independence issue, of course, would have rather generally believed in a considerable measure of general government, or they would not have favored the imperial system; and the evidence introduced has shown that this was especially true where the regulation of trade or commerce was concerned. Belief in the desirability of general government within this field was shared, we have also seen, by some of the men—very likely by a good many of the men—of the revolutionary group; but there were other men within this group, especially among those from the backcountry, who had no real desire for general government at all, and some men, especially from certain of the southern states, who, because of the vastness of the shadowy landclaims of their respective states, were prone to think of those states as themselves embryonic nations. In addition to such men as these, there was the class of petty local politicians everywhere who stood to gain in power and importance from *any* increase of local power. The formation of the revolutionary governments tremendously increased the power and influence of the persons in all these groups. In reference to the issues of continental power, this was clearly true. The exclusion of the loyalists and near-loyalists from influence in the new state governments was in fact the exclusion from influence in the affairs of the country, of a substantial portion of that part of American opinion which favored general government. The inevitable result was to leave the revolutionaries who also favored this mode of government, albeit on a strictly American basis, without a good part of the support upon this issue, which, had the issue of independence not been involved, they ordinarily might have had, and which, in the future, they might normally expect to have when independence should be secured, and the temporarily excluded groups should once more be admitted, as they inevitably would be, to a share in government.

In sum, then, the situation regarding the issue in which we are interested was a temporary and unstable one; for the time being the situation was such as to force the revolutionaries who believed in general government into a working coalition with the "little-nation" and "backcountry" men, and also with the selfish local politicians, all of whom agreed with the revolutionary "general-government" men, upon the issue of the moment: American independence. In circumstances such as those we have described, desire for harmony during the war for that end was, then, almost certain to produce a watering-down of the proposed Articles of Confederation to some point at which the harmony of the revolutionary groups would be assured. There is, therefore, no reason to doubt that something of this sort occurred in the Continental Congress of 1777, substantially in the manner that James Wilson in the Federal Convention said it did, ten years later.

This outcome was not reached, however, without a good deal of struggle; and a view of this struggle increases the certainty of the conclusion as to just what it was that occurred. The beginning occurred while the sessions of Congress were still being held at Baltimore. The occasion was the receipt of a report of the proceedings of the four New England states, in their convention at Providence, which took place late in December of 1776. The convention was called after the Congress had departed from Philadelphia, and the British had invaded Rhode Island. At the time, the New England states seemed thrown very largely upon their own resources, and they accordingly met to determine what to do. In brief, resolutions were passed, recommending to the states participating in the convention that measures be adopted to fix the price of all kinds of labor—agricultural, mechanical, and common—and of all goods, whether of foreign or domestic origin. In addition, measures were recommended to prevent monopoly; to increase taxes and stop further emissions of paper currency; to establish posts; and to facilitate in various ways the defense of the New England states against the British.[13]

It is important to note that the meeting had been agreed to between the states concerned, with some misgivings; at first Connecticut had refused to take part at all.[14] "This state have declined," Governor Trumbull explained, "[because] the honourable Continental Congress were taking up the subject [of stabilizing the currencies] and we had fears that such step would occasion jealousies in the other states, and endanger so cordial a Union."[15] A little later, however, when the exigency of the situation became more extreme, Connecticut changed its mind;[16] yet even then, in the resolution appointing delegates, its legislature was careful to provide that any measures adopted by the convention would be pursued only "until *the whole subject matter* [could] be laid before the Honorable Congress of the United States of America, [and] measures taken and directions given by them thereon."[17] The same precaution was adopted in identical words by the legislature of Rhode Island.[18] The legislatures of these two New England states obviously conceived "the whole subject matter" upon which the convention was to act as being within the competence of the Continental Congress, including, as the reader will observe, measures for the regulation of the *internal* "commerce" of the states concerned. Moreover, the convention that subsequently met appears to have entertained a like opinion, for its final recommendation to each of the assembled states was that it "lay before the Honourable Continental Congress the reasons, occasion and necessity of [the] meeting, and a copy of the [meeting's] proceedings."[19]

In the case of Connecticut, as a precaution in addition to those already mentioned, prior notice of the meeting was given to the Continental Congress by the state's governor. In this notice he expressed the hope that the exigent situation of the New England states would "not only excuse the procedure [they had taken], but obtain the approbation of Congress thereon."[20] A formal report of the convention's meeting, as the convention recommended, and a copy of its proceedings eventually followed and were received by the Continental Congress on January 28.[21]

Three days later the question of the propriety of the New England meeting was taken up in committee of the whole Congress; and no conclusion being reached in the first day's deliberations, consideration in this mode was continued on February 4 and 5. It was then finally resolved:

That it is the Opinion of this Committee that the peculiar situation of the New England States, whose Communication with Congress was in a great Measure cut off, and who were invaded or threatened with an immediate Invasion by the Enemy, rendered the Appointment and Meeting of the [Convention] proper and necessary, and consequently, worthy of the Approbation of Congress.[22]

This resolution was apparently drawn and adopted by the committee on the theory that, because the convention had dealt with continental matters, it was necessarily illegal, until and unless it was approved by Congress. Against this view of the matter, however, Richard Henry Lee had objected that the states "were not yet confederated," and that "therefore no law of the Union [was] infringed";[23] and Samuel Adams had observed that the convention had only exercised "the privilege of freemen."[24] In reply, James Wilson pointed out that "the design in the [convention] of the 4 New England States in sending their proceedings to Congress" was apparently "to demand their approbation." Recognition of a need for such approbation was also "clearly intimated," he said, "by the tenor of the appointments from Rhode Island and Connecticut." The truth of this certainly could hardly be denied, and Wilson concluded by observing that the business the convention had transacted was in its nature "*wholly continental* and of course required the approbation of Congress," as the New England States had seemed to recognize.[25]

With this view of the matter, John Adams entirely agreed. He reminded the delegates that "he [had] lately travelled thro' New England"; and he declared to them "he was sure that the approbation [by] Congress of the meeting [of the convention] would give pleasure to [that body] and their constituents," "Their meeting," said Adams, "was founded in necessity; [and] altho' we [are] not confederated, the same principles of equity and reason should govern us as if we were." "The four New England States [bear] the same relation to the Congress that four counties [bear] to a single State." "The four New England States, or any other four States have a right to meet upon matters wholly indifferent, but they have no right to touch upon Continental Subjects." "*The [convention] from the 4 New England States have touched upon continental Subjects:* [and] therefore the Meeting stands in need of the Approbation of the Congress."[26]

Doctor Benjamin Rush, one of Wilson's colleagues from Pennsylvania, was another speaker. He averred that he "admire[d] the proceedings of the [states] assembled at Providence"; that they were "full of political virtue and wisdom"; and he declared he verily believed "the other States [would] act wisely and virtuously in proportion as [their proceedings] resemble[d] them." Rush maintained, nevertheless, that "the meeting [was] full of great and interesting consequences, and should be regarded with a serious and jealous eye." "Their business [had been] chiefly continental, and therefore they [had] usurped the power of Congress." And "in one instance" they had actually "counterv[ail]ed an express resolution of Congress" by "regulating the price of goods."[27]

The congressional resolution that Doctor Rush had in mind was the one passed by Congress on April 30, 1776,[28] for rescinding the ninth article of "the Association" of the fall of 1774.[29] That article, in the words of the rescinding resolution, had "enjoined the inhabitants of the United Colonies to sell goods and merchandises at the rate they had respectively been accustomed to do for twelve months then last past." The rescinding resolution described this feature of "the Association" as a temporary measure, the occasion for which was now past; and in view of the British blockade at the time existing, it was declared to be reasonable that "adventurers should be encouraged by a prospect of gain adequate to the danger...in importation." It was therefore resolved "that the power [which Congress itself had therefore given to the] committees [under the Association] to regulate the price of goods (in other instances than the article of green Tea) ought to cease." From the plain purpose of this resolution—that prices in general should thenceforth be "free"—Rush was clearly right in his contention that the New England states had "countervailed" this resolution of Congress, unless the resolution for the forming of revolutionary governments, and the Declaration of Independence, had been concerted by the Continental Congress as measures to *diminish* its own power and promote the great end of national *dis*union.[30]

On the basis, at any rate, of the foregoing arguments by Rush and Adams and Wilson, the resolution of approbation received the vote of a majority of the committee of the whole Congress and was reported to the Congress as such on February 5. A committee of five was then appointed to give further consideration to the proceedings of the New England convention, apparently with a view to congressional recommendation to the other states to follow the example set by New England in the regulation of wages and prices. The committee consisted of Richard Henry Lee, Samuel Chase, Roger Sherman, James Wilson, and John Adams.[31] Two days after his appointment to this committee, Adams wrote to his wife,[32] and with the plainest satisfaction, that "the attempt of New England to regulate prices [was] extremely popular in Congress"; that that body would soon "recommend an imitation of it to the other States." He added that he expected "only a partial and temporary relief from [the measure]," but his letter contained not the slightest trace of the vehement disapproval of Congress's proposed action which he expressed a few days later.

A report favoring the recommendation in question was turned in by this committee of five on February 12;[33] but the report of the committee of the whole, implying a right to disapprove the meeting of the New England states, was taken up first and negatived, after a long debate, by what must have been a very scant majority of Congress, in view of the earlier action in committee of the whole. This inference is confirmed by the fact that, on the day following, February 13, the house was equally divided upon a motion to reconsider; and so, on the basis of an equally divided vote, the report of the committee of the whole finally failed.[34] "All the Members," said William Ellery, of Rhode Island, in writing of the matter on February 15, "[had been] agreed that the meeting [of the convention] was right considering the Circumstances: but [they] split upon the Question of [continental] Right."[35] In other words, the near unanimity on the question of continental power, displayed by the Congress in the preceding summer, was by this time quite gone, but obviously there were still many men in the Congress—probably something like a half of that body—who had *not* changed their minds.

The report of the committee of five was taken up the day following. Almost as a matter of course it failed of adoption. Oddly enough, however, most of the opposition came from the very men who had been so urgent to approve the New England meeting immediately previously, that is, from James Wilson, who had so convincingly pointed out the desire of the New England states for approbation; from John Adams, who had been so plainly satisfied with the prospect (though not expecting much economic relief from it) when he wrote to his wife; and from Benjamin Rush, who had so "admired" the proceedings of the New England states and so hoped that the other states would act with similar "wisdom and virtue." Apparently, then, their interest in adopting the New England price-fixing scheme was confined to the setting of another clear precedent of continental power; and when such a precedent proved impossible, the scheme, to them, became suddenly, and miraculously, what some observers at the present day would probably describe as "uneconomic."

Another and more consistent opponent of the committee's report was James Smith, frontiersman, surveyor, and lawyer of sorts, from the back-country of Pennsylvania. Smith had come into Congress after the drawing of the first two drafts of the Articles. He gave it as his view that to recommend the New England program to the other states would be to "interfere with the *domestic police* of each State which were," he said, "of too delicate a nature to be touched by Congress."[36] What the other members thought of Smith's objection is not recorded.

In the end, the doings of the New England Convention were approved, but in such a way as to imply no right of disapproval; and Rush and Adams and Wilson had what was, perhaps, their revenge, of seeing the proposed endorsement of the New England plan whittled down to a mere "reference" of the plan to the other states, with a "recommendation" that the other states do about it what they would.[37]

The next crossing of swords between the factions occurred toward the end of February. The only information we have upon this particular fracas comes to us from Thomas Burke, of North Carolina. Burke had taken the place of William Hooper in the Congress, as the sole representative of North Carolina, of February 4.[38] A young man, not more than thirty years of age, Burke was possessed of great energy, which was to serve him well in his later role as wartime governor of his state.[39] He had, also, some ingenuity, which enabled him to anticipate the essentials of the so-called "great compromise" in the Federal Convention, by which a national legislature was finally made possible for the United States.[40] Burke also had a Dublin University education, which, judging by the remarks of some of the other delegates, he was more than ready to share with them.

On the issue of states' rights against continental power, however, Burke had at this time no judgment at all. His strange blind spot in this respect, which he eventually got over, and which was matter of some amusement to one of his colleagues of a few months later,[41] may be seen from the fact that he thought the power of Congress to fix a national standard of weights and measures would be a most unnecessary and improper power; from the fact that he thought a power in Congress to regulate the alloy of state coins a dangerous power; from the fact that he thought the states ought each to have the right to "remain neuter" in any war declared by Congress, if, as he said, the war was, in any state's opinion, not defensive; and from the fact, finally, that he thought the states should each also have the right, in every war, to reject the ways and means Congress might appoint for the supplying of men, money, and materials; the right to control the cantonment of soldiers within their territories; and sole right to determine whether any of their citizens, accused of desertion from the army, were actually guilty of that offense.[42] More generally, Burke was of the opinion that it was dangerous to entrust "unlimited Power to any man or set of men on Earth"[43] and therefore, he seemed to reason, it was dangerous to entrust any effective power to Congress, though that body was then subject to the continuing limitation that its members could be recalled at any time by those in the states who appointed them. With such views, it is hardly a subject for wonder that Burke quickly became a leader among the anti-national faction which by this time had made its appearance in Congress; and hardly surprising that his genius produced that reservation of state sovereignty in the articles, as finally drawn, which in actual practice turned out be one of the most troublesome defects in that thoroughly troublesome and thoroughly inadequate scheme of government.

From the beginning of his service in the Congress, Burke followed the practice of dispatching a letter to the governor of his state in every post.[44] In these letters, he kept his governor well informed of what was going on, and his habit was to set forth in full detail, for his own, presumably, as well as his governor's benefit, all that "the Delegate from North Carolina," as he called himself, had had to say in the course of the Congress's proceedings. Occasionally, too, Burke would give briefer accounts of what his opponents had said, especially when he thought that he had worsted them, and this was the case on the particular occasion in which we are interested.

A committee of three had been appointed on February 12 to consider the most effective means for discouraging and preventing desertions from the army. The committee consisted of Richard Henry Lee, Samuel Chase, and Jonathan Dickinson Sergeant.[45] On the day following its appointment, the committee reported. It suggested to the Congress a recommendation to the several states to enact laws empowering all constables, ferry-keepers, and freeholders to arrest persons suspected of being deserters and carry them before justices of the peace for judicial determination of the fact. Safeguarding provisions were included as to the degree and kind of proof required for conviction, and it was provided that, in cases of conviction, the persons who had arrested the deserters should be suitably rewarded.[46] When the Congress got around to dealing with this report on February 25, an amendment was moved and carried that the power of the constables and others to act in the premises should go immediately from Congress without the formality and delay of state legislation. When this amendment passed, "the Delegate from North Carolina" arose and "desired to be informed if he might enter his Protest against it. He was informed by the chair that he could not. He then desired to have his dissent entered on the Journal, declaring he was not Apprehensive of any Injury from [the amendment] in the state he represented because he knew it would never be there observed, the People too well knowing the Maxims of their Government, but that as it was as much as his Life was worth to consent to the Congress exercising such a Power, he desired that he might be able to prove that he did not." From pity, perhaps, for the plight of "the [imperiled] Delegate," a motion was then made and carried for reconsideration.[47]

In the course of the reconsideration, James Wilson observed in support of the measure "that every object of Continental Concern was the subject of Continental Councils"—thus providing another bit of evidence as to how the draft by the committee of the whole was read. He declared "that all Provisions made by the Continental Councils must be carried into execution by Continental authority." Wilson pointed out "that the Army was certainly a Continental object, and preventing Desertion in it was certainly as Necessary an object as the raising of it, that nothing could be more Necessary to prevent Desertion than to take Effectual Measures for Apprehending Deserters, that this Power must Necessarily be in the Congress, and that they certainly had Power to authorize any persons in the states to put them in Execution. That the Power of taking up deserters was in every soldier and officer of the army, and that the Congress might make any Justice of the Peace in any state such an Officer and thereby give him that Power, and if by making him an Officer they could give him that Power, they surely could without."[48]

To this straightforward and eminently sensible argument, Burke replied with even more than his usual loquacity. When Burke had finished, Richard Henry Lee—who for some unaccountable reason had been on the other side on the New England commercial convention—observed, with sarcasm, that it certainly "was a Misfortune to be too learned; that he could see no more in [the proposed measure] than he saw every day in the Newspapers, which was advertising and offering a Reward for Deserters." This set "the Delegate from North Carolina" off again. "If the Congress has the power to appoint any Person to decide this Question, the Congress," he said, "has power unlimited over the Lives and Liberties of all men in America." Very suggestively for the present discussion, Burke also maintained that "if any Question related [*sic*] to the *Internal Polity of a state*, it certainly was this [one]."[49] This proposition was certainly unassailable, since the arrest and detention of any man obviously involves the public peace of the community in which he is arrested. But because the case before the Congress also related to "the common Defence," the point made by Burke was nonetheless without any real relevance under the plans for a confederation that had theretofore been in contemplation.

According to Burke, this question of "the jurisdiction of Congress and the States" was "the main question" in the whole debate; the prevention of desertions was largely forgotten. And according to Burke, the "great majority" of the Congress agreed with him, and not with James Wilson. "But it was not deemed prudent," he said, "to decide",[50] although the truth seems to be, as we shall see in a moment, that the question was decided the other way. Instead of the measure Burke had attacked, the Congress adopted a resolution "earnestly recommend[ing] to the [old] committees of observation or inspection *in these United States*" [that is, elected under the Association] that they seek out all deserters in their respective jurisdictions and "convey [them] to the nearest continental officer"; and "direct[ing] all such officers to receive and secure such deserters, that they [might] be safely delivered to their respective regiments, and brought to a speedy trial and exemplary punishment." Provision also was made for rewards, as originally intended, but the civil safeguards with respect to proof were omitted.[51] This strange substitute, it may be added, was apparently concocted to secure the approval of Burke and his faction. In the course of his remarks, Burke had contended that it was entirely different and proper for Congress to use these committees of inspection and observation to carry out their resolves, because those committees, he said, had been "appointed" by what he referred to as "the states" for that very purpose, although they had in fact been elected by the people of the various towns, cities, and counties *at the direction of Congress*.[52] In the end, then, by taking advantage of Burke's ignorance, Congress was able to satisfy him; the proposers of the measure got something somewhat like what they originally had asked; "the Lives and Liberties of the men of America" remained safe; and another continental precedent—of sorts at least—had been created.

Postponement of a clear decision proved, however, a useless device to the nationalist group. As already indicated, the gradual declension in the national character of Congress continued; and when the issue came again to a vote on April 25,[53] the nationalists were either in a minority or in so small and precarious a majority that it seemed inadvisable to the more judicious to insist on the measure of general, national power which this group, still very numerous in the Congress, undoubtedly desired. The vote occurred when the Articles of Confederation were finally taken up, and that article was reached, which, in the words of Burke, "expressed only a reservation of the power of regulating *the internal police*, and consequently resigned every other power [to Congress]." The significance of Burke's description of this article, as indicating awareness of the limited nature of "internal police," will be apparent to the careful reader. The reservation, Burke also said, "left it in the power of the future Congress or General Council to explain away every right belonging to the States and to make their own power as unlimited as they please[d]." In the sense of paramount, free, and exclusive "states' rights," Burke undoubtedly was right. The article did in fact leave it to Congress to regulate everything except "internal police," and to interfere even in "internal police" whenever either "the common defence," "the security of liberty," or "the mutual and general welfare" was in any way concerned. Burke carefully explained the situation to the other delegates, he says, and offered "an amendment, which held up the principle, that all sovereign power was in the States separately, and that particular acts of it, which should be expressly enumerated would be exercised in conjunction, *and not otherwise;* but that all things else each State would exercise all the rights and powers of sovereignty, uncontrolled."

In other words, Burke offered as an amendment what became the second of the Articles of Confederation as finally adopted. According to Burke, in his customary letter to his governor, the matter "was at first so little understood"—that is, of course, by any one but Thomas Burke himself— "that it was some time before [the amendment] was seconded." In view of the materials hitherto introduced, it seems most unlikely that the delay in the seconding of Burke's amendment was due entirely to the cause to which Burke, in his callow vanity, ascribed it; whatever may have been the cause, however, Burke did finally get a second for his amendment, and the debate upon it began.

This crucial debate lasted two days. "The opposition," says Burke, "was made by Mr. Wilson of Pennsylvania, and Mr. R. H. Lee of Virginia." Benjamin Rush was now gone, and John Adams, from some cause, was silent. "In the end," says Burke, "the question was carried for [the] proposition, eleven ayes, one no, and one divided. The no," he tells us, "was Virginia; the divided, New Hampshire." It thus appears from his testimony that Richard Henry Lee, at least a majority of the Virginia delegation, and half the delegation from New Hampshire voted to the end for a general national power for Congress of the kind heretofore described. Burke was greatly elated over the result; "much pleased," as he told his governor, "to find the opinion of accumulating Powers to Congress so little supported." He surmised that "in the whole business [he should] find [his own] ideas relative thereto nearly similar to those of most of the States."[54] In this opinion, he may possibly have been right; yet, if we bear in mind the near unanimity to the contrary in the preceding summer; the closeness of the vote on the New England convention only a few weeks earlier; the "prudent" postponement of a vote on continental power, which Burke himself had recorded still more recently; and the notice of the final action on deserters, it seems somewhat doubtful that the vote on Burke's amendment was the straight-out vote on the

issue of general versus local government that he supposed—a vote un-
distorted by desire for that harmony so imperiously demanded by the times,
and unconfused by the seemingly insoluble question of the western lands and
the related difficulties over contributions to the national treasury and the
legislative suffrage in the Congress.

After this the final "operation [of the articles] through the Congress" dragged out throughout the spring; then through the summer; and then into the
early fall. Every once in a while, the confederation would be brought up, and
a day would be set for considering it; and, once in a while, it would actually
be considered when the day set came around. But nothing at all was accomplished.[55] Prices, meanwhile, were rising by leaps and bounds; the war was
going badly; and complaints and discontent were increasing on every side. In
the New England states, where, as we have seen, desire for union was felt
most strongly, the price-fixing laws of the preceding winter had failed to
work, and the consensus was that blame for the failure lay with the other
states for not enacting similar laws, and with the Congress for not "directing"
concurrent action. In the absence of concurrent action by the other states, the
owners of supplies in the New England states had simply shipped their
merchandise to the unregulated markets of the other states and thereby made
conditions throughout New England even worse than they had been before.
To deal with the situation which had thus arisen, another convention was
called, as already related, to meet at Springfield, on July 30. In this second
convention, the state of New York participated, and the convention began to
look even more like a rival congress than it had before.[56]

In the meeting at Springfield, it was voted, after a few days' deliberation,
that the various price- and wage-fixing laws of the preceding winter should be
repealed; that certain restrictions should be imposed on the transport of
goods "from one State to another"; that taxation should be increased and
made more frequent; and that a copy of the convention's measures should be
transmitted to the Continental Congress, in order that such action might be
taken to obtain concurrence in the said measures by the other states "as [the
Congress] in their great wisdom [should] think meet." On August 6, therefore, Stephen Hopkins, president of the convention, wrote to the president of
Congress, pointing out that the failure of the other states to concur in the
laws enacted in New England, in the preceding winter, had "in a great
measure prevented [those laws from] answering the good purpose for which
they [had been] intended"; informing the Congress that "other measures [had]
now been agreed upon for the same purposes"; and suggesting that, since
"the success of [these measures, also, would] greatly depend upon the concurrence of the United States in the same," the states in convention were
"submit[ting] the whole to the Honourable Congress," for such action in the
premises as the Congress might think proper to take.[57]

This rather pointed Hopkins letter was received by the Congress on August 18, and with it came a copy of the proceedings of the Springfield
convention. These documents were at once referred to a committee of three,

which was enlarged to a committee of eight, on September 10.[58] Judging by the members' letters at about this time, the adoption of a confederacy came suddenly to seem a most essential step in stabilizing the currency, and a most necessary prerequisite to any improvement at all in other branches of finance.[59] The basis of these views was disclosed by Roger Sherman in a letter he wrote, a little later in the fall, to Richard Henry Lee. "Nothing effectual can be done," he said, "to fix the credit of the currency or to raise necessary supplies until some rule of proportion [among the states in the matter of contributions to the national treasury] is adopted."[60] And the need for improvement in these two fields seemed so urgent to the delegates in the Congress that they apparently decided to sink their differences in other respects; agree upon some rule of contribution to the national treasury; and get through a plan of confederation which should at least be adequate to this single, important purpose. Agreement was accordingly reached, late on September 18, "to enter upon the weighty business of the Confederation" on the morning following.[61] Before that morning arrived, however, the Congress was once again in headlong flight from Philadelphia. The departure this time took place in the middle of the night, and by what Thomas Burke described as "universal Consent, every Member Consult[ing] his own particular Safety."[62] The members eventually reassembled at Lancaster, in Pennsylvania, on September 27, but only to determine at once to move a little further on, to York, in that state, about ninety miles from danger.[63] There, "in retirement" on October 1, the members resumed their sessions, hoping for the future to be "permitted to deliberate without interruption."[64] And there, in the backcountry of Pennsylvania, the Continental Congress finally buckled down, a few days later, to what had at last come to seem the *urgent* business of agreeing on a plan of confederation.

The determination of the delegates to agree upon some kind of plan is plainly evident, thereafter, in their altered behavior. Whereas, for months before, they had shown reluctance, or perhaps indifference, in dealing with the subject, and could agree on nothing throughout the summer, they now suddenly evinced an ability to agree and a diligence in relation to the subject which kept them steadily at it until the articles of Confederation were at last completed on November 15.[65] The determination of the members to get something through for the sake of finances is also evident in the way in which they disposed of the three capital questions which previously had caused them such endless trouble. On the very first day, October 7, they voted that each state, in the future as in the past, should have one vote.[66] They then spent nearly a week in debate over modes of contribution to the national treasury and, after various alternatives had been considered, finally voted, on October 14, that state contributions to the national treasury should be in proportion to the total value of lands and improvements in private ownership in the different states.[67] Of the three capital questions, therefore, *only* the issue of contributions was extensively canvassed; questions of the western lands and the mode of voting were both left *in statu quo*.[68] This procedure and this result both strongly suggest that there was a balance of delegates within the Congress which antecedently had agreed to leave the last two matters alone, in hope that something might be gotten through by this procedure which would be of value in the field of finance. The detail of the votes on these questions clearly shows that the delegates who made up this balance of votes within the Congress were principally the delegates from the New England states, which had been so urgent, through their convention, that something in regard to finances must be done.[69] It may be added that, by the time the Articles went forth to the states, a short while later, the Congress also had ready its resolution of November 22, 1777, heretofore mentioned, which called upon the states of the eastern, middle, and southern regions of the country, to meet in conventions for the fixing of wages and prices; which recommended the stoppage of further emissions of the state paper currencies; and which, for the first time, called upon the states to raise money for the support of the war, by current taxation.[70] The conclusion seems sufficiently clear: the Articles were finally adopted in the Continental Congress primarily as a measure of wartime finance.[71]

As for the decisions made by the Congress upon other aspects of the Articles, few of these have any bearing on the subject of the present investigation. It may be noted, however, that, in certain respects *not* involving congressional power, some new provisions were added, which made for a closer peacetime union;[72] but excepting the power over the alloy of state coins, no addition was made to the enumerated sole and exclusive powers of Congress. Instead, certain of these powers which previously had been given were so much cut down as to be virtually destroyed. This was the case with the commercial treaty power. A proviso was added to it, on October 23, which, subject to an exception in favor of treaties made in pursuance of certain outstanding proposals to France and Spain, forbade the making of any treaty which should "restrain the respective States from imposing such imposts and duties on foreigners as their own people [were] subjected to, or from prohibiting the exportation or importation of any species of goods or commodities whatsoever."[73] Subject to the stated exception, this proviso obviously made impossible, as a practical matter, any commercial treaties at all. Significantly, the exception covered treaties which Congress was seeking as a means for supplying the immediate needs of the country growing out of the war.

Fully as destructive as the proviso just noticed was the one added, on October 28, to the power over Indian affairs. This proviso stipulated that the power to "regulate the trade and other affairs with the Indians" should be so exercised by Congress as not to "infringe or violate the legislative right of any State within its own limits."[74] Considering the extent, at this time, of the various state land claims, particularly those of that southern states, it is evident that this proviso made the Indian power almost completely illusory. As grants subject to such provisios were manifestly absurd, the votes in favor of these provisos, especially the vote in favor of the attached to the commercial treaty power, may very well be taken as further proof that there was, at this time, in the Continental Congress, little interest in the Articles, beyond their relation to the country's immediate wartime needs.

The votes in favor of the foregoing provisos may at first seem also to be clear proof of a general aversion to general government in the Congress. The reader should remember, however, that after equal voting was provided on October 7, the Articles of Confederation were, from the point of view of the more extensive and more populous states, simply a proposal to create a general legislature with a "rotten-borough" system of suffrage and representation. All other considerations aside, the larger states could hardly be expected to show much enthusiasm for vesting such a body with extensive or important powers of government.[75] On the other hand, the smaller states' insistence upon an equal vote for all the states in Congress was only what was to be expected, so long as such potential giants as Virginia, North Carolina, and Georgia were continued in the geographic extent they at that time claimed; the smaller states could see for themselves no future under a proportional suffrage, except as appendages to the politics of those potentially enormous states. Some fair solution of the question of the western lands would therefore have been absolutely necessary as a prerequisite to the establishment of general government, even if the desire for such government had been universal; and this being true, it seems quite clear, from the final votes on the Articles in Congress, that no inference whatever can be drawn as to the state of sentiment within that body on the issue of general *versus* local government.

The reasons for the final votes on the Articles cannot now be known. However, the fundamental importance of the western-land question is known; the country's pre-Revolutionary sentiment on the subject of general government is known; and so, too, is the character of the campaign for independence which was carried on before the people in the spring of 1776. In addition, there is the existing clear evidence regarding the sentiment upon this subject in the Congress, which declared independence in the ensuing summer. When all these facts are kept in view, together with the close vote on the first New England convention, in the early part of 1777, and the "prudent" postponement, the certainty appears that there was far more sentiment favorable to general government, in the Continental Congress, in the autumn of that year, than an uncritical examination of the final votes on the Articles might lead one to think.

The land question, it eventually turned out, was also fundamental to any solution of the problem of national finance, for when the Articles of Confederation were submitted to the states, certain of the landless states declined to ratify until the western-land question should be fairly settled. Of these states, Maryland, because of its unyielding pertinacity, was the most important. The position of these states was that the unsettled lands were a public asset; that, if these lands should be secured from Britain as a result of the war, they would have been secured by the exertion of *all* the states and should therefore be available to *all* the states as a means of paying off the national war debt and, in fair proportions, as a means of paying off the state war debts also, and for other purposes after that. In addition to this general public interest in the western lands, there were certain private claims to portions of those lands, the validity of which turned on a solution of the land question in a manner favorable to the powers of the national government. Some of the members of the Congress and of the legislatures of the landless states were interested in these claims, and their private interest undoubtedly had the usual effect upon their view of the public interest. This aspect of the opposition to the Articles as finally framed has received, in recent years, some exaggeration at the hands of the "economic determinists."[76] As the reader can readily see, however, the public interest in the western lands stood on its own merits; and even among congressional delegates from the landed states, the contemporary judgement was that the public interest was the paramount consideration with most of those who were urging the right of all the states to share in the western lands.[77] In any event, the stubborn adherence of Maryland to this position, from whatever cause, kept the Articles from going into effect until March 1, 1781. By that time, the War of the Revolution was near its end. As matters turned out, the Articles of Confederation were not available, for very long, for the urgent purpose for which, as we have seen, they had primarily been intended. For any other national purpose they were quickly discovered to be quite useless.

CHAPTER VIII

Resumé and Conclusions on the
Articles of Confederation

O N THE basis of available materials, the foregoing is in brief outline the history of the framing of the Articles of Confederation by
the Continental Congress. In all the detail of that history, there is
nothing to show that the form of government set up by the Articles was the
kind of government desired by a majority of the American people of the time.
The several versions of the Articles were secretly drawn in Congress; the
votes in that body were in a mode which was undemocratic in a high degree;
and though the Congress that produced the first two drafts may not have
been fairly representative of the country, there is every reason to believe that
the Congress which produced the final draft was very much less so. In
addition, as we have seen, there were various complicating factors which by
themselves make it extremely doubtful that the final votes on the Articles, in
the Continental Congress, were a true indication of the sentiments of that
body or, indirectly, of the American people, on the questions of governmental
organization involved in the Articles.

As for the actual adoption of the Articles by the various states, that process
also was without significance, one way or the other, on the issue in which we
are interested. The process followed, except in New Hampshire and Massachusetts, was an extremely undemocratic one. Except in these two states,
the Articles were not submitted to the people even of the revolutionary
group;[1] they were not discussed in any significant way, or at all to more than
a negligible extent, in the public prints; and they were ratified, *not* by assemblies elected for that purpose by the whole people, but by authority of
the revolutionary state legislatures, chosen by the revolutionary faction only,
whose members had all the extreme bias, so very natural to the members of
such bodies, in favor of their own power and importance. In these circumstances, it may possibly be true that the form of government set up by the
Articles was the form of government which a majority of *the revolutionary
party* wanted; again, it may be that, because of the mode of voting in the
Congress, and the many considerations which confused the essential issue in
1777 not even this was true. Whether true or not, however, there exists no
reason whatever for believing that the government set up by the Articles was

the kind of government which a majority of *the whole American people* of the time desired.

This view of the Articles of Confederation is clearly at some variance from the view held by a great many present-day historians, but it is a view which was common enough late in the eighteenth century when the Articles were in effect. "Our civil and political establishments are essentially defective," declared an able writer in *The New Haven Gazette and Connecticut Magazine*, in 1787, "[because] they are not founded on the free and unanimous choice of the people." "Have the people," he asked, "ever had an opportunity of considering and debating this subject and of making a deliberate choice? Certainly they have not; and no man to this day, knows what form of government is most agreeable to their wishes; only, it is presumed they would not prefer a Kingly government. . . . " He maintained further that "a right in the people to chuse what form of government they think will best promote their publick interest; or, in other words, what form they please, is founded in nature, and cannot be legally superceded, nor vacated." And consequently, he urged, "any form of government [meaning, of course, the Articles and the constitutions of the separate states] set up among a free people upon any other foundation, or, by whatever other means, is an usurpation and illegal."[2]

Precisely this view of the state constitutions and, consequently, of the Articles and of any national constitution based upon them was urged on the floor of the Federal Convention by George Mason, of Virginia. "In some of the states," he said, "the Gov[ernmen]ts were not derived from the clear & undisputed authority of the people. This was the case in Virginia. Some of the best & wisest citizens considered the Constitution [there] as established by an assumed authority. A National Constitution derived from such a source would [therefore] be exposed to the severest criticism." Against this view, it was urged in reply merely that it was too late to question the de facto constitutionality of the existing system: "both the State Gov[ermen]ts & the [Confederation had] been too long acquiesced in, to be shaken."[3] No delegate urged that these bodies had orginated in the choice of the people. Nor is this fact in any way surprising. The delegates in the Federal Convention, unlike the historians of later years, actually could remember the campaign for independence in 1776 and the pre-Revolutionary sentiment of the country. From having lived through the troubled times when the Articles had been adopted, they knew that a large number of men who were in favor of general government had then been excluded from free participation in governmental affairs; they knew that a large number of the most influential Americans who had similar views had then been officers of the army; and they knew that the votes on the Articles had been much confused by various extraneous considerations. It would therefore be astonishing indeed, had the men of the Convention urged that the existing system had originated in the choice of the people.

The men of the Convention, however, knew that the army and its leaders had since returned to civil life; that many of the persons excluded from political activity during the years of war were now again active in their various communities; and that the depressed condition of "commerce" in the three years preceding the year in which they met, together with the chaotic conditions which had, since the peace, arisen from the selfishness and bickering of the thirteen separate states, had alienated many persons from the state system, who, ten years before, perhaps had favored it or, at any rate, had looked with tolerance upon it. In these facts lay the Convention's hope. But the delegates were also fully aware that a certain type of petty politician still abounded in the legislatures of the separate states, and that this class of men was unalterably opposed to any change in the existing system, which, in the words of the writer in the New Haven paper quoted above, was "so admirably calculated to make *a great many* GREAT MEN."[4] This opposition of the state-politician class was the principal obstacle which the Federal Convention had to overcome. They knew that fact full well; and knowing and understanding this and all the other facts just set forth, the men of the Convention gave the best possible proof that they did know and understand these facts, and actually believe them, when they determined to go over the heads of the legislatures to the people of the country, in seeking ratification for the more effective scheme of goverment which they were about to propose.

The decision in favor of this mode of ratification, the reader should clearly understand, was not a decision based upon theory merely; it was based, in addition, upon the Convention's practical judgment that a direct appeal to the people was the most likely means of getting the new constitution adopted. "Whose opposition," asked Edmund Randolph, of Virginia, "will be most likely to be excited against the [proposed new] System?" "That of the local demagogues," he answered, "who will be degraded by it from the importance they now hold.... It is of great importance therefore that the consideration of this subject should be transferred from the Legislatures where this class of men have their full influence to a field in which their efforts can be less mischievous."[5] "I am not for submitting the national government to the approbation of state legislatures," James Wilson, of Pennsylvania, said, "[for] I know that they and the state officers will oppose it. I am for carrying it to the people."[6] "The Legislatures being to lose power, will be most likely to raise objections. The people," argued Rufus King, of Massachusetts, "having already parted with the necessary powers, it is immaterial to them, by which government they are possessed, provided they be well employed."[7] "The people," agreed George Read, of Delaware, "are wrongly suspected of being averse to a General Government. The State Magistrates may disagree; but the people are with us."[8] To the democratic procedure which these delegates proposed, it was then objected by Luther Martin, of Maryland, the arch-representative, in the Convention, of the state-demagogue group, that "the people [had] no right to [sanction the proposed new government] without the consent of those to whom they [had] delegated their power for State purposes." "Through the tongue [of the state legislatures] only," declared this son of liberty, "can [the people] speak; through their ears only, can hear!"[9]

The majority in the Convention were undeterred, however, by Luther Martin's desperate objection. They determined to send the Constitution to the Continental Congress with their formal "opinion" that "it should afterwards be submitted to a Convention of Delegates, chosen in each State by the People thereof, under the Recommendation of its Legislature, for their Assent and Ratification."[10] The effect of this procedure, as the reader will at once perceive, was to impale the petty politicians of the several states upon the horns of a singularly acute and most uncomfortable dilemma. Those distinguished apostles of Democracy, Revolution Principles, and the Rights of Man dared not refuse to call the proposed conventions, lest they thereby open themselves to the charge of recreancy to the very principles they so loudly affirmed; and they dared even less to call the conventions, lest the people agree to the scheme of government the Convention had proposed. They therefore resorted to misrepresentation, subterfuge, and delay; but in the end the conventions were called, and the Constitution was adopted. The result vindicated the judgment of the Federal Convention that the people were with them; and when the Constitution is properly understood, the reader can likewise see that the result also vindicated the judgment of the Continental Congress of 1776 regarding the kind of government desired by the American people of that faraway day.

For the purposes of the present investigation, this last is an important conclusion. It means that the inclusion of the Commerce Clause in the Constitution, whereby, as we have seen, a power was expressed which extended to *all* of the country's "commerce," as that term was then understood, was in no possible way a sudden, unforeshadowed, and inexplicable occurrence. In short, it was not a bolt from the blue. It was, instead, the fulfillment of a long-felt need and widely expressed desire; it was a most natural reversion, in the midst of difficulty, to a previously known mode of government in the field of commerce, one in which there was widespread belief not only among Americans generally, up to the very eve of the Revolution, but within as well as outside the Continental Congress even after that event occurred.

This reversion to the earlier scheme of things was made possible—indeed, inevitable—by the unstable alignment of parties in the American Revolution. Once independence had been secured, those revolutionaries (including all those influential men who were officers in the army, and many of the soldiers)[11] who believed in general government, were certain, sooner or later, to make common cause with the men of the erstwhile excluded groups, who also believed in that mode of government, in order to secure the kind of constitution which all these groups desired. For most of the men of the previously excluded groups, general government on an American plan was not, it is true, the thing that they originally had wanted, but it was, at least, the next best thing from their point of view; and, given independence as an accomplished fact, it was—again from their point of view—the best which they could hope to have. Some of them, no doubt, were embittered and perhaps traitorous, for a time, to an independent America, but abundant evidence shows that many of the neutrals and near-loyalists of the Revolution were prominently concerned in the post-Revolutionary movement which resulted in the adoption of the Constitution.[12] The prints and letters of the time abound with statements to this effect; and the great hubbub over the political activities of Tories in the period just before the meeting of the Federal Convention is unquestionably explained, in very large degree, by awareness among the state-officer class that the neutrals and near-loyalists of the Revolution were about to make common cause with that group of the revolutionaries with whom they previously had agreed upon the subject of general government, in order to overturn the system in the Articles of Confederation which, in a few brief years, had produced so many griefs and difficulties for the country.[13] The story of the long and persistent movement which had this consummation will be recounted in the ensuing pages of this book.

Part II

The Movement for a National Commerce Power in the 1780s

CHAPTER IX

The Revolutionary Origins of the Movement
for a Complete National Commerce Power

COMPLAINT of the inadequacy of the Articles of Confederation began the moment the Articles were completed in the Continental Congress. According to Henry Marchant, of Rhode Island, John Adams then predicted, on the floor of that body, that "before ten years, [the] confederation, like a rope of sand, [would] be found inadequate, and its dissolution take place." "Heaven grant," Adams added, according to Marchant, "that wisdom and experience may then avert what we have most to fear!" Adams told Marchant that Marchant's recollection of the date at which this prophecy was made, was not quite accurate; but the sentiments, he agreed, were his. "I own," said Adams, "[that] after [the] determination [of the mode of voting] and some other [matters], I gave up that confederation in despair of its efficacy or long utility."[1]

The dissatisfaction and apprehension felt by Adams were shared by many others. Even the state legislatures were dissatisfied, loose though the Confederation was, and while most of their complaints were of little consequence, a few were sensible and important. Of the latter character was the complaint made by the legislature of New Jersey, that, "by the sixth and ninth articles, *the regulation of trade* seem[ed] to be committed to the several states within their separate jurisdictions, in such a degree as [might] involve many difficulties and embarrassments, and be attended with injustice to some states in the union." "We are of the opinion," the New Jersey legislature said, "that the *sole and exclusive* power of regulating the trade of the United States *with foreign nations*, ought to be clearly vested in the Congress."[2] This suggestion, along with every other which any of the legislatures made, was voted down by Congress, in June 1778.[3] The action was taken, however, "not so much from an opinion that all the [suggested] amendments [were] improper, as from the conviction," according to the delegates from Maryland, "that if any should be adopted, no Confederation [would] take place, at least for some months, perhaps years; and in that case, many apprehend[ed], none [would] ever be entered into by all the . . . United States."[4]

The effort of the New Jersey legislature to obtain a national power over foreign commerce thus met, at the moment, with no success at all. Yet the desire of the state for a power of this kind continued and, shortly before the Articles were finally adopted, the New Jersey delegates in Congress made another attempt to obtain such a power, extended, however, to include, besides the country's foreign commerce, its entire internal commerce as well.[5] This extension in New Jersey's views seems to have resulted from the repeated failures to accomplish a nationwide regulation of wages and prices by uniform state action in the years 1777–80. The state had been active in these price-fixing attempts from the very first, and it was the first and most ardent advocate of the last of them, in the fall of 1779. Early in October of that year, the New Jersey legislature sent a petition to the Continental Congress, asking that nationwide regulation of all wages and prices be once again recommended to the several states. The need for such a step was declared to be imperative, since no regulation, the New Jersey legislature said, could possibly be effective, unless generally adopted. "As to the impracticability of [price and wage regulation], so much urged by speculators, monopolizers, and others whose minds are vitiated and poisoned by similar views of unreasonable gain, and those who wish to ruin our money and conquer us in that way, it has," said the New Jersey legislature, "not the smallest degree of weight with us; because we are very clear that it does not exist. If [such regulation] is practicable in one state, it is also in another, and of course may be carried through the union; and that it is practicable in one state we are sure, because it has been adopted, and carried into execution in the state we have the honor to represent." The legislature then referred, with regret, to the selfishness exhibited by certain of the states in the attempts at price-fixing theretofore made, but it nonetheless expressed its confidence that the states would now all come into a price-fixing scheme, if Congress would again provide the lead. For the need for price regulation on the former occasions had not, it declared, been "one-thousandth part as evident and pressing" as it had now become.[6]

To the representation thus made by the legislature of New Jersey, there was shortly afterwards added the concurrent sentiments of a convention of the states of New Hampshire, Massachusetts, Rhode Island, Connecticut, and New York, which met at Hartford in the latter part of October of the year in question. This convention declared that, "the circumstances of the States being duly considered, a limitation of the Prices of the principal articles of merchandize and produce [would] have a tendency to prevent the further depreciation of [the] currency"; but "to render such a limitation permanent and salutary, it [was] expedient," it said, "that all the States, or all of them as far westward as Virginia inclusive, should accede [to the limitation]." A convention of "all the States as far westward as Virginia" was therefore proposed as a means for effecting such a general limitation, and Congress was requested to recommend this measure to the respective states.[7] Persuaded, apparently, by the urging of the six states previously mentioned, which together consitituted nearly half the Confederation, Congress once more, and for the last time, recommended nationwide price-fixing through uniform state laws, on November 19, 1779. Besides "laws for establishing and carrying into execution a general limitation of prices," the states were asked to enact "strict laws against engrossing and witholding." The price limitation was to apply, with certain stated exceptions, to "articles of domestic produce, farming and common labor, the wages of tradesmen and mechanics, water and land carriage, [and] articles imported from foreign parts." Prompt action was requested, and it was suggested that the laws to be passed be made effective from February 1, 1780.[8]

New Jersey was among the states which responded promptly. On December 15, it passed an act to prevent engrossing and monopoly,[9] and on December 21 an act to regulate wages and prices.[10] Its next-door neighbors, however, hung back, as Massachusetts had done in the earlier effort of the same kind in the spring of 1778. So on February 26, 1780, twenty-six days after its law took effect, New Jersey suspended the further operation of its price-fixing law "until the adjacent states of New York, Pennsylvania, and Delaware [should] enact and carry into execution laws for establishing a general limitation of prices... on the principles recommended [by Congress]."[11] This condition was never fully met;[12] and on February 3, 1781, after this final Revolutionary price-fixing attempt had failed, John Witherspoon, a New Jersey delegate in Congress, presented a motion there, "that it [was] indispensably necessary that [the body] be vested with a right of superintending the commercial regulations of every State, that none might take place that should be partial or contrary to the common interest."[13] This motion, which was offered in substitution for a committee report suggesting a recommendation to the states to enact an impost for national purposes, also included provision for an impost power in Congress; however strange this may seem, the motion was seconded, and supported on the ensuing vote, by the great architect of the Articles of Confederation as they finally had been drawn: Thomas Burke, of North Carolina. On the other hand, James Madison, of Virginia, who, the historians tell us, was "the Father of the Constitution," was among those who voted *against* the Witherspoon motion. The motion failed by a vote of five states to four. New Jersey, New York, Connecticut, and North Carolina voted in favor of the measure; South Carolina, Virginia, Delaware, Pennsylvania, and New Hampshire, all voted against it. Of the four states not appearing in the vote, Massachusetts was equally divided; Georgia, whose sole representative was for the measure, was not sufficiently represented for its vote to be counted; and Rhode Island and Maryland were at the moment not represented at all. There were also three individual votes in favor of the measure among the negating states. Even as early as 1781, then, a full national power to regulate commerce—though, like the other powers under the Articles, a power apparently, of an indirect character—had much support in Congress.[14]

That this early proposal of a complete congressional superintending power over commerce grew directly from the repeated failures in price-fixing by uniform state action, which had theretofore occurred, appears probable from a number of attendant circumstances. The most impressive of these is the fact that the price-fixing failure had been the only clear and conspicuous failure in commercial regulation before the Witherspoon proposal was made. In addition, it is true there had been a good deal of difficulty in getting the states into line with adequate laws against trading with the enemy, and some confusion and squabbling had occurred over the embargoes upon commerce "from one state to another," which had been rather widely employed to keep up the supply of commodities, and hence to keep down their price, within particular states. These embargoes,* however, were merely a phase of the price-fixing efforts, as, indeed the trading-with-the-enemy laws were, also to a certain extent, since the enemy market, like the American market in unregulated states, was a continual source of difficulty in the price-fixing efforts. In their major aspect, however, the trading-with-the-enemy laws were measures for the common defense; and while the failure in this field probably had something to do with the Witherspoon proposal, the enemy, of course, was a foreign nation, and to the extent that the laws against trading with the enemy were thought of as regulations of commerce, they probably were thought of as regulations of foreign, rather than domestic, commerce, as the subject of commerce was then generally divided. As respects its probable motivation in the midst of war, then, the comprehensive scope of the Witherspoon proposal is hard to account for, except as an outgrowth of the repeated failures in price- and wage-fixing.

That these failures were the generating cause of the Witherspoon proposal is, furthermore, strongly indicated by the language in which the Witherspoon proposal was cast. As we have already seen, the failure of the price-fixing laws was ascribed in New Jersey, as it also was by a large number of men in New England and New York,[15] to the "partial" (i.e., the less than nationwide) character of the laws in question; and the embargoes on commerce "from one state to another," which had resulted from this belief as to the cause of the failure of the price-fixing laws, were regarded, at the time, by a good many men in Congress, and many in the states, as "contrary to the common interest."[16] It also seems significant that the antecedent attempts at price-fixing had all been undertaken as measures to support the currency and the public credit,[17] and that the circumstantial context and apparent purpose of the Witherspoon proposal were the same.

The remaining items of evidence supporting the foregoing view of the origin and motivation of the Witherspoon proposal have to do with the general state of opinion, at the time, regarding the desirability of increasing

*These interstate embargoes by particular states should be distinguished from the general embargo upon the exports of provisions, to be executed by the states, *which was laid by Congress, on June 8, 1778*, as a measure for stamping out trading with the enemy. Journals, XI, 578–79.

the powers of Congress. One of the most interesting items bearing upon this point is a discussion of the weakness of the Articles of Confederation, which appeared in *The* [Trenton] *New Jersey Gazette*, on April 11, 1781. Published, the reader will note, within a few weeks after the defeat of the Witherspoon proposal in Congress, the item was, so far as is known, the first public proposal, anywhere in the country, for amending the then recently adopted Articles so as to vest in Congress full power to act in all cases for the national welfare. The proposal was made by someone who signed himself "A True Patriot," an old contributor to the Trenton *Gazette,* who in the preceding year had urgently advocated the nationwide regulation of wages and prices.[18] "An essential defect [in the existing constitution]" he said, "is the want of necessary power in the collective body of the United States." "It is true," he conceded, "we have a Congress, a Council of the United States." But are they much more than a Council? . . . They say, be it resolved, that such things be recommended to the respective states. Then if a mere majority in either branch of any Legislature gives a negative upon the measure, ten to one if the whole is not void, however necessary it may be." This, of course, was what had happened to the price-fixing scheme which the "True Patriot" had advocated, and Congress had recommended, a short time before. Such failures, the "Patriot" maintained, were fraught with danger to "the chain of union." "Every department in a empire ought to enjoy such powers as [were] necessary for the discharge of its offices for the good of the community. Therefore, all such powers as belong[ed] to the policy* or good and wholesome government of each individual state ought to be and remain unalienable. But the powers by which *the general matters and concerns of the empire* [were] to be managed ought to be lodged in Congress. Agreeable to such general outlines, particulars ought to be squared." The "Patriot" was quite aware, he said, that some might think it "dangerous to entrust Congress with too much power." "I answer," said he, "what is 'too much'? what is necessary for *the well-being and safety of the whole,* cannot be 'too much'!" He therefore urged that a power of the scope he had indicated, ought, in reason, to be given to Congress. There was, it may be added, a good deal more to what the "True Patriot" had to say; but the foregoing exhibits the nature of the power which he had in mind, and the probable relationship to his proposals of the price-fixing failures.

The foregoing writer in the Trenton *Gazette* was the earliest known newspaper advocate of sweeping change in the Articles of Confederation, after the date when the Articles became effective; but a number of proposals of similar scope had been made, albeit in a less public manner, before that date. As these earlier proposals were advanced after the failure of the last of the price-fixing attempts became manifest, but before the Witherspoon motion was made in Congress, they constitute a part of the background of the

*Probably, in view of what followed, a misprint for "polity."

Witherspoon motion. The first of them was a set of resolutions, not communicated to the general public at the time, which was adopted in a convention of the states of New Hampshire, Massachusetts, and Connecticut, held at Boston, from August 3 to 9, 1780. The delegates to this convention were: John Langdon, of New Hampshire, a future delegate to the Federal Convention, whose sentiments in 1776 in favor of a general national legislative power extending to "everything of moment relative to government matters," we have already seen;[19] Jesse Root, of Connecticut, who was soon to vote in the Continental Congress for the Witherspoon motion for a national superintending power over the country's entire commerce;[20] and Nathaniel Gorham, Thomas Cushing, and John Lowell, of Massachusetts. Two of these Massachusetts men, Cushing and Gorham, had been members of the Hartford convention which had recommended nationwide price-fixing in the preceding fall, and Gorham was later also to be a member of the Federal Convention and a member of the committee of that body which selected the language of the Commerce Clause. Assembled primarily to promote the success of the military campaign which was then in progress, and "to cultivate a good understanding and procure a generous treatment" of the French land and naval forces which had then recently landed at Newport, this convention at Boston seized the occasion of its meeting to declare its opinion that is was "essential to [the country's] final safety, to the establishment of public credit, and to put a speedy and happy issue to the present calamitous war, that the union of [the] States be fixed in a more solid and permanent manner; that the powers of Congress be more clearly ascertained and defined; and that *the important national concerns* of the United States be under the superintendency and direction of one *supreme head.*" The convention accordingly recommended to the states which were represented in the convention that they at once "confederate with such of the [other] States as [would] accede to the Confederation proposed by Congress," and, in addition, that Congress be at once invested with "powers competent for the government and direction of *all those common and national affairs* which did not, nor could come within the jurisdiction of particular States." What these affairs were, the convention did not undertake to say, and "commerce," as such, was not actually mentioned, but in view of the prior and subsequent records of the men who were in this convention, and the general opinion as to the "national" character of "commerce," it seems impossible to doubt that "commerce" was such "a common and national affair" within the meaning of the resolutions adopted by this convention.[21]

About three weeks after this convention adjourned, news of its proceedings reached General Washington, whereupon he wrote to Governor Bowdoin, of Massachusetts, commending the convention and expressing the hope that its proposals would be adopted.[22] Five days later, Washington's young aide, Alexander Hamilton, who had penned Washington's letter to Bowdoin for him, dispatched a letter on his own account urging James

Duane, in the Continental Congress, that the time had come for that body to take vigorous action to improve and strengthen the government.[23] As this letter of Hamilton's, with certain other writings of his shortly thereafter, affords a clear proof of the kind of national commerce power which was then being asked, and a clear proof, also, of the correctness of the view here taken of the origin and motivation of the Witherspoon proposal, it will be worth-while to examine in some detail what Hamilton had to say in those writings.

In his letter to Duane, Hamilton declared his belief that Congress ought to be given *"complete sovereignty*, except," he said, "as to that part of internal police which relates to the rights of property and life among individuals, and to raising money by internal taxes." Upon a casual examination, the language employed by Hamilton in this formula of power may seem obscure and uncertain to many readers today, but when the technical, eighteenth-century sense of "internal police" is kept in mind,[24] Hamilton's words are not at all obscure or uncertain. Their meaning was that the taxing power of the states was to be limited to internal taxes, and that the regulatory power of the states was to be limited to those branches of tort and criminal law which have for their object the general security of persons and property, along with the law of estates and devolution of estates, and testimentary law, and the law of husband and wife, parent and child, guardian and ward, and the other topics usually included in the law of persons. Besides these several subjects, there may, perhaps, have been a few other small matters to which, in Hamilton's opinion, the laws of the states might properly extend, but that such other matters were neither numerous nor important seems perfectly clear from Hamilton's language, as does also the fact—inferable from his use of the term "internal police"—that no phase of "commercial regulation" was among them. This last fact is also established by Hamilton's outright statement, made a little further on in his letter, that the national sovereignty ought to include *"all* that relate[d] to *trade*," in addition to "all that relate[d] to war, peace, finance; and to the management of foreign affairs."[25] The state power Hamilton had in mind was, therefore, a power from which would have been excluded "all" public regulations of agriculture, manufactures, and "merchan-dize," and every other branch of what was known in the eighteenth century as "trade" or "commerce." By the same token, there would likewise have been excluded from it "all" those branches of private law which were classified in the eighteenth century as "commercial," for otherwise the "sovereignty" of Congress over *"all* that relate[d] to *trade*" would not have been "complete."

In advocating a national governing power of this extensive scope, Hamil-ton, it is usually supposed, was something of an extremist. The reader will readily see, however, that this view of Hamilton is quite unwarranted. The opinions he expressed in his letter to Duane were manifestly much like the views which previously had been expressed by a great many other men in the spring of 1776;[26] much like the views to which, in a few months more, the

"True Patriot" of the Trenton *Gazette* would be giving voice; and, most important of all, much like the opinions of the Boston convention which Washington had just approved, and from which, it seems clear, young Hamilton derived his belief that the time had come for Congress to act. Beyond all this, the fact that Hamilton's ideas, particularly in the field of commerce, were not out of line with those of other men of the time, may also be inferred from what he had to say on the subject of commerce in a series of papers he wrote and published a few months afterward. And what Hamilton had to say in those papers affords the final element in the proof above-mentioned, that the view here taken of the motives and genesis of the Witherspoon proposal is correct.

The papers in question are Hamilton's "Continentalist" papers.[27] Those papers were written within a few months after the defeat of the Witherspoon proposal in Congress. By some mischance (the nature of which is not known), however, some of them had gotten out of their author's possession shortly after he had written them; and the publication of some of the papers was therefore delayed until the spring and summer of 1782.[28] One of the delayed papers, which appeared in *The* [Fishkill] *New York Packet*, on April 18, 1782, contains the material in which we are interested. It relates to the nature of the opposition which existed, at the time, to the vesting of commercial power in Congress. The opposition had "originated," he said, "in the injudicious attempts made at different times to effect a regulation of prices." "It [had] become a cant phrase," he said, "among the opposers of these attempts, that trade must regulate itself; by which at first was only meant that it had its fundamental laws, agreeable to which its general operations must be directed, and that any violent attempts in opposition to these would commonly miscarry. In this sense the maxim [had been] reasonable but it ha[d] since been extended to militate against all interference by the sovereign; an extreme as little reconcilable with experience or common sense as the practice it was first framed to discredit."[29]

These brief remarks of Hamilton's afford a clear proof of several things of importance in the present discussion. To begin with, they afford proof that Hamilton, like the various writers on price-fixing quoted in an earlier volume,[30] regarded the then recent attempts to regulate the prices of all kinds of labor and goods, as *part* of "the regulation" of "trade," or "commerce." By virtue of this fact, Hamilton's remarks also constitute proof that their author had been advocating a national commercial power extending to the fixing of prices and all other kinds of regulation, in agriculture and manufactures, as well as in "merchandize" and other kinds of economic activity, when he had written to James Duane, in the September before the Witherspoon proposal had been advanced in Congress. In the letter which Hamilton had then written to Duane, as the reader will recall, he had urged that Congress ought to be given "complete sovereignty" over "*all* that related to *trade*"; and that if agriculture, manufactures, and all other branches of economic activity were "trade" to Hamilton, as they appear to have been in the above-quoted passage, then Hamilton, in this letter to James Duane, must have been urging "complete sovereignty" for Congress over "*all* that related to" agriculture, manufactures, and all other branches of economic activity.

The remarks from Hamilton's "Continentalist" papers afford proof, however, of still another important point: that other men, besides Hamilton, must have understood the subject of commercial regulation, at the time of which he wrote, in the same extensive sense as he. This conclusion follows, as to the opposers of a national commerce power, from what Hamilton said was the reason for their opposition. Since a power of the kind which Hamilton had advocated in his letter to Duane, was the thing which these opponents of a national commerce power opposed, the further inference quite certainly follows that a good many other men, besides Hamilton, must have been urging the necessity of such a comprehensive national commerce power, at the time of which he wrote. These several propositions, finally, can be taken to refer only to the Witherspoon motion in Congress, because, at the date when Hamilton wrote his "Continentalist" papers (whether that date be taken as 1781 or 1782), the Witherspoon motion was the *only* effort which had been made to vest Congress with commercial power, *after* the period during which the price-fixing troubles had occurred. The opposition to which Hamilton referred must, therefore, have related to that effort; that being true, the inference follows that the view of the origin and motivation of the Witherspoon proposal here stated is correct.

It should be added that this conclusion does not mean that all the men who supported the Witherspoon motion were advocates of wage and price regulation. That, apparently, was not true. John Witherspoon himself did not favor that species of commercial regulation;[31] and it is not improbable that there were other men who voted for his proposal who did so only with a view to vesting in Congress a power to prevent those "partial," or state, regulations of wages and prices that had theretofore been in force. Indeed, the Witherspoon proposal appears to have been worded with a view to obtaining precisely such support. Nevertheless, in the light of Hamilton's statement as to the nature of the opposition to a national commerce power which existed at the time, the inference seems reasonable that a very considerable part of the support for the Witherspoon proposal must have come from men who desired to make possible an effective nationwide regulation of wages and prices. Apparently the fear of what such men would do with the proposed new power had created the opposition.

As for the suggestions, finally, which Hamilton himself advanced in his "Continentalist" papers, they consisted, not of a proposal of "complete national sovereignty" subject to certain specified exceptions (as in his letter to Duane), but of certain particular national powers which, Hamilton declared, were the absolute minimum that would suffice for the country's welfare. The first and foremost of these was "THE POWER OF REGULATING TRADE, comprehending," said Hamilton, "a right of granting bounties and premiums [upon agricultural products, manufactures, exports, and imports][32] by way of encouragment, of imposing duties *of every kind*"—i.e., apparently, excises, or inland duties, in addition to external, or customs, duties—" as well for revenue as regulation, of appointing all officers of the customs, and of laying embargoes in extraordinary emergencies."[33]

The enumeration of particular component powers which Hamilton thus appended to this proposal of a national "POWER OF REGULATING TRADE," may give rise to some slight uncertainty as to what Hamilton intended his proposal to cover. As in all such cases, there is at least a theoretical possibility that the enumeration of particular component powers was intended to be exhaustive, and not merely, what it seems to have been, precautionary as to those particular elements of a general commercial power which for some reason or other Hamilton thought might be questioned.

That the latter was the true character of Hamilton's enumeration appears from several considerations. In the first place, his emphatic mode of reference to "THE POWER OF REGULATING TRADE" would hardly have been appropriate if the rule-making authority, as distinct from the duty-laying and bounty-paying authority, which was to be comprehended in his proposed national power, was one limited to the "laying [of] embargoes in extraordinary emergencies." Quite apart from this emphatic mode of reference, it is highly unlikely that Hamilton could have been advocating a rule-making authority so very narrowly limited. And if the rule-making authority comprehended in his proposed power *did* extend to any other than this one particular enumerated instance, it must have extended to all that were within the generality with which his proposal was begun. This view of what Hamilton intended by his entire proposal is amply confirmed by the character of the particular component powers which he enumerated. Thus, the embargo power, exercised, as it usually was, in time of scarcity, was plainly related to "the public health," a "police" object; and since various of the state constitutions contained specific "police" power reservations, the reader will easily see that the enumeration of this particular component power must have appeared to Hamilton as absolutely necessary. Much the same will have been true of the power of imposing duties for revenue purposes, and of the power of appointing all officers of the customs. As to the second of these, it must be remembered that, at the time when Hamilton wrote, execution was wholly in the hands of the states, and as to the first, that the pre-Revolutionary disputes with Great Britain had made the whole country conscious of the distinction between the "regulating" of trade and its "taxation." There remains, then, of Hamilton's enumeration only the power of paying bounties and premiums to promote new forms of agriculture and manufactures. At the present day, the necessity for specifically enumerating a power of paying these seems, of course, very slight; but since it was promptly denied, during the Washington administration, that such a power belonged to Congress under the Commerce Clause,[34] there probably was some color of uncertainty in the eighteenth century that the word "regulate" would cover it. The proper conclusion is that Hamilton's enumeration was made solely to make it clear that the power he was proposing was one which would comprehend the enumerated components and would not exclude other particular components from the general power over trade with which his proposal was begun.

The reader may feel that Hamilton's remarks about price fixing, in his "Continentalist" papers, are contradictive of this conclusion, since those remarks, standing by themselves, are open to the interpretation that Hamilton disapproved of that species of commercial regulation. We have seen, however, that in 1774 Hamilton had approved of price regulation, when the regulating had been done *by Congress*;[35] and since it is certain that he had urged a national power extending to that subject, only a few months before, in his letter to Duane, it is not improbable that in his opinion the "injudiciousness" of the price-fixing attempts consisted in their "partial," or less than nationwide, character. In any event, he certainly indicated, in his remarks on the subject, that hostility to a national commerce power, based on opposition to price and wage regulation, was a highly unreasonable attitude. Thus the fact that when Hamilton wrote those remarks he was still advocating a national power extending to that and every other commercial subject, seems virtually certain; and this fact, it may finally be noted, is further confirmed by a letter which he wrote to Robert Morris, a short time before his "Continentalist" papers were written. In the course of this letter, dated April 3, 1781, Hamilton told Morris that "it ha[d] ever been his opinion that Congress ought to have *complete sovereignty in all but the mere municipal law of each State*."[36] In the eighteenth century, "municipal law" was usually defined as "the law which a state makes for its own members."[37] The *mere* municipal law of each State" was therefore probably "the law upon matters which concerned single states only"; the "national sovereignty" which Hamilton had in mind was, in consequence, presumably a sovereignty as to *all* matters which concerned more states than one; and since the whole of "commerce," as we have repeatedly seen, was regarded as one of these matters of "general concern," the warranted conclusion is that the whole of "commerce" was covered by the power which Hamilton had in mind. By way of further corroboration it may also be noted that, after Lord Mansfield's labors on the King's Bench in England, which were nearly complete at the time Hamilton was writing, the whole of the private law of "commerce" was also regarded as lying outside the scope of "municipal law."[38] The fact that Hamilton was still advocating "complete [national] sovereignty" as to "all that related[d] to trade" is very hard to doubt.

Despite this fact, and the fact that many other men besides Hamilton were likewise advocating such a power in 1781, there can be very little doubt—

even in the face of the close vote on the Witherspoon proposal in the same year—that the opposition to a national commerce power must have been rather formidable *at that time.* This opposition, too, it is interesting to note, must have come in the main from the mercantile element, which a few years later became one of the chief elements in the community which advocated such a power. Its opposition to such a change in 1781 is indicated by Hamilton's statement that the opponents of the change were afraid that the power might be used for price-fixing purposes. In the nature of the case, opposition to the proposed new power upon such a ground must have come from the element in the community which would profit most from a free play of prices. That, of course, was the mercantile element; and until the sellers' market enjoyed by that element in 1781 and 1782 had definitely passed away and been replaced by a postwar depression, and until, furthermore, the mercantile element had finally, in 1785, signified its willingness to support a movement for a general power, rather than a partial power devised for its special benefit, the movement for a national commerce power did not really begin to make progress. Certainly, Hamilton's proposals in his "Continentalist" papers made little impression when those papers were published;[39] and his efforts in New York and in Congress, in the winter and spring of 1782-83, to obtain the calling of a national convention and the investing of the nation with what he called "a *general* superintendence of *trade*," though they were supported in Congress by Stephen Higginson, of Massachusetts, and by others of the more vigorous nationalists there, were opposed by James Madison[40] and apparently by a majority in that body, and finally ended in failure.[41] The truth seems to be that, even as late as the spring of 1783, conditions were still very far from ready for any such change.

Despite this fact, writings advocating such a change continued to appear sporadically in the various newspapers. Some of the writings from this earlier period shed a good deal of light on the ideas of the time, so it will be well to look at one or two of them, before we turn to the second major phase of the movement for a national commerce power, which began in the following autumn. The first of these temporarily fruitless efforts that seems worthy of examination is a letter, signed "A Friend to Rhode Island and the Union," which appeared in "*The* [Boston] *Independent Chronicle*, of January 16, 1783. Devoted primarily to a consideration of the then-current proposal of a continental impost, the letter also discussed the regulation of commerce and, in doing so, brought out with unusual clarity some of the reasons which led so many of the men of the time to regard *all* commerce as a unit which was properly a subject for regulation by the nation only. "Commerce," the letter maintained, "is not the local property of any State . . . , unless it can be proved that such a State neither buys nor sells out of its own dominions. But as *the commerce of every State* is made up out of the produce and consumption of other States, *as well as its own*," and "is diffused over and promiscuously drawn from all parts, beyond *as well as within the State*," "its regulation and protection can only be under the confederated patronage of all the States."

That the foregoing statement related to "commerce" in a sense which included what lawyers today call "intrastate commerce" is apparent from the portions in italics. It is also apparent from the nature of "the commerce" which, the item intimated, was, under certain conditions, the "local property" of a single state. The intention of the statement, in the light of the nature of this "commerce," seems to have been that, in the absence of these conditions, the "regulation and protection" of *all* domestic "commerce" (what we call "intrastate" as well as what we call "interstate") ought to be under the national "patronage" *only*. With respect to the country's foreign commerce, the item also pointed out that "the United States [were] accountable to foreign powers for all misconduct committed under their flag, which privileged our commerce abroad, and on the seas"; and concluded from thence that "the regulation of [such commerce] must reside in the same power." Hence, the whole position of the writer was that a state's "commerce" could be regarded as its "local property" and properly subject to its own direction, only if a state could prove that its "commerce"—i.e., its *whole* commerce—was *purely* internal, or domestic, *with respect to itself*. No such proof could be offered by any state, however, because the commerce of every state, as the writer indicated, was connected with that of the others; hence, the whole of the "commerce," both foreign and domestic, of all the states was properly a subject for regulation by Congress only.

Such, typically, were the reasons—when reasons were given—which led the Americans of the eighteenth century to regard the regulating of the entire commerce of the country as a matter of "general concern." Most proponents of change did not, however argue this point. Instead, they simply listed an unqualified general commercial power among their agenda of reform. This was the procedure, for example, of Pelatiah Webster, a retired merchant of Philadelphia, who published a well-known pamphlet there, early in 1783, in advocacy of a stronger and better-constructed national government. "My first and great principle," said Webster, "[is] that the constitution must vest powers in every department sufficient to secure and make effectual the ends of it. *The supreme authority* [i.e., the legislature of the nation] must have the power of making war and peace—of appointing officers both civil and military—of making contracts—of emitting, coining, and borrowing money—*of regulating trade*—of making treaties with foreign powers—of establishing post offices—and in short of doing every thing which the well-being of the Commonwealth may require, and which is *not compatible** to any particular State, all of which require money, and cannot possibly be made effectual without it. [The su-

---

*"Compatible" was apparently used by Webster, in this passage, instead of the more correct world, "competible." The confusion of these two words was common in the eighteenth century. The meaning given to the passage by this word is: "not within the competence of a single state." See *The Oxford English Dictionary* on "compatible" and "competible." It is important to note that all nationwide laws would fall in this category, since no single state, despite the anomalies of present-day corporation law, has any proper competence to legislate for the others. Uniformity, *where the general welfare required it*, was obviously not intended by Pelatiah Webster to be attainable only by the uncertain mode of nationwide uniformity of state action.

preme power] must therefore of necessity [also] be vested with the power of taxation." Webster further proposed, among other things, that the constitution of Congress should be altered by converting it to "two chambers, an upper and lower house, or senate and commons, with the concurrence of both necessary to every act"; that national courts of law and equity should be appointed; and that "every person whatever, whether in public or private character, who [should], by public vote or other overt act, disobey the supreme authority [of the nation]" should be subject to "fine, imprisonment, or punishment for his disobedience." In these last proposals, the reader will observe, Webster, to a certain extent, was a pioneer.

Regarding the scope of Webster's proposed national power "of regulating trade," there was, as might be expected, no direct statement in Webster's pamphlet as to what he meant by it. To Americans of the eighteenth century, this phrase did *not* require explanation; the strong presumption, therefore, is that Webster used the phrase in the extensive sense in which it was then commonly employed. That this was in fact the case is affirmatively shown by certain oblique evidence in his pamphlet. Thus, among other suggestions which were advanced therein, one was that a "chamber of commerce" should be set up, to consist wholly of merchants, and to have the right and duty of advising Congress "concerning all bills before [it] as far as the same [might] affect *the trade of the States*." The considerations adduced to justify this proposal disclose the scope of the national commercial power which Webster had in mind. Merchants, he argued, ought to compose the chamber, because they were not only the best qualified men "to give the fullest and most important information to our supreme legislature, concerning the state of our trade— the abundance and wants—the wealth and poverty, of our people, i.e., their most important interests, but [were] the most likely to do it fairly and truly, and to forward with their influence, every measure which [would] operate to the convenience and benefit of our commerce, and oppose with their whole might and superior knowledge of the subject, any wild schemes, which an ignorant or arbitrary legislature [might] attempt to introduce, to the hurt and embarrassment of our intercourse both with one another, and with foreigners." From the general tenor of this passage, and particularly from its final words, it is obvious that Webster contemplated for his national Congress a commercial power extending to the "intercourse [of Americans] both with one another and with foreigners"; or, in other words, that he contemplated a national power over the entire body of both foreign and domestic trade. By way of corroboration of this inference, it may be added that Webster's discussion also shows that he thought of the interests of "husbandry" and "manufactures" as falling within the advisory functions of his projected "chamber of commerce." This seems a rather clear indication that he regarded those interests as falling within the scope of his proposed national commerce power; but if, in spite of this internal evidence in Webster's pamphlet, and in spite of all the concurrent evidence previously introduced as to the general understanding of a power over trade, there can be any doubt that this was true, there certainly can be none that the interests in question would have fallen—at least for all "national" purposes—within the general power which Webster also proposed for Congress, "of doing *every thing* [not within the competence of any one state] which the *well-being* of the Commonwealth [i.e., the general welfare of the United States—might] require."[42]

To what has been said of Webster's views, it will not be amiss to add that his advocacy of a national governing power extending to all these various economic matters seems particularly interesting in view of the fact that Webster had been, for years, the most untiring "free-trade" advocate in the country. During the years of the Revolution he had written constantly for the Philadelphia papers upon what he termed "free-trade"—that is, in the main, trade at unregulated wages and prices.[43] His plain advocacy of a comprehensive national commercial power, as well as a power to act generally for the national welfare, is conclusive proof that so-called "free-trade" principles were not at all inconsistent (as some modern commentators have wishfully thought) with desire and advocacy, in the case of these Americans of the eighteenth century, of a most ample *national* power over *all* commercial, as well as other, subjects. "Free trade," indeed, in whatever of its many senses the word be taken, was not, and never had been, to intelligent men in the eighteenth century, a synonym for lawlessness and lack of government. Hamilton, we have seen, had intimated as much in his "Continentalist" papers; Pelatiah Webster, plainly, was of the same opinion; and since a complete national commerce power had the obvious advantage, to every intelligent "free-trader," of at least providing an instrument for striking down trade barriers "between state and state," and preventing the states from fostering local monopolies and erecting other obnoxious commercial restrictions, it will be obvious that the "free-traders" of 1787 could quite easily have been ardent advocates of an all-inclusive national commerce power, without in any way being recreant to their "free-trade" principles.

In concluding our survey of the preliminary phase of the movement for a stronger government in the 1780s, it is of interest to note that the general scheme of governmental power urged by Pelatiah Webster still had the support, when Webster was urging it, of the most influential man in the country. Washington, it is true, as commander-in-chief of the Continental armies, had been very diffident in his various *public* utterances, with reference to the subject of increasing the national powers. This was due to his fear that he might appear to his countrymen "to arrogate more than belong[ed] to [him]" in his official position. Although this was true of his various public statements, Washington had never been so reserved in his private letters. These had "teemed," as he himself assured Alexander Hamilton, with sentiments in favor of augmenting the national powers.[44] He was afraid, as he had

explained in a letter to LaFayette, "that local, or state Politics [would] interfere too much with that more liberal and extensive plan of government which
wisdom and foresight, freed from the mist of prejudice, would dictate." And
firmly believing "that the honor, power, and true Interest of [the] Country
must be measured by a Continental scale," Washington accordingly made use
of every private opportunity which came to him, to urge, both by spoken
word and written letter, that the powers of the national government be
increased.[45]

The letters in which Washington advocated, in terms more or less clear,
the grant to Congress of the general national power which Pelatiah Webster
urged, are very numerous indeed.[46] Of his various statements, perhaps the
clearest is that contained in a letter he wrote to Doctor William Gordon, of
Massachusetts, on July 8, 1783. Having expressed his thanks to Doctor
Gordon for congratulations on the peace, Washington turned to a consideration of the future of the country. It now lay, he said, entirely with the states,
either "to make [the] country great, happy, and respectable, or to sink it into
littleness; worse, perhaps, into anarchy and confusion." "For certain I am,"
said Washington, "that, unless adequate powers are given to congress for *the
general purposes of the federal union*, we shall soon moulder into dust, and
become contemptible in the eyes of Europe, if we are not made the sport of
their politics. To suppose that *the general concerns* of this country can be
directed by thirteen heads, or one head without competent powers, is a
solecism, the bad effects of which every man, who has had the practical
knowledge to judge from that I have, is fully convinced of, though none
perhaps has felt them in so forcible and distressing a degree."

"The County of Worcester in Massachusetts," Washington bluntly went
on, "or Gloucester County in Virginia . . . with as much propriety might
oppose themselves to the Laws of the State in which they are, as an Individual State can oppose itself to the Federal Government, by which it is or ought
to be bound.* Each of these Counties has, no doubt, its local polity and
Interests. These should be attended to, and brought before their respective
legislatures with all the force their importance merits; but when they come in
contact with the general Interest of the State; when superior considerations
proponderate in favor of the whole, their voices should be heard no more; *so
should it be with individual States when compared to the Union*."

As to the fears then expressed by state politicians, that there was danger
involved in giving power to Congress, Washington simply ridiculed these.

---

*The reader should constantly bear in mind that the Articles of Confederation expressly
provided that the resolutions of Congress were to be binding upon the states. Article XIII ran, in
part, as follows: "Every State shall abide by the determination of the United States in Congress
assembled, on all questions which by this Confederation are submitted to them. And the
Articles of this Confederation shall be inviolably observed by every State, and the Union shall be
perpetual. . . . "

"For Heaven's sake," he asked, "who are Congress? Are they not the Creatures of the People, amenable to them for their Conduct, and dependant from day to day on their breath? Where then can be the danger of giving them such Powers as are adequate to *the great ends of Government* and to all the general purposes of the Confederation?" "I repeat the word *general**," he added, "because I am no advocate for their having to do with the particular policy of any State, further than it concerns the Union at large." In other words, Washington *was* an advocate of Congress's "having to do with the particular policy of every state as far as it *did* concern the Union at large"; and "the Union at large," he seemed clearly to think, was "concerned" with all "the great ends of government," among which "war" and "commerce" and "justice" undoubtedly were included.[47]

These same sentiments, we may add, had finally been publicly expressed by Washington when he was ready to resign his commission, about a month before he wrote his letter to William Gordon. "It [might] not be necessary or proper," he had said at that time, "for [him] to enter into a particular disquisition of the principles of the Union, and to take up the great question which ha[d] been frequently agitated, whether it [would] be expedient and requisite for the States to delegate a larger proportion of Power to Congress." "Yet it [was] a part of his duty," he insisted, "and that of every true Patriot, to assert without reserve, and to insist upon the following position: That it [was] indispensable to the happiness of the individual States, that there should be lodged somewhere, *a Supreme Power to regulate and govern the general concerns of the Confederated Republic*." "Without [this]," he declared, "the Union [could] not be of long duration."[48] These statements were made in the course of a circular letter Washington had dispatched to the thirteen states, on June 8. The evidence as to the spirit in which this was received in the states is not very plentiful; but, according to Edmund Randolph, in a letter he wrote to Madison on June 28, "the murmur [was] free and general," at least in Virginia, "against what [was] called," said Randolph, "the unsolicited obtrusion of [Washington's] advice."[49] Undeterred, however, Washington's last public act before his retirement was to offer a toast, at the public dinner held upon his actual resignation of his commission, in December, to "Competent powers for Congress for *general* purposes!"[50]

The reader can therefore entertain no doubt that a national power extending to all phases of business, or "commerce," when the national welfare was involved (which may quite well have covered every case), had the full approval and support of Washington in 1783. More generally, it is clear that Washington, like Pelatiah Webster and various other men, desired to revert, to that simple, obvious, and flexible division of power between state and nation which, as we have seen, had been so strongly advocated before the

*Washington's emphasis.

country in 1776; which had at that time been widely desired among the people; and which had, indeed, actually been practiced upon by the Continental Congress during the twenty-one-month period of its existence before independence was declared. Desire for that scheme of power, we shall presently see, was to grow and grow until the Constitution at last resulted; and the Constitution itself, we shall also see, was generally understood, at the time it was proposed, as actually embodying precisely such a simple, obvious, and flexible formula of the national power.

CHAPTER X

The Post-Revolutionary Troubles in Trade with the British and the Resultant Unsuccessful Attempt by Congress to Obtain a Limited Power over Certain Phases of Foreign Commerce

THE materials set forth in the last chapter, together with certain of those set forth in earlier chapters, show that of the two earliest experiences of the commercial inadequacy of the Confederation, one was—predominantly, at least—in the field of what we would now call "intrastate commerce," i.e., the attempts made during the years of the war to regulate the prices of all kinds of labor and all kinds of goods, whether of foreign or domestic origin. Contemporaneous with this commercial failure in the domestic field, and closely related to it, was the somewhat similar failure of the efforts made to stamp out trading with the enemy. This second failure was in the field of what would then have been called our "commerce with foreign nations," though it was a commerce which was, in part, territorially internal to the country. The far better-known instance of the Confederation's inadequacy in the field of commerce, experienced in the troubles with the British after the making of the peace—and this is the only one of these three early failures in commercial regulation ordinarily mentioned in histories of the subject—was therefore not the first, nor even the second, experience of the existing system's commercial inadequacy. This fact deserves emphasis because, when it is taken with other evidence herein presented, it makes quite incredible the common story to the effect that the demand in the 1780s for a national commerce power had its origin in the postwar troubles in trade with the British, and in the barriers to commerce "between state and state" and the various other domestic difficulties which grew out of them. The demand for a national commerce power, it is true, did gain a new strength from those postwar troubles, but the congressional request for commercial powers which grew directly out of the troubles with the British was a request for partial powers *only*, and, precisely because the request was for *partial* powers, a number of the states were disinclined to grant it. The full national power desired by those states had already been demanded in Congress before the revolutionary struggle was over. The demand for such a power was renewed when the troubles with the British arose; it spread when the congressional request for partial powers met with failure; and it was this renewed demand for a full national power, *not* the unsuccessful demand for incomplete national power, to which the Commerce Clause of the Constitution was an answer.

The postwar troubles in trade with the British began early in 1783, when an attempt was made to enter into a commercial treaty with them, after the signing of the provisional peace. In the beginning, the attempt seemed likely to succeed. British merchants were naturally eager to engage once more in commerce with America, and the British government of the time seemed ready enough to take whatever steps were necessary to facilitate such a result. In the belief, indeed, that American laws prohibiting commerce between the countries would not be repealed until Britain had set an example by repealing hers, a bill was introduced in Parliament, which would have given to Americans the same privileges in the trade to Great Britain as British subjects enjoyed, and would have repealed, as to Americans, that part of the British navigation act which applied to foreign nations. The bill, of course, had its opposition in Parliament, and it was opposed, as well, by at least some of the American peace commissioners then present in Europe. These latter took the position that trade between the countries ought to be regulated by treaty; that the subject ought to be covered by provisions forming part of the definitive treaty of peace; and that trade would not be resumed by America so long as any British troops remained at New York or anywhere else within the United States. As a result of the parliamentary opposition to the bill, and possibly in part as a result of the attitude of these American commissioners, the bill was finally dropped; instead, temporary power to regulate the American trade by edict was given to the king in council.[1]

In this state of affairs, the American commissioners in Europe were completely befooled, and their bargaining position with the British entirely destroyed, by a renewed failure of certain of our states to enforce, and the ill-considered action of others in repealing, the laws which had been in effect against trading with Great Britain. As a result of such action or inaction by the various states, American vessels laden with American produce began to appear at various British ports, ready at once to resume trade, and as a consequence the American commissioners were simply laughed at by the British. This development, which seems, oddly enough, to have been unexpected by the American commissioners despite the notoriously lax enforcement of these laws during the period of the war, seemed to vindicate the position taken by the opposition in Parliament.[2] Their position was that there was no need to repeal the navigation act in its application to Americans; no need to enter into any commercial treaty with them; and no need to fear any retaliatory action from them, because of the total incapacity of the states of America to act together. In short, American behavior seemed to prove that Lord Sheffield, the principal spokesman for the British opposition group, was right: that Great Britain had nothing to fear from America as a nation. "It must," said Sheffield, in a pamphlet he published at about this time, "be a long time before [the American states] can engage, or will concur in any material expense. A Stamp Act, a Tea Act, or such act, that can never again occur, could alone unite them; their climate, their staples, their manners, are different; their interests opposite; and that which is beneficial to one, is destructive to the other. . . . In short, every circumstance proves, that it will be extreme folly to enter into any engagements, by which we may not wish to be bound hereafter." It was impossible, he added, to name any advantage which the American states would, or could, give to Britain, in a treaty, more than she would be certain to have without one. "No treaty [could] be made," he maintained, "with the American States that [would] be binding on the whole of them. The act of Confederation [did] not enable Congress to form more than general treaties: at the moment of the highest authority of Congress, the power [to make binding commercial treaties had been] withheld by the several States."[3] Lord Sheffield, as he very easily might, cited chapter and verse from the Articles of Confederation in seeming proof of his assertions.[4]

The faction for whom Lord Sheffield spoke was likewise angry over what they regarded as the needlessly generous terms of the provisional peace. This group, unfortunately, came into power in the British government before the definitive peace was signed, while the commercial relations between the two countries were still unsettled. With this development in British politics, all hope of an early commercial treaty between America and Great Britain came to an end. This became clear early in the summer of 1783, with the appearance of various royal proclamations for regulating the American trade. One of these, which gained especial notoriety, opened up a trade in certain enumerated articles between the United States and the British West Indies, but restricted that trade completely to British-built ships owned by British subjects and navigated in accordance with British laws.[5] The object of this restriction was to embarrass the important American shipbuilding trade, as well as to prevent resumption of the American carrying trade to the islands in question, which the New England and Middle colonies had carried on in the years before the war. In this way, it was hoped, a "spring" might be given to these particular businesses within the British Empire, and a blow, as well, to the prosperity and strength of the newly established American states. For similar reasons, American-caught fish were excluded from the trade to the West Indies, and American whale oil and potash and other articles, from the trade with the British at home.[6]

The second phase of the movement for a national commerce power—the phase of which most is made in conventional histories—may be dated from the early part of September 1783, when knowledge of the royal proclamations for the regulation of British trade with America reached Congress. The knowledge of these measures came through certain letters which arrived from the American peace commissioners. One of these commissioners, John Adams, enclosed with his letter a copy of Lord Sheffield's pamphlet and

strongly urged upon Congress the desirability of procuring an enlargement of
the national powers in order to combat the British restrictions. "A system,"
said Adams, "which has in it so little respect for us and is so obviously
calculated to give a blow to our nurseries of ships and seamen, could never
have been adopted but from the opinion that we had no common legislature
for the government of commerce." "[One] way of influencing England to a
reasonable conduct [would be]," said Adams, "to take some measures for
encouraging the growth in the United States of West India articles; another
[would be] to encourage manufactures, especially of wool and iron among
ourselves." "But the most certain method [would be] to lay duties on exports
and imports by British ships." "What powers Congress should have for
governing the trade of the whole, for making or recommending prohibitions
or imposts," said Adams, "deserve[d] the serious consideration of every man
in America. If a constitutional legislative authority [could] not be given them,
a sense of common danger and necessity [ought, at least, to] give to their
recommendations all the energy upon the minds of the people which they
had six years ago." "[But] perhaps," Adams added, "it will be most prudent to
say little about [all this] at present, and until the definitive treaty is signed
and the States evacuated; but after that . . . , Congress should tell [Great
Britain] that [the United States] have the means of doing justice to themselves." The same line of conduct, the realistic Adams added, might very
well be necessary in the case of "friends" as well as "enemies."[7]

These characteristically militant ideas of John Adams's evoked in the Continental Congress an immediate response. A committee was appointed to
consider the dispatches which had been received from the American commissioners, and the committee reported on September 25 that it considered it "of
the highest importance to counteract [the] systems [which the dispatches
mentioned]." This, it declared, could "only be done by delegating a *general*
Power [to Congress] for regulating [the country's] commercial Interests."
The committee's language seems plain enough, and if Adams's suggestions
are borne in mind, the scope of the committee's recommendation cannot be
regarded as doubtful. The committee also suggested that another committee
be forthwith formed to "prepare an address to the States upon the subject of
Commerce, stating to them the Regulations which [were] prevailing in
Europe, the evils to be apprehended therefrom, and the steps proper to be
taken to guard against and Counteract them."[8] Although it was opposed by
Virginia and Rhode Island and individual delegates from certain of the other
states, this suggestion was promptly approved by a large majority in Congress, and a new committee was appointed, consisting of Thomas Fitz-
Simmons, of Pennsylvania; James Duane, of New York; and Arthur Lee, of
Virginia.[9] On October 9, this second committee reported an address to the
states.[10] An address weaker than the one reported by the committee, however, would be very difficult to conceive, and perhaps as a result of the
character of this address, and the cautionary considerations evoked by it,

Congress did nothing more on the subject of commercial powers until the middle of the following winter.[11]

Before that time arrived, some things had happened to make an open appeal for national commercial powers seem more prudent to Congress and success in such an appeal more probable. The definitive treaty of peace had been received from Europe; the proclamations of the king in council had become generally known; Thomas Paine was once more writing in the cause of "Common Sense"; in some places voluntary associations of merchants were forming to combat the British "system";[12] and some of the state legislatures had even signified a willingness, of their own accord, to vest in Congress powers, though of widely varying scope, for meeting the new situation.

The appeal made by Paine appeared in *The New York Packet* on December 9, and, as in the case of his earlier writings, was copied from newspaper to newspaper, up and down the land, until all who cared to do so must have seen the appeal.[13] Paine began with a simple, straightforward account of what had happened. He admitted the right of any nation "to prohibit the commerce of another into its own dominions." "But as this right belong[ed] to one side as well as the other, there [was]," he maintained, "always a way left to bring avarice and insolence to reason." Lord Sheffield, indeed, appeared "sensible," Paine said, that "he [was] attempting a measure which [could] not succeed, if the politics of the United States [were] properly directed." As Paine pointed out, Lord Sheffield relied, and said very clearly that he relied, on the fact that America was not a nation. "What is this," Paine then asked, "[but] to tell us, that while we have no national system of commerce, the British will govern our trade by their own laws and proclamations as they please. [His lordship has] disclose[d] a truth [to us] too serious to be overlooked, and too mischievous not to be remedied." "[For] the instance now before us is but a gentle beginning of what America must expect, unless she guards her union with nicer care and stricter honor. United, she is formidable . . . : separated, she is a medley of individual nothings, subject to the sport of foreign nations."[14]

Even before Paine's appeal was published, the Virginia House of Delegates had moved, though in a very grudging and inadequate fashion, to effectuate the purpose Paine advocated. On December 4, this Virginia body had resolved, after referring to the king's proclamation on the trade to the West Indies, "that the United States in Congress assembled ought to be empowered to prohibit British vessels from being the carriers of the growth and produce of the British West India Islands *to these United States*, so long as the restrictions [set up by the king's proclamation should] be continued on the part of Great Britain, or to concert any other mode to be adopted by the United States, which [should] be thought effectual to counteract the designs of Great Britain with respect to the American Commerce."[15] The desires of the Virginia deputies extended only to combatting Great Britain, and the power they proposed was a narrow power, even as against Great Britain. For the proposed power extended in a definitive and binding way only to imports from the British West Indies, in which Virginia was without much interest. The power left to the states complete control over all exports, as well as over all imports from points other than the British West Indies, including, of course, all those imports from Great Britain itself, with which Virginia was particularly concerned.

The resolution thus adopted by the Virginia deputies was accorded prompt publicity throughout the country. It appeared, for example, in *The New Jersey Gazette*, of Trenton, on December 23.[16] On the very next day, the New Jersey General Assembly responded unanimously—for "a response" it unquestionably was—"that the United States in Congress assembled ought to be vested with the *exclusive* power of *regulating trade and commerce throughout the United States of America*." Apparently for the purpose of making the utter inadequacy of the Virginia resolution especially clear, the General Assembly then further unanimously resolved "that the United States in Congress assembled ought to be empowered, and ought, when so empowered, to prohibit British vessels from being the carriers of the growth or produce of the British West India Islands to these United States, *or of the growth or produce of these United States to any of the said British West India Islands*, so long as the restriction in the [king's] proclamation [should] be continued by, or on the part of, Great Britain."[17] No careful reader of these three resolves can entertain very much doubt that the New Jersey Assembly knew what it wanted; or that it saw exactly what the Virginia deputies had been about; or that New Jersey, and not Virginia, was in December 1783 still in the lead in the movement for a national commerce power, as it had been in 1778 and 1781.

By this time, however, New Jersey was not alone in the lead. About a fortnight earlier than the New Jersey action, and on the very same day Thomas Paine's newspaper appeal had appeared, the General Assembly of Pennsylvania had adopted a resolution of instructions to its delegates in Congress, and these, though awkward and wordy, were of the same sweeping tenor as the New Jersey resolution. The Pennsylvania resolution read as follows:

Certain measures now pursuing by some European states having a tendency materially to injure *the general trade of America* the attention of this house is naturally turned to the affairs of *Commerce* and are herein struck with an apparent defect in the constitution of Congress for as the local exercise within the states, of the powers of regulating and controlling trade, can result only in discordant systems productive of internal jealousies and competitions, and illy calculated to counteract foreign measures, which are the effect of an unity of Council; this house are clearly of the opinion that the individual as well as the general good will be best consulted, by relinquishing to Congress *all these separate and independent powers*.

And this house are willing and desirous on the part of Pennsylvania to concur in substantiating this idea, by the necessary legal acts.[18]

This resolution of the General Assembly of Pennsylvania obviously lacks the slashing quality characteristic of the resolutions adopted by the legislature of New Jersey. The reference to "the general trade"—i.e., "the whole trade"—of the country, the mention of the "internal" and "foreign" effects of the existing system, and the unqualified use of the general, unqualified, and comprehensive phrase "regulating and controlling trade," on the other hand, permit no doubt as to the sense in which the resolution was intended. For some unknown reason, this Pennsylvania resolution received little publicity, but the resolutions of New Jersey's legislature were published from one end of the country to the other.[19]

The Virginia House of Delegates' resolve actually eventuated in an act of that state, which, in a very temporary way, went somewhat further than the House of Delegates' original resolution: it empowered Congress not only "to prohibit the importation of the growth or produce of the British West India Islands, into these United States, in British vessels," but "to adopt any other mode which [might] most effectually tend to counteract the designs of Great Britain, with respect to the American commerce, so long as the said restriction [i.e., the particular royal proclamation which related to the West India trade] should be continued on the part of Great Britain."[20] The state of New York, soon after, adopted an act of the same tenor;[21] New Jersey, some months later, did the same;[22] and South Carolina, soon after New York had acted, passed an act covering the same subject in somewhat different terms.[23]

On the other hand, instead of concurring in Virginia's temporary act, Maryland passed—or was reported to have passed—an act, or resolution, instructing its delegates in Congress to concur in amending the Articles so as to invest Congress with power "to prevent or prohibit the *importation* [into any of the states] of *all foreign* goods or commodities"—i.e., whether British or not—"in any other than ships or vessels owned by citizens of the United States, or any of them, or such a proportion of seamen citizens of the United States or any of them, as from time to time [might] be agreed upon by nine states in Congress."[24] A short while later, North Carolina issued similar instructions to its delegates in Congress.[25] No power over imports, other than the foregoing, was proposed by either Maryland or North Carolina, and none at all was proposed by either of these states over exports or over any branch of internal trade. As for the remaining states, none of them at this time took any steps to vest the Continental Congress with *any* commercial power at all, temporary or permanent.

The foregoing acts and resolutions (excepting only the last-mentioned act of New Jersey) were adopted by the states in question at different dates through the winter and spring of 1783-84. Long before the last of these acts had been adopted, however, Congress was again at work upon the subject, striving to agree upon the extent of power which the state legislatures should be requested to cede, and upon an address to be used in broaching this subject, which was apparently regarded as touchy. The groveling attempt at an address, drawn up by the committee of the preceding fall, was handed over on January 26 to a new committee, consisting of Arthur Lee, of Virginia; Elbridge Gerry, of Massachusetts; and Jacob Read, of South Carolina. At the same time, the Virginia legislature's act and a motion by one of the Maryland delegates, presumably for the recommendation of a uniform state navigation act, were referred to the committee.[26] The commitment was again renewed on February 6, when Arthur Lee was dropped from the committee, and Hugh Williamson, of North Carolina, and J. T. Chase, of Maryland, were added to it. The Pennsylvania resolution of instruction to its delegates, of December 9, had been read to Congress on that day, and was referred to the committee under the new commitment, either on the date of the new commitment or on April 14.[27] Whether the New Jersey resolves were also among the papers before this committee does not appear from the printed journals of the Congress, but in view of the publicity these resolves had received, they were certainly known to the committee, and were most probably before it. On the date last mentioned, Thomas Jefferson was added to the committee's membership. Eight days later the committee reported a proposal that Congress recommend to the states that they invest it with power, for a term of fifteen years, (1) "to prohibit any goods, wares or merchandise from being imported into or exported from any of the states, in vessels belonging to or navigated by the subjects of any power with whom these states [should] not have formed treaties of Commerce," and (2) "to prohibit the subject of any foreign state, kingdom, or empire, unless authorized by treaty, from importing into the United States any goods, wares, or merchandise, which [should] not [be] the produce or manufacture of the dominions of the sovereign whose subjects they [were]."[28] From the terms of these proposed new powers, they were evidently intended merely for coercing foreign nations into making favorable treaties of commerce with America. They were unfit for use for any other purpose; were quite inadequate to protect any class in the community, except American merchants; and, in particular, were totally unfit for protecting and supporting the infant American manufactures that had sprung into considerable importance in certain of the states during the years of the recent war. Not surprisingly, something less than complete enthusiasm for these powers was exhibited among the several states, when the proposals came to be known outside the halls of Congress.

Besides reporting to Congress the foregoing powers, the committee recommended to Congress that a letter be sent to the states, setting forth the state of Congress's mind in asking for the proposed new powers. Among other things, the committee suggested that Congress should intimate to the states that it had not been its duty, even though it had been its wish, to do anything in the premises before, because its "powers on this head were not explicit"; that it had, however, now become Congress's duty "to take the general sense of the Union on [the] subject [of granting it certain commercial powers]" because various of the states had acted to initiate the subject; but that this duty was, nevertheless, performed by Congress "with reluctance," because it feared, in spite of the prior initiatory action by these states, that the proposals it was making might "be suspected to have originated in a desire of power." Apparently under the influence of this fear, the committee also suggested that the resolutions of the various willing states ought to be sent along with Congress's proposals for new powers, and that Congress go out of its way to refer to these state resolves as containing evidence that "some of the states" were "desirous" that Congress be invested with even *further* powers for the *external* regulation of trade" than Congress itself was asking.[29] The New Jersey resolution, the reader will remember, had proposed, in so many words, that Congress be invested with the power "of regulating trade and commerce *throughout* the United States," and the Pennsylvania resolution had complained of the evils of a "*local* exercise *within the states*, of the powers of regulating and controlling trade," without any suggestion of an "external" or any other qualification in either case. In proposing such a reference to these more liberal state proposals, the committee must have been actuated by a desire to create, in the minds of the legislatures of the more reluctant states, the impression that Congress was certainly not avid or astute to increase its powers. The good sense of the main body of Congress apparently revolted at such transparent posturing, and when the committee's recommendations were eventually sent out as a proposal to the states, they were accompanied by no more than a simple, straightforward appeal for needed powers.[30]

Before that event occurred, the state of Rhode Island, which seems at the time still to have been alarmed lest a national power, such as Congress proposed, would interfere too much with the state's system of imposts, made an attempt to substitute for the committee's proposals a scheme for combatting the British by the old, discredited method of uniform state action. When the committee's proposals came up for action, the Rhode Island delegates moved that action on them be postponed, in order to consider a recommendation that the states pass laws (1) "to restrain *by imposts* or prohibitions, any goods, wares, or merchandize from being imported into them respectively, except in vessels belonging to and navigated by citizens of the United States, or the subjects of foreign powers with whom the United States [might] have treaties of commerce, or the subjects of such foreign powers as [might] admit of a reciprocity in their trade with the citizens of these states," and (2) "to prohibit the subjects of any foreign state, kingdom or empire, from importing into [the states] respectively any goods, wares or merchandize, unless such as [should be] the produce or manufacture of that state, kingdom or empire, whose subjects they [were]." The Congress, however, had apparently by this time had enough of commercial government, or lack of government, by uniform state laws which were but seldom passed by all the states, and on the vote on the question Rhode Island alone voted in the affirmative, although the vote of Connecticut was divided.[31] With the defeat of this Rhode Island proposal, the way was open to act on the proposals of the committee, and these, with a brief accompanying address, were therefore quickly whipped into shape and sent out, under date of April 30, 1784, as the Continental Congress's first, last, and only recommendation to the states for a grant of commercial powers.

While the proceedings which issued in these proposals were dragging along in Congress, talk had continued outside, though not in very lively fashion, about enlarging the national powers. The promising spurt of interest late in 1783 had rather quickly died down, and while some discussion continued throughout the following year, its volume was small, and a good deal of what was said was anything but favorable to a strengthening of the national government. Thus, the Philadelphia pamphlet put out by Pelatiah Webster, in the spring of 1783, had been republished later in that year in Connecticut;[32] and early in 1784, it there evoked a long-drawn-out answer from some one who signed himself "A Connecticut Farmer." This early "states' rights" pamphlet, like most of the writings of that species which have followed it, was indeed a most uncandid performance. The "Connecticut Farmer" accused Pelatiah Webster, among other things, of advocating the subversion of popular government, through the erection over the states of a supreme continental legislature not of an elective character. In support of this accusation, there was nothing at all actually to be found in Webster's pamphlet, but the "Connecticut Farmer" purported none the less to quote from the pamphlet in proof of his accusation. The "Farmer" had the further temerity to declare that the Continental Congress *already* had the power of regulating trade; he quoted from the Articles, apparently in purported proof of this, the provision which gave Congress power to "*regulate the trade* and manage all affairs with the Indians, &c."[33] The authorship of this ridiculous pamphlet is usually ascribed by historians to Roger Sherman, but if there is any evidence to support this view it is never cited and has not been found.

Besides the foregoing pamphlet directed against the whole idea of a stronger national government, there was in 1784 a good deal of commotion in the New England states and, to a certain extent, in the other states, over the action of Congress in voting half-pay to the officers of the Revolutionary army for life and then commuting that half-pay to five years' full payment. Various unofficial county and state "conventions" met in protest over these actions, and with the purpose of stirring up an opposition, based ostensibly upon them, to the recommendation of a continental impost power which Congress had made in 1783. Resentment was also high in certain quarters against the officers of the Revolutionary army for organizing themselves as the society known as the "Cincinnati." They were declared to be an aspiring nobility because of the rule of their society that the right of membership

therein should descend to the members' eldest sons. Some of the opposition
to the Cincinnati was honest, though in a kind of frantic way, but the true
cause of most of the opposition was undoubtedly the fact that the Cincinnati
were known by the state-politician class to be sincerely devoted to the cause
of a strong national government, which many of the state-politician class
opposed.[34] In these circumstances, the remarks of one Connecticut
nationalist, in *The Norwich Packet* of May 13, seemed to strike a sympathetic
chord, at least among the printers, for his remarks were copied from newspaper to newspaper through the various states as far south as South Carolina.
"Your Cincinnati," he said, "[your] state Conventions, rivalships in and
jealousy over particular States, ought all by all means to be totally extirpated,
and [their] substitute be a simple delegation of the most free and extensive
power in Congress, the only legal head which ought to govern the American
empire."[35] These sentiments were certainly unequivocal, but despite the
occasional appearance of such squibs as this, there can be no doubt that
throughout 1784 conditions continued far from ready for the making of any
change.

The general apathy prevalent throughout 1784 accounts for the fact that
the ablest pamphlet of the entire period under the Articles could appear in
that year without attracting any discoverable attention. Entitled *The Political
Establishments of the United States of America, in a Candid Review of their Deficiencies, together with a Proposal of Reformation*, the pamphlet in question was
published at Philadelphia, toward the end of the summer,[36] probably by
someone from Connecticut. At any rate, the author of the pamphlet was
apparently publishing essays on the same general subject in *The New Haven
Gazette and Connecticut Magazine* in the following year, under the pseudonym
"Observator." The pamphlet itself was afterwards republished in the same
New Haven paper, "with additions and alterations," just before the Federal
Convention met in 1787.[37]

The pamphlet was badly printed, and on the whole it lacked that elegance
of style which characterized some other, better-known writings of the period.
A reader of it can readily see, however, that its author had thought about the
subject of government and knew quite well what he was talking about. "The
general idea [of the Confederation]," he said, harking back to the ideas of
1776, "[was] that Congress [should] superintend the *political* interest of the
whole, while the authority of the states [was] confined to the *civil* interests of
their respective inhabitants."[38] Or, as he indicated by his explanations at
another point, the power of the states was to be confined to each state's
"internal police."[39] "But so perfect a division [could] not be made," he said,
"as [might] at first be imagined; for there [was] a necessary connection and
dependence between every kind of public interest, and an intimate correspondence between all acts of legislation. When the powers of government
therefore, [were] divided, as in the [case of the American confederation],
there [were] many things closely connected with the *political* interest of the

nation, which Congress [could] not take cognizance of; others, merely of a *civil* nature, [would] fail of their accomplishment for the want of a more extensive authority than the states respectively [had]; and some rights there [were], claimed by the *civil* powers, which [were] of *general concern*." The very idea of "the division of our *civil* and *political* powers" was a mistake and one of the great "defects in our institutions."[40] Believing this, the author of the pamphlet accordingly maintained that "no reformation or amendment [of the existing system could] answer any effectually good purpose short of the abolishment of our state governments and the forming [of] a constitution, whereby the whole nation could be united in one government."[41] "[He] would not [, however,] be understood," he said, "as rejecting every other kind of institution; subordinate institutions, it [was] possible, [might] be established with great propriety, and to answer useful and necessary purposes."[42] But state sovereignty must go, and a complete national sovereignty be substituted for it.[43]

The manifold considerations which led the author of this able pamphlet to the foregoing conclusions are too numerous for a recountal here. It is sufficient to say that the pamphlet is one of the best existing keys to the meanings attached by eighteenth-century Americans to the words they used in discussing the problems of government. The pamphlet shows a complete grasp of its subject and full foresight of the many difficulties which the dogma of divided power, in the many different shapes which the Supreme Court has given it, has always caused. The ideas of the pamphlet were wasted, however, for the country was not yet, at the time of its publication, in a mood for reform.

In view of the plain lack of popular interest in governmental reform in 1784; the pother over the half-pay, the commutation, and the "Cincinnati"; the open opposition to the continental impost by many men of the state-politician class; and the desire, in certain of the states, for a full, rather than a partial, national power of regulating commerce, it is not at all strange that Congress's proposal, that it be invested with a mere paltry fragment of such a power, received a slow response from the legislatures of the states. By the end of 1784, only Massachusetts,[44] Pennsylvania,[45] Maryland,[46] Virginia,[47] and New Hampshire[48] had taken favorable action. New York, however, in partial deference to the widespread popular agitation which took place in the year following, grudgingly granted the requested powers, early in April of 1785.[49] Connecticut also granted them in the course of that summer,[50] though the powers were in fact too narrow to be a real object of desire to Connecticut, which did all its importing of foreign goods through the ports of neighboring states. As for New Jersey, which had previously spoken so emphatically in favor of the creation of a complete national power, it was in much the same situation as Connecticut, and though it granted the meagre powers which Congress had requested, toward the end of 1785,[51] the contemporary understanding was that it took this action very unwillingly, due to its legislature's belief that the powers Congress had requested were "not extensive enough."[52]

This view of the powers asked for by Congress was apparently also taken in certain of the other states. Thus in Delaware, which was circumstanced much the same as Connecticut and New Jersey, there was the same long delay in granting the requested powers that we have just observed in the case of those two states.[53] In certain of the other states, too, the legislatures omitted to grant the powers that Congress had requested, and instead passed acts to vest that body with powers of a much more extensive nature. Rhode Island, for example, after having passed an act in February 1785 to authorize its delegates in Congress to concur in giving that body power "to regulate, restrain or prohibit" what the legislature described as "foreign Trade,"[54] further authorized its delegates, by an act passed in October 1785, to concur in giving to Congress the remainder of the power "solely" to "regulate, restrain, [and] prohibit, the importation of all foreign Goods," and, in addition, the "sole" power "to regulate *the Trade and Commerce of the respective States, and the Citizens thereof with each other.*"[55] These two acts were afterwards described by the Rhode Island legislature as having been intended, when taken together, to confer upon Congress "the *whole and sole* power of making laws for the *Regulation of Trade.*"[56] The newspaper evidence, of a somewhat indirect character, indicates that it was the general understanding at the time in the other states that Rhode Island was willing to give "entire" or "unlimited" power to Congress over "trade", or "commerce."[57] It is possible, nevertheless, that the wording of these Rhode Island acts may be found troublesome by modern readers; and for the convenience of any who find their interpretation difficult a detailed consideration of their wording, which is of necessity somewhat lengthy, has been provided in the notes at the end of this book.[58]

A short time before these Rhode Island acts were passed, an act of similarly sweeping tenor was passed in New Hampshire. The New Hampshire act was entitled "An Act to vest the United States in Congress assembled with *full* power to *regulate Trade and enter into Treaties of Commerce.*" It began by declaring that "Treaties of Commerce, and a due regulation of Trade, through the United States of America" were become "absolutely necessary"; in conformity with this declaration, it handsomely provided for the vesting of *"full power and authority"* in Congress, "on the part, and in behalf of [New Hampshire], to make and enter into such General Ordinances, and Treaties, *for the due regulation of the Trade and Commerce of the United States*, as [Congress might] Judge best calculated, to promote the weal and prosperity thereof."[59] No comment on the act is necessary, for its meaning appears perfectly clear.

The acts of the Rhode Island legislature were unlike most of the other acts that have been referred to, in that they were by their terms authorizations for an actual amendment of the Articles, though the amendment, if adopted, was to remain in force for twenty-five years only. By the terms of the Articles the

Rhode Island acts were without effect, until Congress should agree to, and all the states concur in, the change which the Rhode Island acts proposed. The New Hampshire act, on the other hand, did not purport to authorize an amendment of the Articles, but merely to grant *aliunde* a temporary power, which was, however, by its own terms expressly conditioned upon the passage of similar acts by all the other states. Neither the acts of Rhode Island nor that of New Hampshire, therefore, had any real effect, for neither Congress nor any of the other states took action to follow the lead provided by New Hampshire and Rhode Island.

Apparently angered by this inaction, New Hampshire, on December 28, 1786, retracted its prior agreement to the partial powers which Congress had proposed on April 30, 1784, and substituted a new act which made the state's own agreement to the partial powers conditional upon agreement by the other states to the "full" power which it had first proposed in its act of June 23, 1785.[60] Something of a similar kind likewise occurred in Rhode Island. Until March 1786, that state had never agreed to the partial powers over foreign commerce which Congress had asked in 1784. At that time, it did at last agree to those powers, but only conditionally, and while the condition imposed was not so drastic as New Hampshire's, it did stipulate that the state's consent to the partial powers should not become effective until Congress should be vested, in addition, with "the Power of preventing any and every of the United States from imposing any Duty or Impost on Goods, Wares, or Merchandize, when transported from one State to another, either by Land or Water."[61] These actions by Rhode Island and New Hampshire sufficiently indicate the complete agreement of those states with the state of New Jersey, that the powers that had been proposed by Congress were "not extensive enough."

The state of Delaware, which was apparently of much the same opinion as Rhode Island and New Hampshire, finally got into line on the requested powers early in the year 1786.[62] Georgia did the same, subject to an exception covering "the negro trade," on August 2 of that same year.[63] South Carolina, however, declined to get into line and, instead, in the spring of 1786, granted to Congress full power, subject to an exception covering "the slave trade," to regulate "all external or foreign trade of the United States."[64] Like the New Hampshire act, this one was conditioned upon concurrent action by the other twelve states, and since none of the other states concurred in it, this relatively liberal act was inoperative to confer upon Congress the narrow powers asked for by that body.

As for North Carolina, the last of the thirteen states then in the Union, it stubbornly declined, throughout the whole period up to the date of its belated ratification of the Constitution in 1789, to go one step beyond the instruction it had issued to its delegates in Congress, early in 1784, for agreement to a limited power over foreign imports only.[65] It remains to be noted, too, that among the foregoing grants of power for limited periods, there was very great diversity as to the dates when the different grants began.

In spite of the fact that some of the state legislatures were ready, even eager, during the years before the Federal Convention to go much further in the granting of commercial powers to Congress than Congress itself had asked, it never proved possible to get the legislatures all into line on the modest grant of powers which Congress requested. Efforts to this end continued through 1786.[66] Yet the probability is, as certain "states' righters" of the time maintained, that some men in Congress did not want to succeed on the powers in question.[67] Certain it is that, long before such efforts were given over, most of the members of Congress had made up their minds that the requested powers would not be adequate, and a scheme for a nearly complete national commerce power had actually been drawn up in Congress, and would very likely have been proposed to the several legislatures, had Congress been able to see how it could ask those bodies (or, at any rate, some of them) for a grant of general commercial power when its previous request for limited powers over foreign commerce had not been granted. In these circumstances, some extralegal step gradually came to seem necessary, and out of this necessity came proposals from various quarters for a national constitutional convention and, in the end, the scheme of the framers of the Constitution, and of certain other men, both in and out of Congress, for submitting that document for approval by conventions specially elected by the people of the states. In view of the extralegal character of these expedients as well as the provision in the Constitution that the government thereby provided should be set up if the Constitution were ratified by nine of the thirteen states then existing, that document may have been, in a certain, very limited technical sense, revolutionary in character.[68] But it was not, as has sometimes been said, counterrevolutionary. The system of government which the Constitution displaced "had not had the sanction of general choice,"[69] so it was not in accord with the Revolution's principles. In rather striking contrast, the system which the Constitution established *with* "the sanction of general choice" was, in all its essential respects, under a true construction, precisely such a system of American continental government as the country had been led to expect eleven years previously, when the Revolution had occurred.

CHAPTER XI

Business Depression and the Popular Agitation of 1785 for a Complete National Commerce Power: Herein of the Origin of the Agitation in the New England and Middle States

THE general popular apathy during 1784 toward the commercial reforms proposed by Congress was apparently in very large degree a by-product of that familiar phenomenon, a postwar boom in business. The coming of peace, which is to be dated for this purpose as the early spring of 1783, let loose upon the country a long-starved demand for foreign merchandise, and as frequently happens in such cases, the demand seemed to nearly everyone much greater than it was. In consequence of this, large numbers of Americans rushed into the merchandising business who never had been in that business before; a host of factors representing British firms crowded into the various towns and cities; and the new adventurers, these British factors, and the older American firms, all in haste to make the largest possible profit from the pent-up demand, ordered out goods from abroad— that is, in the main, from England—in such great quantities that the resulting importations for the six months preceding November 1783 were currently estimated as equal to the total exportable produce of the states over a three-year period.[1] Such a situation was ominous, but despite this fact the much-expanded mercantile class seems to have enjoyed brisk business over a considerable period. After all, the supply of "foreign luxuries" had been long cut off; and those with money—and, apparently, many without—went in for such "luxuries" in a reckless way. The resulting mercantile profits, or apparent profits, were in turn freely spent; a building boom resulted; and many of the other usual marks of a sudden inflation were evident. Even while business was still good, complaints were common that the whole country had "turned to luxury," and these complaints, with a vast amount of other evidence, clearly indicate that the years immediately following the preliminary peace were a quite typical postwar period, a period characterized by free spending and pleasure-seeking, and gay and carefree reaction after the long years of war.[2]

The only trouble was that the mercantile debts to Europe did have to be paid; and since the importations from Europe, chiefly from Great Britain, had so far exceeded what the country could pay for currently in exportable goods (especially after the outlawry, by the British, of many pre-

Revolutionary modes of payment), the practical outcome was that the money of the country had to be exported. Specie exports naturally lessened the effective demand for the goods that had been imported; and since the importations had been much too large anyway, the result was that, by the time the great mass of mercantile indebtedness became due, the whole bubble had burst; goods would not move; and it was seen, too late, that, in the phrase of the day, every one had "over-traded." Mercantile failures then began; the building boom, which for a little while had eased the situation for many members of the artisan group, rapidly faded away; unemployment increased; and as the country was steadily drained of more and more specie to pay the merchants' foreign debts, agricultural prices fell; the troubles of the merchant in meeting his bills were then soon paralleled in the experience of many backcountry farmers; a demand for fiat money and moratory laws arose; violence and insurrection broke out; disunion reared its head; and, greatly helped along at this final state by certain paramount military and political considerations in the southern states, the Constitution at last came to birth out of all this trouble.[3]

At this distance in time it is difficult to determine at just what date the phenomena of depression, or "commercial langour,"* began to manifest themselves and to usher in what may be regarded as the third major phase of the pre-Constitutional movement for a national commerce power. But the sharply different attitude toward proposals of such a power which began to be observable throughout the Northern states in the spring of 1785, suggests that the situation must have become clear in those states, at least to the mercantile and artisan groups, during the preceding fall and winter. Among the merchants, the change in attitude was caused by a sudden fall-off in the demand for imported goods; by consequent ruinous underselling of American firms by the British factors; by spreading failure among the American firms; and by the taking-over and operation of many of these for the benefit of their British creditors. In these circumstances, it began suddenly to seem as if American merchants had walked into a trap of British contrivance; as if the entire merchandising business of the country were about to fall into British hands; and as if the country, in consequence, were about to become as dependent on British commercial dictation by business means, as it had been

---

*It ought perhaps to be noted that, when the men of the eighteenth century complained of "the languishing state of commerce" or "the stagnation of trade," they did not mean to complain of dull times merely in "the trade of merchandize" or in the country's "foreign commerce" but of a general "business depression"—a term, apparently, which was not then in use. See, in this connection, the material cited from *The Pennsylvania Packet*, in note 1 to this chapter, A New York comment upon conditions in Philadelphia, which was reprinted in *The Pennsylvania Packet*, of June 6, 1785, also sheds light on what was meant. "Accounts from Philadelphia mention," the comment said, "that since the Bank has been deprived of its charter, and paper money emitted, *commerce* is most astonishingly facilitated, and the citizens at large experience every conveniency from it, being in equal credit with gold and silver." It is perhaps needless to remark that the Pennsylvania paper currency did not facilitate "foreign or interstate commerce," though it probably did give a temporary fillip to "intrastate trade."

by political means, in the years before the war. In the complaints of the time, "the British factor" therefore played a large and villainous part. And this was as true of the complaints made by the manufacturing groups as it was of those made by the merchants; for, once these two groups had gotten together and made common cause, as they eventually did, to set up an American "system of Commerce," "the British factor" became the common bogey of both: the scoundrelly fellow who was deliberately ruining America's "infant man-ufactures"; who, as the supposed chosen agent of the British government, was striving, through these twin evil activities, to keep America in a de-pendent status with respect to Great Britain, even though America had won the war. That there was some truth in this view, can hardly be doubted; and the great effort necessary to reestablish American prosperity after the long years of the Revolution accordingly seemed, to many Americans, a mere continuation of that struggle: America had won "the war of arms" but, to assure her independence, she had still to defeat Great Britain in "the war of commerce."[4]

Beyond much question, the effects of depression must have been experi-enced first by certain members of the artisan group; for the displacement of various American manufactures that had come into being during the years of the war of course took place before the American importers of "British luxuries" began to notice any falling-off in business. It is therefore not sur-prising that one of the earliest popular expressions in favor of an increase in national powers should have come from "the Artificers, Tradesmen, and Mechanicks of the city of New York." Their views were expressed in an address of welcome that was presented to Congress when that body removed from Trenton to New York, in January 1785. The groups in question de-clared their "entire confidence" in Congress and their "sincere hope" that the legislature of New York would soon coincide with the other States in aug-menting [Congress's] power to every exigency of the union." "Commerce" was not specifically mentioned; but that that subject was uppermost in mind, there can be no doubt.[5]

A short time later, on March 4, the New York Chamber of Commerce presented to the New York legislature a memorial in which it urged in specific and unqualified terms that the power "to regulate trade" ought to be given to Congress.[6] A few days afterward, according to *The New York Packet* of March 7, a second memorial "[was] handing about [the] city for signing," which urged upon the legislature "in the warmest manner . . . the propriety of granting to [Congress] the *sole* power of regulating *the commerce of the United States.*" The legislature responded to these two memorials on April 4, but only by granting to Congress, in the laggard, grudging manner characteristic of so many of the legislatures of the time, the fragmentary powers over foreign trade that Congress had urgently asked nearly twelve months before.[7]

A few weeks after these New York occurrences, sentiments favorable to a complete and exclusive national commercial power were also expressed in

Pennsylvania. The sentiments appeared in a memorial sent to the state's legislature, on April 6, by a committee representing the merchants and traders of Philadelphia. The committee included three men of considerable later importance: Tench Coxe, who was later to be the sole delegate from Pennsylvania to the Annapolis commercial convention of 1786, and Thomas FitzSimons and George Clymer, who were among the state's delegates to the Federal Convention in 1787. The memorial sent to the legislature by this committee reminded the legislature "that it [had] been considered and lamented as a fundamental defect in the constitution of Congress that *a full and entire power over the commerce of the United States*, [had] not been given to that body." The reference, no doubt, was to the Pennsylvania legislature's own resolution to this effect, of December 9, 1783, which has been mentioned earlier.[8] The mercantile committee's memorial went on to declare that, for want of such a "full and entire" commercial power in Congress, the whole country was in "a very singular and disadvantageous situation" with respect to its "commerce with other nations," and that, from the same cause, "the intercourses of the States [were] liable to be perplexed and injured by various and discordant regulations instead of that harmony of measures on which the particular as well as the general interests depend[ed]." Hope was therefore expressed that, in view of the seriousness of these troubles, the Pennsylvania legislature would at once seek to induce Congress to urge upon the states the great need there was for creating such a "full and entire" national power over commerce as the memorial described.[9]

Two days after the date of this memorial from the Philadelphia merchants, the Pennsylvania legislature responded to it. The response of the legislature was favorable, and certainly was expressed in terms potentially covering a complete, though not an exclusive, commercial power for Congress. Yet, in spite of this fact, and of the additional fact that the legislature undoubtedly recognized the need for internal as well as external national power, the terms of its response were not quite so sweeping as those in its instructions to its delegates in Congress, some sixteen months previously. Its opinion was, the legislature said, "that the privilege, in the degree hitherto retained by the States individually, of controuling and regulating their own trade, [was] no longer compatable with the general interests and welfare of the United States." "Reason and experience clearly evinc[ed] that [the] privilege [was] productive of mutual inconveniences and injuries amongst ourselves; [and, likewise, that] the systems of several [foreign] nations . . . [could] not be consistently or effectually counteracted but by a unity of councils." The legislature therefore resolved, in accordance with the suggestion made by the Philadelphia merchants, "that Congress be requested to devise such a system of commercial powers as they ought necessarily to be invested with"; and assurances were given that, if this should be done, Pennsylvania would be willing to grant the powers.[10]

The foregoing occurences in New York and Pennsylvania represent the beginnings of the popular agitation in favor of a national commerce power, which, as we have already intimated, swept over the country in the spring and summer of 1785. The memorials, addresses, and resolutions thus far described were all very widely published in the states in which they originated and in other states as well. They appeared, with some exceptions, in the newspapers of Georgia, South Carolina, Virginia, Pennsylvania, Maryland, New Jersey, New York, New Hampshire, Massachusetts, and Rhode Island, and very likely in the newspapers of the remaining states as well.[11] There can therefore be very little doubt that these several items played their part in the great arousing of the dormant nationalist sentiment of the country that occurred in 1785. But the really important proceedings—the proceedings that were the most widely circulated of all, and which beyond any question had the greatest role in arousing popular sentiment, and in apprising the country of just what it was that the various interested groups wanted—were the proceedings that took place in Boston.

Beyond much question, Boston was the town which had been earliest and hardest hit. Boston had long depended most on the shipbuilding trade, the carrying trade, and the trade with the West Indies; and those trades, along with the fish, lumber, whale oil, and potash of the whole New England region, had all been directly affected by the royal proclamations issued in the middle of 1783. To be sure, there had been a postwar boom in Boston, as there had been in the other towns; but it was shorter-lived in Boston, and grumbling and talk of the necessity of a national commerce power began to appear in the Boston newspapers long before the end of 1784.[12] This talk and grumbling continued through the winter at an increasing rate; and then, in the spring of the year, the men of Boston took action.

The action they took was in accord with a pattern that had become familiar to Americans during the years of the Revolution. At the instance of Stephen Higginson, Caleb Davis, Samuel Breck, and various other Boston merchants, a meeting was called, for April 15, of "all Gentlemen concerned in Trade . . . , to deliberate upon measures proper to be taken, for securing our commerce, and guarding ourselves against plans which [were] forming in Britain to supplant [Americans] in those branches which [were] the great staples of [the] Commonwealth."[13] The intention, of course, was to call a meeting of the "tradesmen and mechanicks," as well as the "shopkeepers and merchants"; but, for reasons which will presently appear, the "mechanical" groups let it be known that they did not think they would be welcome, and therefore had no intention of attending the meeting. So, a second notice was published, which carefully explained that by "Gentlemen concerned in Trade," it had been intended to solicit "the attendance of ALL men of reputation, in EVERY branch of business."[14] At the meeting on April 15, which had been scheduled to take place in "the long room" of the tavern of one Colonel Marston, so many persons appeared (though principally merchants and shopkeepers, it seems)[15] that not all could get in. As many as could, crowded in, elected John Hancock chairman of the meeting, chose a committee to draw up resolutions, and voted to adjourn, to meet again at Faneuil Hall on the morning following.[16] At that session, the committee presented a set of resolutions, which after various amendments was unanimously adopted. The resolutions provided, among other things, that another, larger committee should be appointed; and such a committee was appointed consisting of Hancock, Higginson, Davis, Breck, and eleven other "Merchants, Traders, and others of the town." By the terms of the resolutions, one of the duties of this new committee was to prepare a petition to be sent to Congress, requesting that body "immediately to regulate the trade of the United States, agreeably to the powers vested in them by the Government of [the] Commonwealth"—i.e., agreeably to the fragmentary powers over foreign trade which Congress had requested from the states on April 30, 1784. The committee was also directed to prepare a letter to be sent to the merchants in the other seaports of Massachusetts, soliciting them to send similar petitions to Congress and to seek instructions, in their respective towns, directing their representatives in the next General Court to propose to that body that it urge upon Congress the supreme importance of some early action upon the subject. Most important of all, however, the committee was directed to prepare a letter to be sent to the merchants in the several seaports of the other states, soliciting them to apply to their respective legislatures "to vest such powers in Congress (if not already done) as should be competent to the interesting purposes aforesaid," and to petition Congress to use such powers, when received, to accomplish "the desired effect."

Besides the foregoing program of action, this Boston mercantile meeting also resolved not to have any dealings, either "directly or indirectly," with any of the "British Merchants, Factors or Agents, except such only as [should] be approved by the Selectmen"; not to "let or sell any warehouse, shop, house or any other place for sale of [the] goods [of the said Merchants, Factors, or Agents]"; and not to "employ any person who [should] assist [them] by trucks, carts, barrow, or labor (except in the reshipment of their merchandise)." The meeting also resolved to "discountenance all such persons who [should] in any way advise, aid, or in the least degree, help or support such Merchants, Factors, or Agents, in the prosecution of their business," and to do everything possible "to prevent all persons acting under [themselves] from having any commercial intercourse with [them]." Then, finally, after some other measures not necessary to be noticed here, it was resolved that the persons present in the meeting would "encourage, all in [their] power, the manufactures and produce of [the] country, and [would] in all cases endeavour to promote them." The resolves were then ordered to be printed and distributed among the public, in an effort to gain general support.[17]

The support most desired was undoubtedly that of the local tradesmen and mechanics. Their general refusal to attend the meeting that the mercantile group had called was, of course, not due to any belief on their part that they were not "Gentlemen concerned in Trade." Their refusal was due to their harboring a grievance against the merchants and traders who had called the meeting. As the "mechanical" group viewed the matter, the Boston merchants and traders, with the coming of the peace, had gone in for the importation and sale of "British luxuries" in a thoroughly reckless and selfish way, without the slightest regard to the harm thereby done to the "infant manufactures" of America. By this behavior the merchants and traders, they felt, had shown that they had no real interest in the welfare of American manufacturers; why, then, the Boston tradesmen and mechanics reasoned, should American manufacturers bestir themselves about the troubles of American merchants and traders? The resolve of the mercantile group, respecting the encouragement of American manufactures, was therefore undoubtedly aimed at obtaining the support of the manufacturing element. And the resolution thus adopted, together with the exhortations that appeared at the time in the Boston newspapers for the mercantile and "mechanical" groups to get together,[18] did apparently produce results, for a day or two afterward a meeting of "the Tradesmen and Manufacturers" of the town was called for April 21. The purpose of this meeting, according to the notice of it in the Boston papers, was "to take into consideration what measures [might] be proper for [these "mechanical" groups] to adopt respecting the British Merchants, Factors, &c. . . . and for promoting the manufactures of [the] Country."[19] In the resolutions they adopted when their meeting took place, and in a letter they subsequently sent to the Boston merchants' committee, "the Tradesmen and Manufacturers" signified their willingness to cooperate with the mercantile group, in order "to effect the important purpose of freeing [the country] from the dangerous establishments of British merchants, &c.," whose residence in America was "conceived," they said, "to be destructive both to the mercantile and manufacturing interests." They then went on, however, to point out that "the several branches of [their own] occupations [had] of late been materially affected by European importations"; that the effect upon these occupations of imports of foreign goods was precisely the same, whoever did the importing; and that they accordingly felt "bound to prevent, if possible, those supplies, either by foreigners or [American] merchants." They added that they had "therefore voted a petition, to be presented to the next General Court for this purpose; and as [they] doubt[ed] not the sincerity of [the] declaration [of the mercantile group] 'to encourage the manufactures of this country,' [they] trust[ed] that "the Merchants, Traders, and others" would] support [with their] whole influence any measures calculated to promote so suitable a purpose."[20]

On April 26, the date of the letter sent them by "the Tradesmen and Manufacturers," "the Merchants, Traders, and others" held another meeting;[21] and though no record of what took place at that meeting seems to exist, the tenor of the mercantile group's reply to "the Tradesmen and Manufacturers," the tenor of the petition which they sent to Congress, and the tenor of the letters to the several seaports of the other states, as these were eventually sent out under date, however, of April 22—all indicate that they must have decided at their meeting of April 26, or perhaps at another meeting on the date of their letters, to broaden the basis of their appeal by extending their efforts to the obtaining of a complete national commerce power for Congress, and to the inducing of Congress to set up thereunder a complete American "commercial system." In their letter to "the Tradesmen and Manufacturers," "the Merchant and Traders" assured those groups that their letter had been "interesting and agreeable." "The Merchants and Traders" "rejoiced to find [their] sentiments and views harmonizing with [those of "the Tradesmen and Manufacturers"]"; and they "hoped" that the "united exertions" of the two groups would be "crowned with the desired success." They declared, however, that it was "to the United States in Congress [that they] look[ed] for effectual relief," and that it was "to them [they had] accordingly appealed." "They promised, nevertheless, that they would "cheerfully use what little influence [they had], in promoting and encouraging the [local] manufacturers of [Massachusetts], and for obtaining at the next General Court such restrictions *and excises* as [might] have so happy a tendency."[22] The precise tenor of this promise deserves careful notice: the merchants were willing, it appears, to support "*inland* duties"—i.e., "excises"—upon sales of imported goods, but they were not willing to support "external duties," or "customs"—then frequently called "imposts"—upon importations. The latter, because of the necessity for earlier payment, involved a financial burden that the mercantile group was apparently not willing to assume. It may be added that the distinction between these two kinds of taxes or duties, either of which might be protective, was well established at the time.[23]

The subsequent activities of the Boston mercantile group seem to have been in accord with the foregoing promise. They urged, primarily, the necessity of "full" powers for Congress over all "commerce," and the desirability of setting up under such a power a complete American "commercial system"; but although it is clear that they had little faith in the effectiveness of state regulations, the Boston merchants did not, apparently, oppose regulations by the states on an interim basis. The Boston "mechanical" group, on the other hand, put its emphasis on the need for immediate action by the states as the only agencies empowered at that time to act in the premises; but the proposals of the Boston mercantile group for a continental system were not opposed, and the Boston "mechanical" group, it is well known, came out in favor of the Constitution in the most emphatic terms, when the document was before the country in the winter of 1787-88.[24] It is thus evident that the two groups acted more or less in concert; and out of their concerted activities there came more immediately, in the next General Court, not only a local navigation act and a local system of protection but a proposal for a continental convention for "revis[ing] the confederation, and report[ing] to Congress how far it [might] be necessary, in their opinion, to alter or enlarge the same, in order to secure and perpetuate *the primary objects of the Union*."[25] Those "primary objects," as the reader will recall, were "the common defence," "the security of liberty," and "the mutual and general welfare" of the United States.[26]

As for the petition which the Boston merchants sent to Congress, it preferred the request that Congress make immediate use of whatever powers for the relief of the existing situation Congress might have, and expressed "full confidence" that such power would soon be made available "as alone [could] redress the present, and prevent the impending evils." The resolutions adopted by the merchants accompanied the petition; and the circular letter to the merchants of the seaports in the other states was also sent along to indicate to Congress what powers "the [Boston] Merchants, Traders, and others" considered necessary for the purposes they spoke of.

In the first of these two letters the belief was expressed that "the resources of America, if properly called forth and improved, [were] fully competent to [the] independent and comfortable support [of the country], to the most extensive and beneficial commerce, and, consequently, to [the] national opulence, credit, and dignity." "This cultivation and improvement," the letter conceded, "[would also have to] be directed to its proper end by the wisdom and firmness of the federal government." In the second letter, the one to the seaports outside Massachusetts, the "temporary remedies" that had been attempted by the Boston group were first set forth, after which the following paragraph appeared as the principal appeal of the letter:

Persuaded, however, that the exertions of individual cities, or even states, without the support of the whole confederacy, will be inefficacious, or at most can operate only as a partial relief, and that *nothing short of vesting Congress with full powers to regulate the internal as well as the external commerce of all the States*, can reach the mischiefs we complain of, we would agreeably to the directions of the enclosed proceedings, recommend to you an immediate application to the legislature of your State, to vest such powers in Congress (if they have not already done it) as shall be competent to the great and interesting purpose of placing *the commerce of the United States* upon the footing of perfect equality with every other nation; and to request you also to petition Congress (*when they shall be thus cloathed with authority*) to make such *internal regulations* as shall have that happy effect, encourage an attention to our manufactures, and remove the embarrassments under which our trade at present labours.

The language of the foregoing appeal is undoubtedly plain enough in itself, but an additional indication of the scope of the power being proposed will be seen in the fact that one of the "embarrassments to trade" which the letter "complained of," was "the want of a sufficient [circulating] medium [within the country] to answer the common purposes of life." That "want," then, was one of the "embarrassments to trade" that were to be relieved by *national* "*internal* [commercial] regulations"; or, in other words, by a *national* system of money. And, as the reader will note from the above-quoted paragraph, there were also to be *national* "*internal* [commercial] regulations [to] encourage an attention to manufactures." Among such measures, a system of *national* "excises," or "inland duties," upon sales of imported goods was, no doubt, one; and these most likely were prominent in the minds of the Boston merchants. But by the terms of the merchants' proposal, the power of Congress over "the internal as well as the external commerce of all the states" was to be plenary; and all other "commercial regulations," to the same or any other end, were therefore equally within the proposed power of Congress. The letter to the Massachusetts ports and the petition sent to Congress both accompanied this letter to the ports in the other states; and with the letter to the other Massachusetts ports, both the petition to Congress and the letter to the ports outside Massachusetts were sent. Complete information was thus supplied by the Boston merchants to all persons to whom any of their letters were communicated; and, as already suggested, the tenor of their letters seems to indicate that, at some time subsequent to their April 16 meeting, the Boston merchants must have revised their program of action in the manner previously set forth.

The various proceedings of the Boston mercantile group, and also those of the Boston "tradesmen and manufacturers," together with much of the grumbling and discussion which for months had preceded them, were meticulously reported by the newspapers in other parts of the country. In some of the papers in the other states, the reports of events in Boston began to appear, after a little while, under a special head: "Boston Proceedings" or "Boston Occurrences"; and there were other indications that the "Boston Proceedings" were attracting widespread attention. They were, for example, the subject of frequent comment in the private letters of the time;[27] and the circular letters of the Boston mercantile group, which appeared in the papers as a kind of climax to the entire "Boston Proceedings," were familiarly referred to, both in the private letters and in the discussions which soon sprang up in the various newspapers, as "the Boston merchants' letters," in a manner indicating that they were something everybody knew about.[28] The basis of this assumption can readily be understood if the progress of the letters through the newspapers of the country is followed. The three letters appeared together in most of the newspapers, but in a few of the papers they were printed in successive issues. And the letters were front-page news to a good many printers, which meant, in the eighteenth century, that they were allowed the space usually allotted to paid advertising. That the letters were regarded as important news, there can be no doubt whatever.

The progress of the letters through the newspaper press, so far as that progress can now be traced, was as follows:

May 21 and 28	*The Providence* [Rhode Island] *Gazette*
May 23	*The Boston* [Massachusetts] *Independent Ledger*
May 24 and 31	*The Salem* [Massachusetts] *Gazette*
May 26	*The* [Boston, Massachusetts] *Independent Chronicle*
May 31	*The* [Portsmouth] *New-Hampshire Mercury*
May 31	*The New York Gazetteer*
June 1	*The* [Newburyport, Massachusetts] *Essex Journal*
June 2	*The New-York Journal*
June 2	*The New-Haven* [Connecticut] *Gazette*
June 2 and 16	*Thomas's* [Worcester] *Massachusetts Spy*
June 3	*The* [Philadelphia] *Pennsylvania Packet*
June 3	*The* [Philadelphia] *Pennsylvania Mercury*
June 3	*The* [New-London] *Connecticut Gazette*
June 4	*The* [Philadelphia] *Pennsylvania Journal*
June 4 and 11	*The* [Philadelphia] *Independent Gazetteer*
June 6 and 13	*The* [Hartford, Connecticut] *American Mercury*
June 7	*The* [Springfield, Massachusetts] *Hampshire Herald*
June 8	*The* [Philadelphia] *Pennsylvania Gazette*
June 11	*The Falmouth* [Maine] *Gazette*
June 13	*The* [Baltimore] *Maryland Gazette*
June 27	*The* [Charleston, South Carolina] *Columbian Herald*
June 28	*The* [Charleston] *South-Carolina Gazette and Daily Advertiser*
June 29	*The* [Charleston] *South Carolina Gazette and Public Advertiser*
July 14	*The* [Savannah] *Gazette of the State of Georgia*

The reader will observe that no Virginia, Delaware, or North Carolina newspapers appear in the foregoing list. This does not mean, however, that the Boston merchants' letters were not known and very probably published in those three states. On the contrary, it is definitely known in the case of North Carolina that the Boston letters were sent to the merchants of Edenton and Wilmington within that state;[29] and there is, of course, every reason to suppose the letters were likewise sent to the merchants of Delaware and Virginia, as the resolutions of the Boston mercantile meeting required. In the usual course, the letters probably also found their way into the columns of most of the local newspapers. But there are no known files of Delaware and North Carolina newspapers for 1785, and the fact of the publication of the letters in those two states cannot, therefore, be definitely established. The situation is the same with respect to Virginia, except that there are files of *The* [Alexandria] *Virginia Journal*, which did not print the letters, and incomplete files of *The* [Richmond] *Virginia Gazette, or the American Advertiser*, which probably did.[30] Of the other Virginia papers for the year in question, there are no files known. It may be added that there are, likewise, a considerable number of newspapers through the other states, for which files for 1785 are either lacking or incomplete; and that the total number of papers in which the Boston letters were published was, therefore, in all probability in excess of the number appearing in the foregoing list. That the Boston letters were widely known among the people of every state cannot well be doubted.

CHAPTER XII

The Enthusiastic Response to the Agitation of 1785 in the New England States

IN ADDITION to the fact of the countrywide circulation of the Boston merchants' letters, the importance of those letters appears from the reactions they produced in various of the localities to which they were sent or in which they were published. The reactions to the letters consisted, in part, of newspaper discussions; in part, of resolutions by town meetings, chambers of commerce, and similar groups; and, in part, of recommendations by state governors, and acts or resolutions by state legislatures. Not all these varied expressions of opinion were completely favorable to the Boston merchants' suggestions. Indeed, some of them in the Southern states were apparently unfavorable; others, also chiefly in the South, were indicative of a desire that power be given Congress over foreign commerce only or, in some cases, merely over certain phases of foreign commerce. In one case, the surviving reports of a town meeting that endorsed the complete national power are of a character to indicate that there must also have been in that town some group opposed to anything more than a national power of regulating foreign trade. Despite such evidence of opposition in certain communities—indeed, one might say because of it—these facts are perfectly clear: there was everywhere a complete understanding that a complete national commerce power was being asked for; such a power was everywhere understood as including, besides the foreign commerce of every state, its whole internal commerce; and it was also understood that, if the entire internal commerce of all the states was *not* to be included within a national power "to regulate commerce," some limitation of the power, either to "external commerce" or to "foreign commerce," would have to be plainly expressed. Taken as a whole, moreover, the reactions in the various communities also indicate that in all parts of the country, except only the South, the sentiment in favor of a "full" national power, among the people as distinct from the officers of the states, was very strong indeed. And in not a few of the states the sentiment in favor of a "full" national power prevailed among the state-officer group as well.

In New Hampshire, the earliest of the states to respond to the Boston movement, the reaction was completely favorable. The Boston merchants'

176

letters were published there in *The* [Portsmouth] *New-Hampshire Mercury* of May 31. More than three weeks before that date, however, news of the Boston proceedings appeared in *The* [Portsmouth] *New Hampshire Gazette* of May 6. "Inhabitants of Boston," it was then recorded, "ha[d], in a large and crowded assembly, entered into a number of spirited resolves on [trade]. [And] from the general concurrence of sentiment in the neighboring towns, [it was to be] apprehend[ed that] some decisive measures [would] be quickly adopted." In the same paper, on May 13, 1785, a local appeal appeared, asking national commercial powers of the same scope as those suggested by the Boston merchants. "To such a pitch has British insolence arrived," this local appeal declared, "that added to their prohibiting all American vessels from entering their ports in the West Indies, they will not suffer an American to command a British bottom, unless he can produce a certificate that he served the Britannic Tyrant during the late war." The treatment an American captain had received at Grenada was next recounted, along with various other reported instances of mistreatment of American ships and seamen by the British. The appeal then concluded that "the necessity and importance of investing Congress with *full* powers to regulate *both internal and external commerce,* must [from the occurrences recounted] appear plain and obvious." The "necessity" arising from these occurrences, for investing Congress with "full" power to regulate "internal commerce," may not, however, appear "plain and obvious" to the reader of this book. It may therefore be well to point out that, to eighteenth-century Americans, retaliation against the British inevitably meant getting along, at least for a time and possibly for longer, without the long-customary British manufactures; with such a prospect in view, the necessity of a national power to regulate "internal commerce," including, of course, the power to promote manufactures and otherwise mold and regulate the national economy, was bound to seem to the men of the time a "plain and obvious" thing. Strong evidence that this was the way the matter was viewed may be seen in the action of John Adams, in suggesting measures for promoting manufactures and encouraging new forms of agriculture as eligible means for combatting the British postwar commercial restrictions, when he first had directed the attention of Congress to those restrictions, in 1783.[1] Further circumstances pointing in the same direction are the facts, first, that the foregoing appeal from the Portsmouth *Gazette* was widely copied in the newspapers of the other states, just after it appeared in Portsmouth, and, second, that its republication in the other states nowhere elicited any unfavorable or puzzled comment.[2] It should be said, however, that one newspaper, the anti-national *New-York Journal,* omitted the reference to "internal commerce."[3] In Portsmouth itself, the item was followed, as we already know, by the publication of the Boston merchants' letters on May 31, and about a fortnight afterward, by the appeal of the Philadelphia merchants for a "full and entire" power in Congress over "the commerce of the United States."[4] Thus, on the date in question—June 17—there had appeared in the newspapers of Portsmouth, within the space of six weeks, three separate appeals for a complete national commerce power. Just six days later, the legislature of New Hampshire, sitting in the town of Portsmouth, passed "the Act of June 23, 1785," previously mentioned, "to vest the United States in Congress assembled with *full* power to *regulate Trade* and enter into Treaties of Commerce." As the reader will remember, that act began by reciting that "Treaties of Commerce and *a due Regulation of Trade*" were become "absolutely necessary *through the United States*"; and then made provision for the vesting of Congress "with *full* power and authority, on the part, and in behalf of [New Hampshire], to make and enter into *such general Ordinances*, and Treaties, for the due regulation of *the Trade and Commerce of the United States*, as [Congress might] judge best calculated, to promote the weal and prosperity thereof."[5] In view of the repeated, sweeping language of this New Hampshire act, to say nothing of the three Portsmouth newspaper appeals that had preceded it, the intention of the legislature in passing the act would seem to be open to no uncertainty: it must have been intended as a grant of the "full" national power to regulate "both internal and external commerce," which the Boston merchants, the mercantile committee of Philadelphia, and the local writer in the Portsmouth *Gazette* all had asked. As previously indicated, then, the response in New Hampshire was completely and promptly favorable.

In the state of Rhode Island, the general reaction seems to have been much the same. The Boston merchants' letters were published there, in *The Providence Gazette*, by request of the local merchants, on May 21 and May 28; and the Portsmouth appeal, the Philadelphia merchants' memorial, and most of the other items herein discussed either preceded or followed the Boston letters in the Rhode Island papers. The legislature of the state, the reader may remember, had acted in the preceding February to confer upon Congress power to regulate what that legislature described as "foreign trade"; and after the appearance of the Boston letters and the other items advocating a "full" national power, the legislature took the further action, herein previously described, which it afterwards itself said had been intended, with its earlier action, to confer upon Congress "*the whole and sole* power of making laws for *the Regulation of Trade*." On the basis, then, of the Rhode Island legislature's own statement of its purposes, and the tenor of its acts as elsewhere analyzed in this book, no more doubt seems possible in the case of Rhode Island than in the case of New Hampshire that the general reaction, both in the state's legislature and out of it, was favorable to the proposal of creating a "full" national commerce power, which the letters of the Boston merchants contained.[6]

In the neighboring state of Connecticut, the Boston letters appeared in the newspapers early in June. Most of the items previously mentioned, from New Hampshire, New York, and Pennsylvania, also appeared in Connecticut, either before or after the Boston letters; throughout the summer and early fall, news of the further progress of the movement for a national commerce power was published regularly in the Connecticut papers. Of the local comment, which went considerably beyond most of that in the other states, the most interesting was a series of letters that began in *The New-Haven Gazette* on August 25. Signed "The Observator," the letters were apparently the work of the author of the pamphlet *The Political Establishments of the United States*, which was earlier mentioned as having been published in 1784 at Philadelphia and republished at New Haven in 1787, "with additions and alterations," just as the Federal Convention was assembling. [7]

"Our separate state governments," the first of the "Observator's" letters began, "(each sovereign and independent) which forms the basis of our *political system*, I never could think, would serve the interest of the public." "Nothing more than what has ever been the result of experience," he said, "is required to prove that the *political interest* of a nation, can never be promoted and secured, without the most unequivocal and perfect union; for no measures, however well adapted to promote the interests of the whole, can operate with efficacy among a people, whose *common interests* are partially united; and therefore, it can never be expected that a *system of policy* which establishes so many separate and independent interests, as ours does, can maintain an unanimity in views and measures; nor render any general act of government efficacious." The "Observator" was inclined to concede, however, that there appeared, at the moment, to be little likelihood that "a sacrifice of [that] favourite Hobby-Horse"—state sovereignty—would soon take place. Yet the states, he thought, "might remedy many, if not most of [their existing ills], by entrusting [their] *common interest* in the hands of Congress; and without that much, at least, it [was] vain," he maintained, "[that they should] pretend to a union; for without some institution, invested *with powers as extensive as [their] political concerns—powers free from impediment or controul*—powers capable of preserving a consistency and unanimity, government [in America would] forever remain in a state of confusion and complexity."

"[America's] want of an efficient government, [was] severely felt," the "Observator" went on, "in *all* [the country's] *political interests*, especially in [its] *commerce*." Everyone could see this. "[Yet] the furthest any proposal ha[d] extended, [was] to invest Congress with a power *to regulate our trade*, but even in this, there [did] not appear to be a unanimity." "Should the states, however, agree in [granting commercial power to Congress], it would," said the "Observator," "fall short of what [was] necessary; for *every political interest* of a nation [was] so blended together and dependent on one another, that, unless there [were] a sovereign power *sufficient to govern them all*, the end of public measures [would] be lost, by an interruption in some of their more remote and extensive operations; and therefore if the states should not invest Congress with *full* powers in *all* their *common interests*, their granting [Congress] powers *respecting trade only*, would be but a temporizing, and [would] fail of answering its purpose fully."

In other words, this "Observator," of New Haven, considered the "full and entire" power over "the commerce of the United States," which had been asked by the merchants of Philadelphia—the "full" power, that is, "to regulate the internal as well as the external commerce of all the states," which had been advocated by the Boston merchants—as not enough. There must, he maintained, be more than this: there must be "full" power in Congress over *all* the "political interests" of the nation, among which, as we have seen, "commerce, *internal and external*," in the extensive sense explained in this book, was only one. That this was in fact the precise meaning of the "Observator's" statements appears with certainty from a comparison of his letters and his pamphlet;[8] and his mode of speaking in his letters, without the slightest explanation of the scope of his terms, shows of course that he must have supposed that his readers would, without explanation, understand precisely how extensive "the political interest of a nation" was. In other words, the language which the "Observator" used in his letters was familiar political jargon at the time. This is further shown by the fact that his letter was copied in *The American Herald*, of Boston, on September 12, and afterwards by newspapers in a number of the other states, including *The* [Charleston] *Gazette of the State of South-Carolina*, on November 7. No unfavorable or puzzled comment appeared anywhere.

Another Connecticut writer whose work in 1785 shows how far in advance Connecticut opinion was, was Noah Webster. A young lawyer of Hartford at this period, Webster published a pamphlet there, early in the year, which stands unique among the writings of 1785 in its clear perception of the defects of the existing government and its plain, sensible, matter-of-fact prescription for their cure. "Must the powers of Congress be increased? this question," said Webster, "implies gross ignorance of the nature of government: the question ought to be, must the American states be united?" "And if this [latter] question [was] decided in the affirmative, the next question [was] whether the states [could] be said to be united, without *a legislative head?* or in other words, whether thirteen states [could] be said to be united in government, when each state reserve[d] to itself the sole powers of legislation?" "The answer to all such questions," Webster thought "extremely easy." If the states really wished to be united, "there *must* be a supreme head, clothed with the same power *to make and enforce laws* respecting *the general policy* of all the states as the legislatures of the respective states ha[d] to make laws binding on those states, respecting their own *internal police*."

"The government of the United States," he also said, "[ought to] be formed upon the general plan of government in each of the several states." "The right of making laws for the United States should be vested in all their inhabitants, by legal and equal representation; and the right of executing those laws, committed to the smallest possible number of magistrates [including "judges of courts, justices of the peace, sheriffs, &c."], chosen annually by Congress and responsible to them for their administration." As for the relationship between the states and the nation, Webster maintained that, "as [the] towns and cities [of a state were], as to their general concerns, mere subjects of the state; so the several states [ought to be], as to their own *internal police*, sovereign and independent, but as to *the common concerns of all*, [they ought to] be mere subjects of the federal head." "If the necessity of union [was] admitted, such a system [was] the only means of effecting it. [For,] however independent each state [might] be, and ought to be, in things that relate[d] to itself *merely*, yet as a part of a greater body, it must be a subject of that [greater] body, in matters that relate[d] to the whole."

Regarding the particular powers to be assigned to Congress, however, Webster was not specific. At one point in his pamphlet he intimated that "the general concerns of the continent" could probably be "reduced" to "a few heads." At another point he ventured the opinion that the powers given to Congress by the Articles of Confederation were "perhaps nearly sufficient to answer the ends of [the] union, were there any method of enforcing their resolutions." From this latter statement, taken by itself, the reader might perhaps infer that Webster did not desire a commerce power for Congress, since under the Articles Congress had virtually no power over commerce at all. Webster's desire for a national commerce power, however, appears elsewhere in his pamphlet, with respect to both foreign and domestic commerce, though the quantum of power which he desired for Congress over the two branches of the subject is nowhere actually stated. Besides the foregoing, there is but one other intimation in his pamphlet as to what Webster considered the desirable concrete scope of the national governing power. It is a suggestion that Congress ought to have at least some degree of power to maintain peace and order in the country, a function which Webster significantly referred to as "*general* internal police." Taking this and his other quoted statements together, and remembering that Webster at various points in his pamphlet employed the terms "police" and "policy" for describing respectively the state and national legislative fields, it seems probable, though perhaps not completely certain, that the "few heads" to which he thought "the general concerns of the continent" might be "reduced" were, first, the thing he called "general internal police" and, second, war, trade, and diplomacy; which, as the reader will recall, were the usual "heads"* of what the eighteenth century knew as "policy."[9]

That the views of Noah Webster and the "Observator" of New Haven were fairly representative of the great body of Connecticut opinion in 1785 seems entirely probable. In the beginning of our national history, we have already seen, the Connecticut governor and legislature, in December 1776,

---

*It is perhaps worth noting, in addition to the points touched upon in the text, that Webster advocated the abolition of slavery and declared such action to be "intimately connected"—as, from both a military and commercial point of view, it most certainly was—"with *the policy* of these states."

had both quite readily conceded the domestic as well as the foreign commercial power of Congress.[10] A short while after the period when the "Observator" and Noah Webster wrote, the delegates of Connecticut proposed in the Federal Convention such a complete national commerce power for Congress under the Constitution. In addition, they proposed at the same time that another power be given to Congress, paramount even to the "internal-police" powers of the several states, of legislating in *all* cases for the national welfare.[11] A few months after the adjournment of the Federal Convention, the Constitution, then generally understood to contain such powers, was adopted with negligible opposition in Connecticut.[12] In the following year, the weakening of Congress's powers by amendment was opposed in the state. In the years thereafter, Connecticut remained for long the most staunchly Federalist state in the Union. This series of facts, none of which is open to any question, plainly argues a long-standing nationalist conviction among the people of the state; and since the discussions by Noah Webster and the "Observator" of New Haven, occurring in the very midst of the facts in question, seem to have been in complete accord with all of them, the warranted inference is that the views they expressed were also in accord with the views of most people in Connecticut in 1785.

Nevertheless, the actual response of Connecticut's legislature to the agitations of 1785 extended no further than the grant to Congress, along in the summer, of the fragmentary powers over foreign trade asked for by that body some fifteen months before.[13] The long delay in the grant of these powers was probably due to the same cause that produced a like delay in granting them on the part of the other states, Delaware and New Jersey, which were most similarly situated; that is, the delay was due to the complete inadequacy of the powers for ending the impost-gouging by neighboring states which at the time constituted the chief commercial grievance of these three small states. The states in question were all alike, also, in their failure to do more in response to the agitations of 1785 than to grant to Congress the powers previously requested. All three states were engaged at the time in programs of commercial reprisal against their neighbors for the impost-gouging practiced against them; none was directly concerned in the commercial difficulties with the British which had been so large a cause of the distress in the impost-gouging states; and it was apparently felt, in Connecticut, Delaware, and New Jersey, that they would be more likely to get what they themselves desired, if they did no more than what had been constitutionally requested. The nature and purpose of Connecticut's program of reprisal will be dealt with more fully in connection with the discussion of New Jersey and Delaware.[14] We believe it sufficient at this point to say that, so far as can be told, none of the men from the other states who were most interested in obtaining a full commercial power for Congress felt any doubt that, when such a full national power should be requested by Congress, Connecticut would be found as ready as any of the other states to grant it. The facts of Connecticut's subsequent behavior, already mentioned, show that the men from these other states were undoubtedly correct in this opinion.

As already suggested, the views on governmental reform expressed in Connecticut in 1785 were not completely paralleled in the course of that year in any other state. The nearest to a parallel, at least as to the desirable scope of Congressional legislative power, were certain resolutions adopted on May 19 by the town of Boston, and the resolutions adopted on July 1 by the Massachusetts General Court, calling for a continental convention to revise the Articles. These two sets of resolutions are of particular interest to the argument of this book because they show, in a very striking way, that the sweeping commercial proposals of the Boston merchants were not in advance of, but rather behind, the general body of opinion in their town and state. The resolutions adopted by the town were in the nature of instructions to the delegates to the General Court, that had been elected on the tenth of the month. The instructions directed the attention of the town's representatives to the existing state of American public credit; to the scarcity of "the circulating medium" throughout the country; to the "unequal and unproductive" character of the trade carried on with England; to the baneful activities within the country of "the British factors"; to the menace that had arisen to the continued existence of the American carrying trade; and to the need of the American fisheries for "governmental encouragement and protection." The instructions then went on to express the "earnest wish" of the people of Boston "to see the internal trade of the several states fixed and confirmed on principles of the most perfect equality"; and their "great anxiety" that "the attention of government [might be turned] to the encouragement of agriculture, and to the present reduced state of [the country's] manufactures." "But, gentlemen," the instructions at length concluded, "while we recommend all these circumstances to your notice, and while we contemplate some among the numerous difficulties of our present situation, we look in vain for a power in government adequate to their removal; For it is politically impossible, circumstanced as we now are, from our different views and local attachments, that there should be either concert or decision on many great and national questions, as the measures, of any single state, will probably be opposed and defeated by those of its neighbours, till at length the fabric of our confederacy, by internal dissention, may be convulsed and subverted. To correct these evils, and to add dignity and efficiency to the federal government, your constituents are anxiously solicitous to see the Congress invested *with power competent to our common necessities; to a due regulation of our commerce; and to the adjustment and discharge of our public debt;* and in order to do this, we enjoin upon you to exert your utmost influence with the legislature to request the Supreme Executive forthwith to open a correspondence with the Supreme Executive of each and every other state, to concert the means of national unanimity and exertion."[15]

Shortly after these instructions were issued, an article appeared on June

16, 1785, in *The Independent Chronicle*, of Boston, which opposed and criticized them very severely. This article, entitled "The Warner" and signed "Jonathan of the Valley," seems clearly to have been an elaborate attempt to confuse the public mind as to the hopes and wishes of the Boston merchants and, by a set of subtly contrived, misleading statements, to draw public attention away from their recently published letters. This sly article, taken with a reply which it promptly elicited, is enough to prove—should such proof still seem requisite at this point—that the Boston merchants' letters, and the town's instructions as they related to commerce, were both understood at the time as appeals for precisely the kind of comprehensive national commerce power that this book describes. "The present crisis of our public affairs," "Jonathan of the Valley" began, "is no less important than dangerous. The commercial circle of all America, is violently agitated; fear sits heavy on the sons of commerce, and really they have the highest cause for their dismal apprehensions. The present regulations of the court of London bid fair to ruin the trade of this union; and nothing but vesting Congress with powers adequate to govern *the navigation* of the States, seems to be held out as a remedy." The merchants of Boston in their recent proceedings, he then went on, had , however, been much in error; for, strange as it might seem, they had gone "upon the mistaken idea, that the legislature of [the] commonwealth, by their act of [the] last year [complying with Congress's request of April 30, 1784] had given to Congress sufficient power to remedy the inconvenience they suffer[ed]." That this statement of the position of the Boston merchants was quite unwarranted, at least as to the position they had finally taken, the reader need scarcely be told.[16] But it suited the purpose of "Jonathan of the Valley" to draw a red herring across the trail that led to their letters; and so he represented that the suggestions of the merchants were inadequate, and then falsely purported to go beyond them in his own advocacy of a national power "to govern navigation" only. By these means he doubtless hoped that his own good faith would be made to seem quite certain, and that the interest of his readers in the merchants' letters and proposals would be effectively destroyed.

Having baited this trap for unwary readers, he next turned his attention to the instructions the town of Boston had issued to its representatives in the General Court. He "by no means disapprove[d]," he said, "of the temper or proceedings of that very respectable body"; but he did fear the consequences, "should the ardor of the town spread with its full force through the union." In its consequences, it might, he agreed, very probably "secure [America] against the oppressions of other nations"; but "the remedy [that had been] solicit[ed], *if granted as generally and inrestrictively as they [had] asked it*, would alter totally the form of government" and thereby, he greatly feared, "pull down the goodly fabric of freedom in this western world." *For the town had "ask[ed] Congress to regulate the commerce of the union"*; and would not "a grant of this nature, lay a foundation for *one consolidated government over the whole union*, annihilate all [the] legislatures, and swallow up the separate sovereignty of the States [which had been] so carefully preserved in the confederation?" What was wanted, he insisted, was "a power to pass a navigation act, and [thereby] meet the court of London in the regulation of trade upon their own principles"; but what had been proposed by the people of Boston was "*a general power to regulate trade*." Of the even more general proposal which that town had also made, that Congress be endowed with "power competent to [America's] common necessities," "Jonathan of the Valley" said nothing at all. He seemed to be satisfied to pose, falsely, as a wise and moderate man who wished to steer a middle course with respect to "commerce," between the "reckless" proposals of the town of Boston and "totally inadequate" proposals of the Boston merchants. His lucubrations, it may be added, were shortly afterwards copied in certain antinational newspapers of New York and Philadelphia, in which they were recommended to the public as "an excellent Piece on the impropriety of vesting Congress *with unlimited Powers relative to Trade*."[17]

"Jonathan of the Valley," as already intimated, was answered promptly in Boston. The answer, appearing one week later in the *Independent Chronicle* of June 23, 1785, came from a writer who had long been contributing to the Boston newspapers under the pseudonym of "A Friend of Commerce." "If by [the proposed] *commercial* power," this writer began, "all our *civil* establishments are to be annihilated, Mr. Jonathan is certainly right to speak aloud, though his voice may be as one 'crying in the wilderness.'" "[But] the question," he declared, "[was] whether these states [could] accomplish anything decisive in their commercial concerns, without Congress [were] invested with *a power to produce a general commercial system throughout the whole union*?" The answer to this question, in the opinion of the "Friend of Commerce," was plainly no. And what he meant by "a power to produce a general commercial system throughout the whole union" is inferable from a complaint he had made, in one of his earlier appearances in the same Boston newspaper, that Americans were "too apt to consider [their] importations as the essential branch of [their] commerce; whereas on exports, manufactures, and agriculture, depend[ed their] flourishing as a commercial people."[18]

That the "Friend of Commerce" did not think of "commerce" as signifying only "foreign trade" is also evident from another of his writings, of a few weeks later, in which he invited any reader who felt any doubt as to the "deplorable state" of American "commerce" to "visit [any] merchant in his compting room, or [any] retailer within his shop." "The long hacknied phraises of 'dull times,' 'slow sales,' &c. [were] wrote in characters as legible as they [were] alarming."[19] And in view of this extremely depressed condition of the business of the country, the "Friend of Commerce," in his reply to "Mr. Jonathan," contended strenuously that full power over commerce ought to be granted at once to Congress. There was, he maintained, no more reason for not trusting Congress with this necessary power than there was for not trusting the General Court with its powers. "The argument which forb[ade Congress's] receiving such power would operate equally upon all governments whatever." Such reasoning was "childish." "Government naturally implied[d] a trust, and all we [had] to do, [was], to put our confidence in those, over whom we [had] controul: If we [had] controul over Congress, or the members who compose[d] it, it [was] equally as safe to invest them with powers, as any other body of men [whatever]."[20] This answer by the "Friend of Commerce" to "Mr. Jonathan" was also published in New York;[21] but it did not, so far as is known, appear in Philadelphia.

While the foregoing argument was proceeding in the pages of the *Independent Chronicle*, the Massachusetts General Court, sitting in Boston, was pondering what had better be done in the premises. On May 31, the governor of the state, James Bowdoin, had just delivered a message to it, in which he had called its attention to "the state of [America's] foreign trade, which ha[d] given so general an uneasiness, and the operation of which, through the extravagant importations and use of foreign manufactures, ha[d] occasioned so large a balance against [the country]." "To satisfy that balance," the governor had pointed out, "[the nation's] money [was being] exported, which, with all the means of remittance at present in [America's] power, still f[e]ll very short of a sufficiency. Those means, which ha[d] been greatly lessened by the war, [were] gradually enlarging; but they [could] not soon increase to their former amplitude, so long as Britain and other nations continue[d] the commercial systems they ha[d] adopted since the war." In regulating their trade with America in the manner they had, those nations, said the governor, had of course been within their rights; but "the United States ha[d] the same right, and [could], and ought to regulate their foreign trade on the same principle." "It [was] a misfortune, that Congress [had] not yet been authorized for the purpose by all the States." Massachusetts, the governor intimated, had not itself been thus remiss; but, still, "if there [were] any thing wanting on the part of [Massachusetts] to complete that authority, it [lay] with [the General Court] to bring it forward and mature it. And untill Congress [should] ordain the necessary regulation, [the General Court ought also] to consider what further [was] needful to be done on [their] part, to remedy the evils, of which the merchant, the tradesman and manufacturer, and indeed every other description of persons among [them], so justly complain[ed]."

Having made the foregoing rather diffident suggestions to the General Court, and being encouraged, perhaps, by the cordiality with which they had been received, the governor next informed that body that he considered it "of great importance, and the happiness of the United States," he said, "depend[ed] upon it, that Congress should be vested with *all the powers* necessary to preserve the union, to manage the general concerns of it, and secure and promote its common interest." "That [common] interest, so far as it [was] dependent on a commercial intercourse with foreign nations," the governor now ventured to declare, "[was] not sufficiently provided for"; the matter therefore "merit[ed] their attention"; and if they agreed with him "that Congress should be vested with ampler powers, and that special delegates from the States should be convened to settle and define them," they would, he doubted not, "take the necessary measures for obtaining such a Convention or Congress, whose agreement, when confirmed by the States, would ascertain those powers."[22]

The obvious caution with which Governor Bowdoin had gotten around to this suggestion was apparently unnecessary, for on July 1 the General Court adopted his suggestion in a most full and ample manner. Declaring its belief that "the prosperity and happiness of a nation, [could] not be secured without a due proportion of power lodged in *the Supreme Rulers of the State*," by which it meant Congress, it resolved, as its opinion, that "the present powers of the Congress of the United States were not fully adequate to the great purposes they were *originally* designed to effect," and that it was, accordingly, "highly expedient, if not indispensably necessary, that there should be a Convention of Delegates from all the States in the Union, at some convenient place, as soon as [might] be, for the sole purpose of revising the confederation and reporting to Congress how far it [might] be necessary to alter or enlarge the same . . . in order to secure and perpetuate the primary objects of the Union."[23] Those "primary objects," which Congress "were *originally* designed to effect," were, as the men of the time were fully aware, "the common defense," "the security of liberty," and "the mutual and general welfare" of the entire country.[24]

Upon the General Court's passage of the foregoing resolution, steps were at once taken to inform the Massachusetts delegates in Congress of what the General Court and the people of Massachusetts desired, and urgent "directions" were given them to put the General Court's proposal promptly before Congress and "make every exertion in [their] power to obtain an early calling of the desired convention."[25] Because of certain matters that had come to their attention in Congress, however, the Massachusetts delegates felt dubious of the wisdom of the General Court's proposal, and because of their dubiety they decided not to comply with that body's instructions until they could make known to it the reasons for their doubts and fears. To this end they sent to Governor Bowdoin, on September 3, a lengthy letter for submission to the General Court, in which they urged a great many not very impressive arguments against the wisdom of what they quite correctly described as the legislature's proposal of "a Convention to revise the Confederation *generally*."* They also wrote certain confidential letters to their more intimate friends hinting, rather broadly, at the nature of certain other reasons for their unwillingness to act, "which would [have been] improper to

---

*Underlined in original letters of the delegates upon the subject.

have communicated, but which in [their] opinion [were] of great weight."[26] Ultimately, on November 25, after one of their number had returned to Massachusetts and had had an opportunity of conferring with the General Court, or some of its members,[27] that body voted to suspend, until further notice, the instructions for a general convention which it had adopted so enthusiastically some five months before.[28]

Thus, as the story is usually told, were the patriotic efforts of the Massachusetts governor, the people and merchants of Boston, and the legislature of the state—to the extent that these are known and properly understood—all in the end brought to an absolute nullity by the folly and vanity of the three Massachusetts delegates in Congress. In a future chapter we shall see that the reasons which actuated these three Massachusetts men were anything but vain and foolish. For the present, however, it is sufficient to note that there is nothing in the fact of their undoubted opposition to a *general* revision of the Confederation, or in the fact of the General Court's eventual concurrence in their views, which in any way militates against the conclusions to be drawn at this point. These are, first, that in 1785 the people of Boston desired to see a *complete* national commerce power vested in Congress and, in addition, a "power [in that body] competent to *all* [the nation's] common concerns"; and, second, that the state's legislature, representing the people of the whole state, desired to see Congress invested, generally, with *all* powers necessary to accomplish what had "originally" been intended as "the primary objects of the Union"—i.e., "the common defense," "the security of liberty," and "the mutual and general welfare" of the United States. Views of similarly sweeping scope were likewise held, we have seen, at least by some men in Connecticut; and so far, at least, as the full national power over commerce was concerned, in both Rhode Island and New Hampshire. It therefore seems quite certain that sentiment throughout New England in 1785 was extremely favorable to "vesting Congress with full powers to regulate the internal as well as the external commerce of all the states," as the Boston merchants and other groups then proposed.

CHAPTER XIII

The Response to the Agitation of
1785 in the Middle States

WITH the exception of the more confidential proceedings between the Massachusetts delegates in Congress and the governor and legislature of that state, all the later occurrences in New England which we have just reviewed were reported fully in the newspapers in other parts of the country.[1] The news of these later New England events unquestionably played a part, and apparently an important part, along with the letters of the Boston merchants, in arousing the people in the other states to the various actions they took, or at least attempted, in 1785 for obtaining for Congress full power to regulate commerce. This was the case, for example, in Pennsylvania. The memorial of the Philadelphia merchants on April 6 in favor of a "full and entire" commerce power for Congress had not been presented to the Pennsylvania public at the time when it was sent to the General Assembly; and the same was true of the resolution concurring with the merchants' views, which that body had passed two days afterward. Other items had appeared, however, in the Pennsylvania papers; and among these, during the last week in May, was the demand that had first appeared at Portsmouth, New Hampshire, on May 13 for "investing Congress with full powers to regulate both internal and external commerce." This item was printed in at least two of the newspapers of Philadelphia.[2] Shortly afterward, the Philadelphia merchants' memorial was finally given to the public, together with the reply which the Pennsylvania legislature had made. These documents were published in all the Philadelphia papers.[3] A few days later, a citizens' meeting was called and held at the university in Philadelphia, at which a committee of thirteen persons was appointed (including, among others, Thomas FitzSimons and John M. Nesbitt, of the local merchants' committee), to draw up resolutions on the subject of commerce, to be presented to an adjourned session of the citizens' meetings appointed to be held on June 20.[4] In the days immediately following the appointment of this town committee, the letters of the Boston merchants appeared in at least five of the Philadelphia papers;[5] the instructions of the town of Boston to its delegates in the Massachusetts General Court soon followed;[6] and two days before the date set for the adjourned session of the citizens' meeting, an article was published in *The Pennsylvania Packet* which showed quite plainly that the news of events in Boston and the views of the people there were having a considerable influence in Philadelphia.

The article in the *Packet*, signed with the significant pseudonym "Boston," undertook in a somewhat detailed way to consider the nature of the subject shortly to come before the Philadelphia town meeting. "The committee," the article began, "[would], no doubt, propose such a plan as they [might] conceive best calculated to obtain the important end"—"the prosperity of America"; "but as the intention of the citizens in assembling, [was] to give every individual an opportunity of offering such improvements, as he [might] think proper, the necessity of being prepared for this purpose [was] evident." The subsequent proceedings at the town meeting on the twentieth make these prefatory remarks by "Boston" seem important. Having made them, he launched into his main discussion. *The commerce of a country comprehend[ed]*," he said, "*a great variety of interests*; and, in its ultimate consequences, affect[ed] the whole community: it [was] closely connected with the interests of the farmer, manufacturer, and mechanic, through the medium of the trader. *Every object*, therefore, which ha[d] a *direct* tendency to support *any one, or all of* [*the foregoing*] *interests* c[a]me properly under the notice of the [impending] meeting, and ought to be kept steadily in view [by those intending to attend it]." This declaration, as the reader will at once perceive, is in accord with the eighteenth-century understanding of the phrase "to regulate commerce," as explained in this book; and though "Boston," in the middle of his statement, appears to have shifted unconsciously to some other, more restricted sense of "commerce" (either "trade of merchandize" or "foreign commerce"), he appears to have shifted back again, before its end, to the comprehensive sense with which he had started, and to have been fully aware that, whatever "commerce" might sometimes mean in other contexts, it was to be understood, when used in reference to a sphere of regulation, or government, in the most extensive gainful sense it had.

Having indicated this fact sufficiently to his readers, "Boston" next commended to his fellow Philadelphians the example set by "the patriotic sons of Boston." The Bostonians, he pointed out, had unequivocally declared their desire to "submit to Congress *the controul of the national commerce*, as well as *all other concerns common to all the states*"; and he indicated his opinion that it behooved Philadelphians, and Pennsylvanians generally, to follow Boston's example. In the interim before Congress should obtain such powers, however, it would be necessary for the Pennsylvania legislature to act "to remove every *general* evil." To this end, "additional duties [were required]," he thought, "on such imported articles as interfere[d] with the manufactures and productions of our own country; and an extra duty [ought also to be imposed] on all goods which [should] be imported into [Pennsylvania] in vessels belonging, wholly, or in part, to British subjects; or which, having been so imported into any of the [other] states, [might] afterwards be brought into

[Pennsylvania]." "The necessity of establishing and supporting a circulating medium [also was] obvious"; and to this end, "the president and supreme executive council [of the state ought] to direct the speedy collection of the arrearages of taxes, in order to preserve the full credit of the new [Pennsylvania] money." And "another step deserving [of] attention" was the "extending the inland navigation of the state, as well as [the] repairing and improving the public roads." "These two objects [inland navigation and public roads?] ha[d] a particular reference to [Pennsylvania]," he said; whereas the national commercial power he was advocating would have to do, he explained, with "matters of *a more general concern*, and which respect[ed] Pennsylvania's] *commerce and manufactures** *as connected with the other states in the union*." These last two statements would seem to indicate that "Boston" did not desire for Congress the *"full"* power to regulate "the internal as well as the external commerce of all the states," which was advocated by the Boston merchants. Yet, from his letter as a whole, it is apparent that he desired for Congress "full" power "to regulate commerce," in the extensive sense he had himself described, *in all cases involving the national welfare*; but for some reason or other, he did not seem to think that the national welfare was involved in the establishing of public means of communication in particular states.[7]

Who this "Boston" of Philadelphia was, is not known; but whoever he was, he seems in some way to have known what the town committee was about to propose. A desire to confute his purposes seems also evident in the report made by that committee on June 20. In the course of its report (which, significantly perhaps, was *not* signed by Thomas FitzSimons and one other member of the committee), it was declared to be "presume[d] that [the] resolutions embrace[d] and fully comprehend[ed] the landed, trading, and manufacturing interests of [the] country." The word "interests," however, is an ambiguous term, and in just what sense the "interests" in question were "embraced" and "fully comprehended" in the "resolutions" of the committee was not, perhaps, intended by the committee, or some of its members, to be clear. The committee's "resolutions" included proposals for shutting off all importations of foreign manufactures which interfered with the manufactures of America; proposals for building up new American manufactures and providing in that way a dependable domestic market for the products of the nation's agriculture; and proposals that commercial treaties be sought, with foreign powers, to assure reciprocal advantages to America in her commerce with them. The committee's statement, therefore, could have been taken by a casual reader to mean no more than that "the good" (or "interest") of the landed, trading, and manufacturing "groups" (or "interests") had been considered by the committee in drafting its proposals. Yet the fact remains that there was one other of the committee's "resolutions" which, according to the

---

*"Manufactures," it would seem, was used by "Boston" in this passage in the generic sense which included "agriculture." This seems to follow from his prior statements. Cf. chap. IV, n. 30, Pol. & Con., II, 1281–82.

prevailing usage of the time, "embraced" and "fully comprehended" "the landed, trading, and manufacturing interests of [the] country," in an entirely different sense—i.e., the sense which "Boston" had explained in *The Pennsylvania Packet*. The resolution in which these "interests" were thus "embraced" was one declaring "that nothing but a *full* power in Congress, over *the commerce of the United States* [could] relieve it from its present oppressions." The meaning of this resolution—indeed, the meaning of the entire set of resolutions—was still further thrown into doubt by the preamble with which the committee's report began. In this preamble, it was declared that "the most efficient and proper mode of obtaining the desired relief"—that is, presumably, of "obtaining" a grant of "full" commercial power to Congress— "which the [then] state of [Pennsylvania's] trade and manufactures, *in the relation to foreign nations* require[d], ought to be by application to the [state's] legislature, to whose wisdom and justice, the further consideration of this momentous concern should be submitted."[8] In this declaration, the italicized words (in view of their somewhat awkward character, and the much clearer sense of the passage when they are omitted) appear clearly to have been an interpolation; and their presence in the committee's preamble, seemingly suggesting a limitation of all the committee's proposed resolutions to relationships with foreign nations, almost certainly means that on the committee there were some men who were opposed not only to a complete national-commerce power but to this kind of "general-welfare" commerce power that the writer "Boston" had apparently had in mind in his article in the *Packet*. Furthermore, it seems clear that these opponents of a full national power must either have constituted a majority of the town committee or, perhaps, have been a minority thereof that had, or was feared to have, sufficient support among the body of the town to make their placation, to some extent, seem necessary. The sly and garbling way in which the sentiments of these men appeared in the report suggests, however, that they were not in a position of certain ascendancy among the town at large. Had they been in such a position, these men would undoubtedly have dominated the committee; and had they dominated the committee and not been afraid of the nationalist sentiments of the town, their own anti-national ideas—or, if the reader prefer, their own limited national ideas—would almost certainly have been far more clearly expressed.

The foregoing view of the state of affairs at this Philadelphia town meeting is fully supported by what happened when the resolutions of the committee were put before the citizens. When that occurred, someone in the body of the meeting promptly moved that three additional resolutions be adopted. The first of these asked that the legislature do everything possible to "extend" the "inland navigation" of the state and to "repair and improve" its "public roads." The second complained of the prevalence of tax defaults in the outlying counties and asked that effective measures for the collection of taxes in these regions be taken by the state's officers. These proposals, as we have just seen, were among those which "Boston" had made in his article in the *Packet*. The third additional resolve was a declaration "that the sense of [the] meeting coincide[d] with that expressed by the committee of merchants and traders of [the] city, in their memorial of the 6th of April last, to the general assembly of [the] state,—*so far as the views of that memorial extend*[ed];* And that [the] meeting highly approve[d] of the resolutions of that honourable house, of the 8th of April, in consequence of the said memorial."[9] Bearing in mind the "extent" of "the views" which had been thus expressed by the Philadelphia merchants, the proposal of this third additional resolve from the body of the town meeting undoubtedly means that some of the citizens were displeased with the ambiguities and inconsistencies which had been allowed to creep into the committee's report, and were determined to eliminate or counteract them if they could. The language of the resolve by which this was attempted, as well as the language of the two other additional resolves proposed at the same time quite plainly suggest that "Boston," or someone acting for him, was the proposer of these additional resolutions. This, however, is not known, nor is it directly known whether any of these three additional resolves were adopted. The contemporary newspaper accounts of the town meeting are not clear as to which resolutions were adopted, and since the original of the town's proceedings is apparently lost,[10] any conclusion upon the point must be based upon other evidence.

Evidence sufficient to ground a certain conclusion, however, is supplied by a petition on behalf of this Philadelphia meeting subsequently filed with the Pennsylvania legislature. The petition was filed by a new committee which had been appointed at the close of the adjourned session of the meeting, on June 20. Jared Ingersoll, the chairman of the meeting and a future member of the Federal Convention, was made the chairman of the new committee, and the thirteen members of the original committee, with Ingersoll and seven mechanics of the town, were made the members of it. The new committee was directed to "digest" the town's resolutions into the form of a petition, and then to lay the petition before the legislature at its autumn meeting.[11] This the committee did on September 3. The petition then filed was signed by Ingersoll, *Thomas FitzSimons*, five out of the seven mechanics, and ten out of the twelve other members of the committee, and it was stated publicly, without contradiction, that the failure of the remaining members to sign was due only to absence and lack of opportunity.[12] There can thus be little room for surmise that anything unauthorized was attempted by the second committee; but it may possibly have some significance that two nonsigning members of the second committee who had also been members of the first committee; had both been signers of the somewhat garbled report which the first committee had made. The first paragraph of this petition to the legislature, as printed in *The Pennsylvania Packet* of September 5, read as follows:

---

*Italics in the original newspaper accounts.

The committee, being directed by their fellow-citizens to make representations to your honorable house, upon the several subjects mentioned in the resolutions accompanying this memorial, and under which they were appointed—they beg leave earnestly to press the consideration of these [those?] points which regard our trade and manufactures, as matters of the last importance, affecting immediately or eventually the interest of every particular [i.e., every individual] amongst us, and consequently the prosperity of the state generally: but the committee would observe, that, as, in their apprehensions, nothing short of *a continental system*, could place our commerce upon a respectable and advantageous ground, *whatever state regulations* it might be deemed necessary to adopt, they should *all* give way to such a system. Whenever Congress shall act upon *powers competent thereto*, which the committee intreat your honorable house will by exerting its influence, with the different members of the union endeavour to obtain.

The remainder of the petition dealt with the tax defaults; the public roads and inland navigation of the state were not mentioned. Accordingly, the additional resolve relating to roads and navigation was not adopted; but the additional resolve on tax defaults was adopted, and the same was true of the additional resolve which assimilated the town's resolutions on commerce to the memorial of the Philadelphia merchants, of the preceding April. In other words, from the tenor of the petition filed with the legislature, the final action of the town meeting of June 20 was in favor of the establishment of a complete continental "commercial system," and that any state regulations "respecting" either "trade" or "manufactures" (including, probably, "agricultural," as well as "mechanical," "manufactures") were all to be regarded as interim measures to be superseded by the "continental system," as soon as Congress, when adequately empowered, should take action to establish such a system. And if the inference is well grounded that the proposed resolve on public roads and inland navigation was not adopted, that may mean that the men of Philadelphia in 1785 were desirous that these subjects, as to which the legislature had never shown much interest, should also be handed over entire, along with all other commercial subjects, to the general government of the nation.

The correctness of this general conclusion does not seem open to serious question. The usual accounts of the prevailing sentiments of the time, however, are so very different that it may be well to add to the evidence already adduced a statement by John Dickinson, made in behalf of himself and the other members of the Supreme Executive Council of Pennsylvania, in a message he, as president of the state, delivered to the legislature a few days before the Philadelphia petition was presented. Dickinson, at the time, was dilating upon the great need there was for adding to the national governing powers. He had just listed certain additonal powers which he and the other members of the Supreme Executive Council deemed it desirable that Congress should have and, among others, had mentioned the power "of regulating and protecting commerce." He thereupon added the remark that "many persons [were] now very earnest to have [that power] lodged in Congress *without limitation*."[13] That John Dickinson was a man who understood quite well what an unlimited "power of regulating commerce" was, we have already seen.[14] No reasonable doubt is possible regarding his meaning, and we have, accordingly, this direct testimony of a leading contemporary, given before all factions in the Pennsylvania legislature, to corroborate the general conclusion above stated.

As for the three remaining states of the middle region of the country, the situation in them need not detain us long. Of events in Delaware in 1785 comparatively little is known because of the nonsurvival of any Delaware newspapers for that year. We may confidently assume, however, that the commercial agitations at Boston and elsewhere were all well known to the people of that state by reason of the extensive circulation in Delaware of the newspapers of Philadelphia. We may also take it as certain that the general sentiment of the state was favorable—as was generally believed at the time—to the nationalist commercial suggestions then being made by the men of Boston and other towns. For Delaware in 1785 was no more, commercially speaking, than a dependency of Pennsylvania. Under the governmental arrangements then existing, the state had no proper share in the government of many commercial matters that directly concerned it. By the established course of business, its commerce with foreign nations and the other states went through the port of Philadelphia; its imports, therefore, were subject to imposts by Pennsylvania; and the proceeds of such imposts, though paid in final effect by the people of Delaware, went of course to defray the costs of government in Pennsylvania. This condition of affairs was of course resented in Delaware, as is shown by an act its legislature passed in 1786, whereby New Castle and Wilmington, for twenty-five years, were made free ports for the conduct of external commerce. Merchants taking up their residence in either of these towns were, for the period indicated, exempted from all taxes on their property in trade and all imposts upon their imports and exports. At about the same time an act was also passed in Delaware granting a charter of incorporation to the Bank of North America,* whose Pennsylvania charter was at the time about to be taken away by the Pennsylvania legislature. By this act, it was hoped in Delaware, the bank might be tempted to remove to Wilmington; if this should occur, and the state's free-port policy prove successful, the commercial dependence of Delaware on Pennsylvania might, it was hoped, be diminished or brought to an end. Such a result was, however, extremely difficult for a small community like Delaware to accomplish; this was undoubtedly understood by the men of the state; and this consideration, taken with the known general attitude of the Delaware delegates in the Federal Convention, leads to the conclusion already stated: that the probable attitude of Delaware in 1785 was one of complete approval of the proposals then made for investing Congress with complete commercial power.[15]

*This was the national bank of the Revolutionary period.

In New Jersey, the situation was similar, save that New Jersey, instead of being commercially dependent upon Pennsylvania alone, was split in its dependence between Pennsylvania, in reference to its external commerce from and to the west, and New York, in reference to its similar commerce from and to the east. The early nationalist sentiments of New Jersey with respect to foreign commerce, which had arisen in 1778 from mere foresight of the weakness of the state's commercial situation, we have already noted. We have also seen the state's extreme impatience with the behavior of certain of the other states, when they refused to line up in the nationwide price- and wage-fixing efforts between 1777 and 1780. We have seen its effort in Congress in 1781 to obtain that body's recommendation of a national superintending power over commerce in general; and its legislature's unanimous declaration in favor of a complete national power in late December 1783. These several moves on the part of New Jersey make perfectly clear its long-standing sentiment as to the desirability of a full national commerce power, even before the movement for such a power had gotten under way in some of the other states; and in view of this sentiment and the continuing unfavorable commercial situation in the state, it is certainly not in the least surprising that the meagreness of the powers finally proposed by Congress on April 30, 1784, should have produced in New Jersey a reaction of disgust. The powers of Congress then proposed would have been totally inadequate to afford any relief from the commercial burdens being imposed upon New Jersey by its neighbors; and much less would they have been adequate to the institution of any such general national "commercial system" as New Jersey apparently desired. The state seems accordingly to have decided, when it learned of the meagreness of the powers that Congress had proposed, to try what a little recalcitrance on its own part could do. It accordingly delayed for nearly two years, as already related, in granting the powers Congress had asked. At the same time New Jersey turned its attention to the enactment of local laws for protecting itself against the burdens and exactions of its more favorably situated neighbors. In order to suggest measures to this end, a state commercial convention assembled at New Brunswick in the summer of 1784,[16] and in pursuance of its recommendations the legislature made Perth Amboy and Burlington free ports for external commerce until such time as the Congress of the United States might otherwise provide.[17] Proposals also were advanced, and kept in process in the New Jersey legislature, over a significantly long period, for a system of imposts upon importations coming from other states.[18] Ultimately, as we know, New Jersey gave in along toward the end of 1785, and granted the powers that Congress had requested,[19] but in the following spring the state again resorted to a policy of recalcitrance, when, in resentment against New York, it refused to grant its quota of the national expenses until New York should grant the then-proposed impost power to Congress.[20] This behavior was followed, however, by the grant to its delegates to the national commercial convention at

Annapolis in the ensuing fall, of the most extensive power for proposing amendments to the Confederation that any state in the country granted.[21] The foregoing instances of recalcitrance on the part of New Jersey obviously do not impugn its fundamentally strong nationalist sentiments which were most plainly evident, and generally understood by all Americans, during the whole period under the Articles of Confederation.[22]

As previously indicated in this discussion, the states of New Jersey and Delaware—which latter state delayed even longer than New Jersey in complying with Congress's resolution of April 30, 1784—were not the only states that were so circumstanced as to be made the victims, under the Articles of Confederation, of impost-gouging by their neighbors. The state of New Hampshire, for one, was to a considerable degree so circumstanced with respect to the state of Massachusetts; and New Hampshire, we have seen, showed the same ardor as New Jersey for a complete national commerce power.[23] Connecticut, too, was in such a situation with respect to New York and to a certain extent with respect to Massachusetts and Rhode Island; and though Connecticut, in certain respects was slower to respond, the response, as already indicated, was in the end the same: free ports at New Haven and New London;[24] tariff reprisals against the state's neighbors;[25] and, in the Federal Convention, a proposal of a full national commerce power, and a paramount general power, in the hands of Congress, to act in all cases for the national welfare.[26] In addition, the reader will probably also recall that, when Congress had asked for partial powers over foreign trade, in 1784, the state had shown the same want of interest in those totally inadequate powers as had New Jersey and Delaware. The other chief sufferer from impost-gouging under the Articles was the southern state of North Carolina, which, owing to the peculiar character of its seacoast, was obliged to import and export through South Carolina and Virginia. The impositions of these two neighboring states apparently produced some sentiment in North Carolina in favor of a national commerce power, but, as we shall see in the next chapter, there is no evidence that such sentiment was very extensive. The remote, rural character of the state, and those peculiar factors that arrayed the whole South against the proposal of creating a national "commercial system," were too potent to be overborne by the injustice of the impost situation.

In addition to the foregoing instances of impost-gouging under the Articles, there were a number of other cases in which the practice obtained that are less well known. These other instances, however, were of minor importance—as, indeed, all instances of the practice were—by comparison with that of the state of New York with respect to Connecticut and New Jersey. This was true because it was the deliberate policy of the Clinton government (in office in New York throughout this period) to squeeze as much as possible of its revenue requirements out of the state's less fortunately situated neighbors. This lightened the tax burdens of New York's own citizens and helped the Clintonian faction to remain in power. That the desire of holding on to this iniquitous advantage was the chief cause of the anti-nationalism rampant in New York at the period in question, there can be no possible question. Nevertheless, it would be a mistake to suppose that anything like all the people of the state approved the Clintonian practices. Certain elements of the population were in fact bitterly opposed to them and, throughout the whole period of the impost abuses, were constantly agitating for the establishment of a continental customs systems, a national "commercial system," and an increase generally in the authority of Congress. We have already observed some of this New York agitation with respect to the power over commerce in the early spring of 1785, and, likewise, the very inadequate response to it made by the New York legislature in belatedly granting the meagre powers over foreign trade that Congress had requested about a year before. Later in the spring, when the various occurrences in Boston began to be reported in the New York papers, the agitation for a full national commerce power began again. The most important event in this later agitation was a public meeting held in New York City on June 15, "in consequence of notice given by the Chamber of Commerce and many other citizens, [to take] into consideration the critical state [to which] *the trade of America* [had been] reduced, for want of an adequate power in the supreme authority of the United States *to regulate the same*." It was determined at this meeting, at which Alexander Hamilton was the chief speaker, to appoint a committee "to correspond with the several states in the union and the different counties in [New York], on the interesting subject of *the trade of the United States*." This action was taken, as we learn from the resolutions of the meeting, "in hopes that by a free and reciprocal communication of opinions and sentiments [on the subject], it [might] prove the means of bringing about a measure absolutely indispensable to the true interest of America: that of vesting Congress with *full and ample* powers *to regulate the commerce of the said United States*."[27] The New York committee sent out a letter to the mercantile groups in the other states early in the summer. This letter, though mentioned in the proceedings in some of the other states, was not apparently published anywhere in the newspapers. A second circular, sent out by the New York committee on September 30, appeared, however, in many papers late in the fall. It talked mostly of the trouble with Great Britain; but since it declared in simple, general, and unqualified terms that "the Right of Regulating Commerce" ought to be given to Congress, and urged in justification of this view that "our *commerce, foreign and domestic*, form[ed] the only source of a marine" (i.e., a navy), the scope of the New York committee's views is in no way doubtful.[28]

Despite the temporary dominance in New York of the Clintonian faction, the probability is that at least a very substantial minority among the people of the state agreed with the men of the other Northern states regarding the desirability of a complete commerce power for Congress. It is even possible, indeed, that the Clintonian faction agreed with this view, provided only that the state's revenue from commerce could in some way be preserved. This possibility appears from the fact that on February 22, 1786, a bill was introduced in the New York legislature by Samuel Jones, the floor leader of the Clintonians in the Assembly, "to enable the United States in Congress to regulate trade and commerce."[29] Neither the precise tenor of this bill nor just what happened to it is known; but we do know that in the following year Alexander Hamilton spoke of the bill, in a speech he then delivered on the impost, as if it had proposed a grant to Congress of a general power over trade. He described the bill as one "for granting to congress the power of regulating the trade of the union," and declared that the "legislative authority" comprehended in the bill had gone "to a prodigious extent."[30] The possibility must therefore be recognized that the Clintonians, or at least some of them, may have been willing to go along on the power over commerce, provided that it did not take away from the highly inequitable revenue rights of their state.

Of the seven other Northern states, the three New England states of Massachusetts, New Hampshire, and Rhode Island, appear, as we have seen, to have been in the lead in 1785 in nationalist sentiment upon the subject of a national power over commerce. But no American of the time could possibly have felt any doubt about New Jersey; and no doubt seems to have been felt by anyone about Connecticut or Delaware or Pennsylvania. In the last-named state there were, it is true, a good many men who held views like those of the Clintonians of New York, but men of a more liberal outlook seem to have been in a majority in Pennsylvania, at any rate in and after 1786, not only among the public but in the legislature as well. New York, it would seem, was the only Northern state that held questionable views; and the situation there, apart from the revenue aspect of a power over commerce, was probably not so unfavorable to the grant of such a power to Congress as has generally been supposed. In any case, there can be no doubt that the men of the time who were most interested in obtaining a general commercial power for Congress were pretty confident, for some reason or other, that at the proper time New York could be carried along.

The general view of the situation held by such men late in the fall of 1785, when the agitations for a national commerce power were about over, is well exemplified in two letters written by Rufus King (then in New York, in Congress), on November 2 and 3. King wrote the first of these letters to John Adams in London. "The States eastward of Maryland," he said, were all in agreement with Adams's views upon the subject of commerce. "The eight Eastern states ha[d] common objects [were] under similar embarrassments, [and] would vest adequate powers in Congress," King confidently predicted, *"to regulate external and internal commerce."* "But you very well understand," he dejectedly added, "the false commercial reasonings and ill-founded policy of the other states."[31] The "other states" were the five Southern states, and it seems perfectly clear from the tenor of King's remarks that he was worried about those states only when he wrote his letter to Adams. Yet, in his other letter, written to Caleb Davis on the day immediately following, King spoke of only "seven," rather than "eight Eastern states," as "hav[ing] common commercial interests"; as suffering "similar embarrassments"; and as being ready to "agree in vesting powers in Congress *to regulate external and internal commerce*"; or, as he also phrased it in the course of this second letter, *"power in Congress to regulate trade.."* The reference in this second letter to "seven" rather than "eight Eastern states" may *possibly* mean that King was not quite so sure of all "eight Eastern states" as his letter to John Adams might incline one to think. But in view of the fact that in his second letter he was explaining what a majority of *seven* states could do under the Articles, in spite of the Southern states' "unfederal attitude" with respect to commerce, such an interpretation is probably not correct.[32] In any event, there can be no doubt he was thoroughly convinced that at least "seven Eastern states" were ready to grant to Congress the commercial powers then being widely asked; but of the probable attitude of the Southern states, he was, in this second letter, as he had been in his letter of the preceding day, extremely uncertain and pessimistic.

As to the precise scope of the "power to regulate trade," or the "powers to regulate external and internal commerce," referred to by King in these two letters, the phrases are so obviously comprehensive that uncertainty as to their meaning is hardly possible. First, there is the fact that the second of King's phrases—"to regulate external and internal commerce" was *the precise phrase* used by the Boston merchants in the circular letters they had sent around the country some six months before. There is the further fact that King's second letter was addressed to Caleb Davis, a prominent Boston merchant, who had been one of the leading members of the Boston merchants' committee which had disseminated those letters; and there is the final fact that Davis, at the time King wrote to him, was a member of the Massachusetts General Court and was still extremely anxious to see commercial power vested in Congress.[33] In view of these several facts, and of the additional fact that the meaning of the Boston merchants had been clear in their letters, it is not credible that King would have used the phrases he did in a letter to Davis, *one of the men who had originally used them*, unless he wished to be understood as expressing the view that "Seven Eastern States"—and probably all of them, in view of his letter to Adams—were ready to confer upon Congress the comprehensive power over commerce in general which the Boston merchants had asked.

And Rufus King, the reader should understand, was in an excellent position to know all about this subject. At the time he wrote his letters to John Adams and Caleb Davis, King had for months been a member of a committee in Congress "for giving to the United States *the general regulation of trade*."[34] As a member of that committee, King had had full opportunity, and, in addition, the best of reasons, for conferring with the men in Congress from the other states as to what their respective states would do. In addition, he undoubtedly had had the advantage of seeing and, very probably, studying carefully the detailed evidence that has here been presented, as to what the states of the North would do. Considering the nature of that detailed evidence, together with strong likelihood that King had further evidence that has not survived, and that many other leading men, in both North and South, held similar views,[35] the indicated conclusion is that King was warranted in his belief that upon the subject of full commercial power for Congress the eight Northern states—or the "eight Eastern states," as men then called them—would go along. As for his pessimistic opinion as to the probable behavior of the Southern states, that opinion also was held by a great many others, and was equally well warranted by the detailed evidence, as will be found by the reader from the materials relating to the Southern states, to be presented in the chapters which follow.

CHAPTER XIV

The Partial Success of the Agitation
of 1785 in South Carolina

NEWS of the Northern agitations for the establishment of a national "commercial system" began to appear in the newspapers of the further South in the latter part of June. Of the various items published there, one of the earliest was the April 6 memorial of the Philadelphia merchants' committee, which had declared for a "full and entire" commerce power for Congress. It made its initial appearance in *The* [Charleston] *South-Carolina Gazette and Public Advertiser* of June 22. A few days later, at least three of the other four newspapers of Charleston published it, together with the favorable response that the Pennsylvania legislature had made.[1] A short while thereafter news of the concurrent resolutions of the Philadelphia town meeting also appeared;[2] the statement of the Supreme Executive Council of Pennsylvania eventually followed, that "many persons [were] now very earnest to have ["the power of regulating and protecting commerce"] lodged in Congress without limitation";[3] and the Philadelphia town petition for a complete "continental commercial system" sent to the Pennsylvania legislature in the fall of the year was also fully published.[4] Quite certainly, every interested person in Charleston in 1785 must have been fully aware of what people in Pennsylvania were asking.

The situation in respect to New York and the states of New England was equally fully reported. The occurrences in the first-named state, including the important town meeting of June 15, which came out for "full and ample" power for Congress "to regulate the commerce [or "the trade"] of the United States," were noticed in the Charleston papers at a number of different times through the early summer;[5] the emphatic appeal for "full" power for Congress "to regulate both internal and external commerce," which first appeared in *The* [Portsmouth] *New-Hampshire Gazette* on May 13, was published in Charleston on June 25;[6] and a few days later at least three of the town's newspapers published the letters of the Boston merchants.[7] In all three of the papers reporting the letters, the complaints of the merchants were fully set forth, with their stirring appeal for a power in Congress "adequate" to "call forth and improve the resources of America" and their blunt assertion that, for the great purposes they had in mind, "nothing short of vesting Congress with full power to regulate the internal as well as the external commerce of all the states" would do. Doubt as to what the Boston merchants meant by what they said could hardly have been possible; and that the people of New England were in accord with their views was proved for the men of Charleston, first, by the August 2 publication in the Charleston papers of the full text of the New Hampshire legislature's act of June 23, by which that body had granted to Congress the "full" power over commerce which the Boston merchants and other groups were asking;[8] second, by the publication of the Rhode Island act to the same effect when that act was passed in the ensuing fall;[9] and third, by news that the Massachusetts General Court on the July 1 had moved to obtain a convention of all the states for conferring upon Congress all such powers as were necessary "to secure and perpetuate" "the common defence," "the security of liberty," and "the mutual and general welfare" of the whole country.[10] When the plain tenor of all these Northern memorials, petitions, and resolutions is kept in mind, together with the equally plain tenor of the various acts passed by the New England legislatures, the reader will have no doubt that any one in Charleston could have felt any uncertainty as to what was being asked among the several Northern states of the country.

The Boston merchants' letters appeared in the several papers that published them between June 27 and 29. The first indication of Charleston opinion in accord with the Boston views appeared on July 7 in *The Gazette of the State of South-Carolina*, in an account of an entertainment which William Moultrie, governor of the state, had given on the Fourth of July. At this entertainment, one of the toasts had been: "May the Congress be invested with *full* power *to regulate the trade of the American states!*" In the July 14 issue of the *Gazette of the State* it was observed, however, that "Congress [would] doubtless be invested with full powers to regulate our *foreign* trade"; and in the remaining July issues of the paper in question, a number of brief squibs under Northern datelines appeared, seemingly indicative of a desire in the Northern states for a national power over foreign trade only.[11] While the toast drunk at the Moultrie gathering certainly indicates that there was, from the very first, sentiment in Charleston favorable to the Northern views, there can also be little doubt that, from the very first, opposition to such views existed.

The circular letter from New York was received in Charleston about August 1. When it came, notices were published in the local papers that the Charleston Chamber of Commerce had "received circular letters from the Chamber of Commerce of New York, and from the Committee of Merchants, Traders and Citizens of Boston, relative to the trade of the United States"; that, "wishing to lay the same before the Citizens of the State, [the Charleston chamber] request[ed] a meeting of the Citizens, at the [City] Exchange, on Thursday, the 11th [of August,] to determine on a proper application to the Legislature for a redress of grievances."[12]

According to the newspaper accounts that appeared a few days later, a "numerous and respectable" meeting took place, as a result of these notices, at the time and place indicated; the letters from New York and Boston were read to the assembled citizens; and a report was presented by a committee of the local chamber of commerce "expressing the highest approbation of the proceedings of such of [the other] states as [had] stood forth to rescue the commercial interests of the United States from impending ruin."[13] The "approbation," on the face of the thing, extended to the Boston and New York letters which had just been read, and to the New Hampshire act for vesting Congress with "full" commercial power which had been published a few days previously in the Charleston papers.[14] But the "approbation," the reader will have observed, was the "approbation" of the committee of the Charleston Chamber of Commerce, which had called the meeting, and not that of the assembled citizens. That the citizens did not in fact concur in this "approbation" may be seen from a statement—or from a careful reading of a statement—that immediately followed in the newspaper accounts of the meeting. The statement was that "the purport of the [committee's] report was to recommend to the Citizens, that they should present a memorial to the legislature at their next meeting praying [that body's] speedy interpostion in such manner as [might] seem most effectual to them, and [that,] as this idea met with general approbation, a [Citizens'] Committee [had been] named for that purpose."[15]

To this evidence taken from the Charleston newspapers we may add the further corroborative fact that, during the last week in August, a report was current in Newport, Rhode Island, that the Charleston meeting had failed to act favorably upon the proposals contained in the Boston and New York letters.[16] The interval involved was approximately that required for a voyage from Charleston to Newport; and since the Charleston newspaper accounts, when carefully read, plainly accord with the Newport report, the conclusions seem in order that the Newport report was accurate and that the Charleston newspaper accounts (which were exactly the same in all the Charleston papers) were probably contrived so as not to disclose too clearly what had occurred. Very likely the truth is that there were a good many men in Charleston, who entertained some hope, despite the somewhat disappointing citizens' meeting, that the state's legislature might still be induced to do what the citizens had refused to urge.

The suggested inference is supported by the surviving evidence of subsequent related occurrences. On August 15, the committee appointed at the meeting on the eleventh reported a form of petition to an adjourned session of the citizens' meeting. The precise tenor of the petition then reported is not known, but according to an account of the adjourned session of the citizens' meeting, published in *The Charleston Evening Gazette* on the day it occurred, "the general tenor of [the memorial] was, that the memorialists beheld with regret the misfortune in which [the] country was involved with regard to its *navigation*[, and] that it was essential to the *regulation of this navigation* that Congress should be invested with *more ample powers* than those which that august body was at present possessed of." This part of the petition, which sounds something like "Jonathan of the Valley," was "agreed to *una voce*," according to the *Evening Gazette*; but precisely what additional powers were thereby recommended for Congress, the *Gazette* account unfortunately does not make clear. Instead it goes on to say that "some debate" was occasioned by a recommendation of local measures for the promoting of manufactures; and most of the remainder of the space devoted to the meeting is taken up with a speech by a Dr. Budd, who appears to have been a most zealous advocate of a policy of protection. The turn taken by the debate was probably not considered favorable by the managers of the meeting, for it was apparently decided not to submit the proposed petition to the assembled citizens. Instead, a resolution was proposed, and passed, that copies of the petition "be lodged with the City Treasurer until the 10th of September for the purpose of being signed by citizens of the state."[17] According to a statement in the proceedings of the South Carolina legislature, this petition was eventually "signed by a great number of names" and presented to that body when it assembled late in September.[18] No copy of the petition is known to exist, but from certain references to it in the legislature's proceedings, we may infer that, respecting the enlargement of the powers of Congress, it recommended no more than the empowering of that body "to regulate trade, *with foreign nations*, with whom treaties [of commerce had] not been already formed."[19] The above suggested inference regarding the nature of the action taken at the Charleston meeting on August 11 would appear to be correct: the Northern proposals for a "full and entire" national commerce power were not endorsed at that meeting, nor were they endorsed at the later session of that meeting on August 15.

That the sentiments expressed in the Charleston petition were nevertheless more nationalistic than the majority of the town approved, was intimated in a letter signed "Horatio," appearing on August 29 in *The Gazette of the State of South Carolina*. The letter in question was the first of a series of eight that ran in the *Gazette of the State* until September 26. In the first of these letters, "Horatio" not only cast doubt on the general approval of the Charleston petition, but took occasion to express his own conviction that "thirteen legislatures, pursuing different objects, and viewing the same subject in different lights, ought carefully to avoid delegating any authority which, in the end, [might] be prejudicial to themselves; especially when it [would] be of no essential service to the federal compact." He did not wish, he said, to see the states southward of Maryland bound by the same treaties as those to the "east" of that state. Having expressed these sentiments in a sufficiently straightforward fashion, he nonetheless sought to confuse the issue in the manner so characteristic of "states'-rights" writers, then and since, by declaring that he could see no possible objection to investing Congress, "for a limited time, with power sufficient to regulate the commerce of the whole," provided only it were stipulated that one set of treaties should be made by Congress—i.e., presumably by the Southern states in Congress—to bind the Southern states, and another set—presumably to be made by the Northern states in Congress—to bind the North. As such a stipulation would of course have defeated a most important purpose of the commercial proposals then being advanced—that is, that the whole nation should act together as against foreign nations—"Horatio's" position amounted in fact to opposition to a *national* commercial power for Congress. His remaining letters expressed sentiments of about the same general character as his initial letter.

During September, while "Horatio's" letters were appearing in the *Gazette of the State*, other local writers began increasingly to express opinions of a different kind, in the same and other papers. One such writer in the *Gazette of the State* of September 8, though not expressing himself on the subject of commercial power for Congress, demanded that South Carolina at once impose "a higher duty on all those articles imported from Europe which might be obtained from [its] Sister States." If this were done, "importations from Europe would cease, and encouragement would be given to the American manufacturers to employ a greater number of poor people who [were] at [that] time groaning," the writer said, "under indigence and misery." The end result of such a policy, he further maintained, would be in South Carolina's own interest, since it would be bound to lead to "a greater consumption of [the state's] products, in the sister states." Another local writer in favor of protection appeared in *The Columbian Herald* on September 19; still another in the same paper on September 28; and a third in the issue for October 5. In the September 28 issue of the *Herald*, just as the legislature met, there was also an appeal by "A Countryman" for South Carolinians to vest Congress with power "to regulate [their] trade for 15 years, *the negro trade excepted*."*

Opponents of the policy of protection, it is interesting to note, though probably not wanting in South Carolina in 1785, were nevertheless extremely scarce or lacking in the Charleston papers. Such local attacks upon the Northern proposals as then appeared were mainly directed against the adoption of a continental navigation act, rather than against promoting American manufactures by protection. Typical of such attacks was an item in *The Columbian Herald*, of September 23, by someone signing himself "Caroliniensis." The proposal of an American navigation act, he said, came from interested men in the Northern states, who wished to victimize the South and draw its fabulous wealth into Northern coffers. These views provoked an attack upon their author in *The South-Carolina Gazette & Public Advertiser* of October 1. He was "some Briton," it was said, or "some degenerate American," "some wretch principled to betray the land of his nativity, under the misapplied signature of 'Caroliniensis.'" The attack was

*Italics in the original.

anonymous, being signed sententiously "The Spear of Ithuriel." The "Spear" was in favor of an American navigation act, in favor of protection and support for American manufactures, and in favor of commercial power for Congress; and he expressed himself upon all these subjects, but especially upon the "true" character of "Caroliniensis," in no uncertain terms.

As already indicated, the South Carolina legislature had assembled a few days before the "Spear's" attack appeared. When it was assembled, the Charleston petition was presented to it; and a committee in the House of Representatives had at once been appointed to draw up recommendations for action, if any, to be taken by the legislature on the Charleston petition.[20] During the first week in October, however, opposition developed to taking any action before it was known what the other states of the Union were going to do.[21] Just what occurred thereafter is unclear; but apparently a committee was appointed despite the opposition, at some time prior to October 8, "to bring in a bill for impowering the Congress to regulate *foreign* trade, &c. of [the] state." On that date a bill for that purpose was reported in the House by a committee so described.[22] The bill was considered on October 11, was recommitted, and apparently in the end postponed until the winter session of the legislature, which began in January.[23]

Before this action was taken, Charleston had witnessed the publication of the most elaborate discussion of the subject of vesting commercial power in Congress that appeared in that town. Entitled *A Few Salutary Hints*, the discussion was put out as an anonymous pamphlet in the early days of October.[24] The general position of the pamphlet was that it was folly for the Southern states to continue to "wear [British] manufactures, consume [British] productions, promote [British] trade, starve the New-England men, make [their] negroes work, buy more [from Britain] as [they] could get credit, live luxuriously, and spend [their] days as consumers of British good things." This, of course, was what the British wanted, but the true policy for the Southern states was that suggested by their Northern brethren. In particular, the American navigation act so much desired by the Northern men, "so far from doing an injury" (as, it was declared, "the British" in Charleston maintained) "would at once give a general animation to shipbuilding and other branches of industry through the continent. The cities of America would soon swarm with artificers; her docks and bays resound with the busy noise of ship-wrights and other sons of industry; her ports in a few years would be covered with her own shipping; send forth her own seamen, and receive by thousands, those of Britain, who [were] well known to prefer sailing out of America. Even Charleston herself, instead of having her carrying trade engrossed, and harbour filled with British vessels, would soon be mistress of ships and seamen to carry her own produce to market. Thus the numbers and industry of the Northern states would give security, strength, and splendor to the south; and the wealth of the south, instead of going into British coffers, to answer British purpose against [America], would then enrich ourselves, and reward the laborious inhabitants of the north: and thus would the resources of each part, contribute to add to the strength and glory of the whole empire."

With more particular reference to the military aspect of his subject, the writer of the *Salutary Hints* maintained that *an American navigation act would* "*lay the foundation of the marine of America*, to which," he declared, "every friend of the [American] empire ought to look forward. Britain, in the early state of her marine, [had been] in timber, naval stores, and other resources, as far below what America [then was], as the Thames [was] far inferior in extent and dignity to the Potomack. And as to an arduous spirit of enterprize and galantry in naval affairs, no age or country [had ever] exhibited more signal proofs of it, than the Americans [had] in the [late] war." "It [was] well known," he averred, "that wherever the New-England armed vessels [had] met the enemy with equal numbers of men and guns, they [had] in general dowsed the British colours, and [this] gave us ample confidence to hope, that if we only encourage our own shipping, the thirteen stars of America would one day wave in distant nations, with as much lustre as the ensigns of her enemy."

In view of all these important aspects of his subject, the writer of the pamphlet declared his conviction that Americans must "strengthen the hands of Congress as well with respect of revenue, as *to restrain importations*, credit and commerce from Britain; *and lay a solid foundation for* [*their*] *own* trade, *navigation and manufactures*." The desire of this anonymous South Carolinian for a national commercial power extending in some manner to the promotion and protection of American navigation and manufactures is clear beyond all possible doubt, but since at another point in his pamphlet he declared that he "trust[ed] the assembly [would] invest Congress with the power to regulate foreign trade" (as was then being proposed in that body), the fact may be that he did not wish in these respects to go so far as the men in the Northern states. When it appeared, his pamphlet, we may add, was promptly attacked by "Horatio," the localistic writer previously mentioned; but the author of the pamphlet, taking his cue from the transforming "Spear of Ithuriel," declared, in *The Charleston Evening Gazette* of October 11, that he was "informed" "Horatio" was "a British subject lately admitted as a citizen," and that no credence, therefore, could be given to anything he said.

While these various local items were appearing in Charleston, a considerably larger number of Northern items culled from the Northern newspapers by the local printers were also being published there. This publication of Northern items on commercial regulation and governmental reform, varied occasionally with local comment, continued unabated in volume all through the interval between the autumn and winter sessions of the legislature. The items appearing during this period indicate clearly that a concerted effort was then being made to convince a majority of the people of the state of the expediency of the commercial proposals the men of the Northern states had made. Many of the items employed in this effort were brief squibs interspersed among the news. Such, for example, was what purported to be a news item that appeared in *The Gazette of the State of South-Carolina*, on November 21. It reported, with very dubious correctness,[25] that the merchants of Baltimore, having received the letters of the Boston merchants, were in agreement with the sweeping proposals those letters had made. Another brief item, apparently printed with similar intent, was "an extract of a letter from London" which, it was reported, had been received by "a Virginian" and contained information that "Mr. [John] Adams [was] of opinion that nothing [would] so speedily bring about a [commercial] treaty [with Great Britain], as [the American states'] generally adopting *the measures of the Bostonians and Philadelphians*."[26] And a third brief item, actually taken from a Philadelphia paper, informed South Carolinians, just before the beginning of the winter legislative session, of the great impatience that the South's indifferent attitude on commerce had caused in Pennsylvania.[27]

Besides these briefer items, one Charleston paper published serially[28] the whole of Noah Webster's pamphlet, *Sketches of American Policy*. In the course of this pamphlet, as the reader will no doubt recall, Webster had declared that, unless the American states did not really wish to be united, "there must be *a supreme head*, clothed with the same power *to make and enforce laws* respecting the *general policy* of all the states, as the legislatures of the respective states ha[d] to make laws, respecting their own *internal police*." The reader will also remember Webster's further vigorous statement that "however independent each state [might] be, and ought to be, in things that relate[d] to itself *merely*, yet as a part of [the United States], it must be a subject, in matters that relate[d] to the whole." In Webster's pamphlet there was much more along similar lines;[29] and there was likewise much along similar lines in the first letter of "The Observator," of New Haven, Connecticut,[30] which the same Charleston newspaper had published shortly before Webster's pamphlet.[31] The "Observator" had bluntly declared that a national power to regulate commerce was not enough. "*Every political interest* of a nation [was] so blended together," he had said, "and [so] dependent on one another, that, unless *there* [*were*] *a sovereign power sufficient to govern them all*, the end of public measures [would] be lost, by an interruption in some of their more remote and extensive operations." The states, therefore, if the national welfare was an object, *must* vest Congress "with *full and ample* powers"—"powers," the "Observator" insisted, which should be "*free from impediment and controul*"—"in *all the political interests* of the nation." The "Observator's" strange, eighteenth-century terminology was familiar, and his meaning clear to the people of the further South, as we may infer from the fact that the same terms were used in a Georgia item that appeared in *The* [Charleston] *Columbian Herald*, of January 23, 1786. Like "Observator" in New Haven, the author of this Georgia item was in favor of full power for Congress in the field of "policy," and he spoke of that field as including "whatever might relate [to], *or any way affect* foreign powers." The powers of a state, he thought, should be restricted and should apply only to "those things which relate[d] to the people of the state *only*." Clearly he had the same general idea of the appropriate relationship between state and national power as did "Observator." He also understood, as did "Observator," that "full" power over "policy" signified *full* power, *internal as well as external*, over *the whole* of any subject (such as "commerce") that might in "any way affect foreign powers," as is indicated by the fact that he considered *all* "money matters," which were the specific topic of his discussion, as falling within the field of "policy" or "political" affairs. Thus the probability—indeed, the virtual certainty—is that he regarded such full monetary power as merely an incident of that general power over "commerce" which in the understanding of his time was one grand division of the thing then known as "policy."

The foregoing Georgia item appeared in *The Columbian Herald*, at just about the time the South Carolina legislature reassembled. A few days afterward an article appeared in *The Charleston Morning Post*[32] as specially written for that paper, which avowed its agreement with some unidentified "anonimous writer,"[33] that, "as the United States of America form[ed] one *grand, entire republic*,* composed of a number of small ones confederated for their common safety and advantage, and distinct only for their greater conveniency with respect to legislation and internal police; *the supreme sovereign authority of the whole, ought, most undoubtedly to be lodged in Congress*;—and [that] body should possess such powers and privileges, not incompatible with the happiness of a free people, as usually appertain[ed] to sovereignty, in order to enable them to direct *the common concerns of the United States** upon *uniform principles** so as to afford *equal advantages to each*,* and give energies to the whole." "It [was] obvious to the most superficial observer," the article went on, "that the commerce of the United States *with foreign countries* ought to be regulated and protected by proper treaties"; and since, by the terms of the Confederation, "no separate state [could] treat,[34] either Congress must have this power, or the whole trade of [the] country must lie at the mercy of foreign nations." In view of this plain anomaly in the existing constitutional situation, and the undeniable fact that the Articles were expressly a compact by the several states "to assist each other, against all force offered to, or attacks made upon, them, or any of them, *on account of* religion, sovereignty, *trade* or any other pretence whatever,"[35] the conclusion very plainly was, that, by "the spirit and intention of [the Articles], Congress should be invested with all such powers and authority as [were] necessary to give consistency and efficiency to federal measures, both with respect to the different states in the union, and to foreign countries." The conclusion, as well as the general position of the article that Congress ought to be vested with "the supreme sovereign authority of the whole," clearly meant that, with respect to trade, Congress should be vested with a complete power of regulating both

*Italics in the original.

internal and external commerce. But the article talked mostly of the harassments, restrictions, and injuries, to which "the commerce of the United States *with other nations*" was then subjected, and was perhaps open to the interpretation that the author meant to advocate no more than a power over foreign commerce. Probably he meant to argue primarily for a whole power over trade, together with a general national sovereignty over all matters involving the grand objects recited in the Articles, but secondarily to make clear the extreme anomaly that existed under the Articles with respect to foreign trade and, hence, the especially strong case that existed for giving Congress power over at least that subject.

Whatever may have been the intention of this article in the *Morning Post*, Governor Moultrie lined up with the advocates of a complete national commercial power, in the message he delivered to the South Carolina legislature on February 1. One of the most resolute soldiers of the Revolution, with ideas much like those of the soldiers everywhere, Moultrie advised the legislature to invest Congress with *"full"* power to regulate [the state's] *commerce and navigation.*" He conceded that "such a power [might] be attended, with some disadvantage to [South Carolinians] as a State"; but they ought, he thought, to be willing to "sacrifice some local advantages for the general good."[36] Along with his message, Moultrie also presented to the legislature a letter he had received from John Langdon, president of New Hampshire, asking "whether [South Carolina] agreed with [New Hampshire] in empowering Congress to regulate *the commerce and navigation of the United States.*"[37] The reference, of course, was to the New Hampshire legislature's act of June 23, 1785, which had been published in Charleston and was undoubtedly known to the South Carolina legislators. The sentiment in South Carolina, or in certain parts of the state, however, was apparently still somewhat behind the sentiment in New Hampshire, as we may see from a petition to the South Carolina legislature that was received at this time from the back-country community of Camden. The petition suggested, in consonance with the Charleston petition of the preceding fall, that Congress be invested with power "to regulate the trade of the United States *with Foreign Countries*" only,[38] and the action finally taken by the legislature of the state, as we have seen, was in accord with this back-country view. The act finally passed was carefully entitled by the legislature "An Act to authorise the United States in Congress assembled to regulate Trade of the United States *with Foreign Nations,*" and, as already related in Chapter X, the legislature was careful to confer upon Congress, in consonance with the title of its act, power to regulate *"external or* foreign trade" only. The grant, moreover, was made subject to a proviso that no regulation adopted under it should in any way "affect the slave trade."[39]

Whether the act thus passed was in accord with the majority opinion in the state in 1786 is difficult to say. The evidence here reviewed shows clearly that there was opposition in the state to the grant to Congress of power even over foreign commerce, but it likewise shows that there was in the state an influential group which approved the proposals of the Northern states and would have liked to see those proposals prevail. That the available evidence should point to such a conclusion is not particularly remarkable. Despite the fact that South Carolina was the theater of nullification in the 1830s, its principal town of Charleston was one of those communities in which Federalism* lingered on, and as late as 1828 there were men in the town who believed with unshaken conviction, that Congress had, and ought to have, under a just construction of the Constitution, full power to legislate in all cases for the national welfare. And they were men, it may be added, who were able to defend this conviction with distinciton.[40] It can therefore hardly be considered surprising that the state of which such a community was a part should have shown strong nationalist leanings in 1785; that sentiment favorable to the nationalist views of the Northern states should in fact have reached its peak among the Southern states in South Carolina; and that the act of the state's legislature in 1786 should have been what in fact it was: the most ample grant of national commercial power which any Southern state made before the date when the Constitution was adopted.

Much more important than their relative sympathy with the Northern views, however, are three other facts about the people of South Carolina in 1785, which seem plainly inferable from the events and discussions that have just been recounted. The first of these is the fact that the men of the state had been unquestionably made aware, by the agitations of that year, that a "full and entire" national commerce power was being demanded among the states of the North. The second is the fact, demonstrated by the men of South Carolina through their own behavior, that they were entirely aware that a power of that kind would include "full power to regulate the internal as well as the external commerce of all the states." The third is the fact, clearly demonstrated by the act of the South Carolina legislature, that the men of the state were aware that, if they did not wish their own "internal" trade or commerce to become the subject of any national power "to regulate trade" or "commerce" they might decide to grant, some words unmistakably excluding their "internal commerce" from the scope of such a power would have to be included in the act by which such a national power was granted.

The importance of these three facts, as providing a solid basis of inference as to the original understanding in South Carolina of the Commerce Clause of the Constitution seems obvious, but the significance of these three facts in this important connection can be appreciated fully only when this further fact is brought to view: of South Carolina's four astute delegates to the Federal Convention, three—namely, John Rutledge, chairman of the Federal Convention's Committee of Detail, which selected the language of the Com-

---

*As capitalized here and below, "Federalism" has the eighteenth-century sense of "nationalism," as distinct from "localism," or devotion to "states' rights."

merce Clause; Charles Cotesworth Pinckney; and Pierce Butler—were members of the South Carolina legislature when the act of 1786 was passed.[41] In the light of this fact, any supposition that these three men, or the state they represented, could even possibly have overlooked what in 1787 was the obvious generality of the Commerce Clause is a supposition too improbable to entertain.

CHAPTER XV

The Complete Failure of the Agitation of 1785 in Georgia, North Carolina, Maryland, and Virginia: Herein of Virginia's Proposal of the Annapolis Commercial Convention of 1786

I N THE state of Georgia, the majority sentiment in 1785 was very likely somewhat less favorable to the proposals advanced by the Northern states than was the case in South Carolina. The letters of the Boston merchants reached Savannah early in July and were published there in *The Gazette of the State of Georgia* on July 14. As in South Carolina, however, no action was taken until toward the end of the summer, when the letter from New York arrived. After the receipt of that letter, the men of Savannah, in view of the many other evidences they had had that a serious movement for a national commerce power was at least under way, apparently decided they had better take action. A meeting of the citizenry was therefore called to assemble at the local courthouse on September 8 to debate the question whether the town should petition the Georgia legislature "to give the power of regulating [their] trade into the hands of Congress." When the citizens assembled, those against the proposal prevailed; no petition of any kind was sent to the state's legislature by the men of Savannah.[1]

This unsuccessful effort in Savannah appears to have been the only attempt in the nature of an organized response made in Georgia in connection with the commercial agitations of 1785. The Georgia legislature itself took no notice of the widespread agitations then in progress, and did not in fact, until August 2, 1786, confer upon Congress the meagre powers over foreign trade that Congress had asked early in 1784.[2] Additional striking evidence of the unfavorable attitude of the state may be seen in a letter written by John Habersham, one of the Georgia delegates in Congress, to a friend back home shortly after Habersham's arrival in New York (where Congress was then sitting) at the end of May 1785.[3] The date of his arrival, the reader will notice, fell within the period when the commercial agitations in the New York neighborhood were at their peak. Habersham was apparently much astonished at the nature of these proceedings and those in the neighboring states, and toward the end of June he accordingly gathered up and sent to his friend in Georgia a packet of Northern newspapers containing accounts of the events that were taking place. Referring to these, he said in his letter dated June 24: "You will observe that Town Meetings have been held in

Different parts of these Northern States to consider the present distressful situation of American Commerce." "The result," he went on with manifest amazement, "has been that [the people at these meetings] have agreed to recommend to their respective Legislatures the investing Congress *with full power to regulate Trade*." The italics represent Habersham's emphasis, and his comment was that "this [was] a nice subject to come before Congress"; that "ample, indefinite powers [would] hardly go down." He conceded, however, in the grudging manner characteristic of so many Southerners of the period, that "something" would probably have to be done about granting some kind of power in the field to Congress, but that was all. The Northern demands for a "full" national power Habersham seemed to think were beyond all reason.[4]

Despite these views expressed by John Habersham, and despite the total want of any successful organized response by the people of Georgia in 1785, it is difficult to state precisely how considerable the opposition to the creation of a full national commerce power at that time actually was. A letter, signed "T.G.," that appeared contemporaneously in the Savannah newspaper tends to indicate that even some part of the opposition at the Savannah town meeting of September 8 was composed of men who were fully in favor of broader powers for the national government but were not in favor of the proposal that the Georgia legislature should grant them. In the letter in question, published in *The Gazette of the State of Georgia* on October 13, the suggestion was made that the current commercial exigency was simply "a new proof of the necessity and importance of giving powers in all cases, equal to the duties of those stations in which the public servants [were] placed." The writer of the letter maintained, nevertheless, that the Georgia legislature was totally without power to delegate to Congress, and that, if the legislature were permitted to take such action, it would create a precedent extremely dangerous to the rights of the people of the state. He also urged, with what seems obvious justification, that "if [the] powers [of Congress], or any important one of them, [were] to depend on the laws of the several states from time to time, to be passed or withheld as passion or party [might] prevail, it need[ed] no spirit of prophecy to foresee, that they [i.e., the Congress], must sink into disregard, if not contempt." What was wanted he said, were "powers GRANTED BY THE PEOPLE AND PERMANENTLY FIXED." Moreover, the result of the Savannah meeting, he thought, should not to be regarded as establishing that the people of Georgia were against the granting of commercial power to Congress. The notice of the meeting had been inadequate and few had attended. "[And] whatever men of narrow minds, or not well informed of facts, [might] think, it [was] happily the circumstance of the American Union that the interest of every state [was] promoted by the same measures; and the case [of the commerce of the United States]," he declared, "[might] serve for an example."

Another Georgian who held similar views, but was apparently less particular as to how Congress should receive its powers, was George Walton, chief justice of the state and formerly a member of Congress. Walton's constant habit, as he rode on circuit, was to discourse before the grand juries in the different counties on the existing most urgent need for enlarging the national powers. A good idea of the views he entertained may be obtained from an article, signed "Agricola," which appeared in *The* [Savannah] *Gazette of the State of Georgia* on September 29.[5] In his charge to the grand jury of Chatham County the week following, Walton referred to this article as "a sensible production" that had appeared in the Savannah *Gazette* the week before.[6] The article in question had declared that the "powers [of Congress] ought to go as far as *the general interest extends*, whether it be to *trade*, to religion, or to any other circumstance." The Chatham County grand jury, presumably, was not ready to go quite so far, but it did "present as a great grievance that Congress [had] not powers adequate *to the regulation of our trade*, and earnestly recommend[ed] to the Legislature to grant them such as [might] be sufficient to support the united views of the continent."[7] A similar presentment was made by the Effingham County grand jury a little while later;[8] and Chief Justice Walton was more or less successful in other counties of the state as well.[9]

A final indication of the state of opinion in Georgia in 1785 is a letter signed by "A Citizen," which appeared in the Savannah *Gazette* on November 24. "No scheme of commercial regulation can be ultimately beneficial," this "Citizen" declared, "unless it be continental; because, if it be partial, it must operate against the principles of the Union; and who are the guardians of the continental interest," he asked, "but Congress?" "Nothing appears to me more plain," he also said, "or more certain, than that it is necessary for us [Georgians] to concur in giving *every* degree of respectability, weight, and dignity to the grand federal Council. For, however self-elevated we may be with the pretty idea of our sovereignty, independence and greatness, as a state, was our connection with Congress, that gordian knot of the American Confederacy, once broken, we should immediately sink into insignificancy, and become a prey to the first invader."

Despite the result at the Savannah town meeting, and despite the inaction of the state's legislature, then, it is quite certain there were some (and very likely a good many) men in Georgia in 1785 who agreed spontaneously with the men of Philadelphia, New York, and Boston, and with the men of many smaller Northern communities as well, that a complete national commerce power should be vested in Congress; and some men in Georgia there also were, who agreed that a power to govern *all* the "general concerns" of the United States should be confided to that body. Such men, to be sure, were a minority in the state in 1785; but, as in the case of the men who held such views in the neighboring state of South Carolina, they constituted a substantial and dependable nucleus of nationalist opinion, to which the supervention of any new and unforeseen factor favorable to such views might very easily add enough converts to swing the general opinion of the state that way. Such a new factor did in fact soon supervene to turn the balance in Georgia as well as in the other Southern states, as we shall presently see.

Of the three Southern states not yet mentioned, the state of North Carolina need not detain us long, for little is known of what happened there in 1785, due to the disappearance, in the intervening years, of all the state's newspapers for the year in question. It is known, however, that the legislature of the state took no action in 1785 to grant to Congress any powers over commerce beyond the very fragmentary powers over foreign imports that the legislature had signified its willingness to grant of its own motion early in 1784.[10] Indeed, the state never did take any steps to grant to Congress any commercial powers in addition to these, until its belated adoption of the Constitution in 1789. Besides this complete lack of evidence of any relevant activity in the North Carolina legislature, the records of that body are likewise bare of evidence that any citizens of that state took the trouble in 1785 to petition the legislature upon the subject of commercial power for Congress; and since it is definitely known that the Boston merchants' letters were sent to the men of Edenton and Wilmington within the state,[11] and altogether probable that those letters and many other similar communications were published in the local newspapers, the conclusion seems warranted, in view of the known general attitude of the state throughout the whole formative period of the nation's history,[12] that North Carolina in 1785 was at least as indifferent toward the Northern proposals of a full national commercial power as any state in the Union. The correctness of this conclusion is further supported by the total absence in the surviving newspapers of the other states of any evidence that the commercial agitations of that year evoked any response of any kind in North Carolina.[13]

This extremely indifferent, if not actually hostile, attitude on the part of the state is undoubtedly to be explained in part by certain economic characteristics that North Carolina then had, and by certain peculiar features of the state's geography which were not true of any other state then in the Union. By reason of the extraordinary character of its seacoast, cut off from access to the open sea by a long series of low-lying islands with but few and extremely dangerous passageways between them, North Carolina was without a single, really accessible seaport of its own. In consequence of this, the state had to do its traveling to the other states, and its importing and exporting, mainly through South Carolina and Virginia, and because of this unique inaccessibility, the state as a whole, despite its maritime location, was in reality a *remote* rural region, a kind of back-country on the seacoast, with all the usual characteristics of back-country regions in other parts of the country. The extent to which all this was true we may infer from the fact that, though North Carolina was in 1785 one of the larger states in point of numbers, it had, nevertheless, not a single town that was more than a village; it had no industry save that of "making" its staple "agricultural" products, including naval stores, chiefly by slave labor; and it seems to have had no commercial desires or ambitions, beyond that of exporting these products, and importing needed goods, free of the burdens that its next-door neighbors to the north and south ungenerously imposed upon it. The desire to be free of these burdens later produced in North Carolina some sentiment in favor of the Constitution, and it is natural to suppose that this desire may also have had some such effect in 1785. If it did, however, all evidence of the fact has disappeared: the state as a whole seems in that year to have exhibited the same sort of indifference, or actual hostility, that was found in a greater or less degree in all the remote rural regions of the country, and particularly in all those regions that were tied up, as North Carolina was, to the slavery system.[14]

The situation in Virginia was, of course, in many respects similar to that in North Carolina. A gigantic, sprawling, rural region with a scattered population, Virginia in 1785 was without any towns that were not small, even by eighteenth-century standards; its sole industry, like that of its southern neighbor, was agriculture; and though it probably numbered more opponents of slavery than any of the states to the southward, there can be little doubt it was nearly as firmly tied up to the slavery system as these states. At this point, however, the resemblance of Virginia to North Carolina ends, for, unlike North Carolina, Virginia *did* have accessible seaports, and it numbered among its citizens a considerable body of men who were very anxious to force the growth of the Virginia ports, and Virginian ownership of merchant vessels, by an exclusive Virginian system of commercial regulation. Because of the size of Virginia, this project, unlike the somewhat similar projects in Delaware, Connecticut, and New Jersey, was apparently quite seriously entertained as a possible system of permanent state policy; and the group in Virginia who advocated adopting a Virginian system of commercial regulation, and who professed to see in an American system a dreadful peril for their state in the form of an impending Northern carrying monopoly, included some of the bitterest opponents of the Northern proposals of complete commercial power for Congress which were to be found anywhere.

The existence and strength of this localistic party in Virginia undoubtedly played a major role in 1785 in producing the strange behavior of the neighboring state, and, particularly, of the commercial element in that neighboring state, Maryland. For the commerce of Baltimore—then, as now, Maryland's principal town—was carried on in large part with Virginians, and that being true, a considerable part of the commerce of the town was manifestly threatened by the party in Virginia just mentioned. In addition, the whole of the external waterborne commerce of both the town and the state seemed to lie (in case the Union should not continue) at the mercy of Virginia, thanks to that state's presence on both sides of the mouth of Chesapeake Bay upon which Baltimore lay. Maryland's need for cultivating the good will of its much larger and more powerful neighbor must, therefore, have seemed very obvious, and since, during the months when the commercial agitations were in progress, there also was in progress a most promising project (from a local point of view) for the joint development and regulation by Virginia and Maryland of the commerce of the Potomac and Pocomoke Rivers and the intervening lower parts of Chesapeake Bay,* the reader will hardly find it surprising that the Boston merchants' letters, and the many similar proposals made at the time, produced no known response among Maryland's mercantile element. As a matter of fact, few of these proposals were even published in the Maryland papers; many were not even noticed; and in the light, particularly, of the later easy success of the Constitution in Maryland, the impression is hard to down that the whole agitation of 1785 was deliberately damped down by the Maryland mercantile element, in order to avoid offense to the state's neighbor and customer at the south.

The project mentioned above, for the joint regulation by the two states of the commerce of the Potomac and Pocomoke rivers had been proposed in the Virginia legislature in 1784 by James Madison.[15] Having completed the allowable term of three consecutive years of service in Congress in the preceding fall, Madison had then returned to Virginia and been elected to the legislature shortly afterward. During his service in Congress, as the reader will recall, Madison had been one of those who had helped to defeat the Witherspoon motion of February 3, 1781, which had proposed for Congress a complete commercial power;[16] and two years later, though advocating power to carry into execution the substantive powers—chiefly for the common defense—that Congress already had,[17] Madison had been one of those who had opposed the holding of a general continental constitutional convention (as Hamilton had then proposed), for the purpose, among others, of "vesting in the United States a general superintendence of trade."[18] Madison's opposition, at this period of his career, to a general national power of regulating commerce is clear beyond doubt from his record in Congress; and though in 1784 he favored a continental convention for the limited purpose of vesting in Congress executive powers,[19] there is nothing in fact, or in anything else connected with his record in the years immediately following his retirement from Congress, which in any way conflicts with his record in that body. To the contrary, Madison's continuing hostility—or, if the reader prefer, behavior not reconcilable with a disappearance of his hostility—to a general national power of regulating commerce appears in various of his letters from this period of his career. For example, in a letter written to Jefferson on December 10, 1783, there are hints of the plans he then was making for what he described as "the emancipation" of "the commerce of this country"—i.e., Virginia—from "Phil[adelphi]a & Baltimore," which cities, he said, were exacting from Virginians "a tribute" of "not less than 30 or 40 Per Ct. on all [their] exports & imports."[20] In another letter to Jefferson, in

*The Pocomoke is across the bay on Cape Charles. Its mouth is in Virginia.

the following August, he complained specifically that Virginia's tobacco "ha[d] currently sold 15 or 20 per Ct., at least, higher in Phil[adelphi]a," than it had in Virginia, though, "being [there] as far from the ultimate market," he said, "it [could] not be intrinsically worth more." He also declared that "goods [were] much dearer in Virginia, than in the States"—such as Maryland and Pennsylvania—"where trade [was] drawn to a general mart"; that "even goods brought from Phil[adelphi]a and Baltimore to Winchester & other W[estern] & S[outh] W[estern] parts of Virginia [were] retailed cheaper than those imported directly from Europe [were] sold on tide water."[21] In the course of this letter, his remedy for all these iniquities, or these imagined iniquities, also appeared: a separate Virginian system of commercial regulation which would force the growth of Alexandria and Norfolk as the state's exclusive ports and centers of commerce.[22] This plan, which was obviously inconsistent with a grant to Congress of a complete power of regulating commerce, was the chief cause—at least one of the chief causes—of Madison's interest in the plan for the joint regulation of the commerce of the Potomac and other waters, by Maryland and Virginia, mentioned above.[23]

Madison's interest in that plan arose out of the fact that, by the terms of certain old colonial documents, the southern boundary of Maryland was fixed, though perhaps not with complete certainty, as the south bank of the Potomac River. In view of the nature of Madison's plans, this fact was exceedingly disconcerting. Because his plans contemplated the diminishment of Baltimore's importance as a port, Madison naturally foresaw that Maryland would use this ancient claim to an exclusive jurisdiction over the Potomac River to defeat his plans, at least so far as Alexandria was concerned.[24] If Madison wished to succeed in his plans, therefore, he was faced with the necessity of devising some way of circumventing this serious difficulty. A way to accomplish this object was rather luckily provided soon after by certain plans that Washington, with very different motives, then brought forward for clearing the navigation of the Potomac and connecting its headwaters commercially with those of the Ohio.[25] These plans of Washington's, equally with those of Madison, required some agreement with Maryland for a joint jurisdiction over the Potomac, and since Washington's plans, unlike those of Madison, held forth to Maryland and Baltimore, as well as Virginia, a promise of an increased, rather than decreased, commerce, Washington's plans quite naturally presented themselves to Madison as a convenient stalking-horse for the attaining of his ends. He therefore promoted Washington's scheme in the Virginia legislature; through Washington's efforts the enthusiastic participation of Maryland was obtained; and a joint commission of the two states was finally appointed to draw up an agreement for their joint regulation of the commerce of the Potomac and other waters.[26] A meeting of this joint commission had taken place in the spring of 1785, at about the time when the agitations for a national system of commercial regulation were getting under way among the Northern states.[27]

The report of this commission was, therefore, in general expectation in Virginia and Maryland when the news of the Northern agitations began to be received, and while there can be no suspicion of Washington's motives, the reader can entertain little doubt that the expectation of the Maryland-Virginia commission's report, and the pendency of the project to which that report appertained, had a very great deal to do with the attitude of indifference displayed by both Virginia and Maryland toward the Northern proposals of a *national* "commercial system."

The nature of the Maryland attitude toward the Northern proposals may easily be seen by comparing the newspapers of Maryland for 1785 with those of the states of the North, or even with those of such Southern states as Georgia and South Carolina. It is not, as already intimated, that the Maryland newspapers contained many pieces in opposition to a national commercial power in the year in question, but simply that, compared with the Northern states, and even with the further Southern states, they displayed very little interest in the subject. As for the Virginia response, the newspaper record there has unfortunately in large part disappeared, but from such fragments of the record as have survived, it appears that the state's attitude was at least as disappointing to those interested in a national commerce power as was the attitude of its neighbor, Maryland. Besides the surviving fragments of the Virginia newspaper record, there are certain petitions still in existence, which, probably as a result of receipt of the Boston merchants' letters, were filed with the Virginia legislature in 1785 by the mercantile element in the various towns throughout the state. Those petitions fully corroborate that the Virginia response was as stated, so the factual nature of that response cannot very well be doubted.

There are, in all, five of these Virginian mercantile petitions,[28] all of them filed during November 1785.[29] The high-mark of nationalism in them (as James Madison recognized at the time)[30] is to be found in the petition which was filed by "the Merchants, Traders, and other inhabitants of the Town of Alexandria." This petition, however, went only so far as to urge upon the legislature that it would be "wise, politic and for the general welfare of the United States" if Congress were vested with "certain rights and authorities, *to be properly defined and ascertained*, over the *foreign* Trade and Commerce of the several States." One of the other petitions, that of "the merchants, traders, and others of the town of Suffolk, and County of Nansemond," expressed regret that "all the States [had] not vested Congress with powers that would have enabled them, to have placed our Commercial Interests, on a solid and advantageous footing," but no suggestion was made that Virginia bestow any powers on Congress beyond the very meagre powers over foreign trade which the state had already granted.[31] After declaring that it seemed "uncertain" when suitable national powers would be given (i.e., presumably, by the other states), this Nansemond petition went on to advocate local regulations only. Of the other three petitions, two, coming from the towns of Norfolk and Portsmouth, advocated state regulations without any expressed desire to vest regulatory power in Congress; and the third, from the town of Petersburg, not only advocated state regulations at very great length, but admonished the legislature that Virginia was "possessed of a Valuable Staple, and other Native Commodities of a lucky nature," and "that it [was therefore] a matter of the greatest National Concern [i.e., Virginian concern] that the regulating the Trade of our Country [i.e., Virginia] be not given up to any Power, not amenable to [the Virginia legislature], without such Restrictions, and under such Reserve, as the relative Importance of [Virginia's] Commerce seem[ed] to require, when considered with the Reduced State of [its] Navigation."

The unenthusiastic character of Virginia's response to the commercial proposals of the Northern states had been fully anticipated—indeed, very strikingly exemplified—in a letter James Madison had written on the preceding June 21 to James Monroe, who was then in Congress.[32] In the course of this letter Madison casually remarked to Monroe that he had "observed in a late Newspaper that the commercial discontents of Boston [were] spreading to New York and Philad[elphi]a." Whether they would spread into Virginia, Madison considered doubtful. ["Virginia's] Merchants [were] almost all connected with [Great Britain]," he said, "& [Great Britain] only; and as [the state] ha[d] neither ships nor seamen of [its] own, nor [was] likely to have any in the [existing] course of things, no mercantile complaints [were] heard." "The planters," he conceded, "[were] discontented, and with reason, but they enter[ed] little into the science of commerce [i.e., economics], and rarely of themselves combin[d] in defense of their interests." "If anything could rouse them to a proper view of their situation, one might expect it," he thought, "from the contrast of the market [in Virginia] with that of the other States"—from the higher price, he explained, which Virginia's tobacco commanded at Philadelphia, and the lower prices at which, he said "[he] ha[d] little doubt," imports there sold. Notwithstanding these "facts," of which Madison had long been complaining, it was still proving difficult, he said, "to make [the Virginia planters] sensible of the utility of establishing a Philad[elphi]a or a Baltimore among [them]selves." Many of them, he said, were actively opposing the pending Virginia "port Bill," which aimed, as he put it, at establishing a Philadelphia or a Baltimore among [Virginians]" by "concentrating Commerce at Alexandria and Norfolk." "And the difficulty," Madison assured Monroe, "[was] not a little increased by the pains taken by the [British-dominated Virginia] Merchants to prevent such a reformation." There was a good deal more in a similar vein, but surprising as it may seem to readers of the traditional accounts in American histories, "the Father of the Constitution" had not so much as a single word to say of the desirability of a *national* power of regulating commerce. In fact, the truth seems to be that although Madison knew of the Northern proposals for creating such a power, and in addition knew that a proposal to create such a power was then pending in Congress,[33] he still was interested, when he wrote this letter on June 21, in local Virginia regulations *only*.

Further evidence that Madison at this period was not much interested in the creation of a national commerce power will be seen in a letter to Richard Henry Lee, in Congress, written by Madison a little over a fortnight later. In that letter, dated July 7, Madison not only repeated his complaint (which was, as Lee later explained to him, wholly unwarranted in fact) that "Virginia's staple" was selling at the time at a higher price in the Northern seaports; in addition, he announced his view that there was in actually no prospect of obtaining any such favorable commercial treaty with the British as that to which the Northern men hopefully looked forward. "What," he asked Lee,—obviously in the vein of Lord Sheffield—"could [Britain] get from [America] by concessions which she [was] unwilling to make, which she [did] not now enjoy [without them]?" "The revolution ha[d] robbed [America] of [its] trade with the West Indies, the only one which [had] yielded a favorable balance, without opening any other channels to compensate for it."[34] Lee, who was, from a frantic fear of a Northern carrying monopoly, at this time opposed to a national commerce power and quick, of course, to recognize a potential supporter, wrote back to Madison that "it seem[ed] to [him] clear beyond doubt, that the giving Congress a power to Legislate over the Trade of the Union would be dangerous." "The want of Ships and Seamen [in "the 5 Southern or Staple States"] would expose their freightage & their produce to a most pernicious and destructive Monopoly." He could "say much," he added, "upon this subject," but it was "not necessary, [since he was] sure that [Madison's] good sense reflecting calmly on this subject would sufficiently discern the danger of such an experiment." Very much to his credit, Lee thereupon set Madison right about the higher price at which "Virginia's staple" was selling in the Northern seaports.[35]

Monroe's receipt of Madison's letter of June 21 and, very likely, some inkling from his colleague, Lee, of what Madison had written to Lee on July 7, apparently set James Monroe to thinking. Monroe (who was the real pioneer among Virginians in the ardent advocacy of the national commerce power) was acting at the time as head of a committee which had been appointed in Congress, in December 1784, for "giving to the United States *the general regulation of trade*."[36] Some months previously, this committee had turned in a report in which it had been proposed that the states be asked to invest Congress with a nearly complete commerce power.[37] When Monroe received Madison's letter of June 21, this committee report was still pending before Congress. Upon his receipt of Madison's letter, Monroe, having first ascertained that Madison had been sent a copy of the committee report by William Grayson on May 1, wrote very urgently on July 26,[38] and again on August 14,[39] requesting Madison to express his views upon the proposal contained in the committee report.

Madison finally complied with Monroe's request in a somewhat wordy and circumlocutory letter on August 7. "Viewing in the abstract," he said. "the question whether the power of regulating trade, *to a certain degree at least*, ought to be vested in Congress, it appear[ed] to [him] not to admit of a doubt, but that it should be decided in the affirmative." But Congress, he thought, ought to be practical about these things and avoid recommending to the states what the states, or any of them, would be likely not to grant. And in the present instance he could not "give weight," he said, even to the rather grudging and highly qualified approval of the Monroe committee's report which he expressed in his letter, "by saying that [he had] reason to believe [his sentiments of approval] would be relished in the public Councils of [Virginia]." On the contrary, he "augur[ed] that great difficulties [would] be encountered in every attempt to prevail on the [Virginia] Legislature to part with power." "The thing itself [was] not only unpalatable, but the arguments which plead[ed] for it ha[d] not their full force on minds unaccustomed to consider the interests of [Virginia] as they [were] interwoven with those of the Confederacy, much less as they [might] be affected by foreign politics." On the other hand, the arguments "w[hi]ch plead[ed] ag[ain]st [the proposed national commerce power were]," said Madison, "not only specious, but in their nature of popular; and for that reason, sure of finding patrons."

In addition to all this, there was the fact, Madison again insisted, "that the Mercantile interest which ha[d] taken the lead in rousing the public attention of other States, [was] in [Virginia] so exclusively engaged in British Commerce that what little weight they ha[d would]˙be most likely to fall into the opposite scale." So, look at the matter how he would, he could, so he averred, discern "only [one] circumstance which promise[d] a favorable hearing [in Virginia] to the meditated proposition of Cong[res]s." That was the fact "that the power which it ask[ed would] be exerted ag[ain]st G[reat] B[ritain]." Because of this fact the proposal, he thought, would "be seconded [in Virginia] by the animosities which still prevail[ed there] in a strong degree ag[ain]st [that nation]." The plain import of Madison's whole letter, however, was that this single favorable circumstance would not be enough. On the other hand, he signified his agreement with Monroe that something must be done to relieve the situation in the Northern states. If "seven or eight of the States [should] be hindered by the others" (i.e., by the Southern states and, perhaps, by New York) "from obtaining relief [against Great Britain] by fœderal means, [he] own[ed that he] tremble[d] at the anti-fœderal expedients into which the former [might] be tempted." Yet, for all his trembling, and all the plain import of the Northern demands which were then before the country, Madison seemed to think that somehow the Northern states could be contented and kept in continuing union with the South by some kind of limited power over foreign commerce; perhaps even by a power over that subject for use against Great Britain only, which, as Madison plainly intimated to Monroe, would be the kind of power it would be easiest for Congress to obtain. Madison's letter as a whole, then, leaves no doubt that he was seeking by every argument he could possibly command, to dissuade Monroe and, through Monroe, the other members of Congress, from pursuing the plan which that body then had before it, of proposing to the states the creation of a virtually complete national power over commerce.[40]

There is no known evidence that Madison's letter had any actual effect upon Monroe of lessening the latter's long-standing conviction that a complete national commerce power was a thing which the country very much needed.[41] Despite this fact, however Madison's letter is a singularly important document. It is important, in the first place, because it constitutes so plain a corroboration *from a Southern source* of the general opinion then entertained in the Northern states regarding the probable Southern attitude upon the subject of commercial power for Congress. Madison's opinion of the Southern attitude, which he repeated in letters to Thomas Jefferson,[42] was substantially the same in tenor as the opinions soon thereafter expressed by Rufus King in his letters to John Adams and Caleb Davis, already noted.[43] Madison's opinion, we should also recognize, was quite probably a source of the views that King expressed. King, as the reader will remember, was a member of the Monroe committee on commercial powers in Congress;[44] King and Monroe were rather close at the time;[45] and Monroe wrote Jefferson, at about the date when he must have received Madison's letter of August 7, that he was then maintaining "the most confidential communications" with "the Eastern people" upon the subject about which Madison had written in his letter.[46] It is therefore entirely possible that Monroe may have communicated to King the contents of Madison's extremely dissuasive letter; if he did, it is even easier than it otherwise would be to understand the distrust of James Madison with regard to the subject of commerce, expressed a little later by King and certain other Massachusetts men in contact with King.[47]

Madison's August 7 letter to Monroe is significant in still another important way: it provides the background to the well-known efforts made by Madison and his friends in the Virginia legislature in the ensuing fall to obtain certain limited commerce powers for Congress. Precisely what these powers were is not known, but in a letter to Jefferson written after the close of the legislative session, Madison said the attempt had been "to give [to] Cong[res]s such direct power only as would not alarm."[48] Evidently Madison and his group did act upon the views expressed by Madison on August 7 in his letter to Monroe. The powers, then, could not have been extensive, and the fact becomes quite certain that the November 7 resolution of the Virginia House of Delegates cannot, despite its language, be taken as evidence that an attempt had been made within that body to obtain for Congress complete commercial power. The resolution was "that an act ought to pass to authorize the delegates of [Virginia] in Congress to give the assent of the State to *a general regulation* of the commerce of the United States, *under certain qualifications*."[49] The signification of the words "*a general* regulation" in this resolution was, apparently, only "*a nation-wide* regulation." In the light of Madison's several letters, this much is certain: the words cannot have had reference, at any point in the proceedings, to *the scope* of the nationwide power proposed.

Just how much power the House of Delegates did have in mind when it passed this resolution is not known. It is clear only that this original vote must have been for a grant of some kind of limited power of perpetual duration. This seems the plain meaning of Madison's letter to Jefferson, last mentioned above.[50] The plan of a perpetual grant was, however, shortly afterwards altered to a grant for twenty-five years only, and then, on November 30, after the strontly anti-national Petersburg petition had been received, the duration of the grant was still further reduced to thirteen years.[51] Whether any changes, other that those relating to the duration of the grant, were made after the vote of November 7 is not known. On November 30 the proposed grant, as then reported by committee of the whole, was as follows:

Resolved, that it is the opinion of this committee, That the delegates representing this Commonwealth in Congress, be instructed to propose in Congress, a recommendation to the States in Union, to authorise that Assembly to regulate their trade on the following principles, and under the following qualifications:

1st. That the United States in Congress assembled, be authorised to prohibit vessels belonging to any foreign nation, from entering any of the ports thereof, or to impose any duties on such vessels and their cargoes, which may be judged necessary; all such prohibitions and duties to be uniform throughout the United States, and the proceeds of the latter to be carried into the treasury of the State within which they shall accrue.

2d. That no State be at liberty to impose duties on any goods, wares, or merchandizes, imported by land or by water from any other State, but may altogether prohibit the importation from any State of any particular species or description of goods, wares or merchandize, of which the importation is at the same time prohibited from all other places whatsoever.

3d. That no act of Congress that may be authorized as hereby proposed, shall be entered into by less than two thirds of the confederated States, nor be in force longer than thirteen years.

On the day this report was agreed to, the House of Delegates defeated a motion to increase the duration of the powers proposed in the report. The report was then adopted by the House in the foregoing form.[52]

The extreme meagreness of the national powers under this Virginia resolution is perfectly obvious. Mere partial powers over foreign trade, and those largely illusory because of their inapplicability to acts of Americans, the powers covered by the resolution (despite the greatly increased verbiage used to confer them) were little more in substance, and no greater in duration, than the powers asked by Congress on April 30, 1784, and those powers, as we know, the Virginia legislature had previously granted.[53] In light of this fact, then, the reader will have no cause for wonder that Madison and his group, upon further consideration of the subject, after the day's session was over, reached the conclusion that the measure as adopted was useless, and likely only to annoy and alienate the Northern states which were plainly anxious to see complete power over commerce in Congress.[54] On the following day Madison and his group accordingly moved in the House of Delegates that previous day's action be rescinded, because, they said, it had not "from a mistake contain[ed] the sense of the majority. . . . that [had] voted for [it]." The motion of rescission was promptly passed, whereupon the proposal was again taken up in committee of the whole. Certain changes, the nature of which is not known, were apparently agreed to, but when the committee report containing these changes was brought before the House, the House directed that it "lie upon the table." The attention of the House was then directed to sundry schemes which had been brought before it for the local regulation of commerce by the state, and the proposal for granting to Congress powers over commerce was not again considered.[55]

Among the schemes for the local regulation of commerce to which the Virginia deputies at this point turned their attention, was the scheme that James Madison had promoted, in the legislative session of the previous year, for the joint regulation by Maryland and Virginia of the commerce of the Potomac and Pocomoke rivers and the intervening parts of Chesapeake Bay. The commissioners of the two states who had then been appointed had gone somewhat beyond the authority given them, and turned in a report which, besides covering the matter for which they had been appointed, had recommended to their respective legislatures the adoption of identical regulations upon a number of other commercial subjects. These included rules on the subject of damages in case of foreign bills of exchange; rules of damage and the necessity of protest in case of bills drawn by merchants of either of the states upon merchants of the other; regulations of the value of foreign coins passing current among them; and duties on all imports and exports. The commission's report also proposed, "if these Subjects shou'd be deemed worthy Notice," that as a means of carrying forward this important beginning and "keeping up harmony," as Madison said, "in the commercial regulations of the two states," commissioners should be appointed "to meet [annually], & communicate the Regulations of Commerce & Duties proposed by each State and to confer on such Subjects as [might] concern the commercial Interests of both." When this proposal came before the Maryland legislature, that body, while approving it, added the suggestion that Pennsylvania and Delaware also be asked to participate.[56] This proposal by Maryland naturally suggested the idea of asking all the states to participate, and so, when the matter came up in the Virginia House of Delegates in early December, Madison and his group, in view of the defeat they had just sustained on the subject of an immediate grant of power to Congress, moved as a substitute for the Maryland proposal that a resolution be adopted asking the appointment of commissioners by all the states to draw up a scheme of commercial powers for Congress, as the obvious agency for accomplishing, for all the states, the purpose which the Maryland-Virginia commission had

had in mind for two of them. The motion to this effect was presented by John Tyler (afterwards an opponent of the Constitution),[57] acting at the instance of James Madison.[58] However, as in the case of the proposal urged by this same group for an immediate, but limited, grant of commercial powers to Congress, the motion was tabled.[59] On the other hand, the report of the joint commission, together with the Maryland suggestion of a four-state commission, on uniform state commercial laws, was referred to the House's standing committee on commerce.[60]

That committee was definitely under the control of the most extreme opponents of commercial power for Congress. The plan for the joint regulation by Maryland and Virginia of the commerce of the Potomac and Pocomoke rivers and Chesapeake Bay was therefore favorably reported by the committee and promptly adopted by the delegates.[61] According to Madison, the friends of the Confederation made efforts at this point to induce the House to refer this plan to Congress for approval, as the Articles of Confederation in plain terms required.[62] It is eloquent of the prevailing spirit that these efforts proved futile: it was voted that the plan for the joint regulation should be adopted without compliance with this undoubted constitutional requirement.[63] In consonance with this spirit, the committee on commerce also proposed, on January 13, 1786, that the Maryland suggestion of setting up a continuing four-state commission for maintaining uniformity in *state* commercial regulations, as between Pennsylvania, Delaware, Maryland, and Virginia, be broadened into a resolution requesting all the states to appoint commissioners to meet annually for the purpose of maintaining uniformity in *state* commercial regulations throughout the whole country. This strange proposal—virtually a proposal for another Continental Congress, for commercial recommendations only—was at once adopted by the House and sent to the Senate for approval.[64] The Senate approved the measure on January 17,[65] and on January 30, Patrick Henry, as governor of the state, communicated to the other states, as was his official duty, this little-known anticipation of our well-known modern device of attempting to regulate commerce through a standing body of commissioners on uniform state laws.[66]

This proposal, as the reader will have perceived, was totally inconsistent with what had been suggested and urgently advocated during the preceding spring and summer in the states further north. The Virginia proposal could, therefore, only be interpreted in those states as an expression of complete unwillingness on the part of Virginia to join with the Northern states in the establishment of a *national* "commercial system." It was also, for the reasons suggested in the last paragraph, a slap at Congress and the Union. Some of the more prudent, and perhaps as well, the more national-minded, of the Virginia Delegates were apparently not willing that such an impression of Virginia should be created among the Northern states. They probably "trembled" (as James Madison had "own[ed that he] tremble[d]" in the preceding summer) "at the antifœderal expedients into which the [Northern states might] be tempted" if such an impression of the most important of the Southern states should be created among them. Apparently, then, in order to take the edge off the resolution just adopted, this group, just four days later, called up the Tyler motion that had been "lying on the table" since early in the month before, and in some way obtained its immediate passage. This occurred on the last day of the legislature's session, after the attendance in the House had dwindled somewhat toward the session's close. The earlier resolution calling for commissioners to seek "an uniform system in [American] commercial regulations" through uniform state laws was *not* retracted; a second call was simply added, for another body of commissioners "to consider how far an uniform system in [American] commercial regulations [might] be necessary; and to report to the several states such an act relative to [that] great object as, when unanimously ratified by them, [would] enable the United States in Congress assembled effectually to provide for [such uniformity]."[67] The commissioners appointed by Virginia for this second meeting afterwards named Annapolis as the place for the proposed meeting, and the first Monday in the following September as the time, and since the meeting, such as it turned out to be, was eventually held in accordance with these suggestions, it has come to be known in American history as the Annapolis commercial convention of 1786.

The resolution for the calling of this second convention, or commission, had rather wide support in the Virginia legislature when the resolution passed.[68] This fact may seem to the reader incongruous, as it unquestionably did to James Madison and other Virginians at the time. Just what lay behind the fact of this general support for the second resolution is not known. In one of his letters to James Monroe, Madison promised that "the history of [the resolution should] be [the] subject of some future tête-à-tête [between them]";[69] but, naturally, no record of such a "tête-á-tête" is to be found, and we are therefore thrown back upon such hints as exist in the letters of Madison and others, and upon the manifest probabilities of the situation. In accordance with these probabilities, the motives of the more national-minded and prudent of the Virginia legislature were those already set forth. The probability is that these men pointed out, for their legislative brethren, the extreme danger to the Union that would be likely to result from so bald a refusal to join in the plans of the Northern states, as the resolution four days earlier adopted would be considered in those states to be. Such arguments, it is not unlikely, obtained some support for the second resolution among certain members of the Virginia legislature, who, though they may well have lacked the intelligence to see this probability for themselves, and also lacked any interest in commercial power for Congress, did nevertheless esteem the Union. Beyond such support, the resolution very probably obtained the vote of many of the supporters of the first resolution, merely because they regarded it as a perfectly harmless and extremely convenient dilatory device that was likely, in view of the state of sentiment in Virginia and the other

Southern states, to produce nothing but confusion in the movement for a national commerce power, and consequent ill-will in the Northern states for the Virginia proponents of the second resolution. Such effects were, in fact, among the intermediate results of the second resolution, as we shall presently see, and that such results were feared by the proponents of the second resolution, and that they suspected some of their legislative brethren of the motives just stated, are also facts which appear with certainty from their letters.

In the months that followed, more than one broad hint may be found in the letters of James Madison to James Monroe and Thomas Jefferson that the easy passage of the second resolution in the Virginia legislature was not to be taken as evidence that that body in general was "federal" in its views. "The option," Madison insisted to Monroe (who was not much impressed with the proposed convention), "lay between doing what was done, and doing nothing." There was "both ignorance and iniquity to combat," he said;[70] and in a letter to Jefferson, he spoke of prominent members of the Virginia legislature (including one who was among the Virginia delegates to Annapolis) as having been "bitter and illiberal against Congress & the Northern States beyond example"; as having even suggested that it might be "better to encourage the British than the Eastern marine" if Virginia could not have her own.[71]

The most striking evidence, however, is contained in a letter to Monroe, written by Madison on the day immediately following the adoption of the second resolution. In the course of this letter, Madison referred to the extraordinary increase in the number of the commissioners appointed by Virginia, from the three proposed in John Tyler's original motion to the *eight* provided in the resolution as passed. He adverted to the known "unfederal" character of certain of these additional commissioners; observed dejectedly that "it [was] not unlikely that this multitude of associates [would] stifle the thing in its birth"; and bluntly declared that "by some [in the legislature], it was probably meant to do so." The dejection felt by Madison when he wrote this letter is evident also in the comment he made upon a statement apparently made by Monroe in an earlier letter, that Virginia was still well thought of by the other states in Congress. Madison told Monroe he was glad to hear this, but he added sadly that he "should be more so if [he] saw greater reason for [such esteem]."[72] From this and Madison's other remarks, made in this letter to Monroe, while the occurrences of the day previous were fresh in his mind, it seems sufficiently clear that he was not overjoyed when the Tyler motion passed; that he saw at the time little likelihood that anything good could come out of it; and that he probably was "trembling" once more lest Virginia and the South, in the event, should lose those peculiar benefits for which, it seems clear, Madison principally esteemed the Union.

To these worried views of James Madison's, there may be added the contents of the interesting letter sent out by Edmund Randolph, on February 19, 1786, to notify the governors of the other states of Virginia's desire for the second convention. Randolph, in accordance with Tyler's original proposal, had been made the head of the Virginia commissioners, and since, by the terms of the Tyler resolution, the commissioners had the duty of opening up a correspondence with the other states upon the subject of their appointment, it devolved upon Randolph to write and sign the letter that was sent out for this purpose. The letter he sent was a strange one, indeed. Randolph began by making clear that, in sending out the letter, he was doing only what he had been directed to do. And he was exceedingly careful not to recommend the proposed convention to the other states. Instead, said Randolph, "It is impossible for me to decide how far the uniform system in commercial regulations, which is the subject of [the legislature's] resolution, may or may not be attainable." He could "only venture to declare," he added—in what certainly seems to have been telltale fear that the recipients of his letter might for some reason or other take a contrary view of the subject—"that the desire of such an arrangement had arisen [in the Virginia legislature] from a regard to the federal interests." And then, apparently troubled by the unenthusiastic tone that had crept into his letter, Randolph wound up this strange, floundering performance with an intimated explanation that the only real duties of the Virginia commissioners were to request the concurrence of the other states in the proposed commercial convention, and to suggest to them a time and place for the proposed meeting. He then proceeded to discharge these two duties and to terminate his letter. From the tenor of this rather remarkable communication, the text of which has been reproduced for the reader, in Appendix F to this volume,[73] it seems abundantly clear that Edmund Randolph, after having had a full month to think it over, was still as unhappy over the action of the Virginia legislature as Madison had been the day after the Tyler resolution passed; that Randolph, in fact, was extremely unsure and sensitive about the motives behind the Virginia legislature's action; that he was dubious that any good could come out of it, and extremely anxious that he, Edmund Randolph, should not be understood in the other states as personally advocating their concurrence in it. Should the reader feel the slightest doubt of the entire correctness of this view of Randolph's letter, that doubt can be entirely allayed by comparing its text with the text of the pair of letters (printed in Appendix H hereof)[74] that Randolph sent out only a few months later, when, as governor of his state, with a frightened, and therefore earnest and eager, legislature behind him, he announced to the other states Virginia's readiness to participate in the Federal Convention. The anxious urgency of these later letters and the strikingly different tone of the Randolph letter of February 19 can mean only one thing: when Randolph wrote his letter on February 19, he was painfully aware that, as respected a great many men in the Virginia legislature, the proposal of the Annapolis convention had not been exactly an act of good faith.

If such was the attitude of a moderately national-minded Virginia man who knew the facts, the reader will not be at all astonished that, when the facts—or some of the facts—became known among the Northern men, and they came to understand there was no real prospect of obtaining extensive national commercial powers through the Annapolis meeting, the result was anger and extreme distrust of the men of Virginia.[75] Indeed, if the character of Randolph's letter is kept in mind, along with the fact that, when his letter was received, the governors of the other states had only just received a letter from Patrick Henry, Virginia's governor, proposing, in behalf of the Virginia legislature, the appointment of a set of commissioners to concert "an uniform system of [American] commercial regulations," *according to an entirely different plan*, it would not have been at all remarkable had some of the governors of the other states simply concluded that Randolph's letter was some queer mistake. Very likely the recognition that some such interpretation was not impossible is what led Patrick Henry to dispatch a second letter to the governors of the other states a few days after Randolph's letter was sent out. In this second letter Henry assured the governors that Randolph and the other Virginia commissioners actually had been appointed for the purpose Randolph had mentioned, and then added a request, though in purely perfunctory terms, that the governors would "make such communications [within their governments] as [might] be necessary to forward the views of *this legislature*."[76] No kind of letter from Henry was required by the terms of the Virginia legislature's *second* resolution; and since a merely routine authentication of the appointment of the commissioners would certainly have been sent with or before, rather than after, the letter which Randolph sent out, it seems clear enough that Patrick Henry's second letter was produced by the queerness of the situation in which matters had been left. The governor's second letter, however, only partially cleared up that queer situation. As is plainly to be seen from the words that have been italicized, Patrick Henry's second letter put the whole thing on the Virginia legislature and made no attempt at all to explain away the fact that that legislature, within the space of four days, had recommended to the other states *two* distinct and totally different plans for obtaining "an uniform system" in the country's commercial regulations.

Such, then, was the true nature of the response to the commercial agitations of 1785 which took place in the largest and most important of the Southern states. The realities of the situation make perfectly clear that the attitude of Virginia involved more active hostility toward the Northern proposals of vesting full commercial power in Congress than was true of any other of the Southern states. In North Carolina there was, no doubt, a vast indifference and perhaps some hostility, but that state was not even imaginably in a position, as Virginia was, to set up a state system. As for Maryland, it was rather firmly tied to Virginia's plans, whether it preferred a national plan or not, and taking into account Maryland's subsequent behavior, it seems very doubtful whether that state did in fact prefer the Virginia plans, as Maryland's seeming indifference to the Northern proposals in 1785, taken by itself, might incline the reader to think. In the two remaining Southern states, South Carolina and Georgia, there was, apparently, already in existence in 1785 a considerable body of opinion—though very likely less than a majority in either state—which was favorable to the Northern views. Clearly, the opposition to the idea of creating a complete national commerce power reached its peak in 1785 in Virginia, and this despite the fact that Virginia was the home of Washington and a good many other men of strong and liberal national views.

Nevertheless, the fact cannot be denied that, in all the Southern states, the majority opinion in 1785 was certainly opposed, or at least indifferent, to the proposals advanced by the Northern states. This uniformly negative attitude is to be explained in part by the fact that the South as a whole was a rural region; but inasmuch as the entire country was then predominantly a rural region, the fact of the South's rurality is obviously not enough by itself to explain the very striking difference in attitude toward the proposals in question displayed by the two parts of the country.

The only fact that can explain this difference is that the South as a whole, in contradistinction from the North, was tied to, and desired to be tied —or, at any rate, conceived itself to be tied up beyond all remedy—to the slavery system. The consequences of this fact, as it affected the Southern states' attitude toward the commercial proposals advanced by the North, can hardly be exaggerated. So far as the consequences were of an economic kind, they flowed from the conviction then everywhere held, with a good deal of reason, that slave labor could not in general be employed to advantage, except in agriculture and a few other activities in which the slave's lack of incentive could be compensated by the employment of overseers. This general ineffectiveness of slave labor in the more skilled occupations seemed to commit the South, not only temporarily but permanently, to agricultural— or, at any rate, to extractive—industry. This great difference in the economic prospects of the North and South undoubtedly goes far to explain the differing attitude of the two regions toward the proposals of 1785 for developing a diversified American economy.

Even beyond these purely economic considerations, however, there was one other view equally widely held and equally important: a slave economy was universally recognized in the eighteenth century to be militarily weak. The slaves were looked upon as a potential "fifth column": ever present, ever needing to be watched, and ever available to any enemy who could turn them to account for his own hostile purposes. Southern reactions to this inevitable military consequence of the slavery system were diverse. Some Southerners seemed to think that it provided the best of reasons for the South's agreeing to the Northern plans for developing a strong and diversified national economy. Other Southerners, jealous and fearful of the North, were led by these feelings to oppose the Northern plans. The situation was well understood among Northern men, and no better contemporary statement of the matter is anywhere to be found than that contained in a letter to Rufus King written on February 11, 1786, by General Benjamin Lincoln, of Massachusetts.[77] The date of Lincoln's letter, the reader will observe, was just prior to the period when the Virginia proposal of the Annapolis convention became generally known throughout the Northern part of the country.

"The great question," said Lincoln, "is now agitating in the different states, whether Congress shall be vested with *full and competent powers to regulate the trade of the United States.*" "Some [of the states] determine in the affirmative," he said, "while others are for limiting those powers[; and] each State [acts] as its real or imaginary interest points out." "[Thus] it [was the] interest [of Massachusetts]," he thought, "to be the carriers not only of her own produce, but to become so for her neighbours; [and, hence,] Massachusetts [was] from interest clear in opinion, that Congress ought to be vested with powers to regulate the trade of the United States, and they [would]," he predicted, "be full in sentiment that none of the produce of the United States ought to be carried out in British bottoms." "[But] what," he asked, "probably [would] be the language of the southern states on this point? They ha[d] neither men or vessels to export their own produce, nor d[id] they wish to have them, while their labourers [were] more advantageously employed, as," he thought "they [then] really [were] in the cultivation of wheat, Tobacco, Rice, Indigo, &c; each of [which made] a valuable article of exportation; as also the naval Stores, Flour and Iron with which," he said, "some of those states abound[ed]." "It [could] not be their wish to carry their own produce to market. Their interest rather suggest[ed] to them the importance of increasing the number of purchasers at their own market. They ha[d] felt the blessings of th[at] policy too long, willingly to relinquish it. [Hence,] they [would] not, in [his] opinion, soon shut their ports against so valuable a purchaser as the British merchant."

Such, in brief, were Benjamin Lincoln's views of the *economic* consequences of the South's exclusive addiction to agriculture. Lincoln found this aspect of the matter easy enough to understand, and he found no fault with the South's behavior in the premises. Its addiction to the slavery system, and that part of its behavior which constituted an emotional response to an inevitable *military* consequence of that system, however, were to Lincoln matters of a quite different character. "We are told," he said, with a skepticism born, no doubt, of his service in the South during the Revolution, "that such is the nature of the climate in the Southern States, that the necessary labor cannot be performed there, by white inhabitants, and that to import the blacks from Africa is a measure indispensable." "While these ideas are entertained by, and influence the actions of, the [Southern] states, Slavery," he predicted, "will be continued, and [those states, consequently] remain, in a degree, feeble and defenseless." "We might hence suppose," he very reasonably added, "that policy would suggest to them the propriety of their uniting firmly with the Northern States." "But it has had," said he, "quite a different operation. [The

Southern states] seeing and feeling their own inability, become jealous of the [Northern] States. The moment it is proposed to make the Northern carriers for the Southern States, they startle at the idea and immediately paint in their own minds fleets of ships from the Northern States blocking up their ports." And, had he known the fact, Lincoln might very well have added that James Madison, for one, had had such ideas and been guilty of such startling when he had been in Congress in 1781–83. Madison's letters show that he had then been greatly troubled, even before the Revolution was over, about the large number of ships and seamen that the Northern states had, and much worried, even *before* American independence had been won, about "what [was] to protect the Southern States, for many years to come, against the insults and aggressions of their northern brethren."[78] Lincoln, however, probably knew nothing of James Madison's particular notions, so he only added his own general view that "[the Southern states], at least some of them, suppose[d] that they ha[d] too much fear from the enterprising spirit of the Northern hive, to encourage their marine by making them carriers for the [Southern] States." "They [would], therefore, in [his] opinion, oppose every measure which [would] have a tendency to increase [the Northern] seamen, [though] they m[ight], and probably w[ould], give other reasons for their opposition, while their policy w[ould] not let them utter the true ones."

In view, therefore, of all the foregoing unfortunate considerations, Lincoln could not convince himself that, "while [the] doings [of Congress remained] only recommendatory in their nature," it would do any good "to extend the powers of [that body, even] to the utmost limits contended for by the most sanguine on that side of the question." For the Southern states, in that event, would simply refuse to follow the recommendations of Congress upon commercial matters, just as the states in general had refused to follow them in the past upon other matters universally admitted to fall within congressional competence. "A coercive power" for Congress, and "the means uncontroulable by the United States, of carrying [its] powers into effect" would, Lincoln admitted, be a different matter. But since he could, at the time he wrote, perceive no likelihood that any such powers would be given to Congress, he also could see none of "surmount[ing] the evils under which [the country] labor[ed]" except, he said, "by a division" and the formation of a competent government within each of the resulting parts.

The conclusion thus reached by General Lincoln was a melancholy one, indeed, but it was a conclusion, nevertheless, that had already been reached, at the time he wrote, by many other leading men from the New England region. The Virginia proposal of the Annapolis convention arrested, temporarily, the tendency toward disunion that was involved in such views. But the truth about the Virginia proposal was soon discovered; and the reaction that followed, together with deepening depression in the Northern states, and the continuing recalcitrance upon other matters displayed by the South, added so greatly to the number of men, not only from New England but from the Middle states, who came regretfully to the same conclusion, that, before the arrival of the date set for the Annapolis convention, the continuance of the Union had become seriously endangered. Only then was the South brought around. The principal cause of this eventual change in the Southern attitude was probably a belated recognition of those considerations of safety which Benjamin Lincoln had thought policy would have suggested to the Southerners long before. Besides this cause there were a number of others of a contributory character, without which, in all probability, the change in the South's attitude could never have occurred. To an account of those causes, little considered in American histories, and an analysis of the nature of certain little-known obstacles to governmental reform which had come into existence in certain of the Northern states, our attention will presently be turned.

CHAPTER XVI

The Movement in Congress for Commercial Power: Herein of the Monroe Committee's Report of 1785

THE popular agitations of 1785 and the various proceedings recounted in the foregoing chapters all took place without any official intimation from the Continental Congress that any commercial powers were desired or needed beyond those requested by that body on April 30, 1784. Toward the end of 1784, however, a committee had been appointed in Congress "for giving to the United States *the general regulation of trade*."[1] This committee consisted originally of John Jay, of New York; Elbridge Gerry, of Massachusetts; James Monroe, of Virginia; Richard Dobbs Spaight, of North Carolina; and William Houston, of Georgia. The commitment was renewed, however, on January 24, 1785, and at that time Jay was replaced by William Samuel Johnson, of Connecticut.[2] About six weeks later, Rufus King, of Massachusetts, took the place of Elbridge Gerry.[3] With the exception of Jay and Monroe, all these men, it is important to note, were afterwards members of the Federal Convention.

The committee submitted its report on February 16, 1785.[4] The report proposed an amendment of the ninth of the Articles of Confederation so as to vest in Congress the "sole and exclusive" power of "regulating *the trade of the States, as well with foreign Nations, as with each other*, and of laying such imposts and duties upon imports and exports as might be necessary for the purpose." The proposed new power, however, was to be subject to four provisos: (1) Americans should in no instance be subjected to higher imposts and duties than foreigners; (2) the state legislatures should be free to prohibit the importation or exportation of any species of goods or commodities whatsoever; (3) all duties imposed by the Congress under the recommended power should be collected under the authority, and accrue to the use, of the state in which they were payable; and (4) every act passed in pursuance of the proposed new power must have the assent of nine states in Congress.[5]

A few weeks later, on March 11, Congress called upon the committee to draw up a letter to be sent to the states, recommending the proposals made by the committee.[6] James Monroe first appears at this time as the chairman of the committee, though he may have become such somewhat earlier. On March 28, the committee reported a letter such as Congress had asked.[7] The

237

letter quite naturally dwelt upon the current difficulties in foreign trade which at the moment constituted the most urgent reason for asking for commercial power; and apart from one reference to the "*internal* arrangements" necessary to comply with treaties, and another reference to the necessity of "concert in the *system of policy*, which [might] be necessary to frustrate the designs of those powers who were lay[ing] injurious restraints on [American] trade," the letter, as distinct from the report of February 16, contained nothing which appertained to the internal phase of commercial regulation.

For students of the subject, these facts have apparently had the effect of generally minimizing the importance of the power over internal commerce proposed by the committee; and, together with certain changes in word usage which subsequently occurred, they have made it easy for latter-day writers to assume that the whole grant of power proposed by the committee was no more than a power of regulating foreign and interstate trade. There is, however, no known evidence that, at the time it was suggested, the proposed new power was understood in this incomplete and un-"general" sense. The evidence, instead, shows that it was understood in Congress at the time as in substantial accord with the purpose for which the committee had been appointed; and since there is, under eighteenth-century usage, nothing in the language employed by the committee which requires the assumption that its members had proceeded without regard to the terms of its appointment, the case for the common view as to the scope of the proposed new power apparently reduces to one of present-day word usage only.

The reports in the Continental Congress—i.e., the Monroe committee report of 1785,[8] and the grand committee report of 1786[9]—proposed the vesting of the Continental Congress with the "sole and exclusive" power of "regulating *the trade of the states, as well with foreign nations as with each other*." The italicized words are apparently generally read at the present day as signifying "foreign and interstate trade." In the known contemporary references to the reports in Congress (most of which relate to the Monroe committee's report, rather than to the report in the same terms by the grand committee), there appears no evidence whatever that the commercial proposal contained in them was currently so understood. To the contrary, there is a most impressive amount of evidence in these references that, subject only to its minor provisos, the men in Congress understood the report of the Monroe committee as a substantial performance of the commitment which they had made to the Monroe committee. In other words, the report was understood as proposing a recommendation to the states "for giving to the United States *the general regulation of trade*."[10]

In point of fact, there is not to be found, among contemporary references to this proposal, so much even as a mention of what we today call "interstate commerce," except in a single case. The lone reference to this now familiar subject is contained in a letter which William Samuel Johnson, of Connecticut, wrote to Jonathan Sturges, also of Connecticut, on January 26,

1785.[11] The letter was written by Johnson just two days after he took the place on the Monroe committee previously held by John Jay.[12] In his letter Johnson informed Sturges that it was "in contemp[latio]n [in Congress] to ask of the States to invest Congress with the Power of regulating their Trade as well with foreign Nations *as with each other*."* "The first," he said, "[was] conceiv'd necessary in order to carry into effect the Treaties made and to be made with foreign Powers, the other to prevent Dissentions *between State and State* which might indanger the Union." He then went on to point out that the second provision "might probably overturn the System Conn[ecticu]t ha[d] adopt'd as rela[tiv]e to N[ew] Y[ork], which, it [was] said, [New York would] counteract by regulat[ion]s of her Assembly [then] convening." From the mode of this statement it would appear that the Monroe committee at that date had not yet determined to recommend to Congress that the national power be made "sole and exclusive." But Johnson added, with probable reference to this ultimate recommendation, that "the Idea of many seem[ed] to be that *Comm[erc]e between S[tate] and S[tate]* sho[ul]d be absolutely free." In this statement by Johnson, the phrase "Commerce between State and State" was a plain reference to what we know today as "interstate commerce"; and, consequently, a modern mind finds it easy to assume that this phrase and the phrase of the Monroe committee's report, which Johnson used initially in his letter, were phrases of identical meaning. It is important to observe, however, that Johnson did *not* say this. Instead, he simply spoke of the prevention of interstate "Dissentions," and the establishment of interstate "free trade," as motives which had let to the proposal for investing Congress with power to regulate "the trade of the states with each other." Those motives were entirely consistent with a request by Congress for power over the entire internal, or domestic, commerce of the country; they were, in fact, *much more* consistent with such a request than they were with what Congress is usually supposed to have had in mind. If the men in the Continental Congress deplored intergovernmental "Dissention" in the regulation of commerce (as Johnson implied they did), it is difficult to believe that they would have proposed as a remedy for the "Dissention" which then existed "between State and State" any scheme of power which, without doing away with anything more than a fraction of the "Dissention between State and State," would be certain to result in future "Dissention" of a similar kind between the states and the nation. That "Dissention" in the regulation of the commerce of this country has in fact been the result under the scheme of power which it is generally assumed these men proposed, we know from long experience under the Supreme Court's theories; and since the men in the Continental Congress were rational men, trying (according to Johnson) to get away from essentially similar conditions at the time they acted, it is extremely unlikely, apart from the affirmative surviving evidence of what they

---

*These italics, but not those that follow, indicate underlining in the original letter.

thought they did, that they ever so much as thought of, let alone adopted, a scheme of divided power over the country's internal, or domestic, commerce.

Besides Johnson, there were several other men in Congress in the spring and summer of 1785 who wrote letters referring to the Monroe committee report in substantially the same terms as those used by the report itself, but without adding anything that gives a clue to the sense in which they understood the proposals contained in the report.[13] Some other men in Congress wrote letters referring to the report as proposing that Congress be empowered to regulate "the trade of the United States"[14] or "the trade of the Continent."[15] Prima facie, these expressions covered all "trade," internal as well as external. In addition to such letters, which referred specifically to the Monroe report, there were some others, during the same period, which referred more generally to the desire in Congress, or to the writer's own view, or disagreement with the view, that Congress should be invested with "the power of regulating trade";[16] with "power to regulate commerce";[17] or with "the power to legislate over the trade of the Union."[18] It is to be noted, more particularly, that Richard Henry Lee wrote to some other Virginian, in the fall of the year, that, in his opinion, "the Staple States should be feelingly alive to *the proposed plan* of vesting *powers absolute for the restraint and regulating of Commerce* in a Body of representatives"—that is, the delegates in Congress of the majority of eight Northern states and, probably, Maryland—"whose Constituents," said Lee, "[were] differently circumstanced [from the "staple" states]."[19] It is noteworthy, too, that a little earlier in the year David Howell, of Rhode Island, had written to the governor of his state, that "it seem[ed] to be the opinion *even of Congress*, or of a great majority thereof, that they ought to be vested with power *to regulate commerce generally*," and that "one plan" that was under consideration called for "an alteration of the confederation so as to vest Congress with *the power of regulating trade* without limitation of time."[20]

In evaluating the foregoing expressions, the reader should remember that they were used by the men in Congress at a time when the demand "out of doors" was for a "full and entire" national commerce power; for a national power over "both internal and external commerce"; for a national power extending to "the internal, as well as the external, commerce of all the states"; and the like.[21] It should be remembered, too, that some, at least, of these "outside" demands made specifically clear (if any clarification on the point was necessary) that what was desired was a general power to promote and govern the economic development and activities of the country. The most important of these "outside" demands—the letters of the Boston merchants, which had certainly made this point entirely clear—were, moreover, sent to Congress. They were read to that body on May 11, and thereupon ordered to lie upon the table "until Congress [should] take into consideration the report of [its] Committee [i.e., the Monroe committee], on an application to the States to invest Congress with *the power of regulating trade* under certain provisoes."[22] This order certainly sounds as if Congress understood that the Monroe committee had proposed that, subject only to "the provisoes," Congress be invested with "*the general regulation of trade*," as the committee had been directed to propose, and as the Boston merchants and other groups were asking should be done. In the light, then, of the entire circumstantial context, particularly the fact that the "outside" demands were unquestionably known to, and being watched by, the men in Congress, it is extremely difficult to believe that the sweeping terms contained in the letters then being written by members of Congress were carelessly used.

Nevertheless, it may be conceded for the sake of the argument that, devoid as the foregoing letters are of any evidence of an intended interstate limitation, the sweeping expressions in them do not *specifically* indicate that the Monroe committee's report was understood to extend to what lawyers know today as "intrastate commerce." It is also a fact that, apart from certain letters of the committee's chairman (which will presently be considered separately), there is only one known letter from a member of Congress, during the period in question, which contains anything *specifically* contradictive of an intended interstate limitation. That lone letter was written by David Howell, of Rhode Island, to William Greene, governor of that state, on February 9. In his letter, Howell referred to the Monroe committee as then having under consideration a proposal "to vest Congress with power to regulate both foreign and *coast wise* trade."[23] The "coast wise trade," as the reader is most probably aware, and as the act passed for its regulation during the Washington administration clearly demonstrates, was not a trade which was exclusively interstate in character. Howell's letter, therefore, seems rather clear evidence that no interstate limitation was intended, at the time he wrote. As for the suggestion of some possible maritime limitation, which his letter may be thought to contain, this—if it *was* intended when Howell wrote—was dropped by the Monroe committee, for the committee's report contained no suggestion of any kind of maritime limitation. We may add that Howell's later letter to his governor, mentioned above, shows quite certainly that, in Howell's understanding, a "power to regulate commerce *generally*" was the thing which eventually was proposed by the Monroe committee. Additional corroboration of this view is to be seen in the action of the Rhode Island legislature, in October, in passing the act which it afterwards described as intended to confer upon Congress "the *whole and sole* power of passing laws for the regulation of trade."[24]

The various foregoing letters, all devoid of evidence that an interstate limitation was intended in the Monroe committee's report, and, on the other hand, all entirely consistent with and, indeed, very favorable to the view that a whole power over commerce (subject to the provisos) was the thing in contemplation, are the only known evidence as to how the Monroe committee's report was currently understood by the men in Congress, apart from certain letters on the subject written by the chairman of the committee,

James Monroe himself. Monroe's letters about the committee on commercial powers begin in December 1784, a few days after the committee was first appointed. His first letter on the subject was written to James Madison, on December 18. All that appears from this initial letter is that the original appointment of the committee was the result of a proposal to recommend to the states the investing of Congress with "power to regulate the commercial intercourse of the States with other Powers."[25] The actual commitment—or, at any rate, the recommitment on January 24, 1785—however, was "for giving to the United States *the general regulation of trade*";[26] and the report,[27] as previously indicated, proposed (subject to four separate provisos) that Congress be invested with the "sole and exclusive" power of "regulating the trade of the States, *as well with foreign nations as with each other*," and of "laying such imposts and duties upon imports and exports, as [might] be necessary for the purpose."* One of the four provisos attached to the report stipulated that the consent of nine states in Congress should be requisite to the passage of all commercial regulations. This was put in to please the South, since, by the terms of the proviso, at least one Southern state would have had to consent before any use could have been made of the proposed new power. Some of the Southern states were dissatisfied with this security, and wished to raise the required number of consenting states to eleven.[28] Although these facts throw much light upon the conditions under which the Southern delegates were at that time willing to agree to a national commerce power, this first proviso to the Monroe commitee's report, generated by the South's reluctant attitude, is not of any direct importance in seeking to determine the sense in which the report was understood. A second proviso in the committee's report imposed a minor qualification upon the commercial duty power that was to be given to Congress; a third proviso reserved to the several states the power of prohibiting absolutely the importation into their respective territories, or the exportation therefrom, of any species of goods or commodities whatsoever.† These two provisos, particularly the latter, should be kept carefully in mind in seeking to interpret certain of Monroe's remarks in his letters about his committee's report. The remaining proviso, which stipulated that all duties should be collected under the authority, and accrue to the use, of the state wherein they were payable, is also important for the same purpose, since this proviso affords a key to the meaning of certain remarks of Monroe's, which otherwise might possibly be unintelligible. With these various provisions of the Monroe committee's report clearly in mind, we may turn to the remaining letters Monroe wrote concerning it.

The committee's initial report containing the foregoing proposals was submitted on February 16, 1785.[29] In a supplemental report of March 28, the

---

*This reserved power was afterwards cut down by the grand committee of 1786 to a power to lay embargoes in times of scarcity. Journals, XXXI, 494, 495.

†The reasons for specifying the "impost and duty" power undoubtedly grew out of the character of the pre-Revolutionary controversy with Great Britain.

committee added a covering letter to be sent with its proposals to the legislatures of the states.[30] About a fortnight later, Monroe wrote a letter to Thomas Jefferson, enclosing a copy of the committee's report, which he described to Jefferson as intended "for the purpose of investing Congress with *almost the entire* regulation of *the commerce of the Union*, to the exclusion of the particular States."[31] It will at once be apparent to the reader that, *if* the qualifications contained in the second and third of the above mentioned provisos to this committee's report were the only substantive qualifications of the commercial power which the report proposed for Congress, Monroe's description of the purpose of the report was entirely appropriate. On the other hand, if the report contemplated, *besides* those qualifications, the further qualification that there should likewise be excluded from the proposed new congressional power all the intrastate commerce of each and every state, constituting, of course, in total, the great bulk of the country's commerce, then Monroe's mode of describing the report seems, to say the least, a rather strange one. If this letter of Monroe's stood alone, the mode of description which he adopted in it might, even upon such a view, be explained away. It might be said that the popular agitations for a "full" national commerce power had not really begun on April 12, the date of Monroe's letter;[32] that his words, perhaps, were not intended to relate to the whole of his committee's report, but only to the *foreign* commerce power provided in it; that, in a certain sense, only the *foreign* commerce *of the states* was "*the* commerce *of the Union*"; and that Monroe's language, therefore, was merely careless. Such an interpretation of Monroe's letter seems, of course, a little farfetched, since we have had a good many examples of the use of Monroe's phrase in a general sense,[33] and it would be somewhat odd if his general description had been intended to refer to a part of the report, *only*. If his letter of April 12 did stand entirely alone, the possibility of the foregoing explanation of the phrase which Monroe employed might perhaps be conceded. We may therefore pass on, only noting that Monroe also observed to Jefferson, in this initial letter, that "the alteration wh[ic]h [the] report propose[d] in the whole system of [American] gov[ernment] [would] be great"; that "it [was] in fact a radical change of it."[34]

The next letter to be noted is one which Monroe wrote to Jefferson on the following June 16. In this second letter, Monroe referred to the report made by his committee as having proposed "the *absolute* investment of the U.S. with *the controul of commerce*."[35] In this description, which ignores the provisos as inconsequential, the reader will observe that the qualification "of the Union" has disappeared. Monroe speaks of "commerce" without any suggestion of a limitation, and yet he speaks of "the absolute investment of the U.S." with the "controul" of it. The foregoing hypothetical explanation of Monroe's phraseology in his first letter to Jefferson therefore fails, and the completeness of its failure will be apparent to the reader when he remembers that Monroe, as well as the other men in Congress, knew by June 16, 1785, of the demands from the Eastern and Middle states for "full" power in Congress extending to "the internal, as well as the external, commerce of all the states." As already noted, the Boston merchants' letters had been received in Congress and read to that body on May 11; and of course those letters and many other items of similar import had by that time appeared in the newspapers at New York where Congress was sitting.

The failure with respect to this second Monroe letter of the hypothetical explanation suggested with respect to his earlier letter also seems clear if Monroe's further remarks in his second letter are considered. We may begin with his view, expressed therein, that his committee's report would remedy what he considered a very serious defect in the existing governmental arrangements: the fact that "the political economy of each State [was] entirely within its own direction." "The effect of [the] report," said Monroe, "w[oul]d be to put *the commercial economy* of every state *entirely* under the hands of the union." "The measures necessary to obtain the carrying trade, to encourage domestic by a tax on foreign industry, *or any other ends which in the changes of things* bec[a]me necessary, [would then]," said Monroe, "depend *entirely* on the Union."[36] In assessing the evidential value of these remarks, we should note, to begin with, that they establish that Monroe understood a power "to regulate commerce" as involving, in some degree, the power to "direct" the *"political* economy" of a state or nation.

The question remains, in what degree and in what sense did he suppose this power to be involved in what his committee had proposed; or, in other words, what Monroe meant when he said that "the effect of [the committee] report w[oul]d be to put the *commercial* economy of every state *entirely* under the hands of the union." Here the reader may once more be reminded that the term *"political* economy," according to Adam Smith (to whom, it is interesting to note, Monroe referred in his letter), was used, in the period in which we are interested, to signify that "branch of the science of the statesman or legislator" which sought: "first, to provide a plentiful revenue or subsistence for the people [of a state], or more properly to enable them to provide such a revenue or subsistence for themselves; and secondly, to supply the state or commonwelath with a revenue sufficient for the public services."[37] More shortly stated, a nation's "political economy" included, in the eighteenth century, both its system of "finances" or "taxes," and its system of "public commerce" or "commercial regulations." This usage was the accepted usage among "commercial writers" at the time, and the usage appears to have been quite generally understood among the Americans of the period. The term *"commercial* economy," appearing in the foregoing remarks by Monroe, was also employed occasionally to signify a nation's "commercial system," as distinct from its entire "political economy" which included its "taxes" and other fiscal arrangements. In this connection, it should also be remembered that in its general sense the word "economy" meant, and still means, "a system of order, or government, or management, or regulation";[38] and that the word "political," in its technical eighteenth-century sense, included things which were not "commercial" even in the most extensive sense which "commercial" had in English usage.[39] In the quoted passage from his second letter to Jefferson, then, Monroe was simply saying that, under the scheme of his committee's report, "the Union" would take over "entire" control of the "political economy" of the states, with the exception of their fiscal arrangements. That exception appertained, of course, to the proviso in his committee's report that all duties imposed by "the Union" *for the regulation of commerce* should be collected under the authority, *and accrue to the use*, of the state wherein they were payable.[40] In addition, it may have appertained to the fact that, in all other ways, the report left the fiscal arrangements of the states entirely unaffected. As Monroe had said to Jefferson in an earlier letter, "the revenue & the regulation" were to be kept distinct.[41] With this fiscal exception, then, and subject to the relatively unimportant qualifications in the second and third of the committee's provisos, *the control over the "political economy" of the states*, which was to be given to Congress under the report of the Monroe committee, was, according to that committee's chairman, to be *absolutely complete*. This conclusion can only mean that "the trade of the states *with each other*" did *not* mean "interstate commerce" to James Monroe.

The correctness of this conclusion is additionally evinced by other remarks not yet quoted from Monroe's June 16 letter to Jefferson. In these further remarks, Monroe declared that "the expedience of the measure [for "the absolute investment of the U.S. with the controul of commerce"] turn[ed] on one point (especially to the Southern States): whether the obtainm[en]t of the carrying trade and extention of [American] National resources [were] an object." Monroe seemed to think that this question deserved an affirmative answer; that " 'the giving our own citizens a show in the carrying trade' " would, for example, be " 'otherwise advantageous than as it obtain[ed that] particular object' "; that, " 'in effect,' " it would " 'increase the value of land, the number of inhabitants, the proportion of circulating medium, and be the foundation [of] all those regulations which [were] necessary to turn what [was] call'd "the balance of trade" in our favor.' " "Yet an opinion," he added, "seem[ed] to be entertain'd by the late commerc[ia]l writers and particularly a Mr. Smith on the wealth of nations that the doctrine of the balance of trade [was] a chimera, in the pursuit of w[hic]h G[reat] B[ritain had] exposed herself to great injury." With this strange and radical opinion Monroe, however, seemed not greatly impressed. Neither was he impressed with Southern fears of Northern monopolies. "The regulation of the fishery," he pointed out to Jefferson, "[was] as much under [Congress's] contoul [by the terms of the report], *even without* the bounds of the State*, as the tob[acc]o of Virg[ini]a, and all the States [had] produce, so that [he was] inclin'd to hope that the productions of the South, though disproportionate to that of the East wo[ul]d

---

*So in the reprint of this letter, in Monroe's collected writings. The original of the letter has not been seen. "Even within" would seem more appropriate. Either reading, however, plainly implies intrastate power.

not induce . . . any unequal restrictions." "The subject [, however, was] of great magnitude, and [he] very earnestly desire[d] to hear [Jefferson's opinion] on it before it [should] obtain its fate."[42]

The reader will probably remember that Monroe finally decided to ask James Madison's opinion of his committee's report, as well as Thomas Jefferson's. This occurred after Monroe received from Madison the extremely localistic-sounding letter which, as we saw in the previous chapter, Madison wrote to Monroe on June 21, 1785. In Monroe's reply to Madison's letter may be found still further evidence that Monroe understood the commercial proposals of his committee's report in the sense above set forth, for in his reply Monroe referred to his committee's report as "propos[ing] to invest Congress with power to regulate trade *externally & internally*."[43] This description of his committee's report, almost repeating the words of the Boston merchants, whose letters Madison had referred to in his letter of June 21, will set at rest any lingering doubt that Monroe understood his committee's proposals in the sense that has been set forth. Madison answered Monroe's letter on August 7. The contents of his answer, taken with a letter which he wrote to Jefferson early in the fall, provides still further support for the conclusion we have already drawn upon the basis of Monroe's letters only. In his reply to Monroe, Madison vouchsafed his "abstract" belief that "the power of regulating trade, *to a certain degree at least*, ought to be vested in Congress."[44] The form of this concession would seem to evince that Madison understood the Monroe committee's report as proposing a *whole* power over trade; and his letter to Jefferson, dated October 3, confirms this view, for Madison spoke therein of the Monroe committee's report as "a proposition [which] ha[d] been agitated in Congress, [to] ask from the States *a general & permanent authority to regulate trade*."[45]

It remains only to add that, despite Madison's dissuasive letters of the summer of 1785, Monroe remained completely undisturbed in his view that "the absolute investment of the U.S. with the controul of commerce" was desirable. On January 19, 1786, he again wrote to Jefferson that in his opinion, "every expedient [was] unquestionably inferior to the *complete & absolute* controul over commerce in the hands of the U.S."[46] On the following September 3, he wrote to Madison, at Annapolis, that he "ha[d] always considered *the regulation of trade* in the hands of the U.S. as necessary to preserve the Union."[47] And although Monroe had some misgivings about the Constitution on other grounds, when it was before the country for adoption in 1787 and 1788, he adhered at that time to his old position on the subject of commercial power. He spoke of the desirability of adding to the powers of the existing Congress "the *absolute* controul of *commerce*";[48] and he seemed to believe that the Constitution would give to the new Congress "the *absolute* controul of *trade*."[49]

Such, then, is the remarkable body of evidence as to the views of James Monroe, the chairman of the congressional committee which submitted the report on February 16, 1785, proposing that Congress be invested with power to regulate "the trade of the States, as well with foreign nations as with each other." The evidence establishes not only the scope of the commercial power which, in Monroe's opinion, Congress *should* have, but also the scope of the power which in his opinion Congress *would* have by the terms of the report which his committee had made. The evidence points to but one possible conclusion as to Monroe's understanding of his committee's report, and the only conceivable obstacle to that conclusion is the language in which that report was cast. According to *our modern usage*, there can be no doubt that the words of the Monroe committee's report do mean, and so far as the present writers are aware can only mean, "foreign and interstate trade"; but according to the usage of Americans *in the eighteenth century*, this was not, or at any rate was not necessarily, the case. The key to the syntax of the committee's report, and to the otherwise puzzling remarks about it which Monroe and other men made, is provided by one of the passages heretofore quoted from the pamphlet entitled *The Political Establishments of the United States*. The passage referred to is that which defined "commerce" as "the correspondence and connections *of a nation* with other nations, *and with one another*."[50] The words "state" and "nation," as we already know, were both understood in a vivid multitudinal sense in the eighteenth century.[51] The syntax of the commercial proposal in the Monroe committee's report is, therefore, merely a pluralized form of the syntax of the passage just quoted from the pamphlet. Obviously the "one another" of the pamphlet *can* refer *only* to the individuals of "a nation." The "each other" of the committee report, as understood by Monroe and the other men in Congress, must have referred to *the individuals* of "the states." Very likely such a reference for the phrase "each other" in the committee's report will seem strange and improbable to most modern ears, but it is no stranger or more improbable than such locutions as "the state *are*," and "the state *have done*."[52] It is, moreover, a mode of speaking which manifestly depended upon the same psychological factor: the eighteenth century's vivid multitudinal understanding of the word "state." Unless such a reference is given to the phrase "each other" in the Monroe committee's report, it is impossible to account for all the sweeping statements made about that report by Monroe and the other men in Congress. It should be noted, too, by way of final corroboration, that proposals were offered in the Federal Convention for the casting of the Commerce Clause of the Constitution in the words which the Monroe committee's report had used, and the only known evidence as to the sense in which those proposals were understood in the Convention, points directly to the conclusion that they were understood in that body in precisely the same sense as the similar proposal in his committee's report had previously been understood by James Monroe.

The language of the report of the Monroe committee of 1785, and of the report of the grand committee of 1786, which simply repeated the language of the earlier report and cut down the provisos, is the only known evidence that could even possibly be taken to indicate that there was anything in the nature of a pre-Convention movement to invest Congress with power to regulate foreign and "interstate" commerce *only*. It will not be amiss to add that, while the Monroe committee's report was not communicated to the public until long after the Constitution was adopted, the grand committee report of 1786 did become known in the fall of that year,[53] and the only known public comment upon it tends to indicate that it was read as the Monroe committee's report was read in Congress. The comment in question appeared in *The* [Boston] *American Herald*, of February 20, 1787, one week after the grand committee's report had been published in that paper. Over the signature of "Sidney," the comment attacked the report as an attempt "to consolidate the several States into *one general Commonwealth*." The grand committee report contained, of course, other things besides the commercial proposals to which this comment by "Sidney" may perhaps have related. However, considering the general sense of what "Sidney" said; the sense which the word "consolidate" then commonly had;[54] the scope of "a power to regulate commerce" as then understood; and the fact that "Jonathan of the Valley," in *The* [Boston] *Independent Chronicle*, in the year before, had made an exactly similar attack upon the proposal of a general commerce power as then made by the town of Boston,[55] such a reference for "Sidney's" remarks seems by far the most probable. In this connection, the reader should bear in mind that in his letter to Jefferson of April 12, Monroe himself had said of his report that "the alteration w[hic]h [it] propose[d] in the whole system of [American] gov[ernmen]t [would] be great."[56] The Monroe committee's report contained, of course, nothing but the commercial proposal. Yet Monroe added, in that first letter to Jefferson, that his committee's report was "in fact a radical change of the whole system of gov[ernmen]t."[57] This view seems manifestly in line with the views of "Sidney" and "Jonathan of the Valley"; and that the views of all three men were approximately justified, we know from the vast array of evidence we have had, as to the comprehensive sense in which "commerce" as *an object of government* was then understood.[58]

The two foregoing congressional committee reports of 1785 and 1786 constitute the only known evidence that might be regarded as establishing the existence of a pre-Convention movement for a national commerce power extending to foreign and "interstate" commerce *only*. There was, however, one solitary item, signed "Acirema", originating in *The* [Boston] *Massachusetts Gazette* of May 1, 1786, that was phrased in such terms as would no doubt indicate, to most modern readers, a desire on the part of the writer of the item for a power over commerce of that precise kind. The item, it should be emphasized, is unique, being the only one of its kind found in all the long public discussion of the subject of vesting commercial power in Congress, which stretched over the twelve years between the proposal of the Franklin plan of confederation in 1775 and the drafting and proposal of the Constitution in 1787. The item called upon the printers of the country to "rouse" the people to vest Congress with power "to regulate commerce *between the States*, and with foreign nations." The proposal, however, was also phrased as one for a power in Congress "to regulate the commercial system." Considering the sense in which "commercial system" was used in the eighteenth century, the two proposals could hardly have been equivalents *if* "commerce between the states" meant to the author of the item "interstate trade"; and since there is a good deal of other evidence tending to indicate that "commerce between the states" did not mean "interstate commerce," in the eighteenth century, it may be considered as at least doubtful what the author of this solitary item wanted.[59]

The situation with respect to the "interstate" issue, then, is shortly this: there is a total lack of reliable evidence of any pre-Convention movement to vest Congress with a commercial power extending to, *but limited to*, foreign and "interstate" commerce. The committee reports in Congress in 1785 and 1786, which have generally been regarded as justifying a contrary inference, appear in reality to be evidence of a well-developed movement for the creation of a "full" national power (excepting only certain minor provisos) extending to "the internal as well as the external commerce of all the states." It would, perhaps, be rash to conclude from all of this that *no* contemporary Americans understood these two congressional committee reports as later-day writers have understood them, but if they did, there is a singular lack of evidence indicating this, and a sweeping quality about the surviving comments upon the reports which seems extremely odd *if* the reports in Congress were narrowly understood. And if the reports in Congress *were* narrowly understood, the oddity of the surviving comment is in no way decreased by the character of what was being demanded at the time in the New England and middle states.

Part III

Politics and Events Leading up
to the Failure of the
Annapolis Commercial
Convention of 1786

CHAPTER XVII

Northern Fears of Southern Domination

WHEN the Monroe committee reported to Congress the letter to the states referred to in the preceding chapter, Tuesday, April 5, was assigned for considering it, along with the proposal of the new national power which that letter was intended to recommend.[1] The whole matter was repeatedly postponed, however, and not until July 13 did Congress get around to actually considering the subject. Two days were then devoted to it in committee of the whole, and more time later in the summer. No definite conclusion was reached, however, and, apparently by general consent, the matter was allowed to stand over. The motives for this inaction are rather fully set forth in certain letters written by James Monroe to Thomas Jefferson in the course of the spring and summer. The letters indicate that the friends of the report were in a quandary as to how they had best proceed in order to obtain for their proposal the approval of the thirteen state legislatures as the Articles of Confederation required; that they were extremely fearful of arousing opposition by too precipitate action; and that in the end they decided that the best thing they could do was to wait, in hope that public opinion would soon become even more aroused than it already was, by continuance of the business depression.[2]

These considerations that appear in the letters of James Monroe are also to be found in an exchange of letters that took place between two other members of the Monroe committee: Rufus King and Elbridge Gerry. Gerry had gone home to Massachusetts when King took his place on the committee early in March, and he did not return to Congress thereafter until the first week in July. During this period of Gerry's absence from Congress the exchange of letters with King took place. The first letter in the series worth noting is the one King addressed to Gerry on the first day of May. It conveyed the intelligence that news of the beginning commercial agitations in Boston had just reached Congress. "The flame," King predicted, "will communicate from State to State." "If this well-founded uneasiness is attended to by wise & moderate men, in the several States, it may be improved to purposes the most beneficial, to our national government, as well as to our national commerce." "You understand me," King concluded, "without my adding, too much precipitancy may injure us—moderation and delay have ever served our true interest."[3]

Eighteen days later, however, King had, characteristically, begun to worry, for in a letter he then wrote he confessed to Gerry his complete puzzlement as to "what [should] be done." "A very great uneasiness [was] discoverable," he agreed, "among the Merchants and Traders generally through the States, from the disordered condition of Commerce." "[But] eight States only ha[d] complied with the recommendation of the last year"—which in King's opinion was completely inadequate anyway—"for granting to Congress power [merely] to prohibit certain importations and exportations. Nothing, therefore, from [that] quarter [could] be expected." "[So,] what," he asked Gerry, "[could] be done?"[4] Written from Boston on May 27, Gerry's reply was reassuring in tone. Influenced, very likely, by that town's then recent instructions to its delegates to the General Court,[5] Gerry assured King that, in his opinion, the "commercial Evils" of the country would be be certain, sooner or later, to provide their own remedy. He added that he was not really sorry for the failure of the last year, since the recommendation then made, though the best, no doubt, that could then be obtained, was nevertheless, in his opinion, "vastly inadequate" to the needs of the country.[6]

A few weeks later Gerry returned to Congress, and a short while after his arrival there he and the other two Massachusets delegates received from Governor Bowdoin the letter which conveyed to them the General Court's instructions to move in Congress for "a Convention to revise the Confederation generally."[7] Those instructions, we know, the Massachusetts delegates disregarded, and in our prior reference to the subject we reserved the question of their motives for this inaction. The evidence from the letters of King and Gerry which have just been reviewed makes it clear that so far, at least, as they were concerned, the motive for the disregard of the General Court's instructions was not a want of desire to see commercial power vested in Congress. King and Gerry seem to have been genuinely anxious that Congress obtain such a power; their only concern was how best to proceed to obtain it.

To a certain extent, this cautious attitude regarding the procedure to be followed in seeking the desired national commercial power also appeared in the long letter of explanation which the Massachusetts delegates dispatched to Governor Bowdoin a short while after their receipt of the General Court's instructions.[8] One position taken in that letter was that any attempt to go beyond what the immediate situation imperatively required—i.e., any attempt to obtain for Congress anything more than merely temporary and limited commercial powers—might well result in total disappointment. "Whatever the Disposition of the States may be," the delegates admonished, "it can only be known by their Acts: but the different Views which they have had of the Subject give Reason to suppose, that some Legislatures will think temporary commercial powers eligible under present Circumstances; and should this be the Opinion of but one, an attempt immediately to delegate perpetual commercial powers, must fail, and may prevent a delegation of temporary powers." "In politics as in private Life," the delegates concluded, "by aiming at too much, we oft-times accomplish nothing."[9]

This part of the Massachusetts delegates' joint letter to Governor Bowdoin seems, beyond serious question, to have been a statement of a genuine reason for their failure to act upon the General Court's instructions. It accords in considerable degree with the contents of the confidential letters between King and Gerry of a few weeks before and it is difficult to say, particularly in view of the state of sentiment in the Southern states, that the delegates' judgment as to the complete unfeasibility of the General Court's proposal as a means for obtaining the desired commercial power was wrong in all the circumstances then obtaining.

The other "reasons" they gave for their failure to act, however, were of a rather different character. One of these other "reasons" was that the General Court's proposal was in every way premature: it was too soon in the life of the Confederation, they said, to know what changes in its Articles were desirable. Another "reason" was that the mode of change suggested by the General Court was "not [the mode] *expressly*** pointed out by the Articles of Confederation": strictly speaking, the suggested mode might not be unconstitutional, but it was at least not a mode that would be binding upon Congress, and, hence, all the proposed trouble might turn out in the end to have been taken for nothing. Still another "reason," and the one they dwelt upon the most, was the extremely great danger which they said the "calling a Convention to revise the Confederation *generally*"* would involve.

Such a step might, and very probably would, they declared, produce " a Report which would invest Congress with powers that the honorable Legislature [had] not the most distant Intention to delegate": powers that would convert the existing system of American government into "an Aristocracy": a form of government that would "require a standing Army, and a numerous Train of pensioners and placemen to prop and support its exalted Administration." Under such a government there would be establishments for life, and honors and establishments even for the posterity of those who recommended themselves to it. "These [were] pleasing prospects, which republican Governments [did] not afford. And it [was] not to be wondered at, that many persons of elevated Views and idle Habits in these States [were] desirous of the Change." "Plans," declared the delegates, had been "artfully laid" and "vigorously pursued" with precisely this end in view. "Those plans [were] frustrated, but the same Spirit remain[ed] in their Abettors: And the Institution of the Cincinnati, honourable and beneficent as the views [might] have

*The delegates' emphasis.

been of the Officers who compose[d] it, [would] have," they "feared," "if not totally abolished, the same fatal Tendency." The Massachusetts delegates were "for increasing the power of Congress as far as it [would] promote the Happiness of the people, but at the same Time [were] of Opinion that every Measure should be avoided which would strengthen the Hands of the Enemies to a free Government." And, they very plainly intimated, the delegates could not but think that the General Court's proposal was a measure which would have precisely that most unhappy tendency.[10]

The foregoing "reasons" undeniably sound very much like the vaporings of such newspaper demagogues as "Jonathan of the Valley";[11] and since the Massachusetts delegates, and especially Rufus King, were not exactly men of the character of "Mr. Jonathan," it is difficult to accept their joint letter in its entirety as an actual statement of the real reasons that impelled them to the conduct purportedly explained by their letter. Instead, their letter sounds more like a hodgepodge of all the "reasons," good and bad, that the delegates could think of as at all likely to appeal to or frighten any credulous member of the General Court. Their letter is good evidence that the Massachusetts delegates were opposed to the General Court's proposal of "a Convention to revise the Confederation *generally*,"* but since the "reasons" they adduced in support of their views were on the face of things rather foolish reasons, and the Massachusetts delegates were not very foolish men, a strong inference arises that there must have been some other, better reason for their opposition than the "reasons" they actually gave. This probability, furthermore, is very greatly enhanced by the fact that, despite the intense desire in Massachusetts that commercial and other powers be vested in Congress, the Massachusetts General Court eventually concurred in their delegates' views, and retracted their instructions to move for a general constitutional convention. This did not occur, however, until the following November 25.[12] By that time, Samuel Holten, one of the three Massachusetts delegates in Congress, had returned to Massachusetts, and the General Court, or some of its members, had undoubtedly heard from Holten, by word of mouth, the true reason for his own and King's and Gerry's position.[13]

Further good ground for belief that the Massachusetts delegates had some reasons, other and better than those they gave to justify their seemingly strange inaction is afforded by the fact that so levelheaded a Massachusetts man as Theodore Sedgwick, of Stockbridge, should have come around to their views after just twelve days spent in Congress in the following December. In the preceding June, Sedgwick had been elected as a delegate to Congress, but he did not appear there until December 12.[14] For this purpose he apparently had departed from Massachusetts before November 25; at any rate he had departed without knowing that the General Court had on that date retracted its instructions to move for a general convention.[15] Taking his

---

*The delegates' emphasis.

place in Congress on December 12, Sedgwick continued in attendance there until December 24,[16] whereupon he returned to Massachusetts. Upon his arrival in Stockbridge, and still apparently unaware of the General Court's action of November 25, Sedgwick wrote to Caleb Davis in Boston to report how he felt, after his brief attendance in Congress, about the General Court's proposal of a general convention. Davis, as the reader will remember, had been one of the leading members of the Boston merchants' committee of the preceding spring, and was, when Sedgwick wrote to him, one of the Boston delegates in the General Court under the instructions from the town which we have already noted, and personally just as anxious as he had been in the spring to see commercial power vested in Congress. "The delegates of [the] Commonwealth," Sedgwick explained to Davis, "ha[d] as yet done nothing respecting the instructions of the general court which were designated to procure a revision of the articles of confederation." "Whether the delegates' reasons [were] or [were] not conclusive, the general court [would] determine." "But [could] it be [the] wish [of that body]," Sedgwick strangely asked, "to submit whether the great outlines of the federal constitution [i.e., the Articles] founded in democratical principles sh[ould] be subject to a change and alteration? and might not laying the Subject open to free discussion give birth to new hopes of *an aristocratical faction*—which," he broadmindedly added, "every community possess[ed]?" And then, although his suggestions did not on their face appear to require it, Sedgwick carefully stipulated that he "only propose[d] these queries to [Davis's] private consideration & ma[d]e them to [him] in perfect confidence." "At the same time, [he was] as clearly of opinion as any one," he said, "that it [was] greatly the interest of *the northern States* that Congress should be impowered to regulate our commerce"; and in addition that there ought to be "some more sure mode to supply the Treasury."[17] In this connection, it is significant that Rufus King had likewise written Davis, on November 3, that "the [Massachusetts] delegates [at that date in Congress were] of opinion that the Confederation want[ed] additional commercial powers, and some other additions and alterations." "But if once a power is brought into Existence," King solemnly warned, "who may *generally* revise the confederation, farewel to the present Republican plan."[18] Since Sedgwick's letter was almost an exact repetition of these sentiments of King's, it is perfectly clear that Sedgwick, after only twelve days' attendance in Congress, had come around completely to the views entertained by King and the other Massachusetts delegates. The same thing had happened in the case of Nathan Dane, upon his appearance in Congress, a little earlier than Sedgwick, as we may also infer from the tenor of Sedgwick's letter as this related to the sentiments of the state's delegates then in Congress.

All this bears on the probable significance to Davis of Sedgwick's letter. So does the fact that, even before he had received King's letter of November 3, Davis had received from him another letter, in which King had told him that, "in addition, to the ideas [which the Massachusetts delegates had] communicated in [their] joint letter [to the governor, of September 3], there [were] many reasons in favor of [their] Opinion, which [it] would [have been] improper to have communicated, but which in [their] opinion [were] of great weight."[19] In this other letter, King did not tell Davis what these "additional reasons" were, but in a letter he had written on September 17 to Nathan Dane, while Dane had still been in Boston, King had hinted so broadly at the nature of these "additional reasons" that we shall have no difficulty in inferring them. King's letter to Dane may very probably have been seen by Davis, but whether it had been or not, it seems certain that Sedgwick's letter to Davis, with its apparently groundless repetition of the Massachusetts delegates' fear of "an Aristocracy," must, to Davis, have meant more than Sedgwick's actual words expressed. At the very least, it must have meant to him that the "additional reasons" of which King had spoken in his letter in October really were, in Sedgwick's opinion, "reasons of great weight."

The clue to the nature of these "additional reasons" is contained in the letter King wrote to Dane on September 17. That letter, as the reader will have noted, was written just two weeks after the Massachusetts delegates' joint letter to the governor on September 3. King's purpose in writing to Dane was, he said, to request Dane "to re-examine the motives of the Legislature" in proposing a general convention. He asked Dane to take a look at the delegates' joint letter to the governor and, assuring Dane that he was himself in favor of vesting commercial power in Congress "under proper restrictions, and for a limited Time," he reiterated his opinion that "a convention of Delegates for the express purpose of *a general revision of the confederation*" was a dangerous measure. "The report," he warned, "[would] certainly be a confederation *less republican* than the present one. The large states when the present confederation [had been] adopted, [had] objected to the admission of the smaller ones upon equal rights with themselves. The surrounding Dangers at that period, [had] induced *these States** to give up their objections, and the small States [had] c[o]me in with rights equal to the large ones. But at this time, [were] the question again opened to decision, the same objections would be made, the real inconvenience experienced, *and the increasing principals of aristocracy* would strengthen them; and we should by the measure be thrown," he thought, "into total dissension."[20] The foregoing certainly seems on its face an extraordinary statement for a Massachusetts man to make: that the dreaded danger in the General Court's proposal was that it might lead to a departure from the then existing *un*republican system, whereunder the tiny state of Rhode Island counted in Congress for as much as Massachusetts, which was at that time—reputedly at least—the largest body of freemen in the Union.[21] King's final words tend, it is true, to indicate that *all* he feared was "dissension." This "red herring," however, should not obliterate from

---

*King's emphasis.

our minds King's initial statement in his letter: that a departure from the equality of *state* votes in Congress, presumably in the direction of a system of *state* votes therein proportioned to the respective numbers of the several states, or their respective total wealths, or both, would be a system "*less republican*" than the existing system. Neither should it blur our recollection that King had initially stated that the demand for such a reform "would [now] be strengthened by the increasing principals of aristocracy." These strange statements, which King seemed to expect Nathan Dane would understand, surely require more than a childlike interpretation.

Dane replied to King on October 8, in a lengthy letter. In the main, it was an amplification of his view that "the general received opinion" in Massachusetts was "that Congress ha[d] not sufficient powers to controul the several parts of the Union for the General welfare of the whole," but that "the chief defects and difficulties" which the people of the state desired to see remedied, and which were mainly responsible for the General Court's instructions, were "the want of *a general and uniform power* lodged somewhere to levy and collect monies sufficient to discharge the demands against the United States, and *to regulate trade and commerce*." As for the delegates' joint letter to the governor, Dane said that he had not seen it, because the governor had for some time been absent on a trip to Maine. This fact is important as showing that Dane must have been commenting solely upon King's cryptic statements of September 17, when Dane in his answering letter admitted somewhat doubtingly that "perhaps we [i.e., Massachusetts] ha[d] proposed a most important measure to Congress on our federal policy, without having sufficiently considered *the interests and motives of the different States, of landed and commercial men, of Republican and Aristocratical politicians*, for inducing them to concur or not concur with us, and the consequences to which those interests and motives, called into action, [might] lead." At any rate, "few gentlemen," he was sure, "[had] contemplated the infinite hazard and difficulty there [was], generally, in enforcing a new, or altering the fundamental articles or compacts of government."[22]

In seeking to arrive at some sensible interpretation of King's statements to Dane in his letter of September 17, and of the foregoing comments by Dane upon them, we need to bear in mind that the Massachusetts politicians of the period did not follow the Virginians' practice[23] of writing letters in cipher about touchy political subjects. Because of this fact, and of the then generally prevalent fear that private letters might be pried into *en route*,[24] the Massachusetts men did not feel as free as the Virginians did in expressing themselves on paper about such subjects. Consequently, the Massachusetts men's letters have to be read more carefully, and read with an eye to meanings which are at times only vaguely suggested in them. In the same connection, we do well to bear in mind that neither Rufus King nor Nathan Dane was a member of the demagogic faction in Massachusetts and, we may add, neither was Theodore Sedgwick. Instead, all three men were conservatives; able and sensible men; men of the kind who themselves were afterwards attacked by the demagogic faction as "aristocratic." Therefore, in interpreting their expressed fears of "Aristocracy" we need to find some fear, plausibly so described, which in the known general circumstances of the time was not a foolish fear, a fear, moreover, which was consistent with the known characters of these several Massachusetts men who felt it. The fear should also be one *not* communicated in the Massachusetts delegates' joint letter, and one which it "would [have been] improper," according to an eighteenth-century politician's notions of discretion, "to have communicated [in it]."

Beginning, then, with Dane's reply to King's letter, there appears in it a plain suggestion that, in Dane's understanding, the "Aristocracy" feared by King was one to be found, much more at least, in some states than in others, and that it was an "Aristocracy" connected with the "interests and motives" either of "landed men" or "commercial men." These things follow from Dane's reference to "the interests and motives of the different States, of landed and commercial men, of Republican and Aristocratical politicians, for inducing them to concur or not concur with [the General Court's proposal]." In interpreting Dane's words, however, we must bear in mind that both Nathan Dane and Rufus King were Massachusetts lawyers; that both men numbered prominent Massachusetts merchants—Stephen Higginson, Jonathan Jackson, and Caleb Davis—among their friends and correspondents[25] and, very likely, among their clients; and that Rufus King was shortly to marry into a prominent mercantile family of New York.[26] To suppose in the face of these facts that Rufus King feared—or that Nathan Dane for a moment supposed King feared—an "Aristocracy" of "commercial men" is ridiculous. It is equally ridiculous to suppose that King feared—or that Dane supposed King feared—an "Aristocracy" of the "landed men" (i.e., the independent farmers) of the New England states, New Jersey, or Pennsylvania. Something of a case might perhaps be made for the fear of a "landed Aristocracy" in New York and possibly in Delaware as well, but there can be little doubt the "landed Aristocracy" that Rufus King chiefly feared—and that Dane quite clearly understood that Rufus King feared—was the "landed Aristocracy" of the five slaveholding Southern states of the country. Despite a great deal of foolishness then and since written to the contrary, that was *the only* "Aristocracy" which actually threatened the country. In the circumstances existing in 1785, fear of it was not by any means a foolish fear; it was a fear that was consistent with, and honorable to, the characters of King and the other Massachusetts men who felt it; and it made complete good sense in Rufus King's letter to which Nathan Dane was replying. Furthermore, King's fear of the "landed Aristocracy" of the Southern states was not a matter explicitly communicated in the Massachusetts delegates' joint letter; and there can be little doubt it was a matter that Rufus King would have considered "improper to have communicated" in it.[27]

The circumstances of the time which evince the truth of all these statements are connected with certain notions then entertained regarding the geography and the political and economic future of the various parts of that great region between the Appalachians and the Mississippi which constituted "the West" of the America of 1785. Some of these notions are a little hard for Americans of the present day to credit, but there can be no doubt they were widely entertained at the time in question, and perhaps most particularly among Southerners. Thus, for one thing, the belief was rather widespread that a great part of what later became the Northwest Territory, comprising the present wealthy and populous states of Ohio, Indiana, Michigan, Wisconsin, Illinois, and a good part of Minnesota, was worthless land. This belief did not apply to the more southerly parts of the territory bordering along the Ohio River. The nature of the belief, and the parts of the territory to which it appertained, appear quite clearly in a letter written by James Monroe to Thomas Jefferson on January 19, 1786.[28] "My several routs westw[ar]d," Monroe told Jefferson, "with the knowledge of the country I have thereby obtain'd, have impress'd me fully with a conviction of the impolicy of our measures respecting it." It was proposed, he thought, by the resolution of Congress of April 23, 1784—in the drafting of which Jefferson had had a hand[29]—to divide the Northwest Territory into entirely too many separate districts or prospective states. "A great part of the territory," Monroe went on," is miserably poor, especially that near lakes Michigan & Erie & that upon the Mississippi & the Illinois consists of extensive plains w[hic]h have not had from appearances & will not have a single bush on them, for ages." "The districts therefore within w[hic]h these fall," said Monroe, "will perhaps never contain a sufficient number of Inhabitants to entitle them to membership in the confederacy, and in the meantime, the people who may settle within them will be gov[erne]d by the resolutions of Congress in w[hic]h they will not be represented." Such an arrangement, Monroe believed, would not be satisfactory to the few future settlers of these western regions; it would probably result in a weakening of their attachment to the rest of America, and in the end, perhaps, throw them back into British hands. Monroe therefore suggested to Jefferson that the districts or future states of the Northwest Territory should be reduced in number and increased in size. Such a change in the plans for the territory, he believed, would assure a greater diversity of interests among the people in each of the several districts; would weaken their future localism; hasten their entrance into the Union; and attach them permanently to it. Impressed with these and certain other more peculiarly southern ideas, Monroe moved in Congress that the plans for the territory be changed accordingly. As a result, a committee was appointed to consider his motion, which committee recommended in March, on the precise grounds among others which Monroe had urged upon Jefferson, taking the action he had proposed. Since Congress afterwards acted in pursuance of this recommendation on July 7 to reduce the number of prospective states in the Northwest Territory from the number originally contemplated to "not more than five, nor less than three," the probability appears to be that the beliefs entertained by Monroe regarding the future of the territory were beliefs which were rather generally held.[30] This probability is also evidenced by the fact that, although Monroe seemed in his letter to Jefferson to speak of the whole Northwest Territory from first-hand knowledge, his "several routs westward" had not in fact extended very far into the territory, and he had in fact visited very few of the places he mentioned.[31] This of course means that in his letter Monroe was really passing on to Jefferson the common hearsay of the time, and the inference again follows that the views he expressed were widely entertained.[32]

In sharp contrast with the views thus held of the worth and probable future of much of the territory north of the Ohio were the beliefs, then generally entertained by Southern men and without doubt to a considerable extent by others, respecting the quality and future of the lands lying south of that river, which were all still claimed as parts of four of the five Southern states of the time. Those lands were believed by the Southerners to be the fairest lands in the entire Confederation and certain to be, in the not too distant future, the country's most populous region. A fairly typical view was expressed in "a letter from a gentleman at Nashville, Cumberland River, to his friend at Hillsborough, North Carolina," published in *The* [Philadelphia] *Pennsylvania Packet*, on February 17, 1786. Referring to the soil of the Cumberland settlement, the letter writer said that it was "the richest on the continent of America." "[It] produce[d] tobacco, corn, wheat, &c., [and] rice and indigo could also be cultivated to advantage, though not yet attempted." "You have certainly heard," the writer went on, "of the fertility of Kentucky; yet our country is preferable, our climate being much warmer, and emigrants coming daily from thence to settle among us. We have every reason to expect that in a few years this country will be as thick settled as any part of America, by the number of persons flocking to us from Pennsylvania, Virginia, and the two Carolinas: not less than one thousand families have crossed the Appalachian mountains this fall, in order to settle here and at Kentucky." "[This] great number of [new] families that comes to us each fall, furnishes us," the letter went on, "with a market for our corn: our common crops are from sixty to eighty bushels per acre, and about 2500 lb. tobacco per ditto." "In what part of America," the letter writer finally asked, "can the planter meet with so many advantages?"

As the reader will easily see from the foregoing document, the sanguine Southern estimate of the more southerly lands was based in part upon a belief that those lands were warmer and more fertile; in part upon the fact that the most considerable western settlements of the time were in Kentucky and Tennessee; and in part upon the fact that those settlements were rapidly growing. In addition to these facts and beliefs about these southerly lands, some of which may seem to the reader to be nothing more than the natural enthusiasm and "puffing" of men already on the ground, there was one further, extremely important, and entirely indubitable fact: the more southerly of the western lands lay nearer to the Gulf. This advantage was also enjoyed to some extent by that part of the Northwest Territory lying along the north bank of the Ohio River, but the then current belief as to the uninviting character of most of the rest of that territory, and the extreme remoteness of much of it from saltwater, seemed to disqualify the larger part of that vast region as a future seat of *commercial* agriculture. Thence the inference drawn by Monroe and others that a great part of that territory would always be sparsely peopled. In this connection, the reader must remember that the time was one when railroads had scarcely been dreamed of. In the light of this fact, the Southerners' belief that the southerly lands had a great advantage over most of the northerly lands, thanks to their location, was by no means unreasonable. Moreover, the Southern men's judgment seemed to them definitely confirmed by the movements of population then in progress. As Pierce Butler, of South Carolina, observed in the Federal Convention, "the people & strength of America [were] evidently bearing Southwardly & S[outh]westw[ar]dly."[33] They were "swarming," said Madison, "from the North[er]n & middle parts of the U.S. to the Southern & Western."[34]

These statements by Madison and Butler are to be understood, of course, as relating not merely to migrations into the lands lying south of the Ohio, but also to migrations into the more southerly parts of the Northwest Territory along the Ohio River. In so taking these statements, however, it is worth bearing in mind that not until the July 13, 1787, was there any agreement between the states for the exclusion of slavery from the Northwest Territory.[35] Until that agreement had actually been made, there was considerable expectation among most, but not all, of the Southern men, and corresponding fear among the Northern men, that the South's system of slavery might be extended into the territory, and that the future inhabitants, at least of its choicer portions, might therefore become adherents and supporters of Southern politics. Something of what such a prospect must have meant to the men of the New England and Middle states may be surmised from a letter James Madison wrote to Thomas Jefferson on August 20, 1784.[36] "The vacant land of the United States lying on the waters of the Mississippi"—and this expression meant "on the river and its tributaries"—said Madison, "is perhaps equal in extent to the land actually settled." "If no check is given to emigrations from the latter to the former, they will probably keep pace *at least*," Madison predicted, "with the increase of [the American] people, till the population of both [regions] shall become nearly equal." As it was then generally—and, apparently, correctly—believed that the nation was doubling its population every twenty or twenty-five years, Madison concluded that *within that period* the development he was forecasting would probably be complete. This means, as Madison viewed the matter in 1784, that by some time between 1804 and 1809 "the West" would have "at least" half of the nation's population. If then as the Northern men feared and the Southern men hoped, "the West" became addicted to Southern politics, through introduction of the slavery system into "the West," the result would be that "the South," within the period mentioned, would, politically, have added to its population a number equal to the whole population of the country at the date when Madison wrote. Since at that date the South already numbered about two-fifths of the nation's population,[37] the further consequence would be that *by some time within the period between 1804 and 1809* "the South" and its politics would, in terms of numbers, have a preponderance over "the North" *of something like three to one.*

Perhaps to some readers it will seem incredible that views so extravagant as Madison's could possibly have been widely entertained, but the fact appears to be that they were. Support for this statement is provided by Southern declarations in the Federal Convention that the expected future Southern preponderance over the Northern states was precisely a preponderance of *three to one.*[38] Still more convincing is the acceptance by the Southerners in the Convention of a Constitutional guaranty of the South's "peculiar institution" *extending only through the year 1808*: they counted on the domination of the House of Representatives thereafter.[39] Based upon the indubitable co-gency of Southern action upon this subject, then, it is impossible to doubt that views such as Madison's were widely entertained. In the light of this very great preponderance that was otherwise expected by the Southern men, and the superior estimate that they put upon the more southerly parts of the then unoccupied territory, it seems a further certainty that an ample, early preponderance was still expected by the Southern men *after* the agreement for the exclusion of slavery from the Northwest Territory had been reached. Indeed, without the confident Southern expectation to this effect, it is dif-ficult to believe that the Southerners in Congress could ever have been pre-vailed upon to vote for such an agreement, or that the Southerners in the Convention could have been brought to accept the merely temporary guaranties for the South's "peculiar" system that were contained in the Con-stitution.

As the situation existed in 1785, then, the only flaw in this whole rosy dream of the Southern future was the fact that Spain was at the time still in the Floridas and Louisiana. The whole littoral of the Gulf, westward to the Mississippi and beyond, was in Spanish hands; in short, Spain was on both sides of the mouth of the river which, in the existing and prospective state of the art of transportation, was the only possible commercial outlet for much of the South's western region. There was, however, a right that had belonged to Americans as British subjects before their independence, a right to navigate the Mississippi from its source to the Gulf; in the peace of 1783, this right had been confirmed to Americans as Americans, so far as Britain could confirm it.

The Spaniards, it is true, denied that Britain had any right to confirm this right to Americans, but no American of the time concurred in this view, and there can be no doubt that in all their calculations the Southern politicians of 1785 counted heavily upon this American navigating right in the Mississippi as a means of attracting vast hosts of men into the western lands that were claimed by the Southern states. They counted, too, upon those hosts' becoming, in the natural course of things, "Southern" in their political views. To these expectations, there must be added the fact that most Southerners of the time undoubtedly looked forward to eventual American ownership of the Floridas, to say nothing of Louisiana and the other adjacent North American territory that Spain had. How could Spain, they reasoned, hope to hold the narrow neck and strip of land which were the Floridas, and thereby block up the mouths of the many rivers along the Gulf coast, when the Southern backlands along these rivers should be filled with Americans demanding access to the sea? When America should own the Floridas there would, of course, be even greater reason to expect that the Southern country would eventually, and at no very distant date, contain the majority of the American people and the majority of the national wealth, as well.[40]

Entertaining such pleasing views of the probable future, the South had particularly strong reasons for desiring a change from the existing system of *equal votes for the states* in Congress. In the situation then existing in Congress, the North was in a majority of eight states to five, and because of that majority, in a position technically to maintain indefinitely some kind of *state* majority within that body, through the veto over the admission of new states conferred by its existing majority.[41] On the other hand, if a change could be effected to some other scheme of representation in Congress, whether in proportion to numbers, or total wealth, or both of these combined, the South—it was confidently expected—would in a little while be in a position of dominance. Evidence of desire for such a change among Southern men, and of the sanguine expectations that underlay this desire, is to be found all through the materials surviving from the period. Proof of the desire and the expectations underlying it will therefore be accumulated for the reader as this discussion proceeds, but as a beginning of such proof we may here introduce a single, rather striking passage from a letter to Thomas Jefferson written by James Madison, about the middle of March 1787. In this letter Madison referred to the "expediency" of a change in "the principle of representation in the federal system." Such a change, he said, would be "just," and beyond that he was convinced that it would be "practicable." "A majority of the States," he triumphantly explained to Jefferson, "*conceive*[d] that they [would] be gainers by it. It [was] recommended to the Eastern States by the *actual* superiority of their populousness, and to the Southern by their *expected* superiority; and if a majority of the larger States concur[red], the fewer and smaller States [would have] finally [to] bend to them. This point being gained, many of the objections [then being] urged in the leading States against renunciations of power [to Congress would] vanish."[42] Madison thought so well of his analysis and was so certain of the obtuseness of "the Eastern states" that he repeated his views almost verbatim in a letter he wrote to Governor Randolph, of Virginia, about three weeks later,[43] and again, though without quite the same triumphant sectional emphasis, in a letter to Washington about a week after that.[44]

From these three Madisonian letters it is quite evident that a change to a popular basis of state representation or suffrage in Congress was a leading object with the Southern states at the period in question. It was a leading object thanks to their anticipation that, under such a system, the South's "expected superiority in populousness" over "the Eastern states"—or over "the Northern states," as Madison put it in his letter to Randolph—would in a short time enable the South *to rule the nation*. This being true, the reader will have no great difficulty in divining precisely what Rufus King had in mind when he said in his letter to Nathan Dane on September 17, 1785, that "the increasing principals of aristocracy"—i.e., the current increase in the numbers of men in the Southern states—"would strengthen the objections" against the existing system of *equal* votes *for the states* in Congress.

What may not be equally evident to the reader is the absolute truth of King's further statement, that any conceivable change from the existing *un*-republican system—whether to a system wherein *the states* voted in Congress in proportion to their respective numbers, to a system wherein *the states* voted in Congress in proportion to their respective total wealths, or to a system wherein *the states* voted in Congress in proportion to some combination of these two factors—would be a change to a system "*less*' republican" than the then existing system. Superficially, it may seem that any one of the three foregoing changes would have been (and would necessarily have seemed to a Massachusetts man to be), a change to a *more* republican system. Under the existing system, Rhode Island, though one of the least "numerous," and certainly one of the less wealthy, of the nation's states, nevertheless counted in Congress for as much as Massachusetts, then the most "numerous" of the states in freemen, and certainly not the least of the states in wealth. Nor can there be much doubt that men like Rufus King, Nathan Dane, and Theodore Sedgwick, coming as they did from the most "numerous" and one of the wealthier of the states, would have considered any one of the three foregoing alternative systems as *more* republican than the existing system, *provided only* that the internal constitutions of the thirteen states had all been equally democratic. This, however, was not the case, for the internal constitutions of the Southern states were not democratic at all. They were, instead, aristocratic in a very high degree. The right to vote in them, as James Madison pointed out in the Federal Convention, was "much" less "diffusive" than it was in the North, even among white men;[45] and the whole laboring class of the South was made up, and was intended throughout the indefinite future to be made up, of negro slaves, none of whom voted, or would vote, at all.

As a consequence of these facts, any system that resulted in the control of Congress by the Southern *states* would necessarily result in the control of Congress, and hence control of the destiny of the whole nation, by the comparative handful of slaveholding planters who controlled the Southern *states* under their existing, and probable future, internal arrangements. Those were the men who were at the moment blocking the grant of commercial power to Congress; whose illiberal ideas were committing the South indefinitely to a purely agricultural system; and who might be expected, if they once came to power over the country as a whole, to block all the schemes that the Northern men then had for a strong and diversified national economy. That a man like Rufus King, reared under the democratic and commercial conditions in the New England states, a man who was striving at the moment to obtain an agreement in Congress to exclude slavery forever from the Northwest Territory,[46] should have shrunk from subjecting himself and other New Englanders and other Northerners to the risk of such an outcome hardly seems remarkable. Neither does it seem remarkable that King should have preferred the existing system, unfair though that system undeniably was as between Massachusetts and states like Rhode Island. Despite the fact of such undeniable unfairness, that system did seem to give a fairly certain, though less than absolute, assurance that the control of the powers of Congress, whatever they were, would remain among the states of the free, commercial, and relatively democratic Northern region of the country.[47] As King had said in his letters, "the ["seven" or] eight Eastern states ha[d] common objects"; and hence, under the existing system, Massachusetts had a kind of "virtual representation" though the smaller states of the Northern (or "Eastern") region. The certainty of the continuance of Northern dominance in Congress would of course have been greatly enhanced by an agreement for the exclusion of slavery from the Northwest Territory; and the want of such an agreement, together, probably, with some lingering doubt that the North could in the event actually maintain its ascendancy in Congress upon a merely constitutional basis, should the South grow as the South expected, is undoubtedly the key to Rufus King's own expressed preference in 1785 for a grant of national commercial powers *on a temporary basis.*[48] As the reader can see, King's whole attitude is rational, consistent, and thoroughly understandable, in the light of the considerations we have just delineated; apart from these considerations, growing out of a political and transportational situation long since vanished, his attitude is completely impossible to comprehend.

As for Nathan Dane and Theodore Sedgwick and generally the membership of the Massachusetts General Court, their concurrence in King's views, once they understood the basis upon which his views rested, was nothing more than was to be expected. Despite this fact, it is not improbable that from the very first there were some men in Massachusetts who, upon learning of the South's desires and sanguine expectations, took a different view. For the New England country, the reader should not forget, had long been sterile, or at least as sterile as it was in 1785, but that region had in spite of this fact undeniably grown to be the most populous, the most democratic, and the best-educated region in the country.[49] Reflecting upon these facts, many a Massachusetts man of 1785 must have concluded, when he learned of the Southern views, that the thing to do was to make some concession to the Southern desire for an altered basis of representation in Congress (which incidentally would operate also to the advantage of Massachusetts); to exact in return the South's consent to the full national commercial power desired by the New England and Middle states; and, once obtained, to make a prompt and vigorous use of that power to keep the country as a whole, and New England in particular, prosperous. To an enterprising and thoughtful New England man of the mercantile class—such men, for example, as Nathaniel Gorham and Stephen Higginson and Caleb Davis[50]—such a program must have seemed much the most eligible way for New England to retain its people, for the North to preserve its existing ascendancy in Congress, and for Massachusetts to maintain its enviable position of leadership in the country. This view, or something like it, we shall presently see, is the view to which Rufus King and Nathan Dane themselves eventually came around.

However, not all the men in the Massachusetts General Court who had been taught by King and his colleagues to fear the rise of an aristocratic government dominated by the slave-holding South got over their fears so quickly. This appears from much of the opposition to the Constitution that existed in Massachusetts in 1787 and 1788; it also appears from the action taken by the General Court in February 1787 when it first resolved to participate in the Federal Convention.[51] The resolution then passed laid the Massachusetts delegates appointed to that meeting "under the fetter," as Madison phrased it, "of not departing from the 5th of the present articles of Confederation."[53] "The 5th of the articles" provided for the equal vote of the states in Congress. This "fetter" was afterwards removed, for the General Court had acted in the matter before it was known that Congress, under the lead of the state's own delegates, had voted in favor of an unlimited authority for the convention. "But its having [been imposed] at all," said Madison in a letter he wrote to Washington, "denotes a much great[er] prevalence of *political jealousy* in that quarter [of the Union] than had been imagined."[53] Since a *Massachusetts* vote in favor of retaining the system of equal votes for the states in Congress could not have been an evidence of "political jealousy," except upon the basis here presented, this statement of Madison's, which has come down to us not among his papers but among those of Washington, can only be taken as a contemporary judgment corroborative of the views set out in the foregoing pages. Since Madison's judgment of the General Court's motives appears to be the only one possible, the General Court's action must itself be taken as proof that the views presented in the foregoing pages are correct.

CHAPTER XVIII

The Northern Reaction to the Discovery of the Truth about Virginia's Proposal of the Annapolis Commercial Convention

ON THE basis of the considerations set forth in the preceding chapter, the desire of the Massachusetts delegates in Congress in 1785 was to obtain for Congress some kind of taxing power along with ample commercial power, preferably on a temporary basis, without making any change in the scheme of state representation or suffrage in Congress, and without taking any step that could even possibly produce such a change. The plans that had been formed by at least one of the Massachusetts delegates for accomplishing these ends, or at any rate for obtaining the much-desired commercial power, are disclosed in the two letters, earlier mentioned, which Rufus King wrote to John Adams and Caleb Davis, on November 2 and 3. Of these two letters, the one to Davis contains the more complete statement of King's plans. It was written in answer to a letter from Davis, inquiring of King what he and the other Massachusetts delegates who had refused to follow the General Court's instructions proposed to do in order to extricate the country from the commercial difficulties in which it was then involved. Davis had likewise apparently urged upon King the utter impossibility of accomplishing anything decisive along such lines through "uniform acts passed by the several states." He had apparently also inquired of King whether it was really true, as was rumored in Boston, that he, King, had declared "that if Congress had the power to regulate Trade, they would be without the disposition to do it." In his reply, King assured Davis that he had expressed no such opinion. Instead, he said, he "sincerely wish[ed that Congress] had the power," and was sure, "if they had, [that] something would certainly be done which would be worthy of Execution, and remedial of present perplexities." He doubted, however, that "the Southern States [would] relinquish their partial, and unfederal attitude, concerning commerce, until they [should] find a decided disposition in the Eastern States to combine for their own security." On the other hand, "the moment that this Disposition [was] evident, the Southern States," King thought, "[would] sensibly feel their weakness, and accede to such measures as [might] be adopted by the majority of the confederacy." "The confederation," he reminded Davis, "admit[ted] of alliances between two or more States, provided

269

*the purpose and duration thereof** [were] previously communicated to, and approved by, Congress." And since "the Seven Eastern States h[ad] common commercial interests, [were] under similar embarrassments, would vest power in Congress to regulate Trade, and [were] competent to give the Approbation of Congress to [a] sub-confederation [for this purpose]," the thing to do was to form such a subconfederation. This "would not only remedy all [the] existing Difficulties [besetting the Eastern states], but [would] raise them to a degree of power and Opulence which would surprise and astonish."[1] Besides all this, the measure, King confidently predicted, would soon bring the South around.

About a fortnight after King dispatched this letter to Caleb Davis, Nathan Dane made his first appearance in Congress,[2] and judging by a letter Dane wrote to a friend about seven weeks later, he must rather quickly after his arrival there have fallen in with the plans that Rufus King had made. Indeed, Dane wished, if anything, to go further than King, and work directly and drastically upon the conscious "weakness" of the Southern states, by rather pointedly suggesting to them that their course was one that would very probably lead to a complete separation. "The Southern States," said Dane, "ha[d] much to fear from a dissolution of the present Confederacy. Enervated, disposed over a large territory but little inured to constraint they [were] capable of making perhaps if left to stand alone but little resistance to a foreign enemy or one near home." "Nor [were] their best men," he added, "totally unacquainted with these circumstances. These considerations must press them into Federal measures—they surely must be alarmed *even at the suggestion* of a confederacy of the States north of the Potomac or even the Delaware and give up their opposition to avoid such a measure."[3]

Just a few days before Dane wrote this suggestive letter, his colleague, King, had presented a motion in Congress, that the secretary of that body be directed to report to it the number of states which up to that time had complied with the recommendation of limited powers over foreign trade that Congress had made on April 30, 1784. Presented on January 2, this motion was promptly agreed to, and on January 4 the secretary made a report to Congress on the subject, though not with entire accuracy.[4] A committee was thereafter appointed to consider whether any further action in the matter should be taken by Congress. This committee consisted of John Kean, of South Carolina, chairman; Charles Pinckney, also of South Carolina; William Grayson, of Virginia; Melancton Smith, of New York, a member of the Clintonian party there; and Nathaniel Gorham, a merchant of Massachusetts, who had recently taken his place in Congress, beside Dane and King, as a delegate from that state.[5] Of the five members of this Kean committee, Pinckney and Gorham were probably ready to take immediate steps to obtain extensive reforms,[6] but of the sentiments of the chairman,

*King's emphasis. See Article VI of the Confederation.

Kean, little is known; Grayson, at the time, was undecided what to do; and Smith was quite definitely a "states'-rights" man. The prevailing sentiment of this committee is thus difficult to gauge, but it seems reasonable to suppose that Smith's influence, added to the indecision of Grayson, probably produced less readiness to act than had existed in the Monroe committee of the preceding year.

This supposition is more or less borne out by the committee's report. Although its report of February 28 agreed with the Monroe committee report, that there was "little or no probability of commercial treaties being formed with any European power, other than those already concluded," the causes of this situation were declared to be merely "the want of power in Congress to form a system regulatory of *foreign* commerce." The powers that had been requested by Congress on April 30, 1784, were conceded by the Kean committee to be inadequate, even for this purpose. "Yet many very beneficial effects," the committee thought, "[might] be expected from them." The committee therefore urged that another attempt be made to get all the states to grant the confessedly inadequate powers; in order "that Congress [might] stand exculpated from all inattention [to the subject]," the committee further recommended (in view, no doubt, of the news just then received concerning Virginia's proposal of the Annapolis commercial convention)[7] that the attempt be made at once.[8] The report of the committee was thus undoubtedly a step backward from the report submitted by the Monroe committee in the preceding year, yet it was agreed to by Congress with alacrity;[9] the states were circularized accordingly; and this renewed recommendation by Congress, although meagre and inadequate, was given wide publicity in the newspaper press.[10]

This action of the Kean committee, whatever may have been the motives for it, is difficult to account for in the case of Congress on any straightforward and simple basis. As already indicated, it was at the time known in Congress that Virginia had proposed a convention for the express purpose of concerting a scheme of national commercial powers; presumably, so far as the men in Congress then knew, the idea in Virginia was to concert *bona fide* a scheme of powers more extensive than the powers Congress had previously asked. In such circumstances, it would certainly have been more natural for Congress to have given to the states some indication of the scope of the powers which in its opinion were necessary. Instead, however, Congress merely repeated its old appeal for powers which even the Kean committee admitted were inadequate. Considering, then, that the pendency of the Virginia proposal was almost certain to make the success of Congress's appeal impossible, it seems unlikely that there was much expectation in Congress that its appeal would succeed. Why, then, was it made? The answer probably is that Congress once more desired to pose before the country as less anxious to receive commercial powers than the states were to grant them. Such a maneuver, it will be remembered, had been unsuccessfully urged on Congress in 1784 by the committee which originally drew up the fragmentary scheme of power for which Congress still was asking.[11]

That this rather strange action of Congress was not, in any event, due to any general want of desire within that body for a complete commercial power, is indicated by the Massachusetts delegates' reactions to the conversations stimulated in Congress by Rufus King's motion of January 2. Even Rufus King, though he was as a rule a pessimist where the South was concerned, observed rather cautiously in a letter to John Adams on February 1, that "there [was] some ground to expect that several of the Southern states [would] do what [was] right on the subject of the commercial powers of Congress."[12] King's colleague, Dane, more sanguine by nature, seems to have made up his mind within two days after writing his letter of January 8, that there had been some mistake about the South's intentions on the subject. In a letter to Governor Bowdoin, dated January 10, Dane had reported that "the disposition for vesting commercial powers in Congress appear[ed] to [him] more general particularly in the Southern States than [he had] expected to find it." In view of this fact, it was "unfortunate," he said, that the commercial powers proposed by Congress in 1784 had not been "better digested and more adequate." "There [were] many sensible men who appear[ed] to wish commercial powers to be vested in Congress *to be exercised as occasion [might] require*." This, of course, was merely another way of saying "full" commercial power.[13]

Some ten days later Dane informed another correspondent, albeit inaccurately, that New Jersey, Delaware, South Carolina, and Georgia were the only states which had then not granted to Congress the powers requested in 1784. He added that the men from those states, however, said that they too would soon agree to the powers in question, though "some of them at present object[ed]," he said, "that the powers [were] not adequate to commercial purposes, that more extensive powers ought to be delegated." As for the Southern states, Dane said in this letter that their position was that "they till[ed] the ground and produce[d] their exports and [found] the best market for them when their ports [were] open to all the world; but [that] for the sake of agreeing with [the North] they [were] willing the Northern States should become their carriers *submodo*, but not so as to make to themselves an exclusive right and thereby have it in their power to monopolize at pleasure." Because the Northern men did not really entertain the intentions some Southerners feared, this attitude of the Southern men seemed eminently satisfactory to Nathan Dane.[14]

Expatiating in still another letter on the encouraging character of the whole situation,[15] Dane saw all the country's problems virtually solved. All that was required, he though, was patient persistence. In the letter in which these sentiments appeared, Dane reminded his correspondent, Samual Adams, of the proposal that had been made by New Jersey "many years ago, when the articles of confederation were under the Consideration of the States." New

Jersey had then proposed, Dane said, that "Cong[ress] should have *full power to regulate trade internally and externally* and to lay Duties of impost, etc." But the New Jersey "propositions [had been] rejected by almost every State in the Union; even their Delegates in Congress [had] appeared pointedly against them." In these statements, Dane, a newcomer in Congress, was obviously confusing the Witherspoon motion of 1781, which had in effect proposed "full power to regulate trade internally and externally" and had failed in Congress by a rather narrow margin,[16] with the earlier New Jersey proposal of 1778, which had proposed power only over foreign commerce and had not obtained in Congress any support at all.[17] Dane's confusion of these two measures, however, did not detract from his main point, which was that "experience [had] faithfully taught us we were then mistaken." He would "venter to affirm that more than ¾ of the Community [had since] changed their opinion." "To dissolve our union under these [and various other gratifying] circumstances [which Dane also detailed for Adams's benefit]; to become hostile to each o[the]r, and a prey to the nations of Europe, [this,] to me," said Dane, "would be infinitely worse than annihilation." And apparently he had given up—temporarily, at least—at this date (February 11), all idea of threatening the South with such an unhappy outcome.

Shortly after Dane had reached this high point of optimism about the general outlook, the men in Congress learned of the Virginia proposal of the Annapolis commercial convention. Their first knowledge came to them probably through James Monroe, to whom James Madison had written about the subject on the day immediately following the Virginia legislature's action.[18] At any rate, the men in Congress knew about the Virginia proposal by February 23, well before news of it was published in the New York newspapers on March 2.[19] This fact is established by a letter that Nathaniel Gorham wrote, on the date first mentioned, to Caleb Davis in Boston. "The State of Virginia seem to be sensible," Gorham said, "of [the inadequacy of the commercial powers previously requested] & have appointed a committee to meet the other States in Convention to consider the business." "As the Eastern States are particularly interested in having an efficient power in Congress on this head, I hope," said Gorham, "[that] you [i.e., the Massachusetts Genearal Court] will appoint a Committee to meet them, wither their letter comes in form before you rise or not—more especially as the overture comes from a Southern State." He concluded with the caution that it was important to send "men of good Federal ideas" and of "sufficient commercial knowledge."[20]

Through some agency not known, *The* [Boston] *Massachusetts Gazette* was able to print, "From the VIRGINIA GAZETTE," the text of Virginia's proposal of the Annapolis commercial convention, three days before Gorham's letter about it was written from Congress and ten days before news of it was published in the New York City papers. Patrick Henry's letter about Virginia's earlier proposal of an annual convention for obtaining uniform *state* commercial laws was, on the other hand, not put before the Massachusetts General Court by Governor Bowdoin until March 7. Even then it was put before the General Court in a very peculiar way. The Governor informed the General Court that the Virginia resolution he was handling them had *"given rise to another* in the House of Delegates, of the 21st of January"—a fact he could not have learned either from the Boston papers or from Gorham's letter to Davis. He then described the second Virginia resolution; confessed that "the circular letter" in regard to it "ha[d] not yet been received"; but assured his hearers that there was "by another way" (the nature of which Bowdoin did not specify) "satisfactory evidence that the last mentioned resolution ha[d] been passed by the House of Delegates of Virginia." He then intimated—what was certainly contrary to the tenor of the first Virginia resolution and Governor Henry's covering letter—that that resolution was one of interest to Virginia and Maryland only. Having thus apparently destroyed their interest in the resolution in question, he concluded with a strong appeal "to concur with the proposal of the Legislature of Virginia" *which he had not yet received.*[21]

Thirteen days later, on March 20, Bowdoin was able to announce to the General Court that his previous information had been correct, and in addition to hand them both Edmund Randolph's strange letter of notification and Governor Henry's belated authentication of the Virginia appointments. At the same time, Bowdoin renewed his earlier recommendation that the General Court concur with the Virginia legislature's second resolve;[22] and since that resolve undoubtedly seemed to the General Court almost exactly the thing their delegates in Congress had advised was desirable, that body, apparently, was not impressed by the patent strangeness of the Randolph notification. At any rate, just four days later, on March 24, the General Court did promptly concur with Virginia's proposal. On that day they appointed Rufus King, Theophilus Parsons, James Sullivan, and John Lowell, together with Caleb Davis, Benjamin Goodhue, Tristram Dalton, and John Coffin Jones, to serve as the state's representatives at Annapolis.[23] A good indication of the kind of national power to which the General Court still looked forward may be seen in these facts: the last four men were all Boston merchants; they had all been members of the Boston merchant's committee of the preceding spring; and that committee had called for the vesting of Congress "with full power to regulate the internal as well as the external commerce of all the states." Such a measure, the Boston merchants had declared, was the only measure that could "reach the mischiefs [they then] complain-[ed] of"; and those mischiefs, of course, were in 1786 still afflicting the country in aggravated form.[24]

The General Court's prompt approval of the Annapolis convention seems to have been in full accord with the sentiments of the Massachusetts men in Congress. We may infer this not only from the expressions of their sentiments already reviewed but also from an extraordinarily hopeful letter written by Rufus King to John Adams in London, on May 5. Before that date, delegates had been appointed to the proposed convention by Pennsylvania, Delaware, New Jersey, and Rhode Island, in addition to Massachusetts and Virginia, and, on the date of King's letter, New York also had acted. The New York appointments included such staunch nationalists as Alexander Hamilton, James Duane, Egbert Benson, and Robert R. Livingston;[25] the Delaware appointments such men as John Dickinson* and George Read;[26] and the Pennsylvania appointments such prominent merchants as Robert Morris, Thomas FitzSimons, George Clymer, and Tench Coxe.[27] The last three men, it is again of interest to note, had all been members of the Philadelphia merchants' committee of the preceding spring, which had declared so emphatically for a "full and entire" power over commerce for Congress.[28] It would thus seem quite certain that sentiment in Pennsylvania, like sentiment in Massachusetts, was about what it had been in the preceding year. Reflecting, apparently, upon all these encouraging omens, King told Adams that while the situation for the moment was undeniably bad, there was good reason to look for improvement. He would not deny there had been, and still was, "a criminal neglect," on the part of "several of the states," in their "most important duties to the confederacy"; that "our finances [were] not on that firm basis which the riches of the country [would] authorize"; or that "our commerce [was] almost ruined, because jealousies of an unwarrantable nature ha[d] been disseminated through the more Southern states." But "the people generally through the confederacy," he said, "[were] remark[ing], that we [were] at a crisis"; and he "hope[d] a reform [would] take place." "There [was] good reason," on the basis of facts which he carefully detailed for Adams's benefit, "to expect that our finances, would be strengthened and made certain"; and "a proposition ha[d] originated in Virginia, for a convention of delegates, in September, from the several states, to agree on such commercial regulations as [should] extend the American navigation and promote the trade of the Union." "The most important states," King said, "ha[d] already appointed delegates. And if any thing [could] be concluded from the general reputation of the delegates already appointed, there [was] reason to hope that wisdom [would] govern their deliberations, and that their result [would] produce an union of opinions on the subject of commercial regulations through all the states."[29] From the hopeful tenor of this letter, we may be certain that Rufus King was feeling genuinely optimistic when he wrote it, and the fact that he should feel elated is easily understood when we remember that Virginia's proposal of a *special* convention, limited to the making of commercial reforms, was almost exactly the thing that Rufus King and his colleagues in Congress had desired.

King, however, was not the only optimist in Congress at this time, and the optimism of some of the other men there took a form which King could, at the moment, hardly have approved: they were pushing for a general convention, and some of the evidence suggests, though it does not quite prove, that

*Dickinson sometimes served in public office in Delaware, sometimes in Pennsylvania.

some of the delegates already desired a true constituent convention, a convention of the kind by which some of the state constitutions then in effect had been established. King's colleague, Nathaniel Gorham, was one of those favorable to a general convention. This appears explicitly from a letter he wrote to Caleb Davis, six days after he had passed on to Davis the news of Virginia's proposal of a convention limited to commercial reforms only. In this letter, dated March 1, Gorham informed Davis that "Congress ha[d] now before them a motion for calling a Convention of the States to consider wither they [would] establish a federal Government *with powers adequate to the necessities & happiness of the Union.*" The recent refusal by New Jersey to comply with the requisition of Congress, until New York should accede to the continental impost, "ha[d] suspended any other consideration," said Gorham, "for the present." "I wish," he added, "[that] Mass[achusett]s could see their way clear to request Congress to call a Convention—it would very much strengthen the hands of Congress—if the Court should like the idea they might express their sence in such general terms as to preclude much debate or loss of time."[30] Whether this appeal by Gorham produced any action upon Davis's part is not known, but if it did, the General Court must have squelched it.

Much the same thing happened to James Monroe, upon an appeal he made to James Madison on the same subject. Precisely what Monroe said in his letter to Madison is not known, for Madison did *not* preserve that particular Monroe letter among his papers. From Madison's reply to Monroe, dated March 19, it appears that Monroe had written soon after hearing from Madison of Virginia's proposal of the Annapolis convention, and that in his letter he had urged the desirability of transforming the Annapolis meeting into a general convention with "plenipotentiary" powers. Madison's reply to Monroe was very much in the manner of his reply to Monroe's earlier appeal in the preceding summer about the proposal in Congress for "giving to the United States the general regulation of trade." "The option," Madison informed Monroe, "lay between [the convention proposed] and nothing." The Virginia assembly "would have revolted," he declared—and apparently he meant to be understood as expressing an opinion it would still revolt— "against [Monroe's idea of] a *plenipotentiary* commission to [the state's] deputies for the Convention."[31] What Madison meant by "a plenipotentiary commission" is perhaps not certain, but if he used the phrase as other men then did, and if his letter correctly reflected Monroe's ideas, then Monroe, in his missing letter, must have urged a true constituent convention on Madison.

That this was at the time the accepted sense of the words Madison used may be seen very plainly from the well-known letter written by Alexander Hamilton to James Duane on September 3, 1780. In that letter, as the reader will remember, Hamilton had declared his opinion that Congress should be given "complete sovereignty in *all* that relate[d] to war, peace, trade, finance;

and to the management of foreign affairs"; or, as he also put it, Congress should have "complete sovereignty, except as to that part of internal police which relate[d] to the rights of property and life among individuals, and to raising money by internal taxes." To obtain such power Congress, he suggested, might proceed in one of two ways. "One [was] by *resuming* and exercising the discretionary powers [which]," Hamilton said, "[he] suppose[d] ha[d] been originally vested in [Congress] for the safety of the States." If they did this, however, they would have to "rest their conduct on the candor of their countrymen and the necessity of the conjuncture." A better plan would be to "call immediately a Convention of all the States, with *full authority to conclude finally* upon a General Confederation." The "reasons" for his desire that his proposed convention should be vested with what he called *"plenipotentiary authority"* were, said Hamilton, "that the business [might] suffer no delay in the execution and [might], in reality, come to effect. A Convention [might] agree upon a Confederation; the States individually hardly ever [would]."[32] This type of convention, though for the strictly limited object of investing Congress with powers of execution of the substantive powers it then already had, was later talked of in Congress in the autumn of 1784;[33] and as we shall presently see, such a convention for the purpose of a general revision of the Articles was widely demanded, both in and out of Congress, later in the summer and fall of 1786 and in the winter following.[34] Madison's friend, Henry Lee, still in Congress in the fall of 1786, wrote about the matter at that time in the same terms that Hamilton had used in 1780.[35] If, therefore, Madison employed his words in the same sense as Hamilton and Lee; and if his words correctly reflect what Monroe had urged in his missing letter, the conclusion must be that Monroe, and very likely other men in Congress, were already in the spring of 1786 advocating a true constituent convention for effecting a general revision of the Confederation. This conclusion is, however, not completely certain.

The effect upon Monroe of the foregoing extremely dissuasive letter from Madison, of March 19, is undoubtedly to be seen in his strangely contrasting behavior in Congress a few weeks later. On May 3 Charles Pinckney, of South Carolina, had moved "that a grand committee be appointed [in Congress], To take into consideration the affairs of the Nation." In support of his motion, Pinckney had urged that "our Situation was Such that it necessary To inform the Sates thereof—that it was necessary that Congress should be invested with greater powers and therefore it was Necessary to appoint a Convention for that purpose or that Congress should call on them by requisition for Such powers as was Necessary to enable them to Administer the Federal Government or it must fall—That the Confederation was deficient in powers of Commerce; in raising troops, and in the means of Executing those powers that were given, etc." And, when Pinckney had spoken these truthful words, "Mr. Monroe of Virginia alledged that Congress had full power to raise Troops; and that they had a right to compel a Complyance in every case where they acted agreable to the powers given them by the Confederation; That all the States but N.Y. had invested them with Commercial powers (a member informed that N.Y. past an act for that purpose yesterday)[36] *therefore he saw no occasion for a Convention, etc.*"[37] Monroe's behavior on this occasion is completely out of character with his behavior both previously and subsequently, and while it appears, from certain obscure references by Madison to another letter of Monroe's (which was also *not* preserved by James Madison among his papers), that Monroe had some reasons of his own for his behavior on this occasion,[38] one very probable reason was Madison's extremely dissuasive earlier letter. The correctness of this view is further corroborated in some degree by a letter Monroe wrote Thomas Jefferson a few days afterward. In the course of this letter, Monroe explained to Jefferson that the Virginia delegates thought it their "duty" to promote the Annapolis convention by all means in their power, *"as it [had] originated in [their] state."* "Of its success," he added with obvious diffidence and dubiety, "I must confess I have some hopes. The investigation of the subject will always be of advantage since truth & sound state policy in every instance will urge the commiss[io]n, of the power to the U.S."[39]

To what we have said of Charles Pinckney's motion we should add that, despite Monroe's opposition, it was referred by Congress to a committee of the whole, and that as a result a grand committee was appointed on July 3 "to report such amendments to the Confederation . . . as [would] render the federal government adequate to the ends for which it [had been] instituted." This grand committee resurrected the Monroe committee's report of 1785 on commercial powers, cut down the limited reservations of state power that the provisos to the report had originally contained, and reported it in this revised form to Congress on August 7, as part of a rather extensive scheme of proposed amendments to the Articles. These amendments included, among other novel features, provision for "a federal Judicial Court" with jurisdiction to hear, *inter alia*, appeals from the state courts "in all Causes wherein any question [should] arise respecting any regulations that [might] thereafter be made by Congress relative to trade and Commerce."[40] The report, however, was made at a very bad time, and for this, and probably for other reasons, no action was ever taken upon it by Congress.

The reader will note, further, that Monroe, in his diffident letter to Jefferson, did not greatly diverge from the views of the other Virginia delegates in Congress at the time; at least he did not underrate the optimism of an important delegate regarding the Annapolis meeting. This is indicated by a letter written by this delegate, William Grayson, to James Madison on May 28. The letter referred to Charles Pinckney's motion of May 3, which was then still pending in committee of the whole, with a day set for its consideration. Grayson was "apprehensive," he said, that the motion would "produce nothing." The states, he feared, could never agree even in Congress upon the needed reforms. "Mr. Pinkney who [had] brought forward the motion, [would] be astounded when he [should] meet with a proposition to prevent the States from importing any more of the seed of Cain; N[ew] York and Pennsylvany [would] feel themselves indisposed when they [should] hear it proposed that it [should] become a national compact that the sessions [of Congress should] always be held in the centre of the Empire; and how [would] Delaware R[hode] Island Jersey and some others like to vote (with respect to any new powers granted to Congress) according to their real and not their supposed importance in the Union?" Besides all this, Grayson said, he was convinced that "The Eastern people mean[t] nothing more than to carry the commercial point," and that "there they intended to stop." He was therefore "of opinion [that American] affairs [were] not arrived at such a crisis as to ensure success to a reformation on proper principles; a partial reformation [would] be fatal; things had better remain as they [were] than not to probe them to the bottom. [I]f particular States gain[ed] their own particular objects, it [would] place other grievances perhaps of equal importance at a greater distance. [I]f all [were] brought forward at the same time one object [would] facilitate the passage of another, and *by a general compromise* perhaps a good government [might] be procured. Under these impressions," he then bluntly informed Madison, "I cannot say I think it will be for the advantage of the Union that the Convention at Annapolis produce any thing decisive: as in this event nothing more is to be expected from Massachusetts [etc., etc.]. The State of Virginia having gone thus far, it is matter of great doubt with me whether she had not better go farther and propose to the other States to augment the powers of the delegates so as to comprehend all the grievances of the Union, and to combine the commercial arrangements with them, and make them dependent on each other." "[And] in [that] case," he concluded, "[Virginia's] own objects ought not to be pretermitted."[41]

The foregoing views of William Grayson's are of considerable importance as one of the keys to the nature of certain little-understood proceedings in Congress during the following winter, and to William Grayson's probable part and motives in those proceedings.[42] Besides their importance in these respects, Grayson's views are also important for the light they throw upon the diversity of sentiment that prevailed in Congress in the late spring of 1786 with respect to the Annapolis commercial convention. The Massachusetts delegates there, still apparently in ignorance of the true facts about Virginia's proposal of the limited commercial convention which they themselves had so much desired, entertained at the time very great hopes indeed. Apparently still unaware of the then limited desires and purposes of the "Eastern" men, Monroe, a confirmed enthusiast for a full national commercial power, entertained "some hopes" for the convention's success, though he was apparently not an enthusiast for it. On the other hand, William Grayson, who seems to have surmised correctly what the "Eastern" men wished, was beginning to feel that Madison's highly opportunistic scheme for a special convention, limited to the making of commercial reforms, was a distinct mistake; that only a general convention, fully able to effect a total reform by a process of bargain and compromise, held forth any real hope for the aims of Virginia; and that it was, therefore, better that Madison's scheme should fail. This view of the matter was the view naturally taken by any Southern man able to understand the politics of the time; and this being true, it would be natural to expect that Grayson's desire for a general convention able to deal with the whole subject of governmental reform by a process of bargain and compromise would spread among Southern men.

That something of this kind actually did occur among Southern men, during the summer in question, there can be little doubt, but before this development took place, certain other events supervened, which completely shattered the "Eastern" men's hopeful expectations regarding the Annapolis convention, and thereby set in motion a train of causes which had a very great share in producing the eventual change in the Southern men's attitude that occurred with significant abruptness in the late summer and early fall.

The first of these supervening events was the discovery by the Massachusetts men, shortly after June 1, of the true facts—at any rate, a good many of the true facts—about Virginia's proposal of the Annapolis commercial convention. Exactly how this discovery occurred is not known. Reports of the first Virginia proposal for attaining uniformity in the nation's commercial regulations through a continuing annual commission or convention upon uniform *state* commercial laws had found their way by this time into a few of the newspapers.[43] This fact suggests the possibility that, on seeing these, King and Dane applied to James Monroe to know what they meant, and that Monroe, faced with a direct inquiry, felt compelled to tell them the truth. Another possibility—and this is perhaps the more probable—is that the disclosure occurred in connection with certain violent disagreements that arose between Monroe and King, as members of a committee to which they were both appointed, with Charles Pettit, of Pennsylvania, on May 31.[44] However the event occurred, the fact is certain that King had hold of some, at least, of the facts about the Virginia proposal as early as June 11. This appears from a gloomy letter he then wrote to Jonathan Jackson, of Boston. "I fear," he said, "that the commercial convention proposed to be held in Maryland in September, will go but a little way in effecting those measures essentially necessary for the prosperity and safety of the States. Georgia and South Carolina have not appointed Delegates, and their legislatures will not be in Session before the winter. Maryland has not appointed; although the convention is to be in that State. The Assembly of North Carolina have not elected Delegates, but it is said that the executive of that State has nominated persons for the office." As for Virginia, the last and most important of the Southern states, and the state whence the proposal for the convention had come, "it [was] doubtful," King said, "what [its] real sentiments [were] on the question of commercial powers. This [was] certain, that the proposition for the Annapolis convention, which originated in the Assembly of Virginia, [had] not come from the persons favorable to a commercial system common to all the

States, but from those, who in opposition to such a general system [had] advocated the particular regulations of individual States." King did not explain the basis for his conviction in this respect, but since the actual course of events in the Virginia legislature had been of a character which, if known to King, would have seemed to him to warrant what he said, the natural conclusion is that King had discovered them.[45] King concluded his letter by observing that "the merchants through all the States [were] of one mind, and in favor of a national system," but that "the planters in the Southern States [were] divided in their opinion," and that "it [was] to be feared that the majority [was] against the only plan, which [could] insure the prosperity and honor of the confederacy."[46]

Further and more explicit evidence that the Massachusetts men had somehow come into possession of the true facts as to the state of sentiment in Virginia, and as to the true legislative history of that state's proposal of the Annapolis meeting, is seen in a letter that Stephen Higginson wrote in July to John Adams in London. How Higginson in Boston had learned what he then knew is not known. Higginson was a friend and correspondent of Nathan Dane; and his business partner, Jonathan Jackson, as we have already seen, was a friend and correspondent of Rufus King. The probable inference is that Higginson's source of information was, directly or indirectly, the Massachusetts men in Congress. Higginson's most significant information was that "the Measure [had] originated in Virginia with Mr. Maddison." This is particularly significant because the fact is one *of which there was at the time no public record* in Virginia or any place else, so knowledge of it must have come, directly or indirectly, from some confidential Virginia source. The fact, the reader will at once perceive, is consistent with, but more specific than, King's statement that "the proposition [had] originated in the Assembly of Virginia [with] those, who in opposition to a general system [of commerce] ha[d] advocated the particular regulations of individual States." As we know, James Madison had a long record of opposition to a national commerce power and a long record of sentiments antagonistic to the commercial hopes of the Northern states. That record began in February 1781 with his vote in Congress against the Witherspoon proposal of a full national commerce power. The following year, before the Revolutionary War had yet been won, Madison was in a dither over the great and growing maritime power of the New England and Middle states. At that time Higginson's partner, Jonathan Jackson, had been with Madison in Congress.[47] In 1783 Higginson himself had been in Congress,[48] and Madison had at that time opposed the proposal of a continental convention, which Alexander Hamilton had then made for the purpose, among others, of "vesting in the United States a general superintendence of trade."[49] Higginson on the other hand had supported Hamilton's proposal, and of Madison he had then said, in a letter to Theophilus Parsons, that Madison's only object with reference to the confederacy was the obtaining of military protection for Virginia and its lands, without making any return concession for this protection. This, Higginson declared to Parsons, Madison had plainly disclosed "in an unguarded moment."[50]

Besides these facts of Madison's career in Congress, which were unquestionably known to Higginson, there were his activities in Virginia, upon his retirement from Congress, with the object, as Madison then phrased it, of "emancipat[ing]" Virginia's commerce from "Baltimore and Philadelphia." He had proposed to do this through monopolistic local commercial regulations designed to force the growth of the Virginia seaports.[51] Echoes of these activities of Madison's had no doubt reached Jackson and Higginson in Boston through King and Dane; and the same was very likely true of the dissuasive letters Madison had written to James Monroe, when Monroe had been working in the summer of 1785 to obtain general commercial power for Congress. As was pointed out before, the probability is that some knowledge of Madison's letters was conveyed to King, and possibly to the other members of the Monroe committee, at the time when his letters were received. Taking into account the whole situation then, the reader will not find it at all strange that Stephen Higginson, having some but perhaps not all of the facts as to what had transpired in the Virginia legislature in connection with the proposed Annapolis meeting, should have based his suspicion of the good faith of that proposal chiefly upon the fact of James Madison's connection with it. To Adams, Higginson characterized Madison as "a great Aristocrat," and as "not probably knowing or caring much about commercial Objects." "The ostensible object of [the] Convention is," he said, "the regulation of Commerce; but when I consider the men who are deputed from New York, Pennsylvania, and Virginia, *and the source whence the proposition was made*, I am strongly inclined to think political Objects are intended to be combined with commercial, if they do not principally engross their Attention." Higginson's strictures, as they related to some of the men appointed—men like Hamilton and Egbert Benson—were certainly unjustified, but his discovery of the fact that there was little real likelihood of results from the impending meeting had undoubtedly been a severe disappointment, and his letter has to be read with the fact of such disappointment in mind. He concluded with the wish that "a general regulation of Trade might," in spite of his misgivings, "be effected." "But this," he said, "I rather hope than expect."[52]

Knowledge in Boston of the true facts about Virginia's proposal of the Annapolis convention was apparently not limited to Stephen Higginson. This is indicated by the extreme difficulty experienced there in getting any one to go to Annapolis to represent the state. As a means of dealing with this difficulty, the General Court, on July 6, empowered and "requested" the governor to fill up any vacancies that might occur in the state's delegation.[53] Pursuant to this authority, the governor subsequently issued or offered commissions to Stephen Higginson, Elbridge Gerry, George Cabot, Francis Dana, Samuel Breck, and Thomas Cushing.[54] These six men, with the eight who had first been appointed, made a total of fourteen men to whom commissions had been issued or offered. Most of the fourteen, if not indeed all of them, were intensely interested in obtaining general commercial power for Congress; only the *three* last mentioned, and these very tardily, could be prevailed upon to go to Annapolis to attend the convention.[55]

On the basis of the evidence, then, there can be very little doubt that interest in the Annapolis meeting was at an extremely low ebb in Boston as the time of that meeting drew near. That interest was then still at a low ebb among the Massachusetts men in Congress is evident from a letter that Theodore Sedgwick wrote from thence to Caleb Strong, of Northampton, on August 6. In the course of this letter, Sedgwick informed Strong that "no reasonable expectations of advantage [could] be formed, from the commercial convention [at Annapolis]." "The first proposers," Sedgwick said, "designed none. The measure was originally brought forward with an intention of defeating the enlargement of the powers of Congress." Of this fact, he added, he had "the most decisive evidence." Since the actual facts of the legislative history of the Virginia proposal might well have seemed to Sedgwick—as, indeed, they might seem to anyone—to justify his view, our warranted conclusion is that those facts constituted Sedgwick's "decisive evidence." Sedgwick went on to declare to Strong that, in his opinion, "it well bec[a]me the eastern and middle States, who [were] in interest one, seriously to consider what advantages result[ed] to them, from their connection with the Southern States." "They can give us nothing," he argued, "as an equivalent for the protection which they derive from us, but a participation in their commerce. This they deny to us. Should their conduct continue the same, and I think there is not any prospect of an alteration, an attempt to perpetuate our connection with them, which at last too will be found ineffectual, will sacrifice everything to a meer chimera." He therefore urged upon Strong, afterwards a delegate to the Federal Convention, that the Eastern and Middle states ought "seriously to contemplate a substitute [for the existing confederation]," and "no other substitute [could] be devised," he thought, "than that of contracting the limits of the confederacy to such as [were] natural and reasonable, and within those limits instead of a nominal to institute a real, and an efficient government."[56]

To the foregoing we should add that, at the time Sedgwick wrote, a controversy had begun in Congress that was reminding the Northern men in a most vivid and unpleasant way of the possible costs of "the protection" expected by the South. Although still in its early stages on August 6, this controversy was probably one source of irritation to Theodore Sedgwick.[57] It is perfectly apparent from his letter of that date, however, that his principal complaint was the South's persistent refusal to join with the North in establishing an American "system of commerce," and his firm conviction of Virginian bad faith in proposing the Annapolis meeting was undoubtedly the principal cause of the disgust with the idea of going on with the South, which he felt when this letter was written.

Although there is nothing known specifically of the reactions of the men in the other Northern states to the facts surrounding Virginia's proposal of the

Annapolis convention, the probability is that they were in the end much like those of the men of Massachusetts. This view seems indicated for New York: of six delegates there appointed, only two—less than a quorum—put in an appearance at Annapolis.[58] Likewise this view seems indicated for Pennsylvania: of five men there appointed (including three members of the Philadelphia merchants' committee of the preceding year) only *one*—again, less than a quorum—made the very short trip to Annapolis to represent that state.[59] Thus there appears very little room for doubt that something had come to light since the early spring that had destroyed the Northern men's original high hopes about the Annapolis meeting. While this change in the Northern men's views was not solely a result of the discovery of the facts surrounding Virginia's proposal of that meeting, the evidence indicates that the discovery of those facts was one important factor in producing the change.

CHAPTER XIX

The Quarrel in Congress over John Jay's Proposed Spanish Treaty: Herein of the Proceedings in the Committee of the Whole

O F THE other factors contributing to destroy the Northern men's hopes of good from the Annapolis convention, the chief was the attitude exhibited in Congress by the Southern men toward a certain scheme for a treaty with Spain which John Jay, Congress's secretary of foreign affairs, put before that body in the summer of 1786. The scheme in question had been known, at least to a good many members of Congress, for some months before,[1] and when Jay took steps to put it before that body, there arose at once, between the Northern and the Southern delegates, a bitter controversy over it which continued to rage without recess or abatement almost to the date when the Annapolis convention assembled. In this controversy the Southern men's attitude was such as to make the impending convention seem a hollow mockery to the Northern men, especially when these men learned, as by that time they rather generally had learned, of the circumstances in which that convention had been proposed. In their anger over these exasperating aspects of the situation, the Northern men were in the ensuing controversy led into threats of terminating the union with the South, not only in private conversations with the Southern delegates, but in debates upon the floor of Congress.[2] These threats were very likely in part factitious, but they were also to a considerable degree undoubtedly sincere—a result of anger such as Theodore Sedgwick felt when he wrote his letter to Caleb Strong, of August 6, already noted. Whether these threats were factitious or not, they were apparently taken to heart by the Southern men; were productive of a greatly changed attitude on the part of the South toward the proposals then being made for strengthening the national government; and, along with certain events in the New England states, which by chance happened at a time to give increased point and reality to the Northern threats, they were the main cause of the final phase of the movement for a stronger government that eventuated in the Federal Convention in 1787. All this being true, it is manifestly necessary for the purposes of this book that the controversy in Congress over Jay's proposed Spanish treaty be particularly examined, and that the complicated politics connected with that controversy be completely understood.

285

We have already mentioned the fact that Spain had declined to recognize the right to navigate the Mississippi to the Gulf, which Great Britain had sought to confirm to this country in the peace of 1783. Furthermore, Spain declined to recognize the boundaries of the United States as therein stipulated. The Spanish position on the American navigating right was somewhat technical,[3] but its position on the boundary point was strong. Spanish armies had been in possession of the Floridas, as conquered British territory, in 1782, when the preliminary peace between America and Britain had been signed, and the United States, in a plain but queer recognition of the situation then existing, had agreed by a secret article of the preliminary treaty to accept what had once been the northern boundary of West Florida as the southern boundary of this country, in case Great Britain should succeed in retaining West Florida as against the Spaniards upon the termination of her war against them.[4] The line that America thus agreed to accept was an east-west line running through the point at which the Yazoo River empties into the Mississippi. That line would have been about ninety miles to the north of the thirty-first parallel, which was otherwise agreed upon between Great Britain and America as the southern boundary of the United States.[5] The secret article of the preliminary treaty eventually became known to the Spaniards in some way, perhaps not hard to surmise,[6] and in view of the other elements of the situation it seems reasonable to suppose that the knowledge must have considerably strengthened the Spanish expectation that a peaceful and, to them, satisfactory settlement of the boundary question with America could be secured without much difficulty. They seem, at any rate, to have acted upon this assumption.

Early in the summer of 1784, Spain took steps to serve notice upon Congress that, "until the limits of Louisiana and the two Floridas should be settled and determined," American vessels seeking to navigate the Mississippi would be confiscated. "The King [would] see with great pleasure," it was said in an accompanying letter, "every measure which [should] be taken to consolidate and maintain a good understanding between his Catholick Majesty and the United States."[7] A short while later, Don Diego de Gardoqui was appointed as the first Spanish minister to the United States, with a commission giving him authority not only to agree upon a settlement of the boundary and Mississippi disputes but, by implication at least, to enter into a commercial treaty.[8] A commercial treaty with Spain, it is perhaps needless to say, was at the time an object of great general desire in Congress, and especially was this true among the New England men, who, because of the Roman Catholic allegiance of the Spanish Empire, regarded that empire as a most excellent market for New England fish. When Gardoqui at length arrived early in the summer of 1785, Congress promptly commissioned John Jay to treat with him with respect to commerce and with respect to the other two questions at issue. In its instructions Congress directed Jay, however, "particularly to stipulate" in his plan for a treaty not only the American navigating right in the Mississippi from its source to the Gulf but "the right of the United States to their territorial bounds . . . as established in their Treaties with Great Britain."[9] These instructions, of course, amounted to a virtual negation of Jay's authority to treat with respect to these two subjects. Considering the manner in which the negotiation had developed, and the nature of the object that Spain seemed to have in mind, it is hardly matter for wonder that Jay, as he informed Congress, was "not sanguine that a satisfactory termination of [the] negotiation [was] practicable."[10] He nevertheless undertook the duties Congress assigned; and despite the fact that certain contrary suspicions were later entertained by James Monroe and probably by other Southerners in Congress, there is no known evidence that Jay did not make every effort that lay within his power to bring the negotiation to a successful and generally satisfactory conclusion. His efforts, however, were fruitless, and out of the deadlock that soon developed there finally grew the idea which Jay put before Congress in the summer of 1786.

In spite of the fact that it has generally been regarded as a Northern project, the proposal that Jay then put before Congress almost certainly took its inspiration from George Washington. At any rate, months before Jay's proposal was made, Washington set forth in various of his letters all the ideas which must have made his Spanish proposal seem possible to Jay. As early as March 15, 1785, Washington was writing to the Virginian president of Congress, Richard Henry Lee, urging the extreme desirability of Congress's adopting some scheme for a "progressive seating"—i.e., a progressive settling—of the West. "A progressive seating," Washington said, was "the only means" by which "Law and good Government [might] be administered [in the West], and the Union strengthened and supported by [its settlement] "And unless, *in the scale of politics*, more than one new State [was] found necessary, the unit"—contemplated in the original plan for a settlement to the "west" of the Ohio, which had been drawn by a group of army officers at Newburgh in 1783[12]—"would," he thought, "be found more pregnant with advantages than the decies," which had been adopted in the Jefferson committee's plan in Congress in 1784.[13] What Washington seems to have meant by all this was that the simultaneous settlement of the whole Northwest Territory, and an attempt to organize ten separate governments in it, would most likely lead to a great, mad scramble for the choicest lands wheresoever situated; to consequent scattered settlements in the territory with great unsettled areas lying between them; to extreme localism in government in the scattered settlements; to a resulting increase in the number of local politicians with vested interests in local sovereignty; and to lawlessness and lack of culture in the intervening unsettled regions. All this, Washington firmly believed and said to Lee, would be "more advancive of individual interest"—i.e., of the interest of the few who obtained the choicest lands and the local officers—"than [it would be, of] the public welfare." He therefore concluded with the suggestion, which he no doubt advanced in the hope that it might help to promote his idea of a "progressive seating," that "it [was] more than probable that Mr. Gardoque [would] give Congress a good deal of trouble respecting the navigation of the Mississippi river."[14]

Four months after the date of the foregoing letter, Lee wrote Washington that "the Spanish Minister appear[ed to him] to be well disposed toward [the United States]," and that "Mr. Jay [had been] commissioned by Congress to open negotiations with [him] concerning Mississippi, Boundary, Commerce, &c."[15] Washington replied to Lee's letter on August 22. "However singular the opinion may be," he said, "I cannot divest myself of it: That the naviga- tion of the Mississippi, *at this time*,* ought to be no object with us: on the contrary untill we have a little time allowed to open and make easy the ways between the Atlantic States and the Western Territory, the obstruction had better remain." "There is nothing," he went on, "which binds one Country or one State to another but interest; without this cement the Western In- habitants (who more than probably will be composed in a great degree of Foreigners) can have no predilection for us; and a Commercial connexion is the only tie we can have upon them. It is clear to me that the trade of the Lakes, and of the river Ohio as low as the Great Kanawha if not to the Falls, may be brought to the Atlantic ports easier and cheaper, taking the *whole** voyage together, than it can be carried to New Orleans: but once open the door to the latter, before the Obstructions are removed from the former, let commercial connexions, which lead to others be formed, and the habit of that trade will be established, and it will be found to be no easy matter to divest it: and vice versa." "When the settlements are stronger and more extended to the westward, the navigation of the Mississippi will," Washington concluded, "be an object of importance; and we shall then be able (reserving our claim) to speak a more efficacious language than policy, I think, dictate[s] at present."[16]

The foregoing opinions, which Washington repeated in various of his letters to his friends,[17] had apparently been reached by him, as well as by some other leading Virginians, even before the end of 1784. This appears from various letters of James Madison, the chief of which is one addressed to Thomas Jefferson under date of April 27, 1785. In this letter Madison in- formed Jefferson, who was then in Paris, that he had recently had a letter from LaFayette, "dated on the eve of his embarcation [for France]," in which "the Marquis" had reported that he "ha[d] much conferred with the General upon the Potowmac system," and that "many people [thought] the navigation of the Mississippi [was] not an advantage but . . . the excess of a very good thing, viz. the opening of [America's] rivers." "The Potowmac system," to which LaFayette had referred in the letter Madison mentioned, was the project for clearing the navigation of the Potomac River and connecting its headwaters, in accordance with the policy which Washington later outlined

*Washington's emphasis.

to Lee, with the headwaters of the Ohio. When he wrote to Madison, LaFayette had not seen Washington since about December 1, 1784,[18] so Madison's letter to Jefferson means that before that date LaFayette had obtained from Washington the ideas he mentioned to Madison. "It [was] unlucky," Madison went on in his letter to Jefferson, "that [the Marquis] should have left America with such an idea as to the Missi[ssip]pi. It [might] be of the worst consequ[en]ce, *as it [was] not wholly imaginary*; the prospect of extending the commerce of the Atlantic states to the western waters having given birth to it." Upon Washington's anxious plans for maintaining the strength and unity of the country, through the system of policy which he had explained to LaFayette, Madison's revealing comment was that he "c[ould] not believe that many minds [were] tainted with so illiberal and short-sighted a policy."[19]

These views of Washington's, so thoroughly contemned by Madison, were undoubtedly among the principal considerations which made Jay's scheme for a Spanish treaty seem advisable; and they almost certainly were the views which made that scheme seem possible. By the terms of Jay's scheme, the United States was to agree "to forbear to use the Navigation of the Mississippi River below their territories to the Ocean for twenty-five or thirty years"; in return, Spain was to agree for a similar period to open the ports of her empire to American fish and flour and other products which Americans badly needed to sell, and in particular to purchase ship masts from America with specie.[20] To Jay and the men in Congress who were in favor of his scheme, it did not seem likely, in view of the then existing distribution of population, that the right to navigate the Mississippi to the Gulf would be of much value to Americans within the period of the proposed forbearance; and since the United States, by the terms of Jay's scheme, was not to cede but only to forbear the use of its right—and the right, accordingly, was to be implicitly recognized by Spain—it seemed to Jay and his supporters, if we may judge from their letters and the speeches they made in Congress, that the forebearance, as the *quid pro quo* for an advantageous commercial treaty, was well worthwhile. In addition, Jay's supporters referred to the possibility which Washington had stressed, i.e., that the premature opening of the Mississippi, by promoting remote settlements on the river and its tributaries at points near the Gulf before the intervening territory should be settled, might split the country commercially, perhaps even politically, into two separate parts. Finally, by the time Jay's scheme was proposed in Congress, Spain appeared adamant against opening the river, so it naturally seemed to Jay and his supporters that an immediate insistence upon America's right would amount to an unnecessary courting of trouble with Spain, and this at a time when America was far from ready for a new, costly, and not improbably dangerous war.[21] Yet the fact remained that the commercial advantages of Jay's proposed treaty were advantages which would mainly accrue to the Northern states and, very largely, to the states of New England. In view of the jealousy of New England and of the North in general that prevailed in much of the South of the time, it is difficult to see how Jay could possibly have expected any support for his proposed scheme in Congress, except from the eight Northern states, unless, indeed, he saw in it something he thought would be a *peculiar* object to some one or more of the Southern states. Jay did in fact suppose his treaty held forth such an object to at least one of the Southern states. We may be certain of this because of the absolute necessity then existing under the Articles that the approval of *nine* states in Congress be obtained in the making of all treaties.[22] The only questions are, Which of the Southern states Jay was counting on? and, What could have been the peculiar object which Jay supposed would gain for his scheme some Southern state's support? The answers, despite some historians' obtuseness, are certainly not very difficult to divine: in the beginning at least, Jay was counting on Virginia, and very likely upon Maryland also; and the peculiar object he supposed would gain him these states' support consisted of the considerations set forth in Washington's letter of August 22, 1785, to Richard Henry Lee.

One fact pointing to this answer is that Richard Henry Lee himself was converted to Washington's views at some time between August 11, 1785, and October 11 of the same year[23]—i.e., within the period during which Lee must have received Washington's letter of August 22. A second fact pointing in the same direction is that Jay, also, seems first to have conceived his idea for a Spanish treaty within the same period or very shortly afterward.[24] The temporal relationship between these facts, together with the further fact that Lee was afterwards an extremely stubborn advocate of Jay's proposal,[25] suggests rather strongly that Washington's views were made known to Jay by Lee, and that Lee very likely had some share in working out Jay's plan for a Spanish treaty. If this occurred, we can quite easily understand that the support of Virginia must have seemed very probable to Jay. For Jay was aware—as, indeed, the whole country was aware—of Washington's activities in the Potomac and Ohio project; of the support that project had received from the Virginia legislature; and of the fact that the Virginia legislature was also promoting a similar project with respect to the James River.[26] In the light of these facts Jay most probably considered it of no importance that the Virginia legislature had previously instructed its delegates in Congress not to consent to a cession of the American navigating right in the Mississippi.[27] All other reasons apart, Jay did not propose to *cede* that right but merely to contract to *forbear* its use while its use was unimportant, and while the Virginia legislature's Potomac project, its James River project, and various other similar projects, proposed in Virginia and certain of the other states, were going forward.

The foregoing view of Jay's motives and expectations in advancing his proposal for a Spanish treaty, however, does not rest merely upon the facts and considerations thus far stated. In addition, we have the further, firmly established fact that Jay actually approached one of the Virginia delegates,

James Monroe, upon the subject of support for his projected treaty, when Monroe returned to Congress from one of his "routs westward" in December 1785. We know this from a letter to Patrick Henry, the Virginia governor, written by Monroe on August 12, 1786.[28] The letter was written to inform Henry of what Monroe described as the proposal in Congress to "occlude" the Mississippi and of Jay's scandalous behavior—as Monroe by then viewed what Jay had done—in that connection. Monroe was extremely angry with Jay when he wrote this letter, and there can be no doubt that many of the things he said in it must be taken with some reserve. However, the major fact, somewhat in the nature of an admission against interest on the part of Monroe, is not in any way doubtful: shortly after conceiving his scheme for a Spanish treaty, Jay actually approached Monroe in the hope of obtaining Monroe's support for that project. This action means that Jay did in fact take the view of his project which has been suggested here; that he almost certainly knew of the views of Washington and Richard Henry Lee; and that he must have counted originally upon Virginia, and very likely upon Maryland also, as states that would support his scheme. In its inception, then, Jay's scheme could not have been the first step in an anti-Southern dismemberment conspiracy, as James Monroe afterwards heatedly charged.

When Jay first broached his scheme to Monroe, he explained (according to Monroe) that in his negotiations with Gardoqui they had agreed between them to postpone the Mississippi and boundary questions in order to take up the subject of a commercial treaty. According to Monroe,[29] *but not according to Jay*,[30] Jay had at that time already found out that Spain would be willing to enter into a commercial treaty upon condition of American "forbearance of the use of the Mississippi River for 25 or 30 years." Monroe's statement to this effect appears in his letter to Patrick Henry, previously mentioned. Jay was actively desirous, according to Monroe, to agree to such a "forbearance" as a means of obtaining what he regarded as an advantageous commercial treaty. "Whether he suppos'd I was of his opinion or not," Monroe went on, "or was endeavoring to prevail on me to be so, I cannot tell, but as I expressed no sentiment on the subject he went further and obser[ve]d 'that if the aff[ai]r was brought to the view of Congress they wo'd most probably disagree to it, or if they sho'd approve the project, conduct themselves so indiscreetly as to suffer it to become known to the French and Engl[is]h here and thus defeat it.'" "'To avoid this' [Jay] said," according to Monroe, "'[that] it occur'd to him [as] expedient, to propose to Congress that a Committee be appointed to controul him in the negotiation, to stand to him in the room of Congress and he to negotiate under the Committee.'" Monroe informed Henry that at this point he reminded Jay that the Virginia delegates were bound by instructions not to cede the navigating right in the Mississippi, so they could not concur in such a measure as Jay had in mind. From that date onward, according to Monroe, his communications with Jay on the subject of the Spanish negotiation ceased, but Monroe was aware, so he said, that Jay was making the same communication to other members of Congress— "intriguing," as Monroe angrily put it, "to seduce them to concur in defeating the object of his instructions." Finally, Monroe explained, a letter from Jay had come to Congress on May 29, 1786, alleging difficulties in the negotiations with Gardoqui, and suggesting to Congress the appointment of a committee, such as he had suggested to Monroe some six months before. Jay's letter was read to Congress on May 30.[31] It was at once decided, according to Monroe, that Jay's scheme of a committee "to stand in the room of Congress" was not consistent with the requirement in the Articles that nine states in Congress must consent to all treaties, and on the following day Rufus King, Charles Pettit (of Pennsylvania), and James Monroe were appointed as a committee to consider Jay's letter and make recommendations to Congress as to what action that body should take in the matter.[32]

Jay's letter to Congress did not actually disclose his scheme for a Spanish treaty, but the scheme had apparently been known rather generally among members of Congress for some months before.[33] Jay must have been aware that a good many southerners opposed it. This fact may seem to suggest some doubt as to the nature of Jay's motives in submitting his letter to Congress on May 29; in short, it raises the question whether Jay can possibly have been acting on May 29 in promotion of a dismemberment conspiracy, as Monroe afterwards charged. With reference to this question, direct and specific evidence is, of course, lacking. The reader should, however, note that it is by no means certain just how crystallized the Southern opposition was before Jay's letter to Congress was received, and, further, that on May 29 there were certain new facts in the situation which may very well have encouraged Jay to hope that approval of his proposed Spanish treaty could be obtained after all. One of these new facts was the arrival in Congress of Henry Lee, of Virginia.[34] Though bound by instructions on the Mississippi question, as were his colleagues, Lee's own opinions were in accord with Washington's views and were entirely favorable to Jay's ideas for a Spanish treaty.[35] The views of Henry Lee were very probably known to Jay and his supporters in Congress, and the strong probability is that they regarded Lee as "a friend at court" in Virginia. In addition to Lee's arrival, there were the further important facts that the state of Virginia, on May 29, had but recently—and since Jay's conference with Monroe—proposed the meeting of the national commercial convention at Annapolis; that, on May 29, the happenings in the Virginia legislature leading up to that proposal were still unknown to the men in Congress; and that the Northern members of that body were, therefore, still generally in the optimistic mood induced by Virginia's proposal. In these circumstances, Jay and his supporters probably felt that with three such distinguished and respected Virginians as Henry Lee, Richard Henry Lee (by then out of Congress), and George Washington all on their side, the mere bringing of the Spanish matter before Congress might have the effect, despite the opposition of the other Virginia delegates—Monroe, Edward Carrington, and William Grayson—of producing some change in the Virginia legislature's attitude. Jay and his supporters had particular grounds for their view when the fact became clear from the proceedings in Congress that the proposed treaty had the firmly united support of the Northern states as a measure calculated to promote the trade of America and build up the nation's supply of specie. At any rate, subsequent proceedings in Congress indicate that Jay and his supporters did *on some ground* believe that approval of the proposed Spanish treaty was possible. Of any deep-laid conspiracy on their part to use the proposed treaty to disrupt the Union, as James Monroe afterwards charged, there is no evidence whatever.

The first difficulties over Jay's proposal were encountered in the committee of three that had been appointed on May 31. Monroe, of course, was bitterly opposed to everything that King and Pettit desired. In the end, after two months' delay, these two turned in a report (in which, apparently, Monroe refused to join),[36] recommending their own discharge, a recommitment of the Spanish matter to a committee of the whole, and a request to Jay to appear before Congress and give that body full information upon the subject. These recommendations were made by King and Pettit on August 1; Congress approved their recommendations without delay;[37] and pursuant to Congress's request Jay appeared before that body on August 3. In the statement he then made, Jay explained the kind of commercial provisions that Spain would be willing to insert in a treaty; informed Congress that Gardoqui had consistently refused to recognize either the territorial boundaries claimed by the United States or the American navigating right in the Mississippi; pointed out the advantages to America of continued freindship with Spain and the complete unpreparedness of the United States for involvement in a war; indicated his opinion respecting the boundary question that "it would be better even to yield a few Acres, than to part [with Spain] in ill humour"; and regarding the Mississippi suggested the compromise move (as he had to Monroe in the preceding December), of a contractual forbearance for a limited period as the *quid pro quo* for a commercial treaty. In his statement Jay quite pointedly said that he did *not* know whether Gardoqui would agree to his suggested compromise regarding the Mississippi, because his instructions, he pointed out, had restrained him "from even sounding [Gardoqui] respecting it." For the same reason, he had no precise information as to what Spain's territorial claims would be. He expressed his opinion, however, "that Spain [could] justly claim nothing East of the Mississippi but what [might] be comprehended within the bounds of the Floridas." He added that what was comprehended within those bounds was a somewhat uncertain matter, and suggested, to avoid a rupture, that the dispute over the boundary question might be referred to "impartial Commissioners" if Spain should turn out to be "too extravagant" or "too pertinacious" in her claims.[38]

On the basis of the foregoing statement by Jay and a subsequent resumé, by him, of the evidence in his hands from other sources on the probable extent of Spain's territorial claims,[39] the subject of the Spanish negotiation was taken up by Congress, in committee of the whole, first on August 10 and then over several days between the sixteenth and twenty-third of the month.[40] In the proceedings in committee, the seven Northern states (Delaware being absent) lined up solidly behind Jay's ideas, and the five Southern states, apparently under Monroe's leadership, just as solidly against them.[41] The proceedings were begun by a motion, presented by the Massachusetts men, that the limitations in Jay's instructions be striken out,[42] and this proposal (which the Southerners maintained was in effect to free Jay to negotiate a treaty in accordance with his scheme) served as the basis for the debates in the committee.

In these debates, the Southerners argued that, entirely apart from the sacrifice of the navigating right in the Mississippi, the proposed Spanish treaty was not advantageous for America. The Eastern states—chiefly Massachusetts, they said—"might find a market for the fish"; and Jay's state, New York, might, they insinuated, "more speedily settle her waste land." But these, the Southerners asserted, were small and partial advantages that could not possibly justify the sacrifice involved in the proposed treaty, especially when it was considered that "the sacrifice to be made to obtain [these] advantages was *wholly* at the Expence," as the Southerners insisted, "of the S[outhern] States, which had no share in them." This view of the matter appears most clearly in the remarks of Grayson, of Virginia, as the debates on the treaty have come down to us, but much the same position was taken by Charles Pinckney, of South Carolina.[43] The replies of the Northern men, as these have survived, also indicate clearly that this was the chief burden of all the Southern arguments.[44] This Southern position is comprehensible only upon the view we have earlier presented, that the southern part of the western country, by reason of its nearness to the sea, was then regarded as much the choicest part of the unoccupied lands, and that the Southern politicians of the time were counting upon this fact, and the navigating right so essential to it, to attract the bulk of the nation's population in the western lands claimed by the Southern states.

Convincing the Northerners of the inequity of Jay's scheme because of its expected effect upon the Southern states' claims to the most valuable part of the nation's western territory was naturally a singularly formidable task. The Southern claims, like the somewhat similar claims earlier advanced but for the most part since given up by certain of the Northern states, had little basis in fact or law, and no basis whatever in equity. The loss or postponement for the Southern states of an undeserved revenue from the sale of these choice lands on "the western waters" could hardly have been expected to make much of an appeal to a Northern conscience. Still less, we may quite safely assume, could such an effect have been produced among the Northern men by a detailed explanation of how Jay's treaty might postpone the day when new and populous settlements in the southern West would be demanding, in a language of numbers that could not be denied, either a changed basis of state representation in Congress or admission into the Union as additional Southern states. Since such arguments could not in reason have been expected to influence the Northern men, such arguments were of course not presented. Instead, the Southern speakers urged that the treaty would be unfair to individuals in the Southern states: that "the occlusion of the river," in the words of William Grayson, "would destroy the hopes of the principal men in [them] of establishing the future fortunes of their families." Grayson also argued that the treaty would destroy the value of the Northwest Territory and "thereby deprive the U.S. of the fund on which they depend to discharge the domestic debt"—hardly an exclusively Southern interest— "that it would separate the interest of the western Inhabitants"—still, of course, a small body of men in total numbers—"from that of the rest of the Union and render them hostile to it; [and] that it would weaken if not destroy the union by disaffecting the S[outhern] States when they saw their dearest interests sacrificed and given up to obtain a trivial commercial advantage for their brethren in the East." As for Spain, she "knew her own weakness and would not dare to go to war to secure her unreasonable demands." Grayson then went into an elaborate though not very convincing speculation to show that Spain "would not be supported by any of the commercial nations of Europe [in a war upon America]"; that France would not join Spain in the event of such a war, as many seemed to fear; and that "in case she did, G[reat] B[ritain] would join the United States," as indeed Grayson declared, the Dutch would also. Having finally satisfied himself, if not his hearers, upon these points, Grayson bravely concluded "that the U.S. had nothing to fear from a war with Sp[ain]; that Morgan with 1000 men could penetrate into the heart of Mexico and emancipate all the Sp[anish] provinces—that the inhabitants there were ripe for a revolt and only waited for such an event to shake off the yoke of Spain. That the true policy of the U.S. was to stand firm, to cement and strengthen the Union among themselves, and to assert their right to the navigation of the Mississippi." He wound up by declaring that he had not a doubt, if this were done, that Spain "finally" would open the river, as America desired and as Jay and his supporters contemplated.[45]

Grayson's arguments were answered by Rufus King. King began by "point[ing] out the distressed state of the Eastern States—that they had an ungrateful soil and no staple but what they drew from the Sea. That the fishery depended on a market; [that] the best market was Spain; and [that] this [market] could not be secured but by treaty." "Therefore," he said, "a treaty with Sp[ain is] of the utmost consequence to the E[astern] States." Answering Grayson's argument that the treaty would "destroy the hopes of the principal men in the S[outhern] States in establishing the future fortunes of their families," King declared that refusing [for this reason] to treat upon the terms proposed [was] sacrificing the interest and happiness of a Million [people] to promote the views of [a few] speculating landjobbers." Yet King, apparently, was unable to believe that even "landjobbers" would be injured by the proposed treaty. "[For] if the value of the western lands depended upon the free navigation of the river Miss[issippi], the forceable occlusion by Spain [would] operate as strongly to that effect as a voluntary forbearance for a term of years [by America]." All that was proposed, was "an Agreement to forbear [what] we could not at present enjoy. That the Mouth of the river was in the possession of Sp[ain]. That she now excluded us from the use of the Navigation and would continue to exclude us until we were able to assert our right by arms." "That however some gentlemen might depreciate the power of Sp[ain], she was by no means a contemptible enemy. That[, under "the family compact" of the Bourbons,] F[rance] must favour if not join [Spain, in case of war with America]—that our hopes of assistance from any of the Maritime power[s] of Europe were visionary and ill-founded." "That entering into a treaty, on [the] conditions [proposed, would] give time to the U.S. to acquire strength, arrange their affairs, and strengthen the Union, so that at the end of the term they [would] be prepared to assert their right; whereas by breaking off the treaty, Sp[ain would] be disgusted and strengthen her post[s], to exclude us from the use of the river; the settlers in the W[estern] country, buoyed up with the hopes of assistance, [would then] attempt to force a passage; and the U.S. [would] be precipitated into a war before they [were] prepared." "[And] in such an event," King warned the Southerners, "the existence of the Confederation [would, indeed,] be endangered." "For [those] States," he bluntly informed them, "whose interests [were] now neglected, if not sacrificed, [would] not be willing to incur the expence and danger of a war brought upon them, as they [would] think unnecessarily and prematurely; more especially when they considered that, by this precipitate step, they [had been] deprived of [commercial advantages, which were] the only advantages they could expect from the Union." "In such a case," King finally asked, "would there be found a man east of—where to draw the line he did not know—but [he] would say East of Delaware,[46] who w[oul]d give his vote for war?"[47]

The delegates who spoke for the other Northern states expressed somewhat similar views. Arthur St. Clair, for example, a delegate from Pennsylvania, though apparently agreeing with the Southerners' view that his own state would not derive much direct benefit from the treaty, declared "it [was] not an objection with him that the immediate benefits [would] be reaped by one part of the Union. He consider[ed the treaty] in a national view, and that the benefit reaped by one member [would] redound to the advantage of the whole Union." We are in an agricultural state," he said, "and stand in the need of the manufactures of other nations. To pay for [these] we ought to secure a market for our production. The treaty proposed will give us a new staple by promoting the fisheries. It will encourage shipbuilding and the carrying trade and consequently encrease the number of seamen, without which we cannot be secure or respectable." As for the objection that the proposed treaty would "check the settlement of the Western country," he admitted that it might, and considered that this would be "advantageous to the Union." "Our country," he said, "is too thin of inhabitants; we have not hands sufficient for the cultivation of our lands, much less for manufactures of the most necessary kind. Emigration therefore in our present situation is hurtful, and the settlem[en]t of the western country still more so as civilization and government does not advance with the settlers." He therefore thought the treaty plainly advantageous, and the equivalent for it "ought to be considered an advantage," too, even as it respected the navigating right for which America contended, for by the terms of the proposed treaty Spain was to "yield her exclusive claim and confirm [America's] right."[48]

This view of the effect of the proposed contractual "forbearance" was also urged by William Samuel Johnson, of Connecticut, whose state was another of those, according to the Southerners, which would in no way benefit from the treaty. Referring to the debate before he spoke, Johnson declared, that "the adv[ocate]s for the Treaty seem[ed to him] conclusively to have the argument," unless the Southerners could show that the South would indeed be grievously injured by the treaty. Primarily upon this point, he said, the argument against the treaty had been rested, and since the treaty was in every other way plainly beneficial, the fact of the injury to the South "sho[ul]d be clearly established; which [he] ha[d] not yet seen done." "If gent[lemen] sp[o]k[e] farther upon the subject, they [should] apply themselv[e]s to do this." "[But] at present," he said, "I think, for 20 years, there will be little use for the Miss[issipp]i, and I rely upon this that whenever it shall be really essential to the well-being of that Peop[l]e"—i.e., the settlers on "the Western waters"—"wheth[e]r bef[or]e or after 20 y[ea]rs, Treaty or no Treaty, [the river] will be opened. Neith[e]r Sp[ain] nor U.S. can prevent it. The Peop[l]e will no more be restrained than those migh[t]y Waters can be confin[e]d by a Dam. I do not theref[or]e see the Dang[e]r of the Treaty." He added that he also did not think a decision in favor of it could "ever shake the Union." He "rel[ied] upon the good sense and jus[tic]e of [his] South[er]n Brethern." If the matter were stated to them fairly, as it had been in Congress, they would decide, he thought, as Congress would do: "that it [was] best for the whole, and theref[or]e in a polit[ic]al sense best for every Individ[ua]l [in the country]."[49]

Greatly abbreviated herein, these were the arguments in the committee of the whole over Jay's proposed Spanish treaty. Enough has survived to show that the Northern men were unimpressed by the Southerners' arguments. The fact that Southerners like Richard Henry Lee, Henry Lee, and Washington were also quite unimpressed by all these Southern arguments fortifies the view that as matters stood in 1786 the arguments had very little real merit. Henry Lee, for example, was firmly convinced of the entire good faith of the Northern men's interest in the treaty on commercial grounds, and wrote to Washington in the fall of 1786 warning him against the "erroneous information" which, he plainly intimated, was being circulated in Virginia about the controversy in Congress over the treaty.[50] Richard Henry Lee wrote Washington, as late as July 15 of the following year, still complaining of the commercial benefits lost to the country through the South's opposition to the proposed treaty, in a tone as bitter as any New Englander could possibly have used. "Our Gazettes," he said, "continue to be filled with publications against the Spanish Treaty and for opening the Mississippi, some of them plausible, but generally weak and indecent." This kind of writing would have the effect, he feared, of forcing the country to "discard the friendship for the enmity of a powerful Monarch," and of needlessly "loos[ing it] what [it might otherwise] possess: [its] Share of a Commerce that yield[ed] annually 4 or 5 millions of dollars for Codfish only, independent of the Flour & many valuable Articles of American production used in Spain & not interfering with her own products." This, he added, was "to say nothing of a most lucrative Contraband Trade from the Ocean & on the Mississippi which a friend might wink at, but which a vigilant and powerful enemy [would] prevent." "The argument [on the treaty might]," Lee thought, "shortly thus be stated—Spain [would] not agree to the Navigation within her limits—[could] we force it in 25 years—if we [could] not, why risk, for an unattainable Object, the loss of valuable objects, and the incurring pernicious consequences?" "A Candid and impartial consideration of [the] Subject must," he concluded, "determine the question without difficulty."[51] Washington wrote back that his own sentiments on the subject "had long been fixed, and [were] not dissimilar to those which [Lee had] expressed." In all the circumstances by then arisen, however, Washington told Lee he had come to consider it "a moot point" what had best be done. "The State of Virginia having taken the matter up with so high a hand, [was] not," Washington concluded,[52] "among the least embarrassing or disagreeable parts of the difficulty."[53]

On the basis of the reasons actually advanced in favor of and against Jay's proposed treaty, the advocates for the measure clearly did "have the argument," as Johnson of Connecticut suggested. Consequently, the fact that the Southerners in Congress were so very angry and lined up in a solid block of opposition to the treaty, suggests rather cogently that they must have had other reasons for their opposition than those they actually avowed. The probability of this is considerably enhanced by the fact, certainly not open to any question, that profits from land speculations in the Southern states were by no means confined to Southerners,[54] as well as by the fact that the delegates of Virginia, North Carolina, and Georgia, which together claimed virtually all of the unoccupied southerly lands, were joined by the delegates of South Carolina, whose claim to the lands in question was very limited, and by the delegates of Maryland, which claimed none of those lands at all. The genius of an economic determinist, by assembling data as to the personal landholdings of the South Carolina, Maryland, and Northern men—at the time in question or some time indiscriminately in the future—could perhaps explain away these seemingly suggestive facts; but just how the case of James Monroe could be explained away, under the overly simplistic views of these men, is not easy to see. James Monroe, the ringleader of the Southern opposition, was speculating at this time, along with James Madison, in lands lying in the Mohawk Valley of New York.[55]

The truth of course is that the Southern opposition to Jay's proposed treaty was not at all based upon the immediate personal interests of the Southern men; it was based, instead, upon the intense and impatient political desire of many Southerners of the period to rule the nation, and upon their firm conviction that, with the Mississippi as a magnet, they could soon attract into the southern part of the western country men in sufficient numbers to enable them to do this. To a realization of their hopes, it was of course necessary that there be either a changed basis of *state* representation in Congress or an admission into the confederacy of additional Southern states. If the South actually grew as the Southerners expected, the North, it was perfectly obvious, would find agreement to one or the other or both of these changes increasingly hard to avoid. When the Northerners proposed that the nation contract to forbear the use of its navigating right in the Mississippi River, the Southerners quite naturally imputed to the Northern men a deliberate purpose to defeat the South's desires, and lined up in a solid, angry mass against Jay's treaty.

The correctness of this view of the Southern men's motives appears with clarity in the letters of James Monroe throughout the summer of 1786. At some points in his letters Monroe sounded somewhat like an economic determinist, as, for example, in a letter to Madison, of May 31, wherein he ill-naturedly attributed the behavior of his former friend, Rufus King, to the fact that King "ha[d then recently] married a woman of fortune in New York." "If he secures a market for fish," Monroe told Madison, "and turns the commerce of the western country down [the Hudson] river, he obtains his object"—that is, apparently, his object as a Massachusetts man interested in the Newfoundland fisheries, and his object as the son-in-law of his new, rich, merchant father-in-law in New York.[56] In his letter to Patrick Henry, earlier mentioned,[57] Monroe averred that beyond these "interests," which he described as "of a private kind," there was another object, political in nature, in the proposals offered by Jay and his supporters. In what he had to say upon this political phase of the subject, Monroe waxed so wroth that the reader will find it impossible to doubt that Monroe saw in it the most important aspect of the whole matter.

"The object," he declared, "is to break up, so far as [the occlusion of the Mississippi] will do it, the settlements on the western waters, prevent any in the future, and thereby keep the States southward as they now are—or if settlements will take place, that they shall be on such principles as to make it the interest of the people to separate from the Confederacy, so as effectually

to exclude any new State from it. To throw the weight of population eastward and keep it there, to appreciate the vacand lands of New York and
Massachusetts." "In short," he said, "*it is a system of policy which has for its object
the keeping the weight of gov*[*ernmen*]*t and population in this quarter* [*of the
union*]"—that is, among the eight "Eastern," or northern, states—where it
then was. "And [this system had been] prepared," Monroe concluded, "by a
set of men so flagitious, unprincipled and determined in their pursuits, as to
satisfy [him] beyond a doubt, [that] they ha[d] extended their views to the
dismemberment of the gov[ernmen]t and resolved either, that sooner than
fail it sh[ould] be the case, or, being only desirous of that event, ha[d]
adopted this as the necessary means of effecting it."

Much of the remainder of his letter to Patrick Henry from which these
quotations are taken could very likely pass muster with a casual reader of the
present day as a high-minded, disinterested appeal by Monroe for fair treatment of the *Western* states of the future. A careful reading of his letter,
however, will convince one that Monroe's real interest—his "earnest wish,"
as he expressed it in one of his letters to Madison—was for "the admission of
a few additional States into the Confederacy in the Southern scale."[58] His
paramount concern, in other words, was for the existing South (then often
referred to as "the West") and not for "the West" as we are apt to think of it
today. The opinion which he and other Southerners entertained, of much of
the Northwest Territory, affords the key to how they could feel so sure that
the North's espousal of Jay's treaty proposal was in fact indubitable evidence
of a deep-laid plot to deprive the South of its manifest natural right of
dominance in the nation.[59]

That same opinion, seen in its full circumstantial context, also affords the
key to what seems to have been an important purpose of Monroe's in advancing his proposal early in 1786 to decrease the number and increase the
size of the districts, or prospective states, in the Northwest Territory.[60]
Monroe seems to have assumed—quite correctly, as events later proved—
that the early settlements in the Northwest Territory would be mainly along
the Ohio and its tributaries, and that the men of the settlements, whether
Northerners or not, would therefore be at one with the South on all matters
connected with the opening and development of an American navigation
down the Mississippi River. For this reason, and perhaps for others, Monroe
must have thought there were peculiar benefits for the South in expediting
the admission into the Union of new states from the territory, even upon an
anti-slavery basis.[61] If the new states helped the South to procure and promote the Mississippi navigation, they would, as Monroe saw the matter,
enable the South to grow in wealth and numbers as the South expected. If
that growth occurred, the South would sooner or later, in one way or
another, secure its fervently desired position of dominance in the nation.

Considerations such as these lay behind Monroe's motion to expedite the
admission of new western states, as is apparent from a letter he wrote to

Jefferson on July 16, 1786. Referring to the action of Congress in accord with his motion, nine days before,[62] Monroe observed regretfully that "*the investigantion of [that] subject ha[d] open'd the eyes of a part of the Union* so as to enable them to view the subject [of new states in the Northwest Territory] in a different light from what they ha[d t]heretofore done." The remainder of his letter makes perfectly clear that he particularly meant the Northern states. Whether Monroe's motion had actually been necessary to open the Northerners' eyes is, however, very doubtful, in view of the strenuous opposition to "a *general* Revision of the Confederation," which the Massachusetts delegates in Congress had theretofore displayed.[63] From Monroe's mode of speaking, however, it is clear that he himself regarded not only his motion but all that had previously been done regarding the Northwest Territory as adverse to the interests of the Northern states, most particularly the New England states. This being true, it is surely sufficiently evident that, in acting to expedite the admission of new states from the territory, and to block the countervailing moves by the Northern men, Monroe conceived he was acting in the South's peculiar interest.

These inferences are supported by his further remarks in his letter: that the Northerners were "manifest[ing] a desire to rescind every thing they ha[d t]heretofore done in [reference to the admission of new states from the Northwest Territory], particularly [that they had moved] to increase the number of the Inhabitants which sho[ul]d entitle such States to admission into the Confederacy & to make [their admission] depend on their having one 13th part of the free inhabitants of the U.S." "This"—equitable enough, it would seem—"[together] with some other restrictions they wish[ed] to impose," was plain proof, Monroe seemed to think, that "the policy of [the Northern] men [was] to keep [new western states] out of the Confederacy altogether." He then indicated a fear that these restrictions might be adopted, and declared that, if this should occur, the Virginians would simply deny the power of Congress to determine the numbers requisite for the admittance of the new states into the Union, and would claim for their state, on the basis of its shadowy and then already relinquished claim to the Northwest Territory, the right to veto any decision upon this point by the other states in the Union.[64] All this points to the existence of the same transcendent issue between the North and South which Monroe declared was operative in the affair of the Spanish treaty.

Corroboration of Monroe's opinions upon this point, and of Monroe's and the other Southern men's purposes in the same connection, is likewise provided in certain views expressed by an astute contemporary, Louis Otto, the French *chargé d'affaires* in America at the time. In a letter to Count Vergennes, then the French foreign minister, Otto set forth, on September 10, 1786, what he described as "the ostensible arguments" for and against Jay's proposed Spanish treaty. "But a long acquaintance with the affairs of [America]," he said, "authorizes me perhaps to divine the secret motives of the heat with which each state supports its opinion in an affair which does not appear of enough importance to disturb their harmony." "The true motive of [the] vigorous opposition [of the Southern states was] to be found," he believed, "in the great preponderance of the northern states. Eager to incline the balance toward their side, the southern [were] neglect[ing] no opportunity of increasing the population and importance of the western territory, and of drawing thither by degrees the inhabitants of New England, whose ungrateful soil only too much favor[ed] emigration." "The new territories [would] gradually form themselves into separate governments; [would] have their representatives in congress; and [would] augment greatly," said Otto, "the mass of *the southern states*." New England, as a result of this process, would be "doubly enfeebled," since the shift in population, "on the one hand, [would] deprive her of industrious citizens and, on the other, [would] add to the population of *the southern states*." In these mutually opposed political interests of the North and South Otto saw, as did James Monroe, the most important aspect of the bitter controversy over Jay's proposed Spanish treaty.[65]

Whether Otto and Monroe were right in their views respecting the men of the North is—as might be expected—impossible to establish by direct and specific evidence. Apart from a few brief reports of the Northern men's speeches in Congress, the only direct evidence of their views known to be extant is a letter Rufus King wrote to Elbridge Gerry on June 4, 1786,[66] and then retracted before that day was over.[67] The letter tends to indicate, in spite of its retraction, that King felt a strong interest in the treaty as it related to the economic welfare of Massachusetts, but apart from this the letter on its face indicates only that King, as the leader of the Northern men, took much the view of "occluding" the Mississippi that Washington took. "I am pretty [well satisfied]," he said in his letter, "that the free navigation of [the Mississippi], will [some day] be of Vast importance to the Inhabitants [within] the Territories of the U.S." "[But] should there be an uninterrupted use of the Mississippi *at this time* by the Citizens of the U.S., I should consider every emigrant to [the western] country from the Atlantic States, as forever lost to the Confederacy." If, on the other hand, the western settlers were to be "cut off, for a time, from any connections except with the old States across the Mountains, [he w]ould not despair," he said, "that a government might be instituted, so connecting them with the Atlantic States, as would be highly [beneficial to them both] and promise a considerable [trade]." King added that he realized such opinions were "speculative," and that for this reason he felt "very doubtful of them, when a variety of influential motives, which seem[ed] to promise well for "Massachusetts], authorize[d his] assent." Hence, he concluded, he was writing to Gerry for advice on the subject and was requesting him, before he should give it, to consult with Governor Bowdoin, if he could.

There is, in short, nothing in King's letter that gives the slightest hint of any purpose to defeat the increase of the South's political power in Congress. Yet the letters King had written in 1785, when he *and Gerry* and Samuel Holten had declined to move for a general constitutional convention as the Massachusetts General Court had then asked, certainly suggest rather strongly that Monroe and Otto were right in their views, and that Rufus King along with other Northern men did look with favor on Jay's proposed treaty for the reason—but only among many others—that it would postpone the day when the Northern states would have to choose between disunion and the risk of being governed by the South's "landed aristocracy." This aspect of the matter, of course, was not something that Elbridge Gerry needed to have explained to him; and it would, of course, have been quite as "improper [for King] to have communicated" his thoughts upon this subject in his letter to Gerry, as it would have been for him *and Gerry* and Samuel Holten to have "communicated" their thoughts upon the closely related subject of a *general* constitutional convention in their letter to the Massachusetts governor written nine months before. The absence from King's letter of any direct evidence upon this point can hardly be regarded as impugning the correctness of Monroe's and Otto's view that the Northern men were motivated in the affair of Jay's proposed treaty—though apparently only in part—by a desire to "keep the weight of government and population in [the Northern] quarter [of the Union]." That the Southerners most ardently desired to shift "the weight of government and population" in a southerly direction we have already made apparent.

CHAPTER XX

The Quarrel in Congress over John Jay's Proposed Spanish Treaty: Herein of the Proceedings in Congress

IN THE recounting of the Southern arguments in committee of the whole against Jay's proposed treaty, one argument was omitted: if the Northerners pressed the formation of the treaty Jay proposed, this would cause the failure of the impending convention at Annapolis and a miscarriage of the plans which were then afoot for "giving [to Congress] *the power of regulating trade*." "Should the measure [of the treaty] be pursued," warned William Grayson, "the S[outhern] States [would] never grant [that power, or any of the other] powers which [were] acknowledged to be essential to the existence of the Union."[1] Grayson and other Southerners seemed not to perceive the complete futility of this argument; for if the exercise of the power for the nation's commercial welfare was to be foregone in every case wherein it came into conflict with the political ambitions of the Southern states, there was little reason from the Northern point of view to desire that any national power to regulate commerce be created. By the date when this argument was advanced, moreover, the Northern men had already lost faith in the Annapolis convention as a means of effecting any change, so it is not at all remarkable that this argument advanced by Grayson had no perceptible effect upon the Northern men.

To the contrary, a report was adopted in the committee of the whole on August 23, which recommended that so much of Jay's instructions as required him "particularly to stipulate" the American navigating right in the Mississippi, and the territorial bounds of the United States as established in the Treaties with Great Britain, should be repealed. It was further recommended that Jay, instead, should be instructed that he might agree, subject to certain safeguarding provisos, to a "forbearance of the use" of the Mississippi through Spain's dominions, "for a limited time," provided such an agreement should be found "indispensible" to the conclusion of a treaty with her; that he should "insist" upon the territorial bounds fixed in the public treaty with Great Britain of 1783; but that, if Gardoqui, in turn, should "insist" upon the bounds fixed in the secret agreement of 1782, Jay might then agree with Gardoqui for "the settlement and final decision of [their] disagreement by Commissaries mutually appointed for that purpose." Upon the making of this report, Monday, August 28, was set for its consideration by Congress, and on that date the arguments and parliamentary jockeying began all over again.[2]

The report had been adopted in committee by the vote of seven states only;[3] and the Northerners had there argued that the limitations in Jay's instructions could be repealed—and repealed, according to Monroe, "so as to make [his commission] a new one"—by the vote of that number of states in Congress. The Southerners denied the correctness of this position and informed the Northerners that, if they attempted to proceed on such a basis in Congress, the Southern group "would give notice to [Jay] of the incompetency of his powers, as also to [Gardoqui, in order] to justify Congress in refusing to ratify [Jay's acts] if [Congress] sho'd [afterwards] choose it."[4] In this situation, again according to Monroe, matters had continued in the committee, until Friday, August 18. On that day, the Virginia delegates had proposed a compromise. They proposed that the United States agree to the "occlusion" of the Mississippi River, so far as imports were concerned, but insist upon the opening of the river to American exports and at the same time propose to Spain the payment to her of an agreed *ad valorem* duty upon all American exports passing down the river, in return for the privilege of establishing at New Orleans an American *entrepôt* for handling them. The Virginia delegates also proposed, in this connection, that Jay's commission should be totally withdrawn, and that the whole negotiation should be transferred to Europe, by authorizing Thomas Jefferson and John Adams (then the ministers respectively to France and Great Britain) to go to Madrid to act as commissioners in the premises.[5] The plan, apparently, had originally called for the commissioning of the American *chargé d'affaires* at Madrid;[6] the naming of Adams along with Jefferson was apparently an afterthought calculated to gain Northern support.[7]

The Southerners said at the time that they had for this compromise the support of seven states in Congress, and that they thought they could get more. This appears from a report that Otto, the French *chargé d'affaires*, made to Vergennes, the French foreign minister, on August.[23] It likewise appears from Otto's report that "the leaders" of the Southern faction—that is, presumably, the Virginia men—had taken the extraordinary step of going to Otto; disclosing to him their plans; and, without any authority from any one but themselves, requesting him to ask his government if it would not undertake, in return for participation in the projected American export trade at New Orleans, to supervise Jefferson in the making of an American treaty with Spain, in accordance with the Southerners' views.[8] Thus early do we have evidence of the naive and fanatical faith in France that characterized so many anti-national Virginians during the first three decades of our national history.

The only evidence as to which of the Northern states approved this Virginia plan of compromise is a letter, surviving among Monroe's papers, dated

August 20, in which Lambert Cadwalader, a New Jersey delegate, expressed his approval of it in cordial terms.[9] He thought it "a moot point," however, whether the negotiation ought to be transferred to Europe, so his approval could not possibly have extended to the extraordinary step of approaching Otto. If this step later became known to Cadwalader and the Southerners' other Northern converts (if any), it may perhaps account for Cadwalader's vote against the Virginia plan in Congress,[10] and the plan's failure in the committee.[11]

In any event, nothing in the record shows more clearly the excited state of mind of the Southern men than their taking this step of approaching Otto. Further evidence of their extreme excitement is to be seen in Monroe's belief (probably shared by other Southerners) that Jay and his supporters were prepared to go through with their treaty, on the basis of a vote of seven or eight states only, even if they broke up the Confederacy by doing so.[12] That Monroe and his supporters were intended to draw this inference from what went on in the committee seems altogether probable; once the South's solid, intransigent opposition became clear, the whole Northern strategy was undeniably precisely such a show of Northerners' strength and union, as Rufus King and Nathan Dane had thought of and talked about in their letters during the fall and winter before.[13]

On the other hand, there is no evidence at all that the Northern men actually intended to press the treaty to the point of disunion,[14] nor is there any evidence that they actually desired a dismemberment and were attempting to use the Spanish treaty to bring about dismemberment—as Monroe so confidently charged. Without exception, the Northern men's confidential letters are contradictive of such a view; even to Theodore Sedgwick and the one or two other Northerners who spoke of it, dismemberment was decidedly a second choice.[15] Indeed, the first move they made in Congress after their display of strength and unity—what Monroe feelingly described as "flagitious, unprincipled determination"—was an attempt, as Monroe himself was forced to recognize,[16] to detach the state of Georgia from the Southern interest.

This attempt—utterly inconsistent with Monroe's theories—took the form of a motion, made by Rufus King and seconded by Melancton Smith, of New York, to amend the proposed new instructions to Jay by directing him *not* to form a treaty with Spain, unless the territorial limits of the United States as fixed in the public treaties with Great Britain should be "thereby acknowledged and secured." As the territory that might have been ceded, under the original terms of the report of the committee, was wholly within the claimed limits of the state of Georgia, Monroe's interpretation of the purpose of this Northern motion seems certainly correct. At this point in the proceedings, however, the motion failed, due to the division of the vote of Pennsylvania. William Few, one of the Georgia delegates, voted for it.[17]

A division of the committee's report, and a decision on the first proposed resolution, being thereupon called for, the Southerners proposed, instead, that Jay's authority should be withdrawn. This proposal was of course defeated.[18] The next move was a long and argumentative motion by the Virginia delegates, in which they in effect re-urged substantially the same compromise they had previously urged in the committee. This also was defeated, *not a single northern delegate voting for it.*[49] The committee's first resolution repealing the limitations in Jay's instructions was then adopted, but by a vote of only seven states, as in the committee. This vote took place on August 29.[20]

On the day following, when the committee's second resolution came up for action, the King amendment previously urged, which had had for its object the detaching of Georgia from the Southern interest, was once again moved.[21] The Southerners countered with a motion to postpone, in order to consider a resolution which they brought forward, that it was the sense of Congress that Jay had acquired no authority, through the resolution of the day before, to proceed in his negotiation otherwise than as originally instructed. This motion was defeated.[22] The King amendment was then adopted, seven states to four, with Georgia divided by the favorable vote of William Few.[23] A motion was next presented by Arthur St. Clair, and seconded by Rufus King, to amend still further the second resolution so as to include therein a direction to Jay to obtain, *"if possible,"* the opening of the Mississippi to American exports and the establishment of an *entrepôt* at New Orleans, substantially as the previously defeated Virginia motion had asked.[24] The Virginia delegates moved to amend the amendment so as to make the obtaining of these objects mandatory; but their motion was defeated, and the unamended St. Clair-King amendment was adopted.[25] The second resolution of the committee of the whole, having thus been amended with the plain intent of gaining enough Southern support to assure ratification of the proposed treaty, was then submitted to the vote of Congress. The seven Northern states present in Congress voted for it, but the five Southern states (including, in Georgia, William Few) voted against it.[26] The Northerners' effort to gain by compromise enough southern support to enter into a treaty upon the terms proposed thus failed; the incontestable fact that the effort was made is sufficient to establish that as late as August 30 the purpose of the Northern men was primarily the obtaining of the treaty, and not—as James Monroe so foolishly charged—the destruction of the Union.

Upon the foregoing vote, Nathaniel Gorham, as president of Congress, announced that "the question was lost."[27] This seems at first to have been understood by the Southern men as a ruling that the whole Northern effort had failed, and that Jay's original instructions therefore stood.[28] On the day following (August 31), Gorham announced that what he had intended to say was that the second resolution only had failed; and that the first resolution, repealing the limitations originally put into Jay's instructions, had passed,[29] as had previously been announced.[30] Judging by what afterwards took place, this was a pure maneuver *in terrorem*. There was apparently no intention on the part of the Northern men of claiming, in the face of the specific contrary provision in the Articles, a power of ratifying any treaty by the vote of only seven states.[31] The Southerners, however, had denied the power of the majority to repeal Jay's instructions, and when Gorham explained his ruling of August 30 the Southerners moved a resolution to obtain "the sense of Congress" as to "whether Seven States [had been] competent to [a] partial repeal and alteration [of Jay's instructions]." This motion was set aside, apparently without any explanation by the Northerners, upon a motion of "the previous question."[32] At the time, delegates from twelve states were present in Congress. On the following day, September 1, a rule was adopted, pursuant to a postponed motion of the previous day,[33] that, when a question had been put aside by "the previous question," it should not be in order afterwards formally or substantially to move the same, unless, at the time, there should be the same *or as many states* present in Congress.[34] Having by the adoption of this rule tied up the matter and left the Southerners in what was apparently regarded as a salutary state of doubt as to the true intentions of the Northern states, all the Rhode Island delegates, and enough other Northern men to destroy the quorums of certain of the other states, promptly left Congress.[35]

This action by the Northern group was interpreted by James Monroe as the final evidence either that "Jay and his party" meant to have the treaty, even at the expense of breaking up the Union, or that they were merely using the treaty as a means to a dismemberment as their primary object.[36] On the whole, Monroe tended strongly, and had tended strongly throughout the summer, toward the latter view. He was convinced, he had informed Jefferson as early as July 16, that his former friend,[37] "Jay, ha[d] managed [the Spanish] negotiation dishonestly." Moreover, the Massachusetts delegates who were, Monroe also explained to Jefferson, Jay's principal supporters, were all either unprincipled, illiberal, or not very bright. His former friend, King, the leader in Congress of the Northern group, came in for the first of these angry characterizations; King and Dane together, for the second; and Gorham, for the third.[38] The reasons for Monroe's altered opinions of his former friends came out plainly in the various letters he wrote to other Virginians while the Spanish treaty controversy was going on.

"Certain it is," he told Patrick Henry, in his long report of August 12, "that committees are held in this town [New York] of Eastern men and others of this State upon the subject of a dismemberment of the States east of the Hudson from the Union and the erection of them into a separate gov-[ernmen]t." To what length these committees had gone, Monroe confessed he did not know; but of the truth of what he was passing on to the Virginia governor, he declared that he had "assurances," "founded," he said, "on authentic documents." According to this "authentic" information, the plan for a dismemberment was "talked of in Mass[achusetts] familiarly" and was "supposed to have originated there." "The plan of gov[ernmen]t in all its modifications ha[d] even been contemplated"; and he was "persuaded [that] these people who [were] in Congress from that State (at the head of the [Spanish] business) mean[t] that as a step toward the carriage of [their dismemberment schemes]," for the proposed treaty would, he thought, "so displease some of [the States] as to prepare [them] for [such an] event." In a postscript to his letter, he added that, *in conversations at which [he] ha[d] been present*, the Eastern people [had] talk[ed] of a dismemberment so as to include Pen[nsylvani]a . . . & sometimes all the states south to the Potomack." "I trust," he concluded, "[that] these intrigues are confined to a few only; but by these men"—apparently, the Massachusetts men—"I am assured, [they] are not."[39] This story was repeated by Monroe in a letter he wrote to Thomas Jefferson during the following week;[40] was referred to several times in his letters to James Madison through the late summer and early fall;[41] and was undoubtedly given to Madison in full detail by word of mouth, when that gentleman appeared at New York on a visit, while the controversy over the proposed treaty was in progress.[42]

In Monroe's vague and gossipy accounts of this affair, there is, as the reader will have observed, much to suggest that the Northerners, and particularly the Massachusetts men, had been practicing upon Monroe's credulity, and playing upon the fear which he and other Southerners must certainly have had that the North might withdraw from the Confederacy and leave the South to face the despised Spaniards alone. This must certainly have been the character of the "talk" of "the Eastern people" in "the conversations" at which Monroe had been *permitted* to be "present," and when, to the rather plain indications in Monroe's letters, we add the fact that Rufus King and Nathan Dane had (as we know) actually thought of and talked about just such a step in the preceding winter,[43] the probability that the Northern men were to a considerable extent putting on an act for the benefit of "their Southern brethern" seems rather difficult to doubt.

Yet it is certain that much more than this was involved. By this time, the Northern men, particularly the New England men, were losing patience. From the beginning of the country's post-Revolutionary difficulties in trade the Northern men had been aware that the economic situation of the Northern region, particularly of New England (with the exception, to some extent, of Connecticut), was serious. The men of these states had long regarded as the one feasible remedy for their economic ills the finding of dependable new markets for their goods and services, thereby replacing the markets which they, in particular, had lost as one of the costs of the whole nation's independence. The men of the North had proposed to pursue this remedy partly by seeking advantageous treaties of commerce with other nations, and partly by promoting the internal commerce of the United States. The Northern men were fully convinced a complete national commerce power was requisite for these two purposes; and when such a power had once been obtained, they proposed it should be freely used to establish a complete American "commercial system." Under the system they had in mind, American bottoms—in effect, vessels belonging to the New England and Middle states—would do the carrying for themselves and the Southern states; internal waterways and highways would be extensively developed; and American manufacturers and new forms of agriculture would be promoted—all this in order to provide, so far and as soon as possible, a domestic, and therefore dependable, market for the products of the manufacturing and the agriculture already existing. In these ambitious schemes for the thoroughgoing commercial development of the country, the men of the Northern states were motivated, beyond any possible question, by considerations of their own states' interests; but in addition, and with reason, they saw in the plans they made the general welfare of the whole country.

In these plans, the reader should not forget, military considerations played a distinct and important part. It was as true in the eighteenth century as it is today, that no nation dependent upon other nations for the sinews of war is safe. The development of American manufactures was deemed necessary for this reason, among many others: only by such a step could the newborn nation be assured of a sufficient fund of skill and industry, for the wartime manufacture of the cannon, small arms, shoes, clothing, blankets, and countless other fabricated products constituting the ordinary land armaments and military supplies of the time. In addition, the shipping trade, the carrying trade, and the fishing trade were all deemed essential, because these "branches" served as peacetime "nurseries" for the ships and seamen that were then so easily convertible to the nation's belligerent needs. These paramount needs, to say nothing at all of the economic ills of the Northern region, were not—in the beliefs of the men concerned in these plans— matters which could wait upon the so-called "natural" development of the country.

With a view, therefore, to the accomplishment of these urgent military and commercial objectives, the nationwide effort had been launched in 1785 to bring pressure to bear upon the various state legislatures, to induce those bodies to grant to Congress the complete national commerce power which it was believed was required. That effort had convinced leading men, in both the North and South, that the eight Northern states were ready to agree to the investing of Congress with full power over the subject. In the states of the South, the effort had been a failure. South Carolina, alone among the Southern states, had taken any decisive action, and its action had been limited to the subject of commerce with foreign nations. The proposal of the Annapolis commercial convention which at length was made by Virginia, though encouraging at first, had eventually turned out to have quite the opposite tendency. When all these facts antecedent to the controversy over Jay's proposed treaty are borne in mind, and when the military aspects of the demand for a national commercial power are considered, the reader will experience no difficulty in seeing why the South's stubborn attitude toward Jay's proposal was an extremely exasperating matter to the New England and other Northern men in Congress.

Every one of these men, we may feel quite sure, was fully aware of the really weak and perilous military situation in which the Southern states lay. They were aware that all save one of the Southern states claimed much valuable western land, with scant justice as against the rest of America. They were aware that these Southern states—indeed, the South as a whole—had comparatively few people *and virtually no ships and seamen*, in being or in prospect, to defend that land. They were aware that the Southern states had Spain to the south of them in the Floridas, and Spain to the west of them in Louisiana, and that the great tract of valuable land to which the South laid claim (to some of which Spain also laid claim), lay between. Finally, the Northern men were aware that the South had within itself a vast body of men who were held in slavery, a situation of which the great mass of Northern men morally disapproved, and which was universally recognized to be a situation fraught with extreme military danger. Aware of all these things, the men of the North were naturally also aware that the one thing most Southerners desired from the national union was the military and naval protection which the North could give, with its more diversified free economy; its still greater plans and ambitions in this regard; its ships; and its great numbers of free white men. Since the men of the North were aware that this was true, it is in no way remarkable that many of them were much angered and much disinclined to confer this benefit upon the South when it became apparent, as it seemed to be after 1785, and still more after the revealing events of the spring and summer of 1786, that the South, in general, was quite unwilling to confer upon the North the one return benefit that lay within its power: the benefit of becoming a full-fledged partner with the North in establishing an American continental "commercial system."

This, however, was not all. After the South made known its attitude on the Spanish treaty, there was the further galling fact that the South seemed ready to run the country rashly into war, at the very same time declining to join with the North in establishing the kind of "commercial system" that alone could make successful warfare possible. Still more galling was the fact that the war so willingly risked by the South was a war for a right that the Southerners chiefly prized as a means for drawing away from the North its precious resources in men. Finally, there was for the Northern men the supreme irony of the whole situation: if the war in question should be fought and won, and matters should then work out as the Southerners hoped, the free and democratic Northern states would in the end become a hopeless minority under a national government dominated by the landed, slaveholding "aristocracies" of the South. Such an outcome—to say nothing at all of entering upon a war to promote it—was simply unthinkable to the Northern men, and since the South was at the time very obviously in a weak position, it is as certain as anything well can be that clearheaded Northern men like Rufus King had not the slightest intention of yielding to the South's desires. These facts, then, are the final key to an understanding of the Northern attitude toward the Southern opposition to John Jay's proposed Spanish treaty of 1786; to an understanding of the maneuvering that went on in Congress, toward the end of that summer, with the object, apparently, of convincing the South that, if the South were not very careful, the North might withdraw from the Confederacy and leave the South to face its enemies alone; and to an understanding, finally, of the actual determination of many leading Northern men that, rather than fight for their own enslavement, they would, if necessary, carry out this threat and set up a nation of their own.

Despite all this, it is abundantly clear that no Northern men had actually formulated any program of dismemberment, on the basis of such ideas, in 1786. Certainly no evidence of any kind is known that bears out the suspicions entertained by James Monroe, that John Jay and Rufus King and certain other Northern men had entered upon a secret conspiracy to use the Spanish treaty to disrupt the union, and obtain the organization of a Northern confederacy from which the South should be excluded. To the contrary, convincing evidence that no such conspiracy existed is not hard to find. Such evidence appears, for example, in a letter written by Rufus King, to his friend, Jonathan Jackson of Boston, just two days after the affair of the Spanish treaty was temporarily closed.[44] Dated September 3, the letter discloses a continuing desire on the part of King for such a treaty as Jay had suggested, and a continuing determination to get such a treaty if possible. In the letter, King likewise observes that, "if therefore our disputes with Spain are not settled, we shall be obliged either wholly to give up the western Settlers or join *them** in an issue of Force with the Catholic King." "The latter," King said without hesitation, "we are in no condition to think of, the former would be impolitic for many reasons, and cannot with safety be *now** admitted, although very few men who have examined the subject will refuse their assent to the opinion that every Citizen of the Atlantic States, who emigrates to the westward of the Allegany is a total loss to our confederacy." King's remarks undoubtedly evince that he considered dismemberment *from the ultramontane country* as something that might possibly come "if our disputes with Spain [should] *not* [be] settled." There is nothing in his letter suggesting the slightest desire on his part for that or any other dismemberment, *if* those disputes could be settled; much less is there anything suggesting that he was a participant in any conspiracy to use the proposals to settle the country's disputes with Spain *as a means* to disrupt the Union. On the contrary, in a letter to Elbridge Gerry, on June 4, King had talked hopefully, on the assumption that Jay's Spanish treaty might go through, of instituting a

*King's emphasis.

government "so connecting [the ultramontane] with the Atlantic States, as would be highly [beneficial to them both] and promise a considerable [trade]."[45]

That the subject of "dismemberment," on September 3, 1786, was nothing more than an indefinite, future possibility to Rufus King, in case all other expedients failed, is also shown by what he had to say in his letter to Jackson upon the subject of governmental reform. Some men were still advocating, King said, an increase of the powers of Congress. But this was not, in his opinion, a feasible solution, because the "supposed" opposition in the individual interests of the particular states would be certain to "prevent *Unanimity* in *any* opinion concerning the corroboration"—i.e., the strengthening—"of the Federal Constitution." "Others, and by no means the least respectable [were] answer[ing to these suggestions of "corroborating" Congress,] that nothing [could] be done in our present form [of government]; that the Error [lay] in the original plan." They were proposing to "diminish the number of States; [to] reform their Constitutions, give their Governments more energy, the Laws more stability, the magistrates greater authority and responsibility; [and to] let the *State* Governments *be confined* to matters *merely* internal." In other words, these "others," with whom, it is apparent, King himself agreed, were advocates for the establishment of a *national* government, with power extending to *all* matters *not* "merely internal"; that is, of course, not "*merely* internal," *or domestic*, to the *respective* states. That could only have meant a national government with powers extending even to matters which, though of "internal" concern to a state, were also of concern to any, or all, of the other states; and that was the concept of a national government empowered to act in *all* cases for "the general welfare" of the country, the most inclusive of the objects expressly stated in the Articles of Confederation.

As for the form of this national government thus being proposed, it was to consist, according to Rufus King, of "a vigorous Executive, wise Legislative, and independent Judicial." The advocates of such a change argued, he explained to Jackson, "that a league or confederation between so many small and unequal Sovereignties never did, or [could] answer the views of its Patrons." They illustrated their views from history. And having repeated to Jackson some of the historical instances being used by these men to illustrate their arguments—cases, in the main, of forcible conversion of confederacies into unitary monarchies, to the increased happiness, King said, of the people concerned—King hastened to add that his letter was not to be understood as "an opinion" that "a monarchy would promote the happiness of the people of America—far, very far from it." "But they show this," he declared, "[that] if wise and prudent men *discerning the imperfections of the present Governments*, do not in season and without fear, *propose suitable remedies*, the causes which changed the governments alluded to may, and probably will, change those of America." Then, expressing satisfaction that delegates from Massachusetts would be present at Annapolis, and his "hope [that], extraordinary as [that] measure [was], that it [might] issue more favorably than [he] ha[d] ever expected," he concluded with the sentiment, probably shared at the time by most Northern men: "We must wait events."[46]

In short, just two days after the Spanish treaty matter had been temporarily closed, Rufus King, who, according to James Monroe, was the ringleader, along with John Jay, in a deep-laid Northern plot to use that treaty to disrupt the Union, was actually planning, and writing to his personal friends, not about plans for dismemberment but about plans for organizing a new and better government for the whole United States. And since King plainly said, in his letter to Jackson, that the "unanimity" necessary to "corroborate" the Articles was not, in his opinion, possible of attainment as a practical matter, it is perfectly clear his opinion must have been that any change to a better government would *have* to be effected by *some other means* than the unanimous consent of the thirteen state legislatures, which the Articles of Confederation required. The fact that King had come to this important conclusion, at this early date—a conclusion he had likewise strongly suggested to Caleb Davis, nearly a year before[47]—is an extremely useful key, generally overlooked, not only to the true nature of King's own behavior and purposes, in September 1786, but to the true nature of certain little-understood proceedings in Congress, and King's part in those proceedings, in the following winter.[48] And the conclusion in question, along with the other sentiments appearing in King's letter, constitutes ample proof that James Monroe's suspicions of a dismemberment conspiracy were totally unfounded, so far, at least, as Rufus King was concerned.

Monroe's suspicions of John Jay seem also to have been without foundation. This appears from a letter Jay wrote John Adams, in London, about three weeks before he put the Spanish treaty question before Congress. In his letter, Jay told Adams it was "one of the first wishes of [his] heart . . . to see the people of America become one nation in every respect." "For, as to the separate legislatures," he said, "I would have them considered, with relation to the Confederacy, in the same light in which counties stand to the State of which they are parts, viz., merely as districts to facilitate the purposes of domestic order and good government."[49] As we have not the slightest reason for suspecting the sincerity of Jay's sentiments expressed in this letter, the fact that he expressed them is in itself a sufficient refutation of Monroe's dire suspicions. Jay had expressed similar sentiments in his letters to his friends in earlier years,[50] and in the months that followed he was to be one of those, along with Rufus King, who made a valiant effort to induce the states and Congress to adopt a procedure, in the effort then making for a better government, which would make "one nation" sure.

CHAPTER XXI

The Failure of the Annapolis
Commercial Convention: Herein of the Annapolis
Proposal for the Federal Convention

O N THE third of September, the same day on which Rufus King wrote his letter to Jonathan Jackson, James Monroe wrote one to James Madison.[1] The two letters provide a most interesting comparison. On the date of the letters, James Madison was on his way to Annapolis, and he received Monroe's letter at that place a few days later, while he and others were awaiting the arrival of more delegates to the convention. Madison replied to Monroe's letter on September 11,[2] and since his reply, and the endorsement he added to Monroe's letter for filing purposes,[3] definitely indicate that he believed what Monroe had told him, Monroe's letter is undoubtedly important, not only as it relates to Monroe's own state of mind when the Annapolis convention was assembling, but also as it throws light upon the then state of mind of James Madison and, very likely, of the other Virginia delegates at Annapolis.

Monroe's letter was in the nature of a final admonition to Madison as to what the Massachusetts delegates to the Annapolis convention would be likely to do, and as to how important he had finally come to think that convention was to the future of Virginia. He began by informing Madison that he "consider[ed] the party [in favor of the Spanish treaty], especially Jay and the principal advocates"—by which he particularly meant the Massachusetts men—"as having gone too far to retreat." "They must," said Monroe, "either carry the measure or be disgrac'd (as," he added, "the principal already ha[d] been by the vote of 5 states), and sooner than to suffer this they [would]," he predicted, "labour to break the Union." "I suspect," he went on, "[that] they have already (and indeed have too much reason for my suspicions) [been] intriguing with the principal men in [Pennsylvania and New Jersey] to effect that end in the last resort." "They ha[d] even sought a dismemberm[en]t to the Potowmack," he said, with a certitude that seemed to grow as he told his story, "and those of [Jay's] party [in Congress] ha[d] been sounding those in office [that] far [South]." "To defeat the measure, therefore, completely, [the Southerners] must follow [the] movements [of Jay's party] and counteract them everywhere; advise the leading men [of Pennsylvania and New Jersey] of [the Jay party's] designs, the purposes they

315

[were] meant to serve etc.; and, in the event of the worst extremity, prepare [the leading men of those states] for an union with the Southern states." Monroe warned Madison that "some of those in Pen[nsylvani]a [would] have a contrary affection." "But it must be remov'd if possible; [for] a knowledge that [Pennsylvania] was on [the Southern] side wo'd blow [the] whole intrigue in the air. To bring this ab[ou]t, therefore, [was] an important object to the Southern interest. If a dismemberm[en]t [took] place, [Pennsylvania] must not be added to the eastern scale." "It were as well," he added, "[for the Southerners] to use force to prevent [such an outcome], as to defend [them]selves afterwards." All things considered, he regarded "the convention of Annapolis as a most important era in [American] affairs." "Be assur'd," he said, "[that] the Eastern men mean it as leading further than the object originally comprehended. [And] if they do not obtain that things shall be arrang'd to suit them in every respect, their intrigues will extend to the objects I have above suggested." In these final views, except, in part, with respect to dismemberment, Monroe was quite probably right: the Massachusetts men, if we may judge by King's letter to Jonathan Jackson, did indeed mean to go beyond "the object originally comprehended." Whether Monroe was right or wrong in the views he expressed, he did undoubtedly believe them to be true, and he was correspondingly earnest in his closing admonition that "the convention requir[ed Madison's] utmost exertions, in the changes things [would] infallibly take, as well to obtain good as to prevent mischief." Having finished his letter, and being, perhaps, still troubled by recollections of Madison's attitude toward a full national commerce power during the last two years, Monroe added a postscript in which he declared that he "ha[d] always considered *the regulation of trade* in the hands of the U.S. as necessary to preserve the Union"; that, "without it, [the Union would] infallibly tumble to pieces." He also "earnestly wish[ed] [for] the admission of a few additional States into the Confederacy in the Southern scale."[4]

Taking the various statements in the foregoing letter together, one thing seems clear: the summer's controversy over the Spanish treaty, and the Northern threats of dismemberment growing out of it, had not had a bad effect upon James Monroe. Instead, those events had increased his zeal for the national union and aroused in him a fighting determination that everything possible must be done to keep the states together. Still further evidence that this had been the impact of the summer's events upon Monroe appears in his letter to Patrick Henry of August 12. Writing that letter very soon, apparently, after his "discovery" of the deep-laid "conspiracy" in which he so firmly believed, Monroe told Henry, as he later told Madison, that "it [was] necessary [for Virginians] to contemplate [dismemberment] as an event which [might] possibly happen, and for which [they] should be guarded." "A dismemberment which would throw too much strength into the Eastern Division should be prevented. It should be so managed, (if it [took] place) either that it should be formed into three divisions, or, if into two, that

Pen[nsylvani]a if not Jersey should be included [with the South]." Even as he expressed these views as to what Virginia should do, or try to do, if dismemberment came, Monroe also declared his firm conviction that the whole Northern conspiracy ought to be defeated; that "a dismemberment should be avoided by all the states; and [that] the conduct of wise and temperate men should have in view to prevent it."[5] In a second letter to Madison, while the latter was at Annapolis, Monroe took occasion to explain that "the ablest men [in Congress]"—meaning, of course, the Southerners, with the exception of Henry Lee and possibly one or two more—agreed with his views and "believe[d] and act[ed] on it, in the rejection of the [Spanish] proposition, that it endangered the gov[ernmen]t—and that it [would] most probably induce a change of some kind or other [in the existing constitution]." In consonance with his continuing belief to this effect, Monroe then warned Madison once more that "it [was] well for the Southern States to act with great circumspection & to be prepar'd for every possible event—*to stand well with the Middle States especially*."[6]

From these several letters, it is evident that the effect of the summer's happenings upon James Monroe had been to turn his mind to the idea of "saving the Union" through what he apparently conceived would be a "counter-intrigue" between the Southern and the Middle states. If necessary, this counter-intrigue was to extend to the formation of an independent Southern and Middle state union; but since the Middle states had no conceivable desire to become a hopeless minority in such a union, and the preservation of the existing union was the primary object of Monroe's desires, the effect of Southern or Virginian action in accord with his views would be to open a way to the Middle states, and particularly to Pennsylvania, to play a leading role in forwarding the true Northern aims with respect to changes in the government. That something of this sort actually occurred before the Federal Convention met, there can be no doubt at all.

The Southerner who played the chief imaginary role in this "counter-intrigue" with the Middle states was James Madison. He seems to have agreed completely with Monroe that it was "well for the Southern states to stand well with the Middle states," and upon the termination of his visit to New York, Madison began at once to work toward this end. On his journey from New York to Annapolis to attend the convention, he stopped off at Princeton to confer with John Witherspoon, president of the college there, on the subject of "occluding" the Mississippi. Witherspoon saw the subject, Madison later reported to Monroe, "in the proper light."[7] Hurrying on to Philadelphia, Madison next "conferred freely," according to another report to Monroe, with James Wilson of that city. Wilson most probably was privy to the purposes of the Northern men's moves, and judging by Madison's report to Monroe, Wilson allowed Madison to confer as "freely" as he liked, and gave him in return very little satisfaction, one way or the other, as to what his own views were.[8] Undiscouraged, Madison continued his efforts after his arrival at Annapolis, working there upon Abraham Clark, one of the New Jersey delegates[9] and, very likely, upon others. After the convention was over, Madison rode back to Philadelphia and spent the interval until the date set for the Virginia legislature's meeting in further efforts in behalf of Virginia and the other Southern states.[10]

The Madison documents establishing these facts do not, it is true, indicate specifically that Madison sought to "stand well with the Middle states" upon the subject of governmental reform. His letters, instead, speak mostly of the Spanish treaty. Bearing in mind the long-standing desire of the men of New Jersey for a complete national power of regulating commerce, Clark's connection with the proposal that was soon afterwards issued from Annapolis,[11] and Witherspoon's connection in 1781 with the proposal in Congress of a complete national commerce power,[12] it is hard to doubt that Madison was compelled to represent to these New Jersey men that Virginia would support the creation of such a national power, in order to "stand well" with them at all. And not less, as Madison undoubtedly knew, was certainly necessary with James Wilson, who had been one of those who had favored the early drafts of the Articles of Confederation, in 1776.[13] Merely on the basis of the larger aspects of the situation, then, the undeniable probability is that Madison did make such a representation to the men in question.

The real strength of this probability, however, depends upon another fact, which appears in a still unquoted portion of Rufus King's September 3 letter to Jonathan Jackson. From this part of King's letter, it appears that Madison represented to the New England men in Congress, while the Spanish treaty controversy was going on, that he agreed completely with their desire for a *full* national commerce power and looked forward to advocating such a power in the Annapolis meeting. "Mr. Madison of Virginia," King remarked in his letter, "has been here [in New York] for some time past, he will attend the convention. He does not discover or propose any other plan than that of investing Congress with *full powers for the regulation of commerce foreign and domestic*." The language of this statement deserves our careful notice, for it plainly shows, not only that King still distrusted Madison, on September 3, 1786, but that he apparently had tried, in his conversations with Madison, to draw Madison out and judge for himself what Madison's true intentions and expectations were. Madison, apparently, had come through the test successfully and had not "discovered" to King any plans other than those which he actually "proposed." To King's obvious astonishment, the plan Madison "proposed" was precisely the thing the New England and Middle states long had wanted. Yet King, fully aware of the comprehensive extent of a power to regulate commerce; of the extreme difficulty Congress would have in exercising such a power, under the then existing governmental arrangements; and of the limited commissions issued by the states to their delegates meeting at Annapolis, was apparently not convinced. "This power," he told Jackson, "will run deep into the authorities of the individual States, and can never be well exercised without a federal Judicial." "The reform"—and King's letter otherwise shows that he did not at all oppose "a federal Judicial" or a sweeping general change in the whole form of government—"the reform," said King, "must necessarily be extensive." He concluded with the comment already quoted: "We must wait events."[14]

That King was justified in his continuing skepticism about James Madison's representations to him is shown by one of Madison's confidential letters. Written by Madison on August 12 from Philadelphia, "a few days" after he had terminated his visit to New York, the letter was addressed to Thomas Jefferson in Paris. "Many Gentlemen," said Madison, "both within & without Cong[res]s, wish to make [the] Meeting [at Annapolis] subservient to a plenipotentiary Convention for amending the Confederation." "[His own] wishes," he added, "[were] in favor of such an event"; but he "despair[ed] so much of its accomplishment at the present crisis that [he did] not extend [his] views beyond a commercial Reform." "To speak the truth," said he—and he spoke it, of course, in cipher—"I almost despair even of this." One major reason for his despair was the iniquitous proposal then pending in Congress, to "occlude" the Mississippi. "Passing by the other Southern States, figure to yourself," he said, "the effect of such a stipulation on the Assembly of Virginia, *already jealous of Northern politics*, and which will be composed of about thirty members from the Western waters, of a majority of others attached to the Western country from interests of their own, of their friend[s] or their constituent[s], and of many others who though indifferent to [the] Mississippi, will zealously play off the disgust of its friends against federal measures."[15]

From the passage last quoted, it is quite clear that Madison *feared* the affair of the Spanish treaty would simply worsen the already bad situation in the Virginia legislature, with whose "jealousy of Northern politics" he was only too familiar. This *fear* of Madison's, it would seem, has generally passed muster, in discussions of the subject, as the absolute equivalent of the fact which he feared. It will be no occasion for wonder, should the evidence show that Madison's judgment in this matter, as in some matters previously noted, was bad, and that as they actually turned out his fears and the facts were at variance. As we have seen, the effect the Spanish treaty controversy and the resulting Northern dismemberment threats had had upon James Monroe was exactly the opposite of what Madison feared might prevail in the Virginia legislature: those events had increased Monroe's zeal "to preserve the Union," which, he had once more informed Madison in emphatic terms, could only be done if "the regulation of trade" were given to Congress. The effect upon Madison himself had been similar; on his trip to New York, when the Spanish treaty controversy was going on, Madison had *for the first time* advocated what the Northern men wanted: "full" national power to regulate "both foreign and domestic commerce." In short, reaction by these two leading Virginia men to the Northern threats was almost exactly what Rufus King and Nathan Dane had calculated it would be when they first had begun to think of such threats in the preceding fall and winter. If upon examination the reaction of a good many other Virginia men should turn out to have been about the same, the fact should not occasion any surprise.

The details of the general Virginian reaction to the affair of the Spanish treaty belong to future chapters. The point of interest at the present moment is the state of mind of James Madison and the other two Virginia delegates at Annapolis. In the light of the evidence already introduced, Madison's state of mind seems certain. He was the prey of conflicting fears: the fear, on the one hand, that if something drastic were *not* soon done, the North would withdraw from the Confederacy and leave the South to face its enemies alone, and the fear, on the other hand, that if anything drastic *were proposed* to be done, the Virginia legislature would veto it. His fear of the Virginia legislature was of course chiefly based upon his own sad experience with that body a few months previously, when the modest national commercial powers which he had supposed "would not alarm" it could not be gotten through. Edmund Randolph, another of the Virginia delegates at Annapolis, was perfectly familiar with the difficulties experienced by Madison at that time; and if we may judge by Randolph's strange and diffident behavior when he called the Annapolis convention together, he probably still shared Madison's timorous views when the convention met.[16] Little is known of the views of the third Virginia delegate, St. George Tucker,[17] but there is no reason to suppose that, whatever his views, he was in a position to overbear his two colleagues. The warranted conclusion seems then to be that, however anxious to take decisive action these three Virginians may have been, their knowledge of the sentiments and behavior of the Virginia legislature in the preceding year most probably put a great damper upon what they dared to do in September 1786.

Only two other states besides Virginia had quorums of delegates at Annapolis: New Jersey and Delaware.[18] Delaware was represented by John Dickinson, George Read, and Richard Bassett.[19] On the basis of the general record of the first two of these men over many years, and the particular record of all three in the Federal Convention, they probably were ready to take any reasonable action to improve the government.[20] As for New Jersey, represented by Abraham Clark, William Churchill Houston, and James Schureman, it is sufficient to refer once more to that state's consistently national prior record, and to point out that it had actually empowered its delegates at Annapolis not only to go into the subject of commercial regulation (as Virginia had proposed) but also to take into consideration any "other important matters" as to which they might think a "uniform system" was "necessary to the common interest and permanent harmony of the several states."[21] The delegates from New Jersey, like those from Delaware, were in all probability ready to take any action for which the rest of the convention was prepared.

There remain only the delegates in attendance from New York and Pennsylvania. Those two states were represented at Annapolis by less than a quorum of the delegates they had appointed. Pennsylvania's sole representative was Tench Coxe.[22] Nothing is known of what he did at Annapolis; but judging by his past espousal of a "full and entire" national commerce power as a member of the Philadelphia merchants' committee of 1785, and his future activities in behalf of the Constitution during the ratification campaign, it is impossible to believe that he was a clog on the convention's doings. The two New York delegates, Egbert Benson and Alexander Hamilton,[23] were among the staunchest nationalists in the entire country. A man of courage and high intelligence, Hamilton had long been acutely aware of the defects of the Confederacy, and as early as September 3, 1780, had begun his long series of efforts to obtain some improvement in the government. The reader will recall Hamilton's well-known letter to James Duane, in Congress, proposing that Congress should call upon the states to assemble in a "plenipotentiary" convention "with *full* authority to conclude *finally* upon a *General* Confederation." Although his urgings had then failed, Hamilton had thereafter tried repeatedly, through his writings and through efforts made in the New York legislature and Congress, to get something started, but in each case his efforts had met with failure. Among his most recent activities along such lines, Hamilton had been the leading speaker at the meeting in New York on June 15, 1785, which had called for the vesting of Congress with "full" power to regulate "the commerce of the United States."[24] On the basis of Hamilton's entire past activities, it is impossible to doubt that he was, as has always been supposed, the mainspring of energy in the Annapolis convention; and his friend Egbert Benson agreed with him completely.

Of the twelve men present at Annapolis, then, none could have felt any hesitancy in taking vigorous and forthright steps for the improvement of the government, except the delegates from Virginia. Little is known of what actually took place in the convention. The twelve delegates had arrived at Annapolis by September 11,[25] one week after the date set for the meeting. On that day the convention organized, electing John Dickinson president;[26] according to a letter of Madison's to Monroe written on that day, the delegates had then already determined, "unless the *sudden* attendance of a much more respectable number [took] place, ... to break up the Meeting, with a recommendation of another time & place, & an *intimation** of the expediency of extending the plan to other defects of the Confederation."[27] Madison's use of the word "sudden" would seem to carry at least some suggestion that the delegates had decided to hurry away; and of doing precisely this, they were afterwards accused. For this accusation there was undoubtedly very good ground. The convention had no more than finished its business

*Madison's emphasis.

and adjourned *sine die* three days later, when the representative of North Carolina arrived;[28] the delegates returning to the northward met the Massachusetts men at Wilmington, hurrying to Annapolis, with the Rhode Island men en route behind them, just two days after that.[29] The twelve delegates participating in the Annapolis proceedings were the delegates from the nearer states, and there can be little doubt that, according to the usual practice of that era—a practice based upon the prevailing uncertainties of travel—the delegates at Annapolis did not wait very long for their fellow delegates from the more distant states. This fact naturally suggests the question of whether the Virginia delegates, very likely influenced by Monroe's excited letters, did not somehow contrive to hurry the other delegates away before the Massachusetts and other eastern men could arrive. However probable this fact may seem, there is no known direct evidence.

When the delegates had organized on the eleventh, a committee had been appointed to draw up a report, to be sent to the states having delegates present. This committee reported on September 13.[30] According to a statement later made by Egbert Benson, the report in its original form was the work of Alexander Hamilton, though Hamilton was not, according to Benson, a member of the committee.[31] There is also a story, inherently credible but not too well supported by evidence, that Hamilton's original report was bolder and more forthright in what it proposed than the somewhat vague and wordy document finally adopted. According to this story, Edmund Randolph (no doubt remembering what had happened in Virginia in the previous year) objected to Hamilton's report as going too far; Madison (who also had his own vivid memories of those events) advised the convention "to yield to [Randolph]." "Otherwise," Madison is reported to have said, "all Virginia [would] be against [them]."[32] This story, assuming its truth, suggests the question: what were the points upon which Hamilton was obliged to yield? The probability is that he was obliged to yield upon pointing plainly to a national form of government as the desirable innovation, and to a more feasible mechanism for effecting such a change than the one finally suggested by the Annapolis convention. This probability rests chiefly upon the fact that Hamilton had advocated a true constituent, or "plenipotentiary," convention as the desirable agency of reform as early as September 1780;[33] and also upon the fact that, a few months after the Annapolis meeting, when it became apparent that Virginian sentiment had changed very greatly, Hamilton and Benson *and Madison also*, together with "many [other] Gentlemen, both within & without Cong[res]s," were concerned in an attempt to obtain the substitution of just such a convention in place of the convention proposed by the Annapolis conference. The evidence relating to this little-known attempt will be presented to the reader in Chapter XXV.

The report finally adopted at Annapolis began by pointing out that, besides the states having delegates present, New Hampshire, Massachusetts,

Rhode Island, and North Carolina had also made appointments, but that none of their delegates had appeared. The report added that, so far as the Annapolis delegates knew, no delegates had been appointed by the other four states. In view of these facts it seemed "inadvisable," the report went on, for the convention to proceed with its business "under the circumstance of so partial and defective a representation." The more ample commission that New Jersey had given its delegates was next referred to; the opinion was expressed that this was "an improvement on the original plan"; a recommendation was made that another convention be held, with powers of the kind New Jersey had given; and Philadelphia and the second Monday of the following May were suggested as the place and time for such a meeting.

The delegates also observed in their report that they were "the more naturally led to this conclusion, since, in the course of their reflection on the subject, they [had] been induced to think that *the power of regulating trade [was] of such comprehensive extent*, and [would] enter so far into the general system of the federal government, that, to give it efficacy, and to obviate questions and doubts concerning its precise nature and limits, [might] require a correspondent adjustment of other parts of the federal system." Thus, the Annapolis delegates were quite as fully aware as Rufus King was regarding the "comprehensive extent" of a "power to regulate trade" or "commerce," and the extreme difficulty that would have attended the exercise of such a power under the Articles of Confederation. Apparently believing, as James Monroe believed, that a complete national commerce power was required "to preserve the union," the Annapolis delegates rather plainly implied their approval of such a power and called for a new convention with commissions adequate, not only to proposing it, but to proposing in addition all those other changes in the structure of the government that might be judged necessary to make such an extensive power effective. Indeed, in their actual proposal of a new convention, the Annapolis delegates went, in a vague way, somewhat farther. They urged upon their states that the delegates chosen for the new convention be empowered generally "to take into consideration the situation of the United States; to devise such further provisions as [should] appear to them necessary to render the Constitution of the federal government *adequate to the exigencies of the Union*; and to report such an act for that purpose to the United States in Congress assembled as *when agreed to by them, and afterwards confirmed by the legislatures of every state*, [would] effectually provide for the same." "From motives of respect," copies of this report were sent, not only to the states represented at Annapolis, but to Congress and the other states as well.[34]

The foregoing report was undoubtedly some advance over the proposal the Virginia legislature had sent out so strangely in the preceding January. Unlike the original Virginia proposal, the Annapolis report seemed to assume that a complete national commerce power was necessary, and that there were other important changes that should be made. The nature of these other changes was, however, not at all plainly indicated. The objective of "render[ing] the Constitution of the federal government adequate to the exigencies of the Union" was anything but definite; and there was only the vaguest intimation elsewhere in the plan (if, indeed, there was any intimation at all) in favor of the establishment of a national form of government: "a vigorous Executive, wise Legislative, and independent Judicial," such as Rufus King had informed Jonathan Jackson so many men desired.[35]

Far worse than this, however, was the fact that the new convention was to be merely an advisory body, and that every change it might decide upon was therefore, *by express stipulation in the Annapolis plan*, to be at the mercy of *"the legislatures of every state"* in the country. This, to be sure, was in strict accord with the Articles of Confederation.[36] The men in Congress, however, had had much sad experience with that particular mode of constitutional alteration; in the light of this fact, the reader will not feel suprise that, when the Annapolis plan was put before them, many members of Congress failed to exhibit that complete enthusiasm for the plan which has been felt by so many historians in later years. In consequence of their views, the plan never did, strictly speaking, obtain the approval of Congress. Efforts were instead made to obtain the substitution of some more likely-seeming scheme; and when these efforts failed, the more vigorous nationalists in Congress induced the supporters of the Annapolis plan to agree to certain alterations in the statement of objectives for the proposed convention, and also to an alteration of considerable importance in the procedure suggested for reaching the objectives stated. These alterations, so the more vigorous nationalists hoped, would have the effect of making "the firm national government" they had in mind a little easier of attainment; and since the Federal Convention eventually acted in accordance with these suggestions, it is apparent that the importance of the Annapolis plan has generally been greatly exaggerated. As a plan of change, it was never followed; the plan that *was* followed, was suggested by Congress—somewhat vaguely, perhaps—but at the instance of men most of whom had *not* been present at Annapolis.[37]

Part IV

Politics and Events Leading up
to the Agreement of Congress
and the States to the Meeting of
the Federal Convention of 1787

CHAPTER XXII

Shays' Rebellion and Its Diverse Effects in Different Regions of the Country

TO complete the picture of the disordered conditions out of which the Constitution grew, some account should be given of the further course of the post-Revolutionary business depression in the New England states, which was serious as early as the spring of 1785. We have previously mentioned the fact that of the various regions of the country New England was much the most directly and severely affected by the British orders in council of 1783. The effect of those orders had been to dry up at once and almost completely the ancient sources of remittance for foreign goods, upon which the people of the region had relied in the prewar years; and since New Englanders had undoubtedly ordered out their full share of foreign goods in 1783, the inevitable result was a drain of specie from New England, commencing very soon after the British orders in council were issued. Eventually this phenomenon took place or had repercussionary effects in all parts of the country. Whereas the old markets for the staple goods and services of New England (except Connecticut)[1] were actually and directly cut off by the British orders in council, the effect of those orders in other regions was largely circuitous and delayed, being manifested chiefly in falling prices rather than total absence of market for staple services and products. A consequence of this difference was that New England was first and hardest hit; in the whole period between the peace and the Federal Convention, the phenomena of business depression were more severe and more advanced in the New England states (except Connecticut), than they were in any other part of the country.

As long as the depression in New England affected only the business of the urban groups, the rural population, which even in New England constituted the great mass of the people, remained on the whole indifferent. As more and more specie left the country, and prices (including local agricultural prices) fell, however, the increased burden of public and private debts began to be felt in the rural areas as well as in the towns, and the farmers as well as the urban groups began to demand relief. The relief demanded by the urban groups was the creation of a national commerce power and the establishment

327

thereunder of a complete American "commercial system"; but the relief demanded by the farmers was moratory laws; the right to tender property, instead of cash, in payment of existing debts; "paper-money banks"; partial repudiation of public obligations; and reductions and suspensions of taxes. Although such measures were both supported and opposed in the towns as well as in the country, they were primarily and characteristically rural measures; because of the farmers' great numbers and consequent political power, the measures were enacted into law, in whole or in part, in the various states both in and out of New England.

In New England, however, the urban groups were more numerous and more influential than they were in most other regions of the country; the sentiment against paper money and similar measures was there more strongly entrenched; and the urban groups in New England were consequently able, at least for a time, to deny most of the rural or agrarian demands. Precisely because the depression was so severe in New England, however, the unstable and explosive character of the situation there was merely augmented by these measures of denial.

This appears to have been the state of affairs throughout New England at the beginning of 1786. A little later in that year numerous local "conventions" of an unofficial character, strongly reminiscent of those which a few years before had subverted the British government of the country, were held throughout the rural parts of the New England states; programs for "a redress of grievances" were drawn up at these "conventions"; and then, when the legislatures met later in the spring, efforts were again made to obtain the enactment of the various items in these agrarian programs of relief. These efforts generally were unsuccessful; but at the spring elections in Rhode Island, the agrarians won a sweeping victory and were consequently in a position to put their whole extremist program into immediate operation in that state. As first steps in this direction, the newly elected Rhode Island legislature voted at its May session to suspend the collection of taxes, to organize a state "paper-money bank," and to issue to the people of the state one hundred thousand pounds in paper bills.[2] The bills were in the nature of promises to pay the face amount thereof fourteen years from the date of issue; they were to be "secured," in some obscure manner, through a pledge to the state, by the issuee, of "clear landed real Estates" to double the value of the issued bills; and they were to be apportioned among the citizenry in the ratios used for the last state tax, which had been suspended. The bills, of course, were made a legal tender for payment of all debts, but nonetheless they began to depreciate as soon as issued. To provide additional uses for them and thereby, it was hoped, to keep up their value, the legislature at its June session enacted that the last state tax should be collected, and that another tax of the same amount should be levied, both to be payable in the new bills. It was also provided that an earlier and more moderate tender law, which had allowed the payment of debts in real estate or chattels, should be repealed; and provisions were made whereby the paper money could be paid into court in discharge of debts, in cases wherein the creditors declined the money or contrived to avoid having it tendered to them in person. Finally, it was enacted that all persons should be obliged to accept the new bills at par in payment for any goods they might offer for sale; and that any one who declined to do so, or discouraged the circulation of the bills in any way, should be subject to a fine of one hundred pounds; and, upon a second offense, to a similar penalty and loss of his rights as a citizen, in addition. To assure observance and enforcement of these stringent provisions, it was further enacted that "one Moiety" of all fines for offenses against the paper-money laws should be paid over to persons giving information of, and prosecuting, such offenses.[3]

This Rhode Island "paper-money law" of 1786 was not the first such measure enacted into law in our American states, nor was it the only such measure to get into the statute books of the states during the years of the post-Revolutionary business depression. Pennsylvania, North Carolina, South Carolina, and Georgia had all preceded Rhode Island in the issuance of paper money; and New York and New Jersey issued such money soon after. The paper emissions of these various states, with the tender laws that generally accompanied them, particularly the so-called "pine-barren" laws in the Carolinas, all produced more or less disturbing effects. The so-called "forcing" provisions of the Rhode Island law, added by the legislature at its June session, were, however, of unexampled severity, and their impact on the already bad economic and political situation in Rhode Island was catastrophic. Citizen was immediately set against citizen by the "informer" provisions; and the state was split into two violent and bitter factions by the provisions relating to the acceptance of the paper at par in payments for goods. Indeed, these provisions brought all business in the state to a violent stop. The merchants and shopkeepers, naturally unwilling to accept the depreciated paper at par in exchange for their goods, and also desiring to bring the legislature to a realization that its "forcing" efforts would not work, acted together to close up their places of business as soon as the "forcing" provisions were passed. The farmers of the state, most of whom had pledged their lands for allotments of the new bills, were enraged by this action and at once retaliated upon the townspeople by bringing no produce to market. The resulting scarcity of food soon brought on mob violence in the town of Newport, directed first against those business houses that had closed their doors and then against the neighboring farmers who refused to bring foodstuffs to market. In Providence, the situation became equally serious, but violence was avoided there by taking public steps to obtain from outside the state the supplies needed by persons without stores of food. At this point, too, the Providence business houses apparently reopened, though under some kind of general understanding not to accept the new money at par in payments for goods. Penalties were avoided by legal technicalities and dilatory tactics, whose exact nature is not now clear.[4]

When the Providence business houses reopened, efforts were made to obtain an adequate future food supply from local sources by giving assurances to the nearby farmers that, if they would bring their produce to market in Providence, to be disposed of upon such terms as they and their buyers might agree upon, they might count upon freedom from molestation, and also upon an opportunity of supplying their own needs from the Providence shops upon similar terms. But the farmers, in "convention," voted to support the assembly; urged that body to enforce its paper-money laws; and advised it to add to those laws various new provisions designed to accomplish this end.[5] This advice the legislature promptly accepted, and at its August session passed a law requiring summary trial of all paper-money offenses, without a jury.[6] This enactment apparently caused another shutting of the shops. In September, however, the judges of the superior court refused to follow the new law in the celebrated case of *Trevett* v. *Weeden*, and the shops reopened. The legislature thereupon cited the judges to appear before it and explain the reasons which had led them to so extraordinary a decision. Three of them appeared but, maintaining that they were not accountable to the legislature in the discharge of their duties, declined to give the explanation demanded by the legislature. An effort was then made to dismiss them from office. The effort was a failure; and in December, the June and August enactments that had sought to compel acceptance of the paper money at par in payments for all goods, and to deny the right of jury trial for paper-money offenses, were repealed. The judges, who held their offices under one-year appointments by the legislature, were not, with one exception, reappointed at the end of the year.[7]

Meanwhile another rural "convention," held in September, had recommended to the Rhode Island farmers that they pursue a policy of complete nonintercourse with the local shopkeepers and merchants; to the legislature, it was recommended that a "state trade" be promptly organized to replace these ostracized traders. The proposal was that produce, fish, lumber, and labor, as well as money, be accepted by the state in the payment of taxes; and that the state, having provided itself with vessels, should then carry its tax receipts to the other states and foreign nations and there sell them for cash or exchange them for such articles as the agrarians of Rhode Island desired. In this way, it was hoped, the merchants and shopkeepers might be run out of business completely.[8] This extreme measure was never actually adopted, but it was widely talked of and helped to keep up the spirit of faction and unrest among the people of the state.

Certain other recommendations of this September "convention" met with a more favorable reception and were enacted into law at the legislature's December session. These included regulations for clogging the negotiability of private promissory notes, and others for cutting down drastically the period of limitation for bringing actions upon them. Similar regulations were also made with respect to actions upon book accounts—all, of course, with the object of compelling the use of the depreciated bills.[9] A little later the crowning iniquity was added: paying off the state's public debt with the bills which, by the time this action was taken, had become virtually worthless.[10] During the fall of 1786, an attempt was even made to disfranchise all citizens who should fail to take an oath to accept the state's paper money for all purposes exactly as the legislature might require. By another provision, all persons were to be forbidden to bring vessels into, or take vessels out of, the state, unless they should take the required oath. This was aimed at the merchants; the other hated class, the lawyers, were to be forbidden to practice, unless they also should comply with the requirement of the new law. Breaches of the oath were to be punishable as perjuries. This measure, however, was first submitted to the people and was defeated.[11]

Full reports of all these various Rhode Island acts, and threatened acts, together with the distressing practical effects they had upon the people of the state, were published currently in the newspapers all over the country.[12] In view of the nature of the reported events, it might be expected that the news of them would have been found disturbing by the men in the other states. There is, however, little evidence that this was the case. In the South, the whole matter was virtually ignored; and in the middle states, the troubles of "Rogue Island," as the state soon came to be called, were the subject of jest and abuse, but seldom apprehension. Apparently, the state was too small and too far away for its troubles to seem important. To a certain extent, this same attitude was found among the other states of New England. To the thinking men of those states, however, the underlying cause of Rhode Island's troubles was undoubtedly clear, and with the same underlying cause operative elsewhere in New England, and with the same effects already manifest to a considerable degree, the troubles of Rhode Island, not surprisingly, excited more attention and anxiety in the other New England states than they did in the remoter parts of the country.

This was especially true in the case of Massachusetts, where business was also very bad, and where, furthermore, the agrarian party was numerous. The agrarians in Massachusetts did not at any time obtain control of the local government, but they did succeed in electing to the Massachusetts General Court, in 1786, a good many men sympathetic to their views. These men made strenuous efforts in the spring legislative session of that year to obtain the enactment of the paper-money laws, the tender laws, and the other measures desired by the agrarian and debtor elements. As previously intimated, their efforts were in general a failure; and when, upon the adjournment of the General Court, on July 8, this fact became clear, more "conventions" at once assembled in the outlying counties. As in the case of the earlier meetings, elaborate sets of resolutions were adopted, containing long lists of grievances to be remedied. The desirability of "abstaining from all mobs and unlawful assemblies" and of pursuing "a constitutional method of redress" was in all cases solemnly proclaimed, but when the judges of the common pleas and general sessions appeared at Northampton, to hold the scheduled sessions of those courts in the last week in August, they were met by a mob of fifteen hundred armed men, who took possession of the local courthouse and refused to permit them to do so. Thus began the long series of Massachusetts insurrections known in history as Shays' Rebellion.

The "occlusion" of the courts at Northampton had for its purpose the preventing of all proceedings for the collection of debts and taxes, the foreclosure of mortgages, and similar actions. In the following week, the performance was repeated at Worcester by a mob of three hundred armed men. A short while later, at Great Barrington, eight hundred men not only prevented the holding of the courts but broke open the jail, liberated the prisoners (mostly debtors, no doubt) who were in it, and compelled three of the judges of the court of common pleas to sign a promise not to act in discharge of their offices until the various demands of the agrarians should be met. Similar occurrences took place, or were threatened, in other rural counties; and though Governor Bowdoin acted with promptness to quell the disturbances, through the use of the militia, that body proved too sympathetic with the insurrectionaries, in most of the places where the disturbances occurred, to be of any use. The contemporary opinion was that something like a third of the state was sympathetic:[13] a sufficient proof of the extreme "commercial languor" from which the state then suffered. In such circumstances, the disturbances, of course, spread very rapidly, and after a little while the governor called the General Court into extraordinary session.

That body assembled on September 27. Efforts were at once made to induce it to take steps for the restoration of order, but there were too many sympathizers with insurrectionaries among the General Court's members for such a course of action. Attention was turned, instead, to the passing of a tender act and the taking of certain of the other steps demanded by the agrarian "conventions." The hope was that with the enactment of such measures the insurrectionary outbreaks would subside. Learning that proposals had also been made in the General Court to suspend the habeas corpus and to take various other vigorous steps for the suppression of disorder, the insurgents, however, made the mistake, sometime in October, of circularizing the towns in the state's western counties, urging their selectmen to assemble and arm the local militias, and have them ready for instant action for the defense of Massachusetts' liberties. This rebellious measure, reported to the General Court on November 7, apparently convinced that body of the necessity of vigorous action. Shortly afterward, suspension of the habeas corpus was put through, and at the same time provision, obviously out of necessity, was made for the trial of all persons concerned in the insurrectionary disorders, in counties other than those in which their activities had occurred.

When these vigorous steps were finally taken, the General Court had been in session nearly two months. Although during that time a number of different acts had been passed, which it had been hoped would assuage the agrarian grievances, no diminution in the insurrectionary disturbances had occured. Instead, the disturbances had steadily grown worse. When it finally took the steps just mentioned, the General Court, nevertheless, determined to make one last effort to bring the disturbances to an end, without apprehending and punishing the persons concerned in them. It therefore enacted that all persons previously concerned in the disorders, who should nevertheless take an oath of allegiance to the commonwealth before the ensuing January 1, and who, in addition, should be of good behavior in the meantime, should be pardoned. To give ample opportunity for this act of clemency to have effect, no move, aside from merely preventive ones, was made against the insurgents in the intervening period. The General Court's effort, however, proved completely vain. Few of the disorderly elements took advantage of the opportunity to obtain a pardon; the disorders continued and, indeed, increased and grew worse; the courts were still interfered with; and the insurgent elements, collecting in armed bands in the outlying towns, kept the law-abiding citizenry in apprehension. In the end, order was not restored until well along in February, after a body of militia raised in the "well-affected" areas had been marched into the western counties and had there captured or dispersed the last body of insurgents.[14] It may be added that somewhat similar troubles also broke out in New Hampshire about the middle of September 1786, but these disturbances were less serious, were more vigorously dealt with, and were promptly suppressed.[15] The situation in New Hampshire remained, nevertheless, somewhat unstable and, like the situation in Massachusetts, was a source of worry for many months to come.

These occurrences in Rhode Island, New Hampshire, and Massachusetts, constituting a violent climax to a long period of business depression—a climax which the men of New England, both in and out of Congress, had long been striving to prevent—are unquestionably one of the important factors which must be borne in mind if the political situation out of which the Constitution grew is to be fully understood. In a certain sense, of course, this has long been recognized. Conventional histories usually convey the impression that Shays' Rebellion and, to a lesser extent, the troubles in Rhode Island were among the important forces, if, indeed, they were not *the* most important of all the forces which produced the sentiment that led to the holding of the Federal Convention and the drafting and adoption of the Constitution.

This view is far from correct. Despite the fact that the New England disturbances undoubtedly intensified the desire of the New England nationalist group for a strong, well-organized national government, and perhaps helped to reconcile such men as Rufus King and Nathan Dane to the making of *some* concession to the Southern desire for an altered basis of representation in Congress, it is by no means true that in New England the cause of the Constitution was helped by the occurrences in question. As for the states outside New England, where the outbreak of Shays' Rebellion did produce beneficial effects, the predisposing causes that led to those effects have not in general been fully understood.

The generally entertained theory about the beneficial political consequences of Shays' Rebellion in New England appears to be based upon a number of rather strange misapprehensions. Foremost among these is a failure to understand how strong and general the nationalist sentiment was among all the New England states in 1785; and how strong, indeed, such sentiment had been among those states (with occasional temporary vagaries on the part of particular states), from the very formation of the continental union in 1774. In addition to this, conventional histories display a complete want of understanding of the behavior of Rufus King and the other Massachusetts men in Congress in the years 1785–87. The consequence is that the New England states are commonly regarded as among the laggard states in the movement of the 1780s for "a firm national government." On the other hand, Virginia is, most oddly, regarded as having been the leader of this movement. Such an erroneous conspectus of the general situation requires some catastrophic occurrence as a causative agency to bring the New England states into line in the movement for the Federal Convention. This false requirement appears to be met by the outbreak of Shays' Rebellion, and because of this fact and the various misapprehensions underlying it, the conventional view of the rebellion and its political effects has apparently come to be received.

In justice to the accepted view, we should say at the outset that a few of the surviving items of the contemporary record, taken isolatedly, do seem to support it. One of the chief of these is a letter Stephen Higginson, of Boston, wrote to Henry Knox, in New York, in late November 1786. In this letter, written at the height of the Massachusetts disturbances, Higginson declared: "I never saw so great a change in the public mind on any occasion, as has lately appeared in this state as to the expediency of increasing the powers of Congress, *not merely as to commercial objects, but generally*."[16] The evidentiary effect of this statement, taken literally, is undoubtedly corroborative of the view commonly held as to the salutary political effect of Shays' Rebellion in New England. For various reasons, however, it appears impossible to take Higginson's statement literally. In the first place, we must remember that Higginson himself was an extremely ardent nationalist, very anxious to take advantage of the first opportunity that came along to institute "a firm national government." Such a man would be apt to be a little wishful in his thinking; and when we remember, in addition, that Higginson was a Boston merchant, that his personal contacts will therefore have been primarily with "the [Boston] public," and mainly with that part of the Boston public consisting of other merchants, lawyers, physicians, and clergymen, and other men of intelligence and education, the plain probability is that Higginson's letter was simply a somewhat exuberant report upon "the change" in "the mind" of *this part* of "the [Massachusetts] public" which Higginson best knew.

That the nationalism of this part of "the [Massachusetts] public" was quickened and intensified by Shays' Rebellion, there can be no possible doubt. In recognizing this, however, the reader should bear in mind that this particular part of "the [Massachusetts] public" had rather generally been favorable to "increasing the powers of Congress, not merely as to commercial objects but generally," before Shays' Rebellion occurred. The Boston merchants had come out strongly for the vesting of Congress with "full power to regulate the internal as well as the external commerce of all the states" on April 22, 1785; and some three weeks later the town of Boston had gone the whole way and declared generally to the delegates it elected to the General Court that it desired "to see the Congress invested with power competent to [America's] common necessities; to a due regulation of [the country's] commerce; and to the adjustment and discharge of [the nation's] public debt." This suggestion, we know, was adopted by the General Court a few weeks later, when it called for the assembling of a continental constitutional convention, for "lodg[ing] in the Supreme Rulers of the State"—as the General Court styled Congress—powers sufficient "to secure and perpetuate the primary objects of the Union," which were, according to the Articles, "the common defence," "the security of liberty," and "the mutual and general welfare" of the country. Higginson himself referred to this action of the General Court in another letter to Knox, and declared that "the State [had] entered into the measure of appointing a general Convention, *with much readiness*, [in 1785]"; and since the Massachusetts newspapers of that year contain only the scantiest evidence of opposition to the several proposals of reform just listed, Higginson was certainly correct upon this particular point.[17] If he was also correct in his statement first quoted, and if that statement must be understood with complete literality, then we ought to find that "the [Massachusetts] public," taken as a whole, was even "readier," after Shays' Rebellion, to enter into measures for establishing a fully empowered national government than that public had been before.

This view of the matter demonstrates the utter impossibility of a literal acceptance of Higginson's statement. There is no known evidence of any increased *general* readiness in Massachusetts in 1787 to strengthen the government of the nation. Instead, the absolute certainty is that the contrary was the case. The Constitution was bitterly opposed in Massachusetts in 1787–88; the outcome in the state's ratifying convention was thought by the friends of the Constitution to be extremely doubtful when that body met; and the vote by which the Constitution was finally ratified was uncomfortably close. The causes of this opposition were undoubtedly complex and numerous, but making every allowance for other factors, one of the most important of the causative factors was the factionalizing of the people of Massachusetts resulting from Shays' Rebellion or, to state it more accurately, from the long continuance and gradual deepening of the business depression underlying that unfortunate event.

The situation existing in Massachusetts when that state's ratifying convention met was well sketched at the time by Rufus King in certain letters he wrote from Boston to James Madison. "We make but slow progress in our Convention," King reported in one of these letters. The reason, he explained, was that "same infatuation which [had] prevailed not many months [before] in several Counties of [the] State, and [had] emboldened [the people in those counties] to take arms against the Government." The objections of the persons subject to this influence were "not directed," said King, "against any part of the Constitution; but their opposition seem[ed] to arise from an opinion that [was] immovable, that some injury [was] plotted against them." They appeared to feel "a distrust of men of property or education," and "an apprehension that the liberties of the people [were] in danger." They "complain[ed] that the Lawyers, Judges, Clergymen, Merchants and men of education [were] all in favor of the Constitution–and that for that reason [the supporters of the document] appear[ed] to be able to make the worse appear the better cause." They maintained that, "if [they] had men of [that] description on [their] side, [they w]ould alarm the people with the imperfections of the Constitution and be able to refute the defence set up in its favor; that the system [was] the production of the rich and ambitious; that they discover[ed] its operations and that the consequence [would] be the establishment of two orders in the Society, one comprehending the opulent and great, the other the poor and illiterate." Their opinions, King added, seemed to them only confirmed by "the extraordinary Union in favor of the Constitution," which actually existed, "of the Wealthy and sensible part of [the state]."[18]

From the foregoing analysis by Rufus King, fully confirmed by the report of the Convention's debates, it is sufficiently evident that the cause of the Constitution, in Massachusetts, had not benefitted from the occurrence of Shays' Rebellion, or, rather, from the long-continuance of the causative factors which produced that event. Making full allowance for the fact that the recency of the Revolution probably made people somewhat readier than they would be today to resort to violent action, those factors were undoubtedly the widespread unemployment, the scarcity of money, the foreclosures, the bankruptcies, and all the rest of the distressing features of a long-continuing, constantly deepening business depression. These phenomena gradually embittered the groups in Massachusetts that suffered from them most; and since those groups included a large part of the more ignorant and less intelligent members of the state, it was only natural—and, indeed, quite in accord with common experience—that their resentment became directed against those in their immediate neighborhood who did not seem to be suffering so severely as they. From resentment to suspicion was an easy step; once suspicion was aroused, the groups in question became blindly opposed to anything and everything, including the Constitution, which the more intelligent, the better-educated, and the more prosperous groups proposed or advocated. The Constitution, it seems quite certain, would have been ratified more readily in Massachusetts in 1785.[19]

What was true of Massachusetts was likewise true of the other New England states. In Rhode Island the legislature of its own accord had passed acts in 1785 to authorize its delegates in Congress to concur in amending the Articles so as to vest in that body (as the Rhode Island legislature itself afterwards said) "the whole and sole power of making laws for the regulation of trade."[20] In 1787, when the agrarian party was in power, Rhode Island declined to appoint a delegation to the Federal Convention; it refused to ratify the Constitution when that document was submitted to the people in 1787–88; and it remained out of the Union under the Constitution until 1790. In New Hampshire, making due allowances for the smaller proportion of extremists in the state, the situation was similar. Whereas New Hampshire of its own accord had passed an act in 1785 to invest Congress with "full" power, for fifteen years, "to regulate Trade and Commerce through the United States,"[21] conditions had so changed, when the New Hampshire ratifying convention met in 1788, that a majority of that body were instructed by their constituents not to ratify the Constitution. To be sure, this difficulty was eventually surmounted, and after a second appeal to the people the Constitution was adopted. As in Massachusetts, however, there remained in the New Hampshire convention a suspicious group, of considerable size, that to the very end stubbornly voted against ratification. In Connecticut, alone among the New England states, the Constitution was easily and quickly adopted, but in the Connecticut convention, too, there was a suspicious minority, coming mainly from upper portions of the back-country counties, which stubbornly cast its votes against such action. While it is probably true that Shays' Rebellion in Massachusetts, the short-lived insurrection in New Hampshire, and the prolonged agrarian domination in Rhode Island all had some effect of intensifying nationalist sentiment among New Englanders who already desired a strong national government anyway, it is perfectly clear that the total effect of these events was seriously detrimental to the cause of the Constitution in all the states of New England.

As for the Middle states, if Henry Knox is to be believed, the beneficial effects of Shays' Rebellion among these states was not very great. Knox's views upon this subject are to be found in a letter he wrote to Stephen Higginson on February 25, 1787. Knox, we should explain, was one of the men, "without the Congress," who was not satisfied with the plan of change which had been proposed by the abortive convention at Annapolis, and who, along with a number of others, "both within and without [that body]," was concerned in an attempt in the early weeks of 1787 to obtain the substitution of a more likely-seeming scheme. Stephen Higginson, through Knox, was also indirectly concerned in this effort, and on February 13, 1787, Higginson had written to Knox suggesting that the danger of insurrectionary outbreaks also existed in the other states, and that Knox, therefore, would "no doubt endeavour to draw strong Arguments, from the insurrection in [Massachusetts], in favour of an efficient General Government for the Union."[22] After the effort that Knox and these other men were making had very largely failed, Knox, then in New York as Congress's secretary of war, wrote Higginson, in Boston, in explanation of the failure. "The rebellion," he told Higginson, "ha[d] not had, and probably [would] not have the effect that one would rationally suppose." "All the states possess[d]," he agreed, "the seeds of dissolution in them, which [were] hourly springing up and manifesting themselves to an attentive observer, and in some states [were] nearly ripe; yet such [was] the infatuation produced from a variety of causes that *those more immediately on the spot* [did] not appear to observe them, a few men excepted." "*All*," he said, "seem[ed] to speak of the disorders of Massachusetts as produced by a well-meaning, perhaps, but mistaken policy in the management of her internal affairs." Having written this statement, Knox then remembered that the effort with which he had been concerned had actually had the support in Congress of the Virginia delegates, of one Georgia man, and of several men from the Middle states. So, having written the statement just given, he altered it so that it said "*many* people sp[o]k[e] of the [Massachusetts] disorders," in the manner he had indicated. "In many instances," he explained, "they speak as erroneously of the causes of events that have [been] happening *two or three hundred miles from them* as the British used to do of us during the late war." While protesting that he was not discouraged, Knox then concluded with the fear that "this aptness in the minds of the different states to impute the rebellion in Massachusetts to local causes [would] prevent those measures necessary to the establishment of a force"—i.e., a government—"which could controul events."[23]

The distances mentioned by Knox in the foregoing letter, together with his use of the phrase "those more immediately on the spot," seem to establish that he intended his statements to refer principally to the men of the Middle states, an inference further supported by his mention of Pennsylvania as a particularly egregious instance of all that he had to say. It seems altogether probable that Knox was correct in his views and that a good many men in the Middle states did take a rather smug view of the Massachusetts troubles. For the Middle states had suffered in the depression much as New England had, and while it is undoubtedly true that New England had suffered more, it is not probable that Middle-state men were fully aware of this fact or ready to admit it. So, it is not unlikely they tended to think of themselves as common sufferers with New England who had nevertheless managed to avoid the political and insurrectionary troubles that New England had had; and "being men" (as Knox put it), they naturally were prone to think of themselves as having avoided such troubles by their superior management of their own affairs. To confirm them in this view, there was, moreover, the case of New

Hampshire, which had acted promptly when insurrection had broken out, and had not since had any overt troubles of the same kind. Making all proper allowance for the fact that Knox was disgruntled when he wrote to Higginson, and that he may therefore have exaggerated somewhat in what he said, the strong likelihood is that there was much truth in his view of the opinions and reactions of the Middle states regarding Shays' Rebellion. There is no known evidence that Shays' Rebellion made much difference in the Middle states.

The reaction to this event in the Southern states, particularly in Virginia, however, could hardly have been the same. The Southern states, with the single possible exception of South Carolina, were quite aware that they had turned a very cold shoulder to the appeal of the New England and Middle states in 1785 for a full commerce power for Congress.[24] They were also aware that the New Englanders regarded the insurrections in Massachusetts as a natural outcome of the South's indifferent attitude upon that subject, and the consequent defect, throughout the depression, of any seasonable measures on a national scale to arrest its course.[25] They were likewise aware of the irritation they had caused among the Northern states, particularly the New England states, by their attitude in the preceding summer toward Jay's proposed Spanish treaty. They knew that the Northern irritation, particularly the irritation of the New England men, was due in part, at least, to a desire for the commercial advantages held forth in Jay's proposed treaty. They knew, finally, that even *before* the Massachusetts disorders had broken out, the Massachusetts men had threatened dismemberment on the floor of Congress; that the New Englanders had talked, in the presence of James Monroe (and, we may suppose, in the presence of other Southerners as well) of "a dismemberment so as to include Pen[nsylvani]a and sometimes all the states south to the Potomack"; and that, according to the story James Monroe was passing around, the Massachusetts men had held meetings in New York with men from that state and the other three New England states, and had matured a plan, "in all its modifications," for "the dismemberment of the States east of the Hudson"—which of course was understood to include New York—"from the Union and the erection of them into a separate gov-[ernmen]t."[26] In view of all these circumstances, with rumors such as the foregoing floating around, and with Southerners like Madison and Monroe already believing these rumors even before the Massachusetts troubles had occurred, the outbreak of those troubles must certainly have been viewed among the Southern men as the final evidence that, if they wished the protection which the North could give, they would have to recede from their opposition to the full national commerce power, the complete American "commercial system," and the strong and well-organized national government, which the Northern men wanted. If the patience of the Northerners, and particularly the New Englanders, was nearing its end *before* Shays' Rebellion took place, it will surely have seemed to most Southern men that the end of the Northerners' patience was a very great deal closer, afterwards.[27]

Such a reaction was particularly likely to occur among the men of Virginia. Virginia men—at any rate, Virginians like Madison and Edmund Randolph—were almost certainly aware, through the Virginia delegates in Congress, that the leaking out of the facts surrounding Virginia's proposal of the Annapolis commercial convention had produced among the Northerners, especially the New Englanders, the very result they originally had feared from the legislative history behind that measure: a great loss of confidence in the South's intentions with respect to commerce, and a great loss of confidence in the good intentions of Virginia men, in particular.[28] Virginians like Randolph and Madison must therefore, as Virginians, have had very uneasy consciences; and in these circumstances they must have felt, when they heard of the Massachusetts outbreaks, that it had become essential for Virginia to act quickly and in such a way as to regain, if possible, the lost confidence of the men in the Northern part of the country. At the same time, they probably understood that the economic extremity of the New England states, which the insurrections underlined, gave them the best opportunity they probably ever would have for exacting from the North some concession on the subject of the basis of representation in Congress. If the outbreak of Shays' Rebellion had salutary effects anywhere at all, such salutary effects were certainly felt in the five Southern states, particularly in Virginia.

CHAPTER XXIII

Virginian Approval of the Federal Convention and the Politics of Virginia's Sudden Conversion

I N THE light of the considerations set forth in the preceding chapter, the reader will feel no surprise on learning that the first deliberative body on the continent to approve of the Annapolis plan was the legislature of Virginia. That body was scheduled to meet on October 16, but a quorum in the lower house was lacking until October 23;[1] the members who arrived on time were obliged to wait for James Madison[2] and the other tardy arrivals for quite as long as Madison, Randolph, and various others had previously tarried at Annapolis. During the days immediately following the obtaining of a quorum in the House of Delegates, confidential reports on the Massachusetts outbreaks, of a highly alarmist nature, began to come in to James Madison and other persons in Virginia.[3] Madison's own chief source of information was his friend, Henry Lee, in Congress, who also wrote letters of a similar kind all through the fall to George Washington, St. George Tucker, and perhaps others.[4] On October 19 Lee had written Madison that "the eastern commotions [were] becoming very serious." The announced objects of those concerned in them were not, he said, their real objects; these comprehended the abolition of all debts and an equal division of all property. "The decay of their commerce [in the New England states had] left the lower order unemployed; idleness in this body, and the intriguing exertions of another class whose desperate fortunes [were] remediable only by the ruin of society [had] produce[d] schemes portending the dissolution of order and good government." Considering that Shays' Rebellion was a rural, rather than an urban, disturbance, Lee's diagnosis evidently could not have been completely accurate. There was also reason to believe, Lee went on, that agents of Great Britain were concerned in the affair, and that New England's eventual reunion with that country was an object. To this end, it was supposed, the Massachusetts insurgents were in league with "the Vermontese." The disturbed conditions were, moreover, general throughout New England; and "the U.S. who ought to be able to aid the government of particular states in distresses like these [were, instead,] scarcely able to maintain themselves." What but disaster could be expected, unless something were soon done to strengthen the hand of Congress?[5]

341

The foregoing letter, with the alarming new twist it gave to the dismemberment peril, was received by Madison before the House of Delegates took up the report from Annapolis.[6] There is good reason to believe that the Virginia legislature itself received from its delegates in Congress a similarly alarming official report, signed by Edward Carrington and Henry Lee but not by William Grayson, who, like Patrick Henry, seems to have "smelt a rat" in some of the things that were going on. This report to the legislature, dispatched on the date of Lee's letter to Madison, has somehow not survived,[7] but from various other data still in existence, it is possible to draw a virtually certain inference as to the tenor of the vanished report, at least in its reference to Shay's Rebellion. An inference also is possible that Grayson must have dissented from some of the more alarmist statements about that rebellion in that official report. The evidence which makes these inferences possible consists, in part, of what Lee was writing, and had written, about Shays' Rebellion, on the date of the missing report; it consists, in part, of the behavior of the Virginia legislature at about the date when the missing report must have been received; in part, of a known difference of opinion between Grayson, on the one hand, and Lee and Carrington, on the other, regarding the perils that threatened for Virginia and the Union in consequence of the Massachusetts troubles; and, in part, of a letter that Madison and Grayson afterwards wrote to Rufus King on March 11, 1787.

The letter last mentioned was a response to an inquiry King had made concerning a report which he said was current in Boston to the effect that "'the Commissioners on the part of New York [in a then recent meeting with certain commissioners of Massachusetts had] alarmed the Virginia Delegates [in Congress], with an account that the Commissioners on the part of Massachusetts* were for *a Monarchy*†, and that those Delegates [had] wr[i]t[ten] their Legislature of it, who shut their Galaries and made a most serious Business of the Matter.'"[8] Madison and Grayson assured King that the shutting of the doors of "the Virginia Assembly" had occurred while "Mr. M[adison had still been] in the legislature" in the preceding fall; and that "the doors of the Assembly of Virginia [had been] shut on a letter from Col. Carrington and Col. Lee, which Mr. Grayson saw but did not sign for reasons irrelative to [King's inquiry]."[9] That these remarks referred to the lost report of October 19 is virtually certain, on the basis of other evidence which will now be recounted.

One item of this other evidence is the fact that Henry Lee was not reelected to Congress by the Virginia legislature for the new congressional year beginning November 1786. Angered by Lee's agreement with George Washington, Richard Henry Lee, and the Northern men in Congress on the subject of Jay's proposed treaty with Spain, the Virginia legislature had

---

*The Massachusetts commissioners were Rufus King, John Lowell, James Sullivan, and Theophilus Parsons. Journals, XXXII, 619.

†Emphasis in the original.

passed over Lee in favor of his friend, James Madison, and certain others.[10] Upon hearing of what had occurred, Lee took his "disgrace," as he called it, very much to heart and "hastened from N[ew] York," soon after the news of it had reached him, as he had explained to Madison in a letter from Alexandria on December 20. This had been, said Lee, "about the 20th of Nov[embe]r";[11] that he was aware of his "disgrace" at least by the date he mentioned is otherwise established by the fact that, after a fortnight's non-representation in Congress, due to the expiry on November 3 of its delegates' previous commissions, Virginia was represented, on November 20, by Carrington and Grayson.[12] This fact means either that the new commissions were received on that date, a Monday, or that they had been received on the Sunday or Saturday before. That Lee *thereafter* signed any official report with Carrington, from which Grayson dissented, is extremely improbable. It is also unlikely that the letter Madison and Grayson mentioned in their letter to King was one written while James Monroe had still been present in Congress, for, if this had been the case, Monroe's signature, or nonsignature, would certainly have been mentioned by Grayson and Madison in their letter. Monroe left New York to return to Virginia, apparently, on October 13.[13] It is thus virtually certain that the letter mentioned by Madison and Grayson, in their letter to King, was one sent off between October 13 and November 20. Within that period, so far as is known, there was but one communication by the Virginia delegates to the Virginia legislature: the missing report of October 19[14]—presumably the customary general year-end report on all subjects of interest to the assembling legislature. Since the behavior of the Virginia legislature, at about the time the report in question would have been received, was of a character to raise a rather strong inference that it was then they "shut their doors," the inference is also strong that Madison and Grayson were referring to this missing report in their letter to Rufus King.

The inference that this was the case is strengthened by the extreme improbability that Lee and Carrington would have written to the state's legislature on October 19 without detailing the great dangers to Virginia and the Union, which, their other letters show, they undoubtedly then believed Shays' Rebellion entailed. The inference is also strengthened by the fact that their colleague, William Grayson, is known to have disagreed with their highly alarmist views upon this subject. The nature of these views on the part of Henry Lee has already been indicated by the outline given of his letter to James Madison, bearing the same date as the lost report. Further evidence of Henry Lee's state of mind is contained in the series of five letters he wrote to Washington about the subject between September 8 and November 11.[15] In this series of letters, we need refer only to the last letter in order to round out our knowledge of what Lee's views were, and to form some idea of the sources of information on which his views rested.

In the letter in question, Lee informed Washington that he had just "this moment" been conferring with "Gen[era]l Knox and Mr. King." "Every

day," he said, "[was] bring[ing] new information of the designs and preparations of the Malcontents [of Massachusetts]." "They [were] training their
people, ha[d] officered some considerable bodys and [were] forming connexions with their neighboring states and the Vermontese. [And a] convention ha[d] assembled to devise ways and means of supporting their military
arrangements, and of doing such other things as [might] be necessary for the
prosecution of their intentions." These several steps, so reminiscent of the
course of the American Revolution, were naturally found disturbing by Lee
and the other men in Congress; to add to their anxiety, they had "authentic
information," so Lee said, "that [the Massachusetts insurgents] contemplate[d] a reunion with G[reat] Britain, and it [was] not improbable but
that [their] convention now sitting [would] formally make propositions of
this nature to Lord Dorchester (Sir Guy Carleton) who [had just] arrived at
Quebec with plenipotentiary powers as Governor General of British
America."[16] These fears and rumors, with their disturbing new basis for
Virginian apprehensions of a breakup of the Union, are manifestly the same
fears and rumors which Lee had passed on to Madison on the date of the
Virginia delegates' missing report; the same fears and rumors Lee had
mentioned to St. George Tucker in his letter of the day following; and the
same fears and rumors about which Lee had written to Washington, not once
but several times, since his first letter to Washington on the subject on
September 8. Lee's constant recurrence to these matters is indicative of the
extent to which these rumors and apprehensions were preying on his mind,
and the fact strengthens the inference, already drawn, that Shays' Rebellion
must have been extensively and alarmingly treated by Lee and Carrington in
their missing report to the Virginia legislature.

   William Grayson's disagreement with these alarming views is likewise
clearly established. This is apparent from two letters he wrote to Monroe and
Madison on November 22. That date was just two days after Grayson returned to Congress from a long absence on account of illness during ten
weeks or more before.[17] To Monroe, Grayson wrote reassuringly that "of
course" the Massachusetts men "wish[ed] for a continuance of the Confederation"; that "they look[ed] upon the federal assistance [in suppressing
their rebellion] as a matter of the greatest importance"; and that he "understood" they had been "much more friendly . . . since the late insurrection in
their State."[18] To Madison he wrote that "of course," as he said once more,
Massachusetts "wish[ed] not only for a continuance of the confederation, but
that it [might] be made more adequate to the purpose of government." He
admitted, however, that it was "the belief" in New York, of "people well
informed," that the Massachusetts insurrection "threaten[ed] the most serious consequences, and that the objects [were] more extensive than the mere
stopping the Courts of Justice." It was "supposed," he said, "that Vermont
[was] leagued with [the Massachusetts insurgents], and that they [were]

secretly supported by emissaries of a certain nation." But of this "conjecture," as he called it, Grayson with his usual good sense told Madison that he "ha[d] heard no satisfactory proof."[19]

From the tenor of these two letters written by Grayson so promptly after his return to Congress, it is perfectly clear that he wished to moderate, if he could, the highly alarmist fears of a dismemberment of the Union, which he apparently knew Monroe and Madison entertained. His disagreement with their views and likewise with the equally alarmist but somewhat different views of his colleague, Henry Lee, seems certain; and that he was in disagreement with his colleague, Edward Carrington, at least on the subject of Shays' Rebellion, appears from a letter Carrington wrote to Edmund Randolph, by then the governor of Virginia, just sixteen days after Grayson's two letters to Monroe and Madison were written. Since, moreover, Carrington in that letter repeated to Randolph all the alarming things that Henry Lee had been writing to Madison, Washington, and St. George Tucker, somewhat earlier in the fall, the inference seems to follow that his letter is further good evidence of the probable contents of Carrington's and Lee's missing report to the Virginia legislature, as it related to Shays' Rebellion.

Carrington began his letter with congratulations to Randolph upon his recent election as governor, and then added, disconcertingly: "It may happen that your administration will not glide on without meeting opportunities for the full display of your military as well as political talents and influence in the supreme command." "How far the contagion of the Eastern disorders will spread, may not be [so] proper to conjecture," said Carrington, "from the present quiet state of the other parts of the Empire, as from the experience of human nature and the constitutions of our Governments." "The Fathers of the American Fabric" had apparently supposed, he went on, that "discernment and virtue" were "peculiarly [America's] lot"; but "in the progress of experiment, the fallacy [had been] discovered, and the whole pile must fall if [efficiency in government could] not be supplied." "The spirit of insurgency in Massachusetts, ha[d] proceeded," Carrington said, "to a stage which render[ed] the subversion of that Government an event too probable. The malcontents ha[d] assumed a deliberate and systematic conduct, and every day gain[ed] confidence and numbers. The inefficiency of Government ha[d] been felt [in Massachusetts] by its friends as well as enemies, and many [were] falling in with the measures of the insurgents, who at first [had] show[n] a readiness, and actually turned out to oppose them." "Many of the malcontents," Carrington also said, "ha[d] now openly declare[d] for an abolition of debts, public and private, and a distribution of property." This would ruin the men of property in Massachusetts, and they, of course, would make an effort to uphold the government, but it was much to be feared that they would not be successful.

Carrington next referred to the story, then current in New York, "that a british influence [was] operating in this mischievous affair." "In the progress of the thing," Carrington flatly declared, "this ha[d] happened." "It [was] an undoubted truth that communications [were] held by Lord Dorchester with both the Vermonters and the insurgents of Massachusetts, and that a direct offer ha[d] been made to the latter of the protection and Government of Great Britain, which they at present decline[d], but h[e]ld in Petto, as a last resort, in case future events [might] place them in desparate circumstances." In this connection Carrington also explained to Randolph that the insurgents had "declare[d] it [was] not their intention to touch the continental magazine, which [was] situated at Springfield, in the midst of their country, unless [they were] driven to it to save their lives." But they would probably "think the time arrived for this," he feared, "upon the happening of any conflict." "Here," said Carrington, "[was] felt the imbecility, the futility, the nothing-ness of the federal powers. [For] the U.S. ha[d] no troops, nor dare[d] they call into action, what [was] called the only safe-guard of a free government, the militia of [Massachusetts], it being composed of the very objects of the force"—i.e., the insurgents and their sympathizers. As for the neighboring New England states, "N[ew] Hampshire ha[d] already shown her kindred to the revolters; Connecticut [was] not free from the infection; and the Legis-lative Acts of Rhode Island ha[d] discovered that an opposition to [the Mas-sachusetts insurgents could] be expected from no order of people there." So there was no prospect, Carrington thought, of an adequate protection from any quarter.

"What further events [would] arise out of this unfortunate business, [might] be unfolded in its progress. [His] conjectures [were], that, should an act of violence shortly happen, a civil war must be inevitable, and to accident [America] must trust for the consequences." "But," he concluded, after painting this gloomy picture, "despondency is not a common attendant of mine." He still hoped, he said, that good sense would prevail, and all the existing difficulties be composed. "[Yet] this instance, terminate however it [might, would] doubtless teach the necessity of efficiency in government." "And perhaps it would be best placed in the federal head. Indeed, if [effi-ciency could] not be got in the present form [of government], some other ought immediately to be devised. A change of choice [would] probably be one of wisdom. If it [were] left to accident, we [could] not account for the result."

This remarkable letter was then concluded with an assurance that the communications contained in it were made because Carrington thought it his "duty" to make them; "it being proper," he said, "that [Randolph] be fully informed upon so important a subject." He also declared that he "ha[d] endeavoured to found [his communications] upon the best information, and [could] pledge [him]self for [their] authenticity." With certain exceptions, he left it to Randolph "how far it [might] be proper to suffer [his com-munications] to become public"; but he suggested that "it [might] be well to communicate them *confidentially* to some of the members of the Legislature." Governor Randolph communicated the entire letter confidentially to the entire legislature on December 29.[20] It remains only to add that Carrington observed, in the very last paragraph of his letter, that his "honourable Colleague Mr. Grayson," who had sent very contrary advice to Virginia, "[was] much indisposed and ha[d] been so for some time." "I wish," Carrington said, "to see some of the New Members [of the Virginia delegation to Congress] come forward."[21] If this was not intended to discredit Grayson as a source of information, it almost certainly had this effect.

The foregoing letter, which it is difficult to regard as having been intended by Carrington for any purpose other than that of cancelling the effect of Grayson's letters of two weeks before, can leave little doubt that Carrington and Grayson, quite as much as Grayson and Henry Lee, were in disagreement as to the probable perils for Virginia and the Union as a consequence of Shays' Rebellion. If that should seem to the reader to go too far, then at least it is clear that Carrington and Grayson were in disagreement as to the advisability of writing alarmist letters to Virginia as a means of evoking within that laggard state some action to improve and strengthen the national government.[22] This being true, there also can be little doubt, first, that Madison's and Grayson's statement in their letter to Rufus King on March 11, 1787, did refer to the missing report of the Virginia delegates of October 19; second, that it was that report "which Mr. Grayson saw but did not sign"; and third, that the reason for Grayson's refusal to sign was his dissent from the highly alarmist views about Shays' Rebellion contained in the lost report. The virtual certainty of all this is, finally, indicated by the nature of what went on in the Virginia legislature at about the time when the report was received.[23] In the light of what went on, it must have been then that "the Assembly of Virginia" closed its doors and "made a most serious Business" of the news which it had just received.

The allusion is to the very extraordinary action the Virginia legislature then took upon the report of the convention at Annapolis. That report was put before the House of Delegates on October 30. It was thereupon referred to a committee of the whole house,[24] which recommended four days later, on November 3, that a bill ought to pass for appointing delegates to the new convention at Philadelphia, as the report from Annapolis proposed. This recommendation was immediately approved by the House, and the stunning effect produced within that body by the alarming news from New England, and from Madison, the chief speaker, was registered in this unchallengeable fact: the House of Delegates' vote of approval was *unanimous*.[25] A bill for the purpose covered by the vote was then immediately drawn up and passed in due course of November 9.[26] After some delay due to a recurrent want of a quorum in the Virginia Senate, that body concurred with the House of Delegates on November 23,[27] and on December 4 the two houses, by joint ballot, appointed the state's delegation to the Federal Convention.[28]

All these actions by the Virginia legislature, and the notices about them which Governor Edmund Randolph sent out, are in such marked contrast with what had been done in the state and by Randolph a few months earlier, when the call for the Annapolis convention was issued, that it will be worth our while to examine the state's various proceedings at this later time. The apparent purpose in all that was done was to obtain the attention and regain the confidence of the rest of the country. This appears not only from the nature of the things done but from the contents of certain letters that James Madison wrote to Washington while the legislature's doings were in process. In the earliest of these letters, written on November 8, Madison informed Washington that it was "thought advisable" to give to everything done "a very solemn dress," and to impart to Virginia's approval of the Annapolis plan "all the weight that could be derived from a single State." "This idea [would] be pursued," he said, "in the selection of characters to represent Virg[ini]a in the federal convention"; to this end, the legislature would take "the liberty . . . of placing [Washington's] name at the head of [the list]." He then intimated that, if this should not accord with Washington's desires, it would, nevertheless, be preferable for Washington not to say so right away, since his name at the head of the Virginia delegation would "assist powerfully in marking the zeal of [the Virginia] Legislature and its opinion of the magnitude of the occasion."[29]

This mode of dealing, even for the great ends that were then in view, Washington thought "deceptious";[30] and since his position was such that he did not see how he could serve as a delegate to the proposed convention, he wrote Madison informing him of the fact and explaining the reasons that compelled him to this decision. The Cincinnati were holding their triennial meeting in Philadelphia during the week immediately preceding that which had been set for the convention. Though honored with the presidency of the order, he had, he informed Madison, just begged off from attending their meeting, in a circular letter that he had sent to the various state societies about a fortnight earlier. His "principal reason" for this action, so he later informed Madison,[31] had been a desire to withdraw quietly from the leadership of a society which many of his fellow citizens thought "incompatable with republican principles." But the reasons he had given to the Cincinnati (which, he assured Madison, were also "firm & just"),[32] were that his personal affairs required his presence in Virginia and that his health was such as to preclude the journey to Philadelphia. In these circumstances, he "could not appear, at the same time & place" for another meeting, he thought, "with any degree of consistency," or "without giving offence to a very respectable & deserving part of the Community—the late officers of the American army." And so, he indicated to Madison, the legislature of Virginia must excuse him.[33]

The foregoing letter was received by Madison before the Virginia legislature had made its appointment of delegates to the Federal Convention,[34] and since Washington also had made his wishes known to other members of that body,[35] a number of men in the legislature definitely knew of Washington's unwillingness to serve, when the state's choice of delegates was made. They appear, however, to have been so anxious for the use of his name, and so eager for the confidence which they knew his name would inspire in the Northern states, that they withheld their knowledge from their fellow legislators and joined with them in a unanimous choice of Washington as head of the state's delegation.[36] And then Governor Edmund Randolph took the further step of hurrying Washington's name out before the whole country as appointed in that capacity, without first giving him an opportunity to refuse.[37] The day following this action, Madison wrote to Washington in apology for what had been done. It was considered, he said, that, even though Washington should not actually attend the convention, "the advantage of having [his] name in the front of the [state's] appointment *as a mark of the earnestness of Virg[ini]a*, and an invitation to the most select characters from every part of the Confederacy, ought at all events to be made use of." This consideration, in view of the importance of the occasion, would, Madison hoped, "at least apologize" for the action taken by the legislature and the governor; and perhaps, he added, it might even induce Washington to change his mind.[38] Washington wrote back to both Madison and Governor Randolph, that as matters stood he could not serve; that the situation might conceivably change; but that "the probability of [his] non-attendance [was] too great to continue [the] appointment."[39] Upon being pressed further to serve,[40] he finally wrote to some of his particular friends among the Cincinnati in the other states, explaining what had taken place, and asking their opinion as to whether he might serve without offense to his brother officers.[41] In accordance with their advice that they thought this was possible, particularly the advice of his friend, Henry Knox, Washington eventually decided not to disappoint the expectations that had been raised in the other states, without his consent, by the Virginia governor and legislature.[42] Thus, in the end, his services were obtained for the Federal Convention.

With the same idea of giving to everything done "a very solemn dress," the Virginia House of Delegates had commissioned Madison (apparently the leader in this whole affair) to draw up, in what was considered appropriate form, the act for expressing Virginia's approval of the proposed convention. The act Madison drew up began with a long and elaborate preamble. The gist of it simply was that the Virginia legislature was convinced the Union was in imminent danger,[43] and that the state was ready, in order to prevent this dire event, "to concur in such further concessions and provisions [in the Articles] as [might] be necessary to secure *the great objects for which—[the federal] government [had been] instituted.*" Those "great objects," as all concerned were then fully aware, were the common defense, the security of liberty, and the mutual and general welfare of the country.[44] In short, Virginia's action meant that she was ready to agree to the establishment of a general government for these inclusive national objects.

Besides this much needed reassurance to the rest of the country, Madison incorporated in the Virginia act a small but highly important *departure* from the strict letter of the plan proposed at Annapolis—a departure, likewise, from the strict letter of the House of Delegates' antecedent approving resolve. Whereas both the Annapolis plan and the Delegates' resolve had stipulated in specific terms that no change proposed by the convention should be effective until "agreed to by [Congress] and afterwards confirmed by *the legislatures* of every state," the Virginia act spoke only of the necessity of agreement by Congress and "due" confirmation "by *the several states.*" This difference in wording may, to some modern readers, seem insignificant, in which case several things should be borne in mind. First, on the basis of experience, the mechanism of change was unquestionably of the highest importance to those desiring to establish a national government; second, as we know, the word "state" was then commonly used to mean "the people";[45] and finally, this very subject of the mechanism of change had almost certainly been a matter of difference at Annapolis. It is therefore very difficult *not* to believe that James Madison (emboldened, no doubt, by the unanimous vote of November 3), was trying by this new wording to lay the basis for something other than state *legislatural* ratification. This view, it may be added, is well supported by certain proceedings taking place elsewhere in the country at about this time and later in the following winter.

Governor Randolph sent copies of the Virginia act to the governors of the other states on December 1. In his covering letter, in striking contrast with his very eloquent caution in the previous February, Randolph "*solicited*," without the appearance of any reservation, each governor's "cooperation at this trying moment." He further declared that he felt "a peculiar satisfaction in forwarding the [Virginia] act," because "it breathe[d] a spirit truly fœderal & contain[ed] an effort to support our general government, which [was] now reduced," he said, "to the most awful crisis."[46] It is likewise worth noting that five days later Randolph sent to the governors of the other states a *second* letter with which, once more, he sent a copy of the Virginia act. He craved their pardon "for again intruding on [them] with [that] Act" and for "repeating the request [he had] urged in [his] letter of the 1st instant, that [they] would give a zealous attention to the present American crisis." His apology, he said, was "[his] anxiety for the well being of the fœderal Government, [which would] not suffer [him] to risque so important a consideration upon the safety of a single letter." Randolph then added, with apparent casualness, that "the Gentlemen appointed by Virginia for the convention [were] General Washington, Mr. Patrick Henry, the late Governor,* Mr. George Wythe & Mr. John Blair, two of the Judges of the high court of chancery, Mr. James

---

*Henry eventually declined to serve, because, as he afterwards said, he "smelt a rat" in what had been going on. The probable nature of that "rat" will presumably be apparent to the readers of the present book. The vacant Henry appointment was then offered to Richard Henry Lee, who also declined; whereupon James McClurg, a medical practitioner of Richmond, was appointed.

Madison, a member of Congress, Mr. George Mason, a member of the legislature, and [Governor Randolph himself]."[47] Having dispatched this notice of the Virginia appointments to the other states, Randolph wrote Washington, telling him of his appointment and begging him to accept.[48] On the day following, as already indicated, Madison wrote Washington in apology for what had been done.[49] Giving all due weight to all the attendant circumstances, we can see that the real purpose of Randolph's second letter was nevertheless perfectly clear: to get Washington's appointment before the country, before Washington was given a chance to decline.

The whole manner and substance of the foregoing letters exhibit this highly manifest contrast with the diffident, floundering letter Randolph had sent out in the preceding February about the Annapolis convention,[50] because some great change had in the interim occurred in Virginia, and Edmund Randolph knew it. Letters of Madison, written at about the same time, also attest the fact that some remarkable change had occurred. For example, in his letter to Washington of November 8, Madison spoke, with the utmost satisfaction, of the unanimous vote of the House of Delegates on November 3. He informed Washington that a bill for the purpose covered by the vote was then "depending, *and in a form*," he said, "*which attest[ed] the most federal spirit*," and he confidently predicted, since the bill was then "ready for a third reading," and "no opposition ha[d] yet been made," that it would probably pass.[51] These statements strongly suggest what was certainly true: that Madison had taken courage from the vote of November 3 to go somewhat beyond what was warranted by the literal tenor of that vote. Nearly a full month later, after his act had passed, Madison was still in the same exultant humor. This is shown by a letter he wrote to Jefferson on December 4, wherein he confidently declared that "the evidence of dangerous defects in the confederation ha[d] at length proselyted *the most obstinate adversaries to a reform.*"[52] "The unanimous sanction given by the Assembly to the [Annapolis] Recommendation mark[ed] sufficiently," he said, "*the revolution of sentiment which the experience of one year* ha[d] effected in [Virginia]."*

These last statements in Madison's letter deserve our close consideration. They plainly evince, on Madison's part, a state of mind in striking contrast with the depression he had felt some ten months previously, when his scheme for the Annapolis convention had just gone through. Thereby they help to establish the true character of the sentiments and doings of Virginia at that earlier time. The character of the state's doings at that time is also indicated by Madison's description of the change that had since occurred, as "a revolution of sentiment" in the state. Beyond this, there are these two important facts: first, Madison attributed this change to something in "the

---

*Madison's phrase was "in this country"; but neither the context of his phrase nor the status of the Annapolis plan in the other states, at the time he wrote, permit any other interpretation than that indicated in the text.

experience" of the year preceding; second, the change was one which extended even to "the most obstinate [Virginia] adversaries to [governmental] reform." The full significance of the second of these facts becomes apparent when two further circumstances are brought to view: about half the men who had opposed Madison's modest commercial proposals in the preceding year were still members of the Virginia House of Delegates in the fall of 1786;[53] among them were all save one of the men Madison had then described as "bitter and illiberal against Congress & the Northern States beyond example."[54] The meaning of Madison's statements in his letter of December 4 is this: the cause of "the revolution of sentiment" to which he referred was something that could reach and influence these "bitter and illiberal" men. Now this can only mean that the cause was some *new* factor, in "the experience" of the preceding year, which affected Virginia, *in her own particular interest*, in some extremely important way. Nothing of any other kind, we may feel quite certain, could have "proselyted" the men whom Madison had described before.

Of the few items in the preceding year's "experience" that have not thus far been mentioned, the only one that could possibly be deemed to bear a causal relation to this great change in sentiment is the fact that, during the year in question, there had been some increase in the sentiment in Virginia favorable to paper-money laws, tender laws, and the various other agrarian measures that had been tried, both further south and further north. In Madison's letters of the summer preceding, there are several brief references to this subject. While these show that Madison was somewhat concerned about it, they do not indicate that he was greatly worried about it;[55] and this fact, together with the fact that a vote of the House of Delegates, on November 1, was 85 to 17 against a paper emission,[56] makes it difficult to believe that the growth in Virginia of sentiment favorable to this and other similar measures was what "proselyted" all "the most obstinate [Virginia] adversaries to [governmental] reform" and produced in the states a "revolution in sentiment" upon this latter subject.

A further consideration making such a view improbable is the fact that a similar change of sentiment appears to have occurred in all the states of the South, before the date on which the Federal Convention assembled. Virginia and North Carolina had been the *only* Southern states to send delegations to the commercial convention at Annapolis, but *all* the Southern states sent delegations, and very full delegations, to the Federal Convention at Philadelphia. This fact, taken with the general indifference displayed by the South toward the Northern proposals of a full national commerce power in 1785,[57] is enough to indicate that the thing to be sought in "the experience" of the intervening year, as the cause of this striking alteration in Virginian and Southern sentiment and behavior, is something which affected *the whole South*, and not merely Virginia, in some important way, i.e., in its *sectional* interest; something, in other words, which was important enough to Southern men to prevail over the resentment that Jay's proposed Spanish treaty and the Northern states' espousal of that treaty had, in general, called forth among them. A search through "the experience" of the year in question will reveal nothing which even approximately meets these specifications, *except* the threats of dismemberment growing out of the affair of the Spanish treaty, and the specter of defenselessness raised in Southern minds by these threats. The outbreak of Shays' Rebellion undoubtedly contributed materially to the final result at least in Virginia; but only because of the real or fancied relationship between that rebellion and the dismemberment peril were the troubles in Massachusetts of any great interest to the Southern states. As an imminent insurrectionary threat, those troubles had entirely disappeared before the Federal Convention assembled. The only thing that remained, then, to account for the South's altered behavior was the fear of defenselessness, which had originally been raised among the Southern states by the Northern dismemberment threats made in the summer and fall before.

The affair of the Spanish treaty, and the threats of dismemberment growing out of it, had brought home to the South, in the most emphatic fashion, that it could not eat its cake and have it, too. If the South expected the military and naval protection which the North could provide, it would have to agree to the *quid pro quo*—and, as matters turned out, to the political security—desired by the North. If the South did not agree to these Northern demands, it would have to face up to the probability that the North would withdraw from the Confederacy and leave the South to confront its enemies, particularly the Spaniards, alone. Since, for the time being at least, the military situation of the South was of a highly necessitous nature, the South was not a completely free agent in this matter. It was, therefore, in a considerable degree, compelled to "a revolution of sentiment" and to an agreement to the kind of national government which the Northern states wanted.

In assessing this view of the South's behavior, the reader should, of course, clearly understand that, for large numbers of Southern men, no compulsion to a decision in favor of such a government was necessary. Most clearly was this true of the genuinely liberal, national-minded Southern group (of whom George Washington was the outstanding example) which wanted "a firm national government" anyway. This group, beyond any question, was of considerable size, but it was not a majority anywhere in the South, and most certainly not a majority in Virginia. The adoption of the Constitution in the Southern states and, still more, the *unanimous* vote of the Virginia House of Delegates agreeing to the Federal Convention, must therefore be accounted for as acts in large part by other elements in the Southern community. The motives for these acts upon the part of these other elements in the Southern states are necessarily to be sought in considerations of another kind. One factor going far to account for these actions consists of the military considerations already set forth, but those considerations, important though they were, were not the only factor involved. Another factor was the very definite desire for "a firm national government" on the part of many Southerners who cannot properly be regarded as falling in Washington's group of liberal, national-minded men. These were the men of the extremely sanguine, sectional-minded group, well represented by James Monroe, and by this time also by James Madison, which counted so avidly upon the South's becoming, in a little while, the majority in wealth and numbers in the nation. The desire of this group for a national government was more or less conditioned upon an opening of the way to Southern *domination*. In the end, however, this group had to be content with an opening of the way to Southern *security only*, and for many of those constituting this group, security was not enough. The support of this sanguine, sectional-minded group for the proposed change in government therefore fell off in some degree in the ratification campaign. During the fall and winter following the controversy in Congress over John Jay's proposed Spanish treaty, however, the support of *the whole* of this group—at least in the legislatures—was apparently given to the proposal of a general constitutional convention made by the Annapolis delegates. This and the other considerations earlier mentioned are what lay behind the unanimous vote of the Virginia House of Delegates on November 3, 1786. Since the Constitution was eventually adopted in Virginia and all the other Southern states, the disappointment of the more extravagant hopes of the sectional-minded Southern group was apparently not enough to prevail, with the majority of Southerners, over the other above-mentioned considerations—in some cases, genuinely national; in some cases, merely sectionally prudential. We need only add that it is impossible to quantify, in any way, the influence of these various Southern groups and their views, as causes of the events which they ultimately helped to produce. This much we can say: absent the sanguine expectations of the sectional-minded Southern group, and, still more important, absent the extremely necessitous military situation confronting the South, the Federal Convention would in all probability never have met, at least as a convention of states from all parts of the country. The Constitution, as a constitution for all the thirteen states, would therefore, in all probability, never have been drawn up; and, even more probably, as such a constitution, it could never have been adopted.

The view just stated, which sees in the affair of the Spanish treaty and its sequelae the proximate and finally efficient cause that brought the Southern states to face up to the realities of their own situation, to agree to the assembling of the Federal Convention, and eventually to ratify the scheme or government proposed by that convention, is a view at rather considerable variance from the usual story. In that story, the Spanish treaty (when it is mentioned at all) is treated as a piece of unbelievable Northern folly which came uncomfortably close to totally wrecking the fair plans for a stronger government which James Madison, "the Father of the Constitution," had so carefully laid. The Spanish treaty controversy failed of this result—so it appears in these usual accounts—thanks to the extraordinary magnanimity of Madison and a few other Southerners, and to the fact that the whole country, after years of error, indecision, and constantly increasing chaos, was somehow, suddenly and inexplicably, brought to its senses by the shock of Shays' Rebellion in Massachusetts; by the spectacle of unwisdom displayed by Rhode Island; and by the voice of Virginia persistently crying, throughout all these trying years, in the wilderness. As the reader has now seen, however, Virginia had not been a voice crying in the wilderness for very long. The unquestionably salutary influence of Shay's Rebellion among the Southern states is comprehensible only in the light of the antecedent controversy over the Spanish treaty, the threats of dismemberment which grew out of that controversy, and the Southern ambitions and military fears, upon which this controversy and these dismemberment threats impinged.

As for James Madison's carefully laid plans for a stronger government, the unvarnished truth is that that gentleman had laid *no* plans worthy of the name, before he made his visit to New York while the Spanish treaty controversy was going on. Before that visit, he had been nothing but a drag upon Monroe in the latter's efforts to obtain complete commercial power for Congress. Madison's much praised plan for the Annapolis commercial convention had been a piece of the sheerest opportunism on Madison's part, a piece of opportunism, we may add, which worked out rather badly once the facts about it became known. Only when Madison, on his trip to New York, was confronted with the evil results that had grown from his proposal and had learned of the threats of dismemberment then being made by the Northern men, did he finally accede to the Northern men's view that Congress should be invested with "full powers for the regulation of commerce foreign and domestic."[58] Under the spur of fear, Madison undoubtedly did from that date on work faithfully "to save the Union"; after the convention at Annapolis, Madison also worked faithfully to obtain his own state's approval for the general convention that the Annapolis delegates had proposed. As Madison's own letters show, however, both the desire for a general constitutional convention and the idea of using the Annapolis meeting as a means to promote one had originated *with other men*.[59] If, then, on the basis of his tardy activities in behalf of these ideas of other men, Madison is properly to be regarded as "the Father of the Constitution," he obviously had to be pushed and frightened into his celebrated "paternity" of that document. Upon any realistic basis, the truly fathering influence in all that occurred was the political astuteness and adroit maneuverings of a handful of men of the North.

CHAPTER XXIV

The Opposition to the Annapolis Plan
in the New England States and in Congress

SOME weeks before the foregoing events took place in Virginia, the Virginia delegates in Congress had made a fruitless attempt to obtain that body's approval of the Annapolis plan. The report from Annapolis had been received by Congress, and read before it, on September 20.[1] Nothing was done in reference to the report for the time being; but, on October 2, Monroe wrote Madison that he had it "in contemplation to move [that] day that the report be referr'd to a Committee." He was "persuaded," he said, that "the Eastern States [would] not grant an unlimited commission, but wo'd accede to [the plan of a convention] if its objects were defin'd." "Or rather," he added, "this is the language of those whom [the Eastern states] have here."[2] In another letter five days later, he reported to Madison that when his motion had been presented "it [had been] objected to by the Eastern States"; that it had been withdrawn "for the purpose of a conference with them"; but that he expected they would in the end vote against the proposed commitment.[3] Whether this actually occurred is not known; neither do we know what occurred at the conference. The report, however, was referred to a grand committee on October 11, as Monroe had proposed, but with Nathan Dane, of Massachusetts, as chairman.[4] Of the doings, if any, of this grand committee nothing is known. All we know is that the committee never reported to Congress; that, after Monroe had departed for Virginia, Congress, on October 23, made another appeal to the states for the fragmentary commercial powers it had first requested on April 30, 1784;[5] and that, after this action was taken, some more of the delegates went home. Indeed, so many had gone by the end of the congressional year on November 3, that a quorum was then wanting; and a quorum remained wanting thereafter, with the exception only of January 17, 1787, until February of that year.[6] This want of a quorum would have prevented action upon the Annapolis plan in any case, but quite apart from the difficulty arising from this cause, which itself was possibly controlled, the fact is plain that the plan was not looked upon with much favor in Congress.

According to Henry Lee, of Virginia, the chief doubt related to the efficacy of the plan as a means for actually accomplishing any change. It had been "with difficulty," he reported to St. George Tucker, of the same state, on October 20, "[that] the friends to the system adopted by the convention [had] induced Congress to commit [the] report." "All [the members of Congress were] zealous," Lee said, "to accomplish the objects proposed by the authors of the commercial convention"; that is, apparently, all were at least zealous that a national system of commerce should be established. "Indeed," Lee went on, "their conviction of the inadequacy of the Federal government renders them particularly zealous to amend and strengthen it. But different opinions prevail as to the mode; some think with the Annapolis meeting, others consider Congress not only the constitutional but the most eligible body to originate and propose necessary amendments to the confederation, and others prefer State conventions for the express purpose, and a congress of deputys, appointed by these conventions *with plenipotentiary powers*."[7] The last idea—or, at any rate, a desire for some procedure that would avoid the necessity of referring changes ultimately to the thirteen legislatures—was undoubtedly at the root of what turned out to be the most lasting of the congressional objections to the Annapolis proposal; yet certain contemporaneous letters written by Rufus King, read with his letters of the preceding year, show that there still were other objections, equally serious to King and, very likely, to other Northern men at this time.

The earliest of these letters was written by King, from Philadelphia, on September 17. He had gone there on business for Congress; and having just heard of the disappointing outcome of the Annapolis meeting, he took occasion to communicate this news to the governor of his state. The only result, he informed Governor Bowdoin, was a recommendation for another convention "to be held at Philadelphia in [the next] May, for the purpose of a *general Revision** of the confederation, and a Report to Congress, and also to the several Legislatures."[8] King's "also" seems at least to suggest a dislike for the convention's stipulation for state legislatural ratification; and we know from his letter to Jonathan Jackson, of a fortnight earlier, that he did in fact consider such a mode of change as totally unworkable in practice.[9] This feature of the Annapolis plan, and what must have seemed to King the needless delay of postponing action until nine months later, were clearly among the causes of the bitter disappointment with the Annapolis meeting that his letter to Bowdoin went on to express.[10] Apart from these more obvious objections to the Annapolis plan, King's emphasis upon the words "a *general Revision*" shows that in mid-September 1786 he still entertained the fears of a convention so empowered which he had felt when the Massachusetts General Court had proposed such a convention in the year before. Nor is this all; for it is likewise clear, from his confident reliance merely upon this emphasis to convey his thought, that King believed—as a good many historians of later years apparently have not—that Governor Bowdoin would understand and agree with his fears on the point in question.[11]

*King's emphasis.

On October 2, the day Monroe had presented to Congress his motion for commitment of the Annapolis plan, King wrote to John Adams, in London, confidently predicting that Congress would *not* "interfere [with reference to the plan] in such manner as to patronize the project." He added that he was "fully convinced that [Adams's] opinion"—expressed in an earlier letter—was "just and political"; that is, that "Congress [could] do all a convention [could do], and certainly with more safety to *original principles*." This reference to the "safety of original principles" appears to be further evidence that King still feared "a general Revision." He also explained in this letter to Adams that Congress "[were] now separating"; that "the federal year [would] expire in a few weeks"; and that "little public business"—certainly not the subject of recommending a convention—"[would] receive an examination before the assembling of the next Congress."[12] As Congress afterwards acted in full accord with King's predictions, the probability is that the Northern men had already consulted upon the Annapolis proposal, and had already decided, when James Monroe's motion for a commitment was made, upon the course of action that King set forth in his letter.

The motives for such a course of action by the Northern men, and particularly by the New England men, are not very difficult to surmise. By the date we are now concerned with, their threats of dismemberment, made a few weeks before, had already borne fruit: there was an easily perceptible increased Southern readiness to reform and strengthen the government. This being true, for the Northern states to have shown too great and ready an interest in the proposed new convention would have undoubtedly taken the edge off their recently made threats and, consequently, in all probability, lessened the Southern states' interest in the convention. On the other hand, action by "the Eastern states" to oppose and block congressional approval of the Annapolis plan would rather certainly be interpreted among the Southern men as adding credibility to the earlier threats; and if, in addition, the entire block of states lying "east of the Hudson" could be kept from approving the proposed convention at too early a date, credibility would certainly be lent to "the plan" of "erecting [those states] into a separate government," which, the reader will remember, someone for some reason or other had "disclosed" to James Monroe during the preceding summer. If these various steps could be consummated, the Southern fear that the Union was endangered, and, consequently, the chance that a strong national government could be organized on terms protecting the North against possible future Southern domination, could both, in all probability, be increased.[13]

Given all the circumstances, therefore, the reader will not feel surprise that "the Eastern states" *did* oppose congressional approval of the Annapolis proposal in the fall of 1786; that the New England region turned out to be the last of the three great regions of the country, as Massachusetts was the last of the nation's large and populous states, to agree to that proposal; and that the Massachusetts delegates in Congress, who, as we know, were intensely afraid of eventual domination by the Southern-planter "aristocracy," actually carried their opposition to the Annapolis plan into the Massachusetts General Court. Rufus King was the first to take such action. Departing from Congress shortly after the dispatch of his letter to John Adams on October 2, he appeared before the General Court on the eleventh of the month, and was back again in Congress eight days later.[14] According to reports published in the Boston newspapers and widely copied throughout the country, King opposed the Annapolis proposal in his appearance before the General Court on only two grounds. The first was that the proposal was not constitutional, and the second was that it was not an expedient method for accomplishing a change. Its unconstitutionality—which might better be described merely as extra-constitutionality—arose from the fact that the Articles did not provide for the holding of conventions; and its inexpediency, according to the newspaper accounts, arose, in King's estimation, out of the same fact. "The Confederation," they reported him as saying to the legislature, "was the act of the people. No part could be altered but by consent of Congress and confirmation of the several Legislatures. Congress therefore ought to make the examination first, because if it was done by a convention no Legislature could have a right to confirm it. Did any Legislature sit for such a purpose? No. It must be referred to the people, and then what degree of assent was necessary to make it an article of confederation? Whereas if it was conducted agreeably to the confederation, no such difficulty would exist. Besides, if Congress should not agree upon a report of a convention, the most fatal consequences might follow. Congress therefore were the proper body to propose alterations."[15]

The foregoing argument, as the reader will see, was not completely tight and convincing in all its parts; and the fact that the argument prevailed with the body to whom it was addressed, a body which had shown itself zealous for a general constitutional convention only a few months before, suggests rather convincingly that the newspaper accounts probably did not contain the whole of what King had to say on the subject to the General Court—or, at any rate, to some of its members. The probability of this view is increased by the fact that King had not seemed much troubled about the unconstitutionality of conventions when, in the preceding May, he had written so hopefully to John Adams about the Annapolis *commercial* convention.[16] Its probability is still further heightened by the fact that King had never before shown any strong predilection for a mode of procedure that would assure the submission of constitutional changes to the thirteen legislatures for approval. On the contrary, his letters over a long period had shown a want of confidence in that mode of effecting a reform;[17] and, as the reader will remember, he had argued strenuously, in his letter to Jonathan Jackson only a few weeks before, that a bold departure from the constitutionally stipulated mode of proceeding was necessary. Besides these explicit indications of King's real opinion upon this subject, there is the further fact, which will presently appear, that he was actually ready to depart from the constitutionally stipulated mode of change, in certain proceedings that took place in Congress in the following February and, again, a few months later, in those that took place in the Federal Convention itself. Taking all these facts about King together, and bearing in mind the plain hints of continuing objection to "a _general Revision_" that are to be found in his letter of a little earlier in the fall, it seems impossible to accept the arguments attributed to King in the Boston and other newspaper accounts as accurately representing his true views on the holding of a convention. Instead, the probability is that King was ready, even then, for that or any other step that gave promise of success; but he was at the time fully determined that the basis of suffrage or representation in Congress ought not, under any mode of procedure, to be within the field of possible reforms. That the urging of this view upon the Massachusetts General Court was, moreover, his true purpose in his hurried trip to Boston and back to New York seems clearly inferable from two other facts we already know. The first of these is the fact, established by Monroe's letter to Madison, of October 2, that the representatives of "the Eastern states," _then in Congress_, had declared those states "[would] not grant an unlimited commission, but wo'd accede to [the proposed convention] if its objects were defin'd."[18] The other is that the Massachusetts General Court actually did adopt the device of excepting the fifth of the Articles of Confederation from the field of reform, when it first voted in the following February to participate in the proposed convention.[19] In the light of such facts as these, the probability obviously is high that King definitely advised the General Court to proceed in this way, _at least in the first instance_, when he made his brief visit to Boston in October. The views attributed to King in the Boston papers were most probably intended primarily for the eyes of King's friends from the South in Congress.

The conclusions to be drawn from the views reported in the Boston papers as having been expressed before the General Court a little later in the fall by Nathan Dane are very much the same. Dane took his turn of journeying to Boston, soon after King got back to Congress. Dane appeared before the General Court on November 9. He did not actually affirm, as King had done, that the Annapolis plan was unconstitutional; but he did argue strongly that it was inexpedient, and, in that connection, did maintain that Congress could do all a convention could do. "The States," Dane said, "[could] generally delegate the same men to the known constitutional assembly, that they [might] wish to send to a Convention; and when proper, [they could] direct those full delegations to attend two or three months, for the purpose of fully adjusting [the contemplated] alterations." What reason [could] there be," he asked, "for supposing that the alterations [would] be better adjusted [in a convention] than in Congress?" And as for the argument "that the States [would] probably place more confidence in [a convention's] doings," what room was there for that assumption when "several of the States consider[ed] such a convention highly inexpedient; [when] some States"—New Hampshire, Connecticut and Maryland, no doubt—"[considered such a measure] unconstitutional; and [when] not all the States were agreed"—meaning to exclude Maryland, no doubt—"even in the propriety of a commercial Convention?" In the light of these facts, the long delay in obtaining the continental impost power, which had first been proposed by Congress nearly six years before, and the similar delay in obtaining the partial powers over commerce, which had been proposed by Congress nearly three years before, were not sufficient, Dane said, to justify an inference of a want of confidence in Congress. And considering the progress which amendments for these purposes had actually made with the states, "it must," he thought, "be highly imprudent to submit now to examination, in a different form, the objects contained in [them], and thereby effectually prevent any further progress in compleating these alterations, now almost obtained." The commercial powers thus in prospect, were, he conceded, less than complete; but, "in the present state of our trade and commerce," the powers would be adequate, Dane said, for "many regulations beneficial to the United States, and probably [for] most of those that it [might] be wise at present to adopt." There were "other alterations that time and experience [might] point out to be necessary"; but these, he thought, might gradually be obtained in the same constitutional manner. And as for those "very general and indefinite expressions" contained in the Annapolis report, which "seem[ed]," he said, "to suggest the propriety of submitting the federal system...*in general* to a revision," Dane simply asked the General Court (which had already heard so much, from its delegates, of the perils of such a step) whether they thought "the public mind [was] prepared for [such a fundamental change]." "The first principles of government," Dane solemnly warned them, "[were] to be touched with care and attention."[20]

The foregoing arguments are undeniably more complete, and perhaps more credible, standing by themselves, than those reported in the Boston and other newspapers as having come from Rufus King. Yet the suggestions in them of the dangers to "the first principles of government" in a "general Revision" probably mean that the General Court received from Dane the same advice as to the absolute necessity of limiting the field of possible reforms that they had probably received from Rufus King. Beyond this, the views attributed to Dane in the Boston newspapers, and copied from them into many others, show nearly as great an inconsistency with his previously expressed views, and nearly as great an inconsistency with his opinions and behavior in the months that followed, as we have already noted was present in the behavior and sentiments of Rufus King. It thus seems altogether probable that, as in the case of King, the views attributed to Dane in the various newspaper accounts cannot be accepted as his true and complete views upon the subject on which he spoke.

With respect to a power over commerce, we know, for example, that Dane had thought it "unfortunate," in the preceding January, that the commercial powers requested by Congress in 1784 had not been "better digested and more adequate."[21] We know, too, that he had indicated his sympathy at that time with "the many sensible men" whom he had found in Congress, "who appear[ed] to wish *commercial powers* to be vested in [that body] to be exercised *as occasion [might] require*."[22] And we know, finally, that he had declared his belief to Samuel Adams, a month or so later, that "experience had taught [the country] that [it had been] mistaken," when New Jersey's proposal, that "Cong[ress] should have *full power to regulate trade internally and externally*" had been rejected on February 3, 1781.[23] These earlier statements, made in circumstances in which Nathan Dane had no conceivable motive for a want of candor, undoubtedly indicate the kind of national commercial power he really desired; and that surely means that his reported statements to the General Court, on this particular subject at least, were not his actual views. At most, they probably indicated a desire on his part to damp the ardor of those to whom he spoke, for a generally empowered convention. Again, as in the case of Rufus King, the newspaper reports of his views on this subject were in all probability published primarily for the benefit of the Southerners in Congress.

The probability of this view with respect to the whole of Dane's reported statements on November 9 appears, moreover, when his behavior in the months that followed is brought to view. In the following February, Dane was one of the leaders in the partially successful attempt, then made in Congress, to substitute for the Annapolis proposal some form of convention having general powers, which would not have to refer its work to the thirteen legislatures for approval. This fact establishes that Dane was not unalterably opposed to the idea of a general convention, provided the convention were to proceed in a mode that made its success seem assured, and provided, further (as we must certainly suppose in view of Dane's earlier behavior), that he had some reasonable ground to believe such a convention would not involve the peril of dominance by the planter "aristocracies" of the South. The propriety of these conclusions as to Dane's real opinions upon the holding of a convention is further indicated by a letter he wrote to Rufus King, after King, in discouragement over the disagreements in the Federal Convention in the following July, had written to him that it was becoming uncertain what, if any, results that body would achieve. Dane wrote back that "the Convention must do something." "Its meeting," he admonished, "has all those effects"—i.e., of weakening Congress and concentrating the hopes of the country solely on the convention—"which we and those who did not fully discern the propriety of the measure apprehended."[24] The contrast Dane thus casually drew in a friendly letter, between himself and King on the one hand, and "those who did not fully discern the propriety of [a convention]" on the other, seems sufficient by itself to establish that Dane, as well as King, must have favored the holding of a convention, in the proceedings in Congress in February, but a convention of a kind that would be more likely to achieve reforms than the convention proposed at Annapolis. As for the nature of the reforms for which he hoped, Dane's letter to Nathaniel Gorham, on June 6, is sufficient to establish that what he wanted was a national form of government. The letter in question was written in answer to one Gorham had written from the Federal Convention, which conveyed the information that that body had "agreed"—Gorham believed "unanimously"—"that there ought to be a National Legislative Executive & Judiciary."[25] Dane wrote back that he was "very glad [that] the Convention [had] c[o]me fully into [this] determination."[26] The sincerity of these sentiments is amply corroborated by Dane's behavior in Congress in the following fall, when he was one of the leaders in the efforts then made to assure an unprejudiced submission of the Constitution *to the people*, rather than the state legislatures, for ratification.

Against this consistent body of evidence for Dane's strongly nationalist views, no countervailing evidence is known to exist, except a letter which Christopher Gore, of Boston, wrote to Rufus King, on the twenty-seventh of the following December. "Dane," he reported, "is silent on the [Constitution], and, I believe, mortified that all those he respects in this quarter differ from him on this great question."[27] If we may judge from this letter, Dane must have had some reservation about the Constitution as it finally was drawn; but that it was not a very serious reservation appears from a letter which Dane himself wrote to Henry Knox, from his home in Beverly, on the same day. "The State [of Massachusetts]," Dane reported to Knox, "appear[ed] to [him] to divide on the [Constitution] nearly as it ha[d] on all political questions for several years past—thinking men seem[ed], in general, to be impressed with an idea of the necessity of adopting it or at least something like it. It [would] have substantial friends [in Massachusetts], but not, [he] believe[d] a great many very zealous admirers. [For he] doubt[ed] whether it ha[d] monarchy enough in it for some of [the] Massachusetts men or democracy enough for the others."[28]

The probability therefore appears to be that Dane, like his colleague King, was a man who favored the establishment over the states of "a firm national government," and that he was entirely willing to employ a convention to accomplish that object. Whatever doubt Dane may at first have felt as to the advisability of a convention was undoubtedly related solely to the fear, which he shared with Rufus King, and very likely with other Northern men, that a generally empowered convention might agree to the constitution of a national government, according to some scheme that would lead to Southern domination.[29] But since, as the evidence also shows, Dane finally came around to the view that a generally empowered convention was safe and expedient for the Northern states, the conclusion seems required that he must, on some ground, have concluded that the South would agree, or could be made to agree, to some satisfactory basis of representation in the government that would protect the North from such a result.

That Dane's colleague, Rufus King, had arrived at some such view, as early as January 7, 1787, is evident from a letter he wrote to his former colleague, Elbridge Gerry, on that date. In the letter in question, King spoke of "the anxiety and dissatisfaction concerning the government of these States" as "still continuing." "God only knows," he said, "what will prove the issue." "[But] it is certain," he declared, "that things will not long continue in their present condition. If foreseeing the dangers which hang over us, we do not unite in measures calculated to establish public happiness, I am confident that no man will be able to bear up against calamitous events, which will otherwise force themselves into existence." Referring, next, to the convention appointments then already made in Virginia and Pennsylvania; to the intention of Alexander Hamilton to press for appointments in New York; to the expected nonattendance of Washington, news of which, by that time, had gotten around; and to the continuing opposition to the Annapolis plan by "Jay and others," "not alone because it [was] unauthorized," King said, "but from an opinion that the result [would] prove inefficacious," he finally wound up with an admonition to Gerry, who was then a member of the General Court, that, "if Massachusetts should send deputies, for God's sake, [to] be careful who [were] the men." "The times," King warned, "are becoming critical; a movement of this nature ought to be carefully observed by every member of the Community."[30]

In the foregoing letter, King's doubts of the efficacy of the Annapolis plan seemingly continue, but there is in the letter no trace of the opposition to a generally empowered convention which he previously had expressed. We may, therefore, conclude that by January 7, 1787, the date of this letter, Rufus King had ceased to oppose the proposed convention, though he still remained anxious to alter its procedure so as to make it a more certain instrument for achieving its ends. That Dane, also, had arrived at his change of view at about this same period is indicated by a letter Stephen Higginson wrote to Henry Knox on February 8. In the course of his letter, Higginson expressed his belief that both Dane and King had changed their minds about a convention.[31] This probably means that both men had recently been writing to others of their friends, as King had written to Gerry on January 7. Our final inference thus appears warranted: both these men, who had so long opposed a generally empowered convention, gave up their opposition to such a measure soon after the beginning of January 1787.

The precise considerations that influenced Dane and King in this important change of view are not known. It is possible, but far from certain, that the long continuance of Shays' Rebellion had some share in the result; the impatience of certain men at home in Massachusetts may have contributed; talks with Henry Knox, in New York, probably were a factor; and Alexander Hamilton, according to a statement made by one of his sons, himself claimed credit for Rufus King's conversion.[32] That King had been conferring with Hamilton, as early as January 7, seems inferable from the tenor of his letter to Gerry, of that date. In that letter, however, there is nothing to indicate upon what basis Hamilton's feat, if any, had been accomplished; Hamilton's son had, apparently, no information as to how it had been done; and there is no known evidence from any other quarter that sheds any direct light upon the subject, or any direct light upon the reasons which led King's colleague, Dane, to his similar change of view. Only surmise is possible as to what it was that overcame the very real and sensible fears these two men had so long felt, that a generally empowered convention was dangerous to the continued freedom and welfare of the Northern states.

In view, however, of a certain feature of the Virginia plan afterwards offered in the Federal Convention, the possibility at once suggests itself that some sort of assurance may have been received by Dane and King, and of course by the other Northern men, that Virginia, the largest and most important of the Southern states, would be content, except where fiscal measures were concerned, with a system of representation, or suffrage, in Congress, in proportion to the states' respective numbers of freemen only. The Virginia plan, as originally offered, did actually provide that "the rights of suffrage in the National Legislature"—that is, the rights of suffrage therein by the several states "in their collective capacities"—"ought to be proportioned to [their] Quotas of contribution, or to the number of [their] *free* inhabitants, as the one or the other rule m[ight] seem best in different cases."[33] Whether much significance should be attached to this feature of the original Virginia plan is, however, very doubtful. James Madison at once sought to have the provision expunged from the plan, the day after it was proposed;[34] and there is no evidence that the provision ever had support enough in the Federal Convention to give any real hope of its adoption as the basis of voting in both branches of the proposed national legislature. The presence of the provision in the Virginia plan probably means, nevertheless, that by the date when the plan was proposed, some kind of working agreement had been made upon the point between some, at least, of the Virginia and Pennsylvania men; and, very likely, between them and some of the Massachusetts men, also. The possibility must, therefore, be considered, whether the conversion of King and Dane in the preceding winter may have been secured by some kind of representation from the men of Virginia, that their state would support some such scheme of suffrage, or representation, in Congress, as the Virginia plan at first contained.

The chief reason for doubting that such a representation was made to the Northern men grows out of the letters which James Madison was writing as late as the months of March and April 1787. In those letters, as we have already seen, Madison was apparently counting upon some system of representation in the government to be formed that would commend itself to the South as a whole, because of that region's *"expected advantage"* in populousness over "the Northern states."[35] Since the only thing that would seem reasonably to have met such a specification was some system that took into account the South's slaves, and expected slaves, the probability would seem to be that the above-described feature of the Virginia plan was not yet agreed to, in the months in which Madison wrote. Madison's prompt move for the expungement of the feature from the Virginia plan is consistent with this view; and in the light of this fact, and the tenor of his letters in March and April, the making of any Virginian representation upon this point, *around the first of the year*, seems a most improbable occurrence.

If such a representation nevertheless was made, there is this further difficulty: it is impossible to see how a Virginian representation upon the point could have carried much weight with any Northern man to whom it was made. The Northern men, especially Northerners like King and Dane, were certainly aware that the Northerners desired some system of representation in the proposed new government that would enable them to rule when, as they expected, the South should attain to a "superiority in populousness" over "the Eastern[, or "Northern,"] states." And since there is little reason to suppose that the South expected a superiority in number of *freemen* over the North if the slavery system were continued, and no reason whatever to suppose that the states of the further South, to say nothing of Virginia, were ready to consent to the abolition of that system, the conclusion appears to be warranted that the conversion of King and Dane could not have been the result of any representation by Virginia upon the point in question.

The far more likely supposition is that King and Dane were converted by conferences around the first of the year with men coming into the new Congress from the other Northern states, and by talks at that time with men like Hamilton and Knox and others in New York who were interested in a better government. Such a conclusion is suggested, too, by the claim to having influenced King, which Hamilton made; it is suggested by the general tenor of Henry Knox's letters, and by the program King himself had earlier outlined in his letter to John Adams on October 2. The result of such conferences probably convinced King and Dane that the Northern states could be relied upon to act together, in order to fend off their common peril, which the two Massachusetts men had long feared. In this connection, King and Dane probably recollected the gratifying solidarity shown by the Northern states in the affair of the Spanish treaty during the preceding summer; and remembering, also, the necessitous military situation with which the South was confronted, the Massachusetts men probably concluded that the South, in the event, could probably be forced into some kind of compromise that would protect the North from the Southern-planter domination that they feared. Whether the so-called "great compromise" of the Federal Convention was in any way anticipated in that connection, it is impossible to tell. It should not be forgotten, however, that Thomas Burke, of North Carolina, had anticipated the essentials of that scheme ten years previously, when the Articles of Confederation were being drawn.[36] His idea, probably, had not been forgotten. And the proviso, originally attached by the Massachusetts General Court to its participation in the Federal Convention, *and then quickly withdrawn*, was, to say the least, a fairly plain hint that the equal vote of the states in Congress was not *too* objectionable to the North's most "numerous" state. The records of the Federal Convention tend to indicate that the "great compromise" grew unexpectedly out of the conflicts in the convention, where it was first proposed, apparently, by John Dickinson, of Delaware;[37] but the possibility cannot be entirely dismissed that it, or something like it, may have been thought of beforehand by men like Dane and King, though possibly as a second choice to the Northern domination under the Articles. Regardless of the actual fact upon this point, it is clear that, on some basis or other, both Dane and King were converted, soon after January 1, 1787, from their previous very reasonable fear of a generally empowered convention; and that, beginning at some time soon after that date, they were concerned only that the Federal Convention should meet, and that that body should proceed in some way that would insure success.

CHAPTER XXV

The Movement for a "Plenipotentiary Convention"

THE dissatisfaction felt by Rufus King regarding the procedure of change stipulated by the Articles of Confederation was expressed in various of his letters over a long period before the Annapolis plan was proposed.[1] It was also suggested in his letter to Elbridge Gerry on January 7, 1787, in which he referred to the opposition to the Annapolis plan that was felt by "Jay and others" "from an opinion that the result [would] prove inefficacious."[2] That the Massachusetts and other eastern men were still at that date opposed to the Annapolis plan upon this ground, was definitely stated by Henry Knox, in a letter he wrote to Gouverneur Morris on the same day that King's letter to Gerry was written. Declaring he "most exceedingly wish[ed] Massachusetts and the eastern States would be at [the convention]," Knox explained to Morris that they appeared, however, to regard the measure not only as "irregular" but as "inadequate to our critical situation."[3] The nature of their objection on the latter ground, Knox had explained more fully in a letter he had written to Washington three days earlier. It was supposed, he told Washington, that "the proposed convention" would be "inadequate," unless there should be "an appeal *to the people of every State*, and a request to call state conventions of the people,* for the sole purpose of choosing delegates to represent them in a general convention of all the United States, to consider, revise, amend, or change the federal system in such a manner, as to them should seem meet, *and to publish the same for general observance, without any reference to the parts or states for acceptance or confirmation.*"[4] This proposal was essentially similar to the one mentioned by Henry Lee in his letter of October 20, 1786 to St. George Tucker.[5] The idea of what Lee had therein called "a congress of deputys, with plenipotentiary powers," had not been abandoned, and in view of the things that happened "both within & without Congress" shortly after Knox's letters to Morris and Washington were written, there can be no doubt that the idea still had the support of many different men "both within & without [that body]" at the time.[6]

---

*That is, the state conventions were to be elected by the people "for the sole purpose, etc., etc." Cf. Jay's exposition of the matter, below.

Besides writing about this subject to Morris and Washington, Knox wrote about it to his friends in Massachusetts. Thoroughly agreeing with his colleague, Jay, that the convention proposed at Annapolis would probably "prove inefficacious," Knox was, nevertheless, of the opinion that the meeting would "be attended with good effects." "It [would] approximate the public mind to a general government," he said, "and the more [that] subject [should] be discussed the sooner it [would] be accomplished."[7] In this belief he undertook, soon after the first of January 1787, to canvass various influential Massachusetts men with a view to procuring their support for Massachusetts' participation in the proposed convention. Among the men to whom he wrote were Nathaniel Gorham, James Sullivan, Benjamin Lincoln, and Stephen Higginson. His letter to Gorham has not survived,[8] and that to Sullivan contains no precise reference to the subject of the proposed plenipotentiary convention.[9] In his letter to Lincoln,[10] and in that to Higginson, however, Knox went very fully into the subject, seeking to make clear the doubts and difficulties which, in his opinion, were blocking participation in the convention by the Eastern states and approval of the Annapolis plan by Congress. His letter to Higginson was especially full, because Higginson had for some time been writing to Knox, telling him the existing crisis ought to be used to obtain for the country a better government, and urging him to use his influence among the men in Congress to secure vigorous action to that end. "Congress should be making the necessary arrangements," Higginson had written in the preceding November, "for improving" what Higginson even then believed was an increasingly favorable disposition in the country toward a better government. "They must be prepared," he had said, "not only to support a proper force in the field [to suppress insurrection], but *to consolidate the Several Governments into One, general and efficient.*" But having suggested this move, Higginson had then added that he really was "going too fast," since in his opinion the time for such action had not quite come.[11]

On January 20, Higginson, however, had again written Knox and, in what very probably was unjustified optimism, had informed him that "the feelings of the people in the Country [in Massachusetts were now] generally favorable"; that large numbers of them had taken sides against the insurgents; and that, "should this Spirit pervade the other States, it [would] give rise to Sentiments favorable to the Union." "The moment," he had urged, "must be seised by Congress."[12] But "the moment" when Knox received this letter was toward the end of the long period of no quorum in Congress, which had begun after the third of the preceding November; and in his reply, written on January 28, 1787, Knox tried to make clear to Higginson the various circumstances that made it difficult and indeed impossible for Congress, at "the moment," to act, and the reasons why, in Knox's opinion, it might be better for Massachusetts to concur in the Annapolis plan and not count upon some more heroic measure from Congress.

"The poor, poor federal government," Knox explained to Higginson, "is sick almost unto death—But one feeble sign of life for upwards of two almost three months past—No Congress but for part of one day." "How things [were] to be worked up, so as to produce by ordinary operations a remedy for the numerous existing disorders, or be made adequate to the great purposes of a nation, which, considering its vast resources, ought to be a dignified one, [was]," Knox confessed, "difficult if not impossible to conjecture." "A convention is proposed by Virginia," he said, "and acceded to by Pennsylvania, Jersey, probably New York and South Carolina, to consult on some plan to prevent our utter ruin." "Perhaps," he conceded, "this convention originated, and has been imbued, with ideas far short of a radical reform. Let this have been the case, may it not, notwithstanding, be turned to an excellent purpose? Our views are limited in all things, we can only see from point to point at a time, If men—great men—are sent to the convention, might they not assist the vision of the Southern delegates in such a manner as to induce the adoption of some energetic plan, in the prosecution of which [America] might rise to national dignity and happiness?"

Having propounded this question, Knox proceeded to indicate to Higginson just what, as he saw the matter, such a convention might do. "I have heard," he said, "all that has been said about legal and illegal conventions. I confess I do not find the objections on this point so weighty as some people do. Should the convention agree on some continental constitution, and propose the great outlines, either through Congress or directly to their constituents, the respective Legislatures, *with a request that State conventions might be assembled* for the sole purpose of choosing delegates to a continental convention, *in order to consider and decide upon a general government and to publish it for general observance*, in the same manner as Congress formed, and decided upon the articles of confederation and perpetual union, would not this to all intents or purposes be a government derived from the people and assented to by them as much as they assented to the confederation?" This suggestion, which was afterwards acted upon, may quite possibly not have been Henry Knox's own idea. The action of Madison (not yet in Congress on the date when Knox wrote) in departing from the Annapolis formula when he drew the Virginia act approving the proposed convention[13] suggests the contrary. So do certain other matters soon to be detailed; and the probability seems to be that some scheme such as Knox suggested to Higginson may have been talked of among the delegates at Annapolis in September; and that Knox had very likely picked up the idea in conversations with Hamilton and Benson and others in New York thereafter. Knox concluded his letter to Higginson by asking whether, if the convention proposed at Annapolis were not "the best mode" of effecting a change, it was not at least "the best which [was] practicable"; and whether, if this were the case, "it ought [not] to be embraced?" "The Southern States," he insisted, "are jealous enough already. If New England, and particularly Massachusetts, should decline sending delegates to the convention, it will operate in a duplicate ratio to injure us, by annihilating the rising desire in the Southern States of effecting a better national system and by adding to their jealousies of the designs of New England."[14]*

Higginson replied to Knox's letter on February 8. In his letter, Higginson surmised that Nathan Dane and Rufus King "ha[d] now different Ideas of [the proposed convention]." He also indicated his agreement with Knox that the plan for a convention ought to be "embraced"; but he nevertheless wished that the convention might be "empowered to perfect the system, and give it immediate operation, if nine states in Convention"—that is, apparently, in the Federal Convention—"[should] agree to it, without a reference to Congress, or their Constituents." "Otherwise," he said, "much time must be lost, and perhaps such a difference of Sentiment may arise, as to the report, as may entirely defeat the object." "Next to [vesting the convention itself with this plenary power], I should prefer," said Higginson, "[to] hav[e] their report referred to Congress, and if there approved by nine States, they"—that is, Congress—"to be authorized to give it immediate operation." "But I fear," he went on, "[that] the States cannot be brought to either of these points; their several legislatures perhaps have a right to delegate such powers, either to Congress, or to the General Convention; and if they had the right, so fond are they of retaining power in their own hands, and of having everything appear to originate with, or proceed from themselves, that I doubt much whether they could be brought to the exercise of it." In view of these difficulties, Higginson turned to a consideration of other possible modes of procedure.

Ratification by the state legislatures he dismissed at once as wholly impracticable. "To refer the doings of the Convention to the several Legislatures for adoption," he said, "would be to hazard the object, as much perhaps as to recur to the people at large," because the legislatures, he thought, would "not readily consent to a transfer of any part of their own rights to others." "If the referrence should be made to the people at large throughout the Union, what [could] be expected, considering their discordant views and interests, but a diversity and opposition of Sentiment, that [could] not be done away and which must in all probability prevent their agreeing upon any general system of Government?" In all the circumstances, "the most probable way of meeting with Success," he believed, "would be to have special State Conventions appointed, to whom the report of the general Convention should be referred, and they be directed to report to Congress their dissent or approbation therefor, and if nine of those State Conventions sh[ould] report in favour of the system, Congress sh[ould] be authorized thereupon, to declare it to be the federal Constitution of Government; and the States sh[ould] be compellable to conform to and govern themselves by it." "This mode," said Higginson, "is the most likely to be adopted by the people in the several

*In the manuscript, Knox's draft copy, "New" is written over "it in."

States, as it will give each of them a Voice in the revision of the doings of the general Convention, and it will avoid the difficulties which may probably attend a referrence to Congress, to the several Legislatures, or to the people at large."

The foregoing scheme is somewhat like that which finally was followed, but the idea of using state ratifying conventions was not new with Higginson, as may be seen from a casual reference to the subject by Henry Knox in his letter to Washington on January 4.[15] In his letter to Knox, Higginson, however, made one further suggestion which, though not adopted, is of considerable interest as exhibiting one more device that was probably talked of among the men in New York as a means for avoiding the difficulties foreseen if the constitutionally stipulated mode of adopting changes in the government were followed. The suggestion in question was designed by Higginson to preclude the possibility of prolonged controversy, either by the legislatures or the people of the several states, over the system of government that the contemplated convention might propose. His suggestion was that Congress should immediately "recommend to the several States, to appoint Delegates to the general Convention, and to form their several State Conventions for considering the report of the general Convention." The idea was to get the state conventions formed of men in whom the people had confidence, *before* the constitution to be submitted to them was drawn. If this course were adopted, "the people in the several States, to prevent any doubt or difficulties, might," Higginson also suggested, "at their next elections authorize their several Legislatures, by special instructions, to make the appointments necessary to the purposes above stated." In this way, "the whole business," he thought, "might soon be in train for a speedy and happy issue."[16]

Higginson's letter containing these suggestions was received by Knox at a time when conditions in Congress were such as to make virtually certain that Higginson's ideas were passed on by Knox to others. The strong likelihood is, therefore, that Higginson's ideas were among those considered by the interested men in Congress when the attempt finally was made to displace the Annapolis plan in favor of some more likely scheme. The chief alternative to the Annapolis plan which was then in the minds of the men in Congress was, however, the plan for a true constituent, or plenipotentiary, convention that Henry Knox had described to Washington in his letter of January 4. Knox's colleague, Jay, had also written Washington about this subject on January 7, and since Jay was one of the men most in favor of such a plan,[17] it is desirable that his views about it be put before the reader.

Jay's fundamental position was that "no alterations in the government should be made, nor if attempted, [would] easily take place, unless deducible from the only source of just authority—*the People*."* The authority of the convention proposed at Annapolis was "to be derived," he pointed out, "from

*Jay's emphasis.

the acts of the State legislatures." "Are the state legislatures authorized," he asked, "either by themselves or others, to alter constitutions? I think not; they who hold commissions can by virtue of them neither retrench nor extend the powers conveyed to them." This fundamental principle was really fatal not only to the legitimacy of the scheme of alteration proposed at Annapolis but also to the legitimacy of the scheme stipulated in the Articles; to the legitimacy, perhaps, of the Articles of Confederation themselves; and to the legitimacy of some, perhaps most, of the state constitutions which were then in existence. Jay realized, he said, that perhaps it was not intended that the proposed convention should do more than recommend the changes to be made. [If] so, there [was] danger," he thought, "that their recommendations [would] produce endless discussions, perhaps jealousies and party heats."

"Would it not be better," he inquired of Washington, "for Congress plainly and in strong terms to declare that the present Federal Government is inadequate to the purposes for which it was instituted; that they forbear to point out its particular defects or to ask for an extension of any particular powers, lest improper jealousies should thence arise; but that in their opinion it would be expedient for the people of the States without delay to appoint State conventions (in the way they choose their general assemblies), with the sole and express power of appointing deputies to a general convention who, or the majority of whom, should take into consideration the Articles of Confederation, and make such alterations, amendments, and additions thereto as to them should appear necessary and proper, and which being by them ordained and published should have the same force and obligation which all or any of the present articles now have?"[18] The last few words of Jay's long question were an inadvertency, for, as the rest of his letter shows, what Jay actually proposed was the establishment of a national form of government, consisting of a bicameral legislature, an executive, and a judiciary—in short, a government which would have a "force and obligation" *far superior* to that of the existing Articles: the "force and obligation" of a government derived "from the only source of just authority," or, as he said in his letter, "from *the People*."*

Washington did not reply to Jay's letter for over two months. The probable cause of his long delay was the disconcerting letters Washington was at the time receiving from various men in Pennsylvania, Connecticut, and other states, on the subject of reforming the government.[19] The character of those letters was certainly sufficient to account, in the case of a man in Washington's retired position, for the very discouraged letter he did actually dispatch to John Jay. In his letter, Washington confessed to Jay that he, too, was extremely dubious "how far the revision of the federal system, and giving more adequate powers to Congress [might] be productive of an efficient government," It might be true, he said, "as many seem[ed] to think," that

*Jay's emphasis.

"attempts to alter or amend [the existing system would] be like the proppings of a house which [was] ready to fall, and which no shoars [could] support." But he was afraid, he confessed to Jay, that the public mind was not matured for a change to a national government, or for proceeding in the mode that Jay had proposed. "[His] opinion [was] that [the] country ha[d] yet to *feel** and *see** a little more before [such a change could] be accomplished." Although he acknowledged that "without the means of coercion in the Sovereign"—i.e., in Congress—failure was "more than probable." he "would fain try what the wisdom of the proposed Convention [would] suggest, and what could be affected by their councils."[20] This gloomy letter, so unlike the Washington of a few months later, was totally without effect; before the day on which he wrote it, the attempt had been made in Congress to have a plan like Jay's adopted.

The evidence indicates that, for a brief time early in February, the intention was rather general in Congress simply to endorse the plan for a convention that had been proposed at Annapolis, and the action of the states which up to that time had approved the Annapolis proposal, though in the somewhat amended form that Madison had first gotten through in Virginia. The factor chiefly responsible for the rise of this intention in Congress was, apparently, the progress that the plan had somewhat unexpectedly made. Shortly after the plan had been approved by Virginia, it had also been approved by New Jersey; Pennsylvania had added its approval late in 1786; and shortly after the first of the year Delaware and then North Carolina had acted. News of North Carolina's action reached William Blount, one of the state's delegates in Congress, on February 8.[21] With it came instructions to communicate the news promptly to Congress.[22] Congress recommitted the Annapolis plan to a new grand committee for action, four days later on February 12;[23] and a letter of Rufus King's, of the day before, indicates that such action by Congress had his full approval on that date.[24] The inference is therfore strong that the news of the North Carolina decision is what finally galvanized Congress, including the Massachusetts men, into action.

The importance of North Carolina's action lay in the fact that, with her decision to participate in the convention, there came into existence, at the center of the Confederacy, a nearly solid block of five states which were committed to that measure. Included in this block were three out of the four largest and most populous states of the country;[25] and of the states situated at the center of the Confederacy, Maryland alone remained out of the block and could not, as a narrow sliver at the center of the approving states, continue out for long. The participation of the two other uncommitted Southern states was, moreover, rather well assured by the action of the two largest and least national of the Southern states—Virginia and North Carolina—since everyone was then aware of the superior nationalism, from whatever motives, of

*Washington's emphasis.

South Carolina and Georgia, and that the comparative handful of men in them could never stand alone.[26]

A further consequence of the approving action by North Carolina was that the New England states and New York were left as the only solid block of uncommitted states in the entire country. Those states—"the states east of the Hudson"—were the states about which dismemberment rumors had been most assiduously spread in the preceding summer, and though their non-approval up to the date of North Carolina's action may very likely have had the effect of adding zeal to Southern efforts "to preserve the Union," the situation afterward was different. More was then to be gained by throwing the weight of the "trans-Hudson" group behind the proposed convention, and since adhesion to the Annapolis plan by the five central states undoubtedly made that plan seem far more eligible than it had at first, it is not surprising that the Massachusetts men, upon hearing this news, decided to throw their state's great weight behind the convention, or that Congress in general moved at this point for a blanket endorsement of what up to that time had been done.

The evidence of a sudden decision to this effect by the Massachusetts men—or, at any rate, a decision to this effect by Rufus King—is to be found, as already intimated, in the letter King wrote to Elbridge Gerry, in Boston, on February 11. "For a number of reasons," said King in this letter, "although my sentiments are the same as to the legality of [the] measure, I think [Massachusetts] ought not to oppose, but to coincide with [the proposed convention]." "Events," he said, "are hurrying to a crisis; prudent and sagacious men should be ready to seize the most favorable circumstances to establish a more permanent and vigorous government. Let the appointments [by Massachusetts] be numerous, and if possible let the men have a good knowledge of the constitutions and various interests of the several states, and of the good and bad qualities of the confederation."[27] What the "favourable circumstances" were, that had led him to this sudden decision, King did not, in this hasty letter, take time to say; but since the date of the letter was just three days after the news of North Carolina's action had been received by William Blount, and since, furthermore, King did explain to Gerry, in another letter on February 18, that "all the States South of [New York]" were then, for all practical purposes, committed to the convention,[28] the inference seems fully warranted that the critical importance of action by the five central states earlier mentioned was what moved Rufus King to his decision of February 11.

The question remains just how King could have supposed, in view of his realistic views of ratification by the thirteen legislatures,[29] that the proposed convention held out any hope of a successful reform. No absolutely certain answer to this question is possible, but a clue to the probable answer is provided by the further contents of King's letter to Gerry on February 18. In that letter, having disclosed the situation with respect to "the States South of

[New York]," King added: "But the commissions, or authorities, seem to be different." This fact, apparently, had been discovered by Congress after its appointment of its grand committee on February 12. Having disclosed this circumstance to Gerry, King took back completely the enthusiastic endorsement of the proposed convention that he had sent to Gerry just seven days before. He could "not [now] venture a conjecture," he said, "relative to the policy of [the appointment of delegates by] Massachusetts." The thing was too "problematical." He was still "rather inclined to the measure," but more "from an idea of prudence, or for the purpose of watching, than from an expectation that much Good [would] flow from it."[30] The thing that destroyed his earlier optimism was, therefore, apparently something in the state commissions that destroyed his confidence in ultimate good results, and a study of the commissions should, therefore, disclose the basis of the earlier optimism that King had felt.*

The best-known diversity in the previously issued state commissions—the only instance ever mentioned in conventional histories of the subject—is the one which appeared in the commission issued by the state of Delaware. That state's commission contained a proviso that, in the constitutional changes to be proposed by the convention, there was to be no departure from the principle of equality of voting by the states in Congress.[31] That this proviso was the cause of some dissatisfaction among certain of the men in Congress is entirely probable, but the diversity in the state commissions that caused the most serious concern was undoubtedly over procedure. Madison, the reader will not have forgotten, had departed from the strict letter of the Annapolis plan in drawing Virginia's approving act: he had stipulated for a "due" confirmation of any proposed changes by "the several states," rather than for a unanimous confirmation of them by the "thirteen legislatures," as both the Annapolis plan[32] and the Articles of Confederation required.[33] The example thus set by Virginia had been followed—perhaps as a result of some previous understanding at Annapolis—in the acts of approval by Delaware and Pennsylvania.[34] The New Jersey act said nothing as to the mode of effectuating changes and, therefore, presumably left the matter open.[35] The commission issued by North Carolina, in consonance with the general character of that state's politics during the whole Revolutionary and post-Revolutionary period, had carefully stipulated, however, that its delegates to the convention should have authority only to agree upon and "report such an Act *to the General Assembly of* [*that*] *State, as when agreed to by them*, [would] provide for the [objects which the Annapolis plan recited]."[36] This provision, obviously

---

*King also said, in his letter to Gerry of February 18, that he "fear[ed] Pennsylvania and Jersey [would] be entirely under a *southern Influence*." (King's emphasis). The statement related to the Pennsylvania and New Jersey delegates in Congress. It is possible that King's fears in this respect extended to the convention and hence contributed to the abrupt change of view which he expressed in his letter of February 18. King did not, however, say this; the sequence of ideas in his letter does not support such an inference; and his behavior in Congress, on February 21, as we shall see, points plainly to the inference stated in the text.

devised to keep the making of all changes in the North Carolina legislature's own hands, precluded any move by the convention for an appeal to the people. Inasmuch as such action by the convention had been adumbrated in Madison's Virginia act and, likewise, in the Pennsylvania and Delaware enactments and was certainly not excluded under that of New Jersey, the inference seems to be fully warranted, especially in view of Henry Knox's letter to Stephen Higginson, of January 28, that it was the expectation of an appeal to the people which finally had convinced Rufus King, and probably other men around New York, that reform through *the proposed* convention was practicable.

This inference is greatly strengthened by certain proceedings that were begun about this time in the New York legislature, and by what was going on at the same time in Congress. The happenings in these two bodies also indicate that Rufus King was by no means singular in the pessimism he felt when he learned of the foregoing diversity in the state commissions that had been introduced by North Carolina. The earliest of these corroborative happenings was a difference of opinion as to the course to be pursued, which arose in the congressional grand committee of February 12 after the discovery of the diversity in the previously issued state commissions. The grand committee finally reported to Congress on February 19. It proposed that Congress adopt a resolution expressing its "entire coincidence" with the Annapolis delegates "as to the inefficiency of the federal government and the necessity of devising such farther provisions as sh[ould] render the same adequate to the exigencies of the Union," and "strongly recommend[ing] to the different legislatures to send forward delegates to meet the proposed convention."* Such a resolution, had it ever been adopted, would have left nothing to be desired as a complete and unqualified endorsement of the Annapolis plan. Precisely because this was true, however, the reader will easily see that the proposed resolution could not have been at all satisfactory to those men in Congress who were impressed with the difficulty of obtaining change through unanimous action by the thirteen legislatures. Even though it said nothing expressly about the mode of effectuating any change, the proposed resolution, nevertheless, did plainly incorporate by reference the fatal weakness in the Annapolis plan of referring all such changes to "the legislatures of every state" for ultimate "confirmation." By so doing, the resolution likewise approved the unsatisfactory commission that had just been issued by North Carolina. Quite apart from other less serious deficiencies, then, the fact can hardly be regarded as in any way strange that, when made, the report

---

*The full text of the committee's proposed resolution was as follows: "Congress having had under consideration the letter of John Dickinson esqr. chairman of the Commissioners who assembled at Annapolis during the last year also the proceedings of the said commissioners and entirely coinciding with them as to the inefficiency of the federal government and the necessity of devising such farther provisions as shall render the same adequate to the exigencies of the Union do strongly recommend to the different legislatures to send forward delegates to meet the proposed convention on the second Monday in May next at the city of Philadelphia."

had the support *of a bare majority only* of the grand committee's members.[37]

The identity of the members who voted against the report is not definitely known, nor do we know what considerations led them to vote in the committee as they did. The proceedings, already mentioned, that were begun in the New York legislature at what must have been about the time when the diversities in the state commissions became known, afford a key to the views of those members of the grand committee who voted for the proposal that afterwards eventuated in Congress from the New York proceedings. Since one less then half of the grand committee's members then voted for the proposal in question, the inference seems very strong (except, possibly, in the case of one man)* that the grand committee members who voted for that proposal were the same men who had voted against the committee's report in the grand committee. It also seems probable that the ideas involved in the New York proposal were the ideas these men had earlier advocated in the committee.

The proceedings in the New York legislature (which was sitting at the time alongside Congress in New York) were, according to the son of Alexander Hamilton, instigated by his father.[38] Primary evidence of Hamilton's agency in this matter has not been found, but the fact stated by his son is probable, since the proceedings were begun by William Malcom, a member of the assembly from New York City, who appears from various recorded votes in that body[39] to have been a member of Hamilton's nationalist group and was, according to Hamilton's son, one of his father's particular friends and co-adjutors.[40] The fact is also apparent from the recorded vote of the New York Senate, in the particular proceedings about to be discussed, that those proceedings were sponsored by the New York nationalist party.[41]

Malcom began the proceedings by a notice, given at the end of the day's proceedings on February 16, that he would on the next day move this following resolution:

Resolved (if the honourable senate concur herein) that a committee of this house be appointed to prepare a draft of instructions to the delegates of this state in Congress, directing the said delegates to move in Congress for an act, recommending to the states composing the union, that a convention of representatives from the said states, respectively, be held, and meet at a time and place to be mentioned in such recommendation, *for the purpose of revising the articles of confederation* and perpetual union, between the United States of America; *and reporting* to the United States in Congress assembled, and to the states respectively, *such alterations and amendments* to the said articles of confederation, *as a majority* of the representatives met in such convention *shall judge proper and necessary to render them adequate to the preservation and government of the union.*

---

*Melancton Smith is perhaps an exception. A member of the Clintonian faction, and afterwards an opponent of the Constitution, Smith may have voted for the New York motion only because he was bound by his legislature's instructions.

Malcom explained that he was giving notice of his intention to present such a motion in order "that the members might be prepared on the subject."[42]

To perceive what Malcom had in mind when he presented this motion, the reader must bear in mind that *all* "conventions" were unknown to the Articles and therefore extralegal, whether they were held for the purpose merely of proposing changes to Congress and the thirteen legislatures, or for the purpose of actually making changes under the authority of the people of the states of the country. There was therefore no presumption at all, as an American of today might perhaps suppose, that a merely advisory convention was intended when "a convention for the purpose of revising the articles and reporting alterations and amendments" was proposed. On the basis, indeed, of the then recent past experience of the American people, the presumption was undoubtedly to the contrary. The term "convention" had been widely applied, in the months that preceded the Declaration of Independence, to those extralegal representative bodies which thereafter became the legislatures in many of the states. Such bodies, as "conventions," or "congresses," or even as "legislatures," had drawn up and *"given immediate operation to"* most of the state constitutions then in existence. This had been accomplished, except in the cases of Massachusetts and New Hampshire, without any reference of these constitutions to either the people of the states or any other representative bodies for ratification. In other words, the state constitutions existing in 1787 had almost all been adopted by true constitutent or plenipotentiary bodies, acting in some cases with, and in other cases without, prior special authority from the people.[43] In these circumstances, a proposal like Malcom's would naturally be taken—and must therefore have been *intended* to be taken—as opening the way to such a convention. This would undoubtedly have appeared with particular clarity to a man of the time when he compared the language of Malcom's motion with that of the Annapolis plan which it was intended to supersede. The convention that had been proposed from Annapolis was one to "devise" needed changes and "report" an act *to Congress* for making them which, it was then expressly stipulated, should be effective only when "agreed to, *by [Congress]*, and afterwards confirmed *by the Legislatures of every State*." The Malcom motion proposed a convention, however, in which this stipulation was, under the circumstances, very pointedly omitted. Although the convention proposed in the Malcom motion was also to "report," the things it was to "report" to Congress *and "the states"* were *"alterations and amendments to the articles"* which a majority of the convention "should think proper and necessary."

On the face of the Annapolis plan, then, the convention therein proposed was one *merely to advise* Congress, and the procedure of effectuation therein mentioned was precisely that stipulated in the Articles.* The Malcom mo-

---

*The thirteenth of the Articles of Confederation provided in part: "Nor shall any alteration at any time hereafter by made in any of [the Articles of this Confederation], unless such alteration be agreed to in a Congress of the United States, and afterwards confirmed by the legislatures of every State."

tion pointedly omitted this stipulation; and in view of this fact; in view of the unquestionable normalcy of the plenipotentiary procedure in constitutional conventions at the time; and, above all, in view of *the reaction to its words* which took place a little later in Congress, we may properly conclude that the proposal of such a convention was the true purpose of the Malcom motion. The purpose was the curing of the procedural deficiencies of the Annapolis plan, as those deficiencies had been particularly worsened and emphasized by the unsatisfactory North Carolina commission. The mode by which it was proposed to cure those deficiencies was by opening the way to a recommendation by Congress, at the behest—or the seeming behest—of a state, that a true constituent, or plenipotentiary, convention be called together. Shortly stated, the Malcom motion was an attempt to obtain a convention of the precise kind which John Jay,[44] Rufus King,[45] Stephen Higginson,[46] Alexander Hamilton,[47] Henry Knox,[48] and, as Madison had said, "many Gentlemen, both within & without Congress," had long wanted.[49]

The Malcom motion, however, had still another purpose. The Annapolis plan had envisioned the proposal of such changes as would "render the constitution of the *Federal* Government *adequate to the exigencies of the Union*."[50] This formula, though vague enough, perhaps, to cover almost anything, was open to the objection that it did not suggest with any clarity that a "national" or "continental" or "consolidated" form of government was the desirable innovation. As already indicated, there was nothing else in the text of the Annapolis report that conveyed, at all definitely, such a suggestion. In the Malcom motion, an attempt was made to cure this defect, too, for a formula of change was proposed that comprehended all alterations "proper and necessary to render [the Articles] adequate to *the government of the Union*." By these words, the establishment of a "government of the Union" appears to have been made an express, primary object of the proposed convention, and in order to make this authorization of extensive change completely clear, an alternative formula was added, covering all alterations judged "proper and necessary" for "*the preservation of the Union*." To present-day readers this second formula may seem quite as empty as the formula which had been proposed at Annapolis, but the reader should remember that these words were used at a time when fears of a breakup of the Union were very real. We have seen this clearly in the letters of James Monroe, James Madison, and Henry Lee; and the reader may remember, too, that Monroe had specifically declared to Madison, when the Annapolis convention was assembling, that he had "always considered the regulation of trade in the hands of the U.S. as *necessary to preserve the Union*."[51] This secondary formula of the Malcom motion, we may feel absolutely certain, was not empty verbiage; the formula was a definite proposal that the states should be asked to agree to all changes that might be judged "proper and necessary" *to keep the states together*.

As the Malcom resolution finally went through, however, it was changed from its original form in two respects: the express provision for procedure by majority vote of the "representatives met in [the] convention" was omitted, and the formula of change was altered to that of "render[ing the Articles] adequate to the preservation and *support* of the Union," rather than "the preservation and *government*" thereof, as Malcom had originally proposed.[52] Whether the first of these changes made any difference in the procedure to be followed may be doubted, since procedure by majority vote was the usual mode of procedure, unless some other was specified. Under the second change, however, "the government of the Union," as distinct from the securing of the Union's continued existence, was undeniably no longer to be a primary object to be aimed at by the convention. Nevertheless, if the institution of "a government of the Union" had been determined by a convention acting under the New York formula to be a "proper and necessary" means of keeping the states together, an "alteration" of the Articles to establish such a government would, it is perfectly clear, have been entirely within such a convention's powers. Although the changes made did undoubtedly weaken the proposal somewhat, they did not actually alter what was possible under it, and this is the view of the matter which was taken in the Continental Congress when the New York proposal came before that body.

The New York resolution went through in the state's legislature, in the form just indicated, on February 20.[53] The order of the day in Congress, for the following day, was the consideration of the report which that body's grand committee had made on February 19.[54] That report, as we have seen, had recommended a blanket endorsement of the Annapolis plan. When the report was called up for action on February 21, the New York delegates presented to Congress the resolution which had been passed by their legislature on the day before, and moved a postponement of the grand committee's report, in order to take up as a substitute a resolution drawn in accordance with their instructions.* The New York motion was defeated, but, judging from the fact that the "ayes" and "noes" were called for, this result must have been unexpected. Calling for the "yeas" and "nays" would ordinarily mean that there had been some previous assurance of support for the New York motion, which the vote by states had disappointed, and that the men who had been interested in the New York motion desired to be informed just how their disappointment had come about. The rollcall showed that, besides the New York delegates, Egbert Benson and Melancton Smith, the "ayes" included the two Massachusetts delegates, Rufus King and Nathan Dane, and the two Virginia delegates, James Madison and William Grayson. There

---

*The text of the resolution proposed by the New York delegates was as follows: "That it be recommended to the States composing the Union that a convention of representatives from the said States respectively be held at _____ on _____ for the purpose of revising the Articles of Confederation and perpetual Union between the United States of America and reporting to the United States in Congress assembled and to the States respectively such alterations and amendments of the said Articles of Confederation as the representatives met in such convention shall judge proper and necessary to render them adequate to the preservation and support of the Union."

were also favorable votes by William Samuel Johnson, of Connecticut, and William Few, of Georgia, which divided equally the votes of those two states; and the unfavorable votes of New Jersey and Pennsylvania were cast, in each case, by a bare majority only of their delegations, Lambert Cadwalader, of New Jersey, and Samuel Meredith, of Pennsylvania, having each voted in favor of the New York motion. The only states whose delegations were solidly against the motion were the two Carolinas; the states of New Hampshire and Rhode Island were completely unrepresented in Congress when the motion was made, and Delaware and Maryland each had but a single delegate—that is, less than a quorum—present. The motion, then, was really very nearly successful, and the interesting and significant fact is that, among the delegates supporting the motion, there were five of the eleven members of the grand committee of February 12, whose recommendation, by a bare majority of its members, was pending before Congress when the New York motion was made. This five-man minority of the committee consisted of its chairman, Nathan Dane; and Few, Smith, Cadwalader, and Grayson.[55]

Defeat of the New York motion meant, of course, that there could be no true constituent convention. The supporters of the motion had, therefore, to agree, in the resolution eventually passed, that the convention to be held should be one "for the *sole and express* purpose of revising the Articles of Confederation and reporting to Congress and the several legislatures such alterations and provisions therein *as sh[ould] when agreed to in Congress and confirmed by the states* [be effective for the purpose which the resolution recited]."[56]* In the early stages of the Federal Convention, certain of its members—most of them, apparently, for trading purposes—argued that the foregoing provision of Congress's resolve restricted the Convention's authority so as to preclude its proposing of any departures from *the form* of the existing confederation, and, more particularly, that the foregoing provision completely precluded the proposal by the convention of a *national* form of government.[57] This view, it is well known, was also expressed by some anti-Federalist writers and speakers in the ratification campaign, and, as in the case of so many other anti-Federalist fables, this one apparently has become the the accepted view in American history. This view is nevertheless

*The full text of the resolution of Congress was as follows: "Whereas there is provision in the Articles of Confederation and perpetual Union for making alterations therein by the Assent of Congress of the United States and of the legislatures of the several States; and whereas experience hath evinced that there are defects in the present Confederation, as a mean to remedy which several of the states and particularly the state of New York by express instructions to their delegates in Congress have suggested a Convention for the purposes expressed in the following resolution and such Convention appearing to be the most probable mean of establishing in these states a firm national government. *Resolved* that in the opinion of Congress it is expedient that on the second Monday in May next a Convention of delegates who shall have been appointed by the several States be held at Philadelphia for the sole and express purpose of revising the Articles of Confederation and reporting to Congress and the several legislatures such alterations and provisions therein as shall when agreed to in Congress and confirmed by the States render the federal Constitution adequate to the exigencies of Government and the preservation of the Union."

quite certainly false. The above-quoted provision from Congress's resolution had no such purpose: its purpose was merely to *deny* in an emphatic manner that Congress was recommending "the congress of deputys, with plenipotentiary powers," which the Massachusetts delegates, the Virginia delegates, and many other men, "both within & without Congress," long had wanted, and for which the Malcom proposal from New York had been intended to open the way.

On this precise point, there can be no doubt whatever that the supporters of the New York motion were completely defeated. The only concession made to them, on the point of procedure, was an adherence to the departure from the originally stipulated procedure, which James Madison had initiated surreptitiously in the approving act of Virginia; which had been followed in the acts of Pennsylvania and Delaware; left open in the act of New Jersey; and explicitly precluded in the unsatisfactory act of North Carolina. In other words, the "confirmation" of the changes to be proposed by the convention, in the resolution of Congress as finally passed, was stipulated merely to be by "the states," not by "the *legislatures* of every state," as the Annapolis plan had originally suggested. This concession, the reader will at once perceive, adds weight to the view previously suggested: that the diversity in the state commissions *on this particular point* was what gave rise to the proceedings in the New York legislature, out of which the New York resolution in Congess grew.

Our conclusion that the above-quoted language from the resolution of Congress, of February 21, was not in fact intended to trammel the Federal Convention in the changes it might propose, is corroborated by other provisions in the resolution as finally passed, and since the other provisions that make this clear are likewise departures from the Annapolis plan, and therefore departures also from the congressional grand committee's recommended blanket endorsement of that plan on February 19, the further certainty appears that these other provisions were also concessions made by the majority in Congress to the very substantial minority there who had supported the New York motion. One of these other provisions specified the objects to be aimed at by the Federal Convention: it was to propose such changes as would "render the federal constitution adequate to *the exigencies of Government and the preservation of the Union.*" This formula of change is quite obviously different from that contained in the original Annapolis plan; it is likewise different from the formula of change contained in the defeated New York motion, for it is the substance—indeed, very nearly the exact words—of the formula contained in the Malcom resolution orginally offered to the New York legislature on February 16. The resurrection of this formula in Congress certainly suggests very strongly that the men in that body who supported the New York motion, of February 21, were really in favor of the formula of change that had been contained in the original Malcom motion. This probably means that they—at any rate, some of them—had been concerned, along with the nationalist members of the New York legislature, in concerting the Malcom motion as it was first presented. This accords with the call for the "yeas" and "nays" in Congress, and points quite definitely to preconcerted action. Be this as it may, however, the formula in the congressional resolution as finally passed did undoubtedly once more make the transformation of the existing confederation into a government of the Union, a primary object of the impending convention. In addition, it authorized the convention to propose *every change* requisite to keep the states of the Union together. To make the nature of the hoped-for change completely clear, Congress further declared that the convention was being recommended because it "appear[ed] to be the most probable mean of establishing in these states *a firm national government*."

There is no possibility that the words of the resolution could have been misunderstood, either in Congress or outside, at the time. The fact that they were not misunderstood is indicated by the answers returned in the Federal Convention to the sophistical view of that body's powers which was there presented. "The States in their appointments," said Gouverneur Morris, "Congress in their recommendations point directly to the establishment of a *supreme* government capable of 'the common defence, security of liberty and general welfare.'"[58] "We have powers," said James Wilson, "to *conclude* nothing—we have power to *propose* anything."[59] As for the argument, which certain others made, that a national government was *ex necessitate* beyond the powers of the convention because the state legislatures themselves could not ratify such a change, this, said Alexander Hamilton, had been fully anticipated in the New York Senate, where a proposal to restrict the powers of the New York delegates to changes consistent with New York's constitution had been rejected as an inconvenient shackle. It had been said in answer, Hamilton remarked, that in case of such changes (which would probably be necessary) recourse could be had to the people. "This," he concluded, "[was] reasonable and therefore [left the convention] at liberty to form such a *national* government as [it might] think best adapted for the good of the whole."[60] Since this is the view that eventually was followed, the reasonable supposition is that the contrary argument, as before suggested, was advanced, at least in the main, for tactical purposes only.

The certainty that Morris and Wilson and Hamilton were right in their views, and that the view here presented of the purpose of the New York motion is entirely correct, appears from this further consideration: such a view of the true purpose of the New York motion is necessary to explain with any degree of good sense the presence of the words "sole and express" in the resolution as finally passed. The accepted view—that these words were inserted to preclude the proposal of any changes save such as would still leave the so-called government "federal" in character—is a view which makes the resolution of Congress a meaningless jumble of inconsistent and wholly contradictory provisions. According to this accepted view, Congress is supposed first to have declared it was approving the convention as "*the most probable mean* of establishing in these states a firm national government," and then carefully stipulated that "the sole and express purpose" of the convention was to be of a character to make its proposal of that kind of government a forbidden act. For such a view of Congress's resolution there is only one word: ridiculous. When the choice lies between such a view and a view that makes the resolution of Congress a straightforward piece of sensible draftsmanship, the view having the latter effect must certainly be chosen.

Further corroboration of the view here taken of the proceedings in Congress on February 21 is provided by two contemporary letters about those proceedings, which, fortunately for our latter-day understanding of the proceedings, have survived. One of these letters was written by William Irvine, of Pennsylvania, to James Wilson, of that state, on March 6. Irvine was one of the members of the Congressional grand committee which had recommended a full endorsement of the Annapolis plan on February 19,[61] and judging by the sentiments he expressed in his letter, and his mode of voting in Congress on February 21, Irvine must have been one of the majority members of the committee, and very much against what the supporters of the New York motion had tried to do. "The Eastern Delegates," he said in the course of his letter, had all been very much against "the recommendation for a Convention." Since the official records of Congress show that "the Eastern Delegates" were not (with a single exception*) against a convention such as New York proposed,[62] this statement can only have meant that those delegates, in general, were much against "*the* [particular] recommendation for a Convention" which had issued out of Annapolis, and, as we have seen, this was unquestionably true. In consequence of the opposition of the Eastern men, the measure, said Irvine, had been carried "with some difficulty". "Indeed," said he, "I think they would never have come into it, but that they saw it would be carried without them. Then they Joined, *which has made it*," he said, "*a piece of patch work*."[63]

Irvine's final words plainly attribute to "the Eastern Delegates" all those elements in the resolution of Congress, of February 21, which departed from the sense of the original Annapolis plan and, consequently, from the sense of the blanket endorsement of that plan which the congressional grand committee had proposed. As "the Eastern Delegates" were among those who voted for the New York motion, this is in accord with the views presented here. It is also in accord with the official journals of the Continental Congress, which indicate that the resolution Congress finally passed was the work of the two Massachusetts delegates, Dane and King.[64] And since their "patch work" adhered to the procedural departure from the Annapolis plan first made by Madison, in Virginia; since it employed the precise formula of change that had been contained in the Malcom motion as orginally presented in the New York legislature on February 16; and since, finally, it pointed

---

*Stephen Mix Mitchell, of Connecticut, voted against the New York motion of February 21. He also voted against the resolution of Congress as finally passed.

expressly to "a firm national government" as the desired innovation, this question inevitably arises: Precisely what feature of the New York motion was it that the supporters of that motion were obliged to forego? The only possible answer is that they forewent their plan for a true constituent, or plenipotentiary, convention, for, as our analysis has shown, the supporters of that motion actually got, in the result, *everything else* which the New York motion had contemplated.

The second letter indicating the correctness of this view of the proceedings in Congress on February 21, is a report on those proceedings to be found in a letter written by Henry Knox to Stephen Higginson, of Boston, from New York, on February 25. Knox was not a member of Congress; but he was Congress's secretary of war; he was deeply interested in the effort to obtain a more likely-seeming convention; and he was a close friend of the Massachusetts delegates, particularly Rufus King, whose politics by this time, it appears from King's letters, agreed with his own.[65] It seems quite proper, therefore, to regard Knox's letter to Higginson as a report by a man who knew the facts (in all probability as a result of conversation with King), to another man who, as Knox well knew, was quite as much interested in what had gone on in Congress, as he. "You will have learnt by the last Thursday* post," he said, "that Congress have acceded to the idea of a convention. But you will also see that the report of the convention is to be submitted to Congress and the respective states." "This is all," he next wrote, "that could be effected by—" And, then, changing his mind, he crossed out these words† and wrote: "This is all that Congress conceived itself authorized to do and hope." "But it [was] next to an impossibility," Knox went on, "that all the states should agree to an efficient government." After going into the failure of the more distant states, and particularly the failure of Pennsylvania, to understand that the disorders in New England had had national causes, and after intimating to Higginson that this lay at the root of the failure in Congress on February 21, Knox concluded with a statement that, "although [he was] very far from dispairing, yet [he was] pretty much inclined to think that, if an efficient government [should] be established in any reasonable time, it [would] rather be the effect of accident than design." "And [yet]," he told Higginson, "were it possible to carry your mode of approbation into effect"—i.e., through state conventions—elected by the people—"the road to a good government would be much shorter than it now appears to be."[66] That is what was afterwards done; and taking this letter with the other evidence here presented, no doubt is possible that the proceedings in Congress on February 21 had precisely the character delineated herein.

This last conclusion is singularly important for the present discussion. It means that there was in Congress, on February 21, 1787, far more desire and

*February 22, 1787
†The manuscript is Knox's draft copy.

enthusiasm for a national government than has long been commonly supposed. The supporters of the New York motion were the men, in general, who (from very divergent motives, it is true) were by this time the strongest nationalists in that body; the men, at least, who were most urgent that some vigorous course of action be pursued that would be likely to achieve results.* The opponents of the New York motion were not, however, in general opposed to the establishment of a national government; and since at least seven out of the nine states present in Congress, on February 21, eventually agreed upon a resolution pointing explicitly to a "firm national government" as the desired reform,[67] the conclusion is certain that most of the opponents of the New York motion must have agreed with its supporters as to the objective to be achieved: they differed with them only as to what they thought was the most expedient and probably fruitful procedure. The final conclusion undoubtedly must be that, on February 21, 1787, there was very general agreement among the men in Congress that "a firm national government," rather than what then was known as "a federal government," should be established.

*Melancton Smith, of New York, as already indicated, may have been an exception.

CHAPTER XXVI

James Madison's Memorandum on the Proceedings in Congress on February 21, 1787: Herein of the First Clear Instance of Madisonian Falsification

THE foregoing account of what happened in Congress on February 21, 1787, and the conclusion stated at the chapter's end, are based upon all known items of relevant evidence, save one. The exception—i.e., the only piece of evidence we have not yet considered—is apparently the *only* item of evidence usually consulted by American historians in arriving at the traditional view of these proceedings, The item we have not yet considered purports to be a contemporaneous memorandum of what went on, made by an actual participant in the business: James Madison, of Virginia. The memorandum in question is one among a large number of papers that Madison very deliberately prepared and left for publication after his death,[1] which occurred in 1836, some forty-nine years after the occurrences to which these papers of his related. Before 1836, it is relevant to observe, all the men who had participated with Madison in the proceedings in Congress had died; and this was true, also, of all the men who had participated with him in the work of the Federal Convention—the other subject to which Madison's carefully prepared documents related.[2]

Madison's memorandum of the proceedings in Congress on February 21, 1787, reads in its entirety as follows:

WEDNESDAY, FEBRUARY 21ST.

The Report of the Convention at Annapolis, in September, 1786, had been long under the consideration of a committee of Congress for the last year, and was referred over to a grand committee of the present year. The latter committee, after considerable difficulty and discussion, agreed on a report, by a majority of *one* only, (see the Journal), which was made a few days ago to Congress, and set down as the order for this day. The Report coincided with the opinion held at Annapolis, that the Confederation needed amendments, and that the proposed Convention was the most eligible means of effecting them. The objections which seemed to prevail against the recommendation of the Convention by Congress, were, with some, that it tended to weaken the Federal authority by lending its sanction to an extra-constitutional mode of proceeding; with others, that the interposition of Congress would be considered by the jealous as betraying an ambitious wish to get power into their hands by any plan whatever that might present itself. Subsequent to the Report, the Delegates from New York received instructions from its Legislature to move in Congress for a recommendation of a convention; and those from Massachusetts had, it appeared, received information which led them to suppose it was becoming the disposition of the Legislature of that State to send deputies to the proposed Convention, in case Congress should give their sanction to it. There was reason to believe, however, from the language of the instruction from New York, that her object was to obtain a new convention, under the sanction of Congress, rather than accede to the one on foot; or perhaps, by dividing the plans of the States in their appointments, to frustrate all of them. The latter suspicion is in some degree countenanced by their refusal of the impost a few days before the instruction passed, and by their other marks of an unfederal disposition. The Delegates from New York, in consequence of their instructions, made the motion on the Journal to postpone the Report of the Committee, in order to substitute their own proposition. Those who voted against it considered it as liable to the objection above mentioned. Some who voted for it, particularly Mr. MADISON,* considered it susceptible of amendment when brought before Congress; and that if Congress interposed in the matter at all, it would be well for them to do it at the instance of a State, rather than spontaneously. This motion being lost, Mr. DANE,* from Massachusetts, who was at bottom unfriendly to the plan of a convention, and had dissuaded his State from coming into it, brought forward a proposition, in a different form, but liable to the same objection with that from New York. After some little discussion, it was agreed on all sides, except by Connecticut, who opposed the measure in every form, that the resolution should pass as it stands on the Journal, sanctioning the proceedings and appointments already made by the States, as well as recommending further appointments from other States, but in such terms as do not point directly to the former appointments.

It appeared from the debates, and still more from the conversation among the members, that many of them considered this Resolution as a deadly blow to the existing Confederation. Doctor JOHNSON,* who voted against it, particularly declared himself to that effect. Others viewed it in the same light, but were pleased with it as the harbinger of a better confederation.

The reserve of many of the members made it difficult to decide their real wishes and expectations from the present crisis of our affairs. All agreed and owned that the Federal Government, in its existing shape was inefficient and could not last long. The members from the Southern and Middle States seemed generally anxious for some republican organization of the system which would preserve the Union, and give due energy to the government of it. Mr. BINGHAM* alone avowed his wishes that the Confederacy might be divided into several distinct confederacies, its great extent and various interests being incompatible with a single government. The Eastern members were suspected by some of leaning towards some anti-republican establishment, (the effect of their late confusions,) or of being less desirous or hopeful

---

*Emphasis as in the original publication in *The Papers of James Madison* (Washington, 1840), II, 587-590.

of preserving the unity of the empire. For the first time the idea of separate confederacies had got into the newspapers. It appeared to-day under the Boston head. Whatever the views of the leading men in the Eastern States may be, it would seem that the great body of the people, particularly in Connecticut, are equally indisposed either to dissolve or divide the Confederacy, or to submit to any anti-republican innovations.[3]

To most of our readers, the most striking feature of the foregoing memorandum will probably be the total ignorance it seems to evince on the part of James Madison that the New York motion had any such purpose as that propounded for it by the present writers. Madison states for his readers "the objections which," he says, "seemed to prevail against the [Annapolis proposal]," but he makes not the slightest mention of the fear of its inefficacy which, as the evidence from other sources clearly shows, was at the time the chief objection of the Massachusetts delegates, Dane and King, and of other men, e.g., John Jay, Henry Knox, Stephen Higginson, and others—both in and out of Congress. The memorandum likewise gives the impression that the motives lying back of the New York legislature's instructions were, and were generally suspected in Congress of being, anti-national in character; it insinuates that some of the support the New York motion received in Congress was of this character, too; and the whole style and tenor of the memorandum seem to evince an extreme and obvious anxiety on Madison's part to explain away the fact that he himself had voted for a measure that might perhaps be suspected to have had an anti-national character. In the course of his memorandum, the intimation also is made that among the men in Congress there was no clear understanding of each other's desires and purposes in what was going on. The general impression is certainly conveyed that the New York motion came somewhat unexpectedly before that body, and that the support it received there was entirely casual and haphazard, and certainly not preconcerted. Obviously, these impressions are totally at variance with the account of the day's proceedings which we have just given the reader. This being true, we are faced with the need to inquire whether Madison's memorandum can even possibly be considered a reliable piece of evidence, and if it cannot be so regarded, then what character should be attributed to it.

We shall begin our inquiry into these questions with the problem of the motives lying back of the New York motion; whether, in other words, the motives of the resolution of instructions from the New York legislature, out of which that motion arose, can possibly have been of the anti-national character suggested by Madison. For most Americans today, the best guarantee that this could *not* have been the case is undoubtedly the fact that the resolution, if it did not actually originate with Alexander Hamilton, certainly originated with the nationalist group in the New York legislature of which Hamilton was the acknowledged leader.[4] The reader can entertain no doubt whatever that this fact had precisely the same effect in 1787—at least among the men in Congress who were acquainted with Hamilton or had been with him at Annapolis, as Madison had been. The measure was not, in fact, a Clintonian measure, as is further indicated by the vote by which it passed the New York senate. The vote in the senate was 10 to 9, and a comparison with that body's other recorded votes establishes, in the case of nearly all the men who voted for the measure, that they were of the nationalist, rather than the Clintonian, group.[5] The possibility that the New York resolution grew from anti-national motives must therefore be dismissed, though we should recognize the distinct possibility that fear of confusion in the efforts for reform may have been an important motive with some of the men in Congress who voted against the motion. On this particular point, then, it appears that Madison's memorandum probably discloses *some* measure of truth, but quite clearly not the whole truth, nor even enough of the whole truth to render unmisleading whatever measure of truth *is* disclosed.

The character of the support given to the New York motion in Congress may next be considered. The vote of the New York delegates, regardless of their convictions, was determined by their legislature's instructions, and the vote of Melancton Smith, a member of the Clintonian party in New York, may have been determined by that and by nothing else. The other New York delegate, however, was Egbert Benson, a friend and coadjutor of Alexander Hamilton and a man whose motives were quite beyond suspicion.[6] On the basis of their records as a whole, the same was certainly the character of the two Massachusetts delegates, Dane and King. As for the four lone supporters of the New York motion, from the states of Connecticut, Georgia, Pennsylvania, and New Jersey, all the available evidence indicates that these men—respectively, William Samuel Johnson, William Few, Samuel Meredith, and Lambert Cadwalader—were nationalists, Johnson, very clearly and emphatically so;[7] and nothing is known of any of these men to justify the slightest suspicion of their motives in voting for the New York motion. Apart from the two Virginia delegates, then, all the supporters of the New York motion, with perhaps the single exception of Melancton Smith, appear to have been above suspicion in connection with the cause of organizing a firm national government.

In the case of the Virginia delegates—William Grayson and James Madison—the problem of what they were doing when they voted for the New York motion may most profitably be considered from a slightly different point of view. Is it conceivable, possible, and probable that they voted for "a congress of deputys, with plenipotentiary powers" on February 21, 1787?

In the case of William Grayson, we should at once explain to the reader that he was an opponent of the Constitution in 1787–88, when that document was before the country. After its adoption, moreover, he was identified with the extreme anti-national faction in his state.[8] However, according to a statement of his views made in November 1787, in a letter to Thomas Jefferson's secretary, William Short, Grayson's initial opposition to the Constitution was based in part upon the fact that he thought the national powers thereunder in certain respects deficient; in particular that he thought Congress, "in order to face foreign powers properly and to preserve their treaties and their faith with them, should have had a negative upon the State laws, with sev[era]l other incidental powers." He also objected to the Constitution because of its provision for inferior federal courts; and he complained of the fact that the document did not begin with a comprehensive bill of civil rights.

Grayson's leading objections, however, were of an entirely different order from those just stated. One was that "the representation in the Senate ought to have been in the same proportion as the lower house, except in a few cases merely of a fœderal nature"—i.e., "fœderal" as distinct from "national"—in which cases, whatever they were, he was willing to concede "the little States should be armed with a repulsive quality to preserve their own existence." Another of Grayson's chief objections was that "the power of regulating commerce by a bare majority and that of taxing [would] ruin the Southern States." And a third was that "the proposed method of making treaties, i.e., by two thirds of the Senators *present*,* would be the means of losing the Mississippi forever." In sum, Grayson's principal objections amounted to this: the South—or at any rate Virginia—did not have a sufficient share in the control of the proposed new government. This being true, the reader might quite naturally suppose that Grayson must have thought the Virginia delegates had failed in their duty to the South and their own state. Grayson, however, denied this. The delegates, he said, had been "so circumstanced" that "they could not act otherwise" than they had done, and he declared to Short that he "highly respect[ed] the chief of them."[9] The situation at the time Grayson wrote, then, was simply this: he was very much disappointed with the outcome of the Federal Convention. And *if* that fact and his later anti-Federalism could be regarded as *precluding* a vote by him for a true constituent convention in the preceding February, it would at once have to be conceded, on the basis merely of Grayson's vote, that the New York motion must have had some character other than that here suggested.

Grayson's serious disappointment with the work of the Convention, however, clearly has no such preclusive effect. To the contrary, his letters show that over a long, earlier period he had felt a strong desire for a better government, but along with that desire he had definitely been aware that there would be great difficulty in getting the states to agree to all the changes he believed were necessary to be made.[10] Grayson's general point of view was well expressed in his letter to Madison written on May 28, 1786. Grayson told Madison he feared the states could not then be brought to an agreement upon constitutional reforms, even in Congress. "Our affairs," he had then

*Grayson's emphasis.

said, "are not arrived at such a crisis as to ensure success to a reformation on proper principles." He also warned Madison that "a partial reformation [would] be fatal"; in particular that, if Madison's Annapolis commercial convention produced "anything decisive" in the way of commercial powers, "nothing more [was] to be expected from Massachusetts, [etc., etc.]." Grayson's opinion was that the way to proceed was to wait until matters became more critical, and then to get delegates together with powers "comprehending all the grievances of the Union, and to combine the commercial arrangements with them, and make them dependent on each other." "By a general compromise," he thought, "a good government" might "perhaps be procured."[11] To a man holding such views, a plenipotentiary convention would quite certainly have commended itself as an appropriate agency of reform. The whole history of the Confederacy had been one of adopting measures in Congress, only to have them fail for want of execution in the states. Grayson was familiar with that history; and to a man who was aware, as he was, of the great difficulty there would be in getting the thirteen separate states to agree upon anything, a plenipotentiary convention must obviously have seemed the most eligible device for obtaining what he considered to be "a good government" through "a general compromise." Moreover, there was much in the general situation on February 21, 1787—particularly in the altered behavior of the Massachusetts men—to make Grayson or any other man think that the critical moment was at hand. When it is remembered also that Grayson himself desired a national government *with a negative over the laws of the states*,[12] and in addition to this a system of representation in the national legislature that was certain to be distasteful *to the people* as well as the governments of all the Northern states,[13] the conceivability—indeed, the high probability—that William Grayson did deliberately vote on February 21, 1787, for a plenipotentiary convention is a conclusion singularly difficult to avoid.

The probability that Grayson voted for a plenipotentiary convention is increased by what he had to say in certain letters he wrote between February 21 and the time when the Federal Convention assembled. In the first of these letters, written to William Short on April 16, Grayson noted that "some of the gentlemen of the convention" were in New York on their way to Philadelphia; that he "ha[d] conversed freely with them as to the reform [they desired]"; and that "they [were] for going a great way." "Some of them [were] for placing Congress in loco of the King of G[reat] B[ritain,] [by giving them a negative upon the state laws]—besides their present powers"; and they were also "for giving [Congress] a perpetual duty on imports and exports." Grayson, however, was afraid "[America's] distresses [were] not sufficiently great to produce decisive alterations." So far as the people were concerned," the more slack the government [was], the better [they] liked it: of course they [would] not give up any power which [would] prevent them from being compelled to make satisfaction to their Creditors: They [might] perhaps go as far as granting the regulation of commerce to Congress, under such conditions limitations and restrictions as in all probability [would] render the exercise of the power impracticable." But that was all. He therefore "believe[d] the whole thing [would] terminate in nothing: either the assembly"—i.e., the convention—"[would] not agree, or if they [did] agree, the States [would] not ratify." "Figure to yourself," he said by way of conclusion, "how the States will relish the idea of a negative on their laws [etc. etc.]"[14] To a man with such ideas and at the same time desirous of national governmental reform, a plenipotentiary convention must undeniably have commended itself as a wise and probably efficacious measure.

On May 24, Grayson wrote another letter which adds to the evidence for the conclusion just stated. In this letter, written to Madison after that gentleman had gone to Philadelphia, Grayson seems, for a moment, to have felt more hope. "Entre nous," he wrote, "I believe the Eastern people have taken ground they will not depart from respecting the Convention—*One legislature** composed of a lower-house triennially elected and an *Executive** & *Senate** for a good number of years." "I shall see Gerry & Johnson, as they pass," he added, "& may perhaps give you a hint."[15] Whether he ever did give any hint on this subject to Madison is not known, but in a letter to Monroe, dated May 29 and probably written after Gerry had "passed,"[16] Grayson appears to have reverted to the same cynical mood of discouragement that he had shown in April when writting to William Short. "The delegates from the Eastward," he told Monroe, "are for a very strong government, & wish to prostrate all [the] state legislature[s], & form a general system out of [the] whole." "But I don't learn," he added, "that the people are with them." He then gave a short sketch of conditions in Massachusetts which sounds very much like some remarks later made by Gerry in the Federal Convention.[17] He added his own opinion that conditions were not propitious in the other states, except New Jersey, which he thought would "go great lengths," as well "from motives of Interest" as from a desire for "revenge [upon New York]." Thus he "hardly [thought] much good [could] come of [the Convention]: the people of America [did] not appear to [him] to be ripe for any great innovations." "[And] it seems," he said, "they are ultimately to ratify or reject: the weight of Gen[era]l Washington . . . is very great in America, but I hardly think it is sufficient to induce the people to pay money or part with power."[18] Such, then, were the views that Grayson entertained as the Federal Convention drew near: he was still plainly discouraged by the mode of procedure being followed. Since he had also entertained such views in the preceding year, our conclusion seems warranted: a vote by Grayson on February 21, 1787, for a plenipotentiary meeting was an act entirely probable.

Turning to Grayson's colleague, Madison, one of the most important facts to be considered in his case is the strong disposition he had previously shown

*Grayson's emphasis.

to meet the ideas of the Northern men when faced with their threats to dismember the Union. When he had first experienced these threats in the preceding summer, Madison had responded with advocacy of precisely the "full" power for Congress which the Northern men wanted, namely, "for the regulation of commerce foreign and domestic";[19] and this although he had not before that time shown any disposition whatever to advocate an *extensive* national power over trade.[20] On February 21, 1787, Madison once more faced a similar Northern threat. As his memorandum points out, "the idea of separate confederacies had [then] got into the newspapers." It had got into them through an item in *The* [Boston] *Independent Chronicle* of February 15. This item demanded, in an angry tone, that the New England states at once withdraw from Congress and set up as "the [independent] Nation of New England." "[Massachusetts]," it was said, "ha[d] already made reiterated and strenuous exertions to restore that firmness, confidence, and greatness, which distinguished united America from 1774 to 1782, but to little purpose. It [was] therefore time to form a new and stronger union. The five* states of New England, closely confederated, [could] have nothing to fear. Let then [the Massachusetts] General Assembly immediately recall their Delegates from the shadowy meeting which still [bore] the name of Congress, as being a useless and expensive establishment:—Send proposals for instituting a new Congress, as the Representative of the Nation of New England, and leave the rest of the Continent to pursue their own imbecile and disjointed plans, until they ha[d] experimentally learnt the folly, danger, and disgrace of them."

This proposal of dismemberment, as Madison's memorandum correctly says, was the earliest reference to this subject in any of the nation's newspapers. Quite naturally it was copied quickly by other papers and soon became known in other parts of the country.[21] The proposal, again according to Madison's memorandum, was known in New York on the day the New York motion was considered in Congress.[22] The effect of this knowledge upon Madison may be quite accurately surmised from certain letters he wrote a few days later to friends in Virginia. One of these letters went to Edmund Pendleton, an enthusiastic nationalist at that time, in the hope, apparently, that knowledge of the matters to which the letter referred would spur Pendleton on to redoubled efforts "to save the Union." The dismemberment sentiment, Madison told Pendleton, was spreading. "After long confinement to individual speculations and private circles, [it was] beginning to shew itself in the Newspapers." "The late turbulent scenes in Mass[achuset]ts and infamous ones in Rhode Island, ha[d] done inexpressible injury to the republican character in that part of the U[nited] States; and a propensity towards Monarchy [was] said to have been produced by [those events] in some leading minds." "The bulk of the people," Madison surmised, "[would] probably prefer the lesser evil of a partition of the Union into three more

---

*That is, including the then rebel state of Vermont.

practicable and energetic Governments." "But tho' [this was] a lesser evil, it [was] so great a one, that [he] hoped the danger of it [would] rouse all the real friends of the Revolution to exert themselves in favor of *such an organization of the confederacy, as [would] perpetuate the Union*, and redeem the honor of the Republican name."[23]

The day after writing this letter, Madison wrote another, somewhat similar, to Edmund Randolph, then governor of Virginia. "The existing Confederacy," Madison informed Randolph, "[was] tottering to its foundation." After referring to the desire for monarchy, of which, he said, "many individuals of weight, particularly in the Eastern district [were] suspected," and the "prediction" of "others" that "a partition of the States into two or more confederacies" would soon occur, Madison ventured his own prediction that "it [was] pretty certain that, if *some radical amendment* of the single [confederacy could] not be devised and introduced, one or the other of these revolutions, *the latter no doubt*, [would] take place." "I hope" he admonished, "[that] you are bending your thoughts seriously to the great work of guarding against both."[24]

These letters certainly evince that, at the time the New York motion was considered in Congress, Madison still was reacting to the Northern dismemberment threats as he had reacted to such threats in the preceding summer. In the light of this fact, and the renewal of such threats which had then just come to his knowledge, it seems undeniable that, if there was *ever* a day in James Madison's life when it was probable he voted for a true constituent convention, February 21, 1787, was the day. This probability, furthermore, is greatly enhanced by the precise character of the governmental changes he then, and later, desired should be made. As did Grayson, Madison not only wanted a national legislative negative upon *all* state laws,[25] and a Southern share in the control of the government proportioned in some way to the number of its slaves;[26] he wanted, in addition, a full national power to regulate commerce,[27] and more generally a complete power to act in "all cases requiring uniformity."[28] "*This* national supremacy"—i.e., a national supremacy including a *general* national negative supremacy—he wished to see "extended to the Judiciary departments" also.[29] With reference to the executive sphere, he talked of making "the officers administering the Executive departments"—i.e., the *state* executive departments[30]—"appointable by the supreme Government" as a means of establishing "the National supremacy" in that sphere as well.[31] Regarding the desirable nature of the national executive powers, he said he had not then made up his mind. Clearly, then, what Madison desired was to subordinate the state governments to the government of the nation, *completely*.[32] He was more interested in this than anything else. This being true, it is undeniable that, if he thought at all, Madison must have anticipated the greatest difficulty in obtaining the kind of government which he wished to see, *if* such a government were submitted to the *state legislatures* for ratification.

James Madison must have expected equal difficulties in a ratification *by the people*, as is abundantly clear from the extent and character of his anti-democratic views at this time. While it is entirely true that Madison looked forward to some participation in the government by the general mass of the people in the states, he was extremely anxious to subject their participation to some kind of drastic check. The check that first occurred to Madison was a national council for the revision of all legislation, both state and national.[33] As it appeared in the Virginia plan in the Federal Convention, that council was to consist of "the [national] Executive and *a convenient number* of the National Judiciary."[34] The key to the nature of what Madison desired in his advocacy of this device is the fact that he was at the same time advocating "a *single* executive";[35] for this fact means that *one* of the national judiciary would not have been "a convenient number" in the revisionary council. Two judges, at least, would have been "a convenient number" in the revisionary council, for two judges would have been required to avoid tie votes, and they would have thus outnumbered, and therefore controlled, the executive; and since the national judges were "to hold their offices during good behavior," under the Virginia plan,[36] this means that Madison's desired council of revision was to be one dominated by persons holding office under a virtually permanent tenure. The check which this council would have upon the people's participation in the government was, as the reader will see, an extremely drastic one. Despite Madison's ardent advocacy of this device, however, the Federal Convention disapproved it heartily and repeatedly;[37] and when this occurred, Madison became an advocate, as indeed he had been before,[38] of a national executive "of long duration"[39] and at more than one point advocated,[40] and at one point actually voted for,[41] an executive during good behavior, in each case to be armed, we should add, with the power of the discarded revisionary council—the power, in other words, of vetoing all acts of the national legislature. At a still later time, Madison proposed a *double* veto upon all the national legislature's acts, one to be lodged in the executive, and the other in the national judiciary;[42] and he stood out to the end for a requirement of three-fourths, rather than two-thirds, of both houses of Congress to override the single veto that finally was lodged in the executive.[43]

To the foregoing facts, we should add the following. When Madison's favorite device of a national negative on all state laws was voted down by the Convention on the ground, among others, that it would be extremely cumbersome and inconvenient to have to "send all [state] laws up to the Nat[iona]l Legisl[ature] for approval," Madison urged, in accord with an idea he had entertained at least since March of 1787,[44] that this inconvenience could be avoided, and this *to him* desirable check upon "democracy" in the states still effectively instituted, "by [providing for] *some emanation* of the [national negating] power *into the states*, so far at least, as to give a temporary effect," he said, "to [state] laws of immediate necessity."[45] This long circumlocution simply meant that some national officer was to be on duty in the states to pass upon their acts even of local legislation. The incontestable conclusion is, then, that this "Democratic Republican" of future years was in fact *not* very democratic in his views in 1787; and if all the features of the kind of national government he desired so earnestly to see are borne in mind, together with the fact that the basis of representation he desired in that government was certain to be distasteful to *the people* as well as *the governments* of all the Northern states, the reader will find it extremely difficult to believe Madison was not fully aware that the greatest difficulty was certain to be encountered in obtaining such a government through any submission to the people. The consequence is that a vote by James Madison on February 21, 1787, for a true constituent convention is not an improbable, but a highly probable, act. As for his courage for such a vote, this derived, of course, from "the revolution of sentiment" with respect to the extreme need for national governmental reform, which, we have already seen, he believed had occurred in his own state of Virginia.[46]

If James Madison deliberately voted on February 21, 1787 for a true constituent convention, the certainty is that, in his memorandum, he must also deliberately have misstated the reason for his vote for the New York motion. A little reflection will likewise show the reader that, if such was the fact about Madison's vote, the general impression his memorandum seeks to convey of that day's whole doings in Congress must, in various other respects, have been deliberately untruthful as well. For example, *if* the New York motion was an actual attempt to obtain a true constituent convention, there must certainly have been some statement and discussion of its purpose on the floor of Congress. If such was the purpose of the New York motion, it was a purpose that could not possibly have been accomplished slyly: the proponents and supporters of the motion had to state their purpose and argue their case. Of course, once they had stated their purpose and argued their case, there could not possibly have been any uncertainty and ignorance upon this point among the men in Congress "and particularly [on the part of] Mr. MADISON," as that gentleman's memorandum contrives to suggest. Furthermore, the probability is great that there would have been some antecedent preparation for such a motion. *If*, therefore, the New York motion *did* have the purpose we have suggested in the previous chapter, Madison's memorandum can only be regarded as a document systematically rewritten at a later date to obscure and obfuscate what had gone on in Congress on the day to which it relates. It is, therefore, not surprising that it contains, as altered documents not infrequently do, certain lapses in falsification—in other words, survivals of the original truth—which in themselves give the whole situation away.

For example, Madison's memorandum tells us that William Samuel Johnson, of Connecticut, voted *against* the resolution of Congress which finally passed. Johnson's reason for this vote, according to Madison, was that the resolution that passed was considered by Johnson to be "a deadly blow to the existing Confederation," *without* seeming to be, Madison clearly implies, "a harbinger" of anything "better." However, the only difference between the New York motion, *for* which, according to the official records of Congress, Johnson voted,[47] and the resolution of Congress that finally passed, for which, according to Madison, Johnson did not vote, is that the latter provided, whereas the former did not, that the *"sole and express"* power the proposed convention should have was that of concerting, and reporting to Congress, changes in the government *which were not to be effective* until "agreed to in Congress and confirmed by the states." The New York motion, with its proposal of a convention to "alter" the Articles, however, was every bit as deadly a "blow to the existing Confederation" as the resolution which passed; and since Johnson voted *for* the New York motion, he must have done so (even though the motion had that character) because it seemed to him to be "a harbinger" of something "better." This, in turn, could only have been the case if the convention proposed in the New York motion was some type of convention that appeared to Johnson as being more likely to be effective for the ends proposed than the convention recommended in the resolution that passed. This very plainly means that Johnson, in voting for the New York motion, must have supposed he was voting for a plenipotentiary meeting; a convention, that is, which could make its own decisions effective.

Granted the facts about Johnson which Madison supplies, the conclusion just stated cannot be escaped, except upon the assumption that Johnson's motives were slyly anti-national, and that he voted for the New York motion because he saw it in the light Madison suggests in his memorandum, i.e., something well calculated to "divid[e] the plans of the States" and by so doing "frustrate all of them." Such an assumption would be completely inconsistent with all that is known of William Samuel Johnson's character and all that is known of his public career. The assumption, then, is a highly improbable assumption, whereas the alternative view, namely, that the supporters of the New York motion were voting understandingly for a true constituent convention, is not only probable in the case of Johnson, but probable also in the case of James Madison. Because such an assumption is entirely credible in the case of the other men who voted for the New York motion, this view of what happened deserves our acceptance as the correct view.

Despite the extreme improbability of the contrary view—that Johnson voted for the New York motion with anti-national motives—we may usefully assume that view, in order to demonstrate with a little more certainty that he did *not* do so. Even upon that assumption, these significant questions would still remain: Why is Madison's memorandum so much like "the play of Hamlet, with Hamlet left out"? Why, in other words, is his memorandum so very industriously uninformative? Why, when it obviously purports to detail and explain the doings of the day, does it leave out the one thing that makes what finally was done, intelligible? We refer, of course, to Madison's total failure to explain that the majority in Congress were opposed to a shift to a plenipotentiary convention, and that the resolution finally adopted by Congress was carefully drawn to make clear the fact that the convention it recommended was merely of an advisory character. This view of Congress's resolution is required in order to make that resolution sensible, and such a view of the resolution necessitates the conclusion that the New York motion which had just been defeated *was understood* by the men in Congress to be an attempt to obtain a true constituent convention. This understanding of the New York motion, it is possible to assume, was a mistaken one. The fact that Madison's memorandum so carefully avoids all mention of this unquestionable understanding of Congress, however, when that understanding is so essentially necessary to comprehend what finally was done, points directly to the facts that Congress's understanding was not a mistaken one; that the New York motion actually was a *bona fide* and completely understood attempt to obtain a plenipotentiary convention; and that *his* participation in such an attempt was what Madison was in fact striving earnestly to obscure. In other words, Madison, far from having to explain away an act that might be thought to be anti-national in motive, actually had to explain away (or else obscure) an act that was national and anti-"states' rights" in the highest degree. His seeming concern that he should *not* be thought to be guilty of an anti-national act is the merest "red herring." The true view of what went on in Congress on February 21, 1787, is without any doubt the view presented to the reader in the previous chapter.

In suggesting this as the proper conclusion to be reached we realize, of course, that the corollary proposition—that Madison deliberately rewrote his memorandum on the proceedings in Congress on February 21, 1787—may seem to many readers an improbable one. The plain truth is, however, that the probability is overwhelmingly the other way. A full appreciation of this fact cannot be expected by the reader until he has considered the body of evidence relating to the Federal Convention, for the probability referred to depends, in part, upon the existence of a multiplicity of instances in Madison's notes on the Federal Convention, in each of which the probability of falsification is about what it is with respect to his memorandum on the proceedings in Congress which we have just been discussing. This multiplicity of instances of probable falsification, furthermore, is informed and unified by certain motives for such action which are found recurrently in all the separate instances. By virtue of this fact, the separate instances are transformed into a single compound probability which amounts to a virtual certainty. This being true, obviously no absolutely final judgment should be formed upon Madison's memorandum on the proceedings in Congress on February 21, 1787, until all the other instances of probable falsification have been recounted, and the facts which make falsification probable in each of these other instances are fully understood.

Despite the impossibility at this point of putting before our readers all the relevant evidence as to the probability of falsification by Madison in these other instances, we believe it is possible and desirable to indicate in a preliminary way the nature of the facts upon which depends the probability that James Madison did such acts.

One of the most important of these facts is the singularly inconsistent character of James Madison's public career. In his lifetime, this was a commonplace. His own letters show that he was charged in his later years with having been guilty of gross inconsistency with respect to "almost every important question which ha[d] divided the public into parties."[48] This charge, his letters also show, distressed him greatly; and he wrote long, argumentative letters to prove that his behavior, far from being inconsistent, had been singularly consistent, not only with itself, but with the Constitution as well.[49] These long letters, read—as they usually are—without the slightest reference to the matters of fact to which they relate, have a certain plausibility; but if Madison's statements of fact are checked up at all, it becomes perfectly evident that the charge made against him by his contemporaries was completely justified: in the course of his long life, James Madison had been about as inconsistent, especially on the great constitutional issues of his time, as a public man could be.

His life in this respect divides itself into three well-defined periods. The first comprises the years of his public career before his visit to New York at the height of the controversy over the Spanish treaty in the summer of 1786. Before that trip, Madison, if we may phrase our view mildly, had been a very moderate and cautious nationalist. Valuing the Union and the military and naval protection which it meant for the South, he was nevertheless fearful and jealous of the Northern states, even before the Revolution was over. His record in Congress during his first period of service there shows that he consistently voted *against* every proposal of national power for any purpose other than the common defence and the support of it. Once the Revolutionary War had been fought and won, and Madison left Congress and returned to Virginia, he quickly became a leader in the schemes which soon sprang up for what he revealingly described as "the emancipation" of Virginia's commerce "from Baltimore and Philadelphia." This was to be accomplished by an exclusive local system of commercial regulations to force the growth of the Virginia seaports. Consistently with all this, when Monroe was heading the committee in Congress in 1785 for "giving to the United States the general regulation of trade," Madison concurred in Monroe's plans only "in the abstract" and "to a certain degree" which, as Madison's letters and behavior plainly show, was not very great. His letters also indicate that he considered—or purported to consider—the ends for which the Northern states desired a national commerce power as manifestly impossible to attain; and his response to the great commercial agitation of 1785 was, accordingly, that only enough power should be given to Congress to preserve the Northern states from adopting "anti-fœderal expedients." In all this, we think it fair to say, Madison appears to have been actuated at least as much by fear of the Virginia legislature and Virginia public opinion as he was by fear and jealousy of the Northern states. Both motives, however, were plain in his letters, and whichever of his fears was the stronger, there can be no doubt that, as the consequence of either or both of them, he was at that time a very moderate and cautious nationalist.

All this abruptly ended with Madison's visit to New York during the controversy in Congress over the Spanish treaty in the summer of 1786. In the years that immediately followed—years that witnessed his efforts to promote the assembling of the Federal Convention, his activities in that body when it finally met, his efforts in behalf of the Constitution in the ratification campaign, and the first two years of his service in the national Congress—in these years, we think it equally fair to say, Madison was an *extreme and ardent* nationalist—a nationalist, moreover, who was distinctly anti-democratic in his views. A summary of the facts supportive of these statements has already been presented; for the present, then, it is sufficient to say that this period of Madison's extreme and ardent nationalism lasted only five years, and that it ended as abruptly as it began.

It ended in the early part of 1791 with the controversy in Congress over the first national bank organized under the Constitution. The division of the House of Representatives upon that measure was almost a straight division between the North and the South: only four Southerners voted in favor of the measure, one from South Carolina, two from North Carolina, and one from Maryland.[50] As this statement implies, Madison lined up with the Southerners and, in so doing, repudiated the views in general which he had held in the Federal Convention; the view which was, as his own confidential correspondence shows, his honest belief as to the power of Congress "to provide for the general Welfare";[51] and the views as to the scope of the national commerce power, which he had actually expressed on the floor of Congress less than a year before.[52] In these circumstances, it is not surprising that Madison was promptly attacked as a turncoat by his former associates among the Federalists.[53] The accusation was entirely justified and it undoubtedly rankled. Its truth also made Madison's position in the anti-Federalist party somewhat difficult. The more extreme "states'-righters" among the Southern planters were naturally suspicious of a man who had been so extreme and ardent a nationalist such a very short time previously; the democratically inclined working men and farmers of the Northern states also had their suspicions, and the Southern aristocrats, posing as "Democratic Republicans," absolutely had to have the support of these Northerners. Indeed, Madison's position in this respect seems to have grown worse with the passing years: more and more facts came to light as to what had gone on in the Federal Convention, and in the end Madison's inconsistencies became a commonplace among his contemporaries.

Of the various disclosures about the Federal Convention which proved embarrassing to Madison, perhaps the earliest was one made by Hamilton in 1792. Madison was not named in the disclosure Hamilton then made, but there can be no doubt that it was entirely clear to many men that Madison was intended. Hamilton's disclosure was made in response to the unjustified attacks which the Jefferson-Madison party was then beginning to make upon Hamilton as an advocate in the Federal Convention, so they said, of monarchy. In their attacks upon him they declared that he had "opposed the constitution in the grand convention because it was too republican," and that he had wished instead to institute a monarchy. In his reply, Hamilton denounced all this for what it was: "a gross misrepresentation." He had "never made a proposition to the convention," he said, "which was not conformable to the republican theory"; and "the highest toned"—i.e., the strongest, or most energetic—of any he had made, had "actually [been] voted for," he added, "by representatives of several states, including some of the principal ones, and *including individuals who, in the estimation of those who deem[ed] themselves the only republicans, [were] pre-eminent for republican character.*"[54] His reference, of course, was to Madison's having voted for an executive during good behavior. The attacks upon Hamilton continued, and at last, on February 24, 1802, in the columns of *The New York Evening Post*, Hamilton stated the facts accurately and named Madison as having voted for the measure in question.[55] This controversy, it is clear from Madison's own papers, was on his mind almost to his dying day;[56] he kept returning to it in the years after Hamilton's death, arguing about it on the slightest provocation;[57] and in his notes on the Federal Convention, there is plain evidence of alterations to explain away his own behavior and in a most petty way to discredit Hamilton's.

Another early disclosure which appears to have annoyed Madison occurred in 1808, when he was a candidate for the presidency. The disclosure was made in a pamphlet published by Edmond Genet to promote the rival candidacy of his father-in-law, George Clinton, the notorious anti-Federalist governor of New York. The pamphlet consisted of quotations from the notes on the debates in the Federal Convention which had been taken by Robert Yates, one of the delegates from New York. The quotations disclosed the extreme and ardent nationalistic role which Madison had played in the convention.[58] In Madison's notes on the convention, certain of the speeches in question bear indubitable evidence of alteration; the alterations rather tend to lessen or to moderate Madison's nationalism; and the fact of alteration can be corroborated by evidence form other sources.

Yates's notes were published in full at Albany in 1821, two years after the official journal of the Federal Convention had been published at Boston by order of Congress. The appearance of Yates's notes, plainly confirming the suspicions of Madison which had long been entertained by the more extreme "states' rights" Southerners, were productive of renewed attacks upon him by the men in that group, notably by that garrulous, but nonetheless effective, pamphleteer John Taylor, of Caroline County, Virginia.[59]

Shortly after the publication of the Convention's journal and the notes taken by Yates, and in the midst of the renewed attacks upon him which these drew forth, Madison undertook to prepare for posthumous publication the memoranda he had made of the proceedings of the Continental Congress during his two periods of service therein and the extensive notes he had taken of the debates in the Federal Convention.[60] Considering the circumstances in which Madison did this work, and the sensitiveness which he constantly showed to criticism, the fact is scarcely surprising that the documents, as he finally left them, show plain evidence of the kind of extensive alteration of which we have mentioned some instances. Several of the cases of alteration in his notes on the Federal Convention are strikingly similar to the instance which we have just examined, relating to the proceedings in Congress on February 21, 1787. In his notes on the Federal Convention, Madison frequently appears as participating along with others in some act which, on its face, and sometimes on the basis of evidence surviving from other sources, seems plainly to have been an act of a highly nationalistic, or in some cases of an anti-democratic, character; yet, in his own explanations of what went on, Madison either appears in these same cases to have been blandly unaware that the act in question had such a character, or else is pictured (frequently, with too much protestation) as pursuing some very nonobvious, incredible, and different purpose of his own. In addition to cases of this kind, there are many instances of what appear to be small, but are nonetheless important, alterations to the same general end; there are some plain cases of affirmative interpolation; and, most important of all, there are certain cases of egregious wholesale omission of comment upon matters with respect to which Madison changed sides, and which, as shown by the evidence from other sources, had certainly been discussed.

In very large degree, Madison's undoubted motive in all these alterations was an easily understandable desire for self-justification: a desire to appear in the pages of history as a more consistent and clearheaded man, a man less timid and less subservient to the dominant pro-slavery opinion of Virginia and the Southern states than in actual fact he was. In certain cases there is also a seeming desire to aggrandize his part in the proceedings of the Federal Convention, or at any rate to asperse or derogate from the part taken therein by others. These motives undoubtedly go far to account for most of the things that are found, or not found, in Madison's notes on the convention; but to account for all the alterations they apparently contain, something more is necessary. If this be true, another motive, strong enough to justify to most men the kind of thing he did, undoubtedly existed for Madison when he made the changes in his notes. This was the conviction apparently felt by Madison in his latter days that the theories of the Constitution which public opinion in Virginia and the South had compelled him to adopt for political reasons in his earlier years, were in fact absolutely essential to fend off the ruin of that part of the nation whose welfare he had most at heart. The reader will therefore find it easy to understand that with respect to the documents he left for posthumous publication Madison may have been led into acts which, without this powerful motive, he might otherwise not have engaged in.

As we have previously suggested, Madison's original apostasy was almost certainly the result of selfish, prudential motives. By the spring of 1791, when his apostasy occurred, it was perfectly obvious to everyone that Virginia was anti-Federal, and very likely to remain so for a considerable time. In these circumstances, of course, any politically ambitious Virginian, such as Madison or Thomas Jefferson, was obliged also to be anti-Federal, or else face the virtual certainty of never holding office. Considerations of this kind were the probable motives of Madison's abrupt change of sides in the spring of 1791. Before that year was over, however, an event occurred which in all likelihood began the process of Madison's *actual*, as distinct from his ostensible, conversion.

The event in question was the outbreak, on August 20, 1791, of the great slave rebellion in the French colony of St. Domingue on the West Indian island of Haiti. This rebellion, which, after some twelve years of more or less continuous fighting, eventually led to the establishment of the independent black nation of Haiti, was an extremely brutal and sanguinary affair. The slaves on the plantations of the rich northern plain lying back of the town of Cape François (known after the revolution as Cape Haitien) rose by prearrangement; burned the plantations; slaughtered the men and children among the whites, with many revolting variations of ferocity; raped and slaughtered the women in similar fashion; and drove those who succeeded in escaping these fates into Cape François and others of the larger towns. The besieged whites, on their part, handled with unbelievable barbarity the rebellious negroes who fell into their hands; the surviving accounts, whatever their source, indicate that upon this point there was little to choose between the contending parties. The trouble dragged on, aggravated after a little while by the mismanagement of certain commissioners sent over to the colony from Revolutionary France. The climax, so far as American Southerners were concerned, was the sacking and burning of Cape François in the early summer of 1793. This act, carried out by the rebel blacks of the Haitian backcountry, had actually been instigated by the Revolutionary French commissioners in the course of a quarrel they had with the white inhabitants of Cape François. In the light of this fact, it was generally concluded that safety for white men in the island was at an end, and a general exodus of the white population followed. Many of these refugees came to the United States, most of them in utter destitution; and from this time on what had been the richest of the colonies of eighteenth-century France was, for all practical purposes, lost to her.[61] Without going into details, it seems sufficient to say that the stark horrors of the Haitian rebellion, and the progress of the long-continued fighting which finally resulted in the expulsion of the whites and the independence of the blacks of the colony, were all most circumstantially reported in the American newspapers of the time; that eyewitness accounts of these occurrences were published in this country and extensively circulated among the Southern states; and that the lesson to be learned by the South, from the whole occurrence, was the subject of discussion and declamation by Southerners for forty years or more afterward.[62]

The lesson of the Haitian revolution, according to the South, was the absolute necessity, in the strictest sense, of maintaining the status quo with respect to slavery. To comprehend the nature of this Southern conclusion, and the extent to which the fanatical attitude of mind it involved on constitutional questions was a factor supervening *after* the Constitution was formed, it is necessary to understand that, although the presence of slaves within a country had always been regarded as an element of weakness in case of foreign attack, and although minor troubles with slaves were far from uncommon, the occurrence of slave rebellions upon any extensive scale was an extremely rare thing. In the island of Haiti none had occurred in nearly a hundred years; and none had ever before occurred anywhere *in which the slaves had been victorious*. To state the matter concisely, the Haitian rebellion and revolution were indeed something new under the sun, and the Southerners' conclusion was that the whole thing was a direct consequence of the meddling with the status quo of which the French Revolutionary Convention had been guilty. Its initial mistake, they argued, had been the extending of political rights to the *affranchi*, or freed slaves, of Haiti. This action, there can be no doubt, did produce trouble—more accurately, it added to the seriousness of preexisting troubles—between the *affranchi* and the white inhabitants of St. Domingue; according to the Southern analysis, it and various proclamations of the French Revolutionary Convention had put into the heads of the slaves on the island ideas which they otherwise would not have had, and by so doing had been directly causative of the great slave rebellion of 1791; the subsequent destruction of Cape François in 1793; the many unspeakable horrors connected with these events; and the final utter ruin of the rich French colony in which these events occurred. The Southern conclusion therefore was that the South's only safety lay in an absolute maintenance of the status quo with respect to slavery, a strict policy against all individual emancipations of slaves, and a rigorous denial of any improved status to all free persons "of color" whatsoever.[63]

The highly emotional attitude which Southerners came to have regarding this whole subject may be accurately gauged from the extremely graphic phraseology used by Jefferson in certain letters he wrote about the Missouri question in 1820. That question "filled [him] with terror," he said, "as the knell of the Union." "[There] was not a man on earth who would sacrifice more than [he] would to relieve [the country] from this heavy reproach [of slavery], in any *practicable** way. The cession of that kind of property [was] a

*Jefferson's emphasis.

bagatelle which would not cost [him] a second thought, if, in that way, a general emancipation and *expatriation** could be effected; and gradually, and with due sacrifices, [he thought] it might be." "But as it is," he said, "*we have the wolf by the ears, and we can neither hold him, nor safely let him go. Justice is in the one scale, and self preservation in the other*." Jefferson argued, therefore, that Congress had, and should have, no power to "regulate the condition of the different descriptions of men composing a State."[64] In another of his letters he ventured the opinion that, "if Congress once [went] out of the Constitution to arrogate [such] a right, its majority [might], and probably [would], next declare that the condition of all men within the United States [should] be that of freedom." "In [that] case," he said, "all the whites south of the Potomac and Ohio must evacuate their States, *and most fortunate those who [could] do it first!*"[65] Here, it seems perfectly clear, the ghosts of Cape François, after nearly thirty years, were still gibbering through the mouth of Thomas Jefferson.

The danger from "letting-go the wolf," in the figure of speech employed by Jefferson in his letter, was of course avoided, so far as any theory of the Constitution *could* avoid it, by Jefferson's insistence that Congress had no power "to regulate the condition of the different descriptions of men composing a State." The danger arising from "holding the wolf," in that same figure, however, was *not* thereby avoided. We therefore find Jefferson also arguing in his letters that Congress was likewise without power to determine that "the different descriptions of men composing a State [should] not emigrate into any other State."[66] As applied to the slaves of the Southern states, this meant, in the language of the Constitution (which Jefferson avoided), that Congress could not determine that the slaves of the South should not be "*imported*"—a term of "commerce"—into any other state. The need for this contention arose from the imperious necessity of continuously peopling the newer western states with slaves, if those states were to be saved for the slavery system. A sparsely populated western state in which slavery was allowed might, despite this fact—and quite without the exercise of any national intrastate power—easily be lost to the slavery system if free white men only could migrate into and settle within it. In other words, in Jefferson's figure, the existing Southern states dared not "hold the wolf," lest the slave states become in a little while a hopeless minority in the Union. This dilemma* in which the South was placed is the key, then, not only to the Southern theories of the Constitution but to many of the things that Madison did and said to support them.[67]

The Haitian rebellion and the sheer terror to which that event gave rise among the Southern states had repercussions upon the constitutional theories of Southerners almost at once; but as the years wore on other events abroad, directly connected with the slavery question, greatly added to the South's

---

*Jefferson's emphasis.

fears and fortified the constitutional theories growing out of them. These were the successes, and the threatened successes, of William Wilberforce and others within the British Empire, in their onslaughts upon the slave trade and the whole slavery system.[68] "Never let us forget the [British] West India colonists," said a South Carolina writer of the 1820s, "[for] in their lamentable history we have seen the consequences of the interference with the subject of slavery on the part of the British Parliament." "The value of a slave," he went on to argue, "arises not merely from his bodily capacity for labour, (for he has *volition** and may abscond from the service of his owner,) but from his contentment with his condition, and his attachment to his master's household. Once restive and discontented, under the cruelly fallacious hope, that Congress is to take them and their whole race, under its special cognizance and care, our slaves," he warned, "will not only become a present burden to us, but will create in all of us, whose lot is to live in this [Southern] country, *a solicitude as to the future consequences*, which would be the worst species of slavery for us to endure." The end, he said, if the South were not careful, would be "THE RUIN OF THE SOUTHERN STATES."[69] The only remedy was to see to it, not only that Congress kept its hands off slavery, but that it should not even receive petitions upon the subject or do anything that could, by the remotest chance, give hope to any slave. Indeed, for the purpose of complete safety, the Southern states ought to see to it that Congress was compelled to cease at once from all of its "usurpations on the states" in its exercise, or claim of right to the exercise, of *any* internal power.[70]

The insistence upon such views, which were by no means new in the 1820s, had increased very greatly as the Southern hopes of eventually controlling the House of Representatives had receded. In the years immediately following the adoption of the Constitution the South had grown, but the North had grown faster; and when the year 1808 had come and gone, and the South was still in a minority in the House, the absolute need of some theory of the Constitution that would make national action against slavery impossible rapidly came to seem evident to practically all Southern men. Until the close of the Napoleonic wars, however, the country was largely absorbed in foreign affairs and domestic issues were in the background. Not until the years immediately following 1815 did the Southern sophistical theories of the Constitution, among which Madison's is to be numbered, achieve their full flowering. These theories required, contrary to the most elementary canons of documentary interpretation, that the preamble of the Constitution be held to be completely meaningless; that the judiciary power, and therefore all incidental legislative power, be largely destroyed; that the power "to provide for the general Welfare" and all the other general phrases of the document be explained away; that the power to regulate commerce be narrowed from a general power to a power merely over foreign and "interstate" trade; and that

*Italics in the original.

the latter branch of this emasculated power be in some way still further narrowed so as to preclude completely any national control over the movement of slaves from state to state. In general, it may be said that the Southern theories required that all national power over matters of an internal nature (interstate or intrastate) be absolutely denied or frittered down to uselessness. The states were to be declared sovereign over all such matters, and were in general to be absolutely uncontrollable by the nation.

This general theory of the country's government, so far removed from Madison's ideal when the Federal Convention met in 1787, but so very necessary, according to his later views, for the continued welfare of the Southern states, is the theory of the Constitution which Madison's notes on the Federal Convention were written to support or, at least, to render possible. In suggesting this as the purpose for which his notes were finally prepared, we do not mean to imply that, in the alterations he made, Madison actually attempted to establish a seeming historicity for the Southern theories of the Constitution as the intended meaning of the document. Such an attempt would have involved entirely too great risks, and Madison did not take them. He sought, instead, merely to confuse and obfuscate his record of what had gone on; to write, once more, an industriously uninformative document; and whilst sowing here and there suggestions of the Southern views, to make it seem as though the intended nationalist meaning of the Constitution was never so much as thought of, even in the "secret conclave" that produced it. Because the Federal Convention *had* done its work behind closed doors, with an injunction of secrecy upon its members, Madison's work of obscuring and falsifying the record was, of course, very greatly facilitated and simplified, for the members of the convention generally refrained from letters or speech on what they were doing, and direct evidence *from other sources* as to what went on in the convention is, accordingly, very incomplete. Despite this fact, the task of discovering what Madison did to the records he left is not impossible, and when the available evidence is all gathered up and collated, the fact of falsification by Madison appears so palpably in case after case as to amount in the aggregate to certainty.[71] That being brue, any history based upon an implicit, uncritical acceptance of Madison's notes, including his memorandum of what went on in Congress on February 21, 1787, cannot fail to be in many very important respects false history.

CHAPTER XXVII

The Final Approval by the States of the Meeting of the Federal Convention

LITTLE more need be said to complete the story of the process by which the Continental Congress and the several state legislatures were brought into agreement upon the meeting of the Federal Convention. In Massachusetts, Rufus King's correspondent, Elbridge Gerry, had taken action to obtain that state's participation in the Annapolis plan, four days before the movement for approval got under way in Congress. As a result of a motion presented by Gerry on February 8, a joint committee was appointed on that date, from the two branches of the General Court, to make recommendations on the course of action to be taken.[1] The committee reported on February 22; without, of course, knowing what had taken place in Congress on the day before, it recommended the appointment of delegates with authority extending in express terms not only to changes relating to "the trade and commerce of the United States" but, in addition, to "the common welfare and security" generally. The "alterations and additions" to be made, however, were all to be "consistent with the republican spirit and genius of the [existing] articles"; they were specifically required to be laid before Congress; were to become effective, by specific provision of the authority given, only if they were "recommended" by Congress and "agreed to by the Legislatures of the several States"; and, as already recorded herein, the Massachusetts commissioners were "particularly instructed by no means to interfere with the fifth article of the confederation."[2] The committee's recommendation was adopted by both branches of the legislature on the day it was made; and then, about a fortnight later, after its receipt of Congress's resolution of February 21, the General Court was in some way induced to substitute the language of Congress for that of its original resolve, and the "fetter" which had at first excepted the mode of representation in Congress from the field of reform, as well as the other "fetters" above mentioned, was removed.[3] And thus, it would seem, plain notice was given to the smaller states that the existing "rotten-borough" system of representation in the national legislature was about to be abandoned in the not-so-distant future for some other, and very different, system.

410

In New York, a resolution to appoint delegates was presented in the legislature five days after the passage of Congress's resolution of approval on
February 21. The resolution proposed the appointment of five delegates by
joint ballot of the Assembly and the Senate.[4] The motion passed without
alteration in the Assembly, but in the Senate the number of delegates was cut
from five to three. A motion was also there made to limit the authority of the
New York delegates to changes "not repugnant to, or inconsistent with, the
constitution of [the] state [of New York]," and this limitation, which would
virtually have nullified New York's participation in the convention, very
nearly passed. The vote of the Senate upon it was 9 to 9, and the measure was
defeated only by the vote of the Senate's presiding officer.[5] Thus, the first
skirmish was won by the New York nationalists, but the Clintonians were
not yet beaten and in the end succeeded, for all practical purposes, in nul-
lifying New York's participation in the convention in another way: by the
control which they succeeded in exercising over the appointment of delegates.[6] These were Alexander Hamilton, Robert Yates, and John Lansing.
The character of the two latter men may be inferred from a comment on
them by Richard Platt, of New York, in a letter he wrote to Winthrop
Sargent, of Boston, on May 7. "To judge," said Platt, "from the choice of
New York (where Hamilton is coupled with Judge Yates and Mr. Lansing)
one would imagine our State wish'd no change in the present wretched
system of affairs." Yates and Lansing were men, he added, "of Sterling
Integrity & decent Abilities," but "not sufficiently alarmed with the present
danger" to give much hope that they would give their votes for any radical
change.[7]

Fully aware of the situation in which he would be placed when he got to
the convention, Hamilton made a second effort, on April 16, to have a
delegation of five men appointed.[8] He urged that the two additional delegates
should be selected from among "Mr. Chancellor Livingston, Mr. Duane, Mr.
Benson, and Mr. Jay." His proposal succeeded in the Assembly but failed, as
before, in the Senate.[9] Thus Hamilton was obliged to go to the convention
completely blanketed by his two anti-Federal colleagues. His law practice
obliged him to leave the convention for a short period beginning late in
June.[10] About ten days after he left, his two colleagues, thoroughly disgusted
with the proceedings, withdrew and went home.[11] Hamilton tried afterwards to induce one or the other or both of them to return, but without
success.[12] During most of the convention's sessions, therefore, New York
was unrepresented. Hamilton, however, returned on two or three occasions
and was elected by the convention to its final committee, made up in the main
of distinguished lawyers, which gave the Constitution its final form.[13] The
participation of New York in the Federal Convention was thus largely formal, and apart from Hamilton's service on this final committee, its part in the
framing of the Constitution was extremely small.

The only other state which refused to participate wholeheartedly in the Federal Convention after Congress had approved it was the state of Rhode Island. Still under the rule of the radical faction which had come into power there in 1786, Rhode Island declined to appoint any delegates at all to the convention and therefore had no part whatever in framing the Constitution.[14] The remaining states which had not appointed delegates or were not known to have appointed any, when Congress acted—that is, Georgia, South Carolina, Maryland, Connecticut, and New Hampshire—all eventually appointed them.[15] For financial reasons, however, New Hampshire was very late in doing so, and her delegates did not arrive until the sessions of the convention were about half-over.[16] A quorum of quorums from the other states eventually got together, eleven days after the date which had been scheduled for the convention's meeting.[17] And so, on May 25, 1787, after well over a decade of repeatedly disappointed hopes, the long-desired effort to establish for America "a firm national government" at last got under way.

Part V

The Public Mind on the Eve of the Federal Convention

CHAPTER XXVIII

The Public Mind as Reflected in
Private Letters of the Time

AFTER the failure of the Annapolis commercial convention in September 1786, there was a short period when public discussion of how the government should be improved very nearly ceased. The private letters that have survived from this period are also generally devoid of discussions of the subject, beyond, of course, the speculation, of which we have already had examples, as to whether the Annapolis plan or some other mode of change had best be followed. After the first of the year, when it began to seem more probable than it had at first that another convention would be held, attention began to shift to the question of what particular changes in the government should be made, and letters about this phase of the subject became more plentiful. One of the earliest of these was the letter which John Jay, Congress's secretary of foreign affairs, wrote to Washington on January 7. This was the letter, previously mentioned, in which Jay had suggested that the people be asked to consent to the assembling of a plenipotentiary constitutional convention.

"What is to be done," said Jay, "is a common Question, but not easy to answer." "Would the giving *any** further Degree of Power to Congress, do the Business?" He was inclined, he said, "to think not"; and having given his reasons for this view, Jay added that he "promise[d him] self nothing very desireable from any Change which [did] not divide the sovereignty into its proper Departments—Let congress legislate, let others execute, let others judge" "Shall we have a King?" he then asked. "Not in my opinion," was his answer, "while other Expedients remain untried." But he did think that what he called "a Governor General" would be desirable, who should be "limited in his Prerogatives and Duration." He also thought that "Congress might be divided into an upper and a lower House," "the former to be appointed for Life, the latter annually"; and "the Governor General (to preserve the Ballance) with the advice of a council formed, for that *only** purpose, of the great judicial officers [might] have a Negative on their acts." "What Powers should be granted to the Government so constituted, [was] a Question," he said,

---

*Jay's emphasis.

415

"which deserve[d] much Thought." His own opinion, which his earlier letters show he had long entertained,[1] was: "The more [power], the better—The States retaining only so much as [might] be necessary for domestic"—by which, apparently, he meant "*merely* domestic," or *merely* local—"Purposes; and all their principal Officers civil and military being commissioned and removeable by the *National** Governm[en]t." "These" Jay concluded, "[were] short Hints—Details would exceed the Limits of a Letter."[2]

As the reader will doubtless conclude from the foregoing outline, Jay's ideas in some respects went somewhat beyond what most men of his time were asking, but upon two points his ideas accorded quite closely with those of most of his contemporaries who were not biased in their views by some vested interest in the existing state system. The first of these points was his desire for a national government complete in itself; the second was his desire that the state governments should be subjected, or subordinated, completely to a national government having plenary power; or as Jay expressed it, "the more [power,] the better." The very general accord that existed upon these points may be seen by comparing Jay's views with those to be found in the letters of other men which have survived. In no case does the accord appear more clearly than in the letters of Jay's colleague, Henry Knox, Congress's secretary of war.

In 1783, when the suggestion had been advanced that the Revolutionary army before disbanding should take steps, by force if necessary, to obtain for the country a better constitution, Knox had vigorously opposed such a step. "I sincerely hope," he had written to General Alexander McDougall, "[that] we"—i.e., the army—"shall not be influenced to actions which may be contrary"—that is, would be contrary—"to our uniform course of service for eight years."[3] Knox had also written to Gouverneur Morris asking "why, [when] the present Constitution [was] so defective," Morris and the other "great men" in Congress did "not call the people together and tell them so; that is," he said, "have a convention of the States to form a better Constitution?"[4] This step, which Knox considered "the more efficacious remedy,"[5] was proposed in Congress, as we know, by Alexander Hamilton[6] and supported there by Stephen Higginson and some others.[7] It was opposed, however, by James Madison[8] and apparently by the majority in Congress, since Hamilton's efforts were not successful.

Two years later in 1785, when most of the country was thinking only of adding commerce and taxing powers to the authority of Congress as then set up, Knox was already much concerned over the faulty organization of that body, the only national agency which the country had. To General Samuel Parsons he accordingly wrote, on April 1 of that year, that "a social compact so constituted that a very small minority [could] operate to check the great Majority [could] not be upon durable principles." "These things must work a change," he said. "Our fœderal government must be settled upon more ra-

---

*Jay's emphasis.

tional principles, or some events which we do not at present foresee will compel us to adopt systems which we may at times have contemplated with horror." "I confess," he went on, "[that] I hate the office of kings—It is difficult if not impossible to check or restrain their power—they are, upon natural principles, eternally working to render themselves supreme, to free themselves from every controul of Laws, which they generally consider as made for the lower order of mankind." "When I consider the inestimable value of liberty, I cannot hesitate to prefer a democracy to every other form of government, even if it should not have the same principle of permanency—security to property." "[But] I believe," he concluded, "[that] a republican Government formed upon *national* principles, and those principles propagated and perpetuated by habits, may exist a great length of time."[9]

The sentiments thus expressed by Henry Knox, ardently and sincerely republican as they plainly were, throw a flood of light upon much of the propaganda of the period. Knox, the reader should remember, was the originator and secretary-general of that much-maligned society, the Order of the Cincinnati. In view of this fact, it would seem that Knox's strong republicanism, taken with his boldness and vigor, his ability and forthright character, and the efforts which he constantly was making in behalf of his views, affords a pretty good assurance that the aim of that order in the field of politics was quite sincerely what they professed it was: "An unalterable determination to promote and cherish, between the respective States, that Union and National honor so essentially necessary to their happiness, and the future dignity of the American Empire."[10] With this conclusion the unquestionable republicanism of Washington is of course consistent, and the further conclusion therefore seems in order, that the nationalism of the Cincinnati, and *not* their alleged devotion to monarchy and aristocracy, was what provoked the many vicious attacks that were made upon them at this period. Although some sincere men were participants in these attacks, there cannot be any doubt that in the main they issued from the petty local-politician class which had a selfish vested interest in the existing state system. The technique, of course, was a forerunner of that employed a few years later against Alexander Hamilton and the whole Federalist party by "the aristocrats who call[ed] themselves democrats," when they came into power in the national government at the beginning of the nineteenth century.

The views expressed by Knox in his letter to General Parsons, in 1785, were still entertained by him in 1787. This is clearly indicated by the various letters which, as we have already seen, he wrote in that year to promote the Federal Convention and a reform in the government. In his previously mentioned letter to Washington, of January 4, Knox expressed the opinion that "the subject [of governmental reform] ha[d] not been sufficiently discussed, as yet in publick, to decide precisely on the form of [a new] edifice." "[But] it [was] out of all question," he said, "that *the foundation must be of republican principles*; but so modified and wrought together, that whatever [should] be erected thereon, should be durable, & efficient." "I speak entirely," he went on, "of the federal government, or what would be better *one government** instead of an association of governments—were it possible to effect a general government of this kind, it might be constituted of an assembly, or lower house, chosen for one two or three years a senate chosen for five six or seven years, and the executive under the title of Governor General chosen by the assembly and Senate, for the term of seven years, but liable to an impeachment of the lower house, and triable by the senate. A judicial to be appointed by the Governor General, during good behaviour, but impeachable by the lower house and triable by the Senate." "All national subjects," he concluded, "[should] *be designed and executed by the general government, without any reference to the local governments.*" But those governments should be bound to obey the national laws; and if they did not, Knox believed they should be compelled by military force to do so.[11]

The foregoing "rude sketch"—as Knox called it in his letter to Washington—was obviously more democratic in the proposals it made than were the "short hints" which had been made to Washington by Jay. Despite this fact, Knox and Jay seem to have been completely at one in desiring a supreme national government of plenary powers. These ideas of Knox's appear again, in rather striking form, in what apparently is an outline of a speech, in Knox's handwriting, which is among his papers for the spring and summer of 1787. Presumably, the speech is one which Knox himself delivered. Exactly when, where, and to whom he made the speech is not known. It seems virtually certain, however, that it was made at some gathering in Philadelphia, in the week or ten days following Washington's arrival there for the Federal Convention on May 13. One possible occasion is a dinner held by the Cincinnati, which Washington attended, on May 15.[12] The tenor of the speech is such, however, as to suggest the possibility that it may have been delivered at some off-the-record gathering attended, one may suppose, by various of the more important and influential members of the Convention, together with some of the older important men, nonmembers of the Convention, who, because of the triennial meeting of the Cincinnati, were then present in Philadelphia. That some such gathering probably occurred, and that it was out of the views expressed in the course of the meeting, and Washington's great influence with the Virginia delegation, rather than out of the academic historical researches of James Madison, that the so-called "Virginia plan" for a national government really grew, seems virtually certain when the fact is considered that that plan had, for its most important features, the plainly assured support, from the very first, of *more* than the Virginia delegation in the Convention. Since the document that exists among Henry Knox's papers sounds very much like a speech to such a gathering, the inference is strong that Knox was present at such a meeting, and that in his

*Knox's emphasis.

usual clearheaded and forthright way, he there delivered his sentiments upon the subject for which the Convention had assembled.

In the months that had followed Knox's letter of January 4, to Washington, Knox had apparently become more and more concerned over the faulty constitution of the existing government. "The multiplied parts of the machine," he had written to Stephen Higginson, toward the end of February, "are liable to be deformed by the least accident—nay, so disproportioned are the parts that disorder is inevitable—the whole must be taken to pieces and a new one erected on the basis of public liberty and public happiness—less complex and more effectual and durable."[13] The substance of these sentiments he repeated in the speech above-mentioned. "I am of the opinion," he said, "that the national government ought to possess *full and complete powers within itself* uncontrouled by any state or corporate body *to deliberate, decree, and execute,* [and] that *all* the powers retained by the state governments should be as parts of a whole, and not whole and complete in themselves. If this modification can take place, it may be happy," he said, "for the people at large as a nation—if it is morally impossible, *no other alteration can be devised but the abolition of the state governments* or the annihilation of our hopes founded on our existence as a nation." He also repeated his firm conviction, which, we have seen, he had felt at least two years before,[14] "that a *national republic* [might] be formed, having its powers so nicely balanced, and its checks so established as fully to ensure the great blessings of government." "In order to render [such a government] truly a government of laws and not of caprice,"* he was convinced, however, "that some of its branches should be arranged on the principle of good behaviour, the purest and noblest incitement," he quite truly said, "to proper actions." "Clear I am," he concluded, "that whatever form shall on the whole be thought to be most likely to perpetuate the liberty and [happiness] of the nation, *we should have the fortitude to propose it to the people,* regardless of any consequences which [may] arise from the misinterpretations of bad men."[15]

Considering the tenor of the foregoing remarks by Knox, his speech must be assigned to some such gathering as has been suggested; and the probability of such an assignment is considerably increased by certain further surviving evidence that, from the first, Knox was intimately informed of the nature of "the Virginia plan." "The contents of that plan," Nathan Dane wrote to Rufus King, on July 5, "[had been] known to some [in New York] before the Convention met."[16] Knox was one of those who knew of it, as we may infer with certainty from a letter he wrote to Mercy Warren, wife of James Warren, of Massachusetts, on May 30. In that letter, Knox described certain of the main features of "the Virginia plan" unmistakably; and since Knox had left Philadelphia before May 25,[17] and the Virginia plan was not presented

---

*Knox's pen first wrote "men"; but, with the realism characteristic of the man, he promptly struck it out and replaced it as indicated.

to the Convention until May 29,[18] his knowledge of the plan, on the date of his letter, shows that Knox was one of the persons in New York who, as Dane said, knew of the plan "before the Convention met." That fact, taken with the speech-outline existing among his papers, seems pretty certainly to indicate that Knox was in some way concerned in the preliminary conferences out of which the Virginia plan arose.

Knox began his letter to Mrs. Warren with certain gloomy remarks about the existing state of the American nation. "Private convenience," he said, "paper money, and ex post facto Laws* [were] the main springs of [their] governments." His only hope was the Convention. "Should they possess the hardihood to be unpopular, and propose an efficient National government, free of the entanglements of the present defective state systems, [America might] yet be a happy and great nation." With jocose reference to what he apparently regarded as Mrs. Warren's visionary and impractical ideas on government, Knox then assured her that he realized that his ideas would not usher in that "paradise of humanity," a "government of Laws." He liked such principles, he said, "to be established hereafter." "[But he] wish[ed] at present to try the experiment of a *strong national republic*."† Then he added a statement which seems to point definitely to the Virginia plan: "The state governments should be deprived of the power of injuring themselves or the Nation." The rest of his remarks are also an outline of the essential features of the Virginia plan, with the exception of the council of legislative revision. "The people," said Knox, "have parted with power enough to form an excellent constitution: But it is incorp[ora]ted and diffused among bodies which can not use it to good purpose. It must be concentered in *a national government*, the power of which should be divided between a strong executive, a senate, and assembly. The powers which each should have would be a subject of much discussion and nice detail. The time of the executive, and senate should be such as to give stability to the system. The Assembly to be for one two or three years. A Judicial to be formed on the highest principles of Independency." "This government," he bluntly declared, to the horror, no doubt, of Mrs. Warren, "should possess *every power necessary for national purposes, which would leave the state governments but very little*."

To the above statement Knox added that "every power [of the national government] should be defined with accuracy, and checked according to the highest human wisdom." He likewise declared his belief that "[every] attempt to overleap the bounds of the constitution by those who [were] in the execution of it, should be certainly and severely punished."[19] To some modern readers, these statements may sound like "states' rights", but it is as certain as anything well can be, that Henry Knox was not in the least concerned about what later came to be known as "states' rights." He was, instead, concerned—and there can be no doubt whatever that he was *only*

---

*Needless to say, Knox was not talking about retrospective *criminal* laws.
†Knox's emphasis.

concerned—over the rights of men as individuals, which Knox believed, as, indeed, he had just said to Mrs. Warren, the state governments of the time had repeatedly and outrageously violated. *"One government,"* he had therefore told Washington, in January, was "better" than any "federal government," or "association of governments";[20] and six weeks after the writing of his letter to Mrs. Warren, he admonished Rufus King, then somewhat discouraged over the continuing want of agreement in the Federal Convention, that "the State systems [were] the accursed thing which [would] prevent [America from] being a nation." "The democracy," he told King, "might be managed; nay, it would remedy itself after being sufficiently fermented. But the vile State governments are sources of pollution which will contaminate the American name for ages." "Machines that must produce ill, but cannot produce good, smite them" he urged upon Rufus King, "smite them, in the name of God and the people!"[21]

From the vigor of Knox's language, the reader may be inclined to suppose that Knox was something of an extremist. The vigor, of course, was characteristic of the man; and if he was an extremist, he clearly had much congenial company in 1787. We can infer this, for example, in the case of Rufus King, from Knox's confident call upon him to "smite the state governments"—a call which Knox had issued after King had written that there had been no "progress" in the Convention since Knox and their "very able and sagacious friend Hamilton" had departed on June 29; and that what he meant by "progress" was to be inferred from his "political creed, with which," he said, "you are very well acquainted."[22] Besides the evidence of concurrence in sentiments between King and Knox—and, for that matter, between them and Hamilton—to be seen in these letters, there is the fact of Knox's having repeatedly mentioned King, in his letters of the preceding winter, as his choice, along with men like Stephen Higginson and Benjamin Lincoln, to represent Massachusetts in the Federal Convention.[23] It is also noteworthy that King was Stephen Higginson's first choice for the Convention.[24] In addition, there is King's own long letter to Higginson's partner, Jackson, of September 3, 1786, in which we have seen Rufus King's plainly expressed desire for a national government "with a vigorous Executive, wise Legislative, and independent Judicial," and power extending to all matters not "merely internal" to the particular states.[25] The concurrent desire of King and Knox, as well as Knox and Jay, for a supreme national government with plenary powers is not to be doubted; and Higginson and Hamilton and Benjamin Lincoln all entertained similar desires, as we have already seen from their earlier letters.[26]

Of the surviving private letters of New England men upon this subject, it remains to mention a letter which another prominent Massachusetts man, Samuel Breck, wrote to Henry Knox, on the following July 15. A member of the Boston merchants' committee of 1785 which had sent out the important letters of April 22 of that year,[27] Breck had afterwards been one of the three

Massachusetts men who had undertaken the long, vain journey to Annapolis, in 1786, to represent Massachusetts in the Annapolis convention.[28] In his letter to Knox, Breck expressed his agreement "in the necessity of a National Government"; he declared his "hope that a System resembling [the balanced government of Massachusetts might] be adopted"; indicated his belief that "such a government, operating upon the large scale, must, in a relative view, reduce the powers of each State to that of [Massachusetts'] Counties"; and voiced the opinion that such a government "would extend its authority over all *these Petty states** & increase in the proportion as they [were] augmented by new ones." He concluded by observing that "perhaps there never [had been] a time more favourable for such a Revolution."[29]

Views such as the foregoing were not confined to Massachusetts men. This we may see from certain letters which George Mason, one of the Virginia delegates to the Federal Convention, wrote, on May 20 and 21, from Philadelphia.[30] "The most prevalent idea," Mason reported in these letters—at least, with what he called "the principal states"—"[was] a total change of the federal system, and instituting a great national council or parliament upon the principles of equal proportionate representation, consisting of two branches of the legislature invested with *full* legislative powers upon the objects of the Union." These objects, the reader will not have forgotten, were "the common defence," "the security of liberty," and "the mutual and general welfare of the United States"; and since the Virginia act approving of the convention had spoken of "such farther concessions and Provisions as [might] be necessary to secure [these] great Objects for which [the Federal] Government"—i.e., the Continental Congress—"[had been] instituted,"[31] and since, in addition, "the Virginia plan," when it was presented to the Convention, proposed explicitly this same objective,[32] there is not the slightest possibility that George Mason could *not* have been talking of a *generally empowered* national government when he wrote the foregoing letters. Yet doubt that he was talking of such a government is probably entertained by many students of the subject; and this despite the fact that Mason went on to explain that it was proposed "to make the State legislatures *subordinate to the national* by giving the latter a negative upon *all* such laws *as they* [might] *judge* contrary to the principles and interest of the Union," and that it was proposed "to establish also a national executive, and a judiciary system with cognizance of *all* such matters as depend[ed] upon *the law of nations,*† and *such other objects as the local courts of justice* [might] *be inadequate to.*" Mason, of course, later changed his mind, to a certain extent, about a national legislative power "to provide for the general Welfare"[33] and then, apparently, changed it back again, in the Virginia ratifying convention.[34] When he wrote

---

*Breck's emphasis.

†This, the reader should remember, was then understood to include "the general commercial law."

the foregoing letters, however, Mason, *upon the assumption of "equal proportionate representation" in the National legislature*, was apparently in favor of such a power, coupled, perhaps, with some kind of "internal police" limitation in favor of the states[35] and a bill of civil rights in favor of the people.[36] This being true, any doubt that he was reporting that a generally empowered national government was favored among the delegates of "the principal states" present on May 20 in Philadelphia, is entirely unwarranted. The states then present (not all of which, presumably, were "principal states") were, according to Mason, Virginia, Pennsylvania, the two Carolinas, and New York; and *some** of the deputies from the Eastern states" were also there, he said, though on that date none of them had a full delegation present.

The changes of which Mason spoke in his letters had the approval of James Madison, by the date of the Federal Convention, as we know from what has already been said of Madison's ideas in the preceding chapter. His notions as to what should be done in order to improve the government began to assume a concrete form after he had been in New York, among the men in Congress, for about five weeks. The earliest of his surviving letters which contains anything like a definite scheme of governmental reform is one that he wrote to Jefferson on March 18.[37] Letters to Governor Randolph, of Virginia, and to Washington followed, on April 8[38] and April 16,[39] respectively. Madison's expressions of opinion in these various letters are customarily regarded as extremely important seminal ideas from the brain of the man who "richly deserved" the posthumous title of "the Father of the Constitution." Actually, the letters merely show Madison as veering around, perhaps somewhat haltingly on the point of general affirmative legislative power, to the ideas of governmental reform which were at the time rather generally entertained by other interested men in New York, both in and out of Congress.

Only one of the ideas which he expounded in his letters was, in fact, other than a commonplace among such men, when his letters were written. This was his proposal that "the national Government" should have "a Negative, *in all cases whatsoever*, on the Legislative acts of the States."[40] Even this idea may possibly not have been Madison's own, for it could equally well have originated with one of the other Virginia delegates in Congress, William Grayson and Edward Carrington, both of whom also favored the creation of such a general national negative power.[41] It seems clear, however, that the national negative was a Virginia idea, quite possibly conceived as a device for subordinating the states *completely* to the nation, *without* giving to the nation

---

*Rufus King wrote to Jeremiah Wadsworth, of Connecticut, four days later, that he was "mortified that [he] *alone* [was present] from New England." "The backwardness," he added, "may prove unfortunate." Records, III, 26. Mason may possibly have mistaken Henry Knox and some of the other eastern men among the Cincinnati for "deputies from the Eastern States." He spoke, in his letter of May 20, of "conversations," on the subject of changes in the government, "with the deputies of different States, and with some of the general officers of the late army (who [were t]here upon a general meeting of the Cincinnati)." Records, III, 22.

general *affirmative* power. The device was voted down emphatically by the Federal Convention, not, however, because that body disapproved of complete subordination of the states, but because it considered that that end could be more conveniently accomplished under a general affirmative grant.

A somewhat similar fate overtook another of Madisons's pre-Convention proposals by which he set great store, but which, it is certain, was not his own peculiar invention. This was his proposal of a council of legislative revision.* The scheme of state representation, or suffrage, in Congress, which Madison wished to see, was also not to the liking of the Federal Convention; and his proposal of an appeal to the people as a means of ratification, being the only practicable alternative to a coup d'état after the movement for a plenipotentiary convention was voted down, in February, was the general expectation of all men interested in a better government, at the dates of Madison's various suggestions that such an appeal be made.[42] All that is left of his pre-Convention suggestions is the idea of a supreme national government, consisting of a bicameral legislature, an executive, and a judiciary. As Rufus King wrote Jonathan Jackson that many men wanted such a government, on September 3, 1786, and substantially everyone favored it in Congress, on January 21, 1787, Madison's latter suggestions that such a government should be established were certainly no momentous contribution by "the Father of the Constitution" to the pre-Convention discussion.

As suggested above, there is, also, some uncertainty as to whether Madison, in March and April, had actually come around to the prevailing view of vesting the national legislature with a general affirmative power of legislation. He mentioned particularly, in all his letters, the necessity of giving to the nation "the power of *regulating trade*"—"compleat authority" for the purpose, he said in his letters to Randolph and Washington—and in his letter to Washington, he particularly mentioned certain other powers, also. His statements as to the desirable general scope of the affirmative national legislative power are, however, open to the interpretation that he did wish to see Congress invested with a *general* power to act "in *all* cases," as he said, "which require[d] uniformity"; and that his mention of particular fields, such as that of "trade," was intended merely to exemplify to his correspondents what he conceived such a general affirmative national legislative power would cover.

The other possibility is the one which seems commonly to be assumed: that Madison desired, and intended to suggest when he wrote his letters, a specific and exhaustive enumeration of the national government's *particular* affirmative powers. The nature of these two possibilities may be seen from the language which he used in his letter to Washington. That language is similar, in all essential respects, to the language he employed in his letters to

---

*John Jay, it will be remembered, had advocated such a council in his letter to Washington of January 7.

Jefferson and Randolph. He said in his letter to Washington: "I would propose that in addition to the present *federal* powers, the *national* Government should be armed with positive"—i.e., affirmative—"and *compleat* authority in *all* cases *which require uniformity*; such as the regulation of trade, including the right of taxing both exports & imports,* the fixing the terms and forms of naturalization, &c. ec." In considering the two suggested interpretations of these words, it is important to note that either interpretation would give an affirmative national legislative power *less inclusive* than one extending to "all cases whatsoever," for the latter would of course include a power to legislate for particular states in cases *not* "requiring uniformity." It is thus evident that either of the suggested interpretations would be reconcilable with the fact that Madison used the phrase "in all cases whatsoever" for describing his proposed national negative power. As already suggested, then, there seems to be no way of telling which of the two suggested interpretations of Madison's pre-Convention formula for the national affirmative legislative power is proper. This much is certain: whatever he desired in March and April, Madison had come around to the majority point of view by the time the Federal Convention assembled; as to the position he took in the Convention, the record is entirely clear.

Somewhat the same thing, it is interesting, and likewise important, to note, also happened, though more belatedly, to Thomas Jefferson in Paris. It is not perhaps surprising that Jefferson, far away and out of touch with conditions at home, at first took very little interest in the Federal Convention. Indeed, there is much to indicate that he did not at first even take it seriously. He was, moreover, away from Paris, traveling in southern France and northern Italy, all through the spring before the convention assembled, being absent on this trip from the last day of February till June 10.[43] Madison's letter of March 18 about governmental reforms, and another letter, written on December 27, 1786, by George Wythe, another of the Virginia delegation to the Convention, requesting Jefferson's opinion as to what should be done,[44] were among the accumulated letters which awaited him in June upon his return to Paris from his protracted holiday.[45] For that reason, perhaps, the letters in question received less attention than they might otherwise have had. Wythe's letter was not answered by Jefferson until three months later;[46] and though Madison's letter obtained an answer on June 20,[47] the answer was devoted largely to other matters and contained only a brief expression of Jefferson's approval "of separating the executive business of the confederacy from Congress as the judiciary in some degree was already," and an expression of his disapproval of Madison's pet suggestion of a universal national

---

*The specification of this part of the taxing power as included in the power over trade should be carefully noted. It is doubtless explicable upon the basis of the doubts and difficulties raised by the pre-Revolutionary controversy with Great Britain over the question of whether "the power to regulate trade" included the power to levy such taxes for revenue, and not merely for regulatory, purposes.

negative upon all state laws. Upon Madison's other ideas, Jefferson expressed
no opinion whatever; and that he did not take the Convention very seriously,
at the time, seems manifest from a letter which he wrote to David Hartley,
twelve days later. "I expect," he said, "[that the Convention] will propose
several amendments; that that relative to our commerce will probably be
adopted immediately; but that the others must await to be adopted one after
another in proportion as the minds of the states ripen for them."[48] This same
attitude of mild interest in the Convention was still evident in a letter which
Jefferson wrote to Edmund Randolph, as late as August 3. After inquiring
politely about "your" convention, Jefferson expressed to Randolph the hope
that "at least" they would "persuade the states to commit their commercial
arrangements to Congress, and enable [Congress] to pay their debts, interest
& capital." "The coercive powers, supposed to be wanting in the federal
head, [were] possess[ed]," he assured Randolph, "by the law of nature."[49]

It must have been immediately after his dispatch of this complacent letter
to Edmund Randolph that Jefferson received from Edward Carrington, one of
the Virginia delegates in Congress, a letter which Carrington had written
him on June 9, for on the day following that upon which Jefferson's letter to
Randolph was written, he wrote to Carrington a letter which marked the
beginning of his real interest in the Federal Convention. Carrington had
informed Jefferson that "the prevailing impression as well in, as out of, [the]
Convention, [was] that a fœderal Government adapted to the habits of the
day, [ought to] be formed, whose efficiency [should] pervade the whole
Empire." "And if a work of wisdom [was] prepared, [the people]," Carrington felt confident, "[would] not reject it." Two schemes, he said, were
being talked of. One was "a consolidation of the whole Empire into one
republic, leaving in the states nothing more than subordinate courts for
facilitating the administration of the Laws"; the other was "an investiture of a
fœderal sovereignty with full and independant authority as to the Trade,
Revenues, and forces of the Union, and the rights of peace and War, together
with a Negative upon all the Acts of the State legislatures." "The first idea,"
Carrington thought "impracticable, and therefore [did] not suppose it [could]
be adopted." But the Eastern men were for it, he said, desiring "a total
surrender of the State sovereignties." These two schemes were "the most
moderate of any which obtain[ed] in any general form amongst reflective and
intelligent men"; there was even some talk of monarchy; and since the two
schemes which he had outlined, "ha[d] arisen," he said, "with the most able
men, from an actual view of events," Jefferson ought to "be prepared to
expect them."[50]

In his reply to Carrington, dated August 4, Jefferson protested that "with
all the imperfections of [America's] present government, it [was] without
comparison the best existing, or that ever did exist; it's greatest defect [was]
the imperfect manner in which matters of commerce ha[d] been provided
for." Then repeating his view that Congress had the right of enforcing its

resolutions—e.g., contributions—"by the law of nature," Jefferson explained that, "when two nations ma[d]e a compact"—as, he implied, the states had done—"there result[ed] to each a power of compelling the other to execute it." "Compulsion was never so easy," he said, "as in [America's] case, where a single frigate would soon levy on the commerce of any state the deficiency of it's contributions; nor more safe than in the hands of Congress which [ha]d always shewn that it would wait, as it ought to, to the last extremities before it would execute any of it's powers which [were] disagreeable." He thought it "very material," however, "to separate in the hands of Congress the Executive & Legislative powers, as the Judiciary already [were] in some degree"; and "this [he] hope[d would] be done." But he had to "confess," he informed Carrington, that he "d[id] not go as far in reforms thought necessary as some of [his] correspondents in America." Whether, by this remark, Jefferson meant his friend James Madison is not known. "[His own] general plan would be," he said, "to make the states one as to every thing connected with foreign nations, & several as to every thing *purely* domestic." (In the light of his other remarks, "commerce"—i.e., presumably, *all* "commerce"—was covered by this formula.) He added, however, that "if the Convention should adopt propositions [of the kind which some of his correspondents in America had urged, he should] suppose them necessary."[51]

Carrington's letter must have been much on Jefferson's mind in the days that followed; on August 14 he wrote a letter to Washington, explaining what he thought should be done, and also one in substantially the same terms to another influential Virginian, Joseph Jones. Conceding, once more, that it was desirable "to organise [the federal] head into Legislative, Executive, & Judiciary departments," Jefferson insisted, in both these letters, upon the belief which he had previously expressed to Carrington, that the convention ought "to make [the] states one as to all foreign concerns, [but] preserve them several as to all *merely* domestic." His letters to Washington and Jones indicate, nonetheless, that Jefferson, in the ten-day interval since his letter to Carrington, had made some progress in his thinking. He did not talk in either of these letters of Congress's enforcing its resolutions by "frigates"; he declared instead that it was a "great desideratum" that Congress be given "some peaceable mode of enforcing their just authority."[52] All this he repeated in a letter to one of his European friends, the Count del Vermi, on the day immediately following; and, then, apparently, another thought came to him. To the formula of national power which he had mentioned to Washington, Jones, and Carrington, he added, between the lines of his del Vermi letter, another: "every matter relative to the general mass of our Union."[53] This was the beginning of the end: on September 16, the day before the Federal Convention completed its business, Jefferson finally expressed his approval of a national government with power extending to *any and every* matter not *merely* of concern to a *single* state.

This final step in the development of Jefferson's thinking at this time is to be found in the answer which he finally wrote to the long-unanswered letter of George Wythe. With profuse apologies for his failure sooner to comply with the request which Wythe had made in the preceding December, Jefferson declared, in a kind of self-exculpatory way, that "it would always have been presumption in [him] to have done it." "Your own ideas," he told Wythe, "& those of the great characters who were to be concerned with you in [the Federal Convention] will give the law, as they ought to do, to us all." "My own general idea," he nevertheless explained, "was [*sic*] that the states should severally preserve their sovereignty in whatever concerns themselves *alone*, & that whatever may concern *another state*, or any foreign nation, should be made a part of the federal sovereignty." He then repeated to Wythe the beliefs which he previously had expressed to others about dividing "the federal sovereignty" among three several bodies, "legislative, executive, & judiciary, as the state sovereignties [were]" and about contriving "some peaceable means" "to enforce compliance [with federal measures,] on the part of the states."[54]

From the contents of the foregoing letter, it is sufficiently evident that, at the time the Constitution was drawn, Jefferson finally came around to almost complete agreement with the men who produced that document, with respect to the desirable scope of the national governing power. That this should be true is no way surprising; for, although the power which Jefferson advocated in his letter to Wythe was of course a power of legislating in all cases for "the national welfare" (as the subject of "the national welfare," as distinct from "the welfare of a single state," was then understood), and although the advocacy of such a power was of course entirely out of line with much of Jefferson's *later* behavior, it was not out of line with what Jefferson had stood for in the then not very distant past. The reference, of course, is to the position he had taken in 1775 when, in the Second Continental Congress, he had given his support to Benjamin Franklin's plan for an American confederation. The Franklin plan, it will be remembered, had proposed the creation of a "general Congress" and had suggested that that Congress be invested with power to pass all "such general Ordinances as tho' necessary to the General Welfare, particular assemblies [could] not be competent to [pass]." That Franklin formula was the substantial equivalent of the formula which was set forth by Jefferson in his letter to George Wythe; and when some of the later claims of Jefferson's "states'-rights" party are brought to mind, it is interesting also to remember that Franklin had specifically indicated in his outline of his plan in 1775 that such a national power would comprehend, among other "general Ordinances," all those that might relate to the country's *general* [or entire] *Commerce.*[55]

It ought to be added that, when the Constitution reached Jefferson in Paris a little later in the fall of 1787, he read it, as most men then read it, as a grant of all the powers requisite for accomplishing the objects for which the new government was being "ordained and established," and not merely as a grant of those powers which were *specifically* enumerated in the document.[56] Being a great believer in "paper checks," as distinct from the "structural checks," in which, alone, the Federalists were willing to put reliance, Jefferson advocated the addition to the Constitution, of "a bill of rights providing clearly & without the aid of *sophisms* for freedom of religion, freedom of the press, protection against standing armies, restriction against monopolies, the eternal & unremitting force of the habeas corpus laws, and trials by jury in all matters of fact triable by the law of the land & not by the law of nations."[57] Jefferson advocated, however, no bill of *states'* rights; and it was later proposed that an amendment be added to the Constitution, "explicitly declar[ing] that all powers *not expressly** delegated* by the Constitution [were] reserved to the several states, to be by them exercised."[58] Jefferson objected to this. "It [would] do too much in some instances," he said, "& too little in others. It [would] cripple the federal government in some cases where it ought to be free, and not restrain it in some others where restraint would be right."[59] Whatever views Thomas Jefferson may later have espoused—and possibly have held—and whatever of floundering may be seen in his earlier letters of 1787, there can be no doubt that he was, in the end, when the Constitution was adopted, thoroughly in favor of the same comprehensive national governing power that he had favored when the Franklin plan of confederation had first been proposed in Congress twelve years before.

The same, it is also important to add, was the case with another prominent Virginia anti-Federalist of the near future, Richard Henry Lee. Lee, it will be remembered, had been a leader in the fight in the Continental Congress on April 25, 1777, to retain that body's general powers of acting in all cases for "the common defence," "the security of liberty," and "the general welfare" of the country.[60] After the Articles had been formed, and adopted by the states, Lee, however, opposed the grant of any taxing power to Congress[61] and actually wrote to George Mason, when the Federal Convention was assembling, still opposing, at that late date, the creation of a national commerce power.[62] The key to the seeming inconsistency in Lee's behavior in these several instances is no doubt the fact that the mode of representation, or suffrage, in Congress had not been determined under the Articles on April 25, 1777. The equality of state representation, or suffrage, in Congress that finally was adopted in the Articles created in Congress a kind of "rotten-borough" situation, from a Virginian point of view; and Lee's later opposition to the grant of impost and commerce powers to Congress was no doubt in large measure a reaction to this unsatisfactory situation. This view of his behavior, up to May 1787, is confirmed by the fact that, after he had gotten back into Congress, a little later in that summer, Lee seemed pleased by what he had learned, by a visit to Philadelphia, the Federal Convention was going to do. He had "found the Convention very busy & very secret," he said, in a

---

*The reader should bear in mind that no such amendment ever was adopted. The word "expressly" was left out of the Tenth Amendment, *ex industria*.

letter he wrote on July 14. But "from [a] variety of circumstances," he thought it probable they would propose "a Government not unlike the B[ritish] Constitution—that is, an Execu[tive], with 2 branches composing a federal Legislature, and possessing adequate Tone"—that is, strength. Such a change was "indispensably necessary," he said, "if any government at all [was] to exist in N[orth] America—Indeed the minds of men ha[d] been so hurt by *the injustise, folly, and wickedness of the State Legislatures & State Executives*—that people in general seem[ed] ready for anything."[63] Eight days later he assured another correspondent that "the federal convention [was] proceeding slowly, but [he] hope[d] surely in a practical improvement of our federal Constitution. So far as [he could] judge, the general wish [was] for a ballanced government where the powers [would] be placed independently as in England; and of duration somewhat longer than the present."[64] Another eight days later, in still another letter, Lee again repeated these predictions; and, again, without the slightest trace of rancor.[65] On August 22 he wrote, with the plainest satisfaction, that Congress was expecting "the Report of the Convention . . . about a fortnight [t]hence." "And great," said he, "are the public expectations concerning it. 'Tis expected that a federal Legislature of 3 branches will be recommended, *with independent powers, and supreme for external matters, Revenue, & Commerce*—with an Executive well toned and of reasonable duration.[66]

From the mode of Lee's speech in the last of these several letters, it is perfectly clear that on the date of it he was reconciled to the creation of national powers which at the beginning of the summer he had opposed; and the key to the resolution of his seeming inconsistency is unquestionably the fact that he was *not* reconciled to the vesting of these powers in the Continental Congress, but to the vesting of them in "a ballanced government," in which, he doubtless assumed, Virginia and the South would have enough power *from the start* to be, in his opinion, safe. The Constitution as the Convention finally reported it held forth a *prospect only*, as Lee saw the matter, of Virginian and Southern safety. He therefore opposed the Constitution as it was reported by the Convention, and demanded amendments regulative of the votes required in Congress for the passage of commercial and other regulations.[67] This he did with the purpose of giving to Virginia and the South the safety which, he considered, would otherwise be wanting under the Constitution; for to Lee, whose chief fear was a Northern carrying monopoly, the specific guaranty of the South's "peculiar institution" which the Constitution contained was not enough. The Constitution, it may be added, also provided for a more extensive national legislative power than Lee had expected. It provided, as he read it, and as most men then read it, for a power "go[ing]," on a national basis, "to every object of human legislation"; and since Lee, like Jefferson, was a believer in "paper checks," as well as "structural checks," he demanded the insertion in the Constitution of a comprehensive bill of *civil* rights.[68] But it is immensely significant that Lee, like

Jefferson a few months later, did *not* demand a bill of *states'* rights. That fact means that, provided civil rights were made safe, Lee was not opposed to a generally empowered national government if only it was so constructed that the share of Virginia and the South in the control of it was such, in his opinion, as to make their interests under it safe. From this position, Lee did eventually depart;[69] but there can be no doubt that such was his initial attitude toward the Constitution.

Lee's initial attitude, the reader will by now perceive, accurately reflects an attitude widely held at the time. Apart from a small, but eventually vociferous, group of petty-minded local politicians, who were impressed only by the fact that they stood to lose in a personal way by the adoption of a national system, there was no real opposition to a *generally empowered* national government when the Constitution was drawn, provided only that such a government could be so constituted as to permit both the Northern and Southern regions of the country to feel safe. There were also, on the part of the smaller states, certain fears of a national government dominated by the larger states. In conventional histories, a great deal is made of the small states' fears; some of the fears of the South are, also, generally mentioned; but the fears of the Northern states, *both large and small*, are ordinarily omitted, and statements can even be found that the slavery issue, which gave rise to the Northern fears, was not of much importance in the Federal Convention.[70] The truth is that the slavery issue, with the fears growing out of it, was all-important for the North as well as the South. Without it, and without the consequent fears of the *large* Northern states, the demands of the minor states would undoubtedly have been brushed aside, if, indeed, in the absence of the slavery issue, they would not have been anticipated, and rendered unnecessary, by a complete consolidation.

The essential problem, then, was how the national government which all thoughtful men desired, could be set up *safely*; how it could be set up so as to make it *strong and vigorous*, and yet, at the same time, assure that men in all parts of the nation would feel that their interests were secure. This, it is worthwhile noting, is precisely the view of the matter taken by Nathan Dane when he learned from Nathaniel Gorham, in the early days of the Convention's sittings, that it had been decided to establish "a National Legislative Executive & Judiciary."[71] He was "very glad," he wrote back to Gorham, that the Convention had come "fully" to such a determination. "But in what hands to lodge the Legislative and executive powers so as to collect in the federal Government *the greatest strength and stability*, and *general Confidence*, [was] a work," said Dane, "[which] the Convention, [in his opinion, would] find of vast consideration."[72] There can be no doubt that Dane accurately stated the essential problem; and his expectation that a "vast consideration" would be necessary to solve that problem turned out to be in the fullest degree correct.

CHAPTER XXIX

The Public Mind as Exhibited in
the Newspaper Discussions

1

THE conclusions suggested in the preceding chapter are amply corroborated by the discussions of governmental reform which appeared in the newspapers in the spring and summer of 1787. Brief items suggestive of a radical reform had in fact begun to appear in the preceding winter. The earliest, perhaps, of these briefer items—and certainly one of the most widely circulated—originated in *The* [Newburyport, Massachusetts] *Essex Journal* on December 27, 1786. It suggested bluntly that Congress be invested with "the sovereignty of the continent."[1] Only a few weeks later an item appeared in Boston, demanding irritably that the states of New England withdraw from Congress and set up as "the Nation of New England." This proposal, seemingly at variance with the squib from *The Essex Journal*, was the threat of dismemberment which, coming after the affair of the Spanish treaty, had caused James Madison so much distress when it came to his attention in Congress on February 21. The significant fact is, however, that the declared object of this novel proposal was to get away from what was called "the imbecile* and disjointed plans" of "the rest of the Continent"; there was no expression of an absolute and unconditional desire to dismember the Union.[2]

A much more serious-sounding proposal of dismemberment appeared, however, in *The New-York Journal* on April 5, though, in this instance too, the real object may have been to promote reform on a national basis by arousing fear that the Union was in danger. At any rate, this second dismemberment proposal proceeded, as did the first, upon the assumption that there was general agreement that the Confederation was inadequate, and that some radical change in the form of the government would have to be made. Dismemberment was presented only as something that might possibly be preferred to a single consolidated national republic, which was treated as the only other conceivable reform to be made. "Reflection would have suggested," the item declared, "and our experience has fully convinced us, that there can be only one sovereignty in a government. The notion, there-

*That is, weak; not half-witted.

432

fore, of a government by confederation between several independent States, and each State still retaining its sovereignty, must be abandoned, and, with it, every attempt to amend the present articles of confederation." "Instead of attempting one general government for the whole community of the United States, would it not be preferable," the item asked, "to distribute the States into three republics, who should enter into a perpetual league or alliance for mutual defence?" The reasons adduced to justify this proposal—which was most probably a rather startling one to the people of the states—were the great extent of the country; the great difficulty then existing in travel and communication between its several parts; and the consequent probable difficulty of operating a single national government over its entire extent. The question whether the Union should be dismembered was, the item agreed, a momentous one; but it was a question, the item insisted, which ought to be faced. The item, like the one which had proposed the setting up of "the Nation of New England," was widely copied in the other states.[3]

The two foregoing proposals of dismembering the Union were the only items, other than brief paragraphs interspersed among the news, which appeared in the spring before the date set for the Federal Convention's meeting. With the arrival of that date, a more extensive discussion sprang up, in which one of the earliest items was a brief warning to the anti-national group, which made the rounds of a good many of the newspapers in the latter part of May. Generally printed under a Worcester, Massachusetts, dateline of May 17, it declared that, according to "accounts from the southward and westward" —i.e., accounts from New York and Philadelphia—"one *consolidated** government [was] now fully talked of, to extend from New Hampshire to Georgia." Then, in the manner of "states' rights" effusions throughout our national history, the "hope" was piously added that "there [was] yet that virtue in United States as [would] enable her to support the *free* governments her citizens [now] enjoy[ed]."[4] This trick of confusing "state government" with "freedom," and "consolidation" with "tyranny," was, however, already threadbare in 1787; and except in one brief item in *The* [New York] *Daily Advertiser* of June 2, no answering outcry against "consolidation" anywhere appeared.

Two rather extensive items in opposition to the making of radical reforms had appeared, however, in Philadelphia before this warning item was published. One of these was a pamphlet, entitled *Fragments on the Confederation of the American States*, which first was advertised for sale on May 23.[5] Opposed alike to "a dismemberment of the Union" and to *"a consolidation of the States into one republic,"** the pamphlet declared that "the chief defects of the confederation [were] the non-compliances of the States with fœderal requisitions" and "their feeble and disjointed attempts to counteract foreign regulations injurious to their commerce." To remedy the first of these defects, Congress should be given power, the pamphlet declared, to collect, *but*

---

*Italicized in the original.

not to lay, the taxes necessary to make up the states' quotas of its requisitions. To remedy the second defect, Congress should be given powers to regulate commerce; but the pamphlet did not make clear the precise nature of these powers. The powers should extend, it said, to the setting up of a uniform national system of "duties, imposts, and prohibitions"; to "the collecting, *as well as the imposing* of duties and imposts"; and to the withholding of commercial advantages from foreign nations in order to obtain reciprocal commercial advantages from them. But there ought to be a proviso, the pamphlet also said, that "the right should not be excluded [sic; but probably "included" was meant] to prevent a state from securing itself from a scarcity of provisions by embargoes, or from encouraging the industry of her citizens by bounties or premiums, or from appropriating the revenue arising from its trade." The nature of this proviso suggests that, apart from it, a complete commerce power was meant; but upon this point the pamphlet, as the reader can see, is not entirely clear. The whole proposal was still further obscured by the suggestion of another proviso that, "when one or more States [should] suffer a manifest detriment by the exercise of any of [the powers proposed], a reasonable deduction [should] be made from their quotas of [Congress's] requisitions."

These thoroughly unworkable suggestions, obviously replete with new delays and disputes between the states and Congress, excited no known attention; but the device which the pamphlet suggested for dealing with such disputes and, as well, with the disputes which Congress and the states were already having, did apparently impress a good many men, at least among the printers, as a proposal of some merit. The device suggested in the pamphlet was called "an Equalizing Court." The court was to act as "an umpire," the pamphlet explained, "between Congress and the States"; and was intended to "prevent an oppressive exercise of the powers deposited with Congress [by] interpos[ing] and determin[ing] between the individual state and the federal body upon all disputed points." For the purpose of choosing the proposed court, "the States [were to] be cast as nearly as [might] be, into three equal divisions; the respective legislatures in each division [were then each] to nominate one candidate skilled in *oeconomics and jurisprudence** for judge of the said court"; and from among the nominees in each division one name was then to be selected by lot, and the three men whose names were drawn were to constitute "the Equalizing Court." It was suggested that the judges of the court ought to "continue in office during good behavior, and have a liberal salary incapable of being diminished or taken away." The procedure, it is also interesting to note, was to be one of direct litigation between the state legislatures and Congress. "The court [was] to hear and determine on all appeals made by Congress against a State, or by a State against Congress"; it was "to furnish the State or Congress with a copy of the charge, or complaint;

*Italicized in the original.

cite an appearance; and in case of nonappearance, proceed to judgment." "[The court's] determination [was to] be final and binding upon the parties"—i.e., the states and Congress—and "the confederacy [was] in no case to be allowed to take measures to compel a delinquent State to comply with any of their acts, before the court [should] find a judgment in their favour." The foregoing proposal, remarkable chiefly for the forthrightness with which it proposed a court with functions very like those sometimes claimed, in the field of constitutional law, for the Supreme Court of the United States,* was published in *The Freeman's Journal*, of Philadelphia, and *The Independent Journal*, of New York, on June 6. From those two papers, it was copied by newspapers in virtually all parts of the country.[6]

Cumbersome and ill-judged as its proposals were, the foregoing pamphlet was probably a bona fide attempt to solve the problems of governmental organization facing the country. The same, however, can certainly not be said of the second of the above-mentioned "states' rights" pieces which appeared in Philadelphia as the Federal Convention was assembling. Signed "Z," and published in *The Freeman's Journal* on May 16, the second of these pieces was the plainest kind of attempt to confuse the issues of the day in the minds of the less-informed among the people. "It seem[ed] to be generally felt and acknowledged," the item began, "that the affairs of [the] country [were] in a ruinous situation." The facts of the business depression were then feelingly set forth; the breaches of the public faith resulting from the lack of any federal revenue were carefully catalogued; and the recital at length concluded with the gloomy observation, that "we [were] discontented at home, and insulted and despised abroad." "In this exigency," said "Z," "people naturally look[ed] up to the continental Convention, in hopes that their wisdom [would] provide some effectual remedy." And since it was, "perhaps," "the last opportunity" for establishing in the country "a permanent system of Continental Government," and "much to be feared" that failure would result in "irretrievable confusion," the question, "how the great object of that meeting [was] to be attained, [was] a question which deserve[d] to be seriously considered." With this introduction, which many a sincere Federalist might well have used, "Z" turned to his main discussion.

"There [was] reason to believe [that] some ha[d] indulged the idea of reforming the United States," he said, "by means of some refined and complicated scheme of organising a future Congress in a different form." Such ideas, he assured his readers, were wrong. "The error [was] not in the form of Congress, the mode of election, or the duration of the appointment of members; the source of all our misfortunes [was] evidently in the want of

---

*The reference is to the "states' rights" theory that the Supreme Court was intended "to decide between the Government of the United States and the government of a State whenever any controversy should arise as to their relative and respective powers." Taney, C.J., in *Gordon* v. *United States*, 117 U.S. 697 (1864). Instead, the Court was established to "secure the national rights & uniformity of Judgm[en]ts." John Rutledge, of South Carolina, in the Federal Convention. Records, I, 124.

power in Congress." "To be convinced of this, we [had] only to recollect the vigor, the energy, the unanimity of this country, a few years past, even in the midst of a bloody war, *when Congress [had] governed the continent.*"* This emphatic reference to the time "when Congress [had] governed the continent" was entirely justified, as we know, and it was quite in the manner which a sincere Federalist might have used. A Federalist, however, would have meant by such a reference, *not* the disordered period of the Revolutionary War, but the short period when Congress, as a practical matter, actually had "governed the continent" as to trade, *internal* as well as external, and also as to many other matters, in the twenty-one-month period of Congress's existence before independence was declared.

Our declension from the ideal days "when Congress [had] governed the continent," said "Z," had been gradual. It had been caused by the states' gradually claiming and exercising "the sovereign and absolute right of treating the recommendations of Congress with contempt." This behavior of the states was totally unjustified, and the situation which had resulted was serious and ought to be remedied. "Some, however, [had] weakly imagined that, to remedy these evils, it [was] necessary to annihilate the States, and vest Congress with the absolute direction and *government of the continent*, as one single republic." This would be "impracticable and mischievous," he said; though just why this should be, if it really was desirable, as "Z" previously had said, to "establish a permanent system of Continental government" and have "Congress govern the continent" again, is not easy to see. The proper remedy, "Z" went on, was not what these "weak" and "imaginative" persons proposed; it was to give Congress power to regulate "those things which *alike* concern[ed] *all* the states, such as our *foreign trade* and foreign transactions"; to "invest [them] with the power of enforcing their regulations" of all such matters; but to restrain them from "local and internal regulations, which [they] could not possibly attend to, and to which the States individually [were] fully competent." Except for his insistence that Congress must be confined to those matters that "alike" concerned "all" the states; except for his seeming intimation that, in the sphere of "trade," only "foreign trade" fell within this category; and except, finally, for his desire to hold on to a type of organization which had produced all the evils he professed to condemn, "Z" undoubtedly talked, up to this point in his essay, like a true and ardent Federalist; but to the men familiar with the events and issues of the time, "Z" 's further remarks certainly disclosed, beyond all question, his true character.

"The ocean," said "Z," "which joins us to other nations, would seem to be the scene upon which Congress"—the proper governor, the reader will remember, *of the continent*—"might exert its authority with the greatest benefit to the United States." "No one State," he pointed out, "[could] possibly

*Italics in the original.

claim any exclusive right in [the ocean]." "[And hence] it had long been seen that the States individually [could] not, with any success, pretend to regulate trade [sic]." "So, would it not then be right," he solemnly asked, "to vest Congress with the sole and exclusive power of regulating trade [sic], of imposing port duties, of appointing officers to collect these duties, of erecting ports and deciding all questions by their own authority, which concern[ed] *foreign* trade [sic] and navigation *upon the high seas?*" He was aware, he said, that some would object "that this [was] too small a power to grant to Congress;—that many more [were] necessary to be added to those which they already possess[ed]"; but to such persons, he would "only say, that perhaps they [had] not sufficiently reflected upon the great importance of the power proposed." As for "those [other] persons who had conceived a narrow jealousy of Congress, and therefore [had,] unhappily obstructed their exertions for the public welfare, [and who might] perhaps be startled at the idea [of granting to Congress the power to regulate *"foreign* trade and navigation *upon the high seas"*]"—to such persons he "would answer, that [the] situation appear[ed to him] to be sufficiently desperate to justify the hazarding an experiment of *anything* which promise[d] immediate relief." Having finally, by all this pother, confused the idea of "the general welfare" in the minds, perhaps, of some of his simpler readers; having, also, perhaps, confused in their minds, "the power of regulating trade" with "the power of regulating merely foreign trade and navigation upon the high seas"; and having, perhaps, also made it seem to some such men that even such a limited power was a thing of danger to many thoughtful men, he next purported to assure his readers that, *to him*, the power seemed "necessary and useful," and that he could "not think it would in the least degree endanger [America's] liberties." "The representatives of the States in Congress [were] easily changed," he said, *"as often as we please*[d], *and they must necessarily be changed often."* "Let us then try this [experiment]," he magnanimously concluded, *"for a few years*; and if we find it attended with mischief, we can refuse to renew the power."

The foregoing consummate example of the "states'-rights" art was apparently copied, soon after its original appearance in Philadelphia, by some New York newspaper that could not be found, and then recopied therefrom by *The* [Philadelphia] *Pennsylvania Gazette*, on June 16.[7] It had, however, no further circulation in the country's newspapers and was apparently generally recognized for what it was. In its failure to circulate, the appeal of "Z" was in marked contrast with a strongly nationalist item, entitled "An Address to the Freemen of America," which appeared initially in *The Pennsylvania Journal*, *The Pennsylvania Gazette*, and *The Independent Gazetteer*, of Philadelphia, on May 30. Signed "Harrington," by some one who described himself as "a citizen of Pennsylvania in a retired situation who holds and wishes for no share in the power or offices of his country and who often addressed you, in 1774–1775, upon the interesting subject of the liberties of America," the address in question was apparently the work of Doctor Benjamin Rush, of

Philadelphia.[8] Judging by the tenor of his remarks as "Harrington," Rush had not changed his ideas very much as to the desirable scope of the national governing power since the days, some ten years previously, when he and John Adams, James Wilson, and Richard Henry Lee had fought together to maintain the general governing power of the Continental Congress.[9] Rush's change of view, as in the case of most other men, was chiefly as to the form which the government of the nation ought to have. In his "Address of Harrington," he accordingly came out for a one-man national executive, to be dependent for the tenure of his office upon frequent popular election, and for "*one supreme* legislature," to consist of "two or three* branches." To such a government, Rush maintained, "the eyes of the whole empire [could be] directed"; its "duties [therefore could] be perfectly understood"; its "conduct narrowly watched"; and because of these factors, Rush believed, its "laws [would] be obeyed with cheerfulness and respect." "Upon the narrow scale of a state government," he also said, the violence of factions "[could] never be restrained"; but in a national government, "they [would] check each other."†

As for the desirable scope of the national government's legislative power, Rush boldly declared that "the more [Americans] abridge[d] the states of their sovereignty, and concentre[d] the supreme power in an assembly of the states (for, by this term let us call our federal government), the more safety, liberty and prosperity [would] be enjoyed by each of the states"—that is, of course, by the "states" as multitudes of individual men, not by the "states" as governments.

Rush also drew the attention of his countrymen to the known characters of the men who were met to draw up a new scheme of government for the nation. "Many of them," he reminded his readers, "[had been] members of the first Congress that sat in Philadelphia in the year 1774. Many of them [had been] part of that band of patriots who, with halters round their necks [had] signed the Declaration of Independence on the Fourth of July 1776. Many of them [had been] distinguished in the field and some of them [bore] marks of the wounds they [had] received in [the nation's] late contest for liberty. Perhaps no age or country [had] ever [seen] more wisdom, patriotism, and probity united in a single assembly than [America] beh[e]ld in [the] Convention of the States. [And] who [could] read or hear that the immortal Washington ha[d] again quitted his beloved retirement and obeyed the voice of God and his country by accepting the chair of this illustrious body of patriots and heroes, and doubt of the safety and blessings of the government [the country would] receive from their hands?" "Under the

---

*The "third" branch of the legislature, according to the mode of speaking at the time, may have meant the "executive" veto, or it may have meant some kind of "council of legislative revision."

†This, of course, is the notion which Madison later developed in No. 10 of *The Federalist*. It was at the time a commonplace among the advocates of a national system. Cf. Henry Knox's idea of the durability of a republic on "national principles."

present weak, imperfect and distracted government of Congress—anarchy, poverty, infamy and slavery await[ed] the United States. Under such a government as [would] probably be formed by the present Convention, America [might] yet enjoy peace, safety, liberty and glory."

It was a stirring address, and it was widely copied. Its vogue in fact was remarkable, for it appeared in the newspapers of practically every state in the country, and in many it was published as a "broadside" covering the entire front page.[10] What seems even more remarkable than its widespread publication, however, is the fact that it did not, so far as can be ascertained from the surviving newspaper record, anywhere elicit any angry, dissenting comment. Of all the newspapers in which the address was published, this complete want of dissenting comment is, perhaps, the most remarkable in the case of *The Independent Gazetteer*, of Philadelphia, one of the three papers in which the address initially appeared. The reason for this is that in the ensuing fall in Philadelphia *The Independent Gazetteer* played the leading part in the anti-Federalist campaign against the Constitution. In its columns there appeared, month after month, a steady stream of attacks upon the Constitution and its framers, in large part of a highly vitriolic and scurrilous character. The total want of any reply to "Harrington's Address" when it appeared in that paper is, therefore, a particularly noteworthy circumstance. It strongly suggests that the later abuse in the *Gazetteer* was not in reality a true index of Pennsylvania popular opinion; in other words, the items which appeared in that paper in the course of the ensuing year were not spontaneous responses, on the part of the general body of the paper's subscribers, to what the Constitution contained but in fact a factitious product issuing from a little group of self-interested state politicians and their hirelings, as the Federalists maintained at the time. Just why the *Gazetteer* lent itself to this sort of thing, when the Constitution appeared, is very far from clear, but this fact is certain: *throughout the summer* there appeared in its columns more items of a strongly Federalist flavor than in any other Philadelphia paper.

The want of any spontaneous objection among the people of Pennsylvania to the institution of a national government with general powers is further strikingly evidenced by the other items which appeared in the Philadelphia papers during the spring and summer in question, and by the total absence in those papers of any disapproving comment upon them. In the *Independent Gazetteer*, for example, there appeared, on the day following the publication of "Harrington's address," a letter from some one signing himself "Rustick." "Rustick" bluntly advocated the abandonment of the Articles of Confederation, and "striking out on a different plan." In suggesting this course, he assured his readers that he did not mean that the country "should divide into three separate empires." "Neither," said he, "am I for a monarchy, either limited or absolute. I am for a pure republic, and the more simple the better: As it is a rule in mechanics (and I think it will hold good in frames of government) the more simple the machine, the less liable to be out of order."

In accordance with this principle, Congress, he said, ought to be made "the supreme *executive* head [of the nation], with all those powers that [would] render [America] respectable in foreign states, and other [powers] that [Congress] seem[ed] to possess, but [which could] not, from the defects of the present *form* of government, be put in force." Bearing in mind that "judicial courts" were then often known as "executive courts," and that "adjudication" was then frequently viewed as a part of the "executive process," the probable scope of "Rustick's" suggestion of change in "the form" of the existing government seems obvious. Although he was, as the reader will observe, inexplicit regarding the precise substantive scope of the national legislative power, "Rustick" was very clear and emphatic about the need for a complete general subordination of the states to the nation. To this end, he thought, Congress should be given the power of appointing the state governors. The governors would then be obliged, he said, to act under congressional instructions and would, in consequence, negative all laws in the states that were "contrary to the general interest." Harking back to the ideas of 1775 and 1776, "Rustick" also urged that the several state constitutions should be abandoned, and "one general constitution" substituted, "containing the fundamental principles of liberty and good government." This was the kind of document which the Federal Convention, in his opinion, ought to draw. Yet, despite the unmistakable meaning of such a suggestion, and despite the outcry which arose in the fall, when it was learned that the convention had in fact done *some* of the things which "Rustick" had suggested, "Rustick's" letter, like the "Address of Harrington," evoked no response at all when it appeared.[11]

Short items of an equally pronounced Federalist flavor appeared in the columns of the *Gazetteer* from time to time throughout the summer. "The principal difficulty," said one of these items, "will arise from the [existing] *Officers of Government*. Their interest, it is imagined, will be affected by alterations. Hence, we must expect to hear them cry out, as the crown officers did in the beginning of the war, 'this is not the time for making alterations—alterations are dangerous, and we shall be enslaved by our rulers, &c.'" "But it [was] to be hoped," the item suggestively concluded, "[that] *the people* [would] neither be influenced by such men, nor their connections, in the adoption of a new Federal Government."[12] Brief items expressive of equally staunch Federalist views also appeared from time to time in most of the other Philadelphia papers. The total number of these shorter items was considerable; and their importance, no doubt, likewise so; but more concretely interesting in the present discussion is an elaborate treatment of the whole problem of improving the government, which was published in thirty installments,—also in the columns of *The Independent Gazetteer*—between August 6 and October 2.[13] This production, entitled "An Essay on the Means of Promoting Federal Sentiments in the United States," by "A Foreign Spectator," was copied extensively by the newspapers in other parts of the country;[14] and since the strong inference, therefore, is that the sentiments expressed in the essay were popular sentiments, a detailed examination of the proposals contained in it seems worth our while.

The "Foreign Spectator," the author of this essay, was the Reverend Nicholas (or Nils) Collin, of Philadelphia, a Swedish clergyman, who had resided in New Jersey during the years of the Revolution.[15] A friend of Franklin's, well known to many of the Philadelphia Federalists of the time, Collin was in thorough sympathy with that group's desire for a strong American national government.* His "Federal Sentiments" essay was completely in accord with this point of view; and in the period just after the government was formed under the Constitution, Collin wrote the strongest series of papers which appeared at that time in defense of the "general welfare" power, and against any weakening of the government's powers generally by amendments.[16]

In his earlier essay, Collin declared emphatically that "efficient government [in America] absolutely require[d] a strong federal power"; each necessary branch of such a power, "legislative, executive, and judiciary," should embrace everything, he said, which *the grand interest of the confederacy require[d]*." Although he believed that certain fundamental civil rights might properly be stipulated, Collin maintained that "the grand interest of the confederacy" could not possibly be limited or defined. "Future events [were] unknown—the overseers *must* have powers adequate to *any* eventual situation."[17] But though the powers of the national "overseers" could not be defined because the eventualities to be met could not be predicted, there were some things which, all could see, would necessarily be comprehended. For example, all could see that the national powers must, under all circumstances, extend to the military defense of the country against foreign nations;[18] as, also, to the suppression of all rebellions against the government of the nation, all strife between state and state, and every insurrection within particular states. The militia must, in the light of these considerations, be subject solely to the federal power in all these emergencies, and must therefore be trained under federal regulations.[19] "*External commerce*" would likewise be rather generally the subject of national regulations; and "it [was] evident that *internal commerce* [would] also, in many cases, become a federal object." "There [could] not be a doubt," he added, by way of summary on this commercial point, "[that] federal power, *whenever its interference [was] necessary*, [would] manage *the national commerce* to the best advantage." By "national commerce," Collin here seems clearly to have meant "the nation's whole commerce, both foreign and domestic," for he spoke at length in the

---

*Collin was a member of the Society for Political Enquiries mentioned herein at a later point, which included all but one of the Pennsylvania delegates to the Federal Convention among its members. The society also included such staunch nationalists as Benjamin Rush, Timothy Pickering, William Rawle, Francis Hopkinson, Samuel Powel, and Tench Coxe. Thomas Paine had also been a member of the society before his departure for Europe in the preceding April.

same context about the great facilities of the country for internal navigation; of the need that existed for developing these facilities; of the need for seeing to it that the western country was *gradually* settled; of the need for bringing all the fertile lands of the country under careful cultivation; and of the need for promoting every kind of domestic manufacture.[20] Collin failed to set forth in each particular instance the relationship of the national legislative power to all these ends; his insistence upon a national power "adequate to any eventual situation" could of course only have meant that all these ends, as well as every other, were within that power to whatever extent the needs of "any" particular "eventual situation" might require. Although Collin did not, apparently, contemplate an "exclusive" national power over "commerce," as many other men did, he did contemplate a power in the national government extending without exception to the nation's whole "commerce," whether "internal" or "external" in character.

Other "internal objects" which Collin believed would fall within the scope of a proper national governing power were the establishment of universities, the patronage of learned societies, and the regulation and early abolition of slavery.[21] The several state constitutions, "when properly settled," should also, Collin thought, be guaranteed by the national government; and the guaranty ought to run against "monarchy, aristocracy, and democracy" alike. The last element in this guaranty (which seems to be the guaranty which actually was incorporated in the Constitution) may possibly puzzle some modern readers. But the kind of thing at which the last element of the guaranty was aimed, and which to Collin and a good many others seemed to justify such a guaranty, was the constant assemblings of "conventions," unofficial "town meetings," and the like, and the attempts, which these gatherings then repeatedly made, to interfere with the functioning of duly elected or appointed public officers. In addition to these undeniable abuses, there was the practice, very prevalent at the time in certain of the states, of tying the hands of representatives by "instructions." These things, Collin thought, the national government ought to eliminate within the states; and he thought that the national governing power ought also to interfere in the governments of the states in every case wherein a state "annul[led] the habeas corpus law, tryal by juries, [or] the like institutions, which [were]," he said, "the pillars of *republican* liberty." "[And] if corruption [became] so rife in any state, that a party could establish itself in oppression; the federal power should redress the grievance, even though [the situation] might not threaten the confederacy with danger."[22] To conclude, Collin thought that the national government should have an ample revenue; and he maintained that the taxes necessary to produce that revenue should be laid and collected by the national government itself. "It [was] high time," he said, "to have done with requisitions."[23] Taking Collin's essay all in all, he clearly advocated in the course of it about what other Philadelphia Federalists of the times were asking; and since his essay evoked no angry answers in Pennsylvania or in any other state in which it appeared,[24] the strong inference is that the kind of thing which he and the other Philadelphia Federalists were asking was about what the American public generally desired.

The correctness of this view is fully evinced by the local expressions of opinion which were published in the newspapers outside Philadelphia. In New York, for example, there appeared in *The Daily Advertiser*, on June 8, a letter addressed "to the Citizens of America," which was quite as nationalistic in its proposals as anything that originated in Philadelphia. "In a republican government," the letter declared, "it [was] the undoubted unalienable, and indefeasible right of the majority of the people to amend, alter, or to annihilate their form of government, [whenever it] should be found [by experience] to be inadequate." "Decision, energy and punctuality" could not be expected from "thirteen sovereignties under the direction of a diplomatic Congress"; and since, "if Blackstone [were] to be credited," it would endanger "public liberty" to give Congress all the powers, both executive and legislative, which would be needed for any real improvement, the conclusion followed that some entirely different form of government was requisite. "A monarchial government, under a good King, [was] generally allowed to be the best: and at present the United States [might] probably have it in their power to place on the throne as good a King as ever reigned: But as history [did] not furnish above one good King to half a dozen bad or indifferent ones, it would be purchasing a good King at too dear a rate." Having thus disposed of monarchy, the writer of the letter turned his attention to the subject of "dismemberment." "To divide the United States into three or more independent republics would," he said, "weaken [Americans] too much against foreigners, leave [each resulting republic] too small to be respectable, and expose [them] to continual quarrels [between themselves], which could only be decided by the sword." "*One consolidated republic*, [therefore,] if formed on the best possible plan, would probably be the most happy government." He would therefore "throw out some hints for this purpose, which [might] be improved on."

"The supreme power" (by which the writer of the letter meant "the government of the nation") "[should] be divided," he said, "into two branches, the one legislative, to-wit, a parliament consisting of the delegates of the people; the other executive, to-wit, the supreme executive council. The house of delegates to consist of one member for every two thousand electors in the United States, to be chosen for two years. The supreme executive council to consist of a president and twenty-six counsellors; the president to be chosen by the governors of the different states, to continue in office five years; the counsellors to be chosen by the legislatures of the different states, each to send two, to continue in office four years, and to be chosen biennially." As "the supreme executive council" was to have a veto over all national legislative acts, it resembled somewhat, both in this function and in the mode of its selection, the senate afterwards set up under the Constitution. It was also to have "the sole power of appointing all officers, civil and military," including judges. The judges, it was emphasized, were to constitute "a distinct and separate body" in the government and were to "hold their appointments *quamdiu se bene gesserint*; in which consist[ed]," the writer of the letter declared, "one main preservative of Public Liberty." "The council" was likewise to be possessed of "the prerogative of making peace, and war, or sending and receiving all ambassadors, of making treaties, leagues, and alliances with foreign states and princes, and [would] be *quo ad hoc* the sovereign power." "The house of delegates," however, was to have, as a check on these prerogatives, "the right of impeaching any member of the council" for acts done with "criminal motives."

"With respect to the *interior polity* of the different states," the state governments were to be allowed a *"subordinate* power of legislation; that is, the power of making local ordinances, *not repugnant* to the laws of the supreme"—i.e., the national—"power; but nothing [was to] be attempted that [might] derogate from [the national] sovereignty." "In other words," as the letter further explained (in terms remarkably like a certain speech by James Madison in the Federal Convention),[25] "[the states should] be in the nature of *civil corporations*, with the power of making *by-laws* for their own interior regulation, and suitable to their different emergencies, with such rights and authorities as [might] be given them, by their constitutions; which [were] particularly to provide that all laws, by-laws, usages and customs, repugnant to any law or ordinance made, or to be made, by the supreme power [should] be utterly void and of none effect." As for "the supreme power"—that is, "the national government"—it was to have *"full* power and authority, to make laws and ordinances of sufficient validity to the states, *in all cases whatsoever."*

The foregoing letter was published over the signature of "A West-Chester Farmer." That signature had been the pseudonym used in 1774 and 1775 by the Reverend Samuel Seabury, of New York, a well-known Tory pamphleteer of the pre-Revolutionary period.[26] In 1787, Seabury was the Anglican bishop of Connecticut.[27] Whether he was responsible for the letter outlined above is not known, but his authorship of it is not improbable. It is barely possible, however, that the letter may have been a subtle piece of anti-Federalist propaganda. The signature, "A West-Chester Farmer," someone may have imagined, would arouse unreasoning resentment against all that the letter proposed. Such a possibility, however, seems farfetched, for, as the reader can see from what has been quoted, the letter had all the appearance of a sincere effort for better government. No unfavorable comment upon the letter is to be found in the New York papers, but it will be remembered that a brief dissent from making Congress "the sole governing power of America"—which the "West-Chester Farmer" of course did not propose—had appeared in *The Daily Advertiser* six days before his letter was published.[28]

The letter of the "West-Chester Farmer" was also published in full in *The* [Richmond] *Virginia Independent Chronicle* of June 27, with an acknowledgment that it had been taken "from a New-York paper." The "Address of Harrington" also had been published in the same paper two weeks previously.[29] The Virginians of the time were thus clearly informed of what was being talked of further north, while the Federal Convention was carrying on its sessions. Despite the jealousy and distrust of the North which many Virginians of the time entertained; despite the power which the North would have had under the scheme of the "West-Chester Farmer"; and despite the opposition to proposals for strengthening the national government which had been displayed in Virginia less than two years before,[30] no opposition was voiced in 1787 to the proposals put forth in the foregoing items, either in the *Independent Chronicle* in which they appeared, or in *The Virginia Gazette, or Weekly Advertiser*, the only other Virginia paper of which files for the period in question are still in existence. It may be added that, likewise, there are to be found in the surviving Virginia papers no local proposals of any kind as to what should be done.

The state of opinion further south appears to have been much the same as, inferably, it was in Virginia. In South Carolina the "Address of Harrington" was published in *The* [Charleston] *Columbian Herald* of July 5. Eight days later a scheme of government, somewhat similar to that suggested by the "West-Chester Farmer," was briefly outlined in a paragraph which appeared in *The Charleston Morning Post* of July 13. The paragraph in the *Morning Post* was apparently of local origin and was published as having been received by that paper "from an anonymous correspondent." "We hear," the paragraph began, "that many sensible persons in America, wish that the United States may in future instead of being governed by a different Legislature in each State, and by a Congress, as has been hitherto done, be under the direction of an assembly of the United States and a Senate. Each of [these bodies] to consist of twenty or more representatives from each State with a Governour General and Privy Council, the Governour General to have a power of assenting to or dissenting from the laws made by the said two Houses; the Council to be chosen as well as the Governor General, by these Houses of Legislature." "The Governor General and Council," it was also explained, "[would] execute the Laws, and appoint all officers both Civil and Military through out the States." "The mode proposed for chusing the Members of the Assembly and Senate, [would be] the same," it was said, "as [that] now practised in this State"—i.e., South Carolina—"for sending Members to Congress, or else to divide each State, into so many Districts, and every District to elect and recal its own Members." No dissents were registered in the Charleston papers to this plain proposal of a "consolidated," or "national," form of government; and neither did any appear to the proposals which had been made known to South Carolinians through the publication of the "Address of Harrington" a few days before. It should be said, however, that the files of the newspapers of Charleston for the summer of 1787 are not quite complete, and there may have been some dissents which have not survived.

Of what appeared in the papers of North Carolina during the summer in question, nothing is known, since virtually no North Carolina newspapers for that summer survive. The situation is the same with respect to Delaware, save, of course, that it is certain that all Philadelphia items were known in that state because of the extensive circulation there of the Philadelphia papers. Files of the newspapers of Maryland and Georgia are available; and in them may be found the "Address of Harrington" fully reprinted.[31] The address also circulated in Maryland and Georgia, to some extent, as, indeed, it also did in Delaware and North Carolina and other states, in the June number of *The American Museum*, a monthly magazine of the time having a nationwide circulation. Nothing in the nature of a dissent from "Harrington's Address" could be found in any Georgia or Maryland paper, but an item in the Augusta *Georgia State Gazette or Independent Register*, of July 21, though indicative of local approval of complete general supremacy in the national government, did dissent from the proposal, which, it said, was being considered in the Federal Convention, that the state legislatures be abolished. "We hear with great satisfaction," the item reported, "that the Convention is now assembled, and doing business at Philadelphia." The various "principles" under consideration were: "1st. That the Thirteen States be divided into three distinct Republics, who ought to league together for their common defence, as so many separate governments, independent of each other. 2ndly. If the Thirteen States remain as they are confederated, to lessen their sovereignty, by abolishing their State Legislatures, and leaving the whole laws to be made by the National Congress, Assembly or Parliament. 3dly. The Thirteen States to remain as they are, *except that their laws be revised by Congress*, so as to make the whole act in conformity as of one, and the Executive Power of Congress enlarged." "It [was] much to be wished," the item concluded, "[that] the latter"—which would seem to have been some faint echo of "the Virginia plan"—[might] be adopted."

The scarcity of comment, characteristic of the states of Maryland and Georgia, was also characteristic of New Jersey and the states of New England. The Philadelphia items heretofore noted, though unpublished in New Jersey, were all probably known there, by reason of the state's proximity to Philadelphia. In New England, the "Address of Harrington," the essay of Nicholas Collin, and other significant items from the Philadelphia papers were widely copied. Only one paper, however, among all those published in the strongly nationalist New England states, printed any local item which was really extensive. This paper was *The New-Haven Gazette and Connecticut*

Magazine, which republished, "with additions and alterations," the previously mentioned pamphlet, *The Political Establishments of the United States*, which originally was published in 1784, in Philadelphia.[32] The republication of that pamphlet ran through the issues of the *Gazette* from May 12 to July 12.

The reader may recall that, in the original version of this pamphlet, the author had declared that it was a mistake to try to divide the powers of government into those that were "civil" and those that were "political" in the way in which, he seemed to believe, the Articles of Confederation had sought to do. It was a mistake, he said, because an exact division of power along such lines was impossible. The two classes of powers, and indeed all governmental powers, ran into each other; were, in short, intersecting categories; and no efficient exercise of either set could, therefore, be carried out without encroachment to some extent upon the other. For this and other reasons, the author of the pamphlet had originally maintained that "no reformation or amendment [could] effectually answer any good purpose, short of the abolishment of [the] state governments and the forming a constitution, whereby the whole nation [could] be united in *one government*." These sentiments, he repeated, with additional arguments to support them, when the pamphlet was republished in New Haven in 1787; and he pointedly declared that he still believed "it would be much to the interest and happiness of the people, could they be persuaded to throw all the states into *one grand republic*." In a footnote, however, he conceded that there might be some ground for apprehension that "revisal of the federal system [would] extend no farther than an enlargement of the powers of Congress." If this should turn out to be the case, "a just line" ought nevertheless to be drawn "between the *civil* and *political* powers." And it would be "trifling, temporizing, and sporting with the most important interests of the nation" to vest the national government with less than "full powers in all national concerns, even," he declared, "*to their remotest and most extensive objects*."[33]

Bearing in mind the common eighteenth-century meaning of the words used by the author of this pamphlet,[34] and the concrete evidence which his pamphlet contained as to how he himself used and understood them, there can be no possible doubt that what he proposed was a plenary national supremacy over all matters, save those comprehended in the narrow field then known as "police," a field which, as we know, included no part of "the regulation of commerce," either internal or external. It is important also to note that, even within the field of "police," the author of the pamphlet believed that the national government ought to be able to interfere when necessary to carry out its "political" powers. This is what he meant by vesting Congress with "full powers in all national concerns, even to their remotest and most extensive objects." This scheme of power, the reader of this book will scarcely need to be told, was the scheme of all the early drafts of the Articles of Confederation. The author of the pamphlet was therefore urging that there ought, at least, to be a return to the ideas of the men who had declared the nation's independence: ideas which, as we know, those men had unwillingly abandoned under the stress of circumstances that arose after that event occurred.[35] What the author of the pamphlet really desired, as already noted, was what other Federalists of the time were asking: the organization of a generally empowered government, of national form, with the states continued, if at all, for subordinate, provincial purposes only.

With this brief view of this republished pamphlet in *The New-Haven Gazette and Connecticut Magazine*, we complete our survey of the public discussions of the changes to be made in the government that appeared in the spring and summer of 1787. Much less numerous than the discussions that appeared in the agitation for a full national commerce power in 1785, the discussions of 1787 were, nevertheless, remarkable for their uniformly more sweeping and radical character. The governments of the states should be swept away, these discussions said; or, at least, they should be reduced to definitely subordinate provincial establishments. The legislative power of the nation ought to be general, they also said; and the states ought to have at most the power of legislating *only* in such fields as the national legislature might allow. Such ideas, *and only such ideas*, the reader should understand, were put before the American public *while the Federal Convention was in session*; and since no angry chorus of dissent greeted these ideas; since no attempts were even made to answer them; and since, instead, there was a constant chorus of brief items in the paper, applauding such ideas,[36] it was only natural that the men in the convention should conclude, as George Read, of Delaware, said, that "the people [were] wrongly suspected of being averse to a General Government."[37] In suggesting this conclusion, Read, undoubtedly, was fully aware that a few anti-Federalist pieces had appeared at about the time when the convention had assembled; in particular, he probably was familiar with the highly sophistical appeal of the plausible Mr. "Z" in *The* [Philadelphia] *Freeman's Journal*.[38] But the character of "Z"'s appeal and of the other anti-Federalist pieces that were published was such, no doubt, as to make clear to a man like Read the source from which they came; we may, therefore, confidently surmise that the only effect which these anti-Federalist writings had upon Read and the other men in the convention was to confirm them in the conclusion which Read stated: that "the State Magistrates [might] disagree, but [that] the people [were] with [the convention]."[39]

This view of the state of the public mind was very likely also confirmed for the men of the convention by the violent attacks upon the character of some of them that began to appear with increasing frequency in certain New York and Philadelphia papers toward the end of the summer. There had been some of this sort of thing, indeed, along in the spring; and in July, after John Lansing and Robert Yates, the New York anti-Federalist delegates, withdrew from the convention, the attacks began again in New York; and the New York governor, George Clinton, indulged orally in predictions that mischief and confusion would be the certain result of the Federal Convention's deliberations.[40] These efforts to undermine the public's confidence in the convention drew a protest from Alexander Hamilton in *The* [New York] *Daily Advertiser* on July 21; for a short while afterward, such efforts again seemed to cease. As the summer wore on, however, it became more and more apparent that there was no real popular objection to the institution of a fully empowered national government; and toward the end of August the state-officer group apparently felt compelled to resort once more to their attacks upon the character of the men in the convention.

In Philadelphia, these tactics were begun by Mr. "Z," of *The Freeman's Journal*. His effort appeared in the issue of that paper for August 22. By that date, the reader will remember, the "Address of Harington" and most of the other previously mentioned Federalist pieces had appeared in the Philadelphia and other papers; Nicholas Collin's *Essay on Federal Sentiments* was well under way; and the absence of any spontaneous public objection to "consolidation" had become perfectly clear. In addition, it was by that time generally known that the convention had finally composed its differences, had adjourned to allow a committee to draw a draft constitution, and that the committee had since reported.[41] It was, moreover, also "whispered" in New York, a few days after "Z"'s attack was made, that there had been "some late changes in [the convention's] scheme which [gave] it a higher tone."[42] If these changes, which were initiated on the floor of the convention on August 18 and 20, and were embodied in a supplemental report from the convention's committee on August 22, were "whispered" in New York a few days after "Z"'s appeal was made, it seems a virtual certainty that they must have been "whispered" in Philadelphia almost as they occurred. This consideration, and the other circumstances previously noted, make it easy to surmise the motives with which "Z" and others like him must have acted.

Nothing is so essential," said "Z," "to the happiness of a people, as the possession of a *free* government. Without this, the most fertile country and the mildest climates, become scenes of misery and desolation; but with it, the most rugged regions of the earth are crowned with cheerfulness and plenty." History showed, he went on, that peoples among whom free institutions had been established, had generally enjoyed their liberties unthreatened for a time and then, lulled into security, had eventually lost them to a few scheming individuals. "In Pennsylvania, it ha[d] been [the] peculiar misfortune [of the people], that, as soon as [their] free and excellent Constitution was formed, a Junto also was formed, of men inspired with principles inimical to the rights of freemen." "Hitherto, indeed, [the free constitution of Pennsylvania] ha[d] been preserved, by means of extraordinary care and vigilance; but its enemies [were] still on the watch, and, however they [might] attempt to disguise their intentions, yet every time they [were] entrusted with power, they g[a]ve but too evident proofs of their pernicious intentions." "The people, [therefore,] ha[d] need to be much on their guard;

for, if [they] fail[ed] in [their] vigilance, the liberties of Pennsylvania [would] speedily be no more; and [that] country, like others where liberty once flourished [would] become the seat of despotism and wretchedness."

After this extremely "pathetic" introduction, "Z" turned to the alleged misdoings of "the Pennsylvania Junto." His full catalogue of "the Junto"'s vile misdeeds (set forth, of course, without the slightest attempt at proof) may be found by the curious in *The Freeman's Journal*. For present purposes, the character of his effort will be sufficiently clear from a single one of his many charges: that "the Junto"'s settled policy was "an unlimited license to the importation of foreign goods, by foreigners, and a total disregard to [the state's] own manufactures and navigation." As a result of this policy, the severest sufferings, he said, had been felt in the Pennsylvania iron manufactory, "of late so flourishing and so profitable to [the] state." The reason for "the Junto"'s pursuit of this wicked policy was very simple: "the Head of the Junto ha[d] bought a slitting mill; and the price of iron [had] to be kept down, by importations, in foreign bottoms, from the Baltic, let who [would] starve among ourselves."

"The Convention," "Z" then immediately went on, "[had been] looked up to with eager expectation, for the relief of our distresses"; and "as much [would] probably depend upon the unanimity, with which the people [should] receive their decisions, it was," he said, "of great importance to secure the hearty concurrence of so considerable a State as Pennsylvania." Yet what had "the Junto" done for the attainment of this end? "[They] had confined the choice of Delegates for [that] great State to the city of Philadelphia, and almost exclusively to their own narrow party in the city;—for even the venerable Franklin was excluded, in their first choice." That Franklin had been omitted from the original choice of delegates was true enough, but not for the reasons which "Z" implied;[43] and as for the backcountry regions of Pennsylvania, the representatives from those regions in the General Assembly had expressed an unwillingness to serve in the Federal Convention, at the time the state's choice of delegates was made.[44] The iniquity of "the Junto" went, however even further. They had actually "included in the [state's] delegation a man, who [was] not even a citizen of [the] State; whose interest [lay] in another State; but who ha[d] the sublime merit, of being the ready tool of the great Head of the Junto." Pennsylvanians "on the Susquehanna and the Ohio," "Z" sneeringly added, would no doubt be represented "to the extent of their wishes," by this "citizen of New York"; and if "anything a little unpalatable [should] appear in the [convention's] proceedings," they would no doubt "reflect how fully they ha[d] been represented," and, so, accept what was unpalatable "for the sake of the great good, which [would] result from the whole." At this point, "Z"'s purpose, of course, was accomplished; but he went on for several paragraphs with his catalogue of "the Junto"'s iniquities and finally ended with a moving appeal to "the people" "not to slumber and neglect themselves"; for, "in no State or country, perhaps, was watchfulness ever more necessary, than [it then was] in Pennsylvania."

The foregoing statements by "Z," however unwarranted in their implications, pointed with sufficient clarity to Robert Morris, Continental Superintendent of Finance during the American Revolution, as "the great Head" of the dread "Junto" of Pennsylvania, and to Gouverneur Morris, who had come originally from New York, as his "ready tool." These two men, chiefly because of the known great ability of the latter, occupied within their state in 1787 the position, later held by Alexander Hamilton throughout the nation, of whipping boys to the "states' rights" party of their time. The use of the two Morrises for this purpose in 1787 was not, however, confined to Pennsylvania, though the exact evils to be feared from them, and the exact nature of their supposed relationship to each other, were not quite the same in other states. Thus, in *The* [New York] *Daily Advertiser*, of May 16, a writer signing himself "Eboracus" had seemed to regard Gouverneur Morris as the master and Robert Morris as the "tool"; but he had seen, nevertheless, no probability that any benefit would result from this fact for the state, in which, according to "Z," Gouverneur Morris's interest lay. On the contrary, it was "Z's" own state, according to "Eboracus," that was going to benefit. "There was a state," he said, "which ha[d] a mercantile Doge."* "[This doge,] in the mercantile circle, move[d] as an animal [did] in the narrow circle of instinct, or as a blind horse in a bark mill; but when [this same doge] leap[ed] from the traces and exercise[d] in the field of politics, a bold state jockey, who was called 'the Devil upon one stick'† back[ed] him, bridle[d] him, and put him alternately to an amble, trot, or canter or speed, as he please[d]." When this jockey took control, it was time to beware. For his "adventurous and imposing genius, aided by the plentiful dinners and Mediterranean wines of the Doge," would be certain to "move political puppets," of the kind, it was implied, that were to be found in plenty in the Federal Convention; and "if C[ongress could], with their treasury and assistance from Mr. Discount Tobacco,* move their scenery to Philadelphia, the independency of America [was] lost."⁴⁵ The tropes and thinking in the foregoing outburst were of course somewhat confused; but with the timorous and unthinking the desired impression was probably created by the vague insinuations with which it was replete.

Efforts of the foregoing kind were resumed in New York, soon after the appeal of "Z" appeared in Philadelphia. In the anti-Federalist *New-York Journal*, of September 6, Hamilton was somewhat belatedly attacked for his letter in *The Daily Advertiser* of July 21. Governor Clinton, it was said, never had made such statements as Hamilton had then attributed to him; and Hamilton, it was added, knew it. His purpose in this letter had been to defame and discredit New York's great governor with the people. "An eminent author

*That is, Robert Morris.
†Gouverneur Morris had lost a leg.

ha[d] predicted, that the opulent and ambitious, would never rest contented with the equality established by our democratic forms of government; [and] that this prediction, [was] already in some measure realized, must be obvious to every man of the least discernment." "[For] it [could] not admit of a doubt that a certain lordly faction exist[ed] in [the] state, composed of men, possessed of an insatiable thirst for dominion, and who, having forfeited the confidence of their fellow-citizens, and being defeated in their hopes of rising into power, ha[d], for some time past, empoyed themselves with unremitted industry, to embarrass every public measure. They [had] reprobate[d the state's] laws, censure[d its] rulers, and decr[ied its] government, thereby to induce the necessity of a change, that they [might] establish a system more favorable to their aristocratic views, *in which, honors and distinction [would] not depend upon the opinion and suffrages of the people.*" And to attain this end, "no measure which low cunning [could] devise, or wicked exertion effect," was being omitted by the "lordly faction." So, "every virtuous man"—meaning, of course, the New York governor—"who dare[d] to stand in the way of their ambitious and arbitrary projects, bec[a]me the victim of their keenest resentment, and [was] devoted to destruction." To such motives, and such motives only, was Hamilton's protest in *The Daily Advertiser* to be attributed; it was a trick to discredit a wise and good man who wished to protect "the people" and, by discrediting him, to pave the way for the introduction of an "aristocratic" constitution.

When this performance appeared, Hamilton was in Philadelphia once more, in the Federal Convention; but some anonymous writer sprang to his defense, in *The Daily Advertiser* of September 10, declaring that there had been good reason for the protest which Hamilton had made in July against the New York governor's tactics. This, however, had no effect upon the campaign of innuendo and abuse which the Clintonians had begun; and in *The New-York Journal* of September 13 a complaint appeared that "it seem[ed] to be highly criminal to differ in opinion from a certain Aristocratic junto." The Federal Convention, it was conceded, contained many wise and good men, as "this junto" maintained; but it was "at the same time, also well known, that there [were within that body] too many of a very different character; perfect Bashaws! (saving a want of power) who would trample on the most sacred rights of the people, without the least reluctance or remorse." "The greatest part of the publications [of this junto were] artfully calculated to prepare the minds of the people, implicitly to receive *any form** of government that [might] be offered them." But "Rusticus, of Queens-County," the author of this protest, declared that he "ha[d] too good an opinion of [the American people] to suppose that [they could] receive any form of government, that [would] not effectually secure their just rights and privileges, let it be recommended by any man, or body of men, however wise, learned, or dignified."

*Italics in the original.

This Clintonian campaign of subtle pin-pricks to the popular ego, of constant insinuation against the character of the convention, and of subtle suggestions that an aristocratic constitution was about to be proposed, reached a climax of low scurrility, in *The New-York Journal*, on September 20. On that day, Alexander Hamilton, then probably known to have signed the Constitution, was attacked once more for having sought to prevent the state's governor from "speaking his sentiments in a matter of general concern." In an adjoining item he was referred to, in certain thinly veiled remarks, as "an upstart attorney [who had] palm[ed] himself upon a great and good man,* for a youth of extraordinary genius." "Under the shadow of such a patronage," the item went on, "[this upstart youth had] ma[d]e himself at once known and respected; but being sifted and bolted to the brann, [he had] at length [been] found to be a superficial, self-conceited coxcomb, and [had] of course [been] turned off and disregarded by his patron."[46] At the same time, it was stoutly maintained, as if there were some danger of such a thing happening, that "the free citizens of this continent [would] never consent to have a constitution crammed down their throats." "They ha[d] an undoubted right to examine before they accede[d], and to deny if they [did] not approve." The next day, September 21, the Constitution was published in *The New-York Packet* and *The Daily Advertiser*, but in *The New-York Journal*, then still a weekly, the Constitution did not appear for another six days. By that time, the first number of the Clintonian "Letters of Cato," attacking the new government, was ready for publication, and in the *Journal* of September 27 the Constitution and the first of the "Letters of Cato" accordingly appeared.

By such tactics, then, did the state-officer class in Pennsylvania and New York seek to discredit the Constitution before it was even known. These tactics, fully realizing the apprehension of Henry Knox, that the Constitution would have to run the gauntlet of "the misinterpretations of bad men"[47] seem, at this distance, a rather plain proof that the "states' rights" party of the time was fearful that, on the merits of a proposal to establish "a firm national government,"[48] they could not win before the people. Since the men in the convention were of the opinion that they would have to go to the people in order to win,[49] the common notion that there was widespread spontaneous opposition among the people to the establishment of a national government in 1787 seems quite clearly to be without foundation. Whatever popular opposition to the Constitution finally surfaced was very largely a whipped-up opposition. For the rest, it was an entirely natural popular reaction to the kind of compromise in the control of the government by the various states which had to be adopted. The three-fifths rule of representation in the lower chamber of the national legislature was nowhere popular in the Northern states; and among the larger Northern states, and those that hoped to be large, the equal vote in the Senate was not popular, either. The considerations which reconciled the politicians from the larger Northern states to

*Washington of course was meant.

such an arrangement could not be discussed in public, for the same reasons which made Rufus King and James Monroe and other men in Congress chary about discussing the subject in their letters in 1785 and 1786.[50] Among the general public in the Northern states these considerations were, accordingly, not well understood. In the South there was the same feeling that was found in the North, at least among the Southern states that were already large or hoped to become so, that the equal vote in the Senate was unfair; and there was also a fear, especially among Virginians like Richard Henry Lee, that the South's interests were not safe. The Southern opposition also was natural; and while there were other factors, in both the North and the South, which were responsible for part of the popular opposition, there can be little doubt that, apart from the opposition which was merely whipped up, the foregoing factors were the chief cause of such popular opposition as actually existed. Since such factors were not inconsistent with a desire for "a firm national government" *satisfactorily constituted*, the conclusion on the basis of the public discussions must be much the same as that on the basis of the private letters: among the people of the states, there was no general opposition to "a firm national government," provided only that such a government were so constituted as to make the men of all states feel safe, and provided, further, that the share which each particular state was to have in such a government was such as would seem, to the general run of its nonpolitician citizens, fair and just to it.

2

Turning now to a more particular consideration of the sentiments in 1787 on a power to regulate commerce, we may note, by way of background, that the popular agitations of 1785 for a complete national commerce power had fallen off considerably in the fall of that year, after it became apparent that the agitations had met with failure in the Southern states. In such circumstances, it might be supposed that Virginia's proposal of the Annapolis commercial convention, early in 1786, must have set these public discussions to going again, but for some reason or other no such effect ensued. The public discussions were generally desultory through the whole of 1786; with the exception of a few items which appeared just before the convention, the most extensive discussion was one which originated in *The* [Boston] *Massachusetts Gazette*, on August 22. After noting that a convention would shortly meet "to take into consideration the commerce of these states," the item expressed the hope that the convention would "lay down, as a first principle, that the United States, in the business they [were] appointed to, [were] ONE." Let them "lay aside all local attachments," the item advised, "and every private, sinister view, [and] consider, upon an extensive plan, the advantages of the different climates—the produce of the several soils and waters—and the various branches of agriculture and manufactures natural to each state—and in what manner these may subserve the good of the whole." "It will be evident to men of so much discernment," the item went hopefully on, "that the natural produce and situation of each state are such, that if they can bring them, as it were, to one focus, where they may unite and act together, it must give great energy to the commerce of these states. [For] no part of Europe has so many resources within themselves, or so well situated to answer every kind of commerce, as the United States of America." In view of this fact, the commissioners would surely not disappoint the hopes of the country. "Their own good sense, [their] thorough knowledge of commerce, and the natural advantages of the several states, [would] dictate what [was] best to be done; and by union in their principles, [would] lead them to be adopted by the legislatures of the several states upon the unanimous recommendation of Congress." This rather wishful item—in effect, a proposal for the establishment under Congress of a continental American "commercial system"—was copied extensively in the newspapers in other parts of the country.[51] The same thing happened to a briefer item, originating, apparently, in New York, which insisted, in so many words, that Congress "must" be given *complete and ample* power to regulate *the whole system of commerce.*"[52] And in Virginia a similar desire seems to have been voiced in a Richmond item, which described the impending convention as one called *"to establish commerce, as well foreign as domestic."*[53] As the date set for the Annapolis convention drew near, then, there was some public interest in the meeting, and what there was tended to show that public opinion upon the subject of a national commerce power had in no way changed.

With the failure of the Annapolis meeting, public discussion of creating a national commerce power dropped for a while to an all-time low, probably as a result, at first, of general discouragement and, later, of a shift in popular interest to more sweeping and radical reforms. Brief paragraphs on the desirability of a national commerce power continued to appear, nevertheless, throughout the whole period after the spring of 1785. Intermingled with the news, these brief paragraphs demanded a "full," or "complete," or "absolute," or "exclusive," or "sole and exclusive" national commerce power; or else they made clear in some other emphatic way that the sentiments of 1785 upon this important subject were still the sentiments of the country.[54] Longer discussions of the subject also occasionally appeared, especially in the spring and summer of 1787; and some of these add striking evidence, in one way or another, of what the eighteenth century understood by a power "to regulate commerce," and why it was considered necessary that the whole of that power be handed over to the nation.

Of the longer discussions touching upon such points, much the most informative for a modern mind was the reprint, in *The New-Haven Gazette and Connecticut Magazine*, of the pamphlet, *The Political Establishments of the United States*, previously referred to. "Suppose," said the author of that pamphlet, in the final installment of the reprint, on July 12, "suppose that congress should be invested with ample powers with respect to security and defence, *the navigation and commerce of the nation, in their most extensive, connected, and dependent objects*; what would there be in this, of which we should have reason to apprehend any evil consequences?" His answer was that "it would be granting no new or extraordinary powers"; that the powers proposed were "powers which the assemblies of the states [had] always held and exercised"; and that "all the difference would be, that the powers [would be] lodged in a different place." "And the advantage would be that the measures [of government] would be more uniform, consistent, and efficacious; whereas," he declared, "they are at present neither." "In the one case, there would be harmony; in the other, endless confusion." That desire for the convenience and simplicity of uniform law was one impelling motive for this writer's views seems evident from the foregoing passages; at other points in his pamphlet he spoke of the "extremely intricate and complicated" character of the "operations and influences" of "commerce"; of the fact that the subject extended "to a great variety of subordinate interests and concerns"; and of what he regarded as a necessary consequence: that the whole of that vast and interconnected subject, together with all the other components of what the eighteenth century knew as "policy" was a matter "*of general and equal concern to the [entire] community*," and that it therefore was "absolutely necessary" that "such a system be established, as [would] promote, secure, and regulate [all these "political"] interests, *by the unanimous aid and concurrence of the nation*." He pointed out, also, that "it [was] frequently necessary to call the united strength of a nation into exercise for its defence"; that "a proportion of private property [was] always necessary to be [taken in taxation]"; and that "a due observation of national treaties and *internal regulations* [was] indispensable to promote the general weal and render advantages among the people equal." Since all these governmental ends and purposes were, as he repeatedly insisted, inextricably interwoven and dependent, "the institution of [one] ultimate, decisive counsel and authority [was] essentially necessary, in the formation of a *political* system"—in which, of course, a "commercial system" was included as an indispensable and major component. Under any other scheme, said the author of the pamphlet, the "political system" of the country could not be "complete"; could not be "adequate to the interests and necessities of the people"; could not avoid "a great variety of evils and perplexities"; and could not "render [the] nation flourishing and happy."[55]

That the author of this pamphlet understood the subjects of "commerce" and "commercial regulation" as those subjects are explained in this book is quite evident from the foregoing passages; but because his pamphlet was republished in New Haven on the very eve of the Federal Convention, and because the points on which he touched are of great importance to the thesis of this book, it seems desirable to put in evidence certain further passages from his pamphlet, which are even clearer and more specific upon the points in question than are those we have already quoted. Thus, at one point in the installment of the pamphlet which appeared on May 17, the author observed that "the whole *political* interest of a nation [might] be included and considered under [two] denominations: [that] of War, or that in which the peace and safety of a nation consists,—and [that] of *Commerce*, or the correspondence and connections *of a nation* with other nations, and *with one another.*" The author's mode of expression in this passage, which is obviously another important key to what was meant in the eighteenth century by "a power to regulate commerce," is, as the reader will at once perceive, antiquated throughout. The word "political" would never be used, at the present time, in the limited technical sense in which the author of the pamphlet used it; the word "correspondence" would never now be used to signify "business," which is the meaning of the word in the passage quoted; and few persons today would speak of "the business and connections of a nation *with one another.*" The word "nation" does not signify, to a modern mind, "the multitude of *individuals* of a nation" with sufficient vividness to justify such an expression. We know, however, from the plural-verb usage and other evidence[56] that the opposit was true of "nation," "state," and similar nouns, in the eighteenth century; and hence it follows that this passage from the pamphlet was an entirely natural way for a man of the eighteenth century to say that "commerce," in the sense in which the author of the pamphlet was using it, signified "the business and the economic relationships of *the individuals* of a nation with the *individuals* of other nations, and *with one another.*" More briefly, the passage was a natural way of saying that "commerce" signified, *in that particular connection*, "the whole economic organization"; or, to use another eighteenth-century term, its "whole commercial system."

The particular connection in which the author of the pamphlet was using the word "commerce" in the foregoing passage was, of course, that of government; and at another point in his pamphlet, he was, if possible, even more specific as to what the word signified in that connection. The passage in question, which is also to be found in *The New-Haven Gazette and Connecticut Magazine* of May 17, was as follows:

Commerce, as an object of government, comprises everything relating to the interest and wealth of a nation in general; and therefore extends to every particular interest and property, which may be affected or influenced by trade.—The productions of a country by agriculture and manufacture, is the source of national wealth, and basis of commerce; The husbandman furnishes the means of subsistence, and the raw materials for fabrication and manufacture; The manufacturer and mechanic prepare those raw materials for use, and the merchant, by *commerce*, renders the superfluous productions of a country valuable, which otherwise would be of little worth, and by an exchange of commodities, supplies the people with such articles of foreign produce and manufacture, as are not furnished among themselves, and which may be necessary for carrying on their *various branches of business*, or for the comfort and convenience of the people. In promoting these general interests, by carrying on an (almost) endless variety of business, necessarily derived from them, the learned, the ingenious, the seaman, artificer, and day-labourer, find employment and support. *On the mutual aid and the support of the whole of these, depends the opulence of a nation; and therefore, equally requires the encouragement and protection of government.*

The reader will observe from the italicized portions of the foregoing passage that at one point in it "trade" is apparently used in the sense of "trade of merchandize" and that "commerce" is apparently used at another point in the sense of the foreign "branch" of that particular "commerce," or "trade." Yet the passage also shows in the clearest way that the author of the pamphlet was aware that "commerce" had a peculiar and different meaning when the word was used to refer to the subject of government, and that that peculiar and different meaning comprehended every "branch of [a nation's] business." In estimating the evidential value of the views of the author of this pamphlet, it is important to bear in mind that his statements with reference to the scope of "commerce as an object"—that is, as "an article," or "department"[57]—"of government" are entirely free, as many later contrary statements are not, of every suspicion of untrustworthiness due to political bias on constitutional issues; for his statements were offered, *not* as an interpretation of the Commerce Clause, or any other constitutional or statutory provisions, but as an explication, in the course of a didactic essay, of what a governmental power over "commerce" comprehended. The author's statements, therefore, may confidently be accepted as the best possible kind of evidence as to what the actual understanding of "a power to regulate commerce" was at the time when the Commerce Clause was drawn. It may be added that other passages from this pamphlet show that the author of it had an equivalent understanding of "a power to regulate trade."[58] Comparable statements as to the scope of "trade" or "commerce" as "an object of government" were likewise contained in the original Philadelphia edition of the pamphlet, of 1784, cast, however, in slightly different terms. These may be found as notes to the reprint of the pamphlet, in one of the appendices of this book.[59]

The foregoing discussion from *The Political Establishments of the United States* is, of course, totally irreconcilable with the conventional view that there was an expectation, when the Federal Convention met, that a national power over commerce would be created, extending to, and limited to, foreign, Indian, and "interstate" commerce only. The letters and discussions noted in this and the previous chapter, both those which demanded a complete "consolidation" and those which suggests a national governing power able to act in all cases for the national welfare, are also irreconcilable with such a view. For the former, of course, contemplated a national power extending to every case, and the latter a national power able to act on every subject when the welfare of the nation was concerned. It seems perfectly clear that in 1787 the demand was not for a limited, but for a complete, national power of regulating commerce. The same, we have seen from the materials reviewed in chapters IX–XVI, was emphatically true of the demand for a national commerce power in 1785. And the truth is that there is a total want of evidence that there ever was a group within the country, at any time during the period between 1775 and 1787, which advocated the creation of a national commerce power limited in the peculiar way in which the Supreme Court says the power established by the Commerce Clause was limited by the words in which that clause is cast.[60] In considering this fact, the reader should remember that the opposition to the creation of a national commerce power existed mainly in the Southern states; and that the opposition there (apart from an unwillingness, chiefly in the southernmost states, to concede any power over the slave trade or slavery) appertained peculiarly to the concession of power over foreign commerce. This is apparent from the fact that a Northern monopoly of the carrying trade from the Southern states to foreign countries was the thing chiefly feared. An exception from the national power covering "intrastate" commerce would, therefore, have had no relevance to the chief opposition to a national commercial power which then existed; and since the creation of a national power, subject to an intrastate exception, would of course have meant an actual increase, rather than a decrease, in the possible as well as probable disuniformities in the regulation of the country's commerce, the reader should not be surprised in the least that there was no group in the country which advocated the now familiar power over "foreign-plus-interstate" trade.

That the general desire in 1785 for a full national power of regulating commerce continued into 1787, both in and out of Congress, we have already seen. It may, however, be well to add to the evidence given, a few more very striking bits of evidence corroborative of this fact. In particular, we should put before the reader the letter previously mentioned, which Richard Henry Lee, of Virginia, wrote to George Mason, of the same state, on the eve of the Federal Convention. Mason, it will be remembered, was one of the Virginia delegates to that gathering; and Lee, about to take his seat in Congress, had been offered a place on the Virginia delegation with Mason, but had refused. His letter to Mason was written on May 15. Lee therein took the general position that the current commercial difficulties with the British were being used by interested persons to obtain a power totally disproportionate to those troubles; in short, that the hole did not fit the patch. "The present causes of complaint," said Lee, "are that Congress can not command the money necessary for the just purposes of paying debts, or for supporting the federal government; and that they can not make treaties of commerce, unless *power unlimited, of regulating trade*, be given them." To meet the revenue difficulty, Lee (who previously had opposed the continental impost power) now seemed ready to concede, rather grudgingly, the necessity of some kind of congressional power to tax. "[But] with respect to the want of power to make treaties of trade, for want of legislation, *to regulate the general commerce*,[61] it appear[ed] to [him]," Lee said, "that the right of making treaties, and the legislative power contended for, [were] essentially different things." Having taken this unassailable position, he pointed out to Mason certain small changes which could be made in the Articles, to accomplish the investiture of Congress with "a complete and unlimited right of making treaties of all kinds." "And, so far," said Lee, "I really think [the power asked for] both right and necessary." "But this," he insisted, "is very different from, and in danger far short of, giving *an exclusive power of regulating trade.*" The Northern states could not form for themselves a carrying monopoly against the South by treaty, and therefore the treaty power was safe; "but a legislative right *to regulate trade through the states*,[62] [might]," Lee said, "in a thousand artful modes, be so abused as to produce the monopoly aforesaid." And, then, forgetful of his own contrary sentiments of a decade earlier, and the contrary sentiments of many others at that time, Lee feelingly reminded Mason that, "when the confederation [had been] submitted for consideration, the universal apprehension was, of the too great, not the defective powers of Congress." "Now," he lamented, "the cry is power, give Congress power!"[63]

That Lee was right in his appraisal of the prevailing sentiment in 1787, we have already seen; and his four phrases, carefully chosen to impress upon Mason the extent and magnitude of the commercial power which was being asked, are worthy of careful note; for not one of them was susceptible, upon a straightforward reading, of any interpretation, at the time they were used, but that the commercial power in prospect was to be absolutely complete, extending to every "branch" of the country's "general [or entire] commerce"; or, in other words, to its whole foreign and domestic trade. Lee knew full well what "a power to regulate commerce" was, as we know from the fact that he was a member of the First Continental Congress, in 1774, and from the part which he took in the debates over the Resolutions on Rights and Grievances, which were adopted at that time.[64] Later, in the summer of 1787, however, Lee appeared to be entirely reconciled to what, he apparently found after talking to the men in Philadelphia, was the thing in prospect. The letters he wrote which evince this fact, and the probable reasons which explain his seemingly inconsistent behavior, have already been considered in Chapter XXVIII,[65] but since the last of his still apparently satisfied letters— that of August 22—contains evidence as to the kind of commerce power which he still expected on that date, that part of the letter will bear repetition here. "The Report of the Convention is expected," he wrote, "about a fortnight hence, and great are the public expectations concerning it—Tis expected that a federal Legislature of 3 branches will be recommended, *with independent powers, and supreme for external matters, Revenue, & Commerce*—with an Executive well toned"—i.e., strong—"and of reasonable duration."[66] The mode in which Lee wrote in this letter precludes any doubt whatever that, as late as August 22, he still expected a whole commerce power. From his mode of speaking, it also seems clear that the "Commerce" to which he expected that power would relate was, like "Revenue," something more, according to his understanding, than an "external matter" only.

Wishes or expectations similar to Lee's were expressed in many different quarters. An early bit of evidence from a neutral source was a report sent by Louis Otto, French *chargé d'affaires* at New York, to his principal in Paris, in April. The scheme of reform then generally talked of, he said, included the giving to Congress, of "the right *exclusively to regulate the commerce* of all the states."[67] Toward the end of the summer, a widely copied item from the Philadelphia papers gave plain evidence of the kind of power which was then expected. "Every enterprize, publick as well as private, in the United States, seems suspended," the item said, "till it is known what kind of government we are to receive from our national Convention." "The states neglect their roads and canals," the item went on, "till they see whether those necessary improvements will not become the objects of a national government. [And] *trading and manufacturing* companies suspend their voyages and manufactures till they see how far *their commerce*"—that is, their business—"will be protected and promoted by a national system of *commercial regulations*."[68] In this item, obviously, "commerce" was used to include "manufactures"; and "roads and canals," it was certainly suggested, were likely to become "national objects."

Further evidence from the discussions of 1787 exemplifying this broad understanding of "commerce" may be found in a paper on "A Commercial System for the United States," which Tench Coxe, the Pennsylvania delegate to the Annapolis convention, read at the home of Benjamin Franklin on May 11[69] and published as a pamphlet eight days later in Philadelphia.[70] Coxe's paper also contained evidence that a full commerce power was then hoped for and expected. After referring in the course of his remarks to various particular commercial powers that Congress ought to have, including a general negative on all state commercial laws, Coxe finally concluded with the pointed suggestion that it was, of course, for the convention to decide whether such particular powers only should be given, or "the *general* power of regulating trade."[71]*

This suggestion by Coxe no doubt sufficiently indicates what was in the air in Philadelphia as the convention assembled; but the most convincing piece of evidence, on the eve of the convention, is undoubtedly a letter which came to the convention itself, just as it began its sessions. The letter came from a group of "Merchants, Tradesmen, and others." of the town of Providence, Rhode Island. It informed the convention that it was "the general opinion [in Providence] and, [the writers] believe[d], of the well informed throughout [their] State, that *full* power for the Regulation of *the Commerce of the United States, both Foreign & Domestick* ought to be vested in the National Council."[72] Certainly, a straightforward reading of this statement by these men of Providence requires the conclusion that what they meant by their words "the entire commerce of the country" included what is nowadays known among

---

*The Society for Political Enquiries, to which Coxe read this paper, included among its members all, save one, of the Pennsylvania delegates to the Federal Convention. The exception was Gouverneur Morris, who probably did not care about being lectured to. See *The* [Philadelphia] *Pennsylvania Packet*, April 4, 1787.

lawyers as "intrastate commerce"; and if the troubled conditions which existed within their state are brought to mind,[73] the reader will see at once that it is simply preposterous to suppose that they could, even possibly, have meant anything else. Their situation, it is true, was somewhat peculiar; but the reader will observe that the words they used were the same words which Rufus King had ascribed to James Madison, at the height of the trouble over the Spanish treaty less than a year before;[74] that their words, though not the same words, were nevertheless incontestably equivalent to the words which had been used by the Boston merchants and many other groups, public and private, in the great agitation of 1785;[75] that their words were likewise equivalent, under an eighteenth-century standard, to the words which had been used in Congress in the committee reports of 1785 and 1786; and that their words, finally, were also equivalent to the words which Richard Henry Lee was using, even as they wrote, to warn George Mason of the evils which, as Lee then saw the matter, were about to come to pass.

In addition to these several lines of corroborative evidence, there are, of course, a great host of others which have been put before the reader in the pages of this and the antecedent volumes of this study. Look at the matter how one will, it is impossible not to conclude that these men of Providence who wrote to the Convention as it began its sessions spoke the sentiment of the country generally at the time they wrote. The reasons that lay behind the general consensus which had thus been reached on the subject of commercial power were very different, we know, in the North and South; but due to a complex set of causes which has already been explained, the divergent motives and desires of the two regions had finally been brought together upon the subject, provided only, as in the case of the broader issue of general power, a government could be constructed under which the men from both regions of the country would feel safe. It would seem to follow, then, that, unless the Federal Convention in the course of its proceedings did something entirely different from what the country generally expected at the time when the convention met, they must have provided in the Constitution for a generally empowered government, whose legislature possessed, along with its many other powers, a complete power over the whole commerce of these United States.

Appendices

APPENDIX A

Franklin's Articles of Confederation

Articles of Confederation and perpetual Union, entred into ~~agro~~ *proposed* by the Delegates of the several Colonies of New Hampshire, &c, in general Congress met at Philadelphia, May 10, 1775.

ART. I.

The Name of this confederacy shall henceforth be *The United Colonies of North America.*

ART. II.

The said United Colonies hereby severally enter into a firm League of Friendship with each other, binding on themselves and their Posterity, for their common Defence ~~and Offence,~~ against their Enemies for the Security of their Liberties and Propertys, the Safety of their Persons and Families, and their ~~common and~~ mutual and general Welfare.

ART. III.

That each Colony shall enjoy and retain as much as it may think fit of its own present Laws, Customs, Rights, ~~and~~ Privileges, and peculiar Jurisdictions within its own Limits; and may amend its own Constitution as shall seem best to its own Assembly or Convention.

ART. IV.

That for the more convenient Management of general Interests, Delegates shall be annually elected in each Colony to meet in General Congress at such Time and Place as shall be agreed on in ~~each~~ the next preceding Congress. Only where particular Circumstances do not make a Deviation necessary, it is understood to be a Rule, that each succeeding Congress be held in a different Colony till the whole Number be gone through, and so in perpetual Rotation; and that accordingly the next Congress after the present shall be held ~~in the~~ at Annapolis in Maryland.

ART. V.

That the Power and Duty of the Congress shall extend to the Determining on War and Peace, to sending and receiving ambassadors, and entring into Alliances, [the Reconciliation with Great Britain;] the Settling all Disputes and Differences between

Colony and Colony about Limits or any other cause if such should arise; and the Planting of new Colonies when proper.

The Congress shall also make ~~and propose~~ such general ~~Regulations~~ Ordinances as tho' necessary to the General Welfare, particular Assemblies ~~from their local Circum~~ cannot be competent to; viz. ~~such as may relate to~~ those that may relate to our general Commerce; or general Currency; to the Establishment of Posts; and the Regulation of our common Forces. The Congress shall also have the Appointment of all General Officers, civil and military, appertaining to the general Confederacy, such as General Treasurer, Secretary, &c.

Art. VI.

All Charges of Wars, and all other general Expences to be incurr'd for the common Welfare, shall be defray'd out of a common Treasury, which is to be supply'd by each Colony in proportion to its Number of Male Polls between 16 and 60 Years of Age; the Taxes for paying that proportion are to be laid and levied by the Laws of each Colony. ~~And all Advantages gained at a common Expence~~.

Art. VII.

The Number of Delegates to be elected and sent to the Congress by each Colony, shall be regulated from time to time by the Number of such Polls return'd; so as that one Delegate be allowed for every [5000] Polls. And the Delegates are to bring with them to every Congress, an authenticated Return of the number of Polls in the respective Provinces which is to be annually triennially taken for the Purposes above mentioned.

Art. VIII.

At every Meeting of the Congress One half of the Members return'd exclusive of Proxies be necessary to make a Quorum, and Each Delegate at the Congress, shall have a Vote in all Cases; and if necessarily absent, shall be allowed to appoint any other Delegate from the same Colony to be his Proxy, who may vote for him.

Art. IX

An executive Council shall be appointed by the Congress out of their own Body, consisting of [12] Persons; of whom in the first Appointment one Third, viz. [4], shall be for one year, [4] for two Years, and [4] for three Years; and as the said Terms expire, the Vacancy shall be filled by Appointments for three Years, whereby One Third of the Members will be changed annually. And each Person who has served the said Term of three Years as Counsellor, shall have a Respite of three Years, before he can be elected again. ~~The Appointments to be determined by Ballot.~~ This Council (of whom two thirds shall be a Quorum,) in the Recess of the Congress is to execute what shall have been enjoin'd thereby; to manage the general continental Business and Interests to receive Applications from foreign Countries; to prepare Matters for the Consideration of the Congress; to fill up [*Pro tempore*] ~~general~~ continental Offices that fall vacant; and to draw on the General Treasurer for such Monies as may be necessary for general Services, & appropriated by the Congress to such Services.

Art. X.

No Colony shall engage in an offensive War with any Nation of Indians without the Consent of the Congress, or great Council above mentioned, who are first to consider the Justice and Necessity of such War.

Art. XI.

A perpetual Alliance offensive and defensive, is to be enter'd into as soon as may be with the Six Nations; their Limits to be ascertain'd and secur'd to them; their Land not to be encroach'd on, nor any private or Colony Purchases made of them hereafter to be held good; nor any Contract for Lands to be made but between the Great Council of the Indians at Onondaga and the General Congress. The Boundaries and Lands of all the other Indians shall also be ascertain'd and secur'd to them in the same manner; and Persons appointed to reside among them in proper Districts, who shall take care to prevent Injustice in the Trade with them, and be enabled at our general Expence by occasional small Supplies, to relieve their personal Wants and Distresses. And all Purchases from them shall be by the ~~General~~ Congress for the General Advantage and Benefit of the United Colonies.

Art. XII.

As all new Institutions ~~are Subject to~~ may have Imperfections which only Time and Experience can discover, it is agreed, That the General Congress from time to time shall propose such Amendments of this Constitution as ~~they~~ may be found necessary; which being approv'd by a Majority of the Colony Assemblies, shall be equally binding with the rest of the Articles of this Confederation.

Art. XIII.

Any ~~other~~ and every Colony from Great Britain upon the Continent of North America and not at present engag'd in our Association ~~shall~~ may upon Application and joining the said Association be receiv'd into this Confederation, viz. [Ireland] the West India Islands, Quebec, St. Johns, Nova Scotia, Bermudas, and the East and West Floridas; and shall thereupon be entitled to all the Advantages of our Union, mutual Assistance and Commerce.

These Articles shall be propos'd to the several Provincial Conventions or Assemblies, to be by them consider'd, and if approv'd they are advis'd to impower their Delegates to agree to and ratify the same in the ensuing Congress. After which the *Union* thereby establish'd is to continue firm till the Terms of Reconciliation proposed in the Petition of the last Congress to the King are agreed to; till the Acts since made restraining the American Commerce and Fisheries are repeal'd; till Reparation is made for the Injury done to Boston by shutting up its Port; for the Burning of Charlestown; and for the Expence of this unjust War; and till all the British Troops are withdrawn from America. On the Arrival of these Events the Colonies [shall] return to their former Connection and Friendship with Britain: But on Failure thereof this Confederation is to be perpetual.

Journals of the Continental Congress, 1774–1789, ed. Worthington C. Ford (Washington, 1904), II, 194–99.

APPENDIX B

John Dickinson's Draft of
the Articles of Confederation

Articles of confederation and perpetual union, between the colonies of

New Hampshire,	*The counties of New Castle, Kent*
Massachusetts Bay,	*and Sussex on Delaware,*
Rhode Island,	*Maryland,*
Connecticut,	*Virginia,*
New York,	*North Carolina,*
New Jersey,	*South Carolina, and*
Pennsylvania,	*Georgia.*

ART. I. THE Name of this Confederacy shall be "THE UNITED STATES OF AMERICA."

ART. II. The said Colonies unite themselves so as never to be divided by any Act whatever, and hereby severally enter into a firm League of Friendship with each other, for their common Defence, the Security of their Liberties, and their mutual and general Welfare, binding the said Colonies to assist one another against all Force offered to or attacks made upon them or any of them, on Account of Religion, Sovereignty, Trade, or any other Pretence whatever.

ART. III. Each Colony shall retain and enjoy as much of its present Laws, Rights and Customs, as it may think fit, and reserves to itself the sole and exclusive Regulation and Government of its internal police, in all matters that shall not interfere with the Articles of this Confederation.

ART. IV. No Colony or Colonies, without the Consent of the United States ~~in Congress~~ assembled, shall send any Embassy to or receive any Embassy from, or enter into any Treaty, Convention or Conference with the King or Kingdom of Great-Britain, or any foreign Prince or State; nor shall any Colony or Colonies, nor any Servant or Servants of the United States, or of any colony or Colonies, accept of any Present, Emolument, Office, or Title of any Kind whatever, from the King or Kingdom of Great-Britain, or any foreign Prince or State; nor shall the United States assembled, or any Colony grant any Title of Nobility.

ART. V. No two or more Colonies shall enter into any Treaty, Confederation or Alliance whatever between them, without the previous and free Consent and Allowance of the United States ~~in Congress~~ assembled, specifying accurately the Purposes for which the same is to be entered into, and how long it shall continue.

ART. VI. The Inhabitants of each Colony shall henceforth always have the same Rights, Liberties, Privileges, Immunities and Advantages, in the other Colonies, which the said Inhabitants now have, in all cases whatever, except in those provided for by the next following Article.

468

Art. VII. The Inhabitants of each Colony shall enjoy all the Rights, Liberties, Privileges, Immunities, and Advantages, in Trade, Navigation, and Commerce, in any other Colony, and in going to and from the same from and to any Part of the World, which the Natives of such Colony or any Commercial Society, established by its Authority shall enjoy.

Art. VIII. Each Colony may assess or lay such Imposts or Duties as it thinks proper, on Importations or Exportations, provided such Imposts or Duties do not interfere with any Stipulations in Treaties hereafter entered into by the United States assembled, with the King or Kingdom of Great Britain, or any foreign Prince or State.

Art. IX. No standing Army or Body of Forces shall be kept up by any Colony or Colonies in Times of Peace, except such a Number only as may be requisite to garrison the Forts necessary for the Defence of such Colony or Colonies: But every Colony shall always keep up a well regulated and disciplined Militia, sufficiently armed and accoutred; and shall provide and constantly have ready for Use in public Stores, a due Number of Field Pieces and Tents, and proper Quantity of Ammunition, and other Camp Equipage.

Art. X. When Troops are raised in any of the Colonies for the common Defence, the Commission Officers proper for the Troops raised in each Colony, except the General Officers, shall be appointed by the Legislature of each Colony respectively, or in such manner as shall by them be directed.

Art. XI. All Charges of Wars and all other Expences that shall be incurred for the common Defence, or general Welfare, and allowed by the United States in General Congress assembled, shall be defrayed out of a common Treasury, which shall be supplied by the several Colonies in Proportion to the Number of Inhabitants of every Age, Sex and Quality, except Indians not paying Taxes, in each Colony, a true Account of which, distinguishing the white Inhabitants who are not slaves, shall be triennially taken and transmitted to Congress the Assembly of the United States. The Taxes for paying that Proportion shall be laid and levied by the Authority and Direction of the Legislatures of the several Colonies, within the Time agreed upon by Unites States assembled.

Art. XII. Every Colony shall abide by the Determinations of the United States in General Congress assembled, concerning the Services performed and Losses or Expences incurred by every Colony for the common Defence or general Welfare, and no Colony or Colonies shall in any Case whatever endeavor by Force to procure Redress of any Injury or Injustice supposed to be done by the United States to such Colony or Colonies in not granting such Satisfactions, Indemnifications, Compensations, Retributions, Exemptions, or Benefits of any Kind, as such Colony or Colonies may think just or reasonable.

Art. XIII. No Colony or Colonies shall engage in any War without the previous Consent of the United States assembled, unless such Colony or Colonies be actually invaded by Enemies, or shall have received certain Advice of a Resolution being formed by some Nations of Indians to invade such Colony or Colonies, and the Danger is so imminent, as not to admit of a Delay, till the other Colonies can be consulted: Nor shall any Colony or Colonies grant Commissions to any Ships or Vessels of War, nor Letters of Marque or Reprisal, except it be after a Declaration of War by the United States assembled, and then only against the Kingdom or State and the Subjects thereof, against which War had been so declared, and under such Regulations as shall be established by the United States assembled.

Art. XIV. A perpetual Alliance, offensive and defensive, is to be entered into by the United States assembled as soon as may be, with the Six Nations, and all other neighbouring Nations of Indians; their Limits to be ascertained, their Lands to be secured to them, and not encroached on; no Purchases of Lands, hereafter to be made of the Indians by Colonies or private Persons before the Limits of the Colonies are ascertained, to be valid: All Purchases of Lands not included within those Limits, where ascertained, to be made by Contracts between the United States assembled, or by Persons for that Purpose authorized by them, and the great Councils of the Indians, for the general Benefit of all the United Colonies.

Art. XV. When the Boundaries of any Colony shall be ascertained by Agreement, or in the Manner herein after directed, all the other Colonies shall guarantee to such Colony the full and peaceable Possession of, and the free and entire Jurisdiction in and over the Territory included within such Boundaries.

Art. XVI. For the more convenient Management of the general Interests of the United States, Delegates should be annually appointed in such Manner as the Legislature of each Colony shall direct, ~~or such Branches thereof as the Colony shall authorize for that purpose~~, to meet ~~in General Congress~~ at the City of Philadelphia, in the Colony of Pennsylvania, until otherwise ordered by ~~Congress~~ the United States assembled; which Meeting shall be on the first Monday of November in every Year, with a Power reserved to those who appointed the said Delegates, respectively to ~~supercede~~ recal them or any of them at any time within the Year, and to send new Delegates in their stead for the Remainder of the Year. Each Colony shall support its own Delegates in ~~Congress~~ a Meeting of the States, and while they act as Members of the Council of State, herein after mentioned.

Art. XVII. In determining Questions ~~in Congress~~ each Colony shall have one Vote.

Art. XVIII. The United States assembled shall have the sole and exclusive Right and Power of determining on Peace and War, except in the Cases mentioned in the thirteenth Article—Of establishing Rules for deciding in all Cases, what Captures on Land or Water shall be legal—In what Manner Prizes taken by land or naval Forces in the Service of the United States shall be divided or appropriated—Granting Letters of Marque and Reprisal in Times of Peace—Appointing Courts for the Trial of all Crimes, Frauds and Piracies committed on the High Seas, or on any navigable River, not within the Body of a County or Parish—Establishing Courts for receiving and determining finally Appeals in all Cases of Captures—Sending and receiving Ambassadors under any Character—Entering into Treaties and Alliances—Settling all Disputes and Differences now subsisting, or that hereafter may arise between two or more Colonies concerning Boundaries, Jurisdictions, or any other Cause whatever—Coining Money and regulating the Value thereof—Regulating the ~~Indian~~ Trade, and managing all ~~Indian~~ Affairs with the Indians—Limiting the Bounds of those Colonies, which by Charter or Proclamation, or under any Pretence, are said to extend to the South Sea, and ascertaining those Bounds of any other Colony that appear to be indeterminate—Assigning Territories for new Colonies, either in Lands to be thus separated from Colonies and heretofore purchased or obtained by the Crown of Great-Britain from the Indians, or hereafter to be purchased or obtained from them—Disposing of all such Lands for the general Benefit of all the United Colonies—Ascertaining Boundaries to such new Colonies, within which Forms of Government are to be established on the Principles of Liberty—Establishing and regulating Post-Offices throughout all the United Colonies, on the Lines of Communication from one Colony to another—Appointing General Officers of the Land Forces in the Service of the United States—Commissioning such other Officers of the said Forces as shall be appointed by Virtue of the tenth Article—Appointing all the Officers of the Naval Forces in the Service of the United States—Making Rules for the Government and Regulation of the said Land and Naval Forces, and directing the ~~Marches, Cruises and~~ operations ~~of such land and naval Forces~~—Appointing a Council of State, and such Committees and civil Officers as may be necessary for managing the general Affairs of the United States, under their Direction while assembled, and in their Recess, of the Council of State—Appointing one of their number to preside, and a suitable Person for Secretary—And adjourning to any Time within the Year.

The United States assembled shall have Authority for the Defence and Welfare of the United Colonies and every of them, to agree upon and fix the necessary Sums and Expences—To emit Bills, or to borrow Money on the Credit of the United Colonies—To raise Naval Forces—To agree upon the Number of Land Forces to be raised, and to make Requisitions from the Legislature of each Colony, or the Persons therein authorized by the Legislature to execute such Requisitions, for the Quota of each Colony, which is to be in Proportion to the Number of white Inhabitants in that Colony ~~who are not slaves~~, which Requisitions shall be binding, and thereupon the Legislature of each Colony or the Persons authorized as aforesaid, shall appoint the Regimental Officers, ~~and~~ raise the Men, and arm and equip them in a soldier-like Manner; and the Officers and Men so armed and equipped, shall march to the Place appointed, and within the Time agreed on by the United States assembled.

But if the United States assembled shall on Consideration of Circumstances judge proper, that any Colony or Colonies should not raise Men, or should raise a smaller Number than the Quota or Quotas of such Colony or Colonies, and that any other Colony or Colonies should raise a greater number of men than the Quota or Quotas thereof, such extra-numbers shall be raised, officered, armed and equipped in the same Manner as the Quota or Quotas of such Colony or Colonies, unless the Legislature of such Colony or Colonies respectively, shall judge, that such extra-numbers cannot be safely spared out of the same, in which Case they shall raise, officer, arm and equip as many of such extra-numbers as they judge can be safely spared; and the Officers and Men so armed and equip[p]ed shall march to the Place appointed, and within the Time agreed on by the United States assembled.

To establish the same Weights and Measures throughout the United Colonies.

But the United States assembled shall never impose or levy any Taxes or Duties, except in managing the Post-Office, nor interfere in the internal Police of any Colony, any further than such Police may be affected by the Articles of this Confederation. The United States assembled shall never engage the United Colonies in a War, nor grant Letters of Marque and Reprisal in Time of Peace, nor enter into Treaties or Alliances, nor coin Money nor regulate the Value thereof, nor agree upon nor fix the Sums and Expences necessary for the Defence and Welfare of the United Colonies, or any of them, nor emit Bills, nor borrow Money on the Credit of the United Colonies, nor raise Naval Forces, nor agree upon the Number of Land Forces to be raised, unless the Delegates of nine Colonies freely assent to the same: Nor shall a Question on any other Point, except for adjourning, be determined, unless the Delegates of seven Colonies vote in the affirmative.

No Person shall be capable of being a Delegate for more than three Years in any Term of six Years.

No Person holding any Office under the United States, for which he, or another for his Benefit, receives any Salary, Fees, or Emolument of any Kind, shall be capable of being a Delegate.

The Assembly of the United States to publish the Journal of their Proceedings monthly, except such Parts thereof relating to Treaties, Alliances, or military Operations, as in their Judgment require Secrecy—The Yeas and Nays of the Delegates of each Colony on any Question to be entered on the Journal, where it is desired by any Delegate; and the Delegates of a Colony, or any of them, at his or their Request, to be furnished with a Transcript of the said Journal, except such Parts as are above excepted, to lay before the Legislatures of the several Colonies.

ART. XIX. The Council of State shall consist of one Delegate from each C[o]lony, to be named annually by the Delegates of each Colony, and where they cannot agree, by the United States assembled.

~~The Business and Duty of~~ This Council shall have Power to receive and open all Letters directed to the United States, and to return proper Answers; but not to make any Engagements that shall be binding on the United States—To correspond with the Legislature of each Colony, and all Persons acting under the Authority of the United States, or of the said Legislatures—To apply to such Legislatures, or to the Officers in the several Colonies who are entrusted with the executive Powers of Government, for occasional Aid whenever and wherever necessary—To give Counsel to the Commanding Officers, and to direct military Operations by Sea and Land, not changing any Objects or Expeditions determined on by the United States assembled, unless an Alteration of Circumstances which shall come to the Knowledge of the Council after the Recess of the States, shall make such Change absolutely necessary—To attend to the Defence and Preservation of Forts and strong Posts, and to prevent the Enemy from acquiring new Holds—To procure Intelligence of the Condition and Designs of the Enemy—To expedite the Execution of such Measures as may be resolved on by the United States assembled, in Pursuance of the Powers hereby given to them—To draw upon the Treasurers for such Sums as may be appropriated by the United States assembled, and for the Payment of such Contracts as the said Council may make in Pursuance of the Powers hereby given to them—To superintend and controul or suspend all Officers civil and military, acting under the Authority of the United States—In Case of the Death or Removal of any Officer within the Appointment of the United States assembled, to employ a Person to fulfill the Duties of such Office until the Assembly of the States meet—To publish and disperse authentic Accounts of military Operations—To summon an Assembly of the States at an earlier Day than that appointed for their next Meeting, if any great and unexpected Emergency should render it necessary for the Safety or Welfare of the United Colonies or any of them—To prepare Matters for the Consideration of the United States, and to lay before them at their next Meeting all Letters and Advices received by the Council, with a Report of their Proceedings—To appoint a proper Person for their Clerk, who shall take an Oath of Secrecy and Fidelity, before he enters on the Exercise of his Office—Seven Members shall have Power to act—In Case of the Death of any Member, the Council shall immediately apply to his surviving Colleagues to appoint some one of themselves to be a Member thereof till the Meeting of the States, and if only one survives, they shall give him immediate Notice, that he may take his Seat as a Councilor till such Meeting.

ART. XX. Canada acceding to this Confederation, and entirely joining in the Measures of the United Colonies, shall be admitted into and entitled to all the Advantages of this Union: But no other colony shall be admitted into the same, unless such Admission be agreed to by the Delegates of nine Colonies.

These Articles shall be proposed to the Legislatures of all the United Colonies, to be by them considered, and if approved by them, they are advised to authorize their Delegates to ratify the same in the Assembly of the United States, which being done, the ~~foregoing~~ Articles of this Confederation shall inviolably be observed by every Colony, and the Union is to be perpetual: Nor shall any Alteration be at any Time hereafter made in these Articles or any of them, unless such Alteration be agreed to in an Assembly of the United States, and be afterwards confirmed by the Legislatures of every Colony.

Journals of the Continental Congress, 1774–1789, ed. Worthington C. Ford (Washington, 1906), V, 546–54.

APPENDIX C

The Articles of Confederation

To all to whom these Presents shall come, we the under signed Delegates of the States affixed to our Names, send greeting.

Whereas the Delegates of the United States of America, in Congress assembled, did, on the 15th day of November, in the Year of Our Lord One thousand Seven Hundred and Seventy seven, and in the Second Year of the Independence of America, agree to certain articles of Confederation and perpetual Union between the States of Newhampshire, Massachusetts-bay, Rhode-island and Providence Plantations, Connecticut, New York, New Jersey, Pennsylvania, Delaware, Maryland, Virginia, North-Carolina, South-Carolina, and Georgia in the words following, viz. "Articles of Confederation and perpetual Union between the states of Newhampshire, Massachusetts-bay, Rhode-island and Providence Plantations, Connecticut, New-York, New-Jersey, Pennsylvania, Delaware, Maryland, Virginia, North-Carolina, South-Carolina and Georgia.

ARTICLE I. The Stile of this confederacy shall be "The United States of America."

ARTICLE II. Each state retains its sovereignty, freedom, and independence, and every Power, Jurisdiction and right, which is not by this confederation expressly delegated to the United States, in Congress assembled.

ARTICLE III. The said states hereby severally enter into a firm league of friendship with each other, for their common defence, the security of their Liberties, and their mutual and general welfare, binding themselves to assist each other, against all force offered to, or attacks made upon them, or any of them, on account of religion, sovereignty, trade, or any other pretence whatever.

ARTICLE IV. The better to secure and perpetuate mutual friendship and intercourse among the people of the different states in this union, the free inhabitants of each of these states, paupers, vagabonds and fugitives from justice excepted, shall be entitled to all privileges and immunities of free citizens in the several states; and the people of each state shall have free ingress and regress to and from any other state, and shall enjoy therein all the privileges of trade and commerce, subject to the same duties, impositions and restrictions as the inhabitants thereof respectively, provided that such restriction shall not extend so far as to prevent the removal of property imported into any state, to any other state, of which the Owner is an inhabitant; provided also that no imposition, duties or restriction shall be laid by any state, on the property of the united states, or either of them.

If any Person guilty of, or charged with treason, felony, or other high misdemeanor in any state, shall flee from Justice, and be found in any of the united states, he shall, upon demand of the Governor or executive power, of the state

473

from which he fled, be delivered up and removed to the state having jurisdiction of his offence.

Full faith and credit shall be given in each of these states to the records, acts and judicial proceedings of the courts and magistrates of every other state.

ARTICLE V. For the more convenient management of the general interests of the united states, delegates shall be annually appointed in such manner as the legislature of each state shall direct, to meet in Congress on the first Monday in November, in every year, with a power reserved to each state, to recal its delegates, or any of them, at any time within the year, and to send others in their stead, for the remainder of the Year.

No state shall be represented in Congress by less than two, nor by more than seven Members; and no person shall be capable of being a delegate for more than three years in any term of six years; nor shall any person, being a delegate, be capable of holding any office under the united states, for which he, or another for his benefit receives any salary, fees or emolument of any kind.

Each state shall maintain its own delegates in a meeting of the states, and while they act as members of the committee of the states.

In determining questions in the united states in Congress assembled, each state shall have one vote.

Freedom of speech and debate in Congress shall not be impeached or questioned in any Court, or place out of Congress, and the members of congress shall be protected in their persons from arrests and imprisonments, during the time of their going to and from, and attendance on congress, except for treason, felony, or breach of the peace.

ARTICLE VI. No state, without the Consent of the united states in congress assembled, shall send any embassy to, or receive any embassy from, or enter into any conference, agreement, alliance or treaty with any King prince or state; nor shall any person holding any office or profit or trust under the united states, or any of them, accept of any present, emolument, office or title of any kind whatever from any king, prince or foreign state; nor shall the united states in congress assembled, or any of them, grant any title of nobility.

No two or more states shall enter into any treaty, confederation or alliance whatever between them, without the consent of the united states in congress assembled, specifying accurately the purposes for which the same is to be entered into, and how long it shall continue.

No state shall lay any imposts or duties, which may interfere with any stipulations in treaties, entered into by the united states in congress assembled, with any king, prince or state, in pursuance of any treaties already proposed by congress, to the courts of France and Spain.

No vessels of war shall be kept up in time of peace by any state, except such number only, as shall be deemed necessary by the united states in congress assembled, for the defence of such state, or its trade; nor shall any body of forces be kept up by any state, in time of peace, except such number only, as in the judgment of the united states, in congress assembled, shall be deemed requisite to garrison the forts necessary for the defence of such state; but every state shall always keep up a well regulated and disciplined militia, sufficiently armed and accoutred, and shall provide and constantly have ready for use, in public stores, a due number of field pieces and tents, and a proper quantity of arms, ammunition and camp equipage.

No state shall engage in any war without the consent of the united states in congress assembled, unless such state be actually invaded by enemies, or shall have received certain advice of a resolution being formed by some nation of

Indians to invade such state, and the danger is so imminent as not to admit of a delay till the united states in congress assembled can be consulted: nor shall any state grant commissions to any ships or vessels of war, nor letters of marque or reprisal, except it be after a declaration of war by the united states in congress assembled, and then only against the kingdom or state and the subjects thereof, against which war has been so declared, and under such regulations as shall be established by the united states in congress assembled, unless such state be infested by pirates, in which case vessels of war may be fitted out for that occasion, and kept so long as the danger shall continue, or until the united states in congress assembled, shall determine otherwise.

ARTICLE VII. When land-forces are raised by any state for the common defence, all officers of or under the rank of colonel, shall be appointed by the legislature of each state respectively, by whom such forces shall be raised, or in such manner as such state shall direct, and all vacancies shall be filled up by the state which first made the appointment.

ARTICLE VIII. All charges of war, and all other expences that shall be incurred for the common defence or general welfare, and allowed by the united states in congress assembled, shall be defrayed out of a common treasury, which shall be supplied by the several states in proportion to the value of all land within each state, granted to or surveyed for any PERSON, as such land and the buildings and improvements thereon shall be estimated according to such mode as the united states in congress assembled, shall from time to time direct and appoint.

The taxes for paying that proportion shall be laid and levied by the authority and direction of the legislatures of the several states within the time agreed upon by the united states in congress assembled.

ARTICLE IX. The united states in congress assembled, shall have the sole and exclusive right and power of determining on peace and war, except in the cases mentioned in the sixth article—of sending and receiving ambassadors—entering into treaties and alliances, provided that no treaty of commerce shall be made whereby the legislative power of the respective states shall be restrained from imposing such imposts and duties on foreigners as their own people are subjected to, or from prohibiting the exportation or importation of any species of goods or commodities, whatsoever—of establishing rules for deciding in all cases, what captures on land or water shall be legal, and in what manner prizes taken by land or naval forces in the service of the united states shall be divided or appropriated—of granting letters of marque and reprisal in times of peace—appointing courts for the trial of piracies and felonies committed on the high seas and establishing courts for receiving and determining finally appeals in all cases of captures, provided that no member of congress shall be appointed a judge of any of the said courts.

The united states in congress assembled shall also be the last resort on appeal in all disputes and differences now subsisting or that hereafter may arise between two or more states concerning boundary, jurisdiction or any other cause whatever; which authority shall always be exercised in the manner following. Whenever the legislative or executive authority or lawful agent of any state in controversy with another shall present a petition to congress stating the matter in question and praying for a hearing, notice thereof shall be given by order of congress to the legislative or executive authority of the other state in controversy, and a day assigned for the appearance of the parties by their lawful agents, who shall then be directed to appoint by joint consent, commissioners or judges to constitute a court for hearing and determining the matter in question: but if they cannot agree, congress shall name three persons out of each of the united states, and from the list of such persons each party shall alternately strike out one, the petitioners beginning, until the number shall be reduced to thirteen; and from that number not less than seven, nor more than nine names as congress shall direct, shall in the presence of congress be drawn out by lot, and the persons whose names shall be so drawn or any five of them, shall be commissioners or judges, to hear and finally determine the controversy, so always as a major part of the judges who shall hear the cause shall agree in the determination: and if either party shall neglect to attend at the day appointed, without showing reasons, which congress shall judge sufficient, or being present shall refuse to strike, the congress shall proceed to nominate three persons out of each state, and the secretary of congress shall strike in behalf of such party absent or refusing; and the judgment and sentence of the court to be appointed, in the manner before prescribed, shall be final and conclusive; and if any of the parties shall refuse to submit to the authority of such court, or to appear or defend their claim or cause, the court shall nevertheless proceed to pronounce sentence, or judgment which shall in like manner be final and decisive, the judgment or sentence and other proceedings being in either case transmitted to congress, and lodged among the acts of congress for the security of the parties concerned: provided that every commissioner, before he sits in judgment, shall take an oath to be administered by one of the judges of the supreme or superior court of the state, where the cause shall be tried, "well and truly to hear and determine the matter in question, according to the best of his judgment, without favour, affection or hope of reward:" provided also, that no state shall be deprived of territory for the benefit of the united states.

All controversies concerning the private right of soil claimed under different grants of two or more states, whose jurisdictions as they may respect such lands, and the states which passed such grants are adjusted, the said grants or either of them being at the same time claimed to have originated antecedent to such settlement of jurisdiction, shall on the petition of either party to the congress of the united states, be finally determined as near as may be in the same manner as is before prescribed for deciding disputes respecting territorial jurisdiction between different states.

The united states in congress assembled shall also have the sole and exclusive right and power of regulating the alloy and value of coin struck by their own authority, or by that of the respective states—fixing the standard of weights and measures throughout the united states—regulating the trade and managing all affairs with the Indians, not members of any of the states, provided that the legislative right of any state within its own limits be not infringed or violated—establishing or regulating post-offices from one state to another, throughout all the united states, and exacting such postage on the papers passing thro' the same as may be requisite to defray the expences of the said office—appointing all officers of the land forces, in the service of the united states, excepting regimental officers—appointing all the officers of the naval forces, and commissioning all officers whatever in the service of the united states—making rules for the government and regulation of the said land and naval forces, and directing their operation.

The united states in congress assembled shall have authority to appoint a committee, to sit in the recess of congress, to be denominated "A Committee of the States," and to consist of one delegate from each state; and to appoint such other committees and civil officers as may be necessary for managing the general affairs of the united states under their direction—to appoint one of their number to preside, provided that no person be allowed to serve in the office of president more than one year in any term of three years; to ascertain the necessary sums of money to be raised for the service of the united states, and to appropriate and apply the same for defraying the public expences—to borrow money, or emit bills on the credit of the united states, transmitting every half year to the respective states an account of the sums of money so borrowed or emitted,—to build and equip a navy—to agree upon the number of land forces, and to make requisitions from each state for its quota, in proportion to the number of white inhabitants in such state; which requisition shall be binding, and thereupon the legislature of each state shall appoint the regimental officers, raise the men and cloath, arm and equip them in a soldier like manner, at the expence of the united states; and the officers and men so cloathed, armed and equipped shall march to the place appointed, and within the time agreed on by the united states in congress assembled: But if the united states in congress assembled shall, on consideration of circumstances judge proper that any state should not raise men, or should raise a smaller number than its quota, and that any other state should raise a greater number of men than the quota thereof, such extra number shall be raised, officered, cloathed, armed and equipped in the same manner as the quota of such state, unless the legislature of such state shall judge that such extra number cannot be safely spared out of the same, in which case they shall raise officer, cloath, arm and equip as many of such extra number as they judge can be safely spared. And the officers and men so cloathed, armed and equipped, shall march to the place appointed, and within the time agreed on by the united states in congress assembled.

The united states in congress assembled shall never engage in a war, nor grant letters of marque and reprisal in time of peace, nor enter into any treaties or alliances, nor coin money, nor regulate the value thereof, nor ascertain the sums and expences necessary for the defence and welfare of the united states, or any of them, nor emit bills, nor borrow money on the credit of the united states, nor appropriate money, nor agree upon the number of vessels of war, to be built or purchased, or the number of land or sea forces to be raised, nor appoint a commander in chief of the army or navy, unless nine states assent to the same: nor shall a question on any other point, except for adjourning from day to day be determined, unless by the votes of a majority of the united states in congress assembled.

The congress of the united states shall have power to adjourn to any time within the year, and to any place within the united states, so that no period of adjournment be for a longer duration than the space of six Months, and shall publish the Journal of their proceedings monthly, except such parts thereof relating to treaties, alliances or military operations, as in their judgment require secrecy; and the yeas and nays of the delegates of each state on any question shall be entered on the Journal, when it is desired by any delegate; and the delegates of a state, or any of them, at his or their request shall be furnished with a transcript of the said Journal, except such parts as are above excepted, to lay before the legislatures of the several states.

ARTICLE X. The committee of the states, or any nine of them, shall be authorized to execute, in the recess of congress, such of the powers of congress as the united states in congress assembled, by the consent of nine states, shall from time to time think expedient to vest them with; provided that no power be delegated to the said committee, for the exercise of which, by the articles of confederation, the voice of nine states in the congress of the united states assembled is requisite.

Article XI. Canada acceding to this confederation, and joining in the measures of the united states, shall be admitted into, and entitled to all the advantages of this union: but no other colony shall be admitted into the same, unless such admission be agreed to by nine states.

Article XII. All bills of credit emitted, monies borrowed and debts contracted by, or under the authority of congress, before the assembling of the united states, in pursuance of the present confederation, shall be deemed and considered as a charge against the united states, for payment and satisfaction whereof the said united states, and the public faith are hereby solemnly pledged.

Article XIII. Every state shall abide by the determinations of the united states in congress assembled, on all questions which by this confederation are submitted to them. And the Articles of this confederation shall be inviolably observed by every state, and the union shall be perpetual; nor shall any alteration at any time hereafter be made in any of them; unless such alteration be agreed to in a congress of the united states, and be afterwards confirmed by the legislatures of every state.

And Whereas it hath pleased the Great Governor of the World to incline the hearts of the legislatures we respectively represent in congress, to approve of, and to authorize us to ratify the said articles of confederation and perpetual union. Know Ye that we the undersigned delegates, by virtue of the power and authority to us given for that purpose, do by these presents, in the name and in behalf of our respective constituents, fully and entirely ratify and confirm each and every of the said articles of confederation and perpetual union, and all and singular the matters and things therein contained: And we do further solemnly plight and engage the faith of our respective constituents, that they shall abide by the determinations of the united states in congress assembled, on all questions, which by the said confederation are submitted to them. And that the articles thereof shall be inviolably observed by the states we respectively represent, and that the union shall be perpetual. In Witness whereof we have hereunto set our hands in Congress. Done at Philadelphia in the state of Pennsylvania the ninth day of July, in the Year of our Lord one Thousand seven Hundred and Seventy-eight, and in the third year of the independence of America.

Josiah Bartlett, John Wentworth, Junr August 8th, 1778,	On the part & behalf of the State of New Hampshire.
John Hancock, Samuel Adams, Elbridge Gerry, Francis Dana, James Lovell, Samuel Holten,	On the part and behalf of the State of Massachusetts Bay.
William Ellery, Henry Marchant, John Collins,	On the part and behalf of the State of Rhode-Island and Providence Plantations.

ROGER SHERMAN,
SAMUEL HUNTINGTON,
OLIVER WOLCOTT,
TITUS HOSMER,
ANDREW ADAMS,

} On the part and behalf of the State of Connecticut.

JAS DUANE,
FRA: LEWIS,
WM DUER,
GOUVR MORRIS,

} On the part and behalf of the State of New York.

JNO WITHERSPOON,
NATHL SCUDDER,

} On the Part and in Behalf of the State of New Jersey, November 26th, 1778.

ROBERT MORRIS,
DANIEL ROBERDEAU,
JON. BAYARD SMITH,
WILLIAM CLINGAR,
JOSEPH REED,
  22d July, 1778,

} On the part and behalf of the State of Pennsylvania.

THOS MCKEAN,
  FEBY 22d, 1779,
JOHN DICKINSON,
  May 5th, 1779,
NICHOLAS VAN DYKE,

} On the part & behalf of the State of Delaware.

JOHN HANSON,
  March 1, 1781,
DANIEL CARROLL, do

} On the part and behalf of the State of Maryland.

RICHARD HENRY LEE,
JOHN BANISTER,
THOMAS ADAMS,
JNO HARVIE,
FRANCIS LIGHTFOOT LEE,

} On the Part and Behalf of the State of Virginia.

JOHN PENN,
  July 21st, 1778,
CORNS HARNETT,
JNO WILLIAMS,

} On the part and behalf of the State of North Carolina.

HENRY LAURENS,
WILLIAM HENRY DRAYTON,
JNO MATHEWS,
RICHD HUTSON,
THOS HEYWARD, JUNR.

} On the part and on behalf of the State of South Carolina.

JNO WALTON,
  24th July, 1778,
EDWD TELFAIR,
EDWD LANGWORTHY,

} On the part and behalf of the State of Georgia.

APPENDIX D

The Constitution of the United States

We the People of the United States, in Order to form a more perfect Union, establish Justice, insure domestic Tranquility, provide for the common defence, promote the general Welfare, and secure the Blessings of Liberty to ourselves and our Posterity, do ordain and establish this Constitution for the United States of America.

ARTICLE. I.

SECTION. 1. All legislative Powers herein granted shall be vested in a Congress of the United States, which shall consist of a Senate and a House of Representatives.

SECTION. 2. The House of Representatives shall be composed of Members chosen every second Year by the People of the several States, and the Electors in each State shall have ∧ Qualifications requisite for Electors of the most numerous Branch of the State Legislature.

No person shall be a Representative who shall not have attained to the Age of twenty five Years, and been seven Years a Citizen of the United States, and who shall not, when elected, be an Inhabitant of that State in which he shall be chosen.

Representatives and direct Taxes shall be apportioned among the several States which may be included within this Union, according to their respective Numbers, which shall be determined by adding to the whole Number of free Persons, including those bound to Service for a Term of Years, and excluding Indians not taxed, three fifths of all other Persons. The actual Enumeration shall be made within three Years after the first Meeting of the Congress of the United States, and within every subsequent Term of ten Years, in such Manner as they shall by Law direct. The Number of Representatives shall not exceed one for every thirty Thousand, but each State shall have at Least one Representative; and until such enumeration shall be made, the State of New Hampshire shall be entitled to chuse three, Massachusetts eight, Rhode-Island and Providence Plantations one, Connecticut five, New-York six, New Jersey four, Pennsylvania eight, Delaware one, Maryland six, Virginia ten, North Carolina five, South Carolina five, and Georgia three.

When vacancies happen in the Representation from any State, the Executive Authority thereof shall issue Writs of Election to fill such Vacancies.

The House of Representatives shall chuse their Speaker and other Officers; and shall have the sole Power of Impeachment.

SECTION. 3. The Senate of the United States shall be composed of two Senators from each State, chosen by the Legislature thereof, for six Years; and each Senator shall have one Vote.

Immediately after they shall be assembled in Consequence of the first Election, they shall be divided as equally as may be into three Classes. The Seats of the Senators of the first Class shall be vacated at the Expiration of the second Year, of the second Class at the Expiration of the fourth Year, and of the third Class at the Expiration of the sixth Year, so that one third may be chosen every second Year; and if Vacancies happen by Resignation, or otherwise, during the Recess of the Legislature of any State, the Executive thereof may make temporary Appointments until the next Meeting of the Legislature, which shall then fill such Vacancies.

No Person shall be a Senator who shall not have attained to the Age of thirty Years, and been nine Years a Citizen of the United States, and who shall not, when elected, be an Inhabitant of that State for which he shall be chosen.

The Vice President of the United States shall be President of the Senate, but shall have no Vote, unless they be equally divided.

The Senate shall chuse their other Officers, and also a President pro tempore, in the Absence of the Vice President, or when he shall exercise the Office of President of the United States.

The Senate shall have the sole Power to try all Impeachments. When sitting for that Purpose, they shall be on Oath or Affirmation. When the President
                                is tried,
of the United States ∧ the Chief Justice shall preside: And no Person shall be convicted without the Concurrence of two thirds of the Members present.

Judgment in Cases of Impeachment shall not extend further than to removal from Office, and disqualification to hold and enjoy any Office of honor, Trust or Profit under the United States: but the Party convicted shall nevertheless be liable and subject to Indictment, Trial, Judgment and Punishment, according to Law.

SECTION. 4. The Times, Places and Manner of holding Elections for Senators and Representatives, shall be prescribed in each State by the Legislature thereof; but the Congress may at any time by Law make or alter such Regulations, except as to the Places of chusing Senators.

The Congress shall assemble at least once in every Year, and such Meeting shall be on the first Monday in December, unless they shall by Law appoint a different Day.

SECTION 5. Each House shall be the Judge of Elections, Returns and Qualifications of its own Members, and a Majority of each shall constitute a Quorum to do Business; but a smaller Number may adjourn from day to day, and may be authorized to compel the Attendance of Absent Members, in such Manner, and under such Penalties as each House may provide.

Each House may determine the Rules of its Proceedings, punish its Members for disorderly Behaviour, and, with the Concurrence of two thirds, expel a Member.

Each House shall keep a Journal of its Proceedings, and from time to time publish the same, excepting such Parts as may in their Judgment require Secrecy; and the Yeas and Nays of the Members of either House on any question shall, at the Desire of one fifth of those Present, be entered on the Journal.

Neither House, during the Session of Congress, shall, without the Consent of the other, adjourn for more than three days, nor to any other Place than that in which the two Houses shall be sitting.

SECTION. 6. The Senators and Representatives shall receive a Compensation for their Services, to be ascertained by Law, and paid out of the Treasury of the United States. They shall in all Cases, except Treason, Felony and Breach of the Peace, be privileged from Arrest during their Attendance at the Session of their respective Houses, and in going to and returning from the same; and for any Speech or Debate in either House, they shall not be questioned in any other Place.

No Senator or Representative shall, during the Time for which he was elected, be appointed to any civil Office under the Authority of the United States, which shall have been created, or the Emoluments whereof shall have been encreased during such time; and no Person holding any Office under the United States, shall be a Member of either House during his Continuance in Office.

SECTION. 7. All Bills for raising Revenue shall originate in the House of Representatives; but the Senate may propose or concur with Amendments as on other Bills.

Every Bill which shall have passed the House of Representatives and the Senate, shall, before it become a Law, be presented to the President of the United States; If he approve he shall sign it, but if not he shall return it, with his Objections to that House in which it shall have originated, who shall enter the Objections at large on their Journal, and proceed to reconsider it. If after such Reconsideration two thirds of that House shall agree to pass the Bill, it shall be sent, together with the Objections, to the other House, by which it shall likewise be reconsidered, and if approved by two thirds of that House, it shall become a Law. But in all such Cases the Votes of both Houses shall be determined by yeas and Nays, and the Names of the Persons voting for and against the Bill shall be entered on the Journal of each House respectively. If any Bill shall not be returned by the President within ten days (Sundays excepted) after it shall have been presented to him, the Same shall be a Law, in like Manner as if he had signed it, unless the Congress by their Adjournment prevent its Return in which Case it shall not be a Law.

Every Order, Resolution, or Vote to which the Concurrence of the Senate and House of Representatives may be necessary (except on a question of Adjournment) shall be presented to the President of the United States; and before the Same shall take Effect, shall be approved by him, or being dis-approved by him, shall be repassed by two thirds of the Senate and House of Representatives, according to the Rules and Limitations prescribed in the Case of a Bill.

SECTION. 8. The Congress shall have Power To lay and collect Taxes, Duties, Imposts and Excises, to pay the Debts and provide for the common Defence and general Welfare of the United States; but all Duties, Imposts and Excises shall be uniform throughout the United States;

To borrow Money on the credit of the United States;

To regulate Commerce with foreign Nations, and among the several States, and with the Indian Tribes;

To establish an uniform Rule of Naturalization, and uniform Laws on the subject of Bankruptcies throughout the United States;

To coin Money, regulate the Value thereof, and of foreign Coin, and fix the Standard of Weights and Measures;

To provide for the Punishment of counterfeiting the Securities and current Coin of the United States;

To establish Post Offices and post Roads;

To promote the Progress of Science and useful Arts, by securing for limited Times to Authors and Inventors the exclusive Right to their respective Writings and Discoveries;

To constitute Tribunals inferior to the supreme Court;

To define and punish Piracies and Felonies committed on the high Seas, and Offences against the Law of Nations;

To declare War, grant Letters of Marque and Reprisal, and make Rules concerning Captures on Land and Water;

To raise and support Armies, but no Appropriation of Money to that Use shall be for a longer Term than two Years;

To provide and maintain a Navy;

To make Rules for the Government and Regulation of the land and naval Forces;

To provide for calling forth the Militia to execute the Laws of the Union, suppress Insurrections and repel Invasions;

To provide for organizing, arming, and disciplining, the Militia, and for governing such Part of them as may be employed in the Service of the United States, reserving to the States respectively, the Appointment of the Officers, and the Authority of training the Militia according to the discipline prescribed by Congress;

To exercise exclusive Legislation in all Cases whatsoever, over such District (not exceeding ten Miles square) as may, by Cession of particular States, and the Acceptance of Congress, become the Seat of the Government of the United States, and to exercise like Authority over all Places purchased by the Consent of the Legislature of the State in which the Same shall be, for the Erection of Forts, Magazines, Arsenals, dock-Yards, and other needful Buildings;—And

To make all Laws which shall be necessary and proper for carrying into Execution the foregoing Powers, and all other Powers vested by this Constitution in the Government of the United States, or in any Department or Officer thereof.

SECTION. 9. The Migration or Importation of such Persons as any of the States now existing shall think proper to admit, shall not be prohibited by the Congress prior to the Year one thousand eight hundred and eight, but a Tax or duty may be imposed on such Importation, not exceeding ten dollars for each Person.

The Privilege of the Writ of Habeas Corpus shall not be suspended, unless when in Cases of Rebellion or Invasion the public Safety may require it.

No Bill of Attainder or ex post facto Law shall be passed.

No Capitation, or other direct, Tax shall be laid, unless in Proportion to the Census or Enumeration herein before directed to be taken.

No Tax or Duty shall be laid on Articles exported from any State.

No Preference shall be given by any Regulation of Commerce or Revenue to the Ports of one State over those of another: nor shall Vessels bound to, or from, one State, be obliged to enter, clear, or pay Duties in another.

No Money shall be drawn from the Treasury, but in Consequence of Appropriations made by Law; and a regular Statement and Account of the Receipts and Expenditures of all public Money shall be published from time to time.

No Title of Nobility shall be granted by the United States: And no Person holding any Office of Profit or Trust under them, shall, without the Consent of the Congress, accept of any present, Emolument, Office, or Title, of any kind whatever, from any King, Prince, or foreign State.

Section. 10. No State shall enter into any Treaty, Alliance, or Confederation; grant Letters of Marque and Reprisal; coin Money; emit Bills of Credit; make any Thing but gold and silver Coin a Tender in Payment of Debts; pass any Bill of Attainder, ex post facto Law, or Law impairing the Obligation of Contracts, or grant any Title of Nobility.

No State shall, without the Consent of ^the^ Congress, lay any Imposts or Duties on Imports or Exports, except what may be absolutely necessary for executing it's inspection Laws: and the net Produce of all Duties and Imposts, laid by any State on Imports or Exports, shall be for the Use of the Treasury of the United States; and all such Laws shall be subject to the Revision and Controul of ^the^ Congress.

No State shall, without the Consent of Congress, lay any Duty of Tonnage, keep Troops, or Ships of War in time of Peace, enter into any Agreement or Compact with another State, or with a foreign Power, or engage in War, unless actually invaded, or in such imminent Danger as will not admit of delay.

Article. II.

Section. 1. The executive Power shall be vested in a President of the United States of America. He shall hold his Office during the Term of four Years, and, together with the Vice President, chosen for the same Term, be elected as follows

Each State shall appoint, in such Manner as the Legislature thereof may direct, a Number of Electors, equal to the whole Number of Senators and Representatives to which the State may be entitled in the Congress: but no Senator or Representative, or Person holding an Office of Trust or Profit under the United States, shall be appointed an Elector.

The Electors shall meet in their respective States, and vote by Ballot for two Persons, of whom one at least shall not be an Inhabitant of the same State with themselves. And they shall make a List of all the Persons voted for, and of the Number of Votes for each; which List they shall sign and certify, and transmit sealed to the Seat of the Government of the United States, directed to the President of the Senate. The President of the Senate shall, in the Presence of the Senate and House of Representatives, open all the Certificates, and the Votes shall then be counted. The Person having the greatest Number of Votes shall be the President, if such Number be a Majority of the whole Number of Electors appointed; and if there be more than one who have such Majority, and have an equal Number of Votes, then the House of Representatives shall immediately chuse by Ballot one of them for President; and if no Person have a Majority, then from the five highest on the List the said House shall in like Manner chuse the President. But in chusing the President, the Votes shall be taken by States, the Representation from each State having one Vote; A quorum for this Purpose shall consist of a Member or Members from two thirds of the States, and a Majority of all the States shall be necessary to a Choice. In every Case, after the Choice of the President, the Person having the greatest Number of Votes of the Electors shall be the Vice President. But if there should remain two or more who have equal Votes, the Senate shall chuse from them by Ballot the Vice President.

The Congress may determine the Time of chusing the Electors, and the Day on which they shall give their Votes; which Day shall be the same throughout the United States.

No Person except a natural born Citizen, or a Citizen of the United States, at the time of the Adoption of this Constitution, shall be eligible to the Office of President; neither shall any Person be eligible to that Office who shall not have attained to the Age of thirty five Years, and been fourteen Years a Resident within the United States.

In Case of the Removal of the President from Office, or of his Death, Resignation, or Inability to discharge the Powers and Duties of the said Office, the Same shall devolve on the Vice President, and the Congress may by Law provide for the Case of Removal, Death, Resignation or Inability, both of the President and Vice President, declaring what Officer shall then act as President, and such Officer shall then act accordingly, until the Disability be removed, or a President shall be elected.

The President shall, at stated Times, receive for his Services, a Compensation, which shall neither be encreased nor diminished during the Period for which he shall have been elected, and he shall not receive within that Period any other Emolument from the United States, or any of them.

Before he enter on the Execution of his Office, he shall take the following Oath or Affirmation:—"I do solemnly swear (or affirm) that I will faithfully execute the Office of President of the United States, and will to the best of my Ability, preserve, protect and defend the Constitution of the United States."

SECTION. 2. The President shall be Commander in Chief of the Army and Navy of the United States, and of the Militia of the several States, when called into the actual Service of the United States; he may require the Opinion, in writing, of the principal Officer in each of the executive Departments, upon any Subject relating to the Duties of their respective Offices, and he shall have Power to grant Reprieves and Pardons for Offences against the United States, except in Cases of Impeachment.

He shall have Power, by and with the Advice and Consent of the Senate, to make Treaties, provided two thirds of the Senators present concur; and he shall nominate, and by and with the Advice and Consent of the Senate, shall appoint Ambassadors, other public Ministers and Consuls, Judges of the supreme Court, and all other Officers of the United States, whose Appointments are not herein otherwise provided for, and which shall be established by Law: but the Congress may by Law vest the Appointment of such inferior Officers, as they think proper, in the President alone, in the Courts of Law, or in the Heads of Departments.

The President shall have Power to fill up all Vacancies that may happen during the Recess of the Senate, by granting Commissions which shall expire at the End of their next Session.

SECTION. 3. He shall from time to time give to the Congress Information of the State of the Union, and recommend to their Consideration such Measures as he shall judge necessary and expedient; he may, on extraordinary Occasions, convene both Houses, or either of them, and in Case of Disagreement between them, with Respect to the Time of Adjournment, he may adjourn them to such Time as he shall think proper; he shall receive Ambassadors and other public Ministers; he shall take Care that the Laws be faithfully executed, and shall Commission all the Officers of the United States.

SECTION. 4. The President, Vice President and all civil Officers of the United

States, shall be removed from Office on Impeachment for, and Conviction of, Treason, Bribery, or other high Crimes and Misdemeanors.

ARTICLE. III.

SECTION. 1. The judicial Power of the United States, shall be vested in one supreme Court, and in such inferior Courts as the Congress may from time to time ordain and establish. The Judges, both of the supreme and inferior Courts, shall hold their Offices during good Behaviour, and shall, at stated Times, receive for their Services, a Compensation, which shall not be diminished during their Continuance in Office.

SECTION. 2. The judicial Power shall extend to all Cases, in Law and Equity, arising under this Constitution, the Laws of the United States, and Treaties made, or which shall be made, under their Authority;—to all Cases affecting Ambassadors, other public Ministers and Consuls;—to all Cases of admiralty and maritime Jurisdiction;—to Controversies to which the United States shall be a Party;—to Controversies between two or more States;—between a State and Citizens of another State;—between Citizens of different States,—between Citizens of the same State claiming Lands under Grants of different States, and between a State, or the Citizens thereof, and foreign States, Citizens or Subjects.

In all cases affecting Ambassadors, other public Ministers and Consuls, and those in which a State shall be a Party, the supreme Court shall have original Jurisdiction. In all the other Cases before mentioned, the Supreme Court shall have appellate Jurisdiction, both as to Law and Fact, with such Exceptions, and under such Regulations as the Congress shall make.

The Trial of all Crimes, except in Cases of Impeachment, shall be by Jury; and such Trial shall be held in the State where the said Crimes shall have been committed; but when not committed within any State, the Trial shall be at such Place or Places as the Congress may by Law have directed.

SECTION. 3. Treason against the United States, shall consist only in levying War against them, or in adhering to their Enemies, giving them Aid and Comfort. No Person shall be convicted of Treason unless on the Testimony of two Witnesses to the same overt Act, or on Confession in open Court.

The Congress shall have Power to declare the Punishment of Treason, but no Attainder of Treason shall work Corruption of Blood, or Forfeiture except during the Life of the Person attainted.

ARTICLE. IV.

SECTION. 1. Full Faith and Credit shall be given in each State to the public Acts, Records, and judicial Proceedings of every other State. And the Congress may by general Laws prescribe the Manner in which such Acts, Records and Proceedings shall be proved, and the Effect thereof.

SECTION. 2. The Citizens of each State shall be entitled to all Privileges and Immunities of Citizens in the several States.

A Person charged in any State with Treason, Felony, or other Crime, who shall flee from Justice, and be found in another State, shall on Demand of the executive Authority of the State from which he fled, be delivered up, to be removed to the State having Jurisdiction of the Crime.

No Person held to Service or Labour in one State, under the Laws thereof, escaping into another, shall, in Consequence of any Law or Regulation therein, be discharged from such Service or Labour, but shall be delivered up on Claim of the Party to whom such Service or Labour may be due.

SECTION. 3. New States may be admitted by the Congress into this Union; but no new State shall be formed or erected within the Jurisdiction of any other State; nor any State be formed by the Junction of two or more States, or Parts of States, without the Consent of the Legislatures of the States concerned as well as of the Congress.

The Congress shall have Power to dispose of and make all needful Rules and Regulations respecting the Territory or other Property belonging to the United States; and nothing in this Constitution shall be so construed as to Prejudice any Claims of the United States, or of any particular State.

SECTION. 4. The United States shall guarantee to every State in this Union a Republican Form of Government, and shall protect each of them against Invasion; and on Application of the Legislature, or of the Executive (when the Legislature cannot be convened) against domestic Violence.

ARTICLE. V.

The Congress, whenever two thirds of both Houses shall deem it necessary, shall propose Amendments to this Constitution, or, on the Application of the Legislatures of two thirds of the several States, shall call a Convention for proposing Amendments, which, in either Case, shall be valid to all Intents and Purposes, as Part of this Constitution, when ratified by the Legislatures of three fourths of the several States, or by Conventions in three fourths thereof, as the one or the other Mode of Ratification may be proposed by the Congress; Provided that no Amendment which may be made prior to the Year One thousand eight hundred and eight shall in any Manner affect the first and fourth Clauses in the Ninth Section of the first Article; and that no State, without its Consent, shall be deprived of it's equal Suffrage in the Senate.

ARTICLE. VI.

All Debts contracted and Engagements entered into, before the Adoption of this Constitution, shall be as valid against the United States under this Constitution, as under the Confederation.

This Constitution, and the Laws of the United States which shall be made in Pursuance thereof; and all Treaties made, or which shall be made, under the Authority of the United States, shall be the supreme Law of the Land; and the Judges in every State shall be bound thereby, any Thing in the Constitution or Laws of any State to the Contrary notwithstanding.

The Senators and Representatives before mentioned, and the Members of the several State Legislatures, and all executive and judicial Officers, both of the United States and of the several States, shall be bound by Oath or Affirmation, to support this Constitution; but no religious Test shall ever be required as a Qualification to any Office or public Trust under the United States.

ARTICLE. VII.

The Ratification of the Conventions of nine States, shall be sufficient for the Establishment of this Constitution between the States so ratifying the Same.

The Word, "the," being interlined between the seventh and eighth Lines of the first Page, The Word "Thirty" being partly written on an Erazure in the fif- done in Convention by the Unanimous Consent of the States present the Seventeenth Day of September in the Year of our Lord one thousand seven hundred and teenth Line of the first Page, The Words "is tried" being interlined between the thirty second and thirty third Lines of the First Page and the Word "the" being interlined between the forty third and forty fourth Lines of the second Page.

Attest WILLIAM JACKSON Secretary

Eighty seven and of the Independence of the United States of America the Twelfth In witness whereof We have hereunto subscribed our Names,

G⁰ WASHINGTON—Presid^t
and deputy from Virginia

New Hampshire	{	JOHN LANGDON NICHOLAS GILMAN
Massachusetts	{	NATHANIEL GORHAM RUFUS KING
Connecticut	{	W^M SAM^L JOHNSON ROGER SHERMAN
New York		ALEXANDER HAMILTON
New Jersey	{	WIL: LIVINGSTON DAVID BREARLEY W^M PATERSON JONA: DAYTON
Pennsylvania	{	B FRANKLIN THOMAS MIFFLIN ROB^T MORRIS GEO. CLYMER THO^S FITZSIMONS JARED INGERSOLL JAMES WILSON GOUV MORRIS
Delaware	{	GEO: READ GUNNING BEDFORD JUN JOHN DICKINSON RICHARD BASSETT JACO: BROOM
Maryland	{	JAMES MCHENRY DAN OF ST THO^S JENIFER DAN^L CARROLL
Virginia	{	JOHN BLAIR— JAMES MADISON JR.
North Carolina	{	W^M BLOUNT RICH^D DOBBS SPAIGHT HU WILLIAMSON
South Carolina	{	J. RUTLEDGE CHARLES COTESWORTH PINCKNEY CHARLES PINCKNEY PIERCE BUTLER
Georgia	{	WILLIAM FEW ABR BALDWIN

LETTER OF THE PRESIDENT OF THE FEDERAL CONVENTION,
DATED SEPTEMBER 17, 1787, TO THE PRESIDENT OF CON-
GRESS, TRANSMITTING THE CONSTITUTION

In Convention, September 17, 1787.

Sir,

We have now the honor to submit to the consideration of the United States in Congress assembled, that Constitution which has appeared to us the most adviseable.

The friends of our country have long seen and desired, that the power of making war, peace, and treaties, that of levying money and regulating commerce, and the correspondent executive and judicial authorities should be fully and effectually vested in the general government of the Union: But the impropriety of delegating such extensive trust to one body of men is evident—Hence results the necessity of a different organization.

It is obviously impracticable in the federal government of these states, to secure all rights of independent sovereignty to each, and yet provide for the interest and safety of all: Individuals entering into society, must give up a share of liberty to preserve the rest. The magnitude of the sacrifice must depend as well on situation and circumstance, as on the object to be obtained. It is at all times difficult to draw with precision the line between those rights which must be surrendered, and those which may be reserved; and on the present occasion this difficulty was encreased by a difference among the several states as to their situation, extent, habits, and particular interests.

In all our deliberations on this subject we kept steadily in our view, that which appears to us the greatest interest of every true American, the consolidation of our Union, in which is involved our prosperity, felicity, safety, perhaps our national existence. This important consideration, seriously and deeply impressed on our minds, led each state in the Convention to be less rigid on points of inferior magnitude, than might have been otherwise expected; and thus the Constitution, which we now present, is the result of a spirit of amity, and of that mutual deference and concession which the peculiarity of our political situation rendered indispensible.

That it will meet the full and entire approbation of every state is not perhaps to be expected; but each will doubtless consider, that had her interest been alone consulted, the consequences might have been particularly disagreeable or injurious to others; that it is liable to as few exceptions as could reasonably have been expected, we hope and believe; that it may promote the lasting welfare of that country so dear to us all, and secure her freedom and happiness, is our most ardent wish.

With great respect, We have the honor to be, Sir,

Your Excellency's

most obedient and humble servants,

George Washington, President.

By unanimous Order of the Convention.

His Excellency the President of Congress.

Appendix D

RESOLUTION OF THE FEDERAL CONVENTION SUBMITTING THE CONSTITUTION TO CONGRESS, SEPTEMBER 17, 1787.

IN CONVENTION Monday September 17th 1787.

Present

The States of

New Hampshire, Massachusetts, Connecticut, Mʳ Hamilton from New York, New Jersey, Pennsylvania, Delaware, Maryland, Virginia, North Carolina, South Carolina and Georgia.

Resolved,

That the preceeding Constitution be laid before the United States in Congress assembled, and that it is the Opinion of this Convention, that it should afterwards be submitted to a Convention of Delegates, chosen in each State by the People thereof, under the Recommendation of its Legislature, for their Assent and Ratification; and that each Convention assenting to, and ratifying the Same, should give Notice thereof to the United States in Congress assembled.

Resolved, That it is the Opinion of this Convention, that as soon as the Conventions of nine States shall have ratified this Constitution, the United States in Congress assembled should fix a Day on which Electors should be appointed by the States which shall have ratified the same, and a Day on which the Electors should assemble to vote for the President, and the Time and Place for commencing Proceedings under this Constitution. That after such Publication the Electors should be appointed, and the Senators and Representatives elected: That the Electors should meet on the Day fixed for the Election of the President, and should transmit their Votes certified, signed, sealed and directed, as the Constitution requires, to the Secretary of the United States in Congress assembled, and that the Senators and Representatives should convene at the Time and Place assigned; that the Senators should appoint a President of the Senate, for the sole Purpose of receiving, opening and counting the Votes for President; and, that after he shall be chosen, the Congress, together with the President, should, without Delay, proceed to execute this Constitution.

By the Unanimous Order of the Convention

G⁰ WASHINGTON Presidᵗ

W. JACKSON Secretary

AMENDMENTS TO THE CONSTITUTION

ARTICLE I

Congress shall make no law respecting an establishment of religion, or prohibiting the free exercise thereof; or abridging the freedom of speech, or of the press; or of the right of the people peaceably to assemble, and to petition the Government for a redress of grievances.

ARTICLE II

A well regulated Militia, being necessary to the security of a free State, the right of the people to keep and bear Arms, shall not be infringed.

ARTICLE III

No Soldier shall, in time of peace be quartered in any house, without the consent of the Owner, nor in time of war, but in a manner prescribed by law.

ARTICLE IV

The right of the people to be secure in their persons, houses, papers, and effects, against unreasonable searches and seizures, shall not be violated, and no Warrants shall issue, but upon probable cause, supported by Oath or affirmation, and particularly describing the place to be searched, and the persons or things to be seized.

ARTICLE V

No person shall be held to answer for a capital, or otherwise infamous crime, unless on a presentment or indictment of a Grand Jury, except in cases arising in the land or naval forces, or in the Militia, when in actual service in time of War or public danger; nor shall any person be subject for the same offence to be twice put in jeopardy of life or limb; nor shall be compelled in any criminal case to be a witness against himself, nor be deprived of life, liberty, or property, without due process of law; nor shall private property be taken for public use, without just compensation.

ARTICLE VI

In all criminal prosecutions, the accused shall enjoy the right to a speedy and public trial, by an impartial jury of the State and district wherein the crime shall have been committed, which district shall have been previously ascertained by law, and to be informed of the nature and cause of the accusation; to be confronted with the witnesses against him; to have compulsory process for obtaining witnesses in his favor, and to have the Assistance of Counsel for his defence.

ARTICLE VII

In Suits at common law, where the value in controversy shall exceed twenty dollars, the right of trial by jury shall be preserved, and no fact tried by a jury, shall be otherwise re-examined in any Court of the United States, than according to the rules of the common law.

ARTICLE VIII

Excessive bail shall not be required, nor excessive fines imposed, nor cruel and unusual punishments inflicted.

ARTICLE IX

The enumeration in the Constitution, of certain rights, shall not be construed to deny or disparage others retained by the people.

ARTICLE X

The powers not delegated to the United States by the Constitution, nor prohibited by it to the States, are reserved to the States respectively, or to the people.

ARTICLE XI

The Judicial power of the United States shall not be construed to extend to any suit in law or equity, commenced or prosecuted against one of the United States by Citizens of another State, or by Citizens or Subjects of any Foreign State.

ARTICLE XII

The Electors shall meet in their respective states, and vote by ballot for President and Vice-President, one of whom, at least, shall not be an inhabitant of the same state with themselves; they shall name in their ballots the person voted for as President, and in distinct ballots the person voted for as Vice-President, and they shall make distinct lists of all persons voted for as President, and of all persons voted for as Vice-President, and of the number of votes for each, which lists they shall sign and certify, and transmit sealed to the seat of the government of the United States, directed to the President of the Senate;—The President of the Senate shall, in the presence of the Senate and House of Representatives, open all the certificates and the votes shall then be counted;—The person having the greatest number of votes for President, shall be the President, if such number be a majority of the whole number of Electors appointed; and if no person have such majority, then from the persons having the highest numbers not exceeding three on the list voted for as President, the House of Representatives shall choose immediately, by ballot, the President. But in choosing the President, the votes shall be taken by states, the representation from each state having one vote; a quorum for this purpose shall consist of a member or members from two-thirds of the states, and a majority of all the states shall be necessary to a choice. And if the House of Representatives shall not choose a President whenever the right of choice shall devolve upon them, before the fourth day of March next following, then the Vice-President shall act as President, as in the case of the death or other constitutional disability of the President.—The person having the greatest number of votes as Vice-President, shall be the Vice-President, if such number be a majority of the whole number of Electors appointed, and if no person have a majority, then from the two highest numbers on the list, the Senate shall choose the Vice-President; a quorum for the purpose shall consist of two-thirds of the whole number of Senators, and a majority of the whole number shall be necessary to a choice. But no person constitutionally ineligible to the office of President shall be eligible to that of Vice-President of the United States.

ARTICLE XIII

SECTION 1. Neither slavery nor involutary servitude, except as a punishment for crime whereof the party shall have been duly convicted, shall exist within the United States, or any place subject to their jurisdiction.

SECTION 2. Congress shall have power to enforce this article by appropriate legislation.

ARTICLE XIV

SECTION 1. All persons born or naturalized in the United States, and subject to the jurisdiction thereof, are citizens of the United States and of the State wherein they reside. No State shall make or enforce any law which shall abridge the privileges or immunities of citizens of the United States; nor shall any State deprive any person of life, liberty, or property, without due process of law; nor deny to any person within its jurisdiction the equal protection of the laws.

Section 2. Representatives shall be apportioned among the several States according to their respective numbers, counting the whole number of persons in each State, excluding Indians not taxed. But when the right to vote at any election for the choice of electors for President and Vice President of the United States, Representatives in Congress, the Executive and Judicial officers of a State, or the members of the Legislature thereof, is denied to any of the male inhabitants of such State, being twenty-one years of age, and citizens of the United States, or in any way abridged, except for participation in rebellion, or other crime, the basis of representation therein shall be reduced in the proportion which the number of such male citizens shall bear to the whole number of male citizens twenty-one years of age in such State.

Section 3. No person shall be a Senator or Representative in Congress, or elector of President and Vice President, or hold any office, civil or military under the United States, or under any State, who, having previously taken an oath, as a member of Congress, or as an officer of the United States, or as a member of any State legislature, or as an executive or judicial officer of any State, to support the Constitution of the United States, shall have engaged in insurrection or rebellion against the same, or given aid or comfort to the enemies thereof. But Congress may by a vote of two-thirds of each House, remove such disability.

Section 4. The validity of the public debt of the United States, authorized by law, including debts incurred for payment of pensions and bounties for services in suppressing insurrection or rebellion, shall not be questioned. But neither the United States nor any State shall assume or pay any debt or obligation incurred in aid of insurrection or rebellion against the United States, or any claim for the loss or emancipation of any slave; but all such debts, obligations and claims shall be held illegal and void.

Section 5. The Congress shall have power to enforce, by appropriate legislation, the provisions of this article.

Article XV

Section 1. The right of citizens of the United States to vote shall not be denied or abridged by the United States or by any State on account of race, color, or previous condition of servitude—

Section 2. The Congress shall have power to enforce this article by appropriate legislation.—

Article XVI

The Congress shall have power to lay and collect taxes on incomes, from whatever source derived, without apportionment among the several States, and without regard to any census or enumeration.

Article XVII

The Senate of the United States shall be composed of two Senators from each State, elected by the people thereof, for six years; and each Senator shall have one vote. The electors in each State shall have the qualifications requisite for electors of the most numerous branch of the State legislatures.

When vacancies happen in the representation of any State in the Senate, the executive authority of such State shall issue writs of election to fill such vacancies: *Provided,* that the legislature of any State may empower the executive thereof to make temporary appointments until the people fill the vacancies by election as the legislature may direct.

This amendment shall not be so construed as to affect the election or term of any Senator chosen before it becomes valid as part of the Constitution.

ARTICLE XVIII

SECTION 1. After one year from the ratification of this article the manufacture, sale, or transportation of intoxicating liquors within, the importation thereof into, or the exportation thereof from the United States and all territory subject to the jurisdiction thereof for beverage purposes is hereby prohibited.

SEC. 2. The Congress and the several States shall have concurrent power to enforce this article by appropriate legislation.

SEC. 3. This article shall be inoperative unless it shall have been ratified as an amendment to the Constitution by the legislatures of the several States, as provided in the Constitution, within seven years from the date of the submission hereof to the States by the Congress.

ARTICLE XIX

The right of citizens of the United States to vote shall not be denied or abridged by the United States or by any State on account of sex.

Congress shall have power to enforce this article by appropriate legislation.

ARTICLE XX

SECTION 1. The terms of the President and Vice President shall end at noon on the 20th day of January, and the terms of Senators and Representatives at noon on the 3d day of January, of the years in which such terms would have ended if this article had not been ratified; and the terms of their successors shall then begin.

SEC. 2. The Congress shall assemble at least once in every year, and such meeting shall begin at noon on the 3d day of January, unless they shall by law appoint a different day.

SEC. 3. If, at the time fixed for the beginning of the term of the President, the President elect shall have died, the Vice President elect shall become President. If a President shall not have been chosen before the time fixed for the beginning of his term, or if the President elect shall have failed to qualify, then the Vice President elect shall act as President until a President shall have qualified; and the Congress may by law provide for the case wherein neither a President elect nor a Vice President elect shall have qualified, declaring who shall then act as President, or the manner in which one who is to act shall be selected, and such person shall act accordingly until a President or Vice President shall have qualified.

SEC. 4. The Congress may by law provide for the case of the death of any of the persons from whom the House of Representatives may choose a President whenever the right of choice shall have devolved upon them, and for the case of the death of any of the persons from whom the Senate may choose a Vice President whenever the right of choice shall have devolved upon them.

SEC. 5. Sections 1 and 2 shall take effect on the 15th day of October following the ratification of this article.

SEC. 6. This article shall be inoperative unless it shall have been ratified as an amendment to the Constitution by the legislatures of three-fourths of the several States within seven years from the date of its submission.

Article XXI

Section 1. The eighteenth article of amendment to the Constitution of the United States is hereby repealed.

Sec. 2. The transportation or importation into any State, Territory, or possession of the United States for delivery or use therein of intoxicating liquors, in violation of the laws thereof, is hereby prohibited.

Sec. 3. This article shall be inoperative unless it shall have been ratified as an amendment to the Constitution by conventions in the several States, as provided in the Constitution, within seven years from the date of the submission hereof to the States by the Congress.

Article XXII

No person shall be elected to the office of the President more than twice, and no person who has held the office of President, or acted as President, for more than two years of a term to which some other person was elected President shall be elected to the office of the President more than once. But this Article shall not apply to any person holding the office of President when this Article was proposed by the Congress, and shall not prevent any person who may be holding the office of President, or acting as President, during the term within which this Article becomes operative from holding the office of President or acting as President during the remainder of such term.

Article XXIII

1. The District constituting the seat of Government of the United States shall appoint in such manner as the Congress may direct:

A number of electors of President and Vice President equal to the whole number of Senators and Representatives in Congress to which the District would be entitled if it were a State, but in no event more than the least populous State; they shall be in addition to those appointed by the States, but they shall be considered for the purposes of the election of President and Vice President, to be electors appointed by a State; and they shall meet in the District and perform such duties as provided by the twelfth article of amendment.

2. The Congress shall have power to enforce this article by appropriate legislation.

Article XXIV

1. The right of citizens of the United States to vote in any primary or other election for President or Vice President, for electors for President or Vice President, or for Senator or Representative in Congress, shall not be denied or abridged by the United States or any State by reason of failure to pay any poll tax or other tax.

2. The Congress shall have power to enforce this article by appropriate legislation.

Article XXV

1. In case of the removal of the President from office or of his death or resignation, the Vice President shall become President.

2. Whenever there is a vacancy in the office of the Vice President, the President shall nominate a Vice President who shall take office upon confirmation by a majority vote of both houses of Congress.

3. Whenever the President transmits to the President pro tempore of the Senate and the Speaker of the House of Representatives his written declaration that he is unable to discharge the powers and duties of his office, and until he transmits to them a written declaration to the contrary, such powers and duties shall be discharged by the Vice President as Acting President.

4. Whenever the Vice President and a majority of either the principal officers of the executive departments or of such other body as Congress may by law provide, transmit to the President pro tempore of the Senate and the Speaker of the House of Representatives their written declaration that the President is unable to discharge the powers and duties of his office, the Vice President shall immediately assume the powers and duties of the office as Acting President.

Thereafter, when the President transmits to the President pro tempore of the Senate and the Speaker of the House of Representatives his written declaration that no inability exists, he shall resume the powers and duties of his office unless the Vice President and a majority of either the principal officers of the executive department or of such other body as Congress may by law provide, transmit within four days to the President pro tempore of the Senate and the Speaker of the House of Representatives their written declaration that the President is unable to discharge the powers and duties of his office. Thereupon Congress shall decide the issue, assembling within forty-eight hours for that purpose if not in session. If the Congress, within twenty-one days after receipt of the latter written declaration, or, if Congress is not in session, within twenty-one days after Congress is required to assemble, determines by two-thirds vote of both houses that the President is unable to discharge the powers and duties of his office, the Vice President shall continue to discharge the same as Acting President; otherwise, the President shall resume the powers and duties of his office.

Article XXVI

1. The right of citizens of the Untied States, who are 18 years of age or older, to vote shall not be denied or abridged by the United States or any state on account of age.

2. The Congress shall have the power to enforce this article by appropriate legislation.

APPENDIX E

Letters of Rufus King to Caleb Davis

Reproduced by Permission of the
Massachusetts Historical Society

New York 17th Oct: 1785

Dear Sir,

The laws relative to commerce and navigation passed in the last session of the General Court are disinterested proofs of the disposition of Massachusetts to make considerable sacrifices for the common good—But care should be taken to well observe the extent of such sacrifices, and the effect they may have, where we might not intend them to operate—I will not venture an opinion concerning the policy of a repeal of those laws, in case it shall turn out, as I expect it will, that neither this State nor Connecticut, Jersey nor Pennsylvania, will pass similar Laws to those of Massachusetts—But if the inclosed Report of the Secretary of the United States for the Department of foreign affairs is well founded, and some parts of it I have not heard a doubt started—it will be necessary to make some alterations in the Laws.—I wish you to examine this Report and be obliging enough if you think proper to shew it to such persons of the court as ought to see it—it is a paper unacted upon in Congress, therefore improper to be given to the public—

How you will think of the Delegates for their delay in following the instruction of the Legislature upon the Subject of a convention for the purpose of a general revision of the confederation I do not know—in addition to the ideas communicated in our joint letter to the Governor, which undoubtedly will be laid before the Legislature, there are many reasons in favor of our Opinion which would be improper to have communicated, but which in our Opinion are of great weight. If the Legislature direct us to proceed, we go on under their Directions—

With great respect and Esteem your Ob^t serv^t

RUFUS KING

I inclose two copies, & request the favor that you will present one of them to the President of the Senate with my best respects.

New York 3d Nov. 1785

Dear Sir,

It gives me pleasure to learn that the Report of Mr. Jay concerning certain clauses in the navigation act of Massachusetts came to hand seasonably, to throw some light upon that Subject—I will not pretend to give an opinion relative to the Policy or wisdom of the law—if the Principle is good, the small errors pointed out by Mr. Jay,

497

may be easily rectified—The extract you was good enough to inclose me corresponds with the uniform official communications of the writer—There is nothing more evident than that not only Great Britain, but France are jealous of the commerce, enterprize, and probable naval importance of the United States; and notwithstanding the *apparent* opposition between these two Countries, it would not be surprizing if they united in advancing each the commerce of the other, if thereby they could suppress or injure the commerce of America—England is less jealous of France than of America—The Twenty propositions of the Minister Mr. Pitt for a union with Ireland bear strong features of a jealousy of America—Ireland now enjoys a free Trade—She can admit at her pleasure the Ships, Products and manufactures of America and of other countries—England is eagle-eyed upon the subject. She wishes to make Ireland a part of Great Britain, and to regulate her Trade—for the Twenty propositions are to be *fundamental Articles*, they are to form a constitution, which is to remain superior to any future laws of either Country—Ireland evidently sees through the Policy—and I hope will effectually defeat the System, which is more a combination against America, than a plan of commercial advantage to Ireland or England.

What ought to be the line of conduct in America is not difficult to discover, but what will be her conduct is wholly conjectural—If America could only rouse the spirit which dictated the non-importation agreement, and would universally restrain her commerce to her own ships and mariners, although the embarrassments would be at first, and for a time very considerable, yet a remedy would soon be furnished by the great number of ships, which would be built, and the multitude of men who would become mariners—How far these events, so much to be desired, will take place, by partial measures, and sacrifices, of individual states, is somewhat difficult to determine—But even admitting that the southern and eastern states cannot & will not soon agree in vesting powers in Congress to regulate external and internal commerce, and that the measure will not be effected by uniform acts passed by the several states—yet the Confederation admits of alliances between two or more states, provided *the purpose and duration thereof* are previously communicated to, and approved by, Congress. The seven Eastern states have common commercial interests, are under similar embarrassments, would vest power in Congress to regulate Trade, and are competent to give the approbation of Congress to such sub-confederation, as they might agree upon, and which would not only remedy all their Difficulties, but raise them to a degree of power and opulence which would surprize and astonish— Politicians in Europe see it, and fear it, more than we appear to wish it—

I would not be understood to give any Opinion relative to the Massachusetts act, for, or against, the principle or policy, of it—I have given no opinion concerning it to any one—neither have I given an Opinion, that if Congress had the power to regulate Trade, that they would be without the Disposition to do it—I sincerely wish they had the power; if they had, something would certainly be done which would be worthy of Execution, and remedial of present perplexities—But I have my Doubts whether the Southern states will relinquish their partial, and unfederal, policy concerning commerce, until they find a decided disposition in the eastern states to combine for their own security—the moment that this Disposition is evident, the Southern states will sensibly feel their weekness, and accede to such measures as may be adopted by the majority of the Confederacy—

You very well understand the Character of our countrymen, they will bear and suffer for a time; but there is a point below which they will not sink; The Difficulties we now suffer will cure themselves, the spirit for reform will become, nay it daily is becoming more and more, general through all the States. The remedy must be waited for with *some degree* of Patience—This language will not bear to be communicated— you know whether it is founded in the nature of our Governments, or not—at any rate

I observe it *in confidence*—Some men think that political Difficulties may as readily be rectified as those of a domestic or private nature; but they understand very little of the Genius of the several states composing this Confederacy—The nature of our Governments renders every reform, or alteration, not only difficult, because our local, or state, interests are sometimes in opposition, but subjects it to tedious Delays—

But Sir, I will not add upon this subject—We are anxious for the Opinion of the Legislature relative to a convention for a general revision of the Confederation—the Delegates here are of opinion that the Confederation wants additional commercial powers, and some other additions or alterations—but if once a power is brought into existence under authority of the States, who may generally revise the Confederation, farewel to the present Republican plan—

I will trouble you one moment longer—whoever the Delegates from Massachusetts may be, they ought for the interest of the state *to be together*; if they have that interest in view they will wish it—on this subject, I will observe to you, that I wish the Legislature would authorize by a Resolve their Delegates to take a house furnished /or if unfurnished, to furnish it/at the expense of the State—to the end that they might live together. I say at the expense of the state; the pay allowed the Delegates will not *allow them* to do it—Mr. Gerry & myself have lived together, *and at board*—I assure you that the allowance of the State will not bring the year about—The sum of house Rent to the State would be inconsiderable—Other States give enough to their Delegates to enable them to hire houses, and to live independently of private family arrangements and perplexities—I would not mention this to the court, lest they should think I have some thing of profit in view—if you think the idea would be approved by the court, and you also think it just, perhaps you may move it; but I pray I may not appear in it. I can in the next year, as I have in the past, spend my own money in the Public service—the allowance from almost every state in the Confederacy exceeds that of Massachusetts from twenty to sixty per Cent.

Pray excuse me for mentioning this subject—I will never trouble you or any other man with it in future—I have written on this, as on more important subjects, with great hurry, but entire sincerity—

> With perfect Esteem & Respect
> Your Ob^t Servt
> RUFUS KING

APPENDIX F

Letter of Edmund Randolph to
Gov. Richard Caswell

RICHMOND, VIRGINIA, Feby, 19th, 1786.

SIR:

I do myself the honor of transmitting to your Excellency the enclosed resolution of the Commissioners thereby appointed who have instructed me to open the communication which it directs with the several States. It is impossible for me to decide how far the uniform system in commercial regulations, which is the subject of that resolution, may or may not be attainable. I can only venture to declare that the desire of such an arrangement arose from a regard to the federal interests.

The commissioners of Virginia have therefore only to request the concurrence of your State, and to propose the first Monday in September next as the time, and the City of Annapolis for the meeting of the different deputies.

I have the honor Sir to be,

Your Excellency's most Obt.,

EDMUND RANDOLPH

[State Records of North Carolina, XVIII, 535]

APPENDIX G

Letter of Gov. Patrick Henry to
Gov. Richard Caswell

RICHMOND, Feby. 23, 1786.

SIR:

The General Assembly have appointed Edmund Randolph, James Madison, junr., Walter Jones, St. George Tucker, Merewether Smith, David Ross, William Ronald & George Mason, Esqrs., Commissioners to meet others from the different States in the Union at a time and place to be agreed on for the purpose of framing such regulations of Trade as may be judged necessary to promote the general interest.

I have to request your Excellency's attention to this subject and that you will be pleased to make such communications of it as may be necessary to forward the views of this Legislature.

I am with great regard,

Your Excellency's obedient Servant,

P. HENRY

[State Records of North Carolina, XVIII, 542]

APPENDIX H

Letters of Gov. Edmund Randolph to
Gov. William Livingston

RICHMOND Dec[r] 1. 1786

Sir

I feel a peculiar satisfaction in forwarding to your Excellency the inclosed Act of our Legislature. As it breathes a spirit truly fœderal, & contains an effort to support our general Government, which is now reduced to the most awful crisis, permit me to solicit your Excellency's cooperation at this trying moment.

I have the honor to be

Your Excellency's

Most obed[t] humble Serv[t]

EDM: RANDOLPH

RICHMOND December 6. 1786

Sir

My anxiety for the well being of the fœderal Government will not suffer me to risque so important a consideration upon the safety of a single letter. Your Excellency will therefore excuse me for again intruding on you with the inclosed Act of our Legislature, and repeating the request urged in my letter of the 1st instant, that you would give a zealous attention to the present American crisis.

The Gentlemen appointed by Virginia for the Convention at Philadelphia, are General Washington, Mr. Patrick Henry, the late Governor, Mr. George Wythe & Mr. John Blair, two of the Judges of the high Court of Chancery, Mr. James Madison j[r] a member of Congress, Mr. George Mason, a member of the legislature and myself.

I have the honor Sir, to be, with Sentiments

of perfect respect,

Your most obed[t] Servant

EDM: RANDOLPH

APPENDIX I

Letter of Henry Knox to Stephen Higginson

Reproduced by Permission of the
Massachusetts Historical Society

New York 25th February 1787

Dear Sir

Permit me to render you my sincere acknowledgements for your esteemed favors of the 8th and 13th instant. Your observations and reflections on the nature and present state of government throughout the union are perfectly just and well founded, and evince that you have bestowed a greater degree of attention and thought on the subject, than most other gentlemen with whom I have communicated. We have arrived at that point in politics beyond which the force of our present institutions cannot urge us. Nor indeed can we rest where we are. Borne on the current of events, we are pressed down to our destruction. We know the right, and yet the wrong pursue. The multiplied parts of the machine are liable to be deformed by the least accident—nay so illy disproportioned are the parts that disorder is inevitable.—The whole must be taken to pieces and a new one erected on the basis of public liberty and public happiness—less complex and more effectively durable.

You will have learnt by the last Thursday post that Congress have acceded to the idea of a convention—But you will also see, that the report of the convention is to be submitted to Congress and the respective states. This is all that Congress conceived itself authorized to do and hope. But it is next to an impossibility that all the states should agree to an efficient government. The convention however will be attended with good effects. It will approximate the public mind to a general government, and the more the subject shall be discussed, the sooner it will be accomplished—and were it possible to carry your mode of approbation into effect, the road to a good government would be much shorter than it now appears to be.

I hope you may find it convenient to attend and that you will be chosen, and also our friend Mr. King, Genl. Lincoln, and the other gentlemen whom you mentioned.

The energy of Massachusetts places it in an honorable point of view—The strongest arguments possible may be drawn from the events which have happened in that state, in order to effect a strong general government—But the rebellion has not had and probably will not have the effect that one would rationally suppose— Although all the states possess the seeds of dissolution which are hourly springing up and manifesting themselves to an attentive observer, and in some states are nearly ripe, yet such are the infatuations produced from a variety of causes that those more immediately on the spot do not appear to observe them, a few men excepted.— Pennsylvania for instance who by her deadly parties will ever be imbecille in the hour of intestine danger, will if I am not much mistaken, exhibit a shocking instance of this opinion. But many people speak of the disorders of Massachusetts as produced by a well meaning perhaps but mistaken policy in the management of her internal affairs—In short being men, they speak of the events which have happened in Massachusetts as they speak of other events which have happened within the circle of their immediate cognizance—In many instances they speak as erroneously of the causes of things which have been happening two or three hundred miles from them as the British used to do of us during the late war. This aptness in the minds of the different states to impute the rebellion in Massachusetts to local causes will prevent those measures necessary to the establishment of a force which would controul events. Although I am very far from despairing, yet I am pretty much inclined to think that if an efficient government shall be established in any reasonable time, that it will rather be the effect of accident than design.

You may rest assured that your communications to me shall be confidentially retained and

I am my dear Sir

with great esteem & respect,

Your very humble serv[t]

H KNOX

Stephen Higginson Esq

APPENDIX J

Unusual Abbreviations Used in the Notes

Am. D. Adv.	*Dunlap's* [Philadelphia] *American Daily Advertiser*
Am. Her.	*The* [Boston] *American Herald*
Am. Merc.	*The* [Hartford] *American Mercury*
Am. Mus.	*The* [Philadelphia] *American Museum*
Annals	*Annals of the Congress of the United States* (Washington, 1834)
Ann. Gaz.	*The* [Annapolis] *Maryland Gazette*
Archives	Peter Force, *American Archives* (Washington, 1837–53)
Balt. Gaz.	*The* [Baltimore] *Maryland Gazette*
Bancroft	George Bancroft, *The History of the Formation of the Constitution*, 3d. ed. (New York, 1883)
B. Cont. Jour.	*The* [Boston] *Continental Journal*
B. Ind. Chr.	*The* [Boston] *Independent Chronicle*
Blackstone	Sir William Blackstone, *Commentaries on the Laws of England*, 1st American ed. (Philadelphia, 1771–72)
Bost. Chr.	*The Boston Chronicle*
Bost. Ev. P.	*The Boston Evening Post*
Bost. Gaz.	*The Boston Gazette*
Ch. City Gaz.	*The* [Charleston] *City Gazette*
Ch. Ev. Gaz.	*The Charleston Evening Gazette*
Ch. G. A.	*The* [Charleston] *South-Carolina Gazette and General Advertiser*
Ch. Mng. P.	*The Charleston Morning Post*
Ch. P. A.	*The* [Charleston] *South-Carolina Gazett and Public Advertiser*
Ch. St. Gaz.	*The* [Charleston] *South-Carolina State Gazette and Daily Advertiser*
Ch. Wkly. Gaz.	*The* [Charleston] *South-Carolina Weekly Gazette*
Col. Her.	*The* [Charleston] *Columbian Herald*
Conn. Cour.	*The* [Hartford] *Connecticut Courant*
Conn. Jour.	*The* [New Haven] *Connecticut Journal*
Conn. Rec.	*The Public Records of the State of Connecticut* (Hartford, 1894 and later)
Cumb. Gaz.	*The Cumberland* [Maine] *Gazette*
DHC	*Documentary History of the Constitution of the United States of America* (Washington, 1894)
Elliot	Jonathan Elliot, *The Debates in the Several State Conventions on the Adoption of the Federal Constitution*, 2d (24 cm.) ed. (Washington, 1936)
Ess. Jour.	*The* [Newburyport, Mass] *Essex Journal*
Fal. Gaz.	*The Falmouth* [Me.] *Gazette*
Ga. Gaz.	*The* [Augusta] *Georgia State Gazette*
Gaz. S.C.	*The* [Charleston] *Gazette of the State of South Carolina*
Hamilton	*The Works of Alexander Hamilton* (Federal ed., New York, 1904)

505

Higginson	*Letters of Stephen Higginson, 1783–1804*, in American Historical Association Annual Report 1896, vol. I, pp. 704–841
Jay	*The Correspondence and Public Papers of John Jay*, ed. Henry P. Johnston (New York, 1890–93).
Jefferson	*The Works of Thomas Jefferson*, Federal ed. (New York, 1904–5)
John Adams	*The Works of John Adams* (Boston, 1850–56)
Journals	W. C. Ford et al., *Journals of the Continental Congress* (Washington, 1904–37)
King	*The Life and Correspondence of Rufus King*, ed. C. R. King (New York, 1894–1900).
Knox	Samuel F. Drake, *Life and Correspondence of Henry Knox* (Boston, 1873)
Lee	*The Letters of Richard Henry Lee* (New York, 1911–14)
Letters	E. C. Burnett, *Letters of Members of the Continental Congress* (Washington, 1921–36)
Madison	*The Writings of James Madison* (New York, 1900–1910)
Mass. Cent.	*The* [Boston] *Massachusetts Centinel*
Mass. Gaz.	*The* [Boston] *Massachusetts Gazette*
Md. Jour.	*The* [Baltimore] *Maryland Journal*
Mid. Gaz.	*The* [Middletown, Conn.] *Middlesex Gazette*
Monroe	*The Writings of James Monroe* (New York, 1898–1903)
N. & P. Jour.	*The Norfolk & Portsmouth* [Va.] *Journal*
Newp. Her.	*The Newport* [R.I.] *Herald*
Newp. Merc.	*The Newport* [R.I.] *Mercury*
N.H. Ct. Gaz.	*The New-Haven Gazette* (later *The New-Haven Gazette and Connecticut Magazine*)
N.H. Gaz.	*The* [Portsmouth] *New-Hampshire Gazette*
N.H. Merc.	*The* [Portsmouth] *New-Hampshire Mercury*
N.H. Spy	*The* [Portsmouth] *New-Hampshire Spy*
N.J. Gaz.	*The* [Trenton] *New-Jersey Gazette*
N.J. Pol. Int.	*The* [Elizabeth-Town, N.J.] *Political Intelligencer*
N.L. Gaz.	*The* [New London] *Connecticut Gazette*
Norw. Pack.	*The Norwich* [Conn.] *Packet*
N.Y. Adv.	*The* [New York] *Daily Advertiser*
N.Y. Ind. Jour.	*The* [New York] *Independent Journal*
N.Y. Jour.	*The New-York Journal* (This paper was published for a time during the Revolution, at Poughkeepsie)
N.Y. Mng. P.	*The New-York Morning Post*
N.Y. Wkly. Merc.	*The New York Gazette and Weekly Mercury*
Pa. Chr.	*The* [Philadelphia] *Pennsylvania Chronicle*
Pa. Gaz.	*The* [Philadelphia] *Pennsylvania Gazette*
Pa. Her.	*The* [Philadelphia] *Pennsylvania Evening Herald*
Pa. Jour.	*The* [Philadelphia] *Pennsylvania Journal*
Pa. Merc.	*The* [Philadelphia] *Pennsylvania Mercury*
Pa. Pack.	*The* [Philadelphia] *Pennsylvania Packet*
Ph. Fr. Jour.	*The* [Philadelphia] *Freeman's Journal*
Ph. Ind. Gaz.	*The* [Philadelphia] *Independent Gazetteer*
Pol. & Con.	Crosskey, *Politics and the Constitution in the History of the United States*, vols. I and II (Chicago, 1953)
Po. Fr. Jour.	*The* [Portsmouth, N.H.] *Freeman's Journal*

Prov. Gaz.	*The Providence* [R.I.] *Gazette*
Records	Max Farrand, *The Records of the Federal Convention* (New Haven, 1937)
Sal. Merc.	*The Salem* [Mass.] *Mercury*
Sav. Gaz.	*The* [Savannah] *Gazette of the State of Georgia*
Seabury	Samuel Seabury, *Letters of a Westchester Farmer,* as reprinted in Publications of the Westchester County Historical Society, Vol. VIII (White Plains, N.Y., 1930)
Tucker	ST. GEORGE TUCKER, *Blackstone's Commentaries* (Philadelphia, 1803)
U.S. Chr.	*The* [Providence, R.I.] *United States Chronicle*
Va. Am. Adv.	*The* [Richmond] *Virginia Gazette or the American Advertiser*
Va. Her.	*The* [Fredericksburg] *Virginia Herald*
Va. Ind. Chr.	*The* [Richmond] *Virginia Independent Chronicle*
Va. Jour.	*The* [Alexandria] *Virginia Journal*
Vt. Gaz.	*The* [Bennington] *Vermont Gazette*
Warren–Adams	*The Warren-Adams Letters* (The Massachusetts Historical Society, 1917–25)
Wbg. Va. Gaz.	*The* [Williamsburg] *Virginia Gazette*

Notes

NOTES TO CHAPTER I

1. Listings of the reviews may be found in Jeffrey, "American Legal History, 1952–1954," in *1954 Annual Survey of American Law*, 866, at 881.

2. Maitland, *Collected Papers*, ed. H. A. L. Fisher (Cambridge University Press, 1911), I, 480–97.

3. Ibid., 490.

4. Ibid.

5. McReynolds, J., in *Berger* v. *United States*, 255 U.S. 22, 42–43 (1921).

6. Maitland, *Collected Papers*, I, 492.

7. Holmes, "The Theory of Legal Interpretation," 12 *Harvard Law Review*, 417 (1899).

8. The early attacks upon the national judiciary are discussed in chap. XXIV (Pol. & Con., II, 754–817); other phases of the declension of the national judiciary are treated in chaps. XXV and XXVI (II, 818–937). Chapter XXX recounts the Supreme Court's destruction of the limitations on states' authority contained in the original Constitution and the initial amendments (II, 1049–82); the Fourteenth Amendment is discussed in chaps. XXXI and XXXII (II, 1083–1158) and Crosskey, "Charles Fairman, 'Legislative History,' and the Constitutional Limitations on State Authority," 22 *University of Chicago Law Review* 1–143 (1954).

9. Jefferson expressed this opinion to his fellow ambassador, John Adams, in a letter on August 30, 1787. *The Adams-Jefferson Letters*, ed. Cappon (Chapel Hill, 1959), I, 196.

10. Pol. & Con. I, 84–114.

11. Ibid., 55–69.

12. Ibid., 146–55.

13. Ibid., 123–36.

14. Ibid., 155–72.

15. Journals, I, 68.

16. Pol. & Con., I, 173–86.

17. Ibid., 187–250.

18. 9 Wheat. 1 (1824), discussed in Pol. & Con., I, 250–68.

19. Pol. & Con., I, 295–323.

20. Ibid., 297–300.

21. Ibid., 304–5.

22. Cf. ibid., 316–17.

23. Ibid., 324–51.

24. Records, II, 640; IV, 59.

25. 3 Dall. (U.S.) 385 (1798), discussed in Pol. & Con., I, 342–46.

26. Pol. & Con., I, 352–60.

27. Ibid., at 355–60.

28. Frankfurter, J., in *Graves* v. *O'Keefe*, 306 U.S. 466, 491–92 (1939).

29. Pol. & Con., I, 363–74.

30. Blackstone, I, 59.

31. Pol. & Con., I, 367.

32. Ibid., I, 374–79, 391–401.

33. Ibid., 398.

34. Ibid., 409–562 (chaps. XV, XVI, and XVII).

35. Ibid., 415–67.

36. Ibid., 411–13.

37. Ibid., 486 ff.
38. Blackstone, I, 267.
39. Pol. & Con., I, 524–37.
40. Ibid., 542–57.
41. Ibid., 522–24.
42. Tucker, bk. I, pt. 2, nn. for pp. 249–80, especially nn. 11, 13, and 67.
43. Records, I, 66; I, 92.
44. Pol. & Con., I, 578–609.
45. Blackstone, I, 107.
46. Pol. & Con., I, 610–40.
47. Ibid., 620–25.
48. Records, II, 186 (August 6).
49. Ibid., II, 423–24 (Journal); II, 431 (Madison).
50. Cf. Pol. & Con., II, 984–1002.
51. Ibid., I, 666–67.
52. Ibid., 615–18.
53. Cf. above, n. 28.
54. Cf. above, pp. 5–6.
55. "An impeachable offense is whatever a majority of the House of Representatives considers it to be at a given moment in history; conviction results from whatever offense or offenses two-thirds of the other body consider to be sufficiently serious to require removal of the accused from office." 116 Cong. Rec. H. 3113–14 (Daily ed., April 15, 1970). The fact that Congressman (as he then was) Gerald Rudolph Ford was contemplating the question of the impeachment of a sitting Supreme Court justice in no way diminishes the complete correctness of the views he expressed.
56. Records, I, 97–98 (Gerry); II, 73 (Gorham).
57. Pol. & Con., II, 938–75 (chap. XXVII).
58. Pol. & Con., II, 1002–7.
59. Ibid., I, 675–708.
60. Annals, I, 433 and 441.

NOTES TO CHAPTER II

1. 7 & 8 Wm. III, c. 22, §9.
2. There is a list of these statutes in Pickering, [*British*] *Statutes at Large* (Cambridge [Eng.], 1765), XXIV, 437, under the rubric "Plantations."
3. Professor Gipson's account of "The Great War for the Empire" is contained in vols. VI–VIII of his *The British Empire before the American Revolution*.
4. 6 Geo. III, c.12.
5. 13 Geo. III, c.44.
6. 14 Geo. III, c.19.
7. Ibid., c.39.
8. Ibid., c.45.
9. Ibid., c.54.
10. Ibid., c.83.
11. Professor Gipson presents a concise account of the antecedents of the Quebec Act, commencing with the administration of Lieut. Gov. Guy Carleton appointed in 1768. See *The British Empire before the American Revolution*, XIII, 144–68 (1967).
12. 14 Geo. III, c.83.
13. Journals, I, 76.
14. Ibid., 44.

15. Ibid., 49–51.

16. Ibid., 48.

17. Ibid., 51.

18. Some readers will, perhaps, urge the Albany Plan of 1754 as the proper candidate for this honorable status. The unplanned character of that project, the nonrepresentation of several colonies at the Albany discussions, and the limited purpose and scope of the Plan seem to us conclusive against this view. For a balanced and perceptive discussion of the abortive Albany project, see Gipson, *The British Empire before the American Revolution*, V, 113–66 (1942).

19. Journals, I, 49.

20. Ibid., 50.

21. Ibid., 49.

22. Pol. & Con., I, 146–53.

23. *The License Cases*, 5 How. (U.S.) 504, 582, 583 (1847).

24. Journals, I, 63–73.

25. Ibid., 68.

26. Pol. & Con., I, 155–72.

27. Journals, I, 62.

28. Ibid., 75–81.

29. Brown unpurified sugar (ibid., 77, n. 1).

30. Ibid., 76–77.

31. Ibid., 78, 79.

32. Ibid., 78.

33. Ibid., 79.

34. Ibid., 80. The operation of "the Association," and the work of the committees established pursuant thereto, are subjects of the authoritative monograph by Professor Arthur M. Schlesinger. See his *The Colonial Merchants and the American Revolution* (New York, 1917), 473–540.

35. Journals, I, 76.

36. *Sketches of American Policy* (Hartford, 1785), 3, 4.

37. Seabury, *Letters of a Westchester Farmer* (White Plains, 1930), 69, 73, 83, 86, 90.

38. *Massachusettensis* (London reprint for J. Mathews, 1776), 110, 111.

39. Hamilton, I, 44, 45, and 48.

40. Journals, II, 89–90.

41. Ibid., 91.

42. Ibid., 195. The complete text of Franklin's draft is reprinted in Appendix A hereof.

43. Ibid., 196.

44. Ibid.

45. Clear evidence of this ordinary meaning of "general commerce" may be seen in a pamphlet entitled *Commerce and Luxury*, which was published in Philadelphia, in 1791. According to the pamphlet, "general commerce" was understood as "divi[ded] into home trade and foreign trade" (p. 4). The pamphlet purports to be a reprint of a pamphlet originally published in London. But for this intimation, it might confidently be described as a subtle piece of anti-Federalist propaganda; and perhaps it should be so described anyway, since no evidence of London publication could be found. "The merit of this Work will be acknowledged," its preface says, "by every judicious reader. The republication of it *in this country, at this time*, has been advised by several enlightened patriots. These wish to promote our national commerce on the basis of agriculture and industry, and free from the base alloy of imposition and gaming. They set a proper value on the conveniencies and ornaments of life; but detest that luxury which is the offspring of a frivolous taste, and the mother of

profligacy, dishonesty, poverty—of numberless private and public vices and misfortunes."

The pamphlet itself says: "The division of *general commerce*, into home and foreign trade, is a subject of which the examination may afford greater utility. To discover the advantages of these two branches, it will not be improper to follow their natural progression." In so doing, the pamphlet notes the hunting, pastoral, and purely agricultural stages of economic organization as precommercial; describes the characteristics of a purely "home trade," or system of exchange of goods and services within a single society; and winds up with a discussion of the conditions when such a national system is extended to include trade with other nations. "By examining the progress of commerce," the pamphlet then observes, "we see the clue that leads out of the labyrinth in which most writers, who have attempted to determine the utility or dangers of an extensive [i.e., a far-flung] trade have lost themselves. Let us consider more particularly its advantages and disadvantages and then judge from the facts." There follows a discussion of "the necessity and the usefulness of commerce"—i.e., of some system of division of labor among men. "[But] these advantages," the pamphlet maintains, "do not depend on a trade's being enormously extensive. They might subsist even with only a home trade. Antient history shews us nations, who, though separated from their neighbors and without foreign trade, were powerful and happy, solely by industry, by the culture of their lands, and of the arts, and by an animated circulation of their own productions. Japan is now an indisputable proof of this truth." From hence, of course, followed the conclusion, supposedly unfavorable to the policies of the Washington administration, which was adumbrated in the preface.

Additional evidence that the term meant "commerce in general" or "all commerce," may be found in many different writings; for example, in one of Josiah Tucker's works, of 1750, in which Tucker attempts to show that the power to regulate commerce is most safely entrusted to "landed gentlemen." "As the private interest of the landed gentleman arises," he says, "from the *general commerce* of the place [where his land lies], he can have no partial views in relation to trade. [For] the more persons there are employed in *every branch of business*, the more there will be to consume the produce of his estate. . . . His own interest is connected with the good of *the whole*." *A Brief Essay on the Advantages and Disadvantages Which respectively attend France and Great Britain, With regard to Trade*, reprinted in McCulloch, *Select Collection of Scarce and Valuable Tracts on Commerce* (London, 1857). See pp. 317–21, especially 321.

The same understanding of "general commerce" also appears in Daniel Defoe's *Plan of the English Commerce*, of 1728, a well-known book of Franklin's youth. "We ought," says Defoe, "to distinguish between the Decay of the *General Commerce* of a Nation, and the Decay of any particular Branch of it; because some particular Manufacture may decay, and even wear out, in a Country, and . . . yet at the same Time the *general Commerce* may not at all be decayed or decreased" (pp. 247 and 248).

Finally, reference may again be made to the passage in Lewes Roberts's *Treasure of Trafficke* (1643), cited in Pol. & Con., I, 85, in which the setting-up of a council of "State-merchants or Merchant States-men" was advocated, which was to have "a superintendency over the *generall Commerce* of the kingdom [of England]." This "superintendency," the discussion showed, was one intended to extend, not to "the Commerce of Merchants" only, but to agriculture, manufactures, and the fisheries, and, in short, to every branch of England's gainful activity. Reprinted in McCulloch, *Select Collection of Early English Tracts on Commerce* (London, 1856). See pp. 93–99 of the reprint. The British Board of Trade was such a council of "State-Merchants or Merchant States-men." Thomas Pownall said in 1764 that its powers extended to "the *general trade* of the Kingdom" (*Administration of the British Colonies*, I, 20). Other material on the similar use of "general trade" is collected in Pol. & Con., I, 87.

46. The narrower meanings all seem to arise out of the peculiar exigencies of particular contexts. For example, in Tench Coxe, *A View of the United States of America*

(Philadelphia, 1794), 331 ff., there is a discussion of what the author calls "the apparent or conjectural disproportion between the exports and imports of the United States." Coxe concedes that the country is importing more than it exports; but he maintains that, if all items entering into "the balance on our trade" are taken into account (including what are now called "invisibles"), there can be no doubt that the country is in a prosperous condition. He then says that he will hazard an opinion upon the subject of the country's trade balance which will appear "somewhat singular" but is "of considerable importance": that "the United States, to make the utmost advantage of things in their present improvable situation, should have little or no balance in their favor on their *general commerce*." In this context, it is obvious that "general commerce" means "foreign commerce only," because only items of "foreign commerce," though "foreign commerce" in a somewhat extended sense, enter into the international trade balance. Coxe used the term "general commerce," in this particular context, to emphasize that he meant "foreign commerce" in this extended sense. This appears from his next sentence: "If their exports, *outward freights, sales of vessels and lands*, &c. amount to twenty-four millions of dollars per annum, they [i.e., the American people] will find their true interest in importing the whole value in well selected commodities." The narrower generality of "general commerce," in this particular context, thus arises out of the peculiar characteristics of the context itself.

In a somewhat similar way, in other contexts in which "commerce" is being used to signify "foreign commerce," "general Commerce" is sometimes used to emphasize that "commerce with *all* foreign nations," rather than "commerce with some particular foreign nations," is intended. For an example of this, see *The Political Writings of John Dickinson* (Wilmington, 1801), I, 413. One instance was encountered in which "general commerce" was used to signify "*all* buying and selling, in both foreign or domestic trade," but not "agriculture" or "manufactures": "To ascertain the quality of currency requisite for any Government, we must first enquire the amount of their annual taxes, for the discharge of their foreign and domestic debt; also the sum necessary for their public exigencies; and their *general commerce*, agriculture and manufactures." B. Ind. Chr. July 21, 1787, p. 2, col. 2. Other examples of peculiar uses could no doubt be found; but the foregoing, with those in the text, seem sufficient to indicate the general nature of the usage. In brief, it may be said that the term "general commerce" was always used, either to extend the coverage of "commerce" in a context in which the word had previously been used more narrowly, or to emphasize the generality of "commerce" in the absence of such a context. In the latter case, which is what we have in Franklin's plan, the term seems to have been used to cover all kinds of "commerce," or business, or gainful activity in general.

47. *The Papers of Benjamin Franklin* (New Haven, 1959–), XVI, 243–49, 244.

48. Cf. Pol. & Con., I, 123–28.

49. *Papers of Franklin*, XV, 112.

50. Cf. Pol. & Con., I, 160–63.

51. In a letter to *The London Chronicle*, January 5, 1768 (*Papers of Franklin*, XV, 3–13, 10, 11).

52. *Papers of Franklin*, XVI, 246–47.

53. Journals, II, 196.

54. Ibid., 197.

55. Ibid., 198.

56. Ibid., 196.

57. Jefferson, V, 199.

58. Journals, II, 198–99.

59. Jefferson, V, 200.

60. Ibid. See, however, the reference to "a Committee" in Letters, I, 313.

61. Pol. & Con., I, 155–66.

NOTES TO CHAPTER III

1. Archives, 4th Ser., III, 1715. There are various bits of evidence in the newspapers of the time indicating that it was noised about that a plan of continental government had been proposed. For example, "A Continental Farmer," in Pa. Jour. of December 6, 1775, observes that, "by a late resolve, all Colony distinctions are to be laid aside"; and "A Freeman," writing in *The* [Cambridge, Mass.] *New England Chronicle*, of November 23, 1775, says that the country will "soon break off all kind of connection with Britain, and form into a GRAND REPUBLIC of the AMERICAN UNITED COLONIES." Knowledge that confederation was being proposed in the Continental Congress is also evident from the action of the Maryland convention in instructing the Maryland delegates, on January 11, 1776, that, unless a certain specified proportion of them should think it "absolutely necessary for the preservation of the liberties of the United Colonies," they should "not, without the previous knowledge and approbation of the Convention of [the] Province, assent to any proposition to declare [the] Colonies independent of the Crown of Great Britain, . . . *nor to any union or confederation of the Colonies, which* [might] *necessarily lead to a separation from the mother country.*" Archives, 4th Ser., IV, 654.

2. North Carolina Colonial Records, X, 175, 181, 186, 191, 192.

3. Warren-Adams, II, 429. The letter cited in the text is only one of many which Warren wrote urging the necessity of getting a continental constitution definitely settled. See, for example, the following: To John Adams, November 14, 1775: "The Union is every thing. With it we shall do every thing, without it nothing" (ibid., I, 185). To Samuel Adams, November 18, 1776: "Now I have given you an Account of some of our doings shall I Enquire what your high Mightinesses [the appellation of the States-General of the United Netherlands] are about. Where is your Confederation" (ibid., II, 185). To Samuel Adams, February 2, 1777: "I have great Expectations from the present Spirit of Congress. . . . if I may Conjecture that the forming a General Constitution be one subject [upon which you are busy], I hope to hear soon that it is Compleated" (ibid., II, 444). To Samuel Adams, June 16, 1777: "I want to hear how your Confederation goes on" (ibid., II, 449). There are other references to the subject scattered through the collection of letters referred to. It may be added that, as late as May 5, 1777, Warren was still referring to Congress expectantly as "the Supream Legislative." See his letter to John Adams of that date (ibid., I, 323).

4. "Is it not time for a test act? Will the Continent have one from the Congress?" (ibid., I, 178).

5. "we are well pleased with the Spirit and Resolutions of your Congress. we could only have wished you had suffered us to have Embraced so good an Opportunity to form for ourselves a Constitution worthy of Freemen. all Bodies have their Foibles. Jealousy, however Groundless, may predominate in yours. we have, however, submitted and are sending out our Letters and shall Express our Gratitude by this Conveyance for your kindness and Benevolence to us in this Respect. our Good Major Hawley can be very sincere and your Brother Cushing I suppose likes it. he has relieved me by an Intimation of a probability that you will regulate the Constitution of all the Colonies" (ibid., II, 413). See, also, another letter of Warren's to Samuel Adams, of July 9, 1775: "when are we to see all the Governments, and our own with them, reformed and set upon a Good Bottom. we look for such an Event" (ibid., II, 414). It should be added that Warren later seems to have shifted somewhat on this particular issue. It was apparently a result of his becoming convinced that the aristocratic tendency to the southward might produce a general form of local government that would not be to the liking of New England. Cf. his letter to John Adams, of June 2, 1776, in which he said: "Whether it is best there should be a perfect similarity in

the form and spirit of the several governments in the colonies, provided they are all independent of Britain, is a question I am not determined on. For some reasons it may be best for us there should be a difference. I therefore consider the address to the Convention of Virginia with the more indifference, as it may (if successful) neither injure the publick or us" (ibid., I, 252). The "Address" referred to was Carter Braxton's pamphlet discussed in Chap. IV hereof.

6. Ibid., I, 268.

7. John Adams, IX, 374.

8. See Pol. & Con., I, 592 (Pownall).

9. Cf. n. 42, to Chap. V, Pol. & Con., II, 1291–94.

10. P. 50 (London reprint for J. Almon). The pamphlet is conveniently reprinted in Bailyn, ed., *Pamphlets of the American Revolution, 1750–1776* (Cambridge, Mass., 1965–), I, 418–82. The quoted passage appears at p. 443.

11. Such suppositions do occur. Anyone who will read Merrill Jensen, *The Articles of Confederation* (Madison, 1940) and note the discussion on p. 126 thereof, of the membership of the committee of the Continental Congress which drew the so-called "Dickinson draft" of the Articles of Confederation, will see that it is there assumed that Stephen Hopkins must have been the kind of man who would have opposed the Dickinson draft. It is intimated, however, that Hopkins was in a hopeless minority and probably too old, anyhow, to take care of himself. In actual fact, Hopkins, who was still vigourous enough thereafter to act as governor of his state, was an ardent believer in continental government. Anyone who will read his *The Rights of Colonies Examined*, of 1764, bearing in mind that Hopkins was the delegate who split Rhode Island's vote in Congress, in the fall of 1774, by voting in favor of James Duane's proposals for conceding complete commercial power to the British Parliament, will see that no other conclusion is possible. Stephen Hopkins, in other words, was no "states'-righter."

12. Reprinted in Archives, 4th Ser., IV, 1541, 1551, 1552, 1554, 1559, and 1560.

13. Ibid., 1554 and 1555.

14. Ibid., 1560.

15. Paine's desire for a unicameral legislature appears from the general tenor of the discussion in the introduction to *Common Sense*. In specific reference to the provincial assemblies, his exact words were: "Let the assemblies be annual, with a President only. The representation more equal. Their business wholly domestick, and subject to the authority of a Continental Congress." The words "with a President only" were a kind of stock expression at the period and signified that the "President" was not to be a "Governor"; he was to have a casting-vote only and no veto power. In other words, according to another mode of speech of the time, he was not to be a separate "branch" of the legislature.

16. Paine desired *at least* such exceptions from both provincial and continental power as would "secure freedom and property to all men, and above all things the free exercise of religion." There was to be no concern at all with religion, except for this purpose. Cf. Archives, 4th Ser., IV, 1559.

17. The intercepted letters were printed in Draper's [Boston] *Massachusetts Gazette*, on August 17, 1775.

18. The letters are reprinted in John Adams, II, 411–12 n. Adams regretted the crack at Dickinson, but not "the ideas of independence." In a later insertion in his *Diary* (ibid.), he said, in part: "Irritated with the unpoliteness of Mr. Dickinson, and more mortified with his success in Congress, I wrote something like what had been published, but not exactly. The British printers made it worse than it was in the original. . . . They thought [the letters] a great prize. The ideas of independence, to be sure, were glaring enough, and they thought they should produce quarrels among the

members of Congress and a division of the Colonies. Me they expected utterly to ruin, because, as they represented, I had explicitly avowed my designs of independence. I cared nothing for this. I had made no secret, in or out of Congress, of my opinion that independence was become indispensable, and I was perfectly sure that in a little time the whole continent would be of my mind. I rather rejoiced in this as a fortunate circumstance, that the idea was held up to the whole world, and that the people could not avoid contemplating it and reasoning about it. Accordingly, from this time at least, if not earlier, and not from the publication of 'Common Sense', did the people in all parts of the continent turn their attention to this subject."

Adams's contemporary correspondence rather bears out the above and also the inference in the text hereof that Adams's political notions were not misreported by the Tory printers. In a letter to Mrs. James Warren, of September 26, 1775, he referred to the fate of the intercepted letters as "unfortunate." "I call them unfortunate after the manner of Men," he said, "For, altho they went into Hands which were never thought of by the Writer, and notwithstanding all the unmeaning Noise that has been made about them, they have done a great deal of good. Providence intended them for Instruments to promote valuable Purposes, altho the Writer of them, thought so little of them that he never could have recollected one Word in them, if they had been lost." Warren-Adams, I, 118. In a letter to James Warren, of October 2, 1775, Adams said: "Our Obligations of Secrecy are so braced up, that I must deny myself the Pleasure of Writing Particulars. Not because some Letters have been intercepted, for notwithstanding the Versification of them, they have done good, tho they have made some People grin. This I can Say with Confidence, that the Propriety and Necessity of the Plan of Politicks so hastily delineated in them is every day, more and more confessed even by those Gentlemen who disapproved it at the Time when they were written." Ibid., I, 124. In a letter to his wife, of March 19, 1776, Adams said: "If I can believe Mr. Dana [who had but just returned from England], those [intercepted] letters were much admired in England. I can't help laughing when I write it, because they were really such hasty, crude scraps. If I could have foreseen their fate, they should have been fit to be seen, and worth all the noise they have made. Mr. Dana says they were considered in England as containing a comprehensive idea of what was necessary to be done, and as showing resolution enough to do it." *Familiar Letters of John Adams and his Wife* (New York, 1876), 147. As editor of Adams's works, Adams's grandson said in 1850 that the originals of the intercepted letters were then "in the State paper office in London." He did not intimate that Adams's ideas had been falsified in any way by the Tory printers. John Adams, II, 411 n.

19. Franklin, it will be recalled, had proposed that "each Colony... might amend its own Constitution as [should] seem best to its own Assembly or Convention." It seems questionable whether Adams agreed with this proposal in the summer of 1775. Cf. Warren-Adams, I, 75; and John Adams, IV, 185.

20. Journals, II, 76–78.

21. *Familiar Letters of John Adams and his Wife* (New York, 1876), 134; cf. ibid., 131–32.

22. Ibid., 137.

23. Ibid., 146.

24. Warren-Adams, I, 227.

25. Ibid., I, 222. Cf. ibid., I, 227 and 233.

26. John Adams, IX, 386–87.

27. Warren-Adams, I, 222.

28. Ibid., I, 243.

29. Writing to James Warren, on April 16, Adams said: "We want a Confederation, you will say. True. This must be obtained." Warren-Adams, I, 227. Writing to

Benjamin Hichborn, on May 29, he said: "I wish I could be at home at this important period. But you will remember that all the other colonies have Constitutions to frame, and what is of infinitely greater delicacy, intricacy, and importance, the continent has a Constitution to form. If I could be of some little use at home, I may be of more here at present." John Adams, IX, 380.

30. John Adams, IV, 189, 200.

31. *Familiar Letters of John Adams and his Wife* (New York, 1876), 176.

32. John Adams, IV, 203, 208. The "preface" added to Adams's Virginia letter by his grandson indicates that the Virginia letter was written in January 1776, after George Wythe and Adams had spent an evening together. This is in accord with a note in Adams's hand, dated "Quincy, 21 July, 1811," which was found among his papers. This would make the North Carolina letter subsequent to the Virginia letter. But Adams's memory must have been at fault. He was away from Philadelphia during all of January 1776 and did not get back to Philadelphia until February 8. *Familiar Letters of John Adams and his Wife* (New York, 1876), 131–32. His contemporary account, which makes the North Carolina letter earlier than the Virginia letter, and written, apparently, between the 6th and 27th of March, will be found in a letter to James Warren, of April 20, 1776. Warren-Adams, I, 230; cf. Letters, I, 1viii.

33. Warren-Adams, I, 230.

34. Ibid.

35. *Familiar Letters of John Adams and his Wife* (New York, 1876), 176.

36. Ibid., 199–200; cf. John Adams, IX, 380.

37. Journals, V, 546.

38. Ibid., 433.

NOTES TO CHAPTER IV

1. See n. 26, below.

2. The letters of "The Independent Whig," from which the quotations in the text are taken, will be found in the issues of N.Y. Jour. of February 29, and March 14 and 28, 1776. There was also an earlier introductory number.

3. The statement was made by Paine, in the second of his "Forester" letters, published in Pa. Gaz., of April 10, 1776. The letter was dated April 8, 1776. Paine said: "I am certain that I am within compass when I say one hundred and twenty thousand [copies have been sold]." One of Paine's biographers says that, in the end, the total sale of *Common Sense* "probably" ran to half a million. Conway, *The Life of Thomas Paine*, (New York, 1909), 69.

4. Quoted in M. C. Tyler, *The Literary History of the American Revolution* (New York, 1897), I, 473.

5. See the collection of opinions in Tyler, *Literary History*, 471 ff.; and Conway, chap. VI.

6. See his letters to John Adams, in John Adams, IX, 342 and 641; see also Brown, *Joseph Hawley* (New York, 1931).

7. Archives, 4th Ser., IV, 1191.

8. Ibid., 1220.

9. Ibid., V, 1168.

10. Quoted in Mayo, *John Langdon of New Hampshire* (Concord, 1937), p. 204 n. The original letter is stated to be in the possession of Mrs. Charles Sumner Hamlin, of Washington, D.C.

11. Quoted in Upton, *Revolutionary New Hampshire* (Hanover, 1936), p. 72. Original stated to be among the Josiah Bartlett Manuscripts in possession either of Dartmouth

College or New Hampshire Historical Society.

12. Reprinted in Archives, 4th Ser., V, 96 ff.

13. Evans, *American Bibliography*, V, 277.

14. Reprinted in Archives, 4th Ser., IV, 1133 ff.

15. Ibid., V, 450 ff.

16. See Pol. & Con., I, 146–52.

17. This view is taken in Merrill Jensen, *The Articles of Confederation* (Madison, 1940).

18. See Campbell, *A History of the Commonwealth and Ancient Dominion of Virginia* (Philadelphia, 1860), 646, and Horner, *The History of the Blair, Bannister, and Braxton Families before and after the Revolution* (Philadelphia, 1898), 126.

19. The date is approximately established by a letter of Richard Henry Lee's dated May 12, 1776. Lee I, 190.

20. The Braxton pamphlet appeared in the issues of June 8 and 15.

21. Reprinted in Archives, 4th Ser., VI, 748 ff.

22. The attack was in a letter to Edmund Pendleton, president of the Virginia convention. Lee, I, 190.

23. Letters, II, 345 and 346; and cf. discussion in chap. VII hereof.

24. Braxton grounded this proposal upon a distinction he drew between private and public virtue. This is the part of his pamphlet which was intended as an answer to John Adams's *Thoughts on Government*, which according to Braxton confused the two. Patrick Henry, in a letter to Adams, dated May 20, 1776 (John Adams, IV, 201–02), referred to Braxton's pamphlet as "a silly thing" and said: "His reasonings and distinction between private and public virtue, are weak, shallow, evasive, and the whole performance an affront and disgrace to this country; and by one expression, I suspect his whiggism." This Henry letter, with the other matters referred to in the text, can leave little doubt as to what feature of the Braxton pamphlet it was that had aroused resentment. Cf. also, Warren-Adams, I, 242 and 252.

25. Other than "J. R.," the series was as follows: April 1, 1776 (p. 3, col. 2): "The privilege of choosing provincial deputies is great, but not equal to that of choosing delegates for the American Congress." Neither should be given up by freemen. Quotes *Common Sense*. May 20, 1776: "A Freeman" gives "A Hint" that popular election of members of Congress is now in order "that the people may be legally represented." Uses the words of *Common Sense*. May 27, 1776: Committee of Inspection of the Several Towns of Litchfield County: Election of congressional delegates by the legislature is "not agreeable to the freedom of the times, to the constitution of this colony, nor to the reason or nature of things." "It is the inherent birthright of every member of society, to have his voice in the choice of those into whose hands, he commits the power *of governing and directing* for the good of the community at large." "It appears to us indispensably necessary that the members of congress be annually elected by the impartial, unbiassed, uncorrupted voice of the freemen at large." May 27, 1776: "We hear the town of Canterbury [Ct.], in a full meeting, have unanimously adopted the principles of independence contained in *Common Sense*; and also voted that the delegates for the Continental Congress be elected by the Freemen of the Colony, and not by their representatives." June 3, 1776: "A Freeman" says: "In forming *a new constitution or empire* in America, people cannot be too jealous of their essential rights. Among these the right of the freemen to elect the Delegates to the Continental Congress will doubtless claim a place." "The privilege ought by no means to be given up." June 10, 1776: "J. R." June 17, 1776: "Marcus Brutus" says he thinks all the foregoing "have inadvertently imbibed a wrong idea of a Continental Congress": it is really only a committee of the colonies to execute certain purposes, not a legislature.

26. The notion will be found in several of the items referred to in the preceding note.

27. Cf. the efforts of the Connecticut delegates, Roger Sherman, Oliver Ellsworth, and William Samuel Johnson, to get state legislatural representation in the national legislature. As early as June 11, Sherman proposed, with Ellsworth's backing, proportional suffrage in the House and equal state suffrage in the Senate. Records, I, 196, 201, 204. "Every thing," he said, "depended on [his second proposal]." Ibid., I, 201. And by "everything," he clearly meant a national government with general national power, such as the Virginia plan proposed. Cf. James Wilson, speaking on national powers under the Virginia plan, on June 16 (ibid., I, 252, 260, 265, 269, 270, 277), and Alexander Hamilton's understanding, on June 18, that "the forming a new government to pervade the whole with decisive powers *in short with complete sovereignty* . . . seem[ed] to be *the prevailing sentiment* [of the convention]." On June 21, according to Madison, Johnson said: "Mr. Wilson and the gentleman from Virginia . . . wished to leave the States in possession of a considerable, *tho' a subordinate* jurisdiction. They had not yet however shewn how this c[oul]d consist with, or be secured ag[ain]st *the general sovereignty & jurisdiction*, which they proposed to give to the national Government. . . . He wished it therefore to be well considered whether in case the States, as was proposed, sh[oul]d retain some portion of sovereignty at least, this portion could be preserved, without allowing them to participate effectually in the Gen[era]l Gov[ernmen]t, without giving them each [i.e., their legislatures] a distinct and equal vote for the purpose of defending themselves in the general Councils." The foregoing is sufficiently confirmed by the reports of Yates and Lansing. Ibid., I, 355; cf. ibid., 363, and Strayer, *The Delegate from New York* (Princeton, 1939), 76. Then, on July 17, after the Convention, in committee of the whole, had agreed to the foregoing Connecticut proposals, Sherman read to it his proposed scheme of power. The general welfare power included in Sherman's proposals was adopted in substance, but without the qualified "internal-police" limitation which Sherman desired to include in it (Records, II, 26–27). At the very end of the Convention, Sherman attempted to obtain a guaranty to the states of their equal votes in the Senate, and renewed his efforts to obtain an "internal-police" limitation. His proposals were at first both defeated; but, upon motion of Gouverneur Morris, the guaranty of an equal vote in the Senate was then inserted in the Constitution apparently as sufficient in itself to accomplish Sherman's purpose. Records, II, 630–31.

28. "J. R." is reprinted in Archives, 4th Ser., VI, 798 ff.

29. There is one other statement of "J.R."'s that should perhaps be noted. He says, at one point, that "the General Assembly of each Colony is the Legislature thereof, invested with supreme powers of Government therein, and may not be infringed upon by the General Congress." This is his reason for making the members of Congress "amenable" to the state legislatures for misconduct. Under our modern notions, the passage just quoted, like the passage quoted in the text, is easy to take in an intraterritorially all-inclusive sense; but "J. R."'s "supreme" clearly means only "supreme" within the General Assembly's appropriate sphere, and his "infringe" relates only to infringements on that sphere. The extent of the General Assembly's appropriate sphere would of course depend upon the extent of the powers granted to the General Congress. These, "J. R." says, have not yet been determined; but, as indicated in the text, he thought they ought to "extend to all matters of general concernment." Hence, no congressional act relating to any matter of "general concernment" could possibly "infringe" the "supreme" powers of a general assembly "within" a colony. This is elementary; but "J. R."'s mode of speech was somewhat loose, and it is necessary to spell out the possibilities in order to reach a reasoned decision as to what he meant. It would of course be possible to reconcile his apparent inconsistencies, by assuming that he thought nothing occurring within the territorial boundaries of a colony could possibly be a matter of "general concernment." But that proposition is such manifest nonsense that it seems unwarranted to assume that he

thought it. After all, even war could occur "within" the territorial confines of a colony, as most of the colonies, if they did now know it, were soon to find out.

30. May 30, June 13, and June 20, 1776.

31. The second letter of "Spartanus," from which the quotations in the text are taken, appeared in *The Packet* of July 1, 1776.

32. The second letter, from which the quotations in the text are taken, appeared in Ph. Fr. Jour. of September 29, 1776.

33. The second and third letters of "Spartanus" are reprinted in Archives, 4th Ser., VI, 840 ff., and 994 ff. The first is apparently not in Archives.

34. See descriptions of the letters of "Essex" and of the plan printed in *The* [Philadelphia] *Pennsylvania Evening Post*, of March 5, 1776, in the next note.

35. Besides the items mentioned in the text, there were the following among others:

Letters IV and V of "Essex," a New Jersey writer, appeared in N.Y. Jour. The remaining letters were not found. The letters were addressed: "To the Author of Common Sense." In N.Y. Jour., of March 7, 1776, "Essex" advocated breaking the states up into smaller, more equal units, to facilitate "equal [i.e., proportional] representation" in Congress, thus anticipating a New Jersey proposal made eleven years later in the Federal Convention. "Let objectors consider," he said, "that the strength and happiness of America must be Continental, and not Provincial, and that whatever appears to be for the good of the whole, must be submitted to by every Part. This holds true and ought to be a governing maxim in all societies." He also advocated popular election of congressional delegates. All males over twenty-one years of age, who met a small property qualification, should have the right to vote, as should all widows, also, who paid taxes. Delegates in Congress should vote per capita, he thought, and not by colonies. In N.Y. Jour. of April 4, 1776, "Essex" advocated the abolition of slavery. "But I leave it with Congress," he said, "by whom America must be directed, Independency or not."

"A Lover of Order," in Pa. Jour. of November 22, 1775, said: "As I hope never to see the day when the Continent shall be without a Congress, so I hope in proper season to see a Congress chosen by the people." He went on to protest against the instruction of delegates to Congress by the colonial assemblies and congresses. The delegates were appointed temporarily by these elected bodies as a matter of convenience; but they were, nevertheless, the representatives of the people. The same writer, under the signature of "A Continental Farmer," in Pa. Jour. of December 6, 1775, announced to the public that "by a late resolve [presumably in the Continental Congress], all Colony distinctions are to be laid aside." He also protested again against the Pennsylvania Assembly's instructing the Pennsylvania delegates and again denied its right to do so.

On March 5, 1776, there appeared in *The* [Philadelphia] *Evening Post* what purported to be "Proposals for a Confederation of the United Colonies." In the printing of the plan one, and possibly two, of its provisions were garbled. Nevertheless, the plan seems worth noting, since it quite certainly proceeded from some one in or close to Congress. This is apparent from the fact that the plan is plainly a worked-over version of the Franklin plan, and also from the fact that certain of its worked-over provisions found their way into the initial, committee draft of the Articles of Confederation, in the Continental Congress. The plan purported to be a "covenant" between the several colonies "to act in union . . . for their common defence against their enemies, the security of their LIBERTIES and PROPERTIES, and for their mutual and general welfare." "The Safety of [the] Persons [of the members of the colonies] and their Families," which Franklin had mentioned in his plan as an "object" of the union, and which, presumably, might well have been regarded as the equivalent of "internal peace," was omitted in the plan in *The Evening Post*; and apparently in consonance with this omission, the provision heretofore referred to as the "states' rights" provision of the Franklin plan was expanded to include a provision that "each Colony [should] have the sole direction and government of *its own internal police*." The "General Congress" was described in general as set up "for the management of the common interests and concerns [of the United Colonies]," which "common interests and concerns" presumably were the objects "for" which they had "covenanted" "to act in union." There was also a catalog of various specific things that the Congress could do. "Regulating commerce" was not mentioned; but the last thing in the list was the "appoint[ing] a Committee of Safety and Correspondence to *transmit* such matters in the recess of the Congress, as [might] be judged necessary to commit to them [i.e., to the Committee] for the general welfare of the United Colonies." "But the Congress," it was immediately added, "shall have no authority to impose or leavy taxes, or interfere with *the internal policy* of any of the Colonies." The word "transmit," in the first of the last two quotations is a misprint for the word "transact"; and, in view of the earlier use in the plan of the term "internal police," the term "internal policy," in the second of the quotations, pretty certainly is a misprint for "internal police" or, possibly, its synonym, "internal polity." Read as the original draft of the Articles was read by contemporaries, this plan would have been interpreted as conferring a "general welfare" power on Congress. Cf. discussion in the text hereof, pp. 116–17. This, of course, was in accord with the expectations generally entertained at this time, as can be seen from the materials considered in the text. The plan, though reprinted in a number of other newspapers (Ess. Jour., March 29, 1776; Conn. Jour., April 3, 1776; N.Y. Jour., April 4, 1776; Conn. Cour., April 15, 1776; Bost. Gaz., April 22, 1776), seems nowhere to have elicited any comment, except in Litchfield County, Connecticut. The Committees of Inspection of the several towns in that county joined in a statement disapproving the provision in the plan, that delegates to the General Congress should be "elected by the legislative Assembly, or Convention, of the respective Colonies." "It is the inherent birthright of every member of society, to have his voice in the choice of those into whose hands he commits the power of governing and directing for the good of the community at large." Conn. Cour., May 27, 1776.

The following appeared in Prov. Gaz., of November 23, 1776: "The business of the Continental Congress being continental, it is to see what each state ought to do for the promotion of the cause [of independence] as it is continental; and then to recommend the same to the assemblies of the United States, and also where they would collect the opinion of the Continent, they recommend to the assemblies of the several States to take the minds of their constituents, which when they have done, they communicate to the Congress. By this means they collect the opinion of the Continent, as was done in the question of Independence. The opinion of the continent being thus collected, may consistent with liberty be enacted as a Continental act, and be binding on the whole continent, and not otherwise; for if we have any body of men to legislate for us, by whose edicts were are bound, over whom we have no controul, we are enslaved." The foregoing may sound like the vaporings of an early "states'-righter" but such apparently was not the character of the author, for he proposed that the same procedure of legislation should be followed by the assemblies of the separate states. Rather, he was a doctrinaire democrat, of the kind responsible for the institution of "instructions to legislators," which produced a good deal of trouble in various connections, for both state and nation, during the early period of our national history.

36. Probably a misprint for "polity."

37. The Articles of Confederation appeared in Bost. Gaz., on January 19, 1778.

38. There are many instances in which the "internal police" of cities and towns is spoken of. See, for example, "Philadelphiensis II," reprinted in Am. Her. of December 17, 1787, wherein "a bye-law made by a town-meeting *to regulate its internal police*"

is referred to; or "Philo," in Balt. Gaz. of January 22, 1788, who speaks of the "domestic police" of the town of Baltimore. It may be noted in passing, too, that Montesquieu spoke of "police" as relating to "trifling" maters: "In the exercise of the *police*, it is rather the magistrate who punishes than the law; in the sentence passed on crimes, it is rather the law that punishes than the magistrate. The business of the *police* consists of affairs which arise every instant, and are commonly of a trifling nature. . . . We ought not to confound a flagrant violation of the laws, with a simple breach of the *police*: These things are of a different order." *The Spirit of the Laws* (Worcester, 1802), II, 186.

39. Washington, XVI, 483, 488.

40. Warren-Adams, II, 294, 296; Drake, *Memoir of General Henry Knox* (Boston, 1873), 77, 96, 147.

NOTES TO CHAPTER V

1. Archives, 4th Ser., II, 1244.
2. Ibid., 1253.
3. See Pol. & Con., I, 155–66.
4. Archives, 5th Ser., I, 1391.
5. 14 Geo. III, c. 45.
6. Journals, II, 76–78.
7. Ibid., 83. The letters of James Warren reflect the dissatisfaction which Congress's action caused in the local congress. On June 20, 1775, he wrote to John Adams: "I am well pleased with most of [the Continental Congress's] resolves. I can't however say that I admire the form of government prescribed [for Massachusetts]. But we are all Submission and are sending out our Letters [as directed] for calling an Assembly. I hope we shall have as good an opportunity for a good Government in some future time." Warren-Adams, I, 64. In a letter to Samuel Adams, of June 21, 1775, he said: "we could only have wished you had suffered us to have Embraced so good an Opportunity to form for ourselves a Constitution worthy of Freemen. . . . your brother Cushing . . . has relieved me by an Intimation of a probability that you will regulate the Constitution of all the Colonies." Ibid., II, 413; cf. ibid., I, 177–78, 182–83; II, 427–28; and John Adams, IX, 365.
8. Archives, 4th Ser., V, 1108 ff.
9. Journals, III, 298.
10. See Pol. & Con., I, 147–49.
11. Journals, III, 319.
12. See Pol. & Con., I, 150–52.
13. Archives, 4th Ser., V, 1 ff.
14. Journals, III, 326.
15. See Van Tyne, "Sovereignty in the American Revolution," 12 *American Historical Review*, 529, 539, 540 (1907).
16. Archives, 4th Ser., V, 611.
17. Journal of the General Assembly of South Carolina, March 20, 1776–April 11, 1776 (Columbia, 1906), 23.
18. Archives, 4th Ser., V, 605.
19. Ibid., 614.
20. Ibid.
21. See Pol. & Con., I, 66.
22. Journals, III, 403.
23. None was established in either Connecticut or Rhode Island. The governments of these colonies being wholly elective under their charters from the British crown, no

change was necessary save nonrecognition, for the future, of the royal right of disallowing colonial laws and the appeal to the Privy Council.

24. Journals, IV, 342.

25. Ibid., 357.

26. Ibid., II, 84, 85, 89, 91, 100, 101, 111, 202.

27. Ibid., IV, 277–78.

28. Ibid., 320.

29. Conn. Cour., June 3, 1776, pp. 1 and 2.

30. Archives, 4th Ser., VI, 1628.

31. Ibid., 5th Ser., II, 52 (Pennsylvania) and 286 (Delaware).

32. No new instructions were issued by Massachusetts.

33. Archives, 4th Ser., VI, 1030.

34. Ibid., 1628 and 1629.

35. The Maryland convention, on January 11, 1776, instructed its delegates in Congress that, unless a certain specified proportion of them should think it "absolutely necessary for the preservation of the liberties of the United Colonies," they should "not, without the previous knowledge and approbation of the Convention of [the] Province, assent to any proposition to declare [the] Colonies independent of the Crown of Great Britain, . . . nor to any union or confederation of [the] Colonies, which [might] necessarily lead to a separation from the mother country." Archives, 4th Ser., IV, 654. On May 15, 1776, the convention, for the sake of "the peace and good order of the Province" resolved to dispense with "the usual Oaths to the Government" by public officers, some officers having "alleged scruples to taking [them] during the unhappy differences with Great Britain." Ibid., V, 1584–85. Five days later, Congress's resolution of May 15, 1776, recommending the forming of state governments, was received. The next day, the Maryland convention proceeded to disagree *seriatim*, in testy fashion, with the various statements in Congress's resolve; to claim for the people of Maryland "the sole and exclusive right of regulating the internal Government and Police of [that] Province," which, it apparently conceived, Congress's resolve had infringed; and to renew its instructions to its delegates, already noted. Ibid., 1587–89. These instructions were recalled on June 28, 1776; and at the same time, authority was given to the Maryland delegates "to concur with the other United Colonies, or a majority of them, in declaring the United Colonies free and independent States [and] in forming such further compact and confederation between them . . . as shall be judged necessary for securing the Liberties of America." It was added that Maryland would "hold itself bound by the Resolutions of a majority of the United Colonies in the premises; *Provided*, The sole and exclusive right of regulating *the internal Government and Police* of [the] Colony [were] reserved to the people thereof." Ibid., VI, 1491. A constitution and bill of rights containing a like reservation were adopted on November 3, 1776 (ibid., 5th Ser., III, 144); and one week later, a new appointment of delegates was made to the Continental Congress with authority "to concur with the other United States, or a majority of them, in forming a Confederation." It was added, however, that "such Confederation, when formed, [should] not be binding upon [Maryland] without the assent of [its] General Assembly," and that there should be "reserv[ed] always to [Maryland] the sole and exclusive right of regulating the *internal police* thereof." Ibid., 179.

36. Archives, 4th Ser., VI, 863.

37. Ibid., 963.

38. 14 Geo., III, c. 45. Cf. *Massachusettensis* (London reprint for J. Mathews, 1776): "The good policy of the act, for regulating the government of this province, will be the subject of some future paper" (p. 24). "When the statute for regulating the government arrived, a match was put to the train" (p. 38).

39. Archives, 4th Ser., VI, 1669. It should be noted that no reservation was made by Rhode Island over any "political" affairs, unless "religious" affairs can be deemed to fall in that category. The Rhode Island reservation probably indicates doubt, on the part of the Rhode Island legislature, that "religious" affairs fell in the "civil" category, which, as explained in Pol. & Con., 151–52, was the category which, together with the "political," covered the whole field of government. It may be noted, however, that "concerns of a religious and ecclesiastical nature, so far as they [might] be under the cognizance and control of civil authority," were referred to, in the New York provincial congress, in 1775, as "the most inestimable object of internal police." Archives, 4th Ser., II, 1317. An item in *The* [Worcester] *Massachusetts Spy*, of August 27, 1776 (p. 1, col. 2), also refers to religion as an "object" of "internal police."

40. Archives, 4th Ser., VI, 461.

41. Ibid., 868. The Connecticut reservation is especially noteworthy. Like James Duane's remarks before the First Continental Congress, the language of the Connecticut reservation indicates an awareness that "the administration of Government" (or, as Duane put it, "the Dispensation of Justice civil and criminal") was not included in "internal police," as that term was then frequently used and understood. Second, the reservation of "the right of forming governments for [local purposes]" indicates awareness of the view, widely entertained in 1776, that the forming of such governments should be subject to continental "direction" (see next note). Finally, the inclusion in the Connecticut reservation of the category of "internal concerns" (which should be understood in a sense contrasting with "continental concerns") shows that "internal police" was understood to be a narrow category.

42. To the materials already cited, there may be added, as indicative of the widespread dubiety, in 1776, as to how local governments should be formed, a statement by the New York writer "Spartanus" (referred to in the previous chapter) that "every Province should be viewed as having a right, *either with or without an application to the Continental Congress*, to alter their form of Government in *some* particulars." "Spartanus," it will be recalled, was a writer with strong predilections in favor of local government. The present power of the Congress of the United States "to make all Laws which shall be necessary and proper" for "guarantee[ing] to every State . . . a Republican Form of Government" vests Congress, of course, with a considerable unexercised power over state constitutions at the present time.

43. Cf. n. 41, above.

44. The Connecticut instruction was something like the resolution of Congress of May 15. It directed its delegates to "move and promote, as fast as may be convenient, a regular and permanent plan of Union and Confederation of the Colonies, for the security and preservation of their just rights and liberties, and for mutual defence and security." Then followed the reservation stated in the text. The reader will note that the stated objects of the "Union and Confederation" desired by the Connecticut Assembly *plus* the reserved fields did not add up to the whole field of government, upon any possible interpretation of the reservation. Much the same was true in the case of Rhode Island. See n. 39, above.

45. The Virginia delegation was still voting for the original scheme on April 25, 1777, when the original scheme was finally voted down. See Letters, II, 346.

46. 12 Wheaton (U.S.), 1.

47. Archives, 4th Ser., V, 860.

48. (1) North Carolina, as already related, rejected Benjamin Franklin's plan of confederation on September 4, 1775. (2) As just related in the text, its instructions in the spring of 1776 were the most localistic of all those issued by the various states. (3) Its delegate, Thomas Burke, as we shall presently see, was responsible for the state-sovereignty reservation in the Articles of Confederation as finally adopted. And (4) it at first rejected the Constitution and was very late in adopting it, being the next to last

of the original thirteen states to adopt it.

49. See Crittenden, *North Carolina Newspapers before 1790*, The James Sprunt Historical Studies, vol. 20, no. 1, p. 9: "In the whole period before 1790, none of the six towns in which newspapers were printed had a white population of more than a thousand." See also the same author's *Commerce of North Carolina*.

50. Archives, 4th Ser., VI, 1674.

51. Ibid, V, 605. Cf. n. 26, above.

52. Archives, 5th Ser., I, 1391.

53. Cf. n. 44, above.

NOTES TO CHAPTER VI

1. Journals, III, 454 and 456.

2. Letters, I, 313. There appears to have been, at about this time, some talk of a New England confederacy if the other states declined to go along. According to Samuel Adams, Franklin was ready, in such an eventuality, to throw in his lot with New England. Cf. John Adams, IX, 373.

3. Letters, I, 460, and Archives, 4th Ser., VI, 517.

4. Journals, V, 425.

5. Letters, I, 502 and 517.

6. Journals, V, 431 and 433.

7. Letters, I, 495.

8. Journals, II, 197 (Art. VII).

9. Ibid., V, 546, at 549–50.

10. Letters, I, 517.

11. Edward Rutledge described the plan as drawn by John Dickinson, of Pennsylvania. James Wilson and Benjamin Rush, of Pennsylvania, afterwards supported the scheme of power which the plan embodied. Letters, II, 234. And Thomas Burke, of North Carolina, indicated in his reports to his governor, in the late winter of 1777, that the New Jersey and Maryland delegates were then taking a similar position. Ibid., 249, 257. Virginia's was the sole negative vote when the scheme of confederation was transformed on April 25, 1777, though some of the individual delegates from other states voted similarly. Ibid., 346. On Virginia's attitude, see also ibid., 234, 253, and 279.

12. See ibid., 56; and cf. with South Carolina material set forth in chap. V hereof.

13. Note that "making everything bend to the good of the whole" was in precise accord with South Carolina's instructions to its delegates. Cf. Archives, 4th Ser., V, 605.

14. Journals, V, 546. The complete text of the Dickinson draft is reprinted in Appendix B hereof.

15. Ibid., II, 195 (Art. II).

16. Ibid., 196 (Art. III).

17. Ibid., V, 547 (Art. III).

18. Ibid., 552 (Art. XVIII).

19. By reference to the letter of John Adams to his wife, of July 11, 1776 (*Familiar Letters*, 199, 200), mentioned in chap. III hereof, n. 36, it will be seen that John Adams assumed that "commercial" matters were to be within the power of the Congress.

20. Journals, II, 196 (Art. V).

21. Records, I, 166, 167, 170, and 172; Strayer, *The Delegate from New York* (Princeton, 1939), 40 and 41.

22. It may also be observed that certain remarks of Luther Martin's, who was not in

the Convention on June 8, also are corroborative of the interpretation of the Dickinson draft here presented. Martin was one of the most outspoken representatives of the state-officer class in the Federal Convention. On June 20, he said: "I confess when the confederation was made, congress ought to have been invested with more extensive powers; but when the states [i.e., the revolutionary state legislatures] saw that *congress indirectly aimed at sovereignty*, they were jealous, and therefore refused any farther concessions." Records, I, 347.

23. Records, I, 167 and 172.

24. Ibid., 166.

25. Ibid., 21.

26. Ibid., 59 and 60.

27. Ibid.

28. Ibid., II, 21 and 25. In presenting his proposal, "Mr. Sherman observed that it would be difficult to draw the line between the powers of the Gen[era]l Legislature, and those to be left with the States; [and] that he did not like the definition contained in the Resolution [as reported by the Committee of the whole]" (ibid). The remainder of the proposals and additions made by Sherman on July 17th will be found in Records, III, 615 and 616. Mr. Farrand, for some reason which he does not make clear, seems to think these "Sherman Proposals," which he prints at this point, represent "the ideas of the Connecticut delegation in forming the New Jersey Plan." He scouts Bancroft's statement that the proposals were "presented to the Federal Convention," and Bancroft's opinion that "in importance, [they] stand next to [the proposals] of Virginia." Considering that the Commerce Clause was taken directly from Sherman's proposals, and that the General Welfare Clause, proposed by Sherman, also went into the Constitution, albeit without Sherman's qualified "internal-police" limitation, it would seem that Bancroft was plainly right as to the importance of Sherman's proposals. That he was also correct in his statement that they were presented to the convention seems clear enough from the description of the "enumeration of powers in explanation of his ideas" which, according to Madison, Sherman read when he presented his general formula of power referred to in the text. Records, II, 26. The Sherman proposals may, of course, also have been read to the caucus which concocted the New Jersey Plan, but there is no evidence to that effect.

29. Ibid., II, 26.

30. Ibid., 367. The committee proposed that "the Legislature of the United States [should] have the power *to provide*, as may become necessary, from time to time, *for the well managing and securing the* common property and *general interests and welfare of the United States in such manner as shall not interfere with the Governments of individual States in matters which respect only their internal Police*, or for which their individual authorities may be competent." It will be noted that, in the committee's proposal, Franklin's formula can still be discerned: a Congress "for the more convenient Management of general Interests" with power to "make such general Ordinances as tho' necessary to the General Welfare, particular Assemblies cannot be competent to." Journals, II, 196 (Art. IV and V).

31. Journals, V, 546–56.

32. Ibid., 600, 604, 608, 609, 611, 612, 615, 616, 621, 624, 628, 635, 636, 639, 674–89.

33. Letters, II, 28, 29, 32, 33.

34. Ibid., 44.

35. Cited in n. 33, above.

36. Letters, II, 54. Rutledge said, in part: "*If my opinion was likely to be taken* I would propose that the States should appoint a special Congress to be composed of new Members for [the] purpose [of framing a plan of confederation]—and that no Person

should disclose any part of the present plan." The mode of speech in this passage, taken with the bad temper and bad taste that run throughout the letter and, even more, through his letter of June 29 (Letters, I, 517), strongly suggest that Rutledge and his ideas were not very highly regarded by his fellow delegates. And the tone of his letters is certainly not such as to lead one to conclude that such a lack of regard for him was unjustified.

37. The notes of Adams and Jefferson are printed in Journals, VI at 1069 ff. and 1085 ff., respectively.

38. The draft of the committee of the whole, with the Dickinson draft in a parallel column, is printed in Journals, V, 674–89.

NOTES TO CHAPTER VII

1. Journals, V, 689.
2. Letters, II, 62.
3. Journals, V, 837.
4. Letters, II, 97 and 113.
5. Ibid., 146.
6. The phrase is William Hooper's. Letters, II, 195. He added: "We are obliged, except when the Weather paves the streets to go to Congress on Horseback, the way so miry that Carriages almost stall on the sides of them. When the Devil proffered our Saviour the Kingdoms of the World, he surely placed his thumb on this delectable spot and reserved it to himself for his own peculiar chosen seat and inheritance." There were other similar complaints, though none quite so pathetic.
7. The figures given in the text are based on the data assembled in Letters, I, xli-lxvi, and II, xxxix-lxxiii. See also John Adams's letter to James Warren, of February 17, 1777: "I have the melancholly Prospect before me of a Congress continually changing, untill very few Faces remain, that I saw in the first Congress. Not one from South Carolina, not one from North Carolina, only one from Virginia, only two from Maryland, not one from Pennsylvania, Not one from New Jersey, not one from New York, only one from Connecticutt, not one from Rhode Island, not one from New Hampshire, only one, at present, from Massachusetts. Mr. S. Adams, Mr. Sherman, and Coll. Richard Henry Lee, Mr. Chase and Mr. Paca, are all that remain. The rest are dead, *resigned*, *deserted* or cutt up into Governors, etc. at home." Letters, II, 260. He might have added that some, like Washington, were in the army; and that some others, like Franklin, were abroad on the nation's business.
8. Letters, II, 252 (James Wilson).
9. John Alsop, of New York, is a well-known case in point. He was one of the delegates from New York to the Continental Congress, until after the Declaration of Independence. Disapproving of that step, he resigned his office. Archives, 5th Ser., I, 368, 1428, 1429. Cf. the action of the North Carolina congress on Franklin's plan in September 1775 (North Carolina Colonial Records, X, 175, 181, 186, 191, 192).
10. Governor William Franklin, of New Jersey, a son of Benjamin Franklin, but a Tory, said it was "perhaps best" that conservatives should participate in the pre-Revolutionary proceedings, "as they [might] be a means of preventing [the revolutionaries'] going into some Extravagances." New Jersey Archives, X, 604.
11. Benjamin Rush said in his *Diary*, for April 8, 1777, that "the declaration of independence produced a secession of tories—timid—moderate and double minded men from the counsels of America." Letters, II, 320. "In consequence", he added, "the congress as well as each of the States have possessed ten times the Vigor and Strength they had formerly." It was, however, a "Vigor and Strength" merely for independence, and not, as Doctor Rush had reason to know, a "Vigor and Strength"

for the kind of American continental government that Doctor Rush himself desired. Cf. his *Diary*, for February 4, 1777, in Letters, II, 234.

12. John Adams, X, 63, 110, 193. Thomas McKean, of Pennsylvania and Delaware, agreed with Adams in this estimate. He added that "more than a Third of influential characters were against [the Revolution]." Ibid., X, 87.

13. The proceedings of the convention are printed in an appendix to Conn. Rec. (Hartford, 1894), I, 585–99. Cf. Pol. & Con., I, 179–80.

14. Archives, 5th Ser. III, 845.

15. Ibid., 1077.

16. Ibid., 1142, 1143.

17. Conn. Rec., I, 587.

18. Ibid., 588–89.

19. Ibid., 599.

20. Archives, 5th Ser., II, 1388, 1389. Governor Trumbull sent, with his letter, a copy of the Connecticut resolution appointing delegates.

21. Journals, VII, 65.

22. Ibid., 80, 81, 87, 88, 93.

23. Letters, II, 234.

24. Ibid.

25. Ibid.

26. Ibid.

27. Ibid., 235.

28. Journals, IV, 320.

29. Ibid., I, 75, 78, 79.

30. This view of the Declaration is, of course, not uncommon. Cf. Van Tyne, "Sovereignty in the American Revolution," 12 *American Historical Review* 529 (1907). The theory seems to be that, in declaring "these *United* Colonies" "free and independent *States*," the intention was to declare them "free and independent" of each other, as well as of the British crown. The reliance of those who take this "states' rights" view of the Declaration is the plurality of the word "states," and an assumption that "states," as used in 1776, necessarily meant "state" in the international sense. But, as already pointed out in Pol. & Con., I, 55 ff., "state" was in common use in the eighteenth century to designate members of confederacies and federal unions, of various kinds. The Declaration, it should be remembered, did not say that "these *Thirteen* Colonies" were "free and independent *nations*."

31. Journals, VII, 93, 94.

32. Letters, II, 237. There is no mention of disapproval of the New England scheme of price-fixing, up to this time, by any one. Quite the contrary. See Letters, II, 227, 229, 233, 235, 242. Abraham Clark, of New Jersey, said on February 8: "The four New England Colonies have had a meeting of Committees from their Legislatures to consult measures for their mutual defence and for regulating Trade and Commerce. Their proceedings are before Congress, and I expect will soon Obtain their Approbation, and recommendation will thereupon be sent to N. York, N. Jersey, Pensa. and Maryland to app[oin]t Com[mitt]ees to meet at Phila[delphia] for the purpose of regulating the Price of all Articles of Trade, etc. the Southern States will also be desired to meet for that purpose." Ibid., 242. Thomas Burke, of North Carolina said on February 12 that Maryland and Pennsylvania had been "very solicitous" to get a vote of approval, on that day. Ibid., 249.

33. Journals, VII, 111, 112.

34. Ibid., 118; Letters, II, 235, 249, 255.

35. Letters, II, 255.

36. Journals, VII, 121; Letters, II, 250–53.

37. Journals, VII, 124, 125; Letters, II, 253.

38. Journals, VII, 85, 87.

39. See *The Dictionary of American Biography*, on Burke.

40. Journals, VII, 328.

41. Burke seconded and supported a motion in Congress, on February 3, 1781, to give Congress a complete "superintending" power over all the commercial regulations of the states. See chap. IX hereof. Cornelius Harnett, one of the delegates from North Carolina in fall of 1777, wrote Burke, on November 13: "The child Congress has been big with, these two years past, is at last brought forth—(Confederation). I fear it will by several Legislatures be thought a little deformed,—you will think it a Monster." He wrote to Burke again, on the twentieth of the same month, about what he was pleased to term "your favorite Confederation." Letters, II, 547 and 562.

42. Letters, II, 276, 554, 555, 557.

43. Ibid., 294.

44. Ibid., 235.

45. Journals, VII, 108, 109.

46. Ibid., 115 ff.

47. Letters, II, 275.

48. Ibid., 276.

49. Ibid., 277, 279.

50. Ibid., 275.

51. Journals, VII, 154.

52. Letters, II, 278.

53. Journals, VII, 300. The evidence that the matter was determined April 25 is a marginal notation to that effect, on page 1 of the printed copy of the draft of the committee of the whole, reproduced in facsimile as a frontispiece to Journals, IX.

54. Letters, II, 345, 346.

55. See various statements to this effect in the letters written by members of Congress during this period, in Letters, II. The references to the matter in the Journals during this period are not very illuminating, except that they exhibit the procrastinating tendency mentioned in the text. They are collected under "Confederation" in the index in Journals, IX.

56. Conn. Rec., I, 599–606; Pol. & Con., I, 181.

57. Ibid.

58. Journals, VIII, 650 and 731.

59. Letters, II, 450, 476, 484, 485, 503, 514, 529.

60. Ibid., 541.

61. Ibid., 498.

62. Ibid., 499.

63. Journals, VIII, 755.

64. Letters, II, 506.

65. Journals, IX, 907.

66. Ibid., 778–82.

67. Ibid., 788, 800, 801. Cornelius Harnett, of North Carolina, said, in a letter of October 10, 1777: "Three proposals have been made, one to tax by Poll, another to assess the value of Lands, and the other to assess property in general." Letters, II, 514. Henry Laurens, in a letter written on the same day, said: "the present question is the mode of Taxation; two days have been amused in conning it, some sensible things have been said, and as much nonsense as ever I heard in so short a space." Letters, II, 515. William Williams, of Connecticut, said, in a letter of October 11: "Congress are now upon the mode and proportion of contribution. sundry plans are proposed, that of numbers is very strongly and forceably opposed, and the appearance is at present

against it, but I do not much expect we shall be able to find one attended with so few Exceptions or more equitable, tho I am certain this is far from perfect." Letters, II, 517.

68. Journals, IX, 806–8.

69. Ibid., 779–82, 801, 807, and 808.

70. Ibid., 953 ff.

71. William Williams, in a letter of October 22, 1777, said that Congress "conceived" the measures recommended in the resolution of November 22 (which he referred to as "the plan of a large Taxation") would "go out with much more weight with or after the Confederation." He then referred to the rapidly rising prices and the alarm of the States over the situation, and added that the only remedy was "a firm Union to establish the Credit"; reduction in the amount of paper money; and meeting future expenses by taxation. Letters, II, 529.

72. Interstate privileges and immunities; interstate rendition of fugitives from justice; full faith and credit in other states, for the records, acts, and proceedings, of each state. Journals, IX, 895 and 899.

73. Journals, IX, 826, 827, 833–36.

74. Ibid., 844 and 845. With respect to the paralyzing effect of this "Indian commerce" proviso, as well as that attached to the "commercial-treaty" power, see the views expressed by Alexander Hamilton in the Continental Congress, in June 1783. *The Works of Alexander Hamilton*, Constitutional Edition (New York, 1903), I, 305, 310. Cf. Sheffield, *Observations on the Commerce of the American States*, 6th ed. (London, 1784), 246 and n.

75. Cf. Journals, V, 554 n. 3 (Franklin Protest, of 1776).

76. See Jensen, *The Articles of Confederation* (Madison, 1940).

77. Letters, IV, 507.

NOTES TO CHAPTER VIII

1. New Hampshire and Massachusetts were exceptions. See Jensen, *The Articles of Confederation* (Madison, 1940), pp. 188 and 189, for a brief account of the method followed in these states. Needless to say, only the revolutionaries had any part in the process, even in these states.

2. June 7, 1787, p. 121, col. 2. The item in question was a republication "with additions and alterations" of a pamphlet, published in Philadelphia in 1784, entitled *The Political Establishments of the United States of America in a Candid Review of their Deficiencies, Together with a Proposal of Reformation, Humbly Addressed to the Citizens of America by a Fellow Citizen*. The sentiments quoted in the text hereof are contained in the pamphlet at pp. 15 and 16. In the pamphlet as reprinted in Pol & Con., II, 1179–1205, the quoted passage appears at p. 1192.

3. Records, II, 89.

4. N.H. Ct. Gaz., July 5, 1787, p. 153, col. 2; *The Political Establishments of the United States* (Philadelphia, 1784), p. 21.

5. Records, II, 89. Nathaniel Gorham, of Massachusetts, said (II, 90): "Men chosen by the people for the particular purpose [i.e., ratification] will discuss the subject more candidly than members of the Legislatures who are to lose the power which is to be given to the General Government."

6. Records, I, 379. For other declarations of similar tenor by Wilson, see ibid., 253 and 344.

7. Ibid., 123.

8. Ibid., 137 and 143. Gouverneur Morris took substantially the position of the writer in the New Haven papers. "The sentiments of the people," he said, "are

unknown. They cannot be known. All that we can infer is that if the plan we recommend be reasonable and right; all who have reasonable minds and sound intentions will embrace it." Ibid., I, 529.

9. Records I, 437.

10. Ibid., II, 665.

11. On February 21, 1783, General Knox wrote to Gouverneur Morris, as follows: "The army generally have always reprobated the idea of being thirteen armies. Their ardent desires have been to be one continental body looking up to one sovereign. This would have prevented much heartburning at the partialities which have been practised by the respective States. They know of no way of bringing this about, at a period when peace appears to be in full view. Certain it is they are good patriots, and would forward anything that would tend to produce union, and a permanent general constitution;... but they must be directed in the mode by the proper authority. It is a favorite toast in the army, 'A hoop to the barrel', or 'Cement to the Union'. America will have fought and bled to little purpose if the powers of government shall be insufficient to preserve the peace, and this must be the case without general funds. As the present Constitution is so defective, why do not you great men call the people together and tell them so; that is, to have a convention of the States to form a better Constitution? This appears to us, who have a superficial view only, to be the more efficacious remedy. Let something be done before a peace takes place, or we shall be in a worse situation than we were at the commencement of the war." Drake, *Memoir of General Henry Knox* (Boston, 1873), 77. The omission in the quoted material appears in the printed source used here.

12. William Samuel Johnson, one of the Connecticut delegates to the Federal Convention, is a case in point. He withdrew from public life shortly after the first hostilities between Great Britain and the colonies, and, not being able conscientiously to join in a war against England, lived in retirement in Stratford, Connecticut, until the conclusion of peace. Groce, *William Samuel Johnson* (New York, 1937) 105 ff. From 1784 to 1787, he was a member of the Continental Congress. He took a prominent part in the Federal Convention, especially in the Connecticut effort to effect a compromise between those demanding equal, and those demanding proportional, state suffrage in the proposed national legislature. He was a member of the Connecticut ratifying convention and, in a speech to that body, informed them simply and candidly that the Federal Convention had "gone on entirely new ground"; that "they [had] formed one new nation out of the individual states"; and that "the Constitution vest[ed] in the general legislature a power to make laws in cases of national concern; to appoint judges to decide upon these laws; and to appoint officers to carry them into execution" (Conn. Cour., January 14, 1788).

Tench Coxe, of Pennsylvania, one of the delegates to the Annapolis convention of 1786, is another case in point. He remained "neutral" during the war. But he worked assiduously to help secure the ratification of the Constitution in 1787 and 1788; and his writings in advocacy of the proposed new government were published, and known, far more widely in those years than *The Federalist* papers about which so much has since been heard.

Another case is that of Nicholas Collin, of New Jersey and Pennsylvania. He was another "neutral" during the war. Johnson, *The Journal and Biography of Nicholas Collin* (Philadelphia, 1936), 119 ff. But in 1787 he was among the advocates of a stronger national government. His contribution to the efforts of this group, entitled *An Essay on the Means of Promoting Federal Sentiments in the United States*, appeared in Ph. Ind. Gaz. (August 6–October 23, 1787), before that paper had gone over to the opposition. The *Essay* was copied from thence by N.Y. Adv. and to a certain extent by newspapers in other parts of the country. After the Constitution had been ratified, Collin wrote the most elaborate of the essays in opposition to any amendment of it. His essay ran in *The New York Daily Gazette* between June 3 and July 7, 1789. What other newspapers published the essay is not known, save that it did appear, in part at least, in *The Fayetteville* [North Carolina] *Gazette* while ratification of the Constitution was still pending in that state (See issues for September 14 and 21, and October 12, 1789). In addition, Collin's essay received country-wide publicity in Am. Mus.

Still another supporter of stronger national government from among those who were at least lukewarm toward independence was John Alsop, of New York. A member of the Continental Congress in 1776, Alsop was "willing and ready," in his own words, "to render [his] country all the service in [his] power, as long as a door was left open for reconciliation with Great Britain upon honourable and just terms"; but he resigned from Congress immediately after the Declaration of Independence, because, he said, Independence was "against [his] judgment and inclination." Archives, 5th Ser., I, 368, 759, 977, 1428–31. In 1785, Alsop was one of the men who were active in New York, in the agitation for the grant of commercial power to Congress. See Ch. St. Gaz., June 18, 1785.

There were many other instances similar to the foregoing.

13. A fairly moderate-sounding pamphlet published in Philadelphia, in 1800, under the title of *An Impartial Review of the Rise and Progress of the Controversy between the Parties Known by the Name of Federalists and Republicans*, has the following to say (p. 35): "The whole of the inhabitants, with very few exceptions, who were opposed to the revolution and the establishment of the independency of the United States, and who remained, or have been readmitted as citizens, are here to be noticed as on [the Federalist] side of the party division. To which may be added the greater part of those who reluctantly yielded a passive submission to the general will and public measures in the time of the revolution, to avoid the consequences of opposition, but carefully avoided rendering any services, either in person or by their property, as far as they decently could. It may be just, however, respecting the persons included under this head, to say that, since the treaty of peace with Great Britain, by which the independency of the United States was explicitly acknowledged, they have yielded obedience to the laws, and shown a disposition to support them, in common with other citizens."

NOTES TO CHAPTER IX

1. John Adams, III, 70.
2. Journals, XI, 648.
3. Ibid., 631–56. The most important objections, at the moment, were those relating to the western lands.
4. Letters, III, 314.
5. Journals, XIX, 110.
6. N.J. Gaz., October 13, 1779, p. 3; cf., Letters, IV, 482, 485, 490, 524, and 550.
7. The proceedings of this convention are reprinted in Conn. Rec., II, 562–71.
8. Journals, XV, 1289.
9. N.J. Gaz., January 19, 1780.
10. Ibid., January 12, 1780.
11. Ibid., March 1, 1780.
12. Cf. Conn. Rec., II, 572 ff.; also Letters, V, 4, 16, and 40.
13. Journals, XIX, 110.
14. Ibid., 111.
15. Cf. Conn. Rec., I, 605–6; II, 567; also Letters, IV, 495.
16. Conn. Rec., I, 604–5; III, 562.

17. Cf. chap. VII hereof, text at nn. 58, 59, 60.

18. N.J. Gaz., March 29, 1780. In the course of his remarks, he said: "The stale saying, '*Trade* must regulate itself,' holds good where the requisite circumstances correspond; but ours manifestly indicate an exception to this rule. But say some, 'A general regulation' "—i.e., of all trade—" ' is not possible.'—Why not? Is not interest regulated? Is there not a standard of profits in *trade* which custom has settled in all nations? Whence can this impossibility arise?"

19. See chap. IV hereof, text at n. 10.

20. Journals, XIX, 111.

21. Hough, *Proceedings of a Convention of Delegates from Several of the New England States, Held at Boston, August 3–9, 1780* (Albany, 1867); also reprinted in Conn. Rec., III, 559–64. The Boston convention likewise recommended the assembling of another convention, to include New York and Rhode Island, on the second Wednesday in November, and such a convention eventually assembled at Hartford on November 11. Its recommendations, relating solely to military and fiscal affairs, included a proposal that the states pass laws "to enable Congress to levy and collect [certain] taxes, duties, or imposts, within [the states] respectively," for discharging the interest on the existing continental debt, and also a proposal "that the Commander-in-Chief of the army of the United States be authorized and empowered to take such measures as he [might] deem proper and the publick service [might] render necessary, to induce the several States to a punctual compliance with the requisitions which have been or may be made by Congress for supplies for the year 1780 and 1781." The latter proposal, symptomatic of the growing impatience with the want of executive authority in Congress, was inspired by the delegates of New York, who had been instructed by the state's legislature to propose such a recommendation to the convention. At the same time, that legislature had unanimously resolved that the New York delegates in Congress be instructed "that it [was] the earnest wish of [that] State, that Congress should during the War, or until a perpetual Confederation [should] be completed, exercise every Power which they [might] deem necessary for an effectual Prosecution of the War, and that whenever it [should] appear to them that any State [was] deficient in furnishing the Quota of Men, Money, Provisions or other Supplies, required of such State, that Congress [should] direct the Commander-in-Chief, without delay, to march the Army, or such Part of it as [might] be requisite, into such State; and by a Military Force, compel it to furnish its deficiency." This resolution and the somewhat similar recommendation of the Hartford convention drew forth a very vigorous dissent, in certain quarters, when it became known, See Letters, V, 487 and 488. John Witherspoon was one of the dissenters. The disposition toward radical action manifested in the New York resolution and the Hartford convention's resolution is, therefore, part of the background of the Witherspoon proposal of February 3, 1781, in its financial aspects, as it is also part of the background of certain committee proposals in Congress, later in that year, for investing Congress with additional powers, chiefly of an executive nature. See Journals, XIX, 236; XX, 469–71; XXI, 894–96. As none of these proposals bears directly on the question of commercial power as proposed by Witherspoon, reference to them has been omitted in the text.

22. Washington, XIX, 452–53.

23. Hamilton, I, 213.

24. Pol. & Con., I, 147–52.

25. Hamilton, I, 224.

26. Cf. chap. IV hereof.

27. Hamilton, I, 243 ff.

28. *The* [Fishkill] *New York Packet*, April 18, 1782.

29. Hamilton, I, 269.

30. Cf., Pol. & Con., I, 179–86.

31. Letters, III, 57. Witherspoon said that he "look[ed] upon the scheme [of fixing wages and prices] as impracticable and absurd." "Fixing Prices by Law," he went on, "never had nor ever will have any Effect but stopping commerce and making Things scarce and dear."

32. The scope of the bounty power is indicated by the discussion at Hamilton, V, 273.

33. Ibid., I, 261.

34. Hamilton accordingly rested the bounty proposals he made in his *Report on Manufactures*, upon the "general welfare" clause. Ibid., IV, 150–52.

35. Ibid., I, 45.

36. Ibid., III, 378–79.

37. Blackstone, I, 44; *Robinson v. Bland*, 1 W.Bl. 234, 237. The definition of Justinian was usually quoted: *"jus civile est quod quisque sibi populus constituit."*

38. See Sullivan, *The History of Land Titles in Massachusetts* (Boston, 1801), 337–38: "Personal estate is not fixed to any place or country, and contracts depend on the *jus gentium* (the general law of nations) for their origin and their expositions, rather than on any *municipal regulations* of particular countries." Also, Swift, *A Digest of the Law of Evidence &c., and a Treatise on Bills of Exchange* (Hartford, 1810), 245: "Bills of Exchange . . . constitute a branch of universal commercial law, to be governed by the customs and usages of nations, and not by *municipal law*."

39. The first number of the "Continentalist" papers was copied in Pa. Pack. on August 2, 1781. So far as is known, there was no other copying of the "Continentalist."

40. In a letter to Henry Knox, dated February 8, 1787, Higginson said: "As early as '83, while I was at Congress, I pressed upon Mr. Maddison and others the Idea of a special Convention, for the purpose of revising the Confederation, and increasing the powers of the Union; the obtaining of which, we all agreed to be essential to our national dignity and happiness. But they were as much opposed to this Idea, as I was to the measures they were then pursuing, to effect, as they said, the same thing. They have, however, now adopted the Idea, and have come forward with a proposition to attempt practising upon it." Higginson, 745. Madison's own record of the proceedings in Congress, in the spring of 1783, shows Higginson as acting with Hamilton in an effort to obtain a convention. It contains no intimation that Madison gave any support to the effort. *The Papers of James Madison* (Washington, 1840), I, 430. Higginson, in 1783, considered Madison as scheming, without giving to the other states an adequate *quid pro quo*, "to secure to [Virginia] a valuable territory which [the state] ha[d] no good claim to, and [to] oblige the continent hereafter to guarantee and defend it for them." "Madison," he said, "ha[d] clearly shown [this], in an unguarded moment." Letters, VII, 122–24. Bearing in mind Madison's vote against the Witherspoon proposal, already noted in the text, and other facts as to Madison's later sentiments and behavior, to be noted hereafter, there can be little doubt that Higginson's views in this matter were entirely warranted.

41. Hamilton, I, 291–95, 305–14.

42. Webster, *A Dissertation on the Political Union and Constitution of the Thirteen United States of North-America* (Philadelphia, 1783), reprinted in Webster, *Political Essays* (Philadelphia, 1791), 198–229.

43. These are collected in Webster, *Political Essays* (Philadelphia, 1791), pp. 9, 27, 50, 74, 97, 230, and 269.

44. Washington, XXVI, 276–77.

45. Ibid., 278.

46. See, in ibid., in addition to the letters mentioned in the text, the following: XIX, 131; XXI, 164, 182–83, 320, 379; XXVI, 184, 188, 358; XXVII, 11, 12.

47. Ibid., XXVII, 48–51.

48. Ibid., XXVI, 483, 487–88.

49. Ibid., XXVI, 491 n.

50. Ibid., XXVII, 285 n.

NOTES TO CHAPTER X

1. Wharton, *The Revolutionary Diplomatic Correspondence of the United States* (Washington, 1889), VI, 303–5, 307, 342–43, 358–61, 366, 379, 396–97, 442–44, 447.

2. Ibid., 491–94, 506–7; cf. Journals, XXV, 589.

3. Sheffield, *Observations on the Commerce of the American States*, 6th ed. (London, 1784), 245–47.

4. The provisions relative to trade treaties in the sixth and ninth of the Articles of Confederation were cited. Cf. Hamilton, I, 310.

5. Wharton, *Diplomatic Correspondence*, VI, 541.

6. Ibid., 542 and 552.

7. Journals, XXV, 587; and Wharton, *Diplomatic Correspondence*, VI, 540–42, 545, 552–54, 557–62.

8. Journals, XXV, 618.

9. Ibid., 621–22, 629.

10. Ibid., 661 ff.

11. Ibid., 664 n. 1.

12. For certain resolutions entered into by the merchants of New Haven, Connecticut, see B. Cont. Jour., January 8, 1784, or Pa. Gaz., January 7, 1784. The merchants of Philadelphia circularized merchants in the other states upon the subject. On December 13, 1783, the Marine Anti-Britannic Society met in Charleston, South Carolina, complained of British efforts "to cramp our Trade, discourage our Manufactures, and obstruct the growth of our Marine," and called for "a speedy restoration of our Chamber of Commerce, solely consisting of true American merchants, patriotic planters, and trading Whig-Subjects of our Allies." Ch. Wkly. Gaz., December 19, 1783.

13. No complete list of the papers publishing Paine's appeal was kept. It appeared in the following papers, among many others: N.J. Gaz., December 30, 1783; B. Cont. Jour., January 1, 1784; Va. Am. Adv., January 3, 1784; *The Salem* [Massachusetts] *Gazette*, January 15, 1784; *The* [Worcester] *Massachusetts Spy*, January 1, 1784; Pa. Gaz., December 17, 1783.

14. Paine's appeal will be found in his collected works as the sixteenth number of *The American Crisis.*

15. Virginia House Journal for 1783 (Richmond, 1828), 46.

16. No list was kept of the other papers publishing the Virginia Delegates' resolution. It may be found, however, in B. Cont. Jour., of January 8, 1784, among many other papers.

17. N.J. Gaz., December 30, 1783.

18. Journals, XXVI, 71.

19. A complete list of the papers publishing the New Jersey resolves was not kept. It appeared in the following newspapers, among many others: B. Cont. Jour., January 29, 1784; B. Ind. Chr., January 29, 1784; Ph. Fr. Jour., January 14, 1784; Newp. Merc., February 7, 1784; Pa. Pack., January 10, 1784.

20. Hening, Va. Stat. at L., XI, 313.

21. N.Y. Laws, 1778–1784 (Official Reprint, Albany, 1886), I, 699.

22. *Acts of the Ninth General Assembly of the State of New Jersey* (Trenton, 1784), 125; also printed in Pa. Pack., December 16, 1784. The act was passed on November 4, 1784.

23. Cooper, S.C. Stat. at L., IV, 596.

24. The precise date of the enactment is not known. It was reported as "just passed," and its text printed, in Ch. G. A., March 16, 1784.

25. State Records of North Carolina, XXIV, 561. The date of passage is given as June 2, 1784, in Journals, XXX, 93.

26. Journals, XXVI, 50. The Maryland motion was by James McHenry. The inference as to its probable character is based on a letter he wrote to Washington on the 14th of August 1785. Letters, VIII, 182.

27. Journals, XXVI, 50. The *Journal* says at this point that "the instructions to the delegates of Pennsylvania, of February 5" were referred to the committee when Jefferson was added to the committee, on April 14. *The excerpt* from the instructions to the Pennsylvania delegates, of December 9, which excerpt was dated February 5, is undoubtedly what was meant. Journals, XXVI, 70–71. The footnote on page 71 says the excerpt was referred to the committee on February 6.

28. Journals, XXVI, 50, 269–71.

29. Ibid., 270.

30. Ibid., 321–22.

31. Ibid., 319–21.

32. So stated in the introduction to the answering pamphlet cited in the next note below.

33. *Remarks on a Pamphlet, entituled a Dissertation on the Political Union and Constitution of the Thirteen United States of North-America*, by "A Connecticut Farmer" (New Haven, 1784). See, especially, pp. 12, 14, 17, 26 ff. The pamphlet was first advertised for sale in Conn. Jour., January 7, 1784.

34. Apart from the pamphlet mentioned in n. 33, the most extensive "states' rights" production of 1784 was a series of papers which appeared in Am. Merc. beginning on September 27, 1784. They were directed chiefly against the proposal of a continental impost. There were other items against the impost. See, for example, one in Ph. Fr. Jour., June 2, 1784, which declared that it would mean the establishment in the country of "one mighty monarchy."

35. Norw. Pack. for May 13, 1784, has apparently not survived; but the source of the item was indicated in most of the papers which republished it. See, among others, Newp. Merc., May 22, 1784, and Ch. P. A., July 10, 1784.

36. The pamphlet was advertised for sale in Pa. Gaz., August 4, 1784.

37. The 1787 edition is printed in an appendix to vol. 2 of this work, together with extracts from the 1784 edition wherever the earlier edition shows variant material that seems of interest. Pol. & Con., II, 1179–1205. A comparison of the "Observator's" first letter (Pol. & Con., II, 1206–9) with the pamphlet will show that there can be little doubt that the same individual wrote both.

38. P. 17; see Pol. & Con., II, 1194.

39. P. 6; see Pol. & Con., II, 1181.

40. Above, n. 38.

41. P. 21; see Pol. & Con., II, 1199.

42. P. 23; see Pol. & Con., II, 1201.

43. Above, n. 41.

44. Acts and Resolves of Massachusetts, 1784–85 (Official Reprint), 41. The date of the act was July 1, 1784.

45. Laws of Pennsylvania, 1784, chap. 1108, passed December 15, 1784.

46. Laws of Maryland, 1784, chap. LXVII, enacted at the session beginning in November 1784.

47. Hening, Va. Stat. at L., XI, 388. The act was passed at the May session.

48. Metcalfe, Laws of N.H., 1784–1792, V, 25. The reports in Congress on the

progress of the appeal of April 30, 1784, and the subsequent appeals for the same powers, consistently ignore this act of New Hampshire, as well as the subsequent act of the state, of June 19, 1786, reconsenting to the powers, with a different provision as to the beginning of the fifteen-year term for which the powers were granted. Journals, XXX, 10, 93; XXXI, 907; cf. Metcalfe, Laws of N.H., 1784–1792, V, 158.

49. New York Laws, 1785–88 (Albany, 1886), II, 102. Passed April 4, 1785.

50. Acts and Laws of Connecticut, 1784–90, 317.

51. The New Jersey legislative journal shows that the act was passed November 28, 1785.

52. Letters, VIII, 288, 294.

53. Laws of Delaware, 1777–1797 (Newcastle, 1797), II, 831. Passed, apparently, in January or February 1786.

54. Acts and Resolves of Rhode Island, February 1785, 28.

55. Ibid., October 1785, 10.

56. In a letter explaining Rhode Island's failure to send delegates to the Federal Convention, which was transmitted to Congress in September 1787, the Rhode Island legislature said, in part: "Your Hon. Body informed us that the Powers invested in Congress for the Regulation of Trade were not Sufficient for the purpose of the great national Regulations requisite, we granted you by an Act of our State the whole and sole power of making such Laws as would be effectual for that purpose, other States not passing similar laws it had no effect." DHC, IV, 282, 283. The general position of the legislature was that it was without power to participate "in a Convention which might be the means of dissolving the Congress of the Union and having a Congress without a Confederation." "[The] Convention," it pointed out, "[was] for the express purpose of altering a Constitution, which the people at large," it said, "[were] only capable of appointing the Members [to do]." Ibid., 283, 284. The nationalist minority in the Rhode Island legislature dissented from this view, in an accompanying letter; but they did not dissent from the majority's interpretation of the Rhode Island acts of 1785. Instead, they gave, as one of the reasons for their dissent, "that the Powers mentioned in [the legislature's] Letter to have been invested in Congress, for the regulating Trade were granted by the Legislature of [the] State, as also finally grant-ing the Impost, which [was] inconsistant," they said, "with the Ideas contained in said Letter, That all such powers [were] not in the Legislature, but in the people at large." Ibid., 285. John Brown, Welcome Arnold, and Joseph Nightingale, three of the signers of this minority letter, had also been signers, earlier in the summer of 1787, of a letter sent to the Federal Convention by certain "Merchants, Tradesmen, and others, of [Providence]," in which it was declared to be "the general Opinion [in Providence] and [the writers believe[d] of the well informed throughout [their] State, that full power for the Regulation of the Commerce of the United States, both Foreign & Domestick ought to be vested in the National Council." Records, III, 19.

57. Conn. Cour. of April 21, 1788, noted, in comment upon another letter of the Rhode Island General Assembly's that that body still thought Congress ought to have "the entire regulation of trade." Cf., DHC, IV, 554, 555. To the same effect, see N.Y. Adv., April 25, 1788. Mass. Cent., on April 16, 1788, noted that the Rhode Island legislature had written Congress that it was still willing to give "unlimited power to regulate commerce." N.Y. Jour. on April 25, 1788, referred to Rhode Island's continuing willingness to give "unlimited power for regulating trade."

58. The Rhode Island act of February 1785 was in substantially the same terms as the Maryland and North Carolina acts of the year before. The only substantial difference was the use, in the Rhode Island act, of the words "regulate, restrain, or prohibit," in place of "prevent or prohibit," as in the Maryland and North Carolina acts. The Rhode Island act was thus broader than the Maryland and North Carolina

acts, but, in view of the similarity in wording in other respects, it was probably elicited by them. The Rhode Island act was entitled "An act vesting Congress with the Power of regulating foreign Trade." It applied, as indicated in the text, to "the Importation of all foreign Goods" in any other than ships owned by Americans and navigated by Americans or such proportion of Americans as Congress might stipulate. The Rhode Island act of October 1785 was entitled "An Act in Addition to an Act intituled, An Act vesting Congress with the Power of regulating foreign Trade." It "authorized and empowered" the state's delegates in Congress "to agree to and ratify any Article or Articles, by which the United States in Congress assembled [should] be solely empowered to regulate the Trade and Commerce of the respective States, and the Citizens thereof with each other; *and to regulate, restrain or prohibit, the Importation of all foreign Goods, in any Ships or Vessels owned by any of the States, or by a Citizen or Citizens of either*." The key to the interpretation of the October act is provided by the words printed in italics. These words added to the words of the February act gave *full* power over *all* importations of "all *foreign* Goods." It follows, of course, from the inclusion of the italicized words in the October act that the unitalicized words of that act were not intended to be understood as including what the italicized words covered, or what was covered in the February act; in other words, the unitalicized words of the October act were not intended to be understood as including *any imports* of "*foreign* Goods." In consequence of this, some meaning has to be found for the unitalicized words of the October act, which, when added to the words of the February act and the italicized words of the October act, sum up to what the legislature said it intended to give: a "*whole* and sole" power of passing laws for the regulation of trade. Cf. n. 56, above.

In the eighteenth century, the exports of a state or nation were sometimes spoken of as its "trade," or "commerce." Thus, "Britain's trade in woolens" might stand for its exports of woolen goods; or "Britain's commerce in coals," for its exports of coal. The words of the Rhode Island October act which are italicized above indicate that, in that act, the words "the Trade and Commerce of the respective States" were so used. They included both the exports of the respective states to foreign nations and their exports to the other states of the Union. Power over the latter included, necessarily, power over "interstate" imports; since the "interstate" export of a particular state is, of course, always an "interstate" import to some other. Power over imports of "foreign Goods" would not, however, have been included; hence the necessity for the words of the February act and the italicized words of the October act. We are left, then, only with the question of what was intended, in the October act, by "the Trade and Commerce of the citizens of the respective States with each other." And the only possible answer is that these words signified "the internal, or domestic, trade and commerce of each of the states"; that is, "the trade and commerce of each state's citizens with each other." As the several elements of the February and the October acts add up, under this interpretation, to a "whole and sole" power of regulating trade, it is evident that the suggested interpretation of the October act meets all the conditions of the problem.

It ought perhaps to be added that the suggested interpretation is, apparently, the only interpretation that does meet all the conditions of the problem. In view, however, of the reference to "Ships or Vessels owned by any of the States, or by a Citizen or Citizens of either," which is contained in the italicized portion of the October act, it may seem to some readers that the unitalicized portion of that act could perhaps be interpreted as meaning "the Trade and Commerce of the respective States in their similar capacities, and the Trade and Commerce of the Citizens of the respective States with the Citizens of the other States." It is some objection to such an interpretation that it would disregard the careful punctuation of the October act and would assume a loose, colloquial use of the word "respective"; but it is fatal that the several elements of the February and October acts would not, under such an interpretation, add up to a "whole and sole" power of regulating trade. This would be true, not merely because the "trade and commerce between citizens of the same state" would be wanting under such an interpretation, but because "the exports of the states *to foreign nations*" would likewise be wanting. No power excluding these branches of commerce could possibly be regarded as a "whole and sole" power over trade.

59. Metcalfe, Laws of N.H., 1784–1792, V, 81.

60. Ibid., 203–4.

61. Acts and Resolves of Rhode Island, March 1786, 6.

62. Laws of Delaware, 1777–1797 (Newcastle, 1797), II, 831.

63. Colonial Records of Georgia (Atlanta, 1911), XIX, pt. II, 554.

64. Cooper, S.C. Stat. at L., IV, 720.

65. State Records of North Carolina, XXIV, 561.

66. For subsequent appeals for the powers asked on April 30, 1784, see Journals, XXX, 93; XXXI, 907.

67. N.Y. Jour., September 13, 1787.

68. This aspect of the Constitution has been greatly exaggerated by many writers, chiefly because of the crude misconceptions as to what went on in Congress on February 21, 1787. Cf. chap. XXV hereof. The most revolutionary aspect of the Constitution was the provision for its going into effect upon the ratification of *nine* states, but even this aspect of the Constitution was consented to by Congress, in submitting it to the state legislatures for submission to the people, and by the legislatures, in acting upon the suggestion for such submission. All the state legislatures had acted upon the suggestion, in one way or another, before nine states had ratified. This was true even of Rhode Island. DHC, IV, 554. The kind and mode of change which the Federal Convention proposed were thus impliedly consented to by all the bodies responsible for the Articles, before the Constitution took effect. To speak of the work of the Federal Convention as amounting to a coup d'état, as Benjamin Fletcher Wright, Jr. ("The Early History of Written Constitutions in America," in *Essays in History and Political Theory in Honor of Charles McIlwain* [1936] 344, 371) and Edward Mead Earle ("Introduction," *The Federalist* [New York, 1937], p. ix) have done, is completely unwarranted.

69. *The Political Establishments of the United States of America* (Philadelphia,1784), 15, 18; see Pol. & Con., II, 1192, 1194 n.

NOTES TO CHAPTER XI

1. See a letter from Edward Bancroft to William Frazer, November 8, 1783, printed in Bancroft, I, 331, 333: "The importation of European goods has been so considerable, within the last six months, that the exportable produce of the states probably will not equal it in less than three years; the British are the only manufactures which have afforded any profit; the foreign have sold under prime cost, and there is hardly anything here to pay for them, except a very little Spanish silver, which is daily carried away, and will soon be all gone." Cf. the complaint of "the scarcity of money and the languishing state of commerce" in Pa. Pack., June 4, 1785: "Hard money was very plenty in this country about two years ago; rents and wages were high, and every man was immediately paid for his work.—Two short years have produced a wonderful change.—Rents are falling, tradesmen can hardly be employed—when they [are] employed are not paid; most people are running in debt, while the means of paying those debts are sinking from their sight." "As soon as peace was restored, our merchants, in haste to be rich, ordered out an immense quantity of goods; unfortunately credit was easily obtained, and many a man who is not worth

ten pounds has imported goods to the value of ten thousand. The appointed hour for payment approaches; but the importer has no money; he trusts shopkeepers, the shopkeepers trust the mechanic, or farmer, and the mechanic, or farmer, with their wives and children are cloathed in foreign manufactures, for which they are neither able nor desirous to pay. We have very little foreign trade, and if all the produce of our country could be sold at the best market, it would not pay for half the goods that we import." "Let us be frugal, industrious and temperate, and we shall presently be rich; our mechanics will be employed, we shall be enabled to pay our debts, and hard money will be plenty."

2. See the American newspapers of the time, generally. The spread of the theatre; the building of public dance-halls—or "assembly halls," as they were called; the constant complaints that every "husbandman" thought he had to have "an English broadcloth coat," and that his wife had to have "cork rumps" and all the expensive "British gew-gaws" that went with them, are all symptomatic. The following suggestive item appeared in Ann. Gaz., February 19, 1784: "The Bostonians, from being puritanical, are become the politest people in the world; for besides the theatre which they hope will be established, they have assemblies and dances every week. Some of their favourite dances take their names from the warlike events of late years; such as the Saratoga jig; Sir Henry's minuet; Mrs. Lee's fancy; the big bow wow; push about the loyalists; with some Congress reels, &c." Local Boston complaints about the building there of a great new assembly hall as a cause of the depression may be found in Am. Her., June 13, 20, and 27; July 4 and 11; and August 1, 1785. Typical anti-luxury items may be found reprinted in Am. Mus. (1787), I, 11, 13, 66, 67, 111, 113, 115, 187, and 461.

3. There has been a fashion among certain modern historians with "states'-rights" sympathies to minimize the troubles out of which the Constitution grew. Franklin and some others wrote letters for publication assuring their countrymen that business conditions, in effect, were "basically sound," and that "prosperity was just around the corner." See Am. Mus. (1787), I, 5 and 461. It is not of record that these reassurances were any more effective than some similar reassurances in more recent times. Another item sometimes cited is a letter which Charles Thomson wrote to Thomas Jefferson, in Paris, in contradiction of "the paragraphs with which the European papers [were] stuffed & the pictures they ha[d] drawn of the distress of America." *Collections of the New-York Historical Society for 1878*, 205–6. Thomson's statements, of course, must be heavily discounted in view of his avowed purpose in making them. The shape of events discernible in the records of the time, if these are fully considered, is unmistakably that stated in the text. There is no reliable evidence to the contrary.

4. Lord Sheffield's pamphlet, cited in n. 3, chap. X, is sufficient proof of the British purpose in the policy pursued. See also Edward Bancroft's letter, reprinted in Bancroft, I, 380. The evidence of the general understanding in America of the British policy may be found in almost any American newspaper of the time. A typical appeal was that of "Anti-Britannick," in Mass. Cent., May 4, 1785, who said in part: "Rouse, then, my Countrymen, and convince the British nation, who are your commercial, as well as your national foes, that America is independent!" Another writer in the same paper, on July 9, said: "An independent nation, destitute of manufactures within themselves, is a solecism in politicks."

5. Pa. Pack., March 4, 1785; Md. Jour., March 8, 1785; and other papers.

6. Printed in N.Y. Mng. P., March 10, 1785; Ch. P. A., June 18, 1785; Va. Jour., May 19, 1785; Sav. Gaz., May 19, 1785; Md. Jour., March 8, 1785; and other papers.

7. See n. 49, chap. X hereof.

8. See chap. X hereof, text preceding n. 18.

9. Pa. Pack., June 2, 1785; Pa. Merc., June 3, 1785; Ph. Ind. Gaz., June 4, 1785; Pa. Her., June 4, 1785; Pa. Jour., June 4, 1785; Ph. Fr. Jour., June 8, 1785; Pa. Gaz.,

June 8, 1785; N.Y. Jour., June 9, 1785; N.J. Gaz., June 13, 1785; Newp. Merc., June 18, 1785; Prov. Gaz., June 25, 1785; N.H. Gaz., June 17, 1785; B. Cont. Jour., June 9 and 16, 1785; Va. Jour., June 16, 1785; Col. Her., June 24, 1785; Ch. P. A., June 22, 1785; Gaz. S.C., June 27, 1785; Ch. St. Gaz., June 29, 1785; Sav. Gaz., July 7, 1785.

10. See the newspapers cited in the preceding note.

11. The papers cited in notes 6 and 9 above do not constitute a complete list, even for the states covered. Many files have gaps covering dates when the items in question probably appeared. No files at all survive for the Delaware and North Carolina papers, or for most of the Virginia papers.

12. The writings of "The Friend of Commerce," hereinafter cited, began in B. Ind. Chr., on July 29, 1784.

13. Mass. Cent., April 13, 1785; B. Ind. Chr., April 14, 1785.

14. *The* [Boston] *Exchange Advertiser*, April 14, 1785, explained "the advertisement inserted in yesterday's Centinel"; B. Ind. Chr. of the fourteenth, also added a word in explanation of the notice of the meeting which it carried on that day.

15. Mass. Cent., April 16, 1785.

16. Ibid.

17. Ibid., April 20, 1785; Am. Her., April 18, 1785; B. Ind. Chr., April 21, 1785; Bost. Gaz., April 18, 1785.

18. Mass. Cent., April 16 and 20, 1785. For an appeal for solidarity between farming, mercantile, and mechanical elements, see B. Ind. Chr., April 21, 1785.

19. Mass. Cent., April 20, 1785; B. Ind. Chr., April 21, 1785.

20. The proceedings of the original meeting may be found in B. Ind. Chr., April 28, 1785, and Mass. Cent., April 27, 1785. The correspondence with the mercantile group may be found in Mass. Cent., of May 7, 1785, and Bost. Gaz., of May 9, 1785.

21. Bost. Gaz., April 25, 1785.

22. Mass. Cent., May 7, 1785; Bost. Gaz., May 9, 1785.

23. See, for example, a notice relative to the "excise" law of Connecticut, in 1785, which applied *only* to foreign imports sold at retail or consumed by retailers or wholesalers, within the state, which appeared in Conn. Jour. on April 27, 1785. The usage in this notice, which followed the usage in the law, is in obvious accord with the usage of the Boston merchants in their letter to the Boston mechanical group. There are other examples.

24. Mass. Cent., January 9, 1788; B. Ind. Chr., January 10, 1788.

25. Acts and Resolves of Massachusetts, 1784–85 (Official Reprint), 666.

26. Article III of the Confederation.

27. Letters, VIII, 108, 110; King, I, 90; Jay, III, 153; Madison, II, 147.

28. See, for example, the letter of "A Carolinian," in Newp. Merc., of September 3, 1785.

29. Thomas Farr, of Charleston, South Carolina, to Caleb Davis, of Boston, July 18, 1785: "Two days before I sailed from Charleston I was honoured with a package, enclosing me a letter from a Committee of the Merchants, Traders, and others of Boston, in which is your name, to the Merchants, Traders, and others of Charleston, Georgetown [S.C.], Savannah, Edenton, and Wilmington—that for Charleston I laid before our Chamber of Commerce, from whom you will soon hear, the others I forwarded.—I have no doubt but the good people of the respective places will enter with similar Resolves to that of your." Caleb Davis Papers, Massachusetts Historical Society.

30. The paper in question published all the Boston items leading up to the merchants' letters. A gap follows, in the only two files known to exist, at about the date when the letters probably were published. The files in question are in the Library of Congress and the Virginia Historical Society.

NOTES TO CHAPTER XII

1. See chap. X hereof.

2. Am. Her., May 16, 1785; Bost. Gaz., May 16, 1785; *The Salem* [Mass.] *Gazette*, May 17, 1785; *The* [Windsor] *Vermont Journal*, June 14, 1785; Newp. Merc., May 21, 1785; *The New York Gazetteer*, May 24, 1785; N.J. Gaz., May 30, 1785; Pa. Jour., May 25, 1785; Pa. Pack., May 26, 1785; Ch. P. A., June 25, 1785. The foregoing list is not complete.

3. N.Y. Jour., May 26, 1785.

4. N.H. Gaz., June 17, 1785.

5. See chap. X hereof, text at n. 59.

6. See chap. X hereof, text at n. 58.

7. See App. A, Pol. & Con., II, 1179–1205.

8. For "Observator's" letter, August 25, 1785, see Pol. & Con., II, 1206–9.

9. Webster, *Sketches of American Policy* (Hartford, 1785), 31–48.

10. See chap. VII hereof, text at nn. 15 to 17.

11. Records, II, 21, 25, 26; III, 615–16.

12. The Connecticut convention ratified the Constitution by a vote of 128 to 40. Conn. Rec., VI, 549–52.

13. Acts and Laws of Connecticut, 1784–90, 317.

14. See chap. XIII hereof.

15. B. Ind. Chr., June 2, 1785; Pa. Pack., May 31 and June 13, 1785.

16. The merchants' original resolutions were open to "Jonathan of the Valley"'s objection, but their letters asking "full" power over "the internal as well as the external commerce of all the states" had been published three weeks *before* "Jonathan of the Valley"'s letter appeared.

17. N.Y. Jour., June 30, 1785; Ph. Ind. Gaz., July 9, 1785.

18. B. Ind. Chr., July 29, 1784.

19. Ibid., September 1, 1785; Pa. Pack., September 20, 1785. The "Friend of Commerce" again called upon the country, in this letter, to vest Congress with "full commercial powers."

20. B. Ind. Chr., June 23, 1785.

21. N.Y. Jour., July 7, 1785.

22. Acts and Resolves of Massachusetts, 1784–85 (Official Reprint), 706–10; Bost. Gaz., June 6, 1785; Pa. Pack., June 14, 1785; Ch. Ev. Gaz., July 21, 1785; Ch. P. A., July 21, 1785. The address was also published by a considerable number of other papers.

23. Acts and Resolves of Massachusetts, 1784–85 (Official Reprint), 706–10.

24. Article III of the Confederation.

25. Acts and Resolves of Massachusetts, 1784–85 (Official Reprint), 667–68.

26. Letters, VIII, 188, 206, 218, 245–46; also, Rufus King to Caleb Davis, October 17 and November 3, 1785, in Caleb Davis Papers, Massachusetts Historical Society. The last two letters are reprinted in Appendix E to this volume.

27. Samuel Holten left New York for Boston at some time between November 6 and November 21. Cf. Letters, VIII, 248, n. 1 to letter no. 271, with 257. There is a plain intimation to Holten, in a letter written to him by King on the last-mentioned date, that he speak to the General Court about "complying with the Requisition" and "the affair of the Old money." Ibid., 257. The fact that he had an opportunity to talk to the General Court about the proposed convention may therefore be taken as virtually certain.

28. Acts and Resolves of Massachusetts, 1784–85 (Official Reprint), 789.

NOTES TO CHAPTER XIII

1. Some of the facts about the General Court's move for a convention eventually became public, but not all of them.

2. Pa. Jour., May 25, 1785; Pa. Pack., May 26, 1785.

3. Pa. Pack., June 2, 1785; Pa. Merc., June 3, 1785; Ph. Ind. Gaz., June 4, 1785; Pa. Her., June 4, 1785; Pa. Jour., June 4, 1785; Ph. Fr. Jour., June 8, 1785; Pa. Gaz., June 8, 1785.

4. Suggestions as to the procedure to be followed were contained in Pa. Pack., June 3, 1785. The meeting at the university had occurred the evening before. Ibid., June 6, 1785. See, also, notices of meeting of June 20. Ibid., June 15, 16, 17, 18, 19, and 20, 1785.

5. See list on p. 174 hereof.

6. Pa. Pack., June 13, 1785. Whether any of the other Philadelphia papers published these instructions was not certainly determined.

7. Ibid., June 18, 1785.

8. Ibid., June 21, 1785; Pa. Gaz., June 22, 1785; Pa. Jour., June 22, 1785; Ph. Fr. Jour., June 22, 1785; Pa. Merc., June 24, 1785; N.J. Gaz., July 4, 1785; Prov. Gaz., July 9, 1785; B. Ind. Chr., July 14, 1785; Col. Her., July 4, 1785; and many other papers.

9. Ibid.

10. So reported by the State Library at Harrisburg.

11. Above, n. 8.

12. Pa. Pack., September 5, 1785; Col. Her., October 3, 1785; and other papers.

13. Pa. Pack., August 27, 1785; Gaz. S.C., September 12, 1785; and other papers. The message in which the quoted statement was contained was delivered to the legislature on August 25.

14. Pol. & Con., I, 123–36.

15. Pa. Pack., March 6, 1786, where "A Customer" went into the whole subject; also, Laws of Delaware, 1777–1797 (Newcastle, 1797), II, 831, 838.

16. N.J. Gaz., November 22, 1784; New Jersey House Journal, August 11, 1784.

17. New Jersey House Journal, August 14, 25, 26, 28, 1784.

18. Ibid., August 27, and December 8, 10, and 13, 1784, and November 18, 1785.

19. See chap. X hereof, text at nn. 51 and 52.

20. Letters, VIII, 315, 318, 319, 321–32, 334; Bancroft, I, 485–87.

21. Elliot, I, 117.

22. The view, common amongst historians, that New Jersey must have been localistic in its views because of its connection with the so-called "New Jersey plan" in the Federal Convention, is based upon an entirely inadequate understanding of the facts.

23. See chap. X hereof, text at n. 59.

24. Acts and Laws of Connecticut 1784–90, 268.

25. Ibid., 271.

26. Records, II, 21, 25, 26; III, 615–16.

27. N.Y. Jour., June 23, 1785; Sav. Gaz., July 21, 1785; Gaz. S.C., July 4, 1785.

28. The New York letter appeared in the following papers, among others: Pa. Pack., November 25, 1785; Va. Jour., November 24, 1785; Gaz. S.C., January 5, 1786.

29. New York Assembly Journal 1786, 52.

30. Am. Mus., I, 445, 446.

31. Letters, VIII, 247.

32. Rufus King to Caleb Davis, November 3, 1785, in Caleb Davis Papers, Massachusetts Historical Society; reprinted in Appendix E to this volume.

33. Davis's sentiments at the time are sufficiently evident from King's answering letter.

34. *Journals*, XXVIII, 17 n.; 70 n.; 201. King, it will be found from the last reference, was on the committee at the time of its report on March 28, 1785.

35. John Jay wrote John Adams, in London, on November 1, 1785, as follows: "In a late report I have called the attention of Congress to this serious question, viz., whether the United States should withdraw their attention from the ocean and leave foreigners to fetch and carry for them, or whether it is more their interest to look forward to naval strength and maritime importance, and to take and perservere in the measures proper to attain it. The diversity of opinions on this point renders it necessary that it should be well considered and finally decided. The Eastern and Middle States are generally"—i.e., all—"for the latter system, and though the others do not openly aver their preferring the former, yet they are evidently inclined to it. Hence it is that the most of the leading men in Congress from that quarter do not only not promote measures for vesting Congress with power to regulate trade, but, as the common phrase is, throw cold water on all such ideas." Jay, III, 175–76. On February 22, 1786, he wrote again to Adams as follows: "The public papers will enable you to see the complexion of the times. Federal opinions grow, but it will be some time before they bear fruit; and, what is not the case with most other fruits, they will, to judge from present appearances, ripen slower in the South than in the North." Jay, III, 183. William Grayson, in Congress from Virginia in 1785, sent William Short, on June 15, 1785, a copy of the report of the committee which had been appointed "for giving to the United States the general regulation of trade." His comment was: "Inclosed is the report of a comm[itt]ee for altering the 9th article of the confederation: 8 States will be for it, but whether or not it will suit the 5 Southern States, is a point very questionable: perhaps some modification may be found that will make it more palatable." *Letters*, VIII, 141. See also letters of James McHenry, of Maryland, and Richard Henry Lee, of Virginia. *Letters*, VIII, 180–83. James Madison's opinion on the point, in complete accord with Rufus King's, is discussed in chap. XXI hereof. See Madison, II, 155, 158, 160, 161–62; 178, 180–81.

NOTES TO CHAPTER XIV

1. Col. Her., June 24, 1785; Gaz. S.C., June 27, 1785; Ch. St. Gaz., June 29, 1785.

2. Col. Her., July 4, 1785.

3. Gaz. S.C., September 12, 1785.

4. Col. Her., October 3, 1785.

5. Ch. St. Gaz., June 18, and July 8, 1785; Gaz. S.C., July 4, 1785; Ch. P. A., July 2, 1785.

6. Ch. P. A., June 25, 1785.

7. Col. Her., June 27, 1785; Ch. St. Gaz., June 28, 1785; Ch. P. A., June 29, 1785.

8. Ch. P. A., August 2, 1785, printed the full text. Gaz. S.C., August 4, 1785, gave the essential terms: "Full power to regulate trade and enter into treaties of commerce."

9. Col. Her., January 12, 1786.

10. Ch. P. A., August 13, 1785.

11. See issues for July 18, 21, and 25, 1785. The items were probably all bona fide.

12. Ch. Ev. Gaz., August 3, 1785; Gaz. S.C., August 4, 8, 11, 1785; Col. Her., August 3, 1785; Ch. P. A., August 11, 1785.

13. Ch. Ev. Gaz., August 11, 1785; Gaz. S.C., August 15, 1785; Col. Her., August 12, 1785; Ch. P. A., August 13, 1785.

14. Ch. P. A., August 2, 1785; Gaz. S.C., August 4, 1785.

15. Above, n. 13.

16. In Newp. Merc., of September 3, 1785, certain extracts from the Charleston newspaper accounts of the Charleston town meeting were published at the request of "A [visiting] Carolinian," whose letter to the *Mercury* also was published. He maintained that the extracts refuted the report, which, he said, had been current in Newport "last week," that the Charleston meeting had adjourned without favorable action on the Boston and New York letters.

17. The report in Ch. Ev. Gaz., for August 15 is the most complete. Briefer accounts of the meeting may be found in Gaz. S.C., August 18 and 22, 1785, and Ch. P. A., August 16, 1785.

18. The petition was presented on September 26. Ch. Ev. Gaz., September 26, 1785.

19. Ibid., October 5, 1785, p. 2, col. 1.

20. Ibid., September 26, 1785.

21. Ibid., October 5, 1785, p. 2, col. 1.

22. Ibid., October 8, 1785.

23. Report of consideration of the bill, on October 11, is contained in Ch. Ev. Gaz. of that date. The issue of the *Gazette* for the twelfth is missing from the only file known. Report of the legislature's adjournment is contained in the issue of the thirteenth.

24. The pamphlet was also printed in Pa. Pack., November 8 and 9, 1785.

25. No confirmation of the fact reported could be found in any Maryland source.

26. Ch. Ev. Gaz., December 2, 1785.

27. Gaz. S.C., February 2, 1786.

28. Ibid., December 22, 1785, to February 6, 1786 inclusive.

29. See chap. XII hereof.

30. See chap. XII hereof, text at n. 8.

31. Gaz. S.C., November 7, 1785.

32. February 2 and 3, 1786.

33. The "anonimous writer" was William Barton, of Philadelphia, mentioned in a previous volume (Pol. & Con., I, 94–95, 119). He was the author of the entire article (see Am. Mus., [1787] I, 13), which had been written not for *The* [Charleston] *Morning Post* but for *The* [Philadelphia] *Pennsylvania Evening Herald*, in which paper the article had been originally published on July 29, 1785. Except for the reference to the "anonimous writer" in the version published in Charleston in February 1786, there was no material variance therein from the version originally published in Philadelphia. Probably *The Morning Post* presented the article as having been written for it, in the belief that, if the article were believed to be of local origin, it would have more influence in South Carolina. The article was again published in Charleston, in *The Charleston Evening Gazette* of June 9, 1786, in which, perhaps with the purpose of discrediting *The Morning Post*, it was stated that it had originally been published in *The Pennsylvania Evening Herald*, on the date above given. Further light on the kind of commerce power desired by William Barton may be gleaned from his pamphlet of 1786, *The True Interest of the United States*. See Pol. & Con., I, 94–95.

34. Article VI of the Confederation.

35. Article III of the Confederation.

36. Ch. Ev. Gaz., February 1, 1786; Gaz. S.C., February 6, 1786; Col. Her., February 2, 1786; Ch. Mng. P., February 2, 1786. Governor Moultrie's message was reprinted in a good many northern newspapers. See, for example, Pa. Pack., March

$\bar{8}$, 1786.

37. Ch. Ev. Gaz., February 4, 1786.

38. Ibid.

39. Cooper, South Carolina Statutes-at-Large, IV, 720.

40. See, for example, *Review of a late Pamphlet, under the Signature of "Brutus,"* by "Hamilton" (Charleston, 1828). This pamphlet, considered more particularly herein at a later point, is ascribed in some libraries, even in South Carolina, to James Hamilton, sometime governor of that state. Such ascriptions most probably keep the old governor restless in his grave.

41. Ch. Ev. Gaz., February 3, 1786, p. 2, col. 2, and Gaz. S.C., February 6, 1786, p. 3, col. 2 (Rutledge); Ch. Mng. P., February 1, 1786, p. 2, col. 4 (C. C. Pinckney); ibid, March 2, 1786, p. 3, col. 1 (Butler).

NOTES TO CHAPTER XV

1. No report of the Savannah meeting appeared in the local papers. The facts stated in the text appear in an anonymous letter "to the People of Chatham County," criticizing the results of the meeting, which was published in Sav. Gaz., September 29, 1785. See also, Col. Her., September 14, 1785, and Ch. P. A., October 8, 1785.

2. Colonial Records of Georgia (Atlanta, 1911), XIX, pt. II, 554.

3. Letters, VIII, lxxxvi.

4. Ibid., 151.

5. Also printed in Ch. P. A., October 8, 1785.

6. Sav. Gaz., October 6, 1785.

7. Ibid.

8. Ibid., November 3, 1785.

9. Ibid., December 8, 1785; Pa. Pack., January 24, 1786. Nathan Dane said, in a letter of January 20, 1786, that "the Grand Juries of most of the Counties in [the] State" had made such presentments. Letters, VIII, 287.

10. State Records of North Carolina, XXIV, 561.

11. Thomas Farr, of Charleston, S.C., to Caleb Davis, of Boston, July 18, 1785, in Caleb Davis Papers, Massachusetts Historical Society.

12. See chap. V hereof, text at nn. 47–49.

13. The only North Carolina item found in the papers of the other states, during the period under discussion, was an attack on Congress, signed "Cassius," which was copied in Ch. Mng. P., August 26, 1786.

14. On the singular physical character of North Carolina and the other characteristics mentioned in the text, see Crittenden, *The Commerce of North Carolina*; also, Crittenden, *North Carolina Newspapers before 1790*, in The James Sprunt Historical Studies, vol. 20, no. 1, p. 9.

15. Madison, II, 41, 42; Rives, *History of the Life and Times of James Madison* (Boston, 1866), I, 551.

16. See chap. IX hereof.

17. Journals, XIX, 236; XX, 469–470.

18. See chap. IX hereof.

19. Madison, II, 99–100; cf. Lee, II, 307. It is not usually noted that the convention in question was for a purpose limited as stated in the text; but this is perfectly apparent from the letter of Richard Henry Lee, to which Madison was replying when he expressed his approval of the convention. Lee had written that the convention being talked of in Congress was one "for *the Sole purpose* of revising the Confederation *so far* as to enable Congress *to execute* with more energy, effect, & vigor *the powers assigned to it*, than it appear[ed] *by experience* that they [could] do under the present

state of things." Madison wrote back that, "in general [he] h[e]ld it for a maxim that the Union of the States [was] essential to *their safety ag[ain]st foreign danger, & internal contention*; and that the perpetuity and efficacy of the present system [could] not be confided in." "Should a view of the other States present no objection ag[ain]st the [proposed convention], individually," he concluded, "I w[ould] wish none to be presupposed here." These sentiments appear to accord rather closely with what Stephen Higginson declared Madison had inadvertently disclosed as his sole interest in the confederacy in 1783: getting the other states bound to defend Virginia and her territory, without agreeing to anything which the other states desired, in exchange for such protection. See Letters, VII, 123.

20. Madison, II, 28; cf. Rives, *James Madison*, I, 542–44.

21. Madison, II, 66.

22. Ibid., 57, 65–66; Rives, *James Madison*, I, 543.

23. Madison, II, 41; Rives, *James Madison*, I, 549.

24. Madison, II, 41.

25. Ibid., 48.

26. Ibid., 104–9.

27. Ibid., 137.

28. The petitions are preserved in the Virginia State Library at Richmond.

29. Journal of the Virginia House of Delegates for 1785 (Richmond, 1828), 22, 24, 54.

30. In a letter to Washington, dated December 9, 1785, Madison said, with reference to the mercantile petitions, that a local navigation act, rather than some measure of commercial power for Congress, was "backed by the mercantile interest of most of [the Virginia] towns except Alexandria, which alone," he declared, "seem[ed] to have liberality or light on the subject" (Madison, II, 198). Cf. the somewhat similar statement made by him in a letter to Jefferson, on January 22, 1786. Madison, II, 218. The fact that Madison regarded the Alexandria petition as "liberal" is, of course, evidence, in addition to that referred to in the text, that his notions as to how much power over the subject should be given to Congress were, at this time, very modest indeed.

31. That is, beyond the fragmentary powers which had been asked by Congress on April 30, 1784. See chap. X hereof, text at nn. 26–31.

32. Madison, II, 146.

33. His knowledge of the Northern proposals appears in his letter. A copy of the report of the committee "for giving to the United States the general regulation of trade" was sent to him by William Grayson, on the preceding May 1. Letters, VIII, 110 and 172.

34. Madison, II, 149.

35. Lee, II, 382. With reference to the differential in the price of tobacco in the Virginian and Northern ports, Lee said: "It is true that the price of our Staple has been for some time greater at Phila[delphia] and here [in New York] than in Virg[ini]a—But it is as true that the European price did not warrant the price at these two places as the great losses and bankruptcies of the Adventures plainly prove—Indeed this excess of price at P[hiladelphia] & N[ew] Y[ork] was occasioned by sinking speculators, who to swim awhile longer, would go any length to keep up appearances, by making some remittance to their Creditors abroad—But this business is now chiefly over & here at present there is neither money nor inclination to purchase Tob[acc]o.—The crowd of bankrupts at P[hiladelphia] has, I believe, nearly produced the same effect." In other words, tobacco as a mode of remittance was acceptable by the New York and Philadelphia merchants' creditors in Europe; and the higher price of which Madison complained was due to a temporary artificial demand for tobacco for remittance purposes. Presumably, the tobacco was bought through

local credit arrangements, or by a set-off of sales of European goods against purchases of tobacco at a premium.

36. Journals, XXVIII, 17 n., 70 n., 201.

37. Ibid., XXVIII, 201; Monroe, I, 80 n.

38. Monroe, I, 97.

39. Ibid., 100.

40. Madison, II, 155.

41. Monroe, I, 163.

42. Madison, II, 160 and 178.

43. See chap. XIII hereof, text at nn. 34 and 35.

44. Journals, XXVIII, 201.

45. Monroe was a guest at King's wedding early in 1786. King, I, 130 ff.

46. Monroe, I, 103.

47. Letters, VIII, 389–90, 415–16; Higginson, 733, 734–35; and cf. Higginson, 745, and Letters, VII, 123. This matter is discussed more particularly in chap. XVIII hereof.

48. Madison, II, 218.

49. Journal of the Virginia House of Delegates for 1785 (Richmond, 1828), 25; Madison, II, 193.

50. Madison, II, 218.

51. Journal of the Virginia House of Delegates for 1785, 54 and 66.

52. Ibid., 66.

53. Hening, Va. Stat. at L., XI, 388. The act was passed at the May session.

54. Madison, II, 218.

55. Journal of the Virginia House of Delegates for 1785, 67–68; Madison, II, 196–98, 218.

56. Journal of the Virginia House of Delegates for 1785, 72, 90, 113, 114, 117–19. The resolutions of the Legislature of Maryland and the report of the joint commission are in the Virginia State Library at Richmond. See also Madison, II, 193, 198, 218.

57. Elliot, III, 655.

58. Madison, II, 198, 218; Higginson, 735; cf. Rives, *James Madison*, II, 60.

59. Madison, II, 218. The motion is not recorded in the official journal of the House of Delegates as having been made until the last day of the legislative session, January 21, 1786. It is then definitely recorded as having been made on that day. Journal of Virginia House of Delegates for 1785, 153. Madison's statement upon this point may, nevertheless, be accepted, since it is supported by a similar statement in a letter of his to Washington, dated December 9, 1785, *which has survived among the Washington papers.* Madison, II, 196.

60. Journal of the Virginia House of Delegates for 1785, 72 and 90.

61. Ibid., 113, 114, 117, 118.

62. Article VI of the Confederation: "No two or more states shall enter into any treaty, confederation, or alliance, whatever, between them, without the consent of the United States, in Congress assembled, specifying accurately the purposes for which the same is to be entered into, and how long it shall continue."

63. Madison, II, 211–12; 233. Cf. the insistence of Rufus King, in proposing to Caleb Davis, a system of joint regulation of "internal and external commerce," by "the Eastern States," on the third of the following November, that this was possible, "provided *the purpose and duration thereof*"—King's emphasis—"[were] previously communicated to, and approved by, Congress." Appendix E hereof.

64. Journal of the Virginia House of Delegates for 1785, 140.

65. Journal of the Virginia Senate for 1785 (Richmond, 1827), 94; Journal of the Virginia House of Delegates for 1785, 145. In these citations, the matter is covered by

the references to "resolutions respecting a joint application to be made by Virginia and Maryland to Congress, relative to the defence of Chesapeake Bay." This was the nature of the first of four resolutions, of which that under discussion was one, which the House had sent to the Senate together. See p. 140 of the House Journal.

66. The letter sent out for this purpose may be seen in State Records of North Carolina, XVIII, 511.

67. Journal of Virginia House of Delegates for 1785, 153–54; Madison, II, 218; 223–24.

68. Madison, II, 218 and 223.

69. Ibid., 234.

70. Ibid., 233. Stung, apparently, by Monroe's comments on his convention (Madison did *not* preserve Monroe's letter), Madison, by this time, was springing to the defense, to some extent, of what he had done. His immediate reaction is reflected in his earlier letters.

71. Ibid., 218. In a letter to Monroe, dated December 30, 1785 (ibid., 211), Madison said that "no pains [had been] spared [in the legislature] to disparage the Treaty [of Peace] by insinuations ag[ain]st Cong[res]s, the Eastern States, and the negociators of the Treaty, particularly J. Adams." "These insinuations & artifices," he added, "explain perhaps one of the motives from which the augmentation of the fœderal powers & respectability has been opposed." In other words, according to Madison, the opposition sprang partly from the dislike, among some Virginia planters, of paying their prewar private debts to British creditors, as the treaty required.

72. Ibid., 222 ff.

73. The obvious lack of any syntactically essential reference to "the Virginia legislature" as the source of the "enclosed resolution" is most probably attributable to a copyist's inadvertence by Randolph's amanuensis.

74. The copies of these letters sent by Randolph to Governor Livingston, of New Jersey, are in The Livingston Papers, Massachusetts Historical Society. Cf. the discussion in chap. XXIII hereof.

75. Letters, VIII, 389–90, 415–16; Higginson, 734–35. This matter is discussed more particularly in chap. XVIII hereof.

76. This letter, published in State Records of North Carolina, XVIII, 542, is reprinted in Appendix G hereof.

77. King, I, 156–60.

78. Madison, I, 132.

NOTES TO CHAPTER XVI

1. Journals, XXVIII, 17 n.

2. Ibid.

3. King appears on the committee for the first time on March 11, 1785. Ibid., 148 n.

4. Ibid., 17 n.

5. Ibid., 201–2.

6. Ibid., 148 n.

7. Ibid., 202.

8. Ibid., 17 n.

9. Journals, XXVIII, 205 n.

10. Ibid., 17 n.

11. Letters, VIII, 13.

12. Journals, XXVIII, 17 n.

13. Letters, VIII, 43, 182.

14. Ibid., 15, 125. Jesse Root, of Connecticut, who, when a member of Congress in

1781, had voted for the Witherspoon proposal of a complete commerce power (Journals, XIX, 111), wrote to William Samuel Johnson, on May 28: "Congress must be invested with Competent powers to regulate Trade—to raise a revenue for national purposes and to govern the republic of States or we never can perpetuate our union and free Constitution of Government." Letters, VIII, 125 n. 4.

15. Letters, VIII, 18.
16. Ibid., 199, 200, 244, 286, 418; cf. 151.
17. Ibid., 26.
18. Ibid., 181.
19. Ibid., 231.
20. Ibid., 199.
21. See chap. XI hereof.
22. Journals, XXVIII, 345.
23. Letters, VIII, 24, 26.
24. See chap. X hereof, including the discussion in n. 58 to that chapter.
25. Monroe, I, 56, 59.
26. Journals, XXVIII, 17 n.
27. Ibid., 201.
28. Letters, VIII, 170.
29. Journals, XXVIII, 17 n.
30. Ibid., 202–5.
31. Monroe, I, 67, 68. Jefferson wrote back that he was "much pleased with the proposition to the states to invest Congress with *the regulation of their trade*, reserving its revenue to the states." Jefferson, IV, 415, 418.
32. The date of the Boston merchants' letters was April 22, 1785. The Philadelphia merchants' memorial to the Pennsylvania legislature was dated April 6, 1785, but it did not become generally known until after the date of Monroe's letter. See chap. XIII hereof.
33. Consider, for example, the use of Monroe's phrase in the letter from *The* [Poughkeepsie] *New-York Journal* of February 15, 1779, referred to in Pol. & Con., 183–84.
34. Monroe, I, 75.
35. Ibid., 80–82.
36. Ibid., 84.
37. Smith, *An Enquiry into the Causes of the Wealth of Nations* (Modern Library ed.; New York, 1937), 397.
38. See *The Oxford English Dictionary*.
39. See Pol. & Con., I, 151–52.
40. Journals, XXVIII, 201.
41. Monroe, I, 53, 55. See also Monroe's letter to Madison, of about the same date. Ibid., 56, 59.
42. Ibid., 85–86.
43. Monroe, I, 97.
44. Madison, II, 156.
45. Ibid., 178, 180. In a letter to Jefferson, of August 12, 1786, Madison wrote that South Carolina had not appointed delegates to the convention at Annapolis because it was "supposed [the state] had sufficiently signified her concurrence in a general regulation of trade by vesting the power in Congress for 15 years." Ibid., 262. As South Carolina had given power only over foreign trade, this may seem to cast some doubt upon the meaning of Madison's letter to Jefferson, of October 3. The words of that letter are, of course, ambiguous, if taken by themselves; but considering the agitation which had gone before, and what Monroe had written, their meaning is not

uncertain. As for Madison's letter to Jefferson about South Carolina, it does not appear whether he knew accurately the terms of the South Carolina act. Cf. his ignorance with respect to the appointment of delegates to Annapolis, in a letter written to Jefferson, on the preceding May 12, wherein he says that "most if not all the States, except Maryl[an]d, have appointed deputies for the proposed convention at Annapolis." Ibid., 236, 238.

46. Monroe, I, 112, 116.

47. Ibid., 160, 163.

48. Ibid., 307, 323.

49. Ibid.

50. See this pamphlet as reprinted in Pol. & Con., II, 1179–1205, at 1184.

51. See Pol. & Con., I, 55–69, and II, 1267–74.

52. Ibid.

53. It was apparently given to the press in Charleston, South Carolina, for the first publication seems to have been in Col. Her., on September 25, 1786. It afterwards appeared in a number of other papers, including at least the following: Ga. Gaz., October 21, 1786; N.J. Gaz., November 20, 1786; *The* [Richmond] *Virginia Gazette & American Advertiser*, November 22, 1786; Mass. Gaz., November 24, 1786; Ch. Mng. P., November 29 and 30, 1786; Newp. Merc., December 4, 1786; N. L. Gaz., December 22, 1786; Am. Her., February 12, 1787.

54. James Madison, in his later life, denied that the sense of "consolidation in 1787, was what, he intimated, it later became. Records, III, 464. This can be refuted from his own notes on the Federal Convention, as well as from the notes on the proceedings of that body taken by others.

55. See chap. XII hereof, text at n. 17.

56. Monroe, I, 75.

57. Ibid. Cf. Monroe's later reference to the "deep and radical" change which his committee's report would make, in his letter to Thomas Jefferson, of June 16, 1785. Monroe, I, 84.

58. *The Political Establishments of the United States* (Pol. & Con., II, 1182 ff.).

59. The "Acirema" item also appeared in Col. Her., on June 29, 1789, and in Va. Jour., on August 2, 1786. It probably also was copied in other papers as well.

NOTES TO CHAPTER XVII

1. Journals, XXVIII, 205 n.

2. Ibid., XXIX, 533, 536, 539; Monroe, I, 67, 80, and 103; Letters, VIII, 189.

3. Letters, VIII, 107.

4. Ibid., 121.

5. See chap. XII hereof, text at n. 15.

6. King, I, 100.

7. Acts and Resolves of Massachusetts 1784–85 (Official Reprint), 666–68.

8. See also the delegates' preliminary reply to the governor, of August 18, 1785, in which they explained that, "at the time [they] received [the General Court's] resolves, Congress had, and [at the time they wrote] still ha[d], under deliberation propositions to remedy the commercial embarrassments experienced in many of the states"; but that "the prevailing opinion discovered in the progress of deliberation, gave [them] no cause to expect an adoption of the plan proposed by the Legislature in the resolves referred to." Cf. Monroe, I, 103–4. The "president" referred to in this Monroe letter was Richard Henry Lee, of Virginia, president of Congress, not Samuel Holten, of Massachusetts, chairman of the committee of the whole, as the editor of Monroe's works supposed.

9. Letters, VIII, 206.

10. Ibid.

11. See chap. XII hereof, text at nn. 16 and 17.

12. Acts and Resolves of Massachusetts 1784–85 (Official Reprint), 789.

13. Holten was gone from New York by November 21, at which time King wrote to him in Massachusetts, in the plain expectation that Holten would be conferring with the General Court. Letters, VIII, 257.

14. Ibid., lxxxviii.

15. Theodore Sedgwick to Caleb Davis, January 31, 1786, in Caleb Davis Papers, Massachusetts Historical Society.

16. Letters, VIII, lxxxviii.

17. Above, n. 15. As indicated, Sedgwick's letter to Davis was dated by Sedgwick "January 31st, 1786." In all the circumstances, it seems probable that this was one of those inadvertent misdatings which so commonly occur just after the beginning of a new year, and that the correct date of the letter was January 1, 1786.

18. Rufus King to Caleb Davis, November 3, 1786, in Caleb Davis Papers, Massachusetts Historical Society (reprinted in Appendix E hereof).

19. Rufus King to Caleb Davis, October 17, 1785, in Caleb Davis Papers, Massachusetts Historical Society (reprinted in Appendix E hereof).

20. Letters, VIII, 218.

21. The precise facts as to the comparative numbers of freemen in Massachusetts and Virginia in 1785 are not known, but the general belief was that the number in Massachusetts was considerably the larger. In the Federal Convention, David Brearley, of New Jersey, used an estimate of the numbers of whites in the three largest states as follows: Massachusetts, 352,000; Pennsylvania, 341,000; Virginia, 300,000. Records, I, 573. C. C. Pinckney, of South Carolina, before the House of Representatives of that state, in January 1788, estimated the white population of the same three states as follows: Massachusetts, 360,000; Pennsylvania, 360,000; Virginia, 252,000. Ibid., III, 253. In an "Address to the convention of Virginia," dated May 21, 1788, Tench Coxe, in attempting to show that Virginia would be more than fairly represented in the proposed national House of Representatives, observed in part: "Taking the number of free citizens, which is the proper rule of representation in free governments, Virginia, in the federal representation, would have about as many votes as New York, and fewer than Massachusetts or Pennsylvania." The "Address" was published in Pa. Gaz., May 21 and 28, 1788, and in Va. Ind. Chr., May 28 and June 4, 1788. See also Am. Mus., III, 426, 437 (May 1788).

22. King, I, 67–70.

23. Jefferson, Madison, and Monroe all used it in their correspondence with each other, during the period under discussion. Jefferson, IV, 125–27 (to Madison); 270–72 (to Madison); 370, 371 (to Monroe); Madison, II, 27 (to Jefferson); 34, 38 (to Jefferson); 146, 148 (to Monroe); 160, 162–65 (to Jefferson); Monroe, I, 22 (to Jefferson); 46 (to Madison); 75–76 (to Madison); 109–11 (to Madison); Letters, VIII, 391, 392 n. 2 (Monroe to Jefferson); 403, 404 n. 4 (Monroe to Jefferson). The foregoing references show that the practice, as between these three men, was followed whilst all three were still within the country. There was also a Virginia state cypher, for use by the Virginia delegates in Congress for their official communications to the Virginia governor. Letters, VIII, 421 n. 2 to letter no. 463.

24. The fear is sufficiently evident in King's remarks in his letter to Caleb Davis, cited above, n. 18. See also the remarks of Monroe in Letters, VIII, 421. Many other similar indications in the surviving letters of the period attest the existence of such a fear.

25. See the King letters in Caleb Davis Papers, Massachusetts Historical Society;

also, Higginson, 709, 752, 754, 756, 757, 760; Letters, VIII, 344, 389, 458.

26. King married Mary Alsop, daughter of John Alsop, a prominent merchant of New York, on March 31, 1786. King, I, 130 ff.

27. In the nature of the case, no direct proof of this point can be given, but it will perhaps be sufficient that Monroe was reluctant, without the cover of a cypher, to write to Patrick Henry about what was the Virginia phase of the same matter. See Letters, VIII, 421–25.

28. Monroe, I, 112.

29. Journals, XXVI, 275. For the original committee report with the ten names which Jefferson had thought up for the new states, see ibid., 118, 119–20.

30. Journals, XXX, 131–35, 390–94; cf. ibid., XXXII, 334, 342. The original committee report (Monroe was the Virginia member of the committee) had said that "many" of the proposed states "must probably contain a large proportion of barren and unimprovable lands," and that "many of them [would] not soon, if ever, have a sufficient number of Inhabitants to form a government." Ibid., XXX, 132. The resolution finally adopted said that "some [would] contain too great a proportion of barren and unimproved lands, and of consequence [would] not for many years, if ever, have a sufficient number of inhabitants to form a respectable government, and entitle them to a seat and voice in the federal council." Ibid., XXX, 393–94.

31. Monroe, I, 40–41, 112–13.

32. Not all Southerners, of course, held such views. In this, as in so many other matters, Washington, for instance, showed better judgment. Washington, XXI, 182 and 248.

33. Records, I, 605.

34. Ibid., 585–86.

35. Journals, XXXII, 343.

36. Madison, II, 64, 72.

37. Records, I, 573; III, 253.

38. According to Madison, the following statement was made by George Mason, of Virginia, on July 11, when Gouverneur Morris was endeavoring to get the convention to vest Congress with power "to regulate the number of representatives. . . . upon the principles of [the states' respective] wealth and number of inhabitants": "From the nature of man we may be sure, that those who have power in their hands will not give it up while they can retain it. On the Contrary we know they will always when they can rather increase it. *If the S[outhern] States therefore should have 3/4 of the people of America within their limits*, the Northern will hold fast the majority of Representatives. *1/4 will govern the 3/4.*" Records, I, 578. He also said: "As soon as the Southern & Western population should predominate, *which must happen in a few years*, the power w[oul]d be in the hands of the minority, and would never be yielded to the majority, unless [it were] provided for by the Constitution."

39. Constitution of the United States, Article I, Section 9, clauses 1 and 4; and Article V.

40. In addition to the speech of William Grayson, of Virginia, cited in chap. XIX hereof, text preceding n. 45, see a jingoistic item from Charleston, S.C., dated April 6, 1786, and signed "Fabius," which was reprinted in Am. Mus. III, 433 (May 1788). It advocated war if Spain did not meet America's demands, and talked of conquering not only the Floridas but Louisiana and Mexico, also. But if Spain acceded to America's demands, "it would," the item concluded, "perhaps be more political to postpone to a more remote time, all thoughts of conquest." See also "a letter from captain John Sullivan, [of Georgia,] late of the continental army, to the Spanish minister at New York," reprinted in the same number of the *Museum*, at p. 436. Such citations from Southern sources of this period could easily be multiplied. Even James

Madison dreamed a little of such conquests, behind the shield of his cypher. Madison, II, 68, 69, 70.

41. The consent of nine states was required, by Articles IX and XI of the Confederation, for the admission of new states. Cf. Journals, XXVI, 119 and 278.

42. Madison, II, 324, 327.

43. Ibid., 336, 338, 340.

44. Ibid., 344, 345.

45. The statement is recorded in Madison's notes as made on July 19 in connection with the discussion of the mode of appointing the president of the United States. Madison said he favored election by "the people at large" but observed that "there was one difficulty however of a serious nature attending an immediate choice by the people." "The right of suffrage," he said, "was much more diffusive in the Northern than the Southern states; and the latter could have no influence in the election on the score of the Negroes. The substitution of electors obviated this difficulty and seemed on the whole to be liable to the fewest objections." Records, II, 57. On July 25, after the employment of electors had been voted down for the time being, he said he thought election of the president by the direct vote of "the people at large" the least objectionable of the several other modes of choice which had been suggested. But he repeated two objections, the second of which was that "ar[i]s[ing] from the disproportion of qualified voters in the N[orthern] & S[outhern] States and the disadvantages which this mode would throw on the latter." "[An] answer to this objection," he thought, "was that this disproportion would be continually decreasing under the influence of the Republican laws introduced in the S[outhern] States"—i.e., apparently, that *would be* introduced in them to correct the "disproportion"—"and the more rapid increase of their population."

46. King, I, 39 ff. King introduced his motion to this effect on March 16, 1785. Journals, XXVIII, 164. By the terms of his motion, the prohibition was to be effective immediately. The Jefferson committee's original scheme of 1784 had contained an anti-slavery clause which was to be effective after 1800, but it was voted down. Journals, XXVIII, 118, 119, 275, 277; Jefferson, IV, 330. King's motion was committed to a committee consisting of himself and David Howell, and William Ellery, of Rhode Island. The committee reported April 6, going back to the form of the original Jefferson committee's prohibition. Journals, XXVIII, 164 and 239. Nothing more was done until the enactment of the Ordinance for the Government of the Northwest Territory, on July 13, 1787, when the prohibition went in as King had proposed it in 1785. Journals, XXXII, 343. See also Letters, VIII, 94, 110. In the last reference, William Grayson, of Virginia, wrote Madison, on May 1, 1785, that "Mr. King of Massachusetts ha[d] a resolution ready drawn which he [was] reserv[ing] till the Ordinance [was] passed for preventing slavery in the new State [*sic*]." "I expect," he added, "Seven States may be found liberal enough to adopt it."

47. It has become the fashion among certain historians to speak of the New England states of this period, especially Connecticut, as the stronghold of aristocracy. This was not the view of the men of the time. Connecticut, in particular, was viewed as the model commonwealth by most Americans of the period and was constantly spoken of, as Hamilton spoke of it in *The Federalist*, No. LXXXIII as "the most popular"—i.e., the most democratic—"state."

48. See especially his letter to Dane, of September 17, 1785, p. 258 above.

49. Noah Webster, in his *Sketches of American Policy* (Hartford, 1785), said (pp. 28–29) that, "in New England, it [was] rare to find a person who [could] not read and write." "In the New-England states," he explained, "the poorest children [were] instructed in reading, writing, and arithmetic, at the public expense." "But if [he was] rightly informed," he went on, "the case [was] different in the southern states."

"[There], education [was] not so general. Gentlemen of fortune g[a]ve their children a most liberal education; and no part of America produce[d] greater lawyers, statesmen, and divines; but the body of the people [were] indifferently educated." "The flourishing state of South-Carolina never had an academy till within a few months past." "[And he could] not learn that North-Carolina ha[d] yet any kind of college or academy. A few gentlemen [there] sen[t] their sons to Europe for an education." He also cited the testimony of Revolutionary officers as to the illiteracy of New York and Pennsylvania troops as compared with those from Connecticut. And he argued generally that "a general diffusion of science"—i.e., knowledge—was America's "best guard." Tench Coxe, a Pennsylvanian, writing in 1794, spoke of "the practice of the eastern states, in regard to schools," as "deserv[ing] the most serious attention of the wise and good" in his own state. *A View of the United States of America* (Philadelphia, 1794), 10–11.

50. King's letter to Caleb Davis, of November 3, 1785, reprinted in Appendix E hereof, plainly shows that Davis was impatient. Nathaniel Gorham's writing to Davis, from Congress, to urge a convention shows that he regarded Davis as of his view. Gorham to Davis, March 1, 1786, Caleb Davis Papers, Massachusetts Historical Society. Gorham, at the time, was already favorable to a change in the basis of representation in Congress. Letters, VII, 318. With reference to the "fetter" attached to the original Massachusetts resolution to participate in the Federal Convention, Gorham, then a member of the General Court, wrote to Henry Knox that "Mr. [Samuel] Adams [was] full of doubts & difficulties & finding that he [could] not obstruct the report generally wishe[d] to limit the Commission in such a manner as [Gorham thought would] exceedingly injure the business." Gorham to Knox, February 18, 1787, Henry Knox Papers, Massachusetts Historical Society. Higginson's impatience is evident from his letter to Knox on February 8, 1787. Higginson, 747.

51. Acts and Resolves of Massachusetts 1786–87 (Official Reprint), 447–49.

52. Madison, II, 321.

53. Ibid.

NOTES TO CHAPTER XVIII

1. See pp. 199–200 hereof. The complete text of King's letter to Davis is reprinted in appendix E hereof.

2. Letters, VIII, lxxxvii.

3. Ibid., 282.

4. Journals, XXX, 6–10.

5. Ibid., 87.

6. On Gorham, see letters relating to him, chap. XVII, n. 50. On Pinckney, see Letters, VIII, 321–30, 350.

7. Gorham to Davis, February 23, 1786, in Caleb Davis Papers, Massachusetts Historical Society.

8. Journals, XXX, 87–88.

9. Ibid., 93–94.

10. Congress's appeal was published generally. See, among others, the following newspapers: Ch. Ev. Gaz., June 1, 1786; N.H. Merc., March 15, 1786; N.Y. Jour., May 4, 1786.

11. See chap. X hereof, text at n. 30.

12. Letters, VIII, 297, 298.

13. Ibid., 283.

14. Ibid., 287, 288; see also 293, 294.

15. Ibid., 303–6.

16. See chap. IX hereof, text at nn. 13 and 14.

17. See chap. IX hereof, text at nn. 2 and 3.

18. See chap. XV hereof, text at n. 72.

19. See N.Y. Jour. for that date.

20. Gorham to Davis, February 23, 1786, in Caleb Davis Papers, Massachusetts Historical Society.

21. Acts and Resolves of Massachusetts, 1784–85, 876–77.

22. Ibid., 915.

23. Ibid., 422, 947–48.

24. See the discussion in chap. XI hereof. A list of the members of the Boston merchants' committee was included in most of the newspapers that published the Boston letters.

25. New York Assembly Journal 1786, 175. Leonard Gansevoort and Robert C. Livingston were also appointed. Three were necessary to constitute a quorum of the state's appointments.

26. Elliot, I, 116.

27. Pa. Pack., April 13, 1786. John Armstrong, Jr. was also appointed.

28. See above, chap. XIII, text at nn. 2 and 3. For the membership of the Philadelphia merchants' committee, see Pa. Pack., January 18, 1785.

29. Letters, VIII, 354, 355.

30. Gorham to Davis, March 1, 1786, in Caleb Davis Papers, Massachusetts Historical Society.

31. Madison, II, 231, 233–34.

32. Hamilton, I, 213, 223–25.

33. Richard Henry Lee wrote Madison about the matter on November 26, 1784, saying: "A propos—It is by many here suggested as a very necessary Step for Congress to take—The calling upon the States to form a Convention for the Sole purpose of revising the Confederation so far as to enable Congress to execute with more energy, effect, & vigor the powers assigned it, than it appears by experience that they can do under the present state of things—It has been observed, why do not Congress recommend the necessary alterations to the States as is proposed in the Confederation? The friends to Convention answer—It has been already done in some instances, but in vain. It is proposed to let Congress go on in the meantime as usual" (Lee, II, 307). It seems evident from the purpose Lee stated that a plenipotentiary meeting was intended.

34. See chap. XXV hereof.

35. He said that some were proposing as a mode of reforming the government that "State conventions" be called "for the express purpose" of "originat[ing] and propos[ing] necessary amendments to the confederation," to be followed by "a congress of deputys, appointed by these [state] conventions *with plenipotentiary powers.*" In other words, the several state conventions were to suggest amendments, and the "congress of deputies" was, as Hamilton had said in 1780, to "conclude finally" on the reforms to be made. Letters, VIII, 490.

36. The reference to New York in the quotation, which is taken from Thomas Rodney's diary, probably relates in some confused way to the continental impost power, herein previously referred to at the various points. It was a very limited power of putting the imposts on foreign imports, for revenue purposes only. It had been granted on May 2, 1786, albeit in unsatisfactory form, by the New York legislature. It is not entirely certain, however, that this is what was meant. A bill had been introduced in the New York legislature on February 22, 1786, and, interestingly enough, by Samuel Jones, floor leader of the Clintonian faction in the Assembly, "to enable the United States *to regulate trade and commerce.*" New York Assembly Journal

for 1786, 52. The bill was referred to a committee of the whole on the following day. Ibid. What it covered is not known; but in a long speech on the impost, answering the contention of the opposition headed by Jones, that the legislature lacked power to grant the impost to Congress, Hamilton said, on February 18, 1787: "The hon[orable] member in my eye [Mr. Jones], at the last session, brought in a bill, for granting to congress *the power of regulating the trade of the union*. This surely includes more ample legislative authority, than is comprehended in the mere power of levying a particular duty. *It indeed goes to a prodigious extent*, much farther than on a superficial view can be imagined." Am. Mus., (1787), I, 445, 446. The reference to New York in the quotation from the Rodney diary may, therefore, relate to something that had recently gone on in reference to this Jones bill, in committee of the whole in the New York Assembly. The "commercial" powers requested by Congress on April 30, 1784, had been granted by New York early in April 1785.

37. Letters, VIII, 350–51.
38. Madison, II, 242–43.
39. Monroe, I, 125, 127–28.
40. Letters, VIII, 351, 367, 373–74, 399, 433, 454–55, 462, 471; Journals, XXX, 230, 387 n.; XXXI, 494–98.
41. Letters, VIII, 372–74.
42. See chap. XXVI hereof, text at nn. 8 to 18, inclusive.
43. See Pa. Pack., April 1, 1786, p. 3, col. 1. The first resolution was also published in both Ch. Mng. P., and Ch. Ev. Gaz. of March 8, 1786. It may have appeared in a few other papers, but it was not published generally.
44. Journals, XXX, 323; Monroe, I, 133.
45. See chap. XV hereof.
46. Letters, VIII, 389–90.
47. Letters, VI, xlvi and liii.
48. Letters, VII, lxviii and lxxvii.
49. See chap. IX hereof, text at nn. 40 and 41.
50. Letters, VII, 123.
51. See chap. XV hereof, text at nn. 21 to 23, inclusive.
52. Higginson, 733, 734–35.
53. Acts and Resolves of Massachusetts 1786–87 (Official Reprint), 312.
54. Higginson mentioned some of the later appointments in his letter to Adams in July. Higginson, 735. For the others mentioned, see DHC, IV, 26.
55. DHC, IV, 26; cf. 58.
56. Letters, VIII, 415–16.
57. See the following chapter.
58. Elliot, I, 116; cf. n. 25 above.
59. Elliot, I, 116; cf. n. 27 above. See also, Madison, II, 271, where Madison says, in a letter to Monroe: "Delaware N.J. & Va. alone are on the ground, two commiss[ione]rs attend from N.Y. & one from Pa."

NOTES TO CHAPTER XIX

1. Monroe, I, 132, 138, 145.
2. Ibid., 150; Letters, VIII, 429 (King). Some of the Southerners made similar threats: Letters, VIII, 437 (Grayson). Henry Lee, of Virginia, deplored these threats, saying "he was sorry to find gentlemen talk so lightly of a separation and dissolution of the Confederation." Letters, VIII, 439.
3. Letters, VIII, 448. The Spanish conquest of the Floridas could hardly affect the navigating right appurtenant to unconquered lands lying further up the Mississippi

and its tributaries, especially those in the hands of Spain's cobelligerent, the United States.

4. Wharton, *The Revolutionary Diplomatic Correspondence of the United States* (Washington, 1889), VI, 100.

5. Ibid., 97.

6. Journals, XXXII, 188.

7. Ibid., XXVII, 688–90.

8. Ibid., XXIX, 494, 562.

9. Ibid., 658. Congress had previously hamstrung Jay even more completely. Ibid., 562, 627–29.

10. Ibid., 629.

11. Lee, II, 391.

12. Pickering, *Life of Timothy Pickering* (Boston, 1867), I, 457, 546–49.

13. Journals, XXVI, 118–20, 275–79.

14. Washington, XXVIII, 108, 109.

15. Lee, II, 377.

16. Washington, XXVIII, 230, 231–33.

17. Ibid., 202, 204–5, 207–8, 255, 256, 459, 460.

18. Madison, II, 97.

19. Ibid., 132, 138–39.

20. Journals, XXXI, 467, 477–80.

21. Ibid., 467, 480–84; Letters, VIII, 380–82, 400, 427–30, 434–37, 438–40, 447–49.

22. Article IX of the Confederation.

23. On August 11, Lee wrote to Madison: "Mr. Jay is commissioned to treat with Mr. Gardoqui, but as yet nothing has been done—The exclusive nav[igatio]n of Mississippi will be earnestly contended for by Spain, who to quiet us on that head will probably grant large commercial benefits—But if we remain firm, I incline to think that the Navig[atio]n will be consented to." Lee, II, 382. On October 11, he wrote to Washington: "The negotiation with Mr. Gardoqui proceeds so slowly, and as yet so ineffectually, that I fancy the free navigation of Mississippi is a point that we may take it for granted will not hastily be concluded upon. So that mischiefs from that source are probably postponed to a distant day." Lee, II, 391. Washington's letter of August 22 must have been received in the interim between these two letters, and it would seem reasonable, in view of Lee's later attitude, to conclude that Washington's arguments had changed Lee's views. Cf. below, n. 25.

24. The evidence indicates that Jay had formulated his scheme by about December 18, 1785, when Monroe returned to New York from a western trip, on which he had left on August 25. Monroe, I, 107, 108, 132, 144. How much earlier Jay's plan had been formulated is not known.

25. Lee, II, 425, 426–27.

26. These matters were very widely noticed in the newspaper press.

27. Monroe, I, 144, 145.

28. Ibid., 144. It also appears from a letter he had written to Madison, on May 31. Ibid., 132.

29. Ibid., 144.

30. Journals, XXXI, 480.

31. Ibid., XXX, 323.

32. Ibid. See also Monroe, I, 131–35, 137–38, 146.

33. Monroe, I, 132, 138, 145.

34. Henry Lee had first appeared in Congress on February 1. Letters, VIII, xcviii.

35. Letters, VIII, 400, 417, 481–82.

36. Monroe, I, 153; cf. Letters, VIII, 407.

37. Journals, XXXI, 457.

38. Ibid., 467–84.

39. Ibid., 509–10, 537–52.

40. Ibid., 509, 511, 524–25, 527, 528–29, 531–35, 554. Monroe stated in a letter dated August 10 that Congress "went into a Committee of the whole [on the Spanish treaty] yesterday." Monroe, I, 143. But the letter was apparently misdated. Cf. ibid., 147.

41. Monroe, I, 145–46, 148, 155–56, 158.

42. Ibid., 147, 155; Letters, VIII, 429.

43. Letters, VIII, 427–28, 436–37, 438–39; Journals, XXXI, 935, 941–42, 946.

44. Letters, VIII, 429–30 (King); 439–40 (St. Clair); 447–49 (Johnson).

45. Ibid., 427–29.

46. Delaware was the only one of the eight Northern states not present in Congress when King spoke. According to the speech of the time, "the states *East* of Delaware" included all the other seven "Eastern"—i.e. Northern—states, not excepting Pennsylvania which was *west* of Delaware. Cf. "the *eight Eastern States*," in King's letter to John Adams, of November 2, 1785, referred to above, chap. XIII, n. 34; Nathan Dane's "*north* of the Delaware [river]," in his letter of January 8, 1786, mentioned above, chap. XVIII, n. 3; and "the States as far *westward* as Virginia inclusive," in the proceedings of the Hartford convention of October 1779, referred to above, chap. IX, n. 7.

47. Letters, VIII, 429–30.

48. Ibid., 439–40.

49. Ibid., 447–49.

50. Ibid., 481–82.

51. Lee, II, 426–27.

52. Washington, XXIX, 249–50.

53. There were apparently other Southern men, besides those mentioned in the text, who were in favor of Jay's proposed Spanish treaty. Evidence to this effect may be seen, for example, in a letter of Edward Rutledge, of South Carolina, who had been so excited, in 1776, over the early drafts of the Articles of Confederation. See chap. VI hereof. In a letter written to John Jay, dated November 12, 1786, Rutledge reported that "the majority [in Charleston], with whom [he] ha[d] conversed, believe[d the country w]ould be benifitted by a limited cession of [the Mississippi] to Spain, or rather a cession for a limited time." He added that all were also agreed that the cession should not be permanent. Jay, III, 216, 217, 218. It is evident from the fact of Rutledge's support for Jay's treaty that he had lost some of his earlier fear of "Eastern" dominance in Congress; that he had also gotten over his youthful dislike of a strong national government is indicated by his support of the Constitution in the South Carolina ratifying convention of 1788. Elliot, IV, 388. The reasons for Rutledge's change in sentiment are not known.

54. Cf. *Fletcher* v. *Peck*, 6 Cranch, 87 (1810); Beveridge, *The Life of John Marshall*, III, chap. X.

55. Monroe, I, 139, 169, 172; Madison, II, 265–66.

56. Monroe, I, 135.

57. Ibid., 144, 150–51.

58. Ibid., 160, 163.

59. There were other Southerners who agreed with Monroe's views as to the true purpose underlying the Spanish treaty, as is shown by a letter which Timothy Bloodworth, of North Carolina, wrote to Governor Caswell, of his state, on September 29. In it, he said in part: "it is well known that the ballance of Power is now in the

Eastern States, and they appear determined to keep it in that Direction. This to me is evident from all their Conduct, and in the present measure"—i.e., Jay's proposed treaty—"if carried they will be favoured in their scheme" (Letters, VIII, 474). See also a letter by Bloodworth, to the North Carolina legislature, upon the subject, of December 16, 1786. Ibid., 520. Monroe expressed similar sentiments as regards the Northern purposes underlying the proposed Spanish treaty, in letters to Madison and Jefferson. Monroe, I, 151–52, 153–58.

60. See chap. XVII hereof, text at nn. 28 and 30.

61. Jefferson believed, in 1784, that Monroe would vote for the exclusion of slavery from the Northwest Territory. Jefferson, IV, 330; cf. Journals, XXVI, 247. There is apparently no evidence as to what his sentiments upon this point were in 1786. It is simply assumed that they were the same.

62. Journals, XXX, 390.

63. See chap. XVII hereof, text preceding n. 10.

64. Monroe, I, 140–41; cf. Journals, XXXI, 669, 672, 738.

65. Reprinted in Bancroft, II, 389, 392–93. The punctuation in the text departs from the punctuation in Bancroft, but it is perfectly evident that the punctuation in Bancroft is wrong.

66. Letters, VIII, 380.

67. In a letter written to Gerry, in the "evening" of June 4, King said in part: "I have nothing to add but an apology for a long and incorrect letter written to you this morning upon an interesting subject." Ibid., 383. What occasioned this retraction is not known.

NOTES TO CHAPTER XX

1. Letters, VIII, 438; cf. Henry Lee (ibid., 439) and Charles Pinckney (Journals, XXXI, 945–46).

2. Journals, XXXI, 554, 565–68.

3. Monroe, I, 158.

4. Ibid., 147–48, 155–56. Cf. Timothy Bloodworth's account. Letters, VIII, 520.

5. Monroe, I, 156.

6. Letters, VIII, 440–42.

7. Monroe, I, 156; cf. Bancroft, II, 384–86. The Bancroft reference is to Otto's letter of August 23 to Vergennes, mentioned in the next paragraph in the text. It tends to indicate that the Southerners really wanted to get the matter into Jefferson's hands alone, and to have him act under the direction of America's "great ally." Whatever might have been true of Jefferson, this arrangement would certainly never have worked with John Adams, as the history of the peace negotiation at the end of the Revolutionary War clearly shows.

8. Bancroft, II, 384–86.

9. Letters, VIII, 446.

10. Journals, XXXI, 574, 594.

11. Monroe, I, 158–59.

12. Ibid., 144, 149, 150–51, 152, 157, 162. Monroe also maintained that Jay had no authority from Congress with respect to a commercial treaty. Ibid., 141, 168. But the understanding in Congress *when Jay was appointed* seems to have been that Jay *did* have power extending to such a treaty. Lee, II, 377.

13. See chap. XVIII hereof, text at nn. 1 and 3.

14. Cf. Jay's report on the negotiations he had carried on, later in the fall, after the repeal of the "ultimatum" in his instructions by Congress had taken place. Journals, XXXII, 185, 187.

15. Letters, VIII, 415–16, 458–60.

16. Monroe, I, 159.

17. Journals, XXXI, 568–69.

18. Ibid., 569–70.

19. Ibid., 574–94.

20. Ibid., 595–96.

21. Ibid., 597.

22. Ibid., 597–600.

23. Ibid., 601.

24. Ibid., 601–2.

25. Ibid., 602–4.

26. Ibid., 604–7.

27. Ibid., 607.

28. Monroe, I, 159.

29. Ibid., 159–60.

30. Journals, XXXI, 595–96.

31. Above, n. 14.

32. Journals, XXI, 610–13.

33. Ibid., 609–10.

34. Ibid., 620–21.

35. In writing to Madison about the matter, on September 1, Monroe said that, when this action was taken, "the State of R[hode] Island [was] ab[ou]t to leave the floor which their delegation accordingly did immediately." For the other departures, see the attendance as officially recorded for the days following September 1. Journals, XXXI, 622 ff. See also Letters, VIII, 462.

36. Monroe, I, 160–65.

37. Ibid., 144.

38. Ibid., 140–42.

39. Ibid., 144, 148–51.

40. Ibid., 153, 156–57.

41. Ibid., 151–52, 160–65.

42. Madison was in New York between some date "shortly" after July 15, and some date "a few days" before August 12. See Monroe, I, 139, 140–42, 143; Madison, *II*, 257.

43. See pp. 269–70 hereof.

44. Letters, VIII, 458.

45. Ibid., 380–82.

46. Ibid., 458–60.

47. King said, in part, in reference to the subject of governmental reform: "You very well understand the Character of our countrymen, they will bear and suffer for a time; but there is a point below which they will not sink; the Difficulties we now suffer will cure themselves, the spirit of reform will become, nay it daily is becoming more and more general thro' all the States. The remedy must be waited for with *some degree* [King's emphasis] of Patience—This language will not bear to be communicated—you know whether it is founded in the nature of our Governments, or not—at any rate I observe it *in confidence* [King's emphasis]—Some men think that political Difficulties may as easily be rectified as those of a domestic or private nature; but they understand very little of the Genius of the several states composing the confederacy—the nature of our Governments renders every reform, or alteration, not only difficult, because our local, or state, interests, are sometimes in opposition, but subjects it to odious Delays." Rufus King to Caleb Davis, November 3, 1785, in Caleb Davis Papers, Massachusetts Historical Society, reprinted in Appendix E hereof.

48. See chap. XXV hereof.

49. Jay, III, 194–95.

50. To William Livingston, Jay had written, July 19, 1783: "A continental, national spirit should pervade our country, and Congress should be enabled, by a grant of the necessary powers, to regulate the commerce and general concerns of the confederacy; and we should remember that to be constantly prepared for war is the only way to have peace." Jay, III, 54–55. To Gouverneur Morris, he had written, on September 24, 1783: "I am perfectly convinced that no time is to be lost in raising and maintaining a national spirit in America. *Power to govern the confederacy, as to all general purposes, should be granted and exercised*." (Jay's emphasis.) Jay, III, 82, 85. To James Lowell, he had written, May 10, 1785: "It is my first wish to see the United States assume and merit the character of one great nation, whose territory is divided into counties [printed incorrectly by Johnston as "countries"] and townships for the like purposes." Jay, III, 142, 143. To John Adams, he had written, on February 22, 1786: "The public papers will enable you to see the complexion of the times. Federal opinions grow, but it will be some time before they bear fruit, and, what is not the case with most other fruits, they will, to judge from present appearances, ripen slower in the *South* than in the *North*" (Jay's emphasis). Jay, III, 183. To Washington, he had written, on March 16, 1786: "The [Annapolis commercial] convention proposed by Virginia may do some good, and would perhaps do more if it comprehended more objects. An opinion begins to prevail that a general convention for revising the Articles of Confederation would be expedient." Jay, III, 186–87.

NOTES TO CHAPTER XXI

1. Monroe, I, 160.

2. Madison, II, 270.

3. Madison's endorsement upon Monroe's letter was: "Design of the Eastern States in certain contingencies, to dismember the union, by the line of the Potomac." Letters, VIII, 461, n. 6.

4. Monroe, I, 160–63.

5. Ibid., 144, 148–51.

6. Ibid., 163–65.

7. Letters, VIII, 419, n. 5 to no. 459. The date of Madison's letter to Monroe was August 11 or 12.

8. DHC, IV, 23. This letter of Madison's was written on August 15.

9. Letters, VIII, 464, 476, 512.

10. Ibid., 512; Rives, *James Madison* II, 131.

11. See pp. 322–23 hereof.

12. See chap. IX hereof, text at n. 13.

13. See chap. VI hereof, text at n. 21.

14. Letters, VIII, 458–60.

15. Madison, II, 257, 262–63.

16. See chap. XV hereof, text at nn. 73 and 74.

17. Tucker was currently supposed to have been the author of an essay entitled "Reflections on the policy and necessity of encouraging the commerce of the citizens of the united states of America, and of granting them exclusive privileges in trade," which appeared in the Virginia papers soon after the British order in council in reference to the West India trade was published in 1783. The essay was reprinted in Am. Mus. of September 1787 (II, 265). In a foreward to the reprint, it was explained that "the assembly of Virginia having passed an act, at their next session [in 1783], authorising congress to prohibit the importation of British West India produce, except in American bottoms, it was [then] thought unnecessary to communicate them

[further] to the public, as it was hoped the example set by the assembly of Virginia, would have been followed in the other states." This would seem to indicate that Tucker's ideas of a desirable national commerce power were not extensive, though his essay does seem to go beyond the Virginia act. Cf. the discussion (Pol. & Con., I, 229–30) of his attempts to belittle the internal commercial power of Congress under the Constitution, in his *View of the Constitution of the United States*, which was attached to his edition of Blackstone's Commentaries, in 1803.

18. Madison, II, 271.

19. Elliot, I, 116.

20. Dickinson was the draftsman of the first version of the Articles of Confederation in 1776. Read, though not a member of the Dickinson committee, was present in Congress when the draft of the committee of the whole was gotten out, apparently with general approval, on August 20, 1776. In the Federal Convention, Read was extremely nationalist in his views, at all times, as was the entire Delaware delegation, after the equal vote in the Senate was secured.

21. Elliot, I, 117.

22. Ibid., 116.

23. Ibid.

24. See chap. XIII hereof, text at n. 30.

25. Elliot, I, 116.

26. Ibid.

27. Madison, II, 271.

28. State Records of North Carolina, XVIII, 772.

29. DHC, IV, 26–27; Letters, VIII, 469, nn. 4 and 5 to no. 503, and references there cited.

30. Elliot, I, 116.

31. J. C. Hamilton, *History of the Republic of the United States*, 3d ed. (Philadelphia, 1868), III, 163, referring to "memoir [of Alexander Hamilton] published by Judge Benson."

32. Ibid.

33. See pp. 276–77 hereof. In his letter to Robert Morris, of April 30, 1781, previously mentioned in chap. IX hereof, n. 36, Hamilton again urged a true constituent convention. He said: "I wish to see a convention of all the States, with *full* power to alter and amend, *finally and irrevocably*, the present futile and senseless Confederation." Hamilton, III, 342, 379.

34. Elliot, I, 117–18.

35. Letters, VIII, 458–60.

36. Article III of the Confederation.

37. See chap. XXV hereof.

NOTES TO CHAPTER XXII

1. The advertisements of the time would seem to indicate that Connecticut's chief export was beef, and that it went, in the main, to the Southern states. During the debate in Congress over Jay's proposed Spanish treaty, Charles Pinckney spoke of Connecticut as having an "inconsiderable European commerce." Journals, XXXI, 941.

2. Acts and Resolves of Rhode Island, May 1786, 13–17, 21; Pa. Pack., May 25, and June 5 and 7, 1786.

3. Acts and Resolves of Rhode Island, June 1786, 8–9, 10, 11, 16–19; Pa. Pack., July 19, 1786.

4. Pa. Pack., July 20 and 26, and August 1 and 3, 1786; Newp. Merc., August 7, 1786.

5. Pa. Pack., September 16, 1786.

6. Acts and Resolves of Rhode Island, August 1786, 5–7; Pa. Pack., September 12, 1786.

7. Varnum, *The Case, Trevett against Weeden* (Providence, 1787); Newp. Merc., October 2, 1786; Pa. Pack., October 10 and 24, 1786; Acts and Resolves of Rhode Island, December 1786, 23.

8. Pa. Pack., October 11, 1786; cf. ibid., September 7, 1786.

9. Acts and Resolves of Rhode Island, December 1786, 6, 7, 22, 23.

10. Ibid., 21–22; ibid., March 1787, 11–12.

11. Pa. Pack., October 26 and November 3, 1786.

12. In addition to the foregoing references, see Arnold, *The History of Rhode Island*, 2 vols. (New York, 1859).

13. Minot, *The History of the Insurrections in Massachusetts*, 2d ed. (Boston, 1810), 105. This work was written in 1788.

14. The facts as to Shays' Rebellion stated in the text will be found set forth in ibid. They may also be found in full detail in most of the newspapers of the time, e.g., Pa. Pack.

15. Minot, *History of the Insurrections in Massachusetts*, 46; Pa. Pack., October 3, 1786.

16. Higginson, 743.

17. See chap. XII hereof.

18. King, I, 316–17; DHC, IV, 449–50, 459–60.

19. The analysis of the causes of Shays' Rebellion which is presented in the text is substantially that to be found in Minot, *History of the Insurrections in Massachusetts*. A more succinct contemporary analysis may be found in Mass. Cent. of February 21, 1787. It winds up with an appeal for a national government "fully competent to the general purposes of the Union."

20. See chap. XII hereof, text at n. 6.

21. See chap. XII hereof, text at n. 5.

22. Higginson, 751.

23. Henry Knox to Stephen Higginson, February 25, 1787, in Henry Knox Papers, Massachusetts Historical Society. For the full text, see Appendix I hereof.

24. See chaps. XIV and XV hereof.

25. On this point see Henry Lee's letters from Congress to Washington, in Letters, VIII, 463, 474, 481–83. He wrote in the same vein to Madison; and, as indicated in chap. XXIII hereof, there was apparently an official report to the Virginia legislature, of similar tenor, which is now lost.

26. Monroe, I, 144–51; see chap. XX above, text at nn. 36 to 42.

27. William Grayson was not in agreement upon this point with the other Virginians in Congress. See pp. 344–45 hereof.

28. See chap. XVIII hereof, text at nn. 43 ff.

NOTES TO CHAPTER XXIII

1. Journal of the Virginia House of Delegates, 1786 (Richmond, 1828), 3–4.

2. Madison apparently left Philadelphia for Virginia not earlier than October 15. See n. 13, below. He could not, therefore, have arrived at Richmond on time.

3. That Madison, and probably the Virginia legislature, had received such a report by October 30 is shown by a letter which Madison wrote to his father on that date. Madison, II, 277–78, cf. ibid., 283.

4. Portions of these letters, with the parts about Shays' Rebellion generally omitted, will be found in Letters, VIII, 463, 474, 481, 486, 490, 493, 505. References are also there given as to the location of the originals.

5. Madison Papers, Library of Congress. A portion of the letter, but not that relating to Shays' Rebellion, is printed in Letters, VIII, 489. Cf. Lee's letters to Washington, of September 8, ca. October 1, and October 11, which are similar in content. Letters, VIII, 463, 474, 481–83. See also Knox to Washington, October 23, 1786, and Washington to Madison, November 5, 1786. DHC, VI, 29–32, 33–35.

6. Above, n. 3.

7. Letters, VIII, 489, n. 2 to no. 526.

8. Ibid., 555.

9. Ibid.

10. Madison, II, 289, 294.

11. Letters, VIII, 524.

12. Journals, XXXI, 928–30.

13. Monroe's last recorded presence in Congress was on October 5. Journals, XXXI, 746. He was probably in Congress thereafter, however, since he was still in New York on October 12, intending, as he said in a letter written from thence to Jefferson on that date, to "sit out for Virginia with Mrs. Monroe by land." Monroe, I, 169. The Monroes picked up Madison as a traveling companion at Philadelphia, starting from thence, presumably, on October 15. Cf. Letters, VIII, 476 and 511.

14. The only reference to the report is in Henry Lee's letter to Madison, of the same date. Letters, VIII, 489.

15. Letters, VIII, 463, 474, 481, 486, and 505.

16. Letters, VIII, 505–6.

17. Monroe, I, 165–66; Letters, VIII, 465, 410, 511; Journals, XXXI, 928–30. This absence may seem to preclude the possibility that Grayson "saw but did not sign" the missing report of October 19. But the probability is that that year-end report was sent to Grayson, at Philadelphia, to be signed by him if he agreed, and, in any event, to be sent on by him to Virginia. Carrington went to see Grayson, at Philadelphia, on October 21. Letters, VIII, 493; cf. Journals, XXXI, 891, 893, and 906. He did not, however, take the report with him to Grayson, since Lee's letter to Madison (of the same date as the report) shows that at the time when Lee wrote, the report had already been dispatched. Letters, VIII, 489.

18. Letters, VIII, 510.

19. Ibid., 511.

20. Letters, VIII, 516, n. 4 to no. 558.

21. Calendar of Virginia State Papers (Richmond, 1884), IV, 195. A portion of Carrington's letter may be found in Letters, VIII, 516.

22. Carrington was an extraordinarily astute and able man, in addition to being a staunch nationalist. It is difficult to believe that he was unaware that Shays' Rebellion was being used "for all it was worth" to obtain action from Virginia favorable to an improvement of the national government. There is, moreover, something too much of art in his letter to Randolph. Carrington afterwards wrote Jefferson that he, Carrington, was "rather a zealot" for the Federal Convention. DHC, IV, 122.

23. The time of posts between New York and Richmond in 1786 is not certainly known to the present writers. The commissions to the Virginia delegates in Congress, for the congressional year beginning with November 1786, were voted by the legislature on November 7 and were in the hands of the delegates in New York on November 20; and since that was a Monday, the commissions may have been in their hands late on the previous Saturday. Journal of the Virginia House of Delegates 1786 (Richmond, 1828), 26; Journals, XXXI, 928–30. Assuming the commissions were dispatched from Richmond on the day they were voted, that would indicate eleven to thirteen days between Richmond and New York. Washington consumed five days traveling from Mount Vernon to Philadelphia for the Federal Convention. Washington, XXIX, 213, n. 40; cf. DHC, IV, 165. Monroe speaks of two days from New

York to Philadelphia. Letters, VIII, 476. That would indicate not over ten days from New York to Richmond, for ordinary travelers. Posts, presumably, made better time. It may be noted, however, that Washington was worried in January 1787 lest a letter written from Mount Vernon on December 26 was in a mail robbery at Newark on January 4. Washington, XXIX, 147. That would seem to indicate about nine days from Mount Vernon to New York, or eleven or twelve days from Richmond.

24. Journal of the Virginia House of Delegates, 1786 (Richmond, 1828), 11.

25. Ibid., 21.

26. Ibid., 28.

27. Journal of the Virginia Senate (Richmond, 1828), 10–11, 13, 17.

28. Journal of the Virginia House of Delegates, 85, 86; Journal of the Virginia Senate, 38.

29. Madison, II, 283–84.

30. Washington, XXIX, 115.

31. Ibid., 113–15.

32. Ibid, 114. Washington's letters permit no possible doubt that he was not well. Cf. ibid., 187, 195, 208–9.

33. Ibid., 70–72.

34. Madison, II, 295.

35. Washington, XXIX, 72, 73; 75, 76.

36. DHC, IV, 47.

37. The notice to Washington of his appointment, and the notices to the other states of his appointment, were both dated December 6, 1786. The notice to Washington is reprinted in DHC, IV, 41. The notice sent to Governor Livingston, of New Jersey, is among the Livingston Papers in the Massachusetts Historical Society. For the text, see Appendix H hereof.

38. Madison, II, 295–96.

39. Washington, XXIX, 113 and 119.

40. Madison, II, 300–301; DHC, IV, 47, 54, 59, 63, 94, 96–97, 106, 111.

41. Washington, XXIX, 125, 127–29; 151–53; 170–72; 172–73.

42. DHC, IV, 59, 63–67, 96–97, 97–99, 109–10, 111–12.

43. The act is printed in full in Elliot I, 132, and Records, III, 559.

44. Article III of the Confederation.

45. See Pol. & Con., I, 55–69.

46. Edmund Randolph to William Livingston, Governor of New Jersey, December 1, 1786, reprinted in Appendix H of this book.

47. Randolph to Livingston, December 6, 1786, reprinted in Appendix H.

48. DHC, IV, 41.

49. Above, n. 38.

50. See chap. XV hereof, text preceding n. 73.

51. Madison, II, 283.

52. Ibid., 289, 290. In this letter, which exists only (?) as a draft copy in the Madison Papers, Madison speaks of "the recommendation from the meeting at Annapolis of a plenipotentiary convention." The recommendation was not for a "plenipotentiary convention," as Madison's friend, Henry Lee, used the phrase, or as it was used by Alexander Hamilton. Cf. pp. 276–77 hereof, and the discussion in Chaps. XXV–XXVI. Madison's usage of "plenipotentiary" in this letter to Jefferson casts doubt on what he meant by the term in his letter to Jefferson, of August 12, 1786, and in his earlier letter to Monroe, of March 19, 1786. Madison, II, 231, 233, 257, 262. The Monroe letter to Madison, which would probably settle what was meant in Madison's letter to Monroe, is absent from the Madison papers. The discussion in chapters 0 and 00 shows that in the letter to Jefferson of August 12, 1786, a *general*

convention with *plenipotentiary* powers for the accomplishment of *general* objects undoubtedly was meant. The letter in question is among the Jefferson papers.

53. A comparison of the lists of those voting on the occasions when yeas and nays were called for shows this. See the Virginia House Journal for the years in question.

54. Madison had mentioned the Speaker, Benjamin Harrison, Charles M. Thruston, Francis Corbin, Carter Braxton, and Meriwether Smith. Madison, II, 218. All of these gentlemen, except Braxton, were in the House of Delegates in 1786.

55. Madison, II, 238, 245, 261, 275.

56. Madison, II, 277 and n.; Journal of the Virginia House of Delegates 1786 (Richmond, 1828), 15.

57. See chaps. XIV and XV hereof.

58. Letters, VIII, 460.

59. Madison, II, 233, 262; cf. Letters, VIII, 373–74. Madison, the reader should be reminded, had opposed Hamilton's plan for a general convention with *plenipotentiary* powers in 1783. Higginson, 745; cf. Madison, I, 439. The convention which Madison somewhat faintly approved, in a letter to Richard Henry Lee, in December 1784, was one for *limited* objects, though it was, apparently, to have *plenipotentiary* powers for their attainment. See pp. 368–74 hereof; and cf. Lee, II, 307, and Madison, II, 99–100.

NOTES TO CHAPTER XXIV

1. Journals, XXXI, 677–80.
2. Letters, VIII, 475.
3. Ibid., 476.
4. Journals, XXXI, 770 n.
5. Ibid., 907–9.
6. Ibid., 928–931; XXXII, 1–11.
7. Letters, VIII, 489–90.
8. Ibid., 468–69.
9. Ibid., 458–60.
10. "Foreign nations," he said, "had been notified of this convention, the Friends to a good federal government through these states looked to it with anxiety and Hope; the History of it, will not be more agreeable to the former than it must be seriously painful to the latter." Letters, VIII, 469.
11. The conventional view seems still to be that to be found in Bancroft, that King had "scales on his eyes" and was "narrow-minded." Bancroft, I, 272. Bowdoin's reply, written on October 24, 1785, to the Massachusetts delegates' letter of September 3, is frequently quoted, that, "if in the union discordant principles ma[d]e it hazardous to intrust congress with powers necessary to its well-being, the union [could] not long subsist." Ibid., 199. This is supposed to show a violent difference of opinion between Bowdoin and the delegates in Congress. The Bowdoin letter of October 24 was written, however, before Holten's return to Massachusetts. The King letter quoted in the text can leave little doubt that Bowdoin was sympathetic, once the basis of the views of King and Holten and Gerry was understood. Cf. chap. XVII hereof.
12. King, I, 144; Letters, VIII, 475.
13. Edward Carrington, Virginia delegate in Congress, wrote James Madison, on December 18, 1786: "The dereliction of Massachusetts [with respect to the Federal Convention] is to be apprehended. the delegation of that State prevented the recommendation of the measure from Congress, as suggested by the deputations at Annapolis, and advised its nonadoption in their Legislature." Letters, VIII, 523.

Whether Carrington fully believed what he wrote, may possibly be open to question. He was an astute man. But if he did not believe implicitly all that he said, at least he must have believed that what he was writing would have a salutary effect on Madison and others in Virginia. As previously indicated, Carrington was a staunch nationalist.

14. Letters, VIII, 488; Pa. Pack., October 24, 1786, p. 3, col. 1.
15. Mass. Gaz., October 13, 1786; Pa. Pack., October 21, 1786; Letters, VIII, 478.
16. Letters, VIII, 354, 355.
17. Rufus King to Caleb Davis, November 3, 1785, reprinted in Appendix E hereof; King, I, 97; Letters, VIII, 121, 458–60.
18. Letters, VIII, 475.
19. See chap. XXVII hereof.
20. Mass. Gaz., November 17, 1786; N.Y. Jour., November 30 and December 6, 1786; Letters, VIII, 500.
21. Letters, VIII, 283.
22. Ibid.
23. Ibid., 303–6.
24. King, I, 227–28; Records, III, 54.
25. Records, IV, 63–64.
26. Letters, VII, 603–4.
27. King, I, 265.
28. Nathan Dane to Henry Knox, December 27, 1787, in Henry Knox Papers, Massachusetts Historical Society.
29. See chap. XVII hereof.
30. King, I, 200; Letters, VIII, 526.
31. Higginson, 747.
32. J. C. Hamilton, *History of the Republic of the United States*, 3d ed. (Philadelphia, 1868), III, 239.
33. Records, I, 20.
34. Ibid., 35–36.
35. DHC, IV, 116.
36. Journals, VII, 328; cf. chap. VII hereof, text at nn. 38 to 40.
37. Records, I, 87; III, 554.

NOTES TO CHAPTER XXV

1. Rufus King to Caleb Davis, November 3, 1785, reprinted in Appendix E hereof.
2. Letters, VIII, 526, 527.
3. Henry Knox to Gouverneur Morris, January 16, 1787, in Henry Knox Papers, Massachusetts Historical Society.
4. DHC, IV, 58–59.
5. Letters, VIII, 489.
6. Cf. Madison, II, 262; and see chap. XXIII, n. 52.
7. Henry Knox to Stephen Higginson, February 25, 1787, in Henry Knox Papers, Massachusetts Historical Society. For the full text of this letter, see Appendix I hereof.
8. Gorham's answer, dated February 18, 1787, is in Henry Knox Papers, Massachusetts Historical Society.
9. Henry Knox to James Sullivan, January 28, 1787, Knox Papers.
10. Henry Knox to Benjamin Lincoln, February 14, 1787, Knox Papers; reprinted in Knox, 95.
11. Higginson, 742–43.
12. Ibid., 743–45.

13. See chap. XXIII hereof, text preceding n. 46.

14. A draft copy of Knox's letter to Higginson, of January 28, 1787, is in Henry Knox Papers, Massachusetts Historical Society; the letter is reprinted in Knox, 93–95.

15. DHC, IV, 58, 59.

16. Higginson, 745–49. Higginson wrote further to Knox upon the subject, on February 13. Ibid., 750–52.

17. Letters, VIII, 526, 527.

18. Jay, III, 226; DHC, IV, 54–57. The remainder of Jay's letter to Washington is discussed in chap. XXVIII hereof.

19. DHC, IV, 63–69, 84–88, 97–99.

20. Washington, XXIX, 175–77; Jay, III, 238–39; DHC, IV, 91–93.

21. Letters, VIII, 538; State Records of North Carolina, XX, 602 and 613.

22. State Records of North Carolina, XX, 602.

23. Journals, XXXII, 42 n.

24. King, I, 201; Letters, VIII, 539.

25. The three most populous states were Virginia, Massachusetts, and Pennsylvania. Both Pennsylvania and Massachusetts were generally supposed to outnumber Virginia in number of freemen. If slaves were counted, Virginia was agreed to be the largest of the states.

26. See Records, I, 573, where it is estimated that there were, in all, 120,000 white persons in South Carolina and Georgia. General Pinckney, of the former state, used figures in January 1788, before the South Carolina legislature, that give a total for the two states of 170,000 whites.

27. King, I, 201; Letters, VIII, 539.

28. King, I, 215; Letters, VIII, 541.

29. Rufus King to Caleb Davis, November 3, 1785, printed in Appendix E hereof.

30. N. 28 above.

31. Records, III, 574–75.

32. Elliot, I, 118.

33. Article XIII of the Confederation.

34. Records, III, 565 and 574.

35. Ibid., 563.

36. State Records of North Carolina, XXIV, 791. The stipulation also appears in the Blount and Williamson commissions, printed in Records, III, 570 and 571.

37. Journals, XXXII, 71 n. The vote in the committee seems to have been recorded only by Madison. *Madison Papers* (Washington, 1840), II, 587. As the discussion in the text will show, the subsequent proceedings in Congress tend to corroborate Madison on this point.

38. J. C. Hamilton, *History of the Republic of the United States*, 3d ed. (Philadelphia, 1868), III, 239, 247, 248 n.

39. An inspection of the recorded votes shows Hamilton and Malcom together most of the time. New York Assembly Journal 1787 (New York, 1787); see especially the votes on the impost, on February 15. Ibid., 51–52.

40. J. C. Hamilton, *History of the United States*, III, 161.

41. New York Senate Journal (New York, 1787), 35; cf. votes recorded at 45 and 95.

42. N.Y. Mng. P., February 21, 1787, p. 2, cols. 3 and 4.

43. These matters are summarized in Hoar, *Constitutional Conventions* (Boston, 1917), 2–7. See also the opening discussion in Dodd, *The Revision and Amendment of State Constitutions* (Baltimore, 1910), and in Jameson, *A Treatise on Constitutional Conventions* (Chicago, 1887).

44. Jay, III, 226; DHC, IV, 54-57.
45. Letter to Caleb Davis, on November 3, 1785, reprinted in Appendix E hereof.
46. Higginson, 745 and 748.
47. Hamilton, I, 223–24; III, 378–79.
48. DHC, IV, 59.
49. Madison, II, 262; cf. Letters, VIII, 489–90.
50. Journals, XXXI, 680.
51. Monroe, I, 163.
52. New York Assembly Journal 1787, 55, 59–60; N.Y. Mng. P., February 21, 1787, p. 2, cols. 3 and 4.
53. Ibid.
54. Journals, XXXII, 71 n.
55. Ibid., 71–73.
56. Ibid., 73–74.
57. Records, I, 34, 39, 41, 42, 177–78, 182, 184, 188, 249, 250, 255, 257, 258, 264, 336, 345. Cf. the retort of Charles Pinckney, of South Carolina, to such arguments from the New Jersey delegates: "The whole comes to this: Give New Jersey an equal vote and she will dismiss her scruples, and concur in the Nati[ona]l system." Ibid., I, 255; cf. 261.
58. Records, I, 43 (McHenry's notes).
59. Ibid., 266 (King's notes).
60. Ibid., 294–95.
61. Journals, XXXII, 42 n.
62. Ibid., 72–73.
63. Letters, VIII, 551.
64. Journals, XXXII, 73 and n.
65. In his letters to Benjamin Lincoln and Stephen Higginson early in 1787, Knox mentioned King as one of his choices to represent Massachusetts in the Federal Convention. Above, nn. 7 and 10. In addition to this evidence of agreement in their views, King wrote from Philadelphia to Knox, on July 11, 1787: "I wish it was in my power to inform you that we had progressed a single step since you left us—I say progressed; this expression must be defined by my own political creed, which you are very well acquainted with." Henry Knox Papers, Massachusetts Historical Society. Knox wrote back, on July 15, as indicated on p. 421 hereof. Knox, 95, 96. This reply indicates with sufficient certainty what King's "political creed" was.
66. Cf. n. 7, above.
67. Seven were necessary to action by the terms of Article IX of the Confederation. Actually, all but Connecticut seem to have agreed to the resolution that was passed. *Madison Papers* (Washington, 1840), II, 589. The opposition of Connecticut to the resolution finally adopted is confirmed by letters afterwards written by the two Connecticut delegates, Stephen Mix Mitchell and William Samuel Johnson. Letters, VIII, 567–68, 574–75, 646–47. In the Gratz collection (case 14, box 31), in the Historical Society of Pennsylvania, is a letter from Mitchell (who voted against the New York motion) to Charles Thomson, dated June 6, 1787, which indicates a fear on his part that the Federal Convention might attempt a coup d'état. He said: "Time alone will discover whether a Convention or Congress is to govern in this Country, we [in Wethersfield, Connecticut,] are impatient to know which."

NOTES TO CHAPTER XXVI

1. Records, III, 475, 497; IV, 87.
2. Madison wrote, in 1827, in a letter in which he explained that he intended a

publication of his notes, "posthumous as to others as well as to [him]self," that "it [could] not be very long before the living obstacles to the forthcomings in question, [would] be removed." "Of the members of Congress," he said, "during the period embraced, the lamps of all are extinct, with exception I believe of 2. Rd. Peters, & myself; and of the signers of the Constitution, of all but 3. R. King, Wm. Few and myself; and of the lamps still burning, none can now be far from the Socket." Records, III, 475. Richard Peters was not in Congress on February 21, 1787. It may be noted, however, that he died in 1828. Rufus King died in 1827; William Few in 1828.

3. DHC, IV, 78–81.

4. An inspection of the recorded votes shows Hamilton and Malcom together most of the time. New York Assembly Journal 1787 (New York, 1787); see especially the votes on the impost on February 15. Ibid., 51–52. J. C. Hamilton, *History of the United States*, III, 161.

5. New York Senate Journal (New York, 1787), 35; cf. votes recorded at 45 and 95.

6. See *The Dictionary of American Biography*, on Benson.

7. See ibid., on Meredith, Cadwalader, and Few. Few was a member of the Federal Convention and a signer of the Constitution, but little appears in the records of that body's proceedings to disclose his views. Johnson, of Connecticut, also a member of the Federal Convention and, later, of the Connecticut ratifying convention, had a prominent part in the making of the Constitution. He was a strong nationalist.

8. See ibid., on Grayson.

9. Letters, VIII, 678–79.

10. Ibid., 33, 372–75, 510–11, 581, 600 and n. 3 to no. 661.

11. Ibid., 372–75.

12. Ibid., 581, 678.

13. Ibid., 678.

14. Ibid., 580, 581.

15. DHC, IV, 167.

16. Gerry first appeared in the convention at Philadelphia, on May 29. Records, I, 16 (Journal).

17. Cf. Records, I, 48, 123, 132.

18. DHC, IV, 170–171.

19. Letters, VIII, 458–60.

20. See discussion in chap. XV hereof.

21. The following are a few of the papers which copied it: Mass. Gaz., February 16, 1787; Vt. Gaz., March 19, 1787; Cumb. Gaz., March 2, 1787; N.Y. Ind. Jour., February 24, 1787; Ga. Gaz., May 12, 1787.

22. It has not been possible to check the accuracy of this statement against all the New York papers of the time. See preceding note.

23. Madison, II, 316–20.

24. *Madison Papers* (Washington, 1840), II, 619–20.

25. Madison, II, 326–27, 338–39, 346–47.

26. Ibid., 327, 338, 340, 345.

27. Ibid., 338 and 345–46; cf. 326.

28. Ibid. It is *possible* that Madison, at *this time*, contemplated a specific enumeration of the national *affirmative* powers of legislation.

29. Ibid., 339 and 347. See also Pol. & Con., I, 644–45.

30. There can be no doubt about this: he discussed the need for "a National Executive" separately. See Madison, II, 348.

31. Ibid., 347.

32. That Madison intended the nation to be supreme over the states, even as to their "internal," or "local," affairs, does not admit of doubt. In a letter to Edmund Randolph, dated April 8, he said, in reference to his proposed general national negative on the laws of the states, that "without such a defensive power, every positive [national] power that [could] be given on paper [would] be unavailing"; and, also, that the negative power would "give *internal* stability to the States." Madison, II, 338–39. In a letter to Washington, one week later, he asks: "Might not the national prerogative here suggested be found sufficiently disinterested for the decision of *local* questions of policy, whilst it would itself be sufficiently restrained from the pursuit of interests adverse to those of the whole Society." In suggesting the extension of "the national supremacy" to "the Judiciary departments" (Madison's plural), he argued that, "if those who [were] to expound & apply the laws, [were] connected by their own interests & their oaths with the particular States wholly, and not with the Union, *the participation of the Union in the making of the laws* [might] possibly be rendered unavailing." Madison, II, 346–47. This "participation," it should be remembered, extended, by Madison's own preceding statement, not only to the making of laws "in all cases which require[d] uniformity" but to "the decision of local question of policy." Of the three letters to Jefferson, Randolph, and Washington, which are cited in this and the preceding seven notes, only that to Washington, which is the one most clearly sweeping in its proposals, exists outside the Madison papers.

33. Madison, II, 339. In the letter here cited, supposed to have been written on April 8, Madison speaks of the council as one "including the great ministerial officers."

34. Records, I, 21.

35. Ibid., 70 (King's notes); 74 (Pierce's notes); and 97 (Madison's notes).

36. Ibid., 21.

37. Ibid., 97–110, 138–40, 141, 144–45; II, 73–80.

38. Ibid., 70 and 72 n. (King's notes); cf. 74 (Pierce's notes).

39. Ibid., II, 32–36.

40. Above, nn. 38 and 39.

41. Above, n. 39; cf. Records, III, 368–69, 395–96, 397–98.

42. Records, II, 294–95, 298.

43. Ibid., 586–87.

44. Madison, II, 327.

45. Records, II, 27–28.

46. Madison, II, 289–90.

47. Journals, XXXII, 73.

48. Madison, IX, 471, 473, 475.

49. Madison, IX.

50. Clarke & Hall, *Legislative and Documentary History of the Bank of the United States* (Washington, 1832), 85.

51. Madison, IX, 251, 255.

52. *The Gazette of the United States* and other papers.

53. See, for example, the speech of Fisher Ames reprinted in Clarke & Hall, *Bank of the United States*, 45 ff. Ames said, at the time, in a letter to George Richards Minot, that "many *of the minority* laughed at the objection [to the bank bill] deduced from the Constitution." *Works of Fisher Ames*, (Boston, 1854), I, 95.

54. Records, III, 368–69.

55. Ibid., 395–96.

56. Madison, IX, 451, 454, 455.

57. Ibid. See also Adams, *Life and Writings of Jared Sparks*, II, 31–36; Records, III, 480–81.

58. *A Letter to the Electors of President and Vice-President of the United States*, "By a Citizen of New York [E. C. E. Genet]. Accompanied with an extract of the secret debates of the Federal Convention, held in Philadelphia, in the year 1787, taken by Chief Justice Yates" (New York, 1808). The "extract" is reprinted in Records, III, 410–16.

59. See Taylor, *New Views of the Constitution of the United States* (Washington, 1823). For Madison's immediate reaction, see Madison, IX, 176. He was still answering Taylor eight years later in 1831. Madison, IX, 474–75. For a contemptuous attack on Madison, on the floor of Congress, in 1824, by John Randolph, of Virginia, see *Annals of Congress*, 18th Cong., 1st Sess., 1301. There were many others.

60. Madison, IX, 68–71; Records, III, 446–50.

61. The classical Haitian account is Thomas Madiou, *Histoire d'Haiti, 1492–1799*, 2d ed. (Port-au-Prince, Haiti, 1922), 102 ff., 195 ff., 201, 202. See also H. P. Davis, *Black Democracy*, rev. ed. (New York, 1936). Bryan Edwards, *An Historical Survey of the Island of Saint Domingo, an Account of the Revolt of Negroes in 1791, and a Detail of the Military Transactions of the British Army in that Island in 1793 and 1794* (London, 1796), is an eyewitness account by an Englishman who arrived at Cape François shortly after the initial revolt had gotten under way.

62. John Taylor, "of Caroline," sometime Senator from Virginia, wrote as follows, in 1820, in his *Construction Construed and Constitutions Vindicated* (Richmond), 301: "It is highly edifying, in computing probable consequences, to recollect similar cases. The society of Amis des Noirs in France, zealous for amending the condition of the free people of colour, and believing that a conscious philanthrophy was local information, invested them with unqualified citizenship, wrote the slaves into rebellion, finally liberated them, and these friends of the blacks turned out to be the real murderers of the whites. An intemperate zeal, united with an ignorance of local circumstances, had to bewail the massacre of about forty thousand white men, women or children, of about thirty thousand mulattoes, after they had united with the blacks in that atrocity, of about one hundred thousand of the blacks themselves, and of dividing the residue into tyrants, and slaves to tyrannical laws, always more oppressive than any other species of slavery. These friends of the blacks in France disavowed at first the design of emancipation; but yet their speeches and writings gradually awakened the discontents of the slaves, and excited efforts which terminated in a catastrophe proving them to have been the worst enemies of the whites. This awful history engraves in the moral code the consequences of a legislation exercised by those who are ignorant of local circumstances, and the wisdom of our distinction between internal and external powers. The people of St. Domingo pressed upon the general assembly of France, its ignorance of local circumstances, and consequent incapacity to judge of the case; but as St. Domingo had representatives in that assembly, it persisted in its fanatical philanthrophy, and lost the finest island in the world of its size. The eastern states have as little knowledge of the Mississippi states, as the general assembly of France had of St. Domingo, and therefore the writings of the friends of the blacks in the United States are almost exactly the same, with those which they uttered in France."

See also [Robert J. Turnbull], *The Crisis* (Charleston, 1827, 133: "It was the discussions in the National Convention at Paris, that first lighted up the fires of revolt in St. Domingo; and if we, in South-Carolina, are ever to witness any thing of the kind in our country, it will be solely owing to our DASTARDLY pusillanimity, and our BASE TREACHERY to our vital interests, by suffering Congress to support the Colonization Society [for the settling of freed American slaves in Africa], and thus to acknowledge the jurisdiction over the subject, by a body, who will make us at some future period, if we thus place ourselves in their power, CURSE the day that *ever we entered into union* with the Northern States."

63. See aso [Turnbull], *The Crisis*, 131.
64. Jefferson, XII, 158–59.
65. Ibid., 185, 187–88.
66. Ibid., 159; cf. 165 and 180.
67. See, for example, Madison's theories as to the meaning of "migration" and "importation," in the Constitution; and his theory that the power to regulate internal commerce—merely interstate, according to his interpretation—and the power to regulate foreign commerce, were conferred upon Congress *diverso intuitu*. Madison, IX, 1–12, 22; Records, III, 478.
68. [Turnbull], *The Crisis*, 15, 64, 128–30, 133, 138.
69. Ibid., 138.
70. Ibid., 130–34. At 137, Turnbull says: "In all cases where slavery is proposed to be brought into discussion, let us say distinctly to Congress, 'HANDS OFF—mind your *own* business—attend to your *post-office* and such *matters.*' If this fails, let us separate." See also, Taylor, *Construction Construed and Constitutions Vindicated* (Richmond, 1820); and idem, *Tyranny Unmasked* (Washington, 1822), esp. 188–89.
71. For an analysis of one example, see Crosskey, "The Ex-Post-Facto and the Contracts Clauses in the Federal Convention: A Note on the Editorial Ingenuity of James Madison," 35 *University of Chicago Law Review* 248–54 (1968).

NOTES TO CHAPTER XXVII

1. Massachusetts House Journal 1787, 396.
2. Acts and Resolves of Massachusetts 1786–87 (Official Reprint), 447–49. Apparently news of the completion of the block of five approving states at the center of the Confederation helped along the result, just as it apparently did with the Massachusetts men in Congress. Nathaniel Gorham, a member of the joint committee, of which Samuel Adams was the chairman, wrote Henry Knox, on February 18, as follows: "Your esteamed favour of the 12th I rec[eived]—sensible & bold Men shall be chosen for the convention if I can have any influence in the business—but we have not yet agreed in the Committee to report in favour of the measure—though I have not much doubt but we shall do it—Mr. [Samuel] Adams is full of doubts & difficulties & finding that he cannot obstruct the report generally wishes to limit the Commission in such manner as I think will exceedingly injure the business—I do not however dispair & am rather encouraged to hope the affair will be rightly managed." Henry Knox Papers, Massachusetts Historical Society. The next day Governor Bowdoin sent a message to the General Court informing them of the approving action by North Carolina. Ibid., 973–74. The action by Virginia was also mentioned, though that was already known in Massachusetts through the newspapers. The committee's report and action by the General Court followed three days later.
3. Ibid., 517.
4. New York Assembly Journal 1787 (New York, 1787), 68.
5. New York Senate Journal 1787 (New York, 1787), 44–45.
6. On March 6, 1787. New York Assembly Journal 1787 (New York, 1787), 82–84.
7. Winthrop Sargent Papers, Massachusetts Historical Society.
8. New York Assembly Journal 1787 (New York, 1787), 165–66.
9. New York Senate Journal 1787 (New York, 1787), 95.
10. Records, III, 53–54, 588.
11. Ibid., 588 and 590.
12. Ibid., 70.
13. Ibid., II, 268, 547; III, 588.
14. DHC, IV, 282–87.
15. Records, III, 573, 576, 581, 585, and 586.
16. Ibid., 572 n., 588.

17. Ibid., I, 1.

NOTES TO CHAPTER XXVIII

1. Jay, III, 55, 85, 143, 195.
2. Jay, III, 226; DHC, IV, 54–57.
3. Knox, 79.
4. Knox, 77.
5. Knox, 77–78.
6. Hamilton, I, 305–14; Madison, I, 438–39.
7. Higginson, 745; Madison, I, 439.
8. See authorities cited in the preceding note.
9. Henry Knox to Samuel Parsons, April 1, 1785, Henry Knox Papers, Massachusetts Historical Society.
10. E. Hume, ed., *General Washington's Correspondence Concerning the Society of the Cincinnati* (Baltimore, 1941), 2.
11. DHC, IV, 58, 61–62; Knox, 147. It is dated "14th Jan. 1787" in the last reference.
12. *The Diaries of George Washington, 1748–1799*, ed. Fitzpatrick (New York, 1925), III, 217.
13. Henry Knox to Stephen Higginson, February 25, 1787, Henry Knox Papers, Massachusetts Historical Society, reprinted in Appendix I hereof.
14. Above, n. 9.
15. Henry Knox Papers, Massachusetts Historical Society.
16. King, I, 228.
17. See letter of Rufus King to Knox, giving him news of what happened in the convention on May 25, in Records, IV, 63.
18. Ibid., I, 16, 18–23, 23–24, 24–28.
19. Warren-Adams, II, 294.
20. Above, n. 11.
21. Knox, 95, 96; King, I, 228.
22. Rufus King to Henry Knox, July 11, 1787, Henry Knox Papers, Massachusetts Historical Society.
23. Knox, 95; see also, Henry Knox to Stephen Higginson, February 25, 1787, Henry Knox Papers, Massachusetts Historical Society, reprinted in Appendix I hereof.
24. Higginson, 748; cf. ibid., 743.
25. Letters, VIII, 458–60.
26. Higginson, 743; Hamilton, I, 224–25; III, 378-79; King, I, 156–60.
27. *The* [Boston] *Independent Chronicle*, May 26, 1785.
28. DHC, IV, 26.
29. Henry Knox Papers, Massachusetts Historical Society.
30. Records, III, 22–24.
31. Ibid., 559, 560.
32. Ibid., 20.
33. Ibid., II, 479; IV, 56–57.
34. Elliot, III, 442.
35. Ibid.
36. Ibid. Cf. Records, II, 587–88.
37. Madison, II, 324–28.
38. Ibid., 336–40.
39. Ibid., 334–52.
40. Ibid., 326, 338, 346.
41. DHC, IV, 189–95; Letters, VIII, 678–80.

42. March 18, 1787, is the earliest date of such a proposal by Madison, so far as is known. Madison, II, 326. Stephen Higginson, however, had suggested state ratifying conventions to Henry Knox, in his letter of February 8, 1787. Higginson, 745, 749. And Knox himself had referred casually to state ratifying conventions in his letter to Washington on January 4, 1787. DHC, IV, 59.

43. Jefferson, V, 283.

44. DHC, IV, 48.

45. Jefferson, V, 283 and 338.

46. Ibid., 338.

47. Ibid., 283.

48. DHC, IV, 225–26.

49. Ibid., 241–42.

50. Ibid., 189, 192–94.

51. Jefferson, V, 318–19; DHC, IV, 242–43.

52. DHC, IV, 249–51; Jefferson, V, 331–32.

53. DHC, IV, 252–53.

54. Jefferson, V, 338, 340–41; DHC, IV, 277–78.

55. See chap. II hereof.

56. DHC, IV, 411, 412; Jefferson, V, 368, 371.

57. See authorities cited in the preceding note.

58. Elliot, II, 177. This was "the 1st amendment proposed by Massachusetts" referred to by Jefferson in his letter to Edward Carrington mentioned in the next note.

59. Jefferson to Carrington, May 27, 1788. Jefferson, V, 400, 401; DHC, IV, 631, 632.

60. See chap VII hereof, text at nn. 53 and 54.

61. Lee, II, 341, 344–45.

62. Ibid., 419. Cf. ibid., 382, 383–84.

63. Ibid., 423, 424.

64. Ibid., 427–28.

65. Ibid., 430, 431.

66. Ibid., 432, 433.

67. Ibid., 442 n., 450–55.

68. Ibid. Quite independently of Jefferson, Lee promptly interpreted the Constitution in the same sense. Cf. ibid., 445, 452, and 457, with Jefferson, V, 371.

69. Lee, II, 463–74, especially 471.

70. See, for example, Farrand, *The Framing of the Constitution* (New Haven, 1913), 110.

71. Records, IV, 63–64.

72. Letters, VIII, 603–4.

NOTES TO CHAPTER XXIX

1. The item was copied by the following papers, among many others: Pa. Pack., January 11, 1787; Am. Merc., January 15, 1787; N.Y. Jour., January 25, 1787; Col. Her., February 5, 1787; and Vt. Gaz., March 19, 1787.

2. B. Ind. Chr., February 15, 1787. See pp. 395–96 hereof.

3. The item was copied in the following papers, among others: Ph. Fr. Jour., April 11, 1787; Sal. Merc., April 21, 1787; Ch. Mng. P., May 19, 1787.

4. *The Albany* [N.Y.] *Gazette*, May 24, 1787; N.H. Gaz., May 19, 1787; and many other papers.

5. Pa. Pack. A copy of this pamphlet may be found in the Ridgeway Library, Philadelphia.

6. The extract dealing with "the Equalizing Court" was copied by the following papers, among others: N.H. Merc., June 14, 1787; *The* [Baltimore] *Maryland Gazette*, June 22, 1787; Prov. Gaz., June 16, 1787; Sal. Merc., June 12, 1787; Ch. Mng. P., July 7, 1787; Va. Ind. Chr., June 20, 1787.

7. The *Gazette* published the item as copied from a New York paper.

8. See Benjamin Rush to Richard Price, June 2, 1787, in *Letters to and from Richard Price* (Cambridge, Mass., 1903), 108, 109, where Rush says: "The enclosed newspaper contains an address suited to our present hour of difficulty and danger. The sentiments contained in it will discover its author." Price wrote back, on September 24, thanking Rush "for sending the Address to the States in the Pennsilvania paper." "I see plainly," he added, "from whom it came and I wish it may do good." The Rush Papers, Ridgeway Library, Philadelphia. There was nothing in the Pennsylvania papers near the date of Rush's letter that corresponded to Price's description, except the "Address of Harrington." It should be added that "Harrington's Address" is to be distinguished from a much earlier "Address to the people of the United States," of which Rush apparently sent Price a copy, on April 22, 1786. *Letters to and from Richard Price*, 82; cf. 83–85. This earlier address had been reprinted, *as Rush's work*, in Am. Mus. for January 1787 (I, 8).

9. See chap. VII hereof.

10. The "Address of Harrington" appeared in the following papers, besides those mentioned in the text: N.Y. Ind. Jour., June 2, 1787; *The* [Baltimore] *Maryland Gazette*, June 8, 1787; *The New-York Packet*, June 8, 1787; N.H. Spy, June 9 and 12, 1787; Mass. Cent., June 9, 1787; Conn. Cour., June 11, 1787; Am. Her., June 11, 1787; Am. Merc., June 11, 1787; Sal. Merc., June 12, 1787; Va. Ind. Chr., June 13, 1787; B. Ind. Chr., June 14, 1787; Newp. Her., June 14, 1787; Prov. Gaz., June 16, 1787; *The* [Springfield, Mass.] *Hampshire Chronicle*, June 19, 1787; The N.H. Gaz., June 23, 1787; *The Carlisle* [Pa.] *Gazette*, July 4, 1787; Col. Her., July 5, 1787; Norw. Pack., July 5, 1787; *The Litchfield* [Ct.] *Weekly Monitor*, July 16, 1787; Vt. Gaz., July 30, 1787; Ga. Gaz., August 11, 1787; Cumb. Gaz., September 20, 1787. Many files are wanting or incomplete, and it is probable that the address appeared in other papers also. A few of the papers omitted the portions of the address not relating directly to what the Federal Convention ought to do; but most of them—nearly all in fact—published the whole of it. The address also was published in the June number of Am. Mus., (I, 429–32), which had subscribers in all the states.

11. Ph. Ind. Gaz., May 31, 1787.

12. Ibid., June 20, 1787. This number of the *Gazetteer* also contained a letter from Richard Price to William Bingham, urging the necessity of giving to the general government "due strength and energy," and praising John Adams's ideas of "checks and balances" as expounded in his recently published book, *A Defence of the American Constitutions*.

13. The early numbers of the "Foreign Spectator"'s essay were likewise published in Pa. Gaz., a weekly, beginning with the issue of August 8. With the appearance of the Constitution, after September 17, interest shifted to the concrete merits of that document; and the *Gazette*, not having the amount of space which was available in the *Gazetteer*, a daily, discontinued the "Foreign Spectator"'s abstract discussion.

14. Cf. Collin's contemporary statement in a letter of March 1788, reprinted in Johnson, *The Journal and Biography of Nicholas Collin* (Philadelphia, 1936), 122, 123–24. Collin's statement was entirely correct. No list was kept of the papers in which the "Federal Sentiments" essay was republished. Among the papers that republished the essay, or parts of it, were Mass. Gaz., and N.Y. Adv.

15. Johnson, *Nicholas Collin*.

16. The papers were published under the pseudonym "A Foreign Spectator" in *The*

New-York Daily Gazette, June 3–July 7, 1789. They also appeared in other newspapers and were reprinted as the work of Nicholas Collin, in Am. Mus., 235–36, 303–5,1789.

17. Ph. Ind. Gaz., September 18, 1787.

18. Ibid., September 6, 1787.

19. Ibid., September 11, 1787.

20. Ibid., September 12, 1787.

21. Ibid., September 13 and 17, 1787.

22. Ibid., September 12, 1787.

23. Ibid., September 17 and 18, 1787.

24. There was one complaint, in *The New-York Journal*, that the essay was unfair to "the ladies of America."

25. Records, I, 471. This is one of the speeches which Madison took the trouble to rewrite in his own records.

26. See *Letters of a Westchester Farmer, 1774–1775* (White Plains, 1930).

27. Ibid., 1 and 39.

28. See pp. 433 hereof.

29. Va. Ind. Chr., June 13, 1787.

30. See chap. XV hereof.

31. Above, n. 10.

32. See Pol. & Con., I, 151–52; chaps. X and XII hereof. The pamphlet is reprinted in Pol. & Con., Appendix A.

33. *The New Haven Gazette and Connecticut Magazine*, July 5 and 12, 1787.

34. See Pol. & Con., I, 84–96, 102–14, 146–53.

35. See chap. VIII hereof.

36. Some of these have already been noted in the text, and others will be noted in the succeeding section. Reference may also be made to an item in *The Carlisle* [Pa.] *Gazette*, of August 1, 1787, by "A Citizen of Franklin County." "It is absurd to suppose," said he, "that the states of America, individually, can be sovereign whilst they have a federal head." He also declared that he thought Americans should have done "with jealous fears and groundless apprehensions." "Why should we wish to support the sovereignty of our petty state? when by resigning it in part, we can have the protection of a government, founded on republican principles, equally free, less expensive, and more respectable." How far the separate sovereignties should be resigned, he was willing to leave to the Federal Convention. "They are our representatives legally chosen. Another item, somewhat longer, appeared in N.Y. Adv., of September 3, 1787. Signed "Rough Carver," the item advocated "an energetic, consolidated system of government, calculated on the broad basis of individual and state welfare." In the issue of September 4, the "Rough Carver" concluded his discussion by insisting *"that a collective energy, answering all the purposes of Government, should be lodged somewhere"* (italics in the original); and that, "in no place or body (provided the necessity of Union [were] admitted) [could] this coercion be vested to advantage, but in that created by the general consent of the States." There were many similar expressions of opinion, and many similar expressions of confidence in the convention, most of them in the form of brief paragraphs interspersed among the news.

37. Records, I, 137.

38. May 15, 1787.

39. Records, I, 143.

40. N.Y. Adv., July 21, 1787; cf. ibid., September 10, 1787. Also, Pa. Pack., August 3, 1787.

41. Pa. Pack., July 30 and 31, 1787; Pa. Merc., August 3, and 10, 1787.

42. Records, III, 75.

43. See the signed statement by William Will and five others, members of the Pennsylvania Assembly, in Pa. Pack., October 8, 1787.

44. Ibid.

45. This item was also published in Ch. Mng. P., of June 1, 1787.

46. This attack distressed Hamilton very greatly and led to an application by him, to Washington, for a letter giving the lie to the story that he had "palmed" himself upon Washington and afterwards been dismissed from his services. Hamilton, IX, 423–25. Washington supplied Hamilton with the desired letter on October 18. Washington, XXIX, 290–91. The facts as to Hamilton's resignation as aide to Washington, not completely creditable to Hamilton, may be found in the letter which he wrote to his father-in-law, at the time. Hamilton, IX, 232–37.

47. See p. 419 hereof.

48. This kind of government, as the reader will remember, was carefully specified by the Continental Congress as their fundamental expectation from the work of the Federal Convention when they adopted the final resolution on February 21, 1787. Cf. Chap. XXV hereof.

49. Records, I, 123, 137, 143, 253, 344, 379, 529; II, 89.

50. See chap. XVII hereof.

51. For example, Pa. Pack., September 2, 1786; and *The New-York Packet*, September 4, 1786.

52. N.Y. Jour., July 27, 1786; N.J. Gaz., August 7, 1786; Ch. Ev. Gaz., August 23, 1786; Gaz. S.C., August 24, 1786.

53. Ch. Mng. P., on September 13, 1786, published the item under a Richmond dateline of August 9.

54. Mass. Gaz., June 19, 1786 ("exclusive"); Ch. Ev. Gaz., September 22, 1786 ("fully"); Gaz. S.C., November 16, 1786 ("complete"); Ch. Mng. P., July 7, 1786 ("exclusive"); *The New-York Packet*, June 15, 1786 ("exclusive"); Vt. Gaz., ("ample"); N.L. Gaz., October 20, 1786 ("absolute"); Sal. Merc., July 3, 1787 ("fully"); Pa. Pack., January 13, 1787 ("From a Norfolk [Va.] paper": "public and uniform regulation of trade throughout the United States"); ibid., December 26, 1785 ("commerce, both at home and abroad"); ibid., November 11, 1786 ("sole and exclusive"); Sav. Gaz., November 24, 1785 ("continental system of commercial regulation"); Gaz. S.C., September 12, 1785 ("continental system for regulation of our trade"); Pa. Pack., June 25, 1787 ("one supreme head with power to regulate trade over the whole union"). The foregoing constitute a random sampling. There were many others. There were also countless items asking power "to regulate trade," or "to regulate commerce," without either emphasis or qualification.

55. N.H. Ct. Gaz., May 17, 1787.

56. See Pol. & Con., I, 55–77.

57. See Pol. & Con., I, 150–51, on this use of "object."

58. In the installment of the pamphlet appearing in *The New Haven Gazette and Connecticut Magazine*, on May 10, 1787, the author says that the "political" powers of government "may be considered under the articles of WAR, and of friendship and TRADE." Cf. this with the passage just cited in the text, p. 457, where he says "the whole political interest of a nation may be included and considered under these denominations:. . . War . . . and Commerce. . . ."

59. See Pol. & Con., II, Appendix A.

60. Hughes, C. J., in *Schechter Poultry Corporation* v. *United States*, 295 U.S. 495, 550 (1935) expressed what is undoubtedly still the position of the Court as to *the meaning* of the words of the Commerce Clause, when he referred to "the distinction between the internal concerns of a state and commerce among the several states, which the commerce clause itself establishes."

61. On the use of the phrase "the general commerce," see Pol. & Con., I, 84–89, and pp. 513–15 hereof.

62. The phrase "through the states" of course meant "throughout the states." Cf.

Monroe's objection to the Constitution that it gave to Congress "the right of excise *through* all the states." Monroe, I, 333. This gives the key to the way the phrase "through the states" was used; and in interpreting it in the phrase "the right to regulate trade *through* the states," one should remember that there were shortly to be interior states, and that it was "through" them, as well as "through" the Atlantic states, that the right in question was to be exercised by Congress.

63. Lee, II, 419–22.

64. See Pol. & Con., I, 155–72; chap. II hereof.

65. See pp. 429–31 hereof.

66. Lee, II, 433.

67. Records, III, 15, 16.

68. This item appeared nearly everywhere. The following are some of the papers which published it: Pa. Gaz., August 29, 1787; Mass. Gaz., September 7, 1787; Mass. Cent., September 8, 1787; Conn. Cour., September 10, 1787; N.H. Gaz., September 15, 1787; *The Litchfield* [Ct.] *Weekly Monitor*, September 17, 1787; *The* [Keene] *New-Hampshire Recorder*, September 18, 1787; Cumb. Gaz., September 20, 1787; Col. Her., September 24, 1787.

69. Coxe, *A View of the United States of America* (Philadelphia, 1794), 4. Coxe usually contrasted "commerce" and "agriculture." The following is a typical passage: "The commerce of America, including our exports, imports, shipping, manufactures, and fisheries, may be properly considered as one interest" (p. 7). For other excerpts from Coxe's *View*, see Pol. & Con., I, 87–89, 109–10. It is not of course to be inferred, from passages such as the foregoing, that the welfare of agriculture, according to Coxe's understanding, lay outside the scope of a power "to regulate commerce." The whole burden of his paper on an American "commercial system" was to the contrary.

70. Pa. Pack., May 19, 1787, p. 3, col. 2.

71. Coxe, *A View*, 11, 29–30.

72. Records, III, 18–20.

73. See chap. XXII hereof.

74. Letters, VIII, 458, 460.

75. See chap. XI hereof.

Index

Index

WITHDRAWN